P9-DZZ-304

WITHDRAWN

REDWOOD

LIBRARY
NEWPORT
R.I.

Gift of
Max J. Loudenslager
Vietnam 1970-71
25th INF. DIV. U.S.ARMY

"For those Americans
still serving as POW'S
in Southeast Asia"

CONVERSATIONS WITH THE ENEMY

Other books by Winston Groom
BETTER TIMES THAN THESE
AS SUMMERS DIE

By Duncan Spencer
LOVE GONE WRONG:
The Jean Harris Scarsdale Murder Case

CONVERSATIONS WITH THE ENEMY

The Story of PFC Robert Garwood

by Winston Groom and Duncan Spencer

G. P. Putnam's Sons
New York

Copyright © 1983 by Winston Groom and Robert Garwood
All rights reserved. This book, or parts thereof, may not be
reproduced in any form without permission in writing from
the publisher. Published on the same day in Canada by
General Publishing Co. Limited, Toronto.

The authors gratefully acknowledge permission from the
following sources to quote from material in their control:
   Acuff-Rose Publications, Inc., for lyrics from "Sad Movies
(Make Me Cry)" by John D. Loudermilk. Copyright © 1961
by Acuff-Rose Publications, Inc. International copyright
secured. All rights reserved. Made in U.S.A.
   Ludlow Music, Inc., for lyrics from "Tom Dooley," words
and music collected, adapted and arranged by Frank Warner,
John A. Lomax and Alan Lomax. Copyright © 1947 (renewed
1975) and 1958 Ludlow Music, Inc., New York, N.Y.

Library of Congress Cataloging in Publication Data

Groom, Winston, date.
   Conversations with the enemy.

   1. Garwood, Robert Russell. 2. Vietnamese Conflict,
1961–1975—Prisoners and prisons, American. 3. Prisoners of
war—United States—Biography. 4. Prisoners of
war—Vietnam—Biography. I. Spencer, Duncan. II. Title.
DS559.4.G37G76   1983   959.704'37   82-23007
ISBN 0-399-12715-1

Printed in the United States of America

145194

DS 559.4
.637
G-76
1983

84B
. G899

CONVERSATIONS WITH THE ENEMY

JAN 1 1 1986 A

JAN 1 1986

Prologue

THERE IS a story of how this book came to be, and it began early in the summer of 1979. One afternoon Winston Groom received a call from the editor of the paperback subsidiary of a major publisher. The editor's first question was, Had Groom heard of Robert Garwood, the Marine POW who had only recently been returned from Vietnam, and the second question was, Would he be interested in writing a paperback book about Garwood's experience in connection with a movie that was to be made about the case? All Groom then knew about the story was what he had read in the press: that Garwood was an accused traitor, turncoat, and enemy crossover who allegedly had led Vietcong troops against his own countrymen. Groom felt the story had an unseemly ring to it, and further, that a paperback book in conjunction with a film was simply not his kind of project, and the conversation ended.

Several days later Groom mentioned the matter to his literary agent, Theron Raines, and Raines' reaction was icy, sudden, and strange. "I have to call you back," he said. Soon afterward the phone rang. It was Raines, who surprised Groom by telling him something he had not been aware of: Raines, ironically, had been asked to represent Garwood's literary interests. After the earlier conversation with Groom, Raines had immediately contacted Garwood's attorney, Dermot Foley, about the paperback publisher's proposal and the so-called movie, because he knew nothing about either of them. Raines quickly ascertained that both projects were simply "gun jumpers." In the instance of the "movie," it was one of the oldest scams around—trying to sell something that doesn't belong to you in the first place, a game played frequently in the fast-and-loose Hollywood crowd. The "producers" had contacted Foley and asked him if Garwood would be interested in selling the rights to his story for a film. Although Foley was noncommittal, nevertheless the producers were optimistic. Armed with nothing more than this, the producers then approached the paperback house with the idea of selling them the right to do a book on Garwood based on the movie, and from this they evidently hoped to get enough money, as an advance, to purchase the story rights from Garwood. It was that kind of deal.

Raines then told Groom that in fact he himself had intended at some point to ask Groom if he would be interested in writing a serious, in-depth hardcover book about Garwood. For one thing, Raines knew far more about Garwood's story than the press had reported, because Foley had kept a tight lid on the details he had learned from Garwood and the media knew only what the Marine Corps was putting out. Also, Groom had served as an Army officer in Vietnam and had recently published a novel about it. Furthermore, he was nearing the end of another novel and Raines felt the time might be opportune.

Groom felt the idea was far more interesting in this light but said that he would like to talk with Garwood before making a decision. A week later a meeting was arranged at, of all places, the Larchmont Yacht Club, a venerable and imposing social institution located in the exclusive community in which Foley lived, about half an hour from Manhattan. To say the least, the setting was incongruous: Groom, Foley, and Garwood—freed only a few weeks from fourteen years of incarceration in Vietnamese prison camps—strolling the green lawns past white-clad players on clay tennis courts; the yachts and swimming pools and the other ritzy trappings of one of New York's fashionable suburban playgrounds. There was a buffet for lunch, a table of what Groom recalled as "women's club food"—Waldorf salads, cheeses, fruits, finger sandwiches and such. But not too far away from this the smells of hamburgers and hot dogs wafted from a snack bar lined with youngsters from the swimming pool. In the end, Garwood went into that line and ordered a cheeseburger, french fries, and a Coca-Cola.

His accent then was heavily Oriental, a kind of glottal diction in which the tongue is pressed against the roof of the mouth to form the variations of Vietnamese syllables. The conversation went on for most of the day at the club and later, back at Foley's home, but Groom wanted a chance to get Garwood alone for a while. As it happened, the gasoline shortage was at its peak and Groom needed to fill his tank before returning to New York, so he asked Garwood to go along with him.

It took nearly two hours to get the gas and they had to wait in a sweltering line on a road densely wooded on one side. As the cars inched forward and then stopped, the two of them would get out and go to the edge of the cool woods and Garwood would squat down Oriental-style. He began to tell Groom some of the details that would later help him decide that the story was possible and well worth the telling. At one point, Garwood observed casually, "You see that tree over there," pointing to a thin, tall oak. "I could make a whole house and the furniture to go in it out of that one tree." And then, pointing to a clump of bushes, he said, "I could put that house right there and you wouldn't be able to see it from the road. Matter of fact," he added, "I could probably live in this little woods here for the rest of my life and nobody would ever know I was here."

Later Groom pondered the things that Garwood had told him that day and decided there was certainly another side to the story than the one being told by the Marines and the media. For one thing, Garwood simply did not seem like a traitor; even his brief explanation of his actions did not seem to warrant the allegations then being made about him. Second, his tale was, if nothing else, a terrific adventure, a bizarre combination of *Lord Jim, The Gulag Archipelago,* and *The Man Without a Country.* Groom was not then sure exactly what he would find, but the story certainly seemed compelling.

Not long afterward an agreement was reached in which Garwood would cooperate with Groom on a book. A deal was struck with G. P. Putnam's Sons, publishers who paid a handsome advance for the rights to publish the story. But the problems even then were worrisome.

Most important was that Garwood's court-martial had not even begun to get underway and there was always the danger that the Marine Corps might, if they found out Garwood was being interviewed, subpoena any notes, tapes, or other material or even put Groom on the witness stand. And, Garwood was not in the best emotional or physical health at the time. He had spent half of his life in Asian prison camps and now, back in the United States, was just about as close to a Rip Van Winkle as anyone might expect to find. He was having difficulty remembering specific dates, places, and things, and there was the tremendous pressure of the impending court-martial bearing down—and the penalty for at least one of the charges, desertion, was the firing squad.

The next time Groom saw Garwood was at Camp Lejeune, a sprawling Marine training center in North Carolina. The two of them had days of long, secret sessions with the tape recorder, and it was apparent to Groom that the strain of the pending court-martial was taking its toll. Garwood had also fallen ill from a variety of lingering jungle diseases and had to be hospitalized. But on the bright side, he had divested himself of some of the Oriental affectations he had picked up. He could, he said, now sleep fairly comfortably in a bed with a mattress or sit with ease in a chair, and much of the Vietnamese accent was gone. By this time he had acquired an automobile. Curiously, but not unpredictably, it was a red 1956 Chevy, in which he had installed a tape deck with a collection of 8-tracks from the late fifties and sixties—the Everly Brothers, Fats Domino, Elvis—almost as though he were trying to pick up wherever he'd left off so long ago.

One poignant episode marked the visit. Garwood had just received a letter, a document actually, from a museum of some sort located in Southern California. The letter, phrased formally, requested permission from him to have his portrait painted from a photograph for inclusion in the "museum's collection." Garwood seemed at first flattered and pleased.

9

Groom inspected the letter and suggested he consult with Foley before agreeing to anything. Shortly afterward it was discovered that the museum was actually a kind of rogues' gallery of infamous criminals, the walls of which were decorated with the likenesses of John Dillinger, Al Capone, Jesse James, and so on. Garwood's portrait was to have been there as a sort of Benedict Arnold character—the Vietnam War's most heinous traitor. Naturally, he was crushed.

Meantime, Groom had been trying to secure some press credentials to cover the court-martial, since seating at such trials is difficult except for daily or periodical journalists. He first approached *The New Yorker* through a friend who was one of its writers, Michael Arlen, offering the magazine first crack to serialize the story in exchange for credentials. But the magazine was not enthusiastic about the idea. *Playboy* magazine's executive editor, G. Barry Golson, was, but in exchange he wanted an exclusive interview with Garwood for *Playboy*. Foley was consulted and it was agreed, stipulating however that nothing could appear in print until after the trial. Groom began to organize an interview and finally boiled down a rough draft of some 150 pages.

It was at this point that Foley asked if he could see the interview. Groom reluctantly agreed, deciding no harm could come of it. In this he was wrong. What Groom did not know was that Foley was then embroiled in a violent dispute with another lawyer he had brought into the case to assist him, John Lowe, of Charlottesville, Virginia. This resulted in Foley's being forced to retire from the case and in Groom's coming to the very edge of abandoning the entire project.

Lowe argued that the existence of the *Playboy* interview, even in Groom's hands, might be dangerous to Garwood's defense if the Marine Corps ever got wind of it. So he sought, in a letter to Golson at *Playboy*, sent over Garwood's signature, to discredit the material, claiming that Garwood said he was intoxicated when he spoke with Groom and that the days of tape-recorded interviews were merely in the nature of a "bull session" rather than a true account of what happened.

When the letter came to his attention, Groom was furious, even though Lowe attempted to explain that the disclaimers were merely to "cover Bobby" in case something happened. Groom felt his integrity had been impugned, even that he had been libeled, and began to have serious doubts about the project. Moreover, Lowe, now clearly in charge of his client, refused to permit Groom to have further interviews with Garwood until the trial was over, the delivery date for the book had already passed, and the court-martial had not even started. And as if this was not enough, Garwood shortly afterward was arrested for a sex offense while awaiting his court-martial at Camp Lejeune. Groom then decided it might be best to abandon the book and made preliminary overtures to that end through his own lawyer.

The matter lay in limbo through the fall of 1981 and the winter, though the court-martial had finally begun and was dragging on. Then in the spring,

10

Groom was having lunch in New York with an old friend and former reportorial colleague from the old days at the *Washington Star*, Duncan Spencer. Spencer and Groom had joined the *Star* at about the same time, and Groom's admiration for Spencer's journalistic abilities was great. Furthermore, the two were close personal friends—they had sailed and hunted duck in Virginia together, and had once jointly done a monthly column for a yachting magazine. Spencer had taken a leave of absence from the *Star* to write a book about the Jean Harris–Tarnower murder case. Groom also knew that Spencer was experiencing doubts about returning to the then-foundering *Washington Star*. During the lunch, Groom was lamenting his problems with the Garwood book, but Spencer became enthusiastic and counseled that he should go ahead with it anyway.

Later Groom pondered the situation. He was now alienated from Garwood's lawyers, who had assumed virtually total control over access to their client, and he wasn't sure that situation could be rectified. Yet there was something in Spencer's enthusiasm that made Groom again begin to feel the book could and should be done.

There were still looming problems. There was a tremendous amount of catching up to do if the book was to be delivered soon enough to satisfy the publisher. It had been nearly two years since the contract was signed and very little had been accomplished because of the restrictions Garwood's lawyers had placed on interviews. Also, the new lawyers had decided to proceed with a psychiatric defense and for all Groom knew, the subject of the book was going to be portrayed in court as a crazy man. And then there was the sex charge. But despite it all, Groom felt it was worth a gamble.

What he needed at this point was help, and who would be better than Spencer? He already knew they could work well together. And he also knew Spencer was dubious about returning to the *Star*, which by that time was on its last legs. Most important, he trusted Spencer's abilities implicitly. A few weeks later he approached Spencer with a proposition that they collaborate and Spencer accepted.

The result of that collaboration, this book, was distilled from hundreds of hours of interviews with Garwood and others associated with the case and a voluminous file of tapes, notes, transcripts, and other documents. The original manuscript totaled over 450,000 words, more than twice the size of the present book.

In reading this story, it must be understood that the recollections of many of the principals go back more than fifteen years, and some are obscure, bitter, or self-serving. The authors have attempted as earnestly as possible to reconstruct the events. They realize that precise recollection of conversations is unlikely, and memories and perceptions of events long past are inevitably clouded in one way or another. But the authors firmly believe that this telling is as close to the truth of the Garwood matter as it is humanly possible to get.

Many people assisted in the preparation of this book, but the authors would especially like to express deep and grateful appreciation to the following persons: Kerry Sipe, Douglas Kamholz, Eddie Morgan, Theron and Joan Raines, Keith Korman and Buck, Jerry Roth, Donna Long, Vaughn Taylor, Megan Rosenfeld, Eugene Rosenfeld, Louisa Spencer, Carol Atkinson, Professor Geoff Nulle, Wendy Lipkind, Lee Klein, Dr. James Ryan, Margaret Kendall, G. Barry Golson, Jack and Helen Garwood and, of course, the editors, Christine Schillig and Peter Israel of Putnam's.

1
The Long, Cruel Day

A BOY sat lost on a dirt road in a jeeplike auto called a Mighty-Mite, the motor still running. It was near dusk. There was a Vietnamese fishing village on one side—Cam Hai, a collection of coconut-frond roofs, mud, grass, bamboo, and the long, narrow fishing boats on the beach a hundred feet away.

The boy was a pale, clean-shaven American Marine private. He wore brand new starched and pressed fatigues, brand new spit-shined boots, and a brand new .45 automatic in a patent-leather holster. His Mighty-Mite was brand new too, and he had driven out from the Headquarters Company motor pool, Third Marine Division, at Da Nang, six kilometers distant.

The reason he had the new clothes, the new gun, the new car, was that he was a division staff driver, one of those rear-echelon soldiers who taxies the brass around, and the brass like their drivers neat and clean; he was merely a chauffeur who took officers to the field and to the club. In the autumn of 1965 there was no official air of desperation in Vietnam, no feeling of despair. It was September 28.

The motor idled quietly. The driver, Robert Russell Garwood, barely nineteen, of Adams, Indiana, smoked casually, a tiny cloud of worry in his mind: Where was his pick-up? He had missed rendezvous before, but always it was the same—late is okay, so long as the job gets done.

The job was simple: "Pick up a Marine lieutenant from a reconnaissance company near Marble Mountain," he'd been told.

Marble Mountain, so named by a long-forgotten Marine, sits at the water's edge. It can be seen plainly from Da Nang, a landmark, considered secure in the daytime, but at night a place of danger. At this early point in the war, after

13

the Marines had landed at Da Nang, at China Beach, right smack in the downtown city, the situation seemed well in hand.

Beyond the village to the east there is nothing. Sand dunes and a fringe of palm and coconut trees shut out the horizon. To the west, out of view, are endless rice fields, canals and dikes, which stretch to the mountains, blue and normal, ten miles away. The fields are ripe with grain; it's harvest time and the peasants are working late. From the beach, the village seems almost empty. Old women wearing worn sarongs attend some incomprehensible chores in and around the hooches.

The driver hardly took in the scene. He thought only of the slightly thickening air, the beginning of dusk spreading from the sea as the sun stooped behind the mountains. He figured he had an hour's light, perhaps more.

Minutes passed. The sea lay calm. In the offing were a dozen fishing boats. He watched them idly. In twelve days, Garwood was to be en route to Bangkok for R&R (rest and recreation). After that Okinawa. After that home. He had short-time thoughts.

Only the stillness was oppressive. A wind from the ocean cooled the land's heat. An old Vietnamese, a man of seventy or eighty with a white beard and a little stringy moustache, white hair, the perfect papa-san, came into view. He was waving with one hand. He was smiling. Garwood watched, curious and cautious; it looked strange; he was the only one. Then Garwood began to wake up from his taxi-man's reverie. There were no children.

No children. No black-headed, bright-eyed, naked rug rats running up shouting, "Okay okay, number one number one," begging money, gum, anything. No "Hey Joe, Hey GI."

It still didn't occur to him that he could be in any kind of danger, between the old man and the sea and the childless village in the dunes. He had never been in contact with the enemy in this ghostly war, and neither had most of his friends. He was only a driver at division headquarters, waiting in the motor pool, on standby, going to the bars and the USO in Da Nang, a place of few places, a place overwhelmed by Marines, Air Force, Navy, Australians, and ARVN (an acronym for the South Vietnamese Army). Nor had he spent any time out in the jungles or rice fields. His was a soft job, a job for a man who wanted to stay out of trouble, who kept up his appearance, who did favors for the staff, who took little drives for people, a kind of ingratiating, unambitious character whose sole aim in life was to get out of Vietnam.

The old man waved and then he stopped. But he didn't stop smiling. He came down to the beach in his bare feet, his black shirt and white trousers drifting around his skinny limbs. He was talking what seemed to be French. At least it was not Vietnamese. With his eyes riveted, Garwood watched the old man come over to the jeep, talking. He touched the jeep, gently, and held out his hand to the American boy with the billed cap in drab green.

Garwood said "No . . . no . . ." smiling to show he couldn't speak the language. The old man pointed to Garwood's weapon, the new .45 in the shiny leather holster at his waist. He gestured as if wanting Garwood to give the gun to him.

It now crossed Garwood's mind that the old man was senile. No Vietnamese would ever ask an American for a weapon. It's a kind of taboo. He wondered, inexperienced with this kind of situation.

It was at this instant, while Garwood was bemused, staring at the old man, who continued to point and gesture and talk in futile French, that other presences, like the shadows across a window, moved at the edge of his vision. Like any reactive animal, he looked up from under the bill of his cap, across the bit of sand and away from the lapping sea to the village. But in front of the village, where seconds before there had been nothing, now there were men. And not all men, his eyes quickly took in, but a few young boys, a couple of young girls. The old man, suddenly silent, began to backpedal to the village through the line, no—a semicircle, like the letter "C"—of Vietnamese men, women, and boys that had formed between the new Mighty-Mite and the sea, and in the middle of the curve of the C was Bobby Garwood and his thoughts.

"I hadn't been in any contact with the Viet Cong or the Communists or anything like that," Garwood was later to say of the last normal day of his life. "I hadn't been in any firefights, I hadn't been in combat or anything like that. When I first saw them I sensed kind of a danger, but I had just heard about them, you know, from the grunts. I was pretty ignorant and I figured with their weapons they were probably ARVN out on patrol. The danger I sensed then first was some kind of language barrier but I was worried more about it getting dark than about the danger."

Garwood sat, the motor still running, and stared at the dark eyes surrounding him. He made a friendly gesture, much as the old man had, but none of them smiled, they stood there, their weapons angled toward him.

There had been no response to the gestures, not a word. He had said, "Hello . . . Okay?" It was clearly not okay.

Garwood's mind immediately switched to escape, and the thought flickered before him that there was an opening, and that the opening was toward the sea, and that he'd always known how to swim, from his days as a farm boy in Indiana, and his mind switched from that to the face of his girl, Mary Speers of Indianapolis, and in another instant he found himself watching fascinated as one of the young children, the only one to move, the one to whom his frightened eye turned immediately, slowly and waveringly raised some laughably antique piece of riflery, and on its tip was a long bayonet, making the thing even more ludicrous, until the tiny hole above the bayonet was just a dark, dark period spot, evil in the dusk, surrounded by worn metal and the child's frank, wide eyes, and Bob Garwood found his mouth forming the words, "Oh, shit . . ."

His body was not ordered, for there were no coherent orders to give. He did not remember knowing anything, he was totally unprepared, like a person who goes to court for a traffic ticket and finds himself sentenced to death. But the

15

body knew, and it threw itself, screaming for safety in every muscle and nerve, across the Mighty-Mite, forgetting that the gearshift was there, banging his legs and hanging up and finally hitting the damp sand and trying to bury his face and the rest of his suddenly huge, unmanageable, tender whole body in it . . .

"It was quite strange," he said, "most of these weapons I didn't recognize. That was something else that kinda clicked and—they weren't acting right, they didn't act like ARVNs, who when they see an American, they come right up. They may be cautious at first but they see your uniform and they ask you for a cigarette or they try to start a conversation. These people just froze. Instant panic, I guess, came right over me."

Garwood didn't know what to do. He still didn't when the young boy raised the rifle. "It was bigger than he was," he remembers with a laugh. "He had a problem getting it up and that's probably what saved my life. I realized he was going to shoot . . ."

As he pressed the breast of the moist sand, moments passed, a silent time, and then all hell broke loose; Garwood was funnily reminded of the rifle range at Camp Pendleton, California, where he went through basic training, and the instructor would drop the flag signaling the recruits to start firing. . . . Now the burst continued for about fifteen or twenty seconds, and the firing ceased. He was trying to bury himself in the ground, he was trying to pull out his decorative-up-to-now .45 (which for whatever obscure reason he had made a habit of cocking before going out of the motor pool and then holstering, so he had only to pull back the blued hammer, not use two hands to slide the receiver back). "A lot of flashes went through my mind. I figured there's just too many of them . . . I don't know if they're ARVNs, or what they are, or why they're shooting at me, but I just knew I was going to die. Simple logic told me I just had a pistol."

In the silence after the firing there was nothing, and then a scream, like a child screaming, and for the first time, he looked up and saw the boy coming at him, with the once-ludicrous bayonet, and he pointed the pistol without taking aim and pulled the trigger, and the scream took on a different tone, and looking up from flat on the ground, he heard the clump of the rifle dropping beside him, and Garwood pulled the trigger a second time as another shape lurched from behind the front of the Mighty-Mite, which for some reason had stopped running. The second man slumped and a burst of automatic fire came from behind and a sudden numbness, not wholly unpleasant, took over his right side and he looked at his hand, noticing that the pistol was somehow gone from it, and he was afraid to look, seeing blood quickening on his arm, afraid that there were worse wounds where the numbness was.

Later he was to know that the bullets hit his right forearm and wrist—one, like the trick shot in a Western, hit the face of the Timex automatic wristwatch he'd bought at the PX, while the other bullet entered the top of his right arm halfway between wrist and elbow, exiting on the underside of the arm, passing between the two arm bones with little damage. The wristwatch was implanted in his wrist like a piece of type.

16

Garwood, still on his belly, pushed his face into the sand, his whole left arm still under him, the wounded arm above his head dripping blood. He stuck his face deeper, thinking, "I'm waiting for the bullet in the head and I don't want to see it." There was a lot of screaming, and instead of the hammerblow of death, someone was pulling at his shiny black combat boots, working the laces off, jabbering and yelling. Other hands reached to his belt with a knife and cut the web material, tugging off his trousers, until he was hauled to his haunches in a preposterous position sitting in his boxer shorts looking at the ocean while the crowd, now interested solely in the clothes and no longer in slaughter, fought one another to get off Garwood's fatigue jacket, which contained a letter to Mary Speers, and one from her telling him that she had just gotten an apartment back in California.

Also in the jacket were Garwood's lighter and a fresh pack of Pall Mall unfiltered cigarettes, and in his trousers his leather wallet, keys, cards, some fingernail clippers, and a pair of aviator sunglasses (a style Garwood keeps to this day, glasses that show a mirror face to the world).

They took off the web cartridge belt, which had a first-aid kit, a canteen, two grenades, and a .45 clip holder with two clips, fourteen rounds in all.

Ridiculous events piled on like rags. Work stopped on the jacket as three helicopters, cruising low over the sea at a stately pace, came into view heading towards Da Nang. At the sight of the helicopters, fresh jabbering and screaming erupted. The group, which Garwood saw numbered about thirty, started motioning, pushing, punching and pulling and dragging him to the nearest hooch.

He was thrown onto the dirt floor of the hooch face down—there seemed to be about ten guards, one of whom held a rifle, pressing it against his temple. He could hear shouting and excitement from outside, and it dawned on him that they were trying to hide the Mighty-Mite from the helicopters, but the noise of the helicopters simply faded steadily and mournfully out.

Silence again. Garwood saw feet, saw legs, and from the numbers of them knew the villagers, appearing from nowhere, were crowding in with a swelling babble of voices, and among them were those who kept repeating "VC . . . VC Number one."

They let him sit up. His arm dangled at his side. It hadn't begun to hurt. The gun was removed from his temple, but three silent men aimed weapons at him. The villagers called and pointed to everyone, even the babies and young children, saying "VC . . . VC." They seemed pleased with themselves, and with him.

The villagers crowded close, touching Garwood's black hair. Some pinched earlobes, or his arms—not to hurt so much as out of curiosity to find out what this strange creature was made of. Two young boys approached with bamboo sticks about four feet long; they prodded at Garwood's penis and genitals, poking and laughing, then jumping away and repeating the exercise until the guards warned them off with a rough word. Old women came up to Garwood and spat on him. Pointing to the sky and the ocean, their fingers leveled at him

17

at last. It was explained later to him that the Viet Cong had saved him from death there at Cam Hai, that the villagers wanted to execute him then and there.

He sat there, his legs out in front of him, his arm cradled or hanging down, for most of an hour, until the feeling returned to his arm. It was caked with sand, almost packed with it, so that the bleeding was only a slight seepage. The arm began to throb. Since his capture, Garwood had simply not reacted. He was helpless. Occasionally people would come in and speak what he imagined was French to him, and each time he shook his head.

Darkness rushed in, a tropical darkness complete except for the yellow winks of worn flashlights, candles, and tiny kerosene lamps. He was taken out of the hooch, both arms tied behind by the elbows and a rope passed around his neck, then passed under the arm rope—a type of bondage that became one of the most familiar pictures of Vietnamese captivity. They led him what seemed to be inland, down to a boat on a river, a river he had noted as he motored towards Cam Hai.

They blindfolded him. His head was pressed down into the boat, which had no motor, and his upper body was covered with leaves. He stayed in the boat for about a half hour while unknown men rowed or paddled, he didn't know where or why. He got out of the boat still blindfolded, and they started shoving him across a confusing footing that alternated between thick muck and a slippery foot trail. He was in a rice paddy, and negotiating it so badly in his bare feet that his captors took off his blindfold and led him on. Removing the blindfold didn't do much good; the night was black, though lights glowed in the sky, and he continued to slip and pitch into the mud. "Di Di . . ." they urged. "Go . . . quick."

"I seen why they kept the blindfold on. With it off, I could see the lights and the flares at Da Nang airstrip. I could hear the planes taking off and coming in for a landing and the planes taking off were passing overhead," he recalled. Every time he started to stare at the air base, which he judged now to be only a couple of miles distant, there would be shoves, and harsh whispers to "Di—Di."

For a little over an hour they marched, Garwood unknowing, afraid he was about to be killed immediately. He thought only that if he cooperated with them, the whole group might stumble into one of the patrols. "I was scared. My arm hurt like hell, I was weak. I was exhausted."

They broke into an open space, and the nearly constant flares from Da Nang lit up the path and the open space, and suddenly there were tracers in the air, going "whoomp" into the mud, and it seemed that Garwood was in the middle of his first firefight, green and red tracers, each coming from a different direction with him and his group in the middle. They were all up to their knees in the paddy, and they pushed him down to a slough and he somehow started to run, straight through, it seemed to the stumbling crashing Garwood, the middle of the fire. They made for a clump of banana trees, the only available

18

cover; one of the guards was hit in the foot. He fell down and grabbed the foot, silent: Comrades lifted him quietly and went on. Garwood was free for a moment—but to do absolutely nothing. Seconds later they were at the trees.

They moved all through the night, but there were no more bullets, only the occasional artillery round landing with a deafening shake, once close enough to splatter mud on him. The guards laughed. They had dropped quickly to the ground and left him in his muddy underwear standing like a scarecrow under fire from his own side.

All through the night, the march moved away from Da Nang. The lights and flares grew more distant, the noise of aircraft less, but the terrain remained the same. Rice fields, tiny villages where they stopped, jabbering, where even at night people would come out to poke and pinch. They offered him water and a kind of tea, but he refused. They threw it in his face, angered. Next day he would drink it greedily, but that night he simply stuck his face into the muddy rice field or into a ditch. As the dawn broke, the landscape dissolved into a cold light, the group found itself on a large trail. People seemed bent on normal life, some carrying sacks, some heading to the fields with tools. His feet were sore and bruised but he could still walk. His arm had swollen to a surprising size, and seemed to have lost its function. Most of it ached, too, whenever he jarred it.

The guards would come and go in what appeared to be relays. The wounded guard had simply disappeared.

The march stopped at about midmorning at a stone building, which looked like a temple or a pagoda. It had one large room with a stone floor and an old man lying there; there was incense burning and bowls of rice, apparently a religious offering, and chicken heads, also offered up. The old man was clearly dying. He was skeletal, he was moaning and alone. He could only move his head. No one attended him. Garwood was shoved into the room and pushed over against a wall. There were three or four guards. All had weapons, a ridiculous assortment of ancient gear, and no regular uniform; no military designation at all. Garwood was unable to sleep because everything hurt, and mischief-minded children would dash in and throw stones when the guards turned their backs. On this second morning, it became clear that the day was for holing up, night for travel. Time crawled. Fatigue had overcome fear, but not hunger. The arm was a constant reminder. Finally, he sat down, but the guards would not let him lie. People passed in and out to peer at the muddy prisoner. The march started again in midafternoon.

He was to find the second night march worse than the first. For some reason he could not decipher, people were more abusive the farther they got from Da Nang. Young boys shied rocks at his testicles, or tried to poke sticks up his anus. When he was allowed to lie down on rest stops, the sticks to his unguarded anus were a torment. Peasants seemed angrier, more abusive and aggressive, sometimes shaking and poking knives at him as in pantomime of rage; the guards became, by their relative mildness, almost protectors.

19

The route of march was the same—rice fields, dikes, ditches, villages, hooches. When helicopters passed, he was shoved into the bushes and a gun held to his head. Every hour came a blessed rest. He would sit, head lolling, leaning against a tree when possible. Bugs and mosquitoes were a torment, particularly to head and neck and thighs.

At the end of the second night's march, in the rain, it became surprisingly cold. Roosters crowed, announcing a village, and he was placed in a hooch, face down. A rope was put around his feet, his hands were tied. The neck rope was looped through the elbow and foot ropes and run up to the rafters. He was hogtied, shivering, miserable. But he was able to get some sleep for the first time in over fifty hours. Drifting through semiconsciousness, he shifted his buttocks against the wall. The boys with the sticks were at it again.

From then on, he knew only time and its passage.

For the next ten days Garwood was taken from village to village, always placed in the central square or clearing, arms and neck tied, sitting in his underclothes, no longer white and growing tattered. After the second day, the guards began to give him some things to eat; hot green tea in a bamboo cup, commandeered from local women. The guards would fill their canteens with this tea—it had a bitter taste that seemed to Garwood to make his mouth dry up, but it was a hot drink. Sometimes they would pull a red rice cake out of a pack—a cake that looked like a cooked potato patty wrapped in banana leaves. Garwood wolfed the cakes down, though they were hard to swallow. Then they began to give him salt.

At first there was no communication between the soldier and his captors. He slowly worked out the crudest kind of signal system. He would stop and defecate or urinate by the side of the trail, until he remembered the Vietnamese word "di" for go and used that. The guards, with a smile, would lead him to a more private place.

The wound, of course, was not improving. Its condition began to alarm Garwood on the third day, when a smell worse than mere body odor began to surround him. His arm was actually rotting and giving out the smell, heavy and strong, of decayed meat. Flies would settle, and Garwood was only able to brush them off after the guards loosened his bonds. He knew it was infected. The pain was increasing with a heated throbbing, the arm was about three times its normal size, and movement of his fingers was an agony.

He took to holding his arm theatrically, putting his free hand to his nose. The guards would grin widely at this and say "U.S. number ten," a joke that always got a hearing. Years later, after mastering the language, he learned that many Vietnamese regarded the Americans as men of legendary strength who did not feel any pain, and were like machines in operation. "I don't think they really considered us as humans," he remembered. Montagnards, the tough tiny hill dwellers, later told him that Americans could not be killed. The guards were delighted with any show of pain.

In the villages, the guards would point to the wound and tell the people about it. By the third or fourth day, when the village displays became a regular pattern, Garwood looked anything but heroic. His clothes were stinking, stained with blood, mud, sweat. It was worse than being filthy, he reeked from head to toe. His feet were swollen, cut up, covered with scratches. Elephant grass had made hatch marks on his knees and thighs and many of the smaller wounds carried pus bags that left scars like the pocks of chicken pox on his skin.

But in every village, people would gather around, usually the children first, to examine this human object. Then old women would come up, stony-faced, with the younger women behind them. Finally came the men. They looked at him as if he were a wild animal. Garwood tried to ignore them. He looked at the sky, listened for gun or artillery fire, watched for aircraft. Meanwhile the guards would whip up the crowds, which were at first silent. They pointed at him, made him stand up, motioning angrily. He sat down at another motion. This following of "orders" delighted the villagers, who crowded closer. It was the children who started more hostile acts—they would take pebbles and gently flip them at Garwood, and he would not move. Seeing no reaction, the children began to throw the stones hard. Garwood dodged with his head, trying to keep his face out of their path, but the stones sometimes hit his inflamed arm, making him yelp in pain. "The kids loved that," he remembers.

The crowd always wanted a reaction—but when the children were able to make him wince with poking sticks or stones the guards shouted angrily at them, and they scattered. The older people reacted angrily because of what the guards said to the children, and they showed their anger by squirting jets of betel nut sputum at Garwood from two or three feet away. If one of the jets of red juice hit, the crowd would roar.

But the spitting also infuriated the guards. They motioned as if to say "Look, don't touch," but at times the hysterical old people seemed almost to lose their heads. They attempted to pelt him with skinny fists. Women unwrapped their shawls and tried to flick his eyes with them. The old people seemed to hold the most hatred. Younger women or girls, on the other hand, didn't participate, but hung back and looked on soberly. Young men simply talked among themselves, only glancing at Garwood. Every once in a while a young man would stride up to Garwood, plant a finger at his own breastbone and chant "VC—VC." Pointing the same finger to Garwood, he would say "Number ten, number ten."

The numbers had started at the beginning of the war in the bars, when the language barrier was first surmounted with a numeral system. One and ten seemed much easier than good or bad.

A whole village performance would take an hour, or sometimes longer. He began to feel like a trained bear, a freak show. "Now I know how that damn monkey felt," Bob said to himself. He had begun to talk and hum and sing to himself, and he always sang or hummed the same song, "Sad Movies":

> He said he had to work
> So I went to the show alone

21

They turned out the lights
And turned the projector on
And just as the news of the world
Started to begin:
I saw my darling and my best friend
Walk in.

Whenever Garwood started to sing "Sad Movies," the silence was immediate, and it dawned on him that he might be able to sing his way out of the stones and the sharp pricks of the bamboo sticks of the younger children. So he got in the singing habit, with a repertoire including "El Paso" and "Tom Dooley" ("Hang down your head Tom Dooley, hang down your head and cry, hang down your head Tom Dooley, poor boy, you're bound to die").

On the third day, the guards finally took notice of the stinking mess on Garwood's arm. After a performance of the Garwood show, a young woman came, dressed in a black pajama get-up, rubber Ho Chi Minh tire sandals, a camouflage scarf; Garwood was surprised to see she was clean and good-looking, and she wore her fresh hair down to her waist. He thought at first she was a paramedic, or a Red Cross worker—over her shoulder she carried a box the size of a shoebox. She stopped at the entry to the hooch and simply stared at him. Then she moved slowly over in front of him and looked, without touching, at the arm and the feet. She wore no expression. She said something to the guards and then left for about ten minutes. When she returned, it was with an aluminum basin of very hot water, which she set down on a table next to Garwood. She took out some well-used but clean cloth and with the water-soaked cloth started swabbing his whole arm from the shoulder down, causing the most exquisite stabs of pain.

When he flinched, she gave him a glance of disdain. She cleaned only the area surrounding the bullet holes, and then brought out alcohol, cotton, and a pair of stainless steel tweezers, and with a ball of cotton soaked in alcohol, began to work into the wound. It felt to Garwood as if his whole arm had been thrust into a hot oven. She pushed out dirt and sand, pus, debris and finally was able to pass the point of the tweezers into the entry hole of the wound and out the other side. Garwood squirmed and flinched, and finally felt the relief of passing some kind of threshold—his arm went numb. She poured a chemical, scented solution directly into the hole, plugged both ends with bits of cotton, wrapped the whole with a piece of black cloth and fashioned a crude sling out of a piece of dried banana leaf.

His arms were still bound, but not tightly. She dealt summarily with the wrist wound. Every time Garwood flinched, one of the guards amused himself by making a cutting motion at shoulder level, as if to show that an easier way would be to take the arm off whole.

But the infection was slowed down and the wound began to heal, though it would be two months before the swelling disappeared. The woman ignored the lesser wounds, scratches and blisters. Throughout the treatment she never said

22

a word, and when she was finished she simply rose, turned, and left the hooch. He never saw her again.

Over the next eight days, an average of three to four villages a day received the benefit of the Garwood show. After a while, it became easier for him. He knew that they wanted reaction. He would flinch, and he would sing, and that would have a quieting effect. While he sang the children would laugh, the fierce older people would look quietly on, the hate in their eyes turned for the moment to the loathing curiosity given a mental defective. The guards never fed him in public, but made a show of giving him drinks of the green tea.

He no longer believed he would be killed at any moment. That fear stopped, with its effect of freezing thought and action. He began to notice things. The life of the countryside went on immediately around him. He saw the children tending the water buffalo, riding their thick black necks to grazing places on the edge of the fields. Women carried bamboo water poles with two buckets balanced—the oldest image of the Orient. The rice flats were being plowed up after harvest; mothers with babies strolled by, breast-feeding, or washed laundry, naked kids chewed cane or some vegetable, snot running down their faces, and the village men worked in the fields, or stood in groups talking, being waited upon by their women, smoking their hand-rolled cigars or chewing betel.

On the fourth day, Garwood accepted his first cigarette since his capture. He noted it was a Ruby Queen, one of the few factory-made Vietnamese cigarettes he had seen out in the country. Of the general direction his wandering march was taking, he knew nothing. He seemed to recognize villages and it crossed his mind that he had been there before. The trails followed rivers and streams but continued in the same kind of country, rice marshes and few hills, small fishing boats on the rivers. There didn't seem to be any objective, there didn't seem to be any hurry. What was important seemed to be to show the prisoner to as many people as possible, and to get the maximum credit for his capture.

Garwood noticed an ominous similarity emerging between what he was experiencing and the stories he had heard of capture in Vietnam. In the barrack stories told by his fellow Marines, a prisoner was a short-timer indeed; stripped after capture, he would be marched from place to place, shown to villagers. It would be pointed out that the Americans were not invincible, and the prisoner would be led in by neck rope as an example. But in the stories, there was no goal. After a while the guards would tire of moving the prisoner, feeding him, showing him off to the jeering peasants, and in some hamlet or village or a larger place, it would be shown incontrovertibly that a single bullet could fell the largest, strongest American immediately, and the public education would be complete.

He had been paraded in dozens of villages. He had not been able to answer even the simplest question that could have had military significance. He began to wonder about his value to them. Personnel had shifted too often—some of the guards did not know any longer how he had been captured. He could see no objective to the aimless wandering, and there was no lessening of the hostility shown him by the peasants. He began to think of escape, not as a realist does, but dreamily, remembering with fondness things in Marine life that had once bored or repelled him. He had eaten out of the general's mess at Da Nang, a far better cuisine than the troops had. He thought of steaks, lots of steaks, he thought of fresh fruit. He thought of beer, the staple of his good times in young manhood, and eggs, milk, chocolate milk.

About the fifth day of his captivity, a depression swept over him. Where he had been merely plodding, hoping, glad somehow still to be allowed to live, the full hopelessness of his situation hit him. It was like coming out of shock, out of suspended animation. Instead of being glad to be alive, he began to wonder why they kept him alive. While before he had scarcely believed in his survival, he now felt that he was doomed to another death, far from familiar skies. Dark thoughts ballooned and filled him. The carelessness of death; why hadn't he been shot in the back of the head? What had saved him?

It was an intellectual exercise, more than anything, not unlike the singing. It was a way of ordering the minutes and hours and gaining a tiny foothold on events. He began carefully to watch how the guards behaved. He watched the rivers and streams, knowing that all of them somehow worked their way toward the ocean. And he began to watch planes in the morning, when the rising sun would give him a clear compass bearing on the east, to see which way they tended to fly. He didn't really know what he was hoping to unlock from these meager clues, but it was a system he watched, a real and orderly world that existed outside the life of a live animal, led like a beast, like him.

But the indications were confusing, the rivers full of turns, the airplanes puzzling—which left only the rivers, and on them he began to think more thoroughly. They always led to the coast, to the beach, which must be part of the same shore leading to Da Nang. What if he followed the river by night, rested during the day? Float the rivers in the darkness, his head like a coconut, then find some bank place. He had noticed the luxuriant growth along the river's edge, places either too marshy or too easily flooded to plant, waste places that could hide a man completely. The water was muddy—there would be no way of marking his passage as in a clear stream. If he could keep moving down to the coast, he could practically see, hear, and smell the familiar troopers, the grunts he once had despised, trudging along some trail, cursing to one another, sweating, and then—finding him. He snapped in and out of this reverie many times in the first few days. The miraculous patrol would appear. They'd take him back to Third Divison HQ, past the airfield, the motor pool where he used to complain about the boredom and the taxi-service atmosphere that now seemed like heaven, where you could go to sleep at night and not have to worry about anything, that ugly drab tent city that was either greasy with mud or clouded with dust, but where he'd been waiting for the last day, the day he would board a C-130 bound for Bangkok . . . the end of it all.

The escape plan became a comfort and an exercise—not a reality, because Garwood held his chances at ninety-nine to one against success. Not only was he the only white person within miles, and the only person over six feet, it seemed, in the whole of the country, but he was also without native clothes, with nothing to protect his sorely tired feet, no knowledge of the language beyond "go" and "stop," no money, no weapon, not even a knife or a tool. And he didn't have the slightest idea where he was. And the right arm was still useless.

He had only the rivers. They varied. Some were clear enough to see fish swimming, others silted with red mud. It would have to be a muddy river, it would have to have a medium current. River crossing was usually accomplished by wading or small boats run by a ferryman, an occupation that had become more common since the beginning of the war because of the growing reluctance of people to cross bridges, which were apt to be blown up by either side. The escape would have to be at night and early to give him maximum time and distance before the next light. But the escape as a reality seemed as distant as the old life—of short time, of the R&R, of the return to Mary Speers in Covina, California.

It was the ninth night, or the tenth, when he tried to escape. It was the day Garwood was to have left the war. He was with three guards late in the night, four men alone along a riverside on a trail, quite close to a village on the same side. The river was a large one, perhaps two hundred feet wide. Dimly, a pagoda appeared ahead, a welcome sight, for the guards were in the habit of staying in the religious buildings, with their upturned eaves and the scent of ancient incense, the dim light glowing from a few candles within. It was a good, relatively clean place to rest.

The party stopped before it and the guards motioned him to sit on the stone steps leading from the body of the building, a set of wide brick steps that debouched wetly into the flank of the river, steps going nowhere, for what purpose he could only guess, except that he frequently saw villagers washing their laundry on them. Strange custom, to wash where you prayed, and then like as not go up to the altar and nod fervently, silently to the spirits. He had heard the Vietnamese went to such places to call back their ancestors, and hold conversations with them, asking twice. He'd heard that when they wanted to roast and eat a chicken, the Vietnamese would take the roasted fowl with its head still on to the pagoda, and with rice in bowls and incense, would ask the ancestors to share the food. They'd leave it there for the ancestors to have their chance to feed, and then take it back to eat themselves. Two birds with one stone. Plus all the flies and bugs, he thought. This night, there were only a few bowls of rancid-looking rice within.

It was chilly and there were dozens of mosquitoes, so that even the sensation of cooling off after the hot march was uncomfortable because his arms were bound. Then he began to shiver. Two of the guards, instead of settling in for a nap, stringing hammocks in the trees, strode off to the town. No matter what the hour, he had noticed, these guards were able to rouse someone and get food, get water, get news of the trail ahead. He was left with a single guard, a young man scarcely more than a boy who had been on the trail for two days. The youth carried a carbine, a standard military-issue weapon. The youth also had a number of American ID cards, eight or so in all, he had shown Garwood, in what seemed an attempt to prove that he had killed Americans. But like so much of the Vietnamese braggadocio, it had backfired. Garwood simply didn't believe him. He knew the cards could be stolen, and were a common item of barter because they gave access to the PX.

He judged the youth to be about fifteen or sixteen, slight—he might have weighed a hundred pounds—but he could hump along the trail with his carbine, cartridge belt, two magazines, a canteen, a couple of grenades, knife, and cloth hat with the older men. He was small but tough, a little string bean.

Garwood had feigned complete indifference to the show of the cards; but had noted that the boy seemed very proud of what he was doing. He hoped it was his first experience as a guard, and he could hardly keep from smiling to see the young man preen, checking his gear, wiping his hair into order and generally pulling himself together before entering a village.

He did what the other guards told him to do. Now they had gone.

Garwood lay down on the steps with a groan, trying to adjust to the discomfort of lying, bound, on the narrow steps, which meant lying on his side facing the river, about twelve feet away. It swept past the stone with a sucking noise, a great liquid muscle with an energy of its own, flowing restlessly down to the ocean. The young guard sat above, facing the river, his rifle across his lap, muzzle pointed away.

Minutes passed. There was no chance of sleep with the mosquitoes. He tried to flinch them off when he could. It was about twenty minutes later that he felt something on his foot. His first thought was "fucking snake." But it was only a small river frog.

Garwood jerked to a sitting posture and saw with surprise that the boy had not moved at all. This was rare. Usually the young guard was so keen that with the slightest change of position or noise from his prisoner he would quickly and thoroughly check the ropes and generally remind himself that all was secure. He didn't move. Garwood turned right over, curious. He thought the kid was playing possum, possibly hoping that he would make a break. To kill an escaping prisoner would be quite a feather in his bonnet.

There was no movement. He was motionless, a slim torso silent and absolutely still in the dim light from the whitewashed pagoda, so dim Garwood could not make out his features or see if his eyes were closed. Garwood was fully awake and on his buttocks. He eased himself back down to the attitude of sleeping, and without thinking of the consequences, he slid his buttocks down to the next step, and pulled down his torso, causing an intense and unexpected pain to lace through his right arm. He rested, he did it again, and soon was at the last step before the water. He hesitated there for several seconds, watching the dim form on the steps and thinking that if the boy did wake up, he'd simply tell him he had to piss. And he thought with some satisfaction of what would happen to the youth as he slipped into the current, avoiding any splash. His arms were bound, but blessedly loose.

He found that the water was barely over his crotch, with about a foot of mud over the more solid footing beneath. The current was a lazy caress. Half kneeling, his feet under him, he propelled himself downstream, trying to put distance between himself and the pagoda. There was no immediate hiding place nor did he want one. Only distance.

The first problem was the rope. It was impossible to move it on the right arm, because of the swelling and stiffness of his mending muscles. But he found that the binding of his left arm was looser in the water, and by relaxing his muscles, he could move the rope down past his left elbow, and at the cost of intense pain, from the right arm. Once the rope was down past the elbow, it was simple to slip it off his wrist, and for all purposes he was free—free with one useless arm. He didn't even bother to move the knots on his wounded arm, sensible only of the need to keep moving downstream, moving, half-swimming, half-wading along the bank. He knew it was after midnight, but there seemed to be no moon and progress was good. He never heard the youth awake, there was only the sucking silence of the water in its banks.

He kept moving. The water pressed into his wound, stinging it. He would move twenty-five yards, stop and listen and move on. After a few hours, almost imperceptibly, it became easier to see things and he realized in panic that it was the inexorable daylight. Ahead was a clump of bushes on the same bank, forming a little cove. Downstream was a small sampan, using the clump as a mooring. Garwood was on the clump before he knew it, and before he could avoid it. There was a noise from within, probably the uneasy sleep of a boatman jarred awake by some unusual sound, for the next event was the glare of a flashlight full in his face from a few feet away, and oaths, he imagined, and excited shouts. He cursed, froze. He did not see the weapons as much as he sensed them. He knew he would be an open target in the water in the growing gray light of dawn. There were more lamps, splashing, hands on his shirt and on his tortured arm, and he was dragged, limp with exhaustion, limp with the number of people who had come, it seemed, from nowhere to push him to the riverbank, where they forced him to lie face down, ignoring the wretchedness of his wound.

He remembered thinking that if he had both arms he might have made it. He could have swum, he would not have had to rely on wading near the bank, near the clump that proved so dangerous.

He lay still on the bank, soaked and gathering what strength he could. There seemed to be no clue in the attitudes of these people that his escape had been discovered. They shouted angrily at him in an incomprehensible language. One put a gun to his head, clearly threatening to shoot if he wouldn't talk. But he could do nothing except shake his head. They hauled him to his buttocks and continued to harangue him to no effect.

Then a fresh excitement was heard, and parting the crowd of villagers was the young guard. Hopping with rage, he rushed up to Garwood without a word, lifted his carbine and pushed it strongly into his face. He was able to duck, catching the blow on the forehead, where it made a large gash, causing blood to flow freely. Consciousness seemed to close down briefly, for the next thing he knew, he was on his back, arms bound again, eyelids sticking with blood and the rusty taste of it in his mouth. He thought only that he was still alive, to his own amazement. The young guard had disappeared, never to reappear again.

He was led to a hooch the size of a chicken coop, guarded and left to himself. He noted the guards were women, women with rifles. He was fed tea, but his scalp wound was not attended. This time, there were to be no more neophyte guards. Four older men, all carrying AK-47s, highly prized semiautomatic Russian guns. AK-47 rifle owners were the toughest, most professional fighters of the VC, he had heard. These guards were to stay with him, never leaving him alone with only one.

The guards now behaved differently, they were more like veteran soldiers. There was never again a show in a village, but instead what seemed a deliberate effort to avoid villages, and an effort to avoid people, to allow no repetition of the group scenes that had become familiar. When close to a village, children would run out as always, but a word or two from the stern guards would send them scampering back and away. The trails that they used were smaller, less traveled, and the pace slightly quicker. But they let their prisoner rest more frequently, though they seemed indifferent to the pain he suffered in his bare, raw feet. The new guards also removed the neck rope, which greatly decreased Garwood's discomfort. Every disjointed step, stumble or halt had meant a painful tug to the neck.

These four men were to remain his constant, silent escorts to his first South Vietnamese prison camp. They did not take rice from villagers, did not pound on hooches for food. They slept on the ground, two guards in hammocks while two men kept watch.

Different too, was the mode of travel. They kept to their little-traveled routes by daylight, camped as soon as night fell, ate regular meals cooked by the trail.

And they headed straight for the mountains. The group climbed swiftly out of the paddy district, through a sparsely farmed district of smallish forest trees, into real jungle, high jungle, protected from the sun by the triple canopy typical of Southeast Asia. Taller trees, under them small trees, and above the heads of the travelers the understory through which led small paths, apparently of ancient use. The land leech, about the size of a pencil, abounded in this forest, and dropped onto the passersby. Garwood's seminakedness made him an easy victim, while the guards tied rubber bands around their cuffs and would brush the leeches off their feet with a curious shuffle step. Garwood found if he stopped to knock or pluck or rub them off, more would get on him. It wasn't worth it, in spite of the discomfort.

Then the mountain proper. Arms tied loosely, the last day was an upward-bound ordeal. The first rocks appeared, the dirt underfoot was slippery, the exertion extreme. Rest stops were increased to one every half hour. The guards moved effortlessly, not even breathing hard, the sweatbands of their green field caps barely soaked through. It was close to dark but there was no camping on the trail that night. All at once a camp was there, like an inland town in the jungle foliage. It was all but invisible; there were three hooches, larger than village hooches and above the ground on stilts. The bamboo was still green and the huts seemed freshly made. There were no old women, no children, and the men had guns. For the first time he saw others in the same position as he. There were ARVN troops there, or at least men in ARVN fatigues, penned up behind a fence, gathering curious and blank-faced as the new arrival, still in his original white cotton BVDs and undershirt, stumbled in blinking his eyes, one arm still clearly swollen and disfigured. Blood clotted his head in a dark mat and his beard hung seedily around his chin and cheeks. His legs were crisscrossed with brown and red scratches, his nails broken, his lips crusted, his eyes crazed and sunken. And he seemed to sense, as he looked around him with the air of a strange animal in hostile surroundings, that he was the only North American at the camp.

It was the time near dusk, and under the jungle canopy the air darkened quickly, but unlike any villages he had seen, here there were no streams of smoke rising from fires. At least, he thought to himself, it is a rest. But rest of a different kind, he was to find. In the middle of the clearing was a raised bamboo box, itself on stilts. It looked like a cage, made of large bamboo poles about six inches apart, hand-lashed in position by some sort of reed or ropelike vine, and it flew through his mind that this thing looked exactly like the cages that circus acts kept their beasts in, only made of bamboo. There was no roof, no thatch, just more bamboo bars, and the floor the same. It was about six feet square. The guards who had brought him to the camp simply and blankly motioned him toward the cage, and made it clear he was to get inside. One of them swung open a door, which was fastened to the box with a chain and an old padlock.

He stepped up to the cage and crawled into it. He thought nothing, except that he was glad to stop, even here. And he was even gladder that a guard was unbinding his arms completely, for the first time since his capture twelve days before. Resting his back against the side of the cage was a luxury. The pain of his feet was forgotten for a moment. After a few minutes, a guard he had never seen before came over and thrust a loosely bundled handful of clothing through the bars. It was a pair of black shorts and a T-shirt made of fine woven cloth. He wearily put the garments on over his unspeakable shorts and shirt. He knew that the evening's chill would come, as it always had. He was used to his own smell. He didn't care; but the guard did, and the man began to gesture and shout, clearly shaking his head, and Garwood wearily began to take the new clothes off, only to hear fresh shouts and headshakes. He put the clothes back on again and the guard left in disgust.

He fell into the first real sleep in many days, and when he woke, it was to a guard's voice. The man brought a bowl of rice and some tea, and with the bowl came a foul fish sauce with an unmistakable odor, which permeated the area. Garwood's stomach heaved gently. He placed the bowl and the bamboo cup in one corner of his quarters and went back to sleep. Incurious, the guard walked off. When he woke again, shivering, it was morning, damp and biting, and the whole camp was in a fever of activity.

There seemed to be about ten or fifteen ARVN prisoners, and he noted with surprise that all had at least a part of their uniforms, and most of them had boots, regular issue, and some had tennis shoes. He felt the strange longing of a man without shoes for the comfort and protection that these men had—even looking mournfully at wooden sandals that some of the ARVNs wore. The guards wore pajamas of many colors—blue, black, gray—with long sleeves, and loose, long trousers, and all of them wore the famous Ho Chi Minh tire tread sandals, the straps made of innertube, cunningly held together without stitching or metal clips.

Garwood still could not muster an appetite for the cold rice and fish sauce. He sat, he shivered, he looked at the life around him. Two older men approached the cage a few minutes after he woke. He immediately identified them as officials, from their gray hair and the deference shown by the guards, who came to a semblance of attention when the two passed. But their dress was similar to the guards', only a shinier, newer-looking material, and each carried a sidearm with a web belt, and a satchel like a woman's purse was slung from one shoulder.

These officers gazed curiously at the new prisoner, talking to each other like tourists at a gallery, in an unnerving manner that excluded his human existence. They pointed to his wounded arm, and to his feet, but never met his eye. They might have been judging a piece of meat or a stand of vegetables for all the real contact they tried. He made no reaction but quietly watched their movements.

Whatever the reason for the official visit, two guards arrived at the cage about twenty minutes after the older men had strolled away. They told him to get out, and led him hobbling down a path to a stream that flowed by the camp. At the stream, there was a rock, a worn piece of cloth, and a sliver of soap, and the guards motioned for him to make use of these things.

He found the water ice-cold, and in spite of the filth of his body, he was reluctant to give up his body warmth on so cold a morning. He gingerly worked on his neck and arm, able to use only one hand to hold soap or cloth—but he was finally able to give a general cleaning to his whole body in the little stream. He took the chance to wash his foul underclothes but when he tried to use soap on them, the guards motioned him not to. He beat them and rubbed them on the rocks as best he could, and then laid them to dry, donning his new clothes. He realized suddenly that he was washing for the first time since the day on the beach.

The next morning, he awoke feeling uneasy and scared. He had become nauseated, his appetite had fled. There was a strong bitter taste in his mouth and his body was chased with bouts of high fever and chills. He was boiling and shivering, hot without sweating, cold without actually being cold—all his strength seemed to have fled. He lay helpless in the cage, unable to vomit, in a twilight world. The guards seemed to take no notice. His morning rice was left untouched and the guard grew angry when he refused to touch it. The guard took it away and brought back one of the camp officials who had visited the first day. This time, the official actually entered the cage, put his hand on Garwood's leg, and then left. A guard appeared with a rush mat, which the quaking Garwood curled up in. This infuriated the guard, who made violent motions until he realized that he was supposed to sleep on top of the mat, not huddle under it. The next seven days were spent half conscious, he noticed only that the tea suddenly had sugar in it, and after the third day, they gave him white tablets of fierce bitterness. He lamely took the tablets, one per day, but could not eat food. Just to look at it made him want to vomit.

Every day at noon, so regularly he began to prepare for it, he would be swept by the chills and the fever, the draining of strength, and then fall into an exhausted state that led to deep sleep. Then the attacks became lighter and he found himself able to take some rice. There was also some medical attention given to his arm, a dressing changed every third day. But when he came out of the weakness, his bowels were suddenly caught in the fire of dysentery. He could not move fast enough to get out of his cage, but squatted or lay miserably naked from the waist, defecating through the bottom bars, his body racked by convulsions. Between the gripings of his bowels he would drift away into deep sleeps that came closer and closer to complete unconsciousness—sleeps that did not refresh and were interrupted only by the nightmarish pains in his belly. After a few days of the dysentery he gave up trying to sit. He could no longer bother. The guards hardly came by, repelled by the stench and the filth everywhere. He looked forward only to the sleeps, during which he would dream narcotically, seeing himself at school, at home, the dreams so real and so fresh that they took the place of the waking time and the pain and the stink, which itself became the hallucination, and the dream the reality.

The guards seemed to show some alarm at the condition of their prisoner, whose fleshy body was fast fading to a skeletal wreck. They brought rice broth, a milky, starchy watery soup sweetened with sugar, and they put banana leaves on top of the cage to make a shade. They gave him other medication of a different taste. They tried to keep him awake to separate him from his precious sleeps, and one guard in particular, like the village boys, took pleasure in poking his buttocks and testicles with a sharp stick, laughing when the miserable Garwood jerked clumsily to wakefulness.

He didn't care that he seemed to be going down into unknown depths. All that seemed to matter were the blessed dreams, the feelings of freedom and peace, of being in another place. One day, as he lay in a stupor, he heard a strange echo. It was a correct-sounding voice, clear and sharp, in perfect English, saying, "Hello . . . hello . . . Wake up. You must wake up."

He took little notice. He did not know what it was but it was little stranger

31

than much of the traffic in the dusty corridors of his mind at that point. "Hello . . . Hello . . . Wake up. Get up. Get up." The voice persisted until he opened one eye to it.

He focused on a man who was with one of the camp officials. The man, whom Garwood had never seen before, was speaking and creating the sound of clear English words. The man was in his early fifties, or looked it, with thinning gray hair. He was thin and small in stature, and he wore the official garb for the higher-ups of the camp. Pistol, satchel. He had thick, horn-rimmed glasses and on his feet were plastic shoes or sandals, clearly factory-made. He was the first person in the camp Garwood had seen with glasses. It swirled through Garwood's mind that at last he had met the Gestapo of Vietnam, their version of intellectual torturer, the forcer of doctrine, deadlier than a man with mere guns and bullets.

"Get up. Sit up," the man commanded.

Garwood lurched to an elbow and flopped back down again. "Okay, okay," the man said, with a smile. "It's okay."

The English was perfect. "Well, Bobby, how are you feeling today? How *are* you today?" The diction was better than Garwood's own. He was shocked into awareness. How did this man know his nickname? Every card he possessed had Robert Russell Garwood on it. Why Bobby, the name he was known by among intimates, and not Bob, which was far more common? He felt a sliver of fear caused by this perfectly normal-sounding voice.

He looked at himself. Total disaster. Scrawny legs stained with feces, no trousers, sunken belly, the stench rising off him like a cloud, and this man was greeting him as if it were a pleasant day at church, in the spring weather, or a simple courtesy.

The English speaker wore a look of friendly indifference and mild interest, as if one was not a reeking fly-blown prisoner in a bamboo cage and the other not a Communist, not the enemy.

Garwood looked at him as if he were crazy. The man asked him again how he felt. Garwood whispered, "I feel ill. I feel weak." The man asked him how long he'd been ill. "Since the first day of capture," was the answer. He asked Garwood, "Can you get up, Bobby? Get up and move around."

Garwood shook his head, told him he was too weak. The man responded calmly, "That's because you sleep too much."

Garwood met this advice with unbelieving silence. Sleep was the only salvation. The man said something in Vietnamese to a companion, turned slowly to the supine Garwood and said, "Well, Bobby, you just keep on resting, and I'll see you later."

He watched him walk away and thought to himself, "Shit, where did that guy come from?" It seemed part of the more frequent hallucinations, dreams that took place between sleeping and waking. And it seemed perfectly sensible that someone would be talking perfect English in this strange camp where he was kept like a dying animal, not tortured but firmly locked in a bamboo cage.

That same afternoon, less than an hour later, a small group of ARVN

32

prisoners, an apparent work detail under the direction of two guards, gave other evidence of Garwood's special status. They cleaned under his cage, using rice-stalk brooms to scrape and sweep the doleful little piles of excrement, and sweep as well the bare earth for about ten feet around the cage. They avoided Garwood's eyes as they went about the seamy task.

In the evening, meat came with the rice. It was not exactly meat, but a piece of pork fat about the size of a domino, boiled to an unappetizing suet-gray and very salty. There was also a banana. He tried to eat it, and ate some of the rice, this time mercifully without sauce.

The visitor came again the next day, but didn't speak. Better food continued, but Garwood hardly noticed it. He remained in the world of half-wakened dreams, mixed reality and sickness for another week, but now there was some stability to the illness. There were ups and downs, times he could not move from his bed of bowel-inflamed pain, but some longer periods of near normalcy. In two weeks he had lost a large amount of body weight, and was never really to recover it in Vietnam. He grew used to it, and continued to survive never really feeling well, but well enough to function at some level. About ten days after the first visit from the English speaker, he found he was able to sit up, then stand in the cage. The state of his body disturbed him, and the advice of the English speaker came back to him. He was still sleeping the long, exhausted sleeps. A little bit at a time, his interest in the world revived, his bowels subsided. The English speaker seemed to have left the camp, or at least he no longer visited. Before the officer had left, he wrote out a list of English words, spelled out phonetically in Vietnamese characters, for the use of the guards, and they began to greet him with "Get up," or "Go," "Stop," or "No sleeping," "Time to eat," "Water," "WC," "Yes," "No," to which Garwood responded.

The life of the camp became clearer. Food was carried in by the guards in sacks—rice, sometimes a pig, or a chicken, or the square five-gallon cans filled with the fish sauce. Activity began at daybreak. First to rise were the guards. They would shuffle past Garwood's cage with a nose-wrinkle of disgust, washcloth in one hand, toothbrush in another. They seemed excitable and eager to talk in the morning. He soon discovered the strategic location of his own raised cage, which could be seen from any corner of the camp. It was never out of sight of some pair of eyes, and he suffered the discomfort of being watched in every movement.

After the guards washed and had their own breakfast, one guard would blow a whistle from the center of the camp, and the ARVNs would stumble quickly into a line, and each speaking a word (he presumed it was a name), would file down to the stream without talking. They would come back after a quarter of an hour accompanied by the ever-present guards. A big pot of rice, prepared in one of the guards' hooches, was lugged into the stockaded compound by one of the ARVNs, and each man would use some makeshift implement—tin can, banana leaf, bamboo cup—into which a trusty from the ranks of the prisoners doled out a dollop of rice. The ARVNs continued to police Garwood's cage and scrape away the evidence of his lingering illness.

Garwood tried to talk to them but the men shook their heads—they could not understand even the simplest English, not even "What's your name?" He had noticed some of them smoking cigarettes, and failed in his attempts to get one.

The guards, who seemed well supplied with cigarettes, would taunt him, offering a cigarette between the bars of the cage, then snatching it from reach of Garwood's fingers. Then they would light them, blow smoke in his face and laugh merrily.

Each time an American plane went overhead (still an almost daily occurrence) the guards would sight their weapons at it and pantomime shooting, then laugh at Garwood. One day an L-19 observer plane flew over low, throwing grenades out in an attempt to start movement below. But the guards merely watched, warily confident they and their camp could not be seen from above the thick umbrella of trees.

There were only two meals a day, and he found himself adapting fairly easily to that, and even to the fish sauce. The monotony of the rice was sometimes varied by a leafy cooked vegetable that looked like boiled spinach of large leaf, but tasted of nothing at all. There was never any meat, just bits of salted pork fat, no starch. Once a week, there would be a bit of sugar cane and once in a while a guard, passing by the cage, would toss a banana to Garwood and he would eat it hungrily, sometimes looking up to find two or three had gathered just for the sight of him eating it.

He was given a wash every other day, but no exercise. It was still impossible for him to contemplate his situation beyond the amazement he sometimes felt in just being alive. He figured he must have been more healthy than he had thought before capture, in spite of the fact that he had not done organized athletics in the Marine Corps, and he looked with some fondness, now, on the once-despised morning calisthenics that the fifty or so men of the Headquarters Battalion Motor Pool had grumbled of.

There was no one to talk to. He felt completely withdrawn. He had never understood why he was in Vietnam. He worried that the Marine Corps might not know where he had been when he disappeared, though there had been a slip of paper in his pocket, now long gone, his "trip-ticket," which he had intended to turn in to his dispatcher at the end of the day.

He had been told at the motor pool the day of his capture to report to G-2, the intelligence section, by 1600 hours (4:00 P.M.) for a run. But orders from G-2 were habitually oral. He had been responsible for entering the run to Marble Mountain in his trip ticket. The person who gave him the order would have to remember it precisely if he were to remember where Garwood had been sent.

That afternoon he had driven up to the G-2 headquarters, a building across from the headquarters of the Third Marine Division commander, Major General Lewis Walt, who had been a sometime passenger of Garwood's, and with whom he had joked and shared treats, like beer and steaks, at functions to which he had driven the general. A Marine captain came out of the building and asked Garwood, "Where the hell have you been?" He was angry and

Garwood told him he'd been at the motor pool. " Who released you to return to the motor pool?" the captain asked. "They've been looking all over for you. You're late." He said to report immediately to a recon unit just set up at Marble Mountain, pick up a lieutenant with recon, take him to the airstrip, drop him off at operations, report back to G-2. "Got that?"

All Garwood said was, "Yes sir." He didn't like the captain's bawling tone. He knew he should have stayed at G-2 until secured for the day, but wanted to get his gear ready for the R&R that was coming up in twelve days. It was a short-timer's malinger.

That captain would have to remember who Garwood was supposed to get and where he was supposed to have gone. How long might it have been before his absence was discovered? With dismay, Garwood knew it could be as long as the next morning. Things that day had been somewhat slack, particularly for a 4:00 P.M. run when he was due off duty at 6:00 P.M. Though he had been on normal twenty-four-hour standby, usually he was not called out after working hours more than twice a week. Would they send a patrol out? God only knew.

He cursed himself for taking the run. He had wanted it, too. G-2 was usually something soft.

He succumbed to the dictates of the time. He could not, he decided, make any plan until he knew more. It was all he could do to get through each day. He had never been questioned. His dog tags were still on his neck. No one had asked to see them. His clothes, identity card, wallet, all were still in the village where he had been captured, as far as he knew. He hung low.

It was about two weeks after that first contact—if such it could be termed, the cool and correct examination, the friendly words, the other-worldly nature of the thing—that the English-speaking official returned to the bamboo cage that had become Garwood's home. He appeared unchanged, wearing the "official" getup and the pistol and the dark-rimmed glasses, and unchanged also were the cheerful inquiries. But he added one, with some satisfaction: "Has your treatment improved at all, Bobby?" he asked. "How are you?"

The eyes were mild, but not friendly, not sympathetic. They were colder than the voice, and the voice itself had got a new edge to it, as if he now expected an answer, and a favorable one. These were the kind of nuances Garwood could easily pick up. All his life he had been extremely sensitive to what other people wanted—at the motor pool he found it natural to win favor and security with the little favors that a man with a vehicle and a general's flag can perform. Now he had the strong feeling that this man was not all that mysterious, that perhaps he wanted to be told that Bobby loved it here, that he'd been treated like a guest.

"Under the circumstances," said Garwood, sitting in his black pajamas on the rush mat and all too aware of the foul reek coming from the ground beneath, "I'm feeling better."

The man's eyes remained cold. Garwood had expected some reaction, at least, from the first English sentence he could remember uttering with a hope

35

of being understood. But there was none. "Well, Bobby," he said, "maybe now you can begin to see and appreciate the lenient and humanitarian policies of the South Vietnam National Front for Liberation towards prisoners." Garwood thought simply that if this was lenient and humanitarian, where were the tough spots? Back in the States, he thought, they'd treat a dog far, far better than they'd treated him.

2
A Father Figure

ROBERT RUSSELL GARWOOD's father, Jack Russell Garwood, is not an arresting figure. True, he has a limp, the result of a youthful motorcycle accident, true he has a large pot belly, myopic eyes and a cigarette dangling from the side of his mouth. But he is small and graceless, a hard little man, a silent man filled with the impatience of long frustration and a failed, poverty-riddled life. Personal misfortune and time have not washed the harshness out of him.

Jack Garwood, Sr., survives "by the third." It simply means that if all has gone well in the main post office, five miles away across the pure corn fields at Greensburg, Indiana (about forty-five miles southeast of Indianapolis), the Social Security check will arrive at his trailer more or less on time—the third of the month—and he can add the sum to the paltry salary his enormous present wife, Helen Raines Garwood, earns as a cook at a Greensburg nursing home.

Yet there is a certain jaunty "grandeeship" to the father of all the Garwoods, like the air of a self-styled pirate reduced to captaining one lifeboat and dressing in rags, but still—there is always the chance of plunder. Ideas for a big deal still swim in his mind and shine out of the dim little eyes through the stream of cigarette smoke. Like his son, he is slim-hipped despite his big belly, fond of Navy-type jeans and a broad black belt, which trusslike seems to support his stretched gut. His chin disappears into his wide neck in close furrows.

The trailer is in the constant state of disorder produced when women work and men stay home in a society where men would be shamed to be seen picking up or washing dishes or sweeping, or even making up the stale beds they had lain in while their wives went off to work. The trailer squats sullenly beside

37

astoundingly straight tracks that ream off into the distant horizon like rifle sights.

Jack's domestic arrangements are harried. He lives with Helen, a kind and self-conscious woman who reacts so violently to any outside threat that she seems hysterical to strangers. She is like a young girl entrapped in a three-hundred-pound, fifty-four-year-old body, maddeningly demanding, submissive and seemingly coy in turns. He deals with her moods by reacting to her, as he does all women, the way he might respond to a dog that can and sometimes will bite.

But there are frequent visits from the other children, who have continued to circle the Garwood compound at Adams either from inertia or from a sense of curiosity about their father. Jack Jr. lives within earshot, across the railroad tracks. Once married, he has lived with girlfriends and has a steady job at the nearby Federal-Mogul bearing plant.

Jack Jr. is acknowledged by family members to be the "best of the bunch" among the males, and exhibits a profile that the rest would envy. Never in trouble with the law, not involved with drugs, not out of work. Among the daughters, Sharon Garwood Messenger is considered the standout. The first daughter of Helen Raines, she is softening into a model of her broad-beamed mother, fighting a weight problem, and has established herself as a church-woman, a good mother. She and her husband, Ken, who was one of the youths young Bobby Garwood grew up with, are considered the model couple by the others.

Less can be said about Don Garwood, Bobby's younger full brother, and his only full sibling, a man who served time in prison for a robbery he claims he had nothing to do with, but during which he was shot in the foot. The rest of the Garwoods have a grudging respect for Don's ability to get a job any time he wants one and their comments about him are tinged with fear and a little annoyance. He is accused of "always having his hand out." He lives in Indianapolis and has two children.

Bobby is the oldest, next comes Don, then Sharon, Jack Jr., Steve—a huge brute of a boy, rough-tongued, ribald, and sometimes out of work, whom Bobby describes as lazy. His sister, Linda, her dime-store prettiness fading, is sly and filled with intrigues, pouty and impatient of the baby she has produced. She married Keith, a young Marine she met while Bobby Garwood was on trial at Camp Lejeune. Keith, with Jack Jr.'s help, has work at the Mogul ballbearing plant. Linda, Bobby's "pet," was "always wild, always wanting to party," according to Bobby. "She hasn't sowed her wild oats yet." The youngest sibling, Geoffrey, was in trouble for a break-in in the fall of 1982 according to Bobby Garwood. He is also unemployed at eighteen, lives with his parents at the trailer, is bitterly resented by the rest of the Garwood bunch for the way his father spoils him. "He's got a car, he's got everything he wants, and all he has to do is ask Dad," Garwood says sourly. "I didn't have no car."

If there is one thing in life that brings them all together (besides sex) it is automobiles. Most of Jack Sr.'s ideas revolve around them, and in the eyes of his children he is a regular wizard in the used car department. Whatever the bunch lacks in worldly goods, they do not lack cars (nor do they lack guns, which occupy a hallowed place on the plywood fascia paneling of the trailer, hanging on a wooden rack like some sort of male shrine).

There are cars everywhere around the trailer—cars, engines, transmissions. Jack Sr., who was a garageman in some former career, boasts that he has never spent over two hundred dollars on "one of the things" in his life, keeps a stable of the dead and wounded so that the living can continue to limp forward. He and Helen drive a huge and gas-intensive station wagon of the "Vistacruiser" type of ten years ago, and though breakdowns are frequent, they are not serious.

The cars around the trailer are other people, in fact. Their conditions and hopes occupy the center stage in the livelier conversations of the Garwood men, a constant source of pain, amusement, joy, banter, and opinion. It would be no exaggeration to say that the members of the Garwood clan know many more facts about the V-8 engine than they know about women in general, more perhaps than about the women they live with; certainly, on the surface of it, the cars seem much more interesting.

Jack Sr., for instance, can remember exactly the configuration of the Indian motorcycle he was driving when in 1939 he had a wreck that crippled him. He almost died at the Greensburg Hospital, and all because of the twin gas tanks slung over the cycle's main beam between his knees, which made him lean down to switch from one tank to the other—the fatal moment of inattention, a tree, and the future was different.

All he can remember about Bobby and Don, though, is that they were "pretty normal kids."

What is normal? To have one child an ex-con, none of the rest graduating from high school, some of them marrying early, marrying pregnant brides or being pregnant brides themselves, at times out of work, out of money, out of luck, and surprisingly, out of tune with the community in which they live.

That profound out-of-tuneness is what makes the chaotic Garwood family such a standout in a tiny Middle Western community like Adams. It may be true that every town has a family like them, but still that is a great uniqueness; perhaps they describe it best when they joke about being "white trash," the term Bobby Garwood uses frequently to describe their poverty and arrogance, and the pity of it all. In Garwoodian terms it is a brave statement, the opposite of their usual racist machismo, but then the inevitable sly reasons for it crop up.

It would be impossible to shove the Garwoods into some neat societal box, and searching the ranks of Robert Coles' raw Appalachians or lonely brought-North blacks is fruitless. The Garwoods are a singular family, sharing with others only two things—poverty, and a peculiarly American rootlessness and confusion.

What makes them different? It is perhaps their mobility, symbolized by the cars they all worship and even the least of the males owns, their untiedness to the land, though they labor like heavy birds to get far away only to return to Adams or Indianapolis. It is also their ability to adapt and survive unmolested (except occasionally by the law). The poor white farmer is tied to his hillside, his share, his acreage, his living, and the poor black likewise, poor urban people are tied to their neighborhoods, or perhaps fenced in by their lack of mobility and their ignorance. The Garwoods have only small shares of these limiting characteristics. Though they are not well read, they watch, they watch television craftily and they assimilate the offerings there into desires and an image of the world. In that image, they are not exactly victims, but are among the totally deserving poor. When Jack Garwood, Sr., tells how he didn't have time to take care of the two boys, and frequently left them with his mother, he recalls with heavy sighs "workin' two jobs" and his son insists that the father worked hard all his life to "keep food on the table"; yet there is not the slightest trace of this energy left in the man of sixty-two, though Garwood says in the last year or two, his father strove successfully to lose about fifty pounds.

Of the many visions of the family available to the legal team assembled to defend Bobby Garwood against court-martial charges, the one chosen is most at odds with the present reality. It was carefully elicited from the psychiatrists in court that Jack Sr. was an overbearing and brutally suppressive father, a drunkard, and that young Bob's life was some kind of Dickensian hell. In fact, the Garwoods agree that their father, whatever his faults, was drunk only once or twice in his life, at New Year's parties, and that his proudest boast now is that he was always able to keep food available for them.

It made Jack Garwood furious, more furious than the accusations and the slurs on his son's honor, his son's betrayal of the nation, to hear it said, and allowed to be repeated, and even reinforced by his son's silence on the subject, that at times during the youth of the two senior Garwood boys, Don and Bobby, they had to receive food as charity. "The hinges on the icebox were always hot in my house," he said with rueful virtue. The slander made him begin to mistrust even television.

Jack Sr. says he had little time for the young Bobby Garwood while he was growing up, and when the young man reached some maturity, the father found him hard-headed and rebellious. It is one consistent thread to Bobby Garwood's character that it has always been reactive rather than active; a character that remains more or less inert, or is guided by like spirits until there is something to kick against.

The effect on the father was one of shock. A man who has always felt virtuous, if not successful, he thought his son owed him complete obedience and he remains to this day completely nonplused by Bobby Garwood's "hard-headed" behavior as a rather ordinary petty rebel. The result is ambivalence. In the months after the court-martial, Jack Sr. was heard to grumble to visitors that he'd had a wish that Bobby wouldn't visit so often back to the trailer and Adams, because of all the trouble and commotion and the inevitable gathering of the "old gang," including the rest of his children, which put a strain on Helen and himself.

40

But then he will lapse into a kind of mannered sentimentality, hawking his parenthood like some disheveled mother and telling Bobby in lament that he never got to see him alone during the Christmas of 1980. Bobby had brought his latest girlfriend to meet the family, always a bad move. Garwood's parents, she said, "treated me like a snotty society bitch . . ."

3
Mr. Ho

THE ENGLISH-SPEAKING Oriental man was still standing outside Garwood's cage, smiling.

Garwood stared at him stupidly. He had never heard of this South Vietnam National Front the man spoke of. He had never been exposed to the Communist line or propaganda of any sort before, and amazingly, his Marine training had included no course of instruction in how to deal with such methods except the bare and stark statements of the code of conduct (a copy of the code follows the Epilogue).

"Bobby, you sleep too much," he continued. "You sleep too much and you must learn how to live here in the jungle. You do not move around enough. We lack many things here in the jungle. Food, clothing, shelter. But the forest supplies us with shelter. I know that conditions here are very hard for you. It is not what you are used to. But we, the Vietnamese who were born and grew up in this country, are forced to live in the jungle and the forest merely because of U.S. imperialist invasion of our country.

"But the Vietnamese people, headed by the South Vietnam Front for Liberation, are determined at any cost, at any sacrifice to fight and drive U.S. aggressors out of their country." Garwood began to see that the man's English, after all, might only be rote phrases memorized. He went on, "You were sent here as cannon fodder of the U.S. imperialist warmongers and U.S. capitalists to kill the Vietnamese people, destroy their homeland and even to shed your own blood for them. . . . The Vietnamese people have a history of fighting aggression for over four thousand years . . . the Vietnamese soil has been greatly enriched by the blood of aggressors, and now our soil is being more enriched by the blood of the American aggressor."

The man simply rattled off this address while Garwood looked on in amazement. Not only did he not understand half of what was said, the things he did understand were completely wrong. Yet the man spoke as if he expected his listener to fully understand what he was saying, as if the two men were on the same wavelength.

"My name is Mr. Ho. I am a cadre of the South Vietnam National Front for Liberation. I live in Da Nang City. My family is well known in Da Nang. I went to school in England and France, studying English and history, and have taught in the Da Nang schools and colleges, subjects of English and American history. Therefore I will conduct some classes in Vietnamese and American history to help you to understand why you are where you are today. Anything you don't understand, feel free to ask me."

Garwood suddenly had the absurd vision of going to class here in the camp. He looked around as if to find the comforting brick walls and painted classrooms of Arsenal Tech in Indianapolis. And then he thought with glowing resentment, "This guy is going to teach me about America? This guy is going to teach me American history? This guy is ignorant as shit. I'm not going to let him tell me about my own country."

"Do you need anything?" Mr. Ho then asked. Garwood was able to have his first real chuckle of the experience. "Well, I would like my rights according to the Geneva agreements," he said simply and straightforwardly, enunciating the words slowly. He had at least heard of that.

Ho's face creased and flushed darkly. "First of all," he shot back with an angry motion of one hand, "you must understand that we do not recognize the Geneva agreements. We are not bound by any law, simply because U.S. aggressors invaded our country in an undeclared aggression against our people and homeland. Therefore *you* are not considered a prisoner of war, and cannot enjoy the international policy as a prisoner of war, but fall under the policy of a criminal of war. Criminals of war cannot expect anything because criminals of war are criminals who plunder, murder, rape, destroy maliciously and without any feeling whatsoever. Therefore any treatment that criminals of war receive other than death is considered to be lenient and humanitarian."

Ho went on: "What religion are you?"

Garwood said, "Methodist."

"You are taught in your religion from your Bible, 'an eye for an eye.' From the reports we have received, it is a pure and simple fact you, yourself, have murdered our people." Garwood thought immediately of the bloody face, the shot from the pistol, the boy on the beach. "You came to our country unwelcome. Therefore you are trespassing. You invaded our homes, and when our children confronted you, you maliciously murdered a child and attempted to murder another one before you were stopped by the people's forces."

Ho was clearly very angry. "By rights, under your law, an eye for an eye, we should have, justly, taken your life that very instant. But instead, we let you live and hope that you would realize what you had done and beg for repentance and forgiveness from the Vietnamese people."

It was a speech, with variations, which Garwood was to hear, out of various mouths but with whole phrases intact, for many years to come. This first time, it shocked him.

For the first time, he realized that his action in taking out his .45, a purely instinctive reaction to the threat posed by the ring of riflemen at the fishing village, had been completely twisted in a cartoon manner. It was as if something ridiculous had become the truth.

"So you see," Ho said with heavy finality. "You have no right to demand anything of the Vietnamese people. We have let you live, but for how long will depend solely upon your progress in understanding and acknowledging what is U.S. imperialism and why we great, heroic Vietnamese people have been fighting heroically and courageously against invaders for over four thousand years. And when you truly repent, and beg forgiveness, for your crimes against the Vietnamese people, and if you are progressing and truly repent, then the Vietnamese people, because of their lenient and humanitarian nature, have no alternative but to return you to your people and country."

And he said, "If you truly want to return to your country and your people, you will strive hard to be a progressive American, and cease being cannon fodder for the U.S. capitalist warmongers."

"Mr." Ho, as he preferred to be called, had leveled a barrage of words at Garwood, saving the best for last: "It's so easy to die here in the jungle. It takes a lot of strong will and determination to live.

"If you die here in the jungle, you will only serve to enrich the soil as so many hundreds of thousands have done in the past."

He listened. It was more like a threat. Garwood thought, This guy means no bullshit. If you have the wrong attitude, they'll just take you out and put a bullet in your head.

He was too frightened to say anything. It would be too easy to say the wrong thing, he thought. It came across loud and clear, he thought, that he was not going to mention any Geneva agreements again. That had really set Mr. Ho off.

The lesson was apparently over, and Ho, leaving Garwood to his thoughts, turned without a word of good-bye and walked back toward the kitchen, talking in Vietnamese to another official who had observed the "history lesson."

Other results of the lecture came the same day. It was not his regular day to wash, but that afternoon a guard came by and motioned him out of the cage. His first reaction was, "Oh, damn. They're going to shoot me now. I've insulted this bastard and they're going to shoot me . . ." The guard merely led him to the washing rock by the stream and motioned him to wash, which he did with the relief that only those under threat of execution can know. He noticed that the swelling on his right arm was reduced considerably, though small amounts of fluid and pus were still in the two arm wounds. The head wound from the guard's rifle butt seemed to be scabbing over nicely. Back at the cage, he noticed that it had been swept and the grounds tended, and there was a new rush mat to lie on. He got resignedly into the cage and found a bamboo cup of condensed milk. It was hot. There was also a coconut bowl containing white rice, no sauce, with brown sugar on it. It was the best meal he had eaten since his capture.

And after the meal, one of the guards, not the one who had made a practice of tormenting him with cigarettes, delivered another special gift.

It was a French-made Ruby Queen cigarette, and it tasted good but smelled like perfume. He smoked it very carefully, accepting a light from the guard.

The night passed, about his twentieth in captivity, without incident. Come morning, the guard motioned him from the cage early. He took him to a freshly made structure, resembling a lean-to of fresh bamboo, under which there was a small wooden table. Somehow it reminded Garwood of an American picnic table. On it were a pot of tea, a tin cup, some loose cut tobacco and some cigarette papers, and a kerosene lamp, small and low, and it was lit.

The guard beckoned him to sit down on the bench beside the table. He had sat there for about ten minutes, not daring to touch anything, when two men, Mr. Ho and the camp official who usually attended with him, came under the little structure. The guard beckoned him to stand up. Garwood stood. He motioned him down, spoke quickly to the guard and the guard left.

"Good morning," Ho said, "how are you feeling this morning?"

"A little better."

"You have to learn to take care of your health as best you can," he said. He sat across from Garwood, the camp official beside him.

Garwood had a feeling he knew what was coming. But he had no idea what was expected of him. Progressive? How to become a "progressive American"? He had already ceased being "cannon fodder for the warmongers" and was worrying mightily how to avoid becoming cannon fodder for the other side. The entire setup puzzled and baffled him. As far as the war went, he knew as little as—no, even less than—the lowliest grunt who had been in the field. He had worked hard to find the softest, safest job he could and he was the envy of most of his fighting colleagues for having it.

Ho snapped him out of his reverie by laying three or four pieces of paper on the table. Garwood had no idea what these documents were, but Ho did not simply throw them down. He laid them importantly, almost reverently, on the surface. He adjusted his glasses fussily, picked up one of them and began to speak. "You being in the military, I am sure are well accustomed to following rules and regulations. Therefore it will be nothing new to you that we have drawn up rules and regulations that you will be required to abide by and obey in this camp. How well you abide by and obey these rules and regulations will have great determination upon your status as to whether you are progressive or nonprogressive." He leaned forward fixedly. "Also, it will be determined how lenient and how humane our treatment will be to you."

He commenced reading: "Number one, you will stand at attention or sit at attention when any member of the camp, be it cadre or guards of the SVNFL, approaches. Number two, before leaving your quarters for anything, you must

45

first seek permission from the guard on duty, both leaving and entering. Number three, absolutely prohibited to make any contact, verbal or otherwise, with any or all of the other prisoners in the camp. Number four, you must maintain oral hygiene twice a week."

Garwood, who had had neither the equipment nor the chance to brush his teeth since his capture, asked, "What's it mean, oral hygiene?"

Ho said, "You must wash your body and your clothes at least twice a week." Garwood thought with some satisfaction, "I must have been getting to him after all . . ."

"Number five," continued Ho, "you must use WC for all body waste. Number six, never try or make any attempt to escape. Number seven, cannot keep any kind of food in living quarters. Have to eat all rations you are given. Number eight, in case of air raid, must follow guard's instructions and directions. Number nine, you must try hard to learn Vietnamese customs and language. Number ten, no singing of U.S. imperialist songs."

He listened silently as Ho asked with his chill politeness if the prisoner had any questions. "What are U.S. imperialist songs?" Garwood asked.

Ho said, "All U.S. songs are of a capitalistic nature. Exploitation of the masses. Therefore they are prohibited."

"Can I whistle?"

"I am not here to play games with you. If you want to sing, or like to sing, I am sure that the guards will be more than happy to teach you some progressive revolutionary songs."

He thought to himself, progressive revolutionary songs, oh, shit, what if I sing "Mary Had a Little Lamb," and asked, "Are there any progressive American revolutionary songs?"

Ho answered, "Oh, yes," he said, "Que Sera, Sera," he motioned grandly. "This is a song I often teach to my Vietnamese students. Do you know this song?"

He nodded. "Yes, I know the song."

"Yes," continued Ho. "There is another, 'John Brown's Body Lies a-Moldering in the Grave.'"

The camp official, name yet unknown to Garwood, then whispered something to Ho. Ho turned again. "And what songs were you singing on your way to the camp? It has been reported to me that you sang quite often."

"'Tom Dooley,'" Garwood told him. "It's an American folk song."

"Tell me the words of this song," Ho demanded.

"Hang down your head, Tom Dooley," Garwood said, "Hang down your head and cry, Hang down your head Tom Dooley, poor boy you're going to die. . ."

"This song is typical of the American culture," Ho said when Garwood had recited all the verses of the Dooley ballad, "sex and violence. What was the other song you sang coming to the camp?"

"'Sad Movies,'" Garwood said, and when he had recited the words, Ho said, "The only songs you know are of sex. Don't you see? This is U.S. capitalists' way of introducing sex and violence so that your mind is preoccupied and that you

46

are totally unaware of the political situation in the United States."

Garwood was profoundly aware that he had never run into a person of Ho's particular stamp of mind before.

But the time of introductions and banter was over. "What is your full name?" Ho asked.

"Robert Russell Garwood."

"What branch of the service are you in?"

"The United States Marine Corps."

"What is your rank?"

"Private."

After this answer Ho took on a kindly look: "You must understand that any and all questions that we ask you, we already know the answers to. We only want to see just how progressive and what is your attitude, to see if you are grateful that we have let you live."

He pushed the tin teacup across. It had been filled by the other official, with a smile, and the other official also rolled a curious cone-shaped cigarette and handed it to him.

Garwood looked on blankly. He had been telling the truth. How can you be "progressive" about your rank?

After Garwood had taken a few sips of tea and a puff on the cigarette, which made him long for the luxury of a Ruby Queen, Ho leaned forward and asked pointedly, "Now, what was your rank?"

"I said private."

"Private what?"

"Private, E-one."

"Enlisted, you are enlisted?"

"Yes, enlisted one. E-one."

"Oh, you are enlisted number one. You are sergeant?"

"No. I am a private."

"Private what?"

"Private E-one."

"You are private sergeant?"

"I am not a sergeant."

"You are an officer?"

"I am not an officer."

Ho picked up his papers with a quick, impatient movement. His eyes rose craftily up to the prisoner's level. "According to the report, when you were captured, you were driving a new jeep, you had on new uniform. You had new boots. You had a new pistol. And you are a private? I was not born yesterday."

Garwood looked at him hopelessly. What the fuck am I supposed to say, he thought. It still had not dawned on him that Ho was utterly convinced he was an officer.

"Is there a difference between enlisted and officers?" Ho asked.

"Yes."

"Are their uniforms different?"

47

"No."

"You are lying," Ho said sadly. "I know for a fact they are different."

"I'm sorry," Garwood said, "you must have seen some different uniforms than I have."

"It is not important. I am just trying to find out if you are being honest with us. If you truly appreciate our lenient humanitarian policy shown towards you." Ho and the other official talked for a few minutes. Garwood smoked quietly.

"What is your unit?"

Garwood did not answer. He did not know whether such an answer was allowed under the code of conduct, which he knew only in general to prohibit giving information other than name, rank, serial number.

"What is your unit?"

"I'm a driver," Garwood answered, hoping this would fulfill both the code and his desire to please.

"You are a driver? What is G-2?"

Immediately, it all clicked in his mind. I see where this fucker's coming from now, he thought in a mild panic. They probably think I'm Intelligence Corps. G-2 is Intelligence Corps. This means they found the trip ticket with G-2 on it. And it is going to be impossible for me to explain that I'm not really G-2, just a driver for it, and how the hell do they know so much anyway?

His consternation must have showed. Ho had a wide and complacent grin. He thinks he's got me now, Garwood thought.

He made no answer to the question. Ho continued, "You are being very obstinate. Any information or news we could get from you or that you know could be of no value to us. You see, we know everything about you. Already we know everything about you. I'm going to give you the rest of the day to think about my question and I hope for your sake and well-being you will be more cooperative tomorrow. We have nothing to lose, you have everything. It is your life, not ours.

"You may go back now." He stood up. He said something to the guard and Garwood went back to his cage. What the hell can I do now, he thought—they evidently have their mind made up. They're convinced I'm with some intelligence outfit, and even if I did tell them the truth, they'd never believe me anyhow.

What if he said nothing? What if he deliberately lied in such a way that later it would be clear he was trying to deceive, but that Ho would be satisfied and the execution staved off. What if he was to simply assemble in his mind a storehouse. A saleable store of little bits. Words, phrases, disconnected information, perhaps about the Mighty-Mite, perhaps about boots, holsters, the life of the motor pool. With this he would have an almost endless store of answers that would seem to be giving. But there would be follow-up questions. Perhaps then he could refuse to answer, remain silent at least. If asked where he lived, he would say California, not Indiana. He had lived in California, at Camp Pendleton. If asked about his parents, he would say that his parents were both dead and that his family was really wealthy. Perhaps there could be some ransom deal. If he didn't give anything, he was afraid conditions would go back to the way they were, or even worse, to the dysentery, the malaria, the unconscious wavering near total weakness.

That night he thought in his cage, and for the first time he decided that time was the only hope. He would try to maintain his health. He would learn to wait. He would try to kill time, the hours and days, buying it by whatever means in the sure knowledge that the war would be over. It wasn't even called a war, he thought hopefully, it was called a conflict, a police action, and it was just beginning. He hadn't even really been a soldier, just a driver.

But how to keep from going crazy? There could be no relaxation of his mental guard. He must remember what he had told Ho, what he hadn't told him. Meanwhile he was in a complete quandary about time. The Viet Cong—if this indeed was what these people were—had no amusements as he knew them. He had never seen them reading, loafing, dating, or hanging out. There were no bars, there was no drinking for that matter. Yet at times they were clearly off duty, when they would appear half-dressed. They whittled things—spoons, ladles, chopsticks, and other small objects—from bamboo with homemade hunting knives, wicked-looking things as much as eight inches long in the blade. Or they would endlessly weave baskets, which were used for every task, carrying supplies, shifting dirt—there were no wheelbarrows or other devices of modern man at the camp. These baskets, too, were of bamboo, like the punji stakes they also manufactured. These were very sharp slivers and stakes of bamboo, which were used both for war and for hunting. They were everywhere around the camp, mute warnings not to go off the trail. The traps were cunningly arranged. One would send the three-foot lance of a sharpened stake whizzing out about belly level when a branch was touched. Another trap was a three-foot pit thickly clustered with sharpened stakes and hidden with a false cover so lifelike that there could be no instant to draw back. Only when they were freshly built could they be noticed. Even an animal would be seriously wounded because the stakes were so sharp and only three inches from one another. The guards hunted a type of deer, which seemed to him larger than the variety seen in Indiana, and wild pigs, monkeys—all of which they ate—but though he would see the hunting parties bringing game into camp and could smell the cooking of it, the meat never seemed to trickle down to his level of society.

It was the isolation he found hardest to bear. When he thought of it, it was like a blank wall stretching in front of him to two horizons, puzzling and blinding. He got used to it quickly on one level. He would talk to himself, he would find within himself an observer, another voice talking to himself. Shit Garwood, why didn't you refuse the run? You didn't refuse the run because you couldn't risk a write-up with only twelve days to go before the R&R. Any write-up could have messed things up.

Mr. Ho was waiting in the lean-to the next day. The official was with him, and a third person, who Ho politely introduced as "One of my English students from Da Nang—who has just come over to the side of the revolution."

He was about twenty-one, thin, very well-dressed, wearing a ring and a watch. Good clothes, plastic shoes like Ho's, and other signs showed that he was not a peasant but perhaps the son of an official or a shop owner. He sat in a leisurely way, almost slouched, observing casually.

"Good morning, Bobby, how are you today?" Ho half-asked in greeting. He always seemed bright and cheerful at the beginning, but when he talked to the official in Vietnamese, his tone changed completely—he grew stern, authoritative. The man had parts, and he wasn't afraid to show them.

After the preliminaries, Ho asked, "Have you pondered in your mind what we discussed yesterday and have you come to a decision?"

"Yes. But first I would like to ask you some questions."

Ho's eyes jerked up. His hand flew to his dark-rimmed glasses and he steadied them, leveling a withering glance at Garwood over them.

"All right. I will be fair about this. You may ask a question."

"What are my rights and do I have any rights as far as answering any questions?" Garwood asked.

"Yes. You have the right to answer the questions, to disregard the questions, or to be silent. We understand that you have been schooled and it has been implanted in your brain and your way of thinking capitalistic ideals, and we cannot expect you to understand us overnight. But, again, you must show some kind of willingness in trying to understand the Vietnamese people, the struggle, Vietnamese history and why we are fighting against U.S. imperialism. Because if you do not take any interest in trying to understand us, that only tells us, the Vietnamese people, that you have no wish to be a progressive American and have resolved yourself only for the purpose of being cannon fodder and serving the interests of the lackeys of the U.S. war machine."

Garwood thought, What the hell is he saying—war machine and lackey? I'm just a United States Marine, a private to boot, and I only want to get my ass home, get married—get a job.

After his filibuster, Ho acted patient.

"Today, we will start afresh. First, your full name is Robert Russell Garwood."

"Yes."

"You are a member of the United States Marine Corps?"

"Yes."

"You are with the Third Marine Division."

Garwood said, "Yes," but thought, shit, that's the only damn division in Vietnam.

"You came from Okinawa?"

"Yes." Garwood thought, Shit, how'd he know that? Then he realized the Third Marine Division had been stationed in Okinawa since the Second World War.

"How many men are there in the Third Marine Division?"

"I don't know."

50

"You don't know? That's hard to believe. You really expect me to believe you do not know how many men there are in your unit?"

"No, I don't know."

"Why don't you know?"

"First of all I'm a private, and I don't know that information. In the second place, I was never real interested. I didn't care."

"You still insist that you are a private?"

"Yes."

"Private what?"

Garwood rolled his eyes. "I'm a private in the United States Marine Corps."

Ho lowered his voice. "Are you married?"

"Yes." He thought: Here goes, it's the old family man thing. You tell the guy with a gun you've got a family . . .

"Do you have any children?"

"No."

"What is your wife's profession?"

"She doesn't do anything at all."

"What is your wife's name?"

"Linda Sutton." Forgive me, Linda, from the sixth grade at Indianapolis, for the notes we passed and the walks home from school.

Ho asked about Garwood's parents.

"They are both dead."

"What was your father's profession?"

"My father owned a printing company."

"How many workers did your father have working for him?"

"About two, maybe three hundred."

Ho talked excitedly to the other official, who took on a look of disgust, as if he had seen a reptile.

"So," said Ho, "you are of the bourgeoisie class?"

"What class?"

"Your family is rich?"

"No, not rich, but not poor."

"But your father has two or three hundred people working for him; in my country we would consider him a landlord. He had over two hundred, he exploited the proletariat. The masses. Your father was a capitalist."

"I never thought of it that way."

"No," Ho said, with kindness in the tone, "because you are blinded by the capitalist ideas of your father and money."

Garwood realized he was getting into deep water. His intention had been to paint himself as a ransomable son of a rich family. Instead, Ho regarded him as the quintessence of the enemy.

"Your father has been responsible for many sufferings," Ho said sternly. "People like your father in Vietnam will soon be ultimately wiped out and the proletariat masses will enjoy freedom to work for themselves, for the good of the country, not for the good of one individual.

51

"How many brothers and sisters have you?"

"Only one sister."

"If your father and mother have died, who does the money go to?"

"It was to be equally shared, fifty-fifty, between me and my sister."

"Whose money is that?" Ho said with a sharp motion of his finger.

"It belonged to my father."

"Wrong. It belongs to the people."

Garwood said nothing. His mind was going a mile a minute trying to invent another turn to get Ho's chariot off this road.

"What do your friends call you back home—Robert, Bob, or Bobby?"

"Most of my friends know me as Bobby."

"Well, Bobby, how would you like to write a letter to your friends back home so that they will not be caught up in the same situation as you are now, in the quagmire of Vietnam. You can help save your friends' lives by making them understand that to serve as cannon fodder of the U.S. government only and ultimately leads to a horrible and dishonorable death on the faraway shores of Vietnam."

"I can't write. My arm isn't right yet. It's too swollen."

"No problem," said Ho with a smile. "I just happen to have a draft with me." Like a magician before children he pulled out a sheet of fresh white paper, neatly typed. Garwood looked around for the typewriter. It seemed more than strange to see a typed page in the middle of the prehistoric camp.

Ho shoved it across the table, where it skidded to rest like a white leaf, perfect and from another world. "Fellow Soldiers Appeal," it read. He noted the type was in blue ink: his favorite color. The first thing that struck him was the "soldier."

I ain't no soldier, he thought. I'm a Marine. He read through it with increasing amazement. He read over it and looked up. Ho had a big grin on his face, as if this was his masterpiece, a stroke so brilliant that anyone would be humbled by it.

"I'm sorry, I can't sign this," Garwood said.

Ho looked upset—or acted the part. "Why not!" he said.

"Two reasons why not. The first one being it's against the code of conduct, secondly, I don't believe what's written here. These are not my beliefs."

"Code of conduct!" Ho spat. "I know all about your code of conduct. But you see, your code of conduct does not and cannot apply here. Let me remind you once again, you are not considered to be a prisoner of war. We do not recognize Geneva Accords. Geneva Accords do not apply to Vietnam. Simply because United States invaded Vietnam in an undeclared war of destruction . . ."

Ho stopped and looked at Garwood. "The United States . . . If I was to come to the United States, come to your home, kill your father, rape and murder your mother and sister, burn your house down. Would you get angry?"

"Yes."

"That is exactly what the United States has done in Vietnam. You have come into our homeland, you have raped our mothers and our sisters. You have killed our fathers. You have burned down our homes, you have destroyed our lands with bombs and shells so we cannot plant our rice crops freely. You have come into my home and driven me to live in the mountains like an animal. Why, just ask yourself? What are you doing so many thousands of miles from your home, here in Vietnam? What has Vietnam done to the United States? Vietnam did not come to the United States. You came here. Uninvited."

Nothing Ho said was of the least comfort to Garwood. Trying to accommodate, he had only made the man more furious.

"You, personally, have the blood of the Vietnamese people on your hands. In United States, in your own country, if you had murdered someone, what would be the penalty?"

"Life in prison or execution," Garwood said reluctantly.

"Not only are you guilty of murder, you are an accessory to all the atrocities and crimes the U.S. has brought to our country. You are part of that machine. The U.S. government and its warmongers have committed crimes and atrocities far more atrocious than those of Nuremberg or the Nazis of World War II. Yet you expect to be treated fairly and according to the Geneva Agreements? It is completely absurd and ridiculous that you would even make such a suggestion or demand.

"But, we understand that they have pulled the wool over your eyes," Ho smiled at this lively turn of phrase, "and blinded you. But we, the Vietnamese people, believe that everyone is allowed at least one mistake. And therefore we will help to re-educate you so that one day you can return to the proletariat class of your country with your head held high."

Garwood was beginning to get a glimmer. He was really a teacher. Almost an evangelist. He hadn't asked any real questions of military value. For instance, while he knew little of tactical value, Garwood knew exactly where the intelligence command for the whole First Corps was located, and the names of most of the top officers. He had learned their names, he'd had to, just to know who to pick up and who to smile at. He knew there was a meeting planned in October in Da Nang. General William Westmoreland would be there, and the location was to be First Corps headquarters at Da Nang.

But Ho had not been logical. Either that, or he didn't understand what G-2 was.

He did not know it then, but Ho was to be an on-and-off visitor for the first five years that Garwood was to spend in South Vietnam. It was a standoff. Ho remained suspicious, but since Garwood knew so little about the larger issues of the war, his answers seemed at least partly to satisfy Ho. He never learned who Ho was, really, to the Viet Cong. Their relationship simply survived without going anywhere. Much as did Garwood's daily life.

It was four days later, though in truth there were more and more times when with the best memory in the world, it would have been difficult to number the days in the bamboo cage. There was time when he lived in the cage, and there was time after the cage, the time when he moved to Camp II, as he knew it in his own reckoning.

But it was some time after the enigmatic questioning about G-2 that, at mid-morning, the grave-faced guards led him out of his cage and through the camp and over a low hill, beyond which he saw another creek, not the washing creek.

As the creek came into view, he saw a clear stream bounded by rocks and a small clearing. Other prisoners were already there, some fifteen of the ARVNs, arms untied, silently waiting, and as he approached, they turned to look at him. Someone had erected benches of the crudest kind. They were made of two bamboo legs tied together—gook bleachers, he thought bemusedly. He sat down on one of them, separated from the ARVNs, as the guards motioned him. He saw Ho there, a little above him, on a bench also, and it struck him that this was unlike any of the simple events he had experienced since his life as a normal human being ended and the half-world of imprisonment began. For the first time there were layers, there was something not self-contained, something prepared that did not have a direct outcome in front of itself.

He thought it was a ceremony or a meeting, or perhaps some of the silly histrionic indoctrination that Ho had been leading him to. Guards were stationed in a perimeter, and the whole looked like an outdoor theater: Where the stage would be, there was only a crude table with two bamboo seats.

Then four guards marched out two prisoners. Each of the captives wore blindfolds, they looked like Vietnamese but it was impossible to tell whether they were ARVNs. They had no boots, and they were dressed in black blouses and loose trousers, the same outfit he was wearing. They had come over the hill; he had seen the guards before. He thought the prisoners were probably from the camp. They were led to the table in the awful helplessness of the blind, and sat down there like mental patients.

He heard a voice from behind: "Bobby," the voice of Ho said confidentially, "these two are cruel agents."

Garwood turned around with a puzzled expression. "They are agents of the Saigon government. They have committed many atrocious crimes against the Vietnamese people and fatherland; their hands are stained with too much blood of the Vietnamese people."

The prisoners, still blindfolded, sat dejectedly at the table, flanked by guards. It had the strange look of a picnic. The ARVN prisoners sat as silent as rocks, their eyes on the two, or shifting nervously to the guards.

A person Garwood had never seen before strode down the gently sloping forest floor to the table and the prisoners. He turned, one hand on the table, and addressed the blindfolded men in Vietnamese. It was a short speech, and after it the two men nodded. The ARVNs sat still. He faced the audience and for the first time Garwood noticed that in his right hand the man had a short-barreled revolver; it appeared to him to be a snub-nosed .38 revolver, a television detective's gun. The man held the gun up, pushed in the ejection rod, and flicked out the cylinder, and like an amateur magician, he held the ugly little weapon up to show there were no bullets in it. He turned his attention to the gun and carefully, with an exaggerated gesture, inserted one bullet, rolled the cylinder on his leg, and placed the gun on the table.

Garwood turned to Ho. "I don't want to watch this."

"What do you think will happen?" Ho asked.

"I know what's going to happen," he said. "Those two men down there are going to be forced to play Russian Roulette."

"Why do you call it *Russian* Roulette?" Ho snapped in a severe voice. Garwood just shrugged.

"Don't let it disturb you, Bobby. All we want to show you is that the agents of lackeys of the Saigon government, their number one objective in life is the U.S. dollar. When that has been taken away from them, they are completely helpless. These two are very stubborn and obstinate. They know their fate and expect the worst, so anything other than the worst happens to them. . . . Don't be afraid. Nothing is going to happen."

Garwood knew there was one bullet in the gun. As did everyone else on the slope, save perhaps the impenetrable Ho.

The master of ceremonies down by the table picked up the hand of the prisoner on the left like a dishrag and put it on the gun. He wouldn't pick it up, but at the touch of the metal, the man began to quaver and shrink away. He seemed to fall completely away from his dejected stolidity.

The officer in charge merely grabbed the prisoner's hand with his own, forced it to the man's head at the temple and pulled the trigger. The sharp, dull click floated on the air and the prisoner pushed the gun away with loathing, his whole body wilted. The gun was down on the table and the other, without hesitation, swept the gun to his head (how he saw where it was Garwood did not know) and again the click sounded faint but loud in the silence.

The silence was complete, except the background noise of a bird in the jungle. Very slowly the left prisoner lifted the gun, without force this time, and held it to his head for what seemed a long time. When the click came there was an audible release of breath from some of the ARVNs. Garwood was riveted by the scene. He had begun to half-believe Ho's words that no one would get hurt. This is just psychological, he thought. Some kind of play to get these men to break down in front of the prisoners. Or why were they blindfolded so they couldn't see if there were bullets in the damn gun?

The stoical prisoner unhesitatingly picked up the gun and put it to his temple and pulled the trigger and for a mini-second it seemed as if the game could continue, but the man's head jerked sideways just like he'd been stung by a bee on the ear and the boom filled the whole area, a shocking sound. The man's body sat there for a couple of seconds and it began to take on a monstrous life, quivering insanely as it fell forward, first onto the table and then, still fumbling and shaking as if to rid demons from head to toe, to the ground.

Garwood was in shock. He had never seen anything like this before in his life. He only knew he wanted to get away from this place of ungainly and wretched torture. A guard blocked his way, and he blindly stumbled into his upheld rifle, which he used as a barrier. He stopped, stunned. Ho said something in Vietnamese and the guard let him pass and Garwood walked straight to his cage and climbed in and sat in one corner.

Ho never made any reference to the incident again, unless it was with one of his favorite homilies, a phrase he repeated with variations and always in the same tone. "It is so easy to die here in the jungle, but it takes a lot of will and determination to survive."

Garwood sat in his cage in a state of barely controlled hysteria. It was the only thing he could do. Except for one. He could try once more to escape. There would be more death games, there would be more letters. They would never let up. And if he cooperated, they would have all the more reason to kill him, he thought. They could never let it be known how the letter was written, or how the "roulette" game was arranged with guards and blindfolds and an audience. This time it would have to be totally different from the first escape, the escape in the river. But he did have his arms free. On the other hand, looking down at his shrunken belly and his rapidly wasting limbs, the regime of dysentery, malaria, and no exercise had left only half the strength, if that, of his body at capture.

The roulette game had shaken the fog from his mind. Death was imminent. He saw himself shaking, shrinking away from the cool and confident shape of the gun, and he heard that crashing boom.

The next time he saw Ho, he asked to be allowed to relieve himself in a dug hole about fifty yards from his cage, which had been used by the guards, but not by prisoners. It was a simple hole with bamboo logs on either side making the roughest sort of privy seat. Ho agreed. It was a step. He had been using the cage while the dysentery raged, and when his gut calmed, he was allowed to use the latrine of the other prisoners, near their compound.

The guard's hole was near a rivulet that fed into the bathing stream. Ho was surprised, and indicated that he had thought Garwood was already making use of the facility. He acceded.

The procedure was that when Garwood wished to make one of his hurried and painful trips to the latrine, he would yell at the guard, "Di Di . . . WC," and each time a guard would unlock the padlock. Finally one guard told him how to say it correctly. "Di cau," he learned, means take a shit.

He began to notice the individual guards. They were not all alike. Some were slow, some hyperefficient. One guard, if he went to the jakes for more than five minutes, would start barking at him. "Bob . . . Bob," he would shout, but it came out "Bop." Others would allow more time. Two would take no apparent notice of how long he took. He began to take rough time trials, sitting on the latrine for longer times. The place was almost private and the guards, who had got in the habit of stopping on the trail that led to the place, left him alone—most of them.

From the latrine, all he could see was the stream and dense foliage. He knew that the jungle was strewn with punji sticks. He had no shoes, but his feet were healed at least. He thought that there were only two ways out of the camp. The trail or the stream.

The river was fast-flowing, clear, bordered with rocks, some of them boulder-sized, whitish in color. He decided on the stream.

His chance came one evening near dusk. By chance, the guard on duty, a man who carried a rifle, was one who regularly allowed him about twenty minutes at the toilet. This time, he stepped directly to the stream. He had no food, no weapon, and he didn't know where the stream led.

He waded across the slippery rocks in knee-deep water. Mostly it was shallower. It was a shockingly short time before he tired and had to stop and sit down. His knees were shaking and it grew hard to keep his balance. He fell more than once, painfully bruising himself. As dark came, he found himself cursing and stepping on through the stream bed, making agonizingly slow progress.

He had been gone about a few hours (who knew?) when he heard rifle shots off in the distance. He did not know whether it was the guard discovering his absence; he didn't know what it was. He decided to crawl along the stream bed, getting some help from his wounded arm, but not much. The rests were more frequent. But there were no more shots. The creek that rushed noisily past him shut out the usual sounds, leaving only the sound of his shallow breathing and his splashing and the knocking of the shifting rocks he could no longer see, but had to feel; the water was cold enough to numb him, but he kept creeping on.

At first light he got a shock. There seemed to be human voices ahead of him, downstream and below. He peered around for a hiding place and found a large rock on the edge of the bank with something of an overhang. He pulled up handfuls of grass from the riverbank and crouched under the rock, arranging the foliage into a screen of sorts. There was little time for care—the bare earth where he had torn out the grass could be seen all too clearly. When the guards appeared, they seemed almost casual. They did not really search but walked, their sandals making it easy, directly to him. Almost kindly they pulled the screen of shrub and grass away and motioned him to get up. Only then did he see the telltale clouds of dirt streaming down from his hiding place. All they had to do was look at the stream and see the dirt and they knew I was above them, he thought. All they had to do was walk up to where the stream of dirty water ended. His head ached miserably.

The guards were angry, but they did not shout as usual. They hacked a path across to the trail, which was only a two-hundred yard hike from the riverbank. With one guard in front and one behind, they started up the path. Garwood's feet were mushy from their immersion and cold with numb pain. When he fell, they would vent their rage, making him rise painfully to his feet alone.

It had taken all night for him to crawl down the stream to the rock, but after only an hour of stumbling slowly up the trail, he began to recognize the steepness. The guards, whose signal shots were answered by the camp's own, pushed him ahead, and he broke into the clearing of the camp, to be shoved directly back into his cage. He fell asleep almost immediately.

The guard was doubled. He was roughly wakened after what seemed a short time to face the camp official, and he was hauled out and taken across the stream where a hole, about seven feet deep and shaped like a latrine trench, had been dug. They told him in gestures to get in the hole, which was only about three feet across at the top, but opened somewhat wider below. He wearily thought *They're going to bury me alive!* and he shook his head and pulled back.

One of the guards from behind stroked him hard with his rifle butt, collapsing him to his knees, and the guards pushed and pulled him into the hole. He fell to the bottom, knees bent, and when he looked up through a shower of loose dirt, it was to see a barricade of bamboo logs, with some heavy object on it, being dragged across, shutting most of the light.

The hole was damp, clearly freshly dug, and he was barely able to sit in an Oriental crouching position at the bottom of it. He was to spend five nights and six days in the hole, but on the fourth day he felt rain coming in. It was urine, by the smell of it, but he was never to find out whose. He was free only to stand up or squat, and was fed once a day. His own feces soon became a problem.

On the sixth day, the barricade was pulled back and a small bamboo ladder thrust down. He was barely able to climb out into the air, and into a circle of guards, including the camp official and some people he had never seen before. They took him to the stream to the bath area and instructed him to bathe, even giving him soap. After the bath, they gave him a meal—rice and the tasteless vegetable, and some sugar. No one said a word, the guards simply watching. One guard treated his arm wound, which was now scabbed and emitting some fluid. The group took him back to the middle of the compound, to his blessed cage, he thought wearily. But instead they led him to the front of the cage, where two stout bamboo stakes were driven into the ground with grooved boards fitted into them. Stocks. He was made to lie on his back, and his feet were held securely about six inches above his body, while his ankles were securely locked into place with two boards lashed together. He found that because of the sharp hardness of the bamboo, any movement cut his ankles. He lay there. It was seven days and he lay in his own excrement staring at the sky, shivering when it rained, but no longer bothered by the mosquitoes. He refused to eat, partly from nausea and partly to reduce the odor his body could not contain. When he was let out, he was too weak to get into the cage himself. But he knew why they had let him out. Ho had returned.

"Bobby," Ho was to tell him after he had somewhat recovered from the escape and its sequel, "this was a very foolish thing."

Ho also told him that there could be little medicine spared for his complaints—dysentery, malaria, and the lingering arm infection. "The first priority is the revolution, the National Front for Liberation soldiers; the second priority for medicines are for the Vietnamese people who support the NFL and their cause. Therefore it is very hard for us to acquire any medicine for your illnesses. Due to your stubbornness and foolishness." Garwood, in a new flood of consciousness, said nothing. He didn't care that much; it seemed to him that all his strength, his will, even the power to think about anything had been drained from his body. He wanted only to be left alone, to find some dark place.

But that evening there was a cup of condensed milk in the now-familiar coconut half-shell and the pills, one for malaria, one for dysentery.

"If you will try," Ho said in the days to follow, "we will try." He asked Garwood to cooperate and they would find the medicine. "It is not in the policy to do this, Bobby," he said. "It is in the attitude of humane gesture on our part." He also asked Garwood to sign the Fellow Soldiers Appeal. He thought about it: If any of our troops pick it up it will be for souvenir purposes only. No piece of propaganda has ever affected our troops, it's too damn ridiculous. Anyone who picked it up would know I did it under pressure.

As a last resort, he signed it. From then on, there was an improvement. Milk was a daily ration, as well as medicine. Within about two weeks of signing the document, he was able to walk around again. Quite to his surprise, one day, he was given back his old Marine uniform, but not his boots. Instead, he was given a pair of Ho Chi Minh sandals. They gave him back his leather billfold, minus the money (about two hundred dollars for his R&R), but with the pictures of his father and mother and Mary Speers. They put a floor in his cage. When they showed him the pictures, he cried. He realized he had forgotten completely about the other world. He was as surprised as by anything in his life that the clothes had been returned to him, and the pictures. It touched him in an unsuspected quarter. He had thought they were lost, little that they were, like the rest. When they were returned, it was almost too painful. Instead of cheering him, it only depressed him. He had grown almost used to the life with death. And now life was calling him again in these paper photographs, the simple green outfit, the fragrant leather of the wallet. Or perhaps it wasn't quite that; he had been content in his little world of pain and sickness. It was tolerable, even in the black pajamas. Now it was less tolerable. He began to hope that he would never return to the world of the wallet and the pictures.

Another event, as bizarre as it was unlooked-for, came after the signing to shake him from his daydreams. One day, remarkably sunny and clear, the guards took him away from the camp down the mountain but to the other side—away from the trail he had climbed so painfully almost two months before. He couldn't think what was happening, but somehow he knew that he was not being taken out for execution. Even these people had a respect for death. They were pleasant, almost jovial that day and he did not worry.

He was amazed how easy it had become to walk in his sandals, but the unaccustomed downhill pace was agony. He wasn't used to the odd-shaped shoes and the rubber straps skidded and bit on his ankles; after a full three hours, they came to a stop. It was down in the paddy belt, with the usual huts crowded together on the high ground left uncultivated. There were numbers of soldiers, too, or at least, civilians with guns. For the first time, he saw armed Vietnamese doing nothing—not marching, simply sitting around. They wore black pajamas, and he noticed with curiosity that they were mostly barefoot, and he wondered whether these were men too poor to afford even the ubiquitous tire sandals. Their weapons were a motley collection, few of them automatic, and most appeared to be of U.S. manufacture.

The guards, who seemed to know several of the others, sat Garwood under a tree, unguarded. Who is going to run, Garwood thought, with thirty armed gooks and a rice field? There was also a team of what appeared to be cameramen, carrying what appeared to be a movie camera of vintage design with a pair of reel-cases like ears poking from the top. The men, khaki-clad, also carried still cameras.

The head of the camera crew was clearly in charge, not only of his fellow cameramen, but of the soldiers. The guards, after about an hour, came over in a jocular mood, telling Garwood in motions to take his sandals off, and they marched him knee-deep into the rice plants. The guards stepped back and it crossed his mind like a darkening shadow that perhaps this was where he was going to die. There were people on the dike on all sides and the guy with the camera was yelling to a small group of armed men—perhaps a dozen—urging them to move. The small group, pointing their weapons at Garwood, clumsily crashed into the marsh. The guards were shouting also, motioning, "Bop . . . Bop . . . Bop," they called, making frantic motions with their hands as if raising them in surrender, and he suddenly realized this was what they wanted him to do. Terrified, he put his hands up and waited. There was nowhere to run and no chance of running. Then, with hands up and the people all around him, he was marched at bayonet point out of the paddy, up the now damp and muddy bank, before he noticed the man with the camera crouching and moving between the men now "guarding" him in an exaggerated way, and he heard the whir of the spring-loaded camera as the cameraman pushed the blind eye of the lens right into his face. They were filming him. He realized with a wave of disgust that the march and the charade, and the bitter terror, so sharp, were just part of the play that was to feature him. He looked down at his muddy fatigues, noting that there was no name on them. They crowded him over to the tree where he had sat and waited and, smiling, offered him rice and pork fat. So this is what the Vietnamese movie star gets paid, he thought. A woman brought him a cigarette, and he took it. She went away angrily when she found he could not talk the language.

There was no retake. The cameramen seemed satisfied after a very few moments of filming. None of them spoke to him. After he had finished his meal one guard came over to him, exhibiting a black-toothed grin. "Cinema," the man said with great satisfaction. Garwood nodded resignedly. In a little while they gave him back his shoes and marched him back up the mountain, back to the cage he was beginning to know as home.

He thought of the signing of the letters and realized the feelings he had about that were most uncomfortable. And after he got better he had a new thought, which he would not have had before. It was gratitude. Gratitude towards his captors, who had not killed him when they might have in the twinkling of an eye, the wink of a muzzle, the tiny boom of a few flakes of powder in the jungle. And why not? Might he not outlast this war he never really knew?

He began to think of his ultimate survival for the first time.

Now he thought a new thought. Wait. Simply wait, surviving in any way he could. Survival, he thought, could become the whole and complete object of his everyday existence. He would live through every day simply to get to the next in the faith that some day the war would end, and there would be no more reason to keep him. Ho had told him that, on occasion, the Front did release prisoners. "A prisoner's release is based on his progressiveness, his willingness to accept the responsibilities of his actions and crimes against the Vietnamese people and country and beg forgiveness," he had said.

Garwood had not believed it. It sounded like more propaganda. But he knew that whatever Ho said, the war would end. Every war he had ever heard of had ended. There would be a prisoner exchange, and he would be one of those exchanged.

4
The Garwood Place

THE HUMAN PART aside, the location into which Bobby Garwood dropped as the result of a mysterious pregnancy was a dull yellow brick building, Greensburg's Decatur Memorial Hospital. It is the same now as it was the day he was born, just as the main square at Greensburg remains the same.

The day was April 1, 1946, a joke that Bobby frequently uses. He was a child of the Cold War, born in the same year that the United States and the Truman administration formulated the policies that were to remain basically the same for our time: East-West tension under the cloud of atomic war.

But in the Garwood circle, there was little of that atomic reality, only the strange little family of Jack and Ruth, Bobby's parents, and Jack's mother, Grandmother Clark, in the white clapboard house that Bobby remembers as having a black roof—probably of tin, like others in the hamlet.

The mother and the father and the grandmother—these are the figures of Garwood's early memories, soon to be joined by the stepmother. Of the two women, the grandmother is by far the best remembered. She had lived most of her life in Staten Island, New York, and had worked as a charwoman in Manhattan. Her husband, Bobby's grandfather, had simply disappeared, and she alternately used her own surname, Clark, and that of Garwood. Her character and her symbol are rugged simplicity itself: "Poor but proud is what she was and what she taught us," Garwood had said.

Jack had certainly been married at least once before, and he has at least two other children, though he maintains Ruth was his first wife. But even his eldest son is not sure how many children there are, or how many marriages, or how many women "he lived with" before Ruth Buchanan.

The mother herself had previous children "taken from her by the court," according to a still-resentful Jack Garwood, Sr. The "two boys," as Bobby and Don came to be called, were brought up in the Baptist faith, quite strictly, according to Bobby, though he believes his mother was Jewish, a strain by which he explains his dark hair and deep-set eyes. If Ruth was Jewish, there is little sign of it. Jack Sr. and his son do not know her maiden name. It was Buchanan when she married into the Garwood clan and Macmillan when she died and was laid to rest.

They were not really "country" people, though the small piece of ground at Adams where Grandmother Garwood's house stood was purchased in the thirties—perhaps as insurance, or as the quiet cottage of retirement dreams. But for the matriarch, retirement was anything but quiet, with her son bobbing in and out, leaving two young boys and a wife of whom she didn't approve, and all the while she, a woman alone, struggled with her own crippled son, "Buddy" Clark, who was a virtual invalid all his life. She had become a fretful, strict, interfering set of wronged virtues by the time young Bobby got to know her.

Young Garwood's early youth was that house and that older woman, a porch amid the sea of corn in the summer, amidst the wide, gentle hillocks and the huge sky in the winter.

His first memory is that of his mother, Ruth, picking him up, and he has a picture of himself, as a smiling and chubby child, being hoisted to the left shoulder of the attractive, slim and dark-haired Ruth Garwood in his family album. In the background is a white house, and on the porch another woman, perhaps his grandmother, obscured by Ruth's body. The porch is latticed with the kind of ornate fretwork seen in the town, and the peace of the country and the harsh farm light from that Indiana sky are there like a bleach or a blanket.

Garwoods never really *own* anything, they sit for a while like ships at anchor. But that's not right either, for a ship means something organized, ordered, able, worthy, possibly profitable, but above all, together. The Garwood world would be a raft, a collection of logs somehow strung together, bound together and here. In Decatur County.

But there are connections, a string of them, which, if they don't supply cause and effect, supply clues to the family. Robert Russell Garwood grew up near where his grandmother lived out the last one-third of a long and unhappy life.

It is a plain piece of ground near the railroad tracks at Adams, Indiana, a tiny town that would look a lot more like the postcard ideal of America if it were not for the presence of the Garwood family. Like the Snopeses of Faulkner's imaginary Mississippi county, the Garwoods brought to Decatur a new reality against which most of the other residents came to measure themselves, and compared to the Garwoods, they found themselves good. Or at least a lot better than the family that neighbors look down on, and that Bobby himself in his few unguarded moments calls "a little better than white trash."

This is flat land, unbelievably rich and level, and one family owns most of the arable acreage of the county; the tilth is so sought by the plow and the corn drill and the soybean that the towns are pushed into little precincts, as if they were forts where people could shop and cars could be parked and coffee could be served in a somewhat urban setting—in the midst of a green battle where wave upon wave of corn, so green it startles the eye, is waving over the shoulder of the road, crowding, growing, pushing, it seems, the fields right into the living rooms.

Such a vista surrounds Adams, which like so many other points in the huge plowed demesne of Indiana has no hill higher than the mound made by the ballast heaped on the railroad line or the muck piled by generations of river and stream flooding, no vantage better than that to be gained by an ascent on a windmill or to the top of a house inevitably crowned with a lightning rod. From such a place one may see—more of the same, more copses, more clumps of trees at the corner of a field, screening a house from the sublime heat of summer and the swish of the air, which one could see would easily swarm in the winter into a gale with hundreds of miles of unbroken fetch. But the feeling is just as it is on the deck of a ship at sea—the sudden realization, not that the sea is so vast, but that one's neighborhood in it, one's visible area, is so small.

The railroad moves past Garwood's childhood like a ruler, but a kindly one. It alone can give some scale to things, to the endless tedium of things here. At least on the railroad, something happens. Trains come and go, and the roadbed itself is a principal playground of the town.

Adams is made up of white clapboard homes, a few streets, dictated by the shape of the surrounding cornfields, a grain shipping depot now defunct, and a few failed and failing shops, most of which have succumbed to the easy access of Greensburg, five miles south on Route 421.

The trailer where the Garwoods live is hard on the railroad, so close that the garden someone planted and never tended seems to be dusted with coal hunks the size of golf balls. The coal is thick on the ground, but, of course, no one in Adams would think of burning it in a trailer. It is irregular coal; it came there when a freight car bearing twenty tons of the stuff overturned and spread its contents on the ground. The owners of that coal never bothered to remove it, and the railroad bulldozers simply shoved it around, like bad boys spreading the dirt rather than picking it up, and now it provides a wide black road stretching half a mile down the track, and the coal road is a popular place for the teens of Adams to ride back and forth, their off-track bikes sounding enraged and nasal, practicing the hot-doggery of motorcycles in the country.

Garwood's trailer once moved and lived, so that now in 1981 it is teeming with life, the life of Jack Garwood's lusty blood carried down two generations in a family where an un-pregnant bride is not uncommon, and where the patriarch is happy to state his natural "Maxim of Courtship" for the benefit of Garwood females and girlfriends and old ladies: "Mommy's baby," he will chuckle, "Daddy's maybe?"

When Bobby Garwood moved away from Adams at age sixteen, there was no trailer parked by his grandmother's house, a house now gone in a town in which few things are actively torn down: In Adams most things rot into the prairie.

But for some reason, now beyond recall, the house of Garwood's youth was torn down and there remains only a weedy lot.

The trailer was moved to its new site after Bobby was captured. Grandmother Clark, Bobby's childhood female nemesis, never talked much about her own husband; he was "no good," the term Garwoods still use for one who has either deserted his family, done time in prison, or got some money. He was a rambling man, Jack Garwood says, giving the title the most romance possible; for there are few in the family who are as little known as the great progenitor of them all.

It is known, however, that the late Grandmother Garwood, nee Clark, lived out whatever existence she knew as the wife of the Garwood grandfather in Staten Island, across the Upper Bay from Battery Park, Manhattan. Later, after the dissolution of her own marriage by death, divorce, or desertion, she came to Indiana and lived there with her two sons, Jack and "Uncle Buddy," now dead also, who was a sufferer from some sort of dimly understood palsy that caused him to be a lifelong invalid, and in turn earned Garwood the unpleasant duty of taking care of a man his father's age who could not eat by himself and could not control his own body's eliminations.

Bobby has learned to speak darkly of his duties as guardian to the incapacitated Uncle Buddy. His lawyers have made sure of that in re-creating, for the specific use of the jury, Garwood's terrible early life. But whether it was that terrible, particularly in regard to the crippled uncle, is a complete dispute— one of those 360-degree misunderstandings not infrequent in his story. Because Jack Garwood says clearly that taking care of the invalid was no big deal, and that for many years he did it himself. The explanation of Uncle Buddy's illness, sometimes ennobled as cerebral palsy and sometimes characterized as a kind of cretinism, is also traced back to a traumatic event. "Caught his head in the car door," Bob Garwood says, "pretty much of a vegetable."

If Robert Garwood's life had patches to it, so did the father's, for almost as soon as he set off on life's course, he was the victim of a terrible motorcycle accident that split open the right side of his body and left him limping for the rest of his life.

It could not have been all roses for Granny Garwood, what with her one invalid son whose head got caught in the car door, and another who was made lame for life by a motorcycle wreck. She comes down in memory as a slight woman, irascible, used to having her own way, or at least so fearful of losing her one card, control of the eldest boy, that she put on a strong front—which is sometimes enough.

She insisted on two things: that she would never live in a nursing home and that her invalid son would not be taken from her. In fact, he was eventually put in an institution, but for a while they lived together in the house at Adams, the mother and the son in the same room and Bob with his own room. For young Bobby Garwood it should have been a fine time of life, one would have thought, except for the several elements already gathering about him, or borning in his young character.

Bobby Garwood didn't come to Adams of his own choice. It was perhaps the first concrete evidence of his helplessness, a helplessness that marks his life throughout its brief course, an inability to avoid the control exercised over him by others. It didn't matter so much who was in the driver's seat—whether it was his father, his stepmother, his grandmother, the juvenile court, the Marine Corps, the Vietnamese, or most recently his squadron of lawyers. It was always the same, always the situation in which Garwood, the innocent, yearning to be free, found himself embroiled by his own actions in a situation from which he would not or could not escape.

Like father, like son. It is not hard to imagine Bobby Garwood in his father or vice versa. What Jack Garwood was like as a father is anyone's guess, and Bobby's opinion is softened by time and changed necessarily into the cliché ruthlessly fostered by his lawyers before his court-martial to gain a sympathy of a particularly corny kind. According to the testimony the lawyers deliberately drew out from the psychiatrists, Jack Garwood was a tyrannical, temperamental, overbearing, and hard-drinking father who ruled with an iron hand, causing his son to run away and rebel. But in fact, Jack Garwood is almost weakly sentimental about his children, the kind of father who threatens thunder but ends up only drizzling a little punishment out in the form of "grounding" or trying to keep his kids in check. So slender was the muscle of Jack Garwood's control over his eldest son that he quickly abrogated it to the local juvenile authorities. Bobby Garwood, who proved to be a model prisoner and who claims an ability to get along with anyone, was too much for him to handle.

Of Ruth Buchanan, Bobby Garwood's real mother, Jack will not say a word of good. For her, he reserves that sly and special insult: "Dick gets hard, brain gets soft."

Garwood, senior, has no particular regard for women, and he expects to be treated in roughly the same way. Women of his acquaintance in Adams and elsewhere in his circle are expected to respect certain male prerogatives. Women wait on men, bringing them food, cleaning up after them, humoring them, maintaining a distance that would pass for respect, except that at a slightly closer inspection it dissolves into a fear that is very close to loathing and disdain.

The men, for their part, try to keep the slender edge that they are afforded by their physical strength, by their harsh sexual mastery, by their necessary function as fathers of the children around which these women build their days. But in the modern time, it is not real: The men do not need to be strong and Jack Garwood's huge-gutted body and lax arms have little relation to what he must once have been—quick and powerful.

Ruth Buchanan is treated with a lively loathing by the man who was once her husband; it's totally unlike Bobby's own mythologizing of her. According to Garwood senior, she was the archetype of the loose country woman—hopping from man to man and bar to bar. Drawing the details out of Jack Garwood on the subject of this woman would daunt a Catholic inquisitor. But the strong impression from his side is that he was done wrong, and that she "screwed around."

Jack Garwood had quickly found out that life was to be no skating party—and it's clear that he was not the master of the house. The marriage lasted only four years. But in fact it was shorter than that, because the divorce laid "on docket for a year." Jack got custody of the two boys, according to him, "Because the judge knew her pretty well."

Ruth Garwood ran off. But it wasn't as neat as that. She ran off with another man, deserting her two children, Bobby, four, and his baby brother. During the end of the marriage, Jack Garwood moved out as well and left the two children with their grandmother—an event with large consequences for young Bobby, who was deprived at once of both mother and father. Things only went well between Garwood's parents for a year, and whoever was in the right, there was blame on both sides.

"She never even showed up for the trial," Jack says. "In fact, she was sitting over there in a tavern when I got the divorce . . . with this guy."

But Jack Garwood had already met his next wife. He had been spending time in Michigan as a gas station attendant and met his present wife, Helen, a waitress of sixteen, or was it 17? Jack can't really remember.

Helen Raines Garwood is an enormous woman who dwarfs her husband with her bulk. At fifty-four she is not yet suffering from the maladies inevitably caused by carrying a body at least twice as large as nature intended on one's frame, and her skin and her carriage are still lively. But she appears to be literally drowning in excess weight. A shy, self-conscious woman who once knew beauty, a good cook, a devoted, hard-handed mother, Helen is stubborn, frightened, almost illiterate and inexpressive, but in her narrow range of words and stories a good, if defensive, historian.

Helen says that Jack now is just as Jack was then, except that he was a little thinner. To get some of her flavor; she seems like a teenager of about fifty, still using her eyes to coquette and her hands to fidget, so that if you could see through the enormous cocoon, there would be a simple young Midwestern girl, who answers a question about what her husband was like in 1949 by saying "What was Jack like? Just like he is now, thinner and younger . . . I don't know. I just liked him, just liked him."

The trailer that is now Bob Garwood's only home, since it contains his father and some in-laws and a half-brother or two—does not really exist in his life. It's the kind of thing that sometimes connects, this memory that Bobby Garwood wants so much. He will almost create memories for you to show he remembers. But he never saw the blue-and-white trailer there where it is, that odd-shaped, completely American vehicle that is only a trailer in that all its grotesque length could be hauled down the road by a truck, and its architecture is limited by the legal maximum for the road. When Bobby left for the Marine Corps in 1963 there was no trailer—he had lived on Takoma Avenue, Indianapolis, in a house since torn down for a park, the only house the Garwoods ever owned for a long time, corresponding to the only job Jack Garwood ever had for a long time, which was that of a printer in Indianapolis.

The Adams little Bobby Garwood knew is gone forever, with all its people. His mother dead, his grandmother also, the house where he was small gone. But the wandering Jack Garwood somehow homed out there and will stay (unless he gets some money to move to better quarters).

Even the school that Bobby went to is gone, and only a school cornerstone remains, a lopsided landmark coming into the tiny hamlet, at least until it is hit by a car or rolled into the river or stolen for its Gothic letters. The wooden building beside the trailer is falling gracefully to bits, settling slowly down on its haunches, its roofline sloping and the gray siding falling away. The Garwood approach to maintenance is to move on—even a few yards.

There is a major problem with Bobby Garwood's memories of his youth, and that is that he is never sure that his lawyers want him to discuss what he remembers. Even now, when the trial is over and Garwood is free to wait the outcome of an administrative hearing that will decide whether he is entitled to almost $150,000 in back pay, even now while he is trying to set up some kind of anonymous new life for himself, he's unsure what is okay for him to remember and what is not.

Despite the original ferocious picture of the father—the hard-drinking, unthinking punitive, harsh old man with whom young Garwood warred—in the end all the elder Garwood seems to be guilty of is a chaotic life, inertia, poverty, and weakness. If there is anyone in the family who is a hard drinker, it is Bobby Garwood himself, who as a frightened and wimpy young Marine away from home deliberately tried to turn himself into an alcoholic in Okinawa, once falling out of a top bunk and getting a concussion.

In the end all Garwood senior is guilty of is a kind of chill, perhaps a disgust, that his children have all turned out so much like him. Behind that is the fact that he didn't really want to have them all—they just came, the tricks of the universe. Jack Garwood, Sr., whispers, "Wish that Bobby would settle down, you know, because every time he comes out here, all the friends, and everyone has to come, and make a big thing about it. It's not that I don't like him, it's just . . ."

But his father never went for the money, no. He just let it lie there. "I don't think I ever really did (lose hope) because there's been a lot of people told me I'd get that money. I shouldn't let the government get it," he said, "the money the government was putting away for him each month."

After seven years, a person is legally considered dead, even in a case like this, Garwood's father said, and after 1973, when he was told nothing by the government (though by this time at least a dozen POWs who had known Garwood and knew he was alive when they last saw him had been debriefed), he might well have gone to a lawyer to try and spring that money.

It must have been hell, living in that trailer, getting the financial statements that showed that Garwood had over $147,000 piled up in the bank for him. "I

68

said that's shit. I said no," Jack Garwood recalled of this moment, surely a proud one now. "I said, well if I get it, I'll surer 'n hell spend it and when he comes home (which he did) of course then *he* ain't got it. Anyhow, he ain't got it yet, but he still has hopes of it."

What Bobby Garwood remembers, in the balance, is that his youth was terribly busy and scrabbling just beyond being poor. There was almost certainly a lot of friction between the father and the son from early in Bobby's life.

The chief reason for this was and is Garwood's ambivalent attitude about his mother, a woman whom his father can barely talk about without gutter asides, a woman who clearly dumped him, leaving with another while he was stuck with his own irascible mother and two small boys.

If there is a tender note, it is Garwood's fable that he spent years tracing down and finding his mother, finally meeting with her and presumably reconciling a few months before he left to go abroad as a Marine. His father says this is complete hogwash, that indeed his real mother lived only a few miles away from Greensburg. Whatever the truth, neither man will change his story.

In addition, Bobby resented Helen, his defensive, youthful stepmother, a woman of hysterical temperament and long-buried frustrations. The reason his parents divorced was never clear to him. "My mother said my father was drinking and beating her," Garwood said, "and my father said it was her drinking and gallivanting around. My grandmother said it was both of them."

The boys were left in Adams with their grandmother, who by all accounts was a grim, ignorant, determined, religious, and selfish woman. Jack Garwood, Sr., had found a job in Indianapolis as the manager of a filling station. Later he found work as a printer, work that at last began to take the shape of a career. Jack Garwood liked the challenge of printing, the difference of every job. It was a stable time, relatively.

5
A Friendship

BOBBY, still in his cage, was trying to imagine what his mother and his fiancée, Mary Speers, were going through, but he could not. Mary was a very high-strung and sensitive person. His mother's first husband had been killed in World War II, and her brother had been killed in Korea. But she never talked about it and when he left for Vietnam, making a Hobson's choice between a juvenile home and the Marines, his mother had not wanted him to go at all. She hugged him fiercely at the airport and said, "Bob, I feel something very strange is going to happen. Please be careful. Please come back to us."

He told her nothing was going to happen. It was so like the World War II movies he had seen. What was he supposed to say? "I'm not a grunt," he said. "I'm not in a combat unit. There's nothing for you to fear."

From reverie to the cage.

He'd signed the document, and he was already feeling guilty about that. Now the man wanted him to beg forgiveness. But the document could be thought of as an aggressive act, a defensive act. He thought some good could come out of that signing. What if it was distributed widely, the Fellow Soldiers appeal? Wouldn't it be a positive proof that he was still alive? There would be real hope, not just daydreams, for his family, and his name would be on a list much better than that catchall "missing in action." He would be called Prisoner of War.

But just as soon as things began to improve at the first camp, he was to leave it.

He was sitting in his cage when the guards told him to get out. The weather had begun to change. Each afternoon, the clouds would gather—or sometimes there would be no clouds, so he often told himself "this is the most fucked-up weather I've *ever* seen"—and the rain would pelt down. Sometimes it would last for four or five hours, then stop as quickly as it had begun. He was glad they had put a leaky roof over his cage. The jungle was damper, cooler, and never dried out completely. He didn't know it, but the monsoon season had come. He stood outside his cage that day, uncertain as always, dressed in fatigues and sandals.

"*Di . . . Di,*" the guards said, "Go." And he stepped off down the trail in the odd swing of the sandal-wearer, down the mountain.

He had no idea he was leaving for the last time. It was only later that he noticed a guard had bundled up his other clothes, the black pajamas and T-shirt and the remnants of his skivvies, into a ball the size of a grapefruit.

The march began early in the morning and was to last twelve days. It was like going twelve rounds every day, sick and dizzy, against an opponent both younger and smaller. It would begin before dawn, with the guards squatting beside a tiny fire of bamboo leaves and stalks lit with a Zippo lighter, one of the most common pieces of equipment in the East. They'd cook the rice in a small mess kit, using a little water to make it stick together. The stuff was then bundled into balls as big as snowballs and packed in banana leaves for the day's ration.

They started with the gray light; there was frequently mist but seldom rain. The guards, burdened with heavy packs containing rice, cooking pans, salt, fish sauce, ammunition, and change of clothes, hung their guns from their necks. Their equipment was stuffed in rough satchels that reminded him of the gunny sacks oats came in. Their pace was short and choppy, like the step of a pony, but though Garwood was taller and presumably stronger, he had trouble maintaining their steady economical gait. On the flat, his longer stride compensated, but on the hills he strained, even without a pack or weapon.

About every two hours, by his rough reckoning, there was a rest stop. Garwood was learning what it was like to live in a free-fire zone. There was evidence every day that the war was going on, though it was unclear who was fighting whom. It was just clear that immense energy was being unleashed on a jungle whose mere passive power of swallowing up energy was a million times more immense. The jungle simply devoured men and arms and noise and remained brooding, growing, eternal.

Jet planes and mortar rounds went overhead daily, and also, with their distinctive warble and whistle, 105-mm howitzers, with a range of over fifteen miles, were shooting—something. There was no pattern, no order, no battle. The guards showed no concern at all at most of the signs of war, and it was only when aircraft came overhead that they dropped into a soon-familiar routine. Wordless, they would push him into the shrubbery and, unshouldering their carbines, would point them at his head and motion him to keep still. Their only fear of U.S. military might seemed to be that Garwood would somehow manage to signal to an aircraft. Then they would march on as if nothing had happened.

On the fourth day out, as Garwood plodded on toward dusk, the little group was trudging across a rice paddy dike when an enormous explosion tore the air apart. A shell, apparently a 105, had landed in the paddy less than fifty feet away. The sound of it hitting could be heard distinctly before the explosion, which threw hundreds of pounds of mud into the air. All four men were splattered with mud, and Garwood, half-falling, half-knocked to the ground, was unsure if he had been hit. In the ringing silence after the round he heard the hateful sound, far off, of the 105 firing again, a dull little boom like a piece of wood struck by a tiny hammer. Then the whistle of the second shell and another muddy, ground-shaking explosion, this one about two hundred yards away.

The guards, muddy and tense, grinned and laughed hysterically. The pattern appeared to be "walking" away from them. The path of the shells moved on. There was no way the U.S. gunner could have seen them. He was firing coordinates. The guards made a joke of it. One pointed to a crater: "Merican," he said happily. Then to the other, "Merican." This seemed to be a great joke, and Garwood realized the joke part was that the guards clearly felt the Americans were trying to kill one of their own. Garwood did not think it too funny. For about half an hour the march was accompanied by the more and more distant firing of the howitzer, and fifteen seconds later, the "bam" of the round hitting. At first amazed that he had not been hit by shrapnel, he soon realized that there was no shrapnel that could result from a round's landing in this muck. The dreaded artillery weapon was almost useless in paddy land.

In general, he knew he was traveling north, but at an easterly angle. The terrain was basically the same—blinding foliage, the occasional rice paddy area, hilly ridges, and always the trail, a beaten path on which few travelers were met. On one of the last days of the march, the group suddenly saw a Vietnamese obliviously pedaling toward them as they marched down a paddy dike.

With head down, the man pedaled furiously and only when he was about twenty feet away did he lift his eyes and see Garwood's pale face, matted beard, and lank hair sandwiched between the smaller, lower heads of the guards. The man's eyes widened and he kept pedaling, transfixed, and sailed off into the paddy with a large splash. Garwood's feet hurt, his body hurt, his stomach ached for a good meal, and his spirit was ground to a nub by the endless tedium of the march. But all four men laughed their full as the peasant, bedraggled as a spaniel in a swamp, tugged his bicycle out of the muck, still staring in shock at the American's face.

There were no words exchanged. He realized that he had not laughed since capture, and he wondered what was happening to him, laughing like a hyena on the edge of a rice paddy deep in enemy territory. Earlier in the day he had been singing loudly to himself as they trudged along; the guards seemed to enjoy that. Now they were almost a band of comrades with their own joke. Against regulations he was singing "Sad Movies" when he glanced at the guard who habitually walked beside him. The guard caught the glance and made one of the world's oldest international gestures, twirling a figure at his temple with a knowing smile. At another point on the march they had walked past a water

72

buffalo and the animal made its curious lowing, mooing sound, like the first try of a child's trumpet. The guards, who had been treated to Garwood's version of "Tommy and Laura," doubled up with laughter and for an hour after, they mooed to each other, pointing at the prisoner.

Yes, the march had been a bundle of laughs, he thought bitterly. Or was he simply retreating into a simpler world? Perhaps the guards were right. The tenth day freaked him out altogether, to the point he thought he was literally going crazy. The march took them through high hilly country, and at about midday, before the break, they crossed a river. Coming across the stream the other way was a man such as Garwood had never seen before.

Medium height, dark-skinned but golden brown, long-haired, wearing only a scanty black breechclout, nothing else, and carrying a spear. The man's jaw worked steadily at something. He was barefoot, and his feet seemed extraordinarily large and flat. The guards took little notice of this strange man, who looked like prehistoric exhibits Garwood had seen in museums. But the wild man—cannibal was the immediate thought—seemed as shocked by Garwood as Garwood was by him. He stopped in midstream, spear by his side, and simply stared. On both arms, he wore metal bracelets, seemingly copper, and around his neck a silver or aluminum decoration like a necklace. His mouth and lips were like a bloody gash from the betel he was chewing. The figure was extraordinarily well-muscled and looked as strong as a bull. He walked over the slippery rocks without even looking, as if he were on a smooth road, while Garwood slipped and stumbled.

Where in the hell are they taking me? he thought. He had never seen anyone remotely like this character, this young wild man who could not belong to the modern world, but was confidently staring at an American as if *he* was the odd one. But the guards simply shouldered on stolidly. Later Garwood was to know other members of the Montagnard race, the hill people of Vietnam. Ignorant, illiterate, clever, tied absolutely to their land, they did not understand the value of money, but only that of tools and weapons. Garwood had never even heard of these people who were to become legendary later in the war.

The effect was deeply unsettling. He had never thought that he could be taken out of time as well as space. He had brief sobering visions of himself with his head spitted on a pole and his body being cooked on a rack. The Montagnard terrified him, with his confident look and the masterful body.

But it was clear that he survived in this terrain, while Garwood was being systematically destroyed by it. He estimated his weight had gone from 187 to about 120, and the long march had made him weaker rather than fitter. He was getting short of breath and dreaded getting up again after the rest stops; he would drink copiously of the water the guards offered from the streams or collapse against a tree or rock. His feet were in terrible shape again, in spite of the sandals, which did not protect his toes from the elephant grass, which would slide between them and cause stinging, shallow cuts. There simply was not enough to eat. Rice, salt, an occasional banana. There were clusters of

73

bananas on the trees and it tormented him that the guards ignored this plenty and only took bananas from people who had already picked them. He was to learn much later that there is literally not one banana tree in the country that does not belong to someone, or some tribe, or some village, jealously guarded and not to be picked.

One of the worst aspects of the march was the lack of communication. He did not know whether they were almost to their destination or just beginning a trek to the moon, so the day of the Montagnard, when the guard stopped and rested in a village populated by people much like the wild man, he was only puzzled.

They spent that night in a long low shed-house made entirely of bamboo, filled with the stench of human bodies and dirty clothes, and not at all improved by the fact that pigs and chickens were penned up in an enclosure made from the stiltlike foundations of the house. It seemed that ten or twelve families lived in the same building, with only screens or bamboo boundaries between the tiny apartments, each of which had its own fire for cooking, adding to the smell. The smoke had turned the inside of the roof a shiny black, and among the bamboo rafters above the fireplaces, people had hung such disparate items as bones, chicken heads, dried rats, corn remarkably like American corn, and tobacco leaves.

Garwood was dazed and his mind wandered further into fantastical and lurid imaginings. He turned a corner and saw an enormous iron pot, precisely like the cartoon pot of the cannibal-missionary cartoons; he began to laugh again.

The women were bare-breasted, but repellent, with sagging paps dangling clumsily and mouths stained red with betel. In the middle of the shedlike common house was a wide room, and Garwood was shown to part of it. It had a plaited bamboo floor, a large fireplace set on a pile of dirt; fatigued beyond caution, he lay down on the bamboo. He fed well that night, on roasted corn that had been tossed into the fire by the women. There was also soup made of vegetables with an undefinable taste. It had part of a frog in it.

Several days later, journey's end came as abruptly as the trip had started. As with everything else, there was no warning. The trail simply ran into a small collection of houses—four of them, two completely surrounded by tied, sharpened bamboo poles, about eight feet high, and the other two normal hooches, similar to those he had seen in the paddies—frames made of wood, walls of bamboo and mud. They seemed almost like home. There were about twenty ARVNs in the compound surrounded with bamboo walls. He noticed a further barrier of punji stakes stuck in the ground, stretching completely around the two hooches. There was one gate, and it was guarded by an armed man. He was astounded because the guards of the new camp seemed unsurprised, as if they were expecting him. But how? There was no electricity, no radio visible, no telephone in this prehistoric fastness. Yet he felt almost glad. There was reason and order in the world again. It was another camp.

He was set on the ground in front of the prisoners' compound. He noticed that the whole camp was placed on the side of a hill, and the sky was visible only through the branches of the high trees. It was also older than the previous camp—judging from the mud-splattered yellow look of the bamboo, and the grounds that had no grass but only dry trampled dirt.

"Bob," the guard called. "Your name Bob?" he asked.

The guard led him to his new home. It was clear already he was the only American and that he was to live in isolation. But at least it wasn't a cage. From the floor to elephant-grass ceiling, it measured about nine feet. Along one side was a long shelf, instantly recognized as a bed for many people, stretching the full twenty feet of the structure. There were no windows, only three doorways on either end and at the side.

The guard left him. He lay down. An hour later a woman appeared beside him. She looked at him and looked around, wrinkling her nose.

"Number ten, number ten," she said.

It looks okay to me, he thought, and I've sure as hell been in a lot worse places than this.

She looked at his arm, feet, and legs, and shook her head. She left without another word. The next visitor was one of the older men, who motioned Garwood to take off his fatigues. Under his old Marine Corps outfit, he wore his black T-shirt and shorts. Garwood started to get out of these also, but he motioned no. He was given long-sleeved black pajamas and he was not to see the fatigues again for two years.

The main difference he found at Camp II was that the place was well-organized, clean, and more relaxed. One reason for the lighter atmosphere was that the camp, wherever it was, was far from most military traffic, though still within the free-fire zone (which at that point in the war included just about the whole of South Vietnam). There were no more momentary panics as aircraft noises loomed, no artillery rounds booming in the distance. The daily routine was fixed. Dawn brought a whistle, at which everyone, guards and prisoners alike, was required to turn out for a half hour of calisthenics, followed by breakfast and washing up. Special rules were imposed on him—curiously, he did not resent them. He was told, "All discussion and thoughts of escape are prohibited." Violations of the regulations, he was told, would have serious consequences. He was told he could not communicate with the ARVNs, who were called "Puppet Troops," and he was instructed to inform on any of them who tried to communicate with him. He had to ask permission to leave his hooch for any reason, was forbidden to make fires, had to bathe at least twice a week, and wash clothes at the same time. Sleep in the daytime was forbidden. He was to stand at attention when any guard, officer, or cadre member entered the compound or hooch; he was told to stay in the hooch whenever an aircraft was heard or spotted and there was to be no leaving the hooch after dark. Sickness or health problems must be reported immediately to the guards or the nurse. He was told he could not keep any food, but must eat all of every ration received.

It was much like the Marine Corps, he mused.

The camp leader, Ninh, was in command of an inadequate store of English, but he made up for it in other ways. Tall, thin, neatly dressed and fastidious, he seemed to have based his self-image on a movie about the British officer corps. He always ate alone. He walked stone-faced, never showed himself frustrated or sympathetic, but merely observant. In his hand was an unfiltered cigarette of his own manufacture. His hair was always combed and he affected matched pajama outfits—three of them, either green, powder-blue, or black. On occasion, he wore glasses with steel or silver rims, which added a look of scholarly surprise to his frozen features. He seldom used the language of propaganda and made no effort to persuade Garwood to become a "progressive American." Around his shoulder he carried a leather pouch, but he had no weapon.

Garwood began to lead a life of real isolation for the first time in his young life. For days on end he would speak to no one, and no one would speak to him beyond the motions and commands that were the bare essentials of a life of perfect order. He did not share the ARVNs' work duties, which as far as he could see amounted to camp maintenance, fuel gathering, digging bomb shelters, and general cleaning and improvement. He nursed his wounds, he thought of home, he wondered how he had gotten into this. So far away, so far out of his grasp did the old world seem that he began to fear that he would never see an American again. Naturally sentimental, he wept tears for his own situation, warned himself about the heat of self-pity, homesickness, loneliness. He daydreamed of Mary and found it difficult to remember precise things about her. Her face, once so easy to recall, became vague on examination. It was the smile he remembered, the sound of her voice, not the contour of her face. He tried to remember their dates, her clothes. Most of the time he spent in the hooch, walking the dirt floor, picking up the rush broom and sweeping endlessly, lost in thought. He played with ants, building tiny barriers for them to climb, trying to force them off their path. Then he would bomb the ants with pebbles.

One day he sat on the edge of his bed, bombing the ants with stones. They were hard to hit—he would usually hit only about two out of six. The guard came in and in a moment took the whole thing in. He grew suddenly angry, shaking his head, he abruptly took the stones away and flung them out of the hooch.

He thinks I'm the mad bomber, Garwood thought. Why is he doing this? Has he seen his own village bombed by American planes? That's it. Why else would he be upset about rocks squashing ants?

But he almost liked the intrusion of the guard. It was something, and so much of his time was nothing. Time got lost. The war got lost. He was not interested in anything, he found. His lassitude grew. He loathed his meals— rice and salt and manioc, or cassava or komi, a starchy root of several names, which tasted chalky and caused gas. The rainy season progressed. It was December and he was continually cold, with the stiffness of inactivity. He had a second sleep mat now, made from rice stalks. So many simple things he yearned for. An American blanket with stripes that weighed about ten pounds, really heavy. Some pepper, just for the taste of it. Toilet paper instead of leaves. A fork, a knife, or a spoon. He would have rushed out and bought soap. He thought of the food he had thrown away and hated, like liver, turkey stuffing, beets, sweet potatoes—the waste filled him with empty sadness. The mess hall steaks that you had to chew for an hour, the stale jokes about them; those mess hall hamburgers, burnt on the outside, cool on the inside; the pasty clammy bread and the pats of butter, either too hard or too soft—paradise lost forever. And beer. Strohs and Budweiser, the one a tiny bit sharp and sour, the other icy and thin and good.

The rain would come every afternoon. There were leaks that he fought by poking fresh leaves into the wet places. But the rain was endless and repetitive. He remembered one day that he had missed Thanksgiving. It was probably cold in Indianapolis, perhaps snowy. He sat by the door, looking out, watching the water streaming off the bare dirt. It deadened all sounds except the soft sopping hits of the drops on the leaves, it deadened him. It was the same as the time in the first camp where reality and the sleep and dreams so entwined they confused him.

It had rained all day. He sat, head on his knees, knees drawn up to his sunken chest, waiting. He heard voices at the camp gate, but leadenly he did not move. More voices, movement over the sodden ground. Still he didn't look up, and felt rather than saw an alien presence stumbling and dragging into the doorway. A dripping figure.

He looked up. He saw a face, a tall body. It was a Westerner, very thin, gray speckled beard, partly blonde. Garwood's dull mind could not react. The man had a piece of plastic around his shoulders and over his head. No shirt, no tags, black shorts plastered to his bony hips and flip-flops on his feet. His feet were huge, either swollen or something else, he didn't know. He had a stick, and he had long hair. His eyes were clutched in a fierce squint as if it were too bright in the dim hooch.

"Oh, my God," the figure breathed out. "Please tell me you're an American."

Garwood stared dumbly. He saw and did not believe. He said nothing, but got slowly up, his joints stiff and unused. His feet were drawn toward the other man, who he noticed for the first time had a guard behind him. He grabbed at the hand of the newcomer. It seemed natural.

"I am an American," he said. The two men fell into each other's arms in a clumsy embrace. Garwood, cold himself, felt the other man's body as far colder and trembling, wet. The guard did nothing, merely watched indifferently. Garwood helped the man, who seemed to be in some physical difficulty, moving with unnatural clumsiness and slowness, out of his plastic. There were still some land leeches on the man's feet, and Garwood plucked them off, scraping them loose with a fingernail.

Garwood found himself talking, fast, as if another person were talking and he were watching from a few feet above and apart, or as if he were imagining himself doing something else. It had the feel of a dream. He was telling him to

77

take his clothes off. He looked half-dead. Bones were pushing through his skin everywhere and marks from past leeches were evident. The man was thinner than Garwood could believe, with veins standing out all over his head and limbs as if the rest of the fabric had shrunk away, leaving the wires and pipes only. He took off his dry camp shirt with long sleeves, and a pair of black shorts, and donned himself the spare black T-shirt. He had to help the man dress. His hands were bony and elongated and seemed to move unwillingly, like the wandering hands of an old man. He could see he was practically a skeleton. The guard remained, making no move to help. Garwood was asking stupidly, "Are ya cold . . . are ya in pain anywhere? Are ya hungry?"

The man answered in a deep slow voice without regional tone, "Nah, I'm just very tired." The guard spoke quickly and the man turned slowly and answered in what appeared to Garwood to be perfect Vietnamese. He worked with the man for about twenty minutes while the guard watched. He busied himself, ridiculously tucking in his clothes, while the stranger swayed on his feet. He sat him down on the bed, wrapped him in his rice mat, though it seemed to do little to decrease the tremors that shook the bones of the older man.

The rain continued. The guard did nothing, even when the camp commandant came in, and later the woman who was known as the nurse. The commandant spoke to the tall man in Vietnamese and he replied. In half an hour the man's tremors diminished. He pulled one of the long and bony hands from under the mat and stuck it out.

He turned his ruined face to Garwood and said, "I'm William F. Eisenbraun," as if answering an interrogation. The voice was flat, dead-tired. "Captain . . . U.S. Army Special Forces . . . Advisory Command."

Garwood told the man who he was, found himself using the same ritual formula: "Private Robert Russell Garwood, United States Marine Corps, Third Marine Division, captured September 28, 1965." He found he wanted to phrase it that way. It was kind of Stanley and Livingstone. It made him feel a bit more like a part of the real world and not this jungle zoo.

Garwood wanted him to sleep, but he wanted to talk. "Hey, Captain, you want to get some sleep, there's plenty of time to talk. Time is one thing they've got here." But inside, Garwood was dying for a chat—even with an officer.

"Cut out the captain shit," Eisenbraun said. "You're the first American I've seen in six months, and we might as well go by a first-name basis. Most of my friends call me Ike. What d'you like to be called?"

"Well, my family knows me as Bobby, but most of my friends know me as Bob. But you ought to get some sleep."

The doorway darkened with two figures. The commander was back and with him, one of the guards. He pointed to Garwood. The commander said, "Follow the guard." Garwood had the sharp sinking feeling that the tiny conversation the two men had had was to be the only one. He got up, not really moving. But the guard took his arm and led him down to the other "open" hooch outside the stockade. There the nurse handed him a pair of black pajamas, two mats, a bowl, and a cup. His spirits rose uncertainly. She said "Ike." Garwood bowed in the Oriental manner and almost ran back to the hooch with his bounty. The commander was talking to the new prisoner in Vietnamese, and Ike translated. "Now there are two of you," he translated. "You will have to learn to take care of each other, and to help each other. There is one law, one rule that I want to stress. There is no rank or seniority between you two. You are both prisoners; therefore the only person in command that either will answer to is me." Eisenbraun spoke with the same flat slow tone he had used earlier, apparently telling exactly what the commander, Ninh, was saying. "The only person who issues orders here is me—and if I see any violations of this order, then we will have to separate you. Is that clear?"

Almost under his breath, Eisenbraun murmured, "Don't answer, just nod your head yes." In the tall man's eyes was a fear of what Garwood might say.

Ninh turned and left after a parting comment to Eisenbraun, which he did not translate. "Don't let it bother you," Ike told him as the commandant disappeared into the rain. "We've both gotta be careful about what we say around the guards and the camp personnel. Survival depends on it. There is a good chance that we can survive, but we gotta stick together."

Ike told Garwood, "The first thing you'll have to do is to start learning the Vietnamese language." Garwood was surprised and thought, Shit, as long as he knows it, that's one of us, why isn't that good enough?

"It's a benefit," Ike said. "It's a better chance for us. If I get sick. If we get separated. You've got to understand what these people are saying, and if you know the lingo there are damn few surprises on their side, at least as far as I've known. You help your chances of survival, you don't hurt them."

He told Garwood to look at their situation realistically. "We could be home tomorrow, or we could rot in jungle camps for the next ten years. We gotta prepare ourselves for the latter, that way, anything else is a benefit, like a gift. You have got to learn the basic fundamentals of how to survive." Ike said he had been in the camps for six months after his outpost was overrun at Pleiku.

He told the Marine that he had been to jungle warfare school and had been in Vietnam for several years, compared with Garwood's brief months.

"Where are you from?" Garwood asked. He was from Southern California, had a daughter and a wife at home. He was a professional soldier, about thirty-four years old. He'd already done close to seventeen years in the service from enlisted man to officer. A mustang who had taken college courses while in the Army, then bucked through Officer's Candidate School.

As the man talked, Garwood had a chance to examine him. He had deep, sunken blue eyes, surrounded with purple pits. His ears were huge, his nose large and pointed, his chin craggy. He wore a straggly beard and his hair was clearly thinning. His emaciation was extreme, his teeth yellow. He looked the wreck of a once strong man in whom some energy still burned, but whose body was simply betraying him. He looked to Garwood like the pictures he had seen of the survivors of Nazi concentration camps whose bone structure was plain, whose skin lay stretched along their joints.

But this man seemed to have his mind still in perfect order.

Garwood told him where he was from. He had to restrain himself, he was bursting with talk about his experiences. But he could see that when the effort of speaking was not made, Ike's eyes faded and his eyelids started to drop over the dreadful-looking eyes. He finally curled up on the bench after Garwood had given him the mats and showed him the coconut bowl.

He sat there watching the man sleep. The officer was snoring deeply, sleeping the careless sleep of complete exhaustion, his limbs inert. Garwood lay down under his own mat, shivering against the damp and cold. Ike woke in the late afternoon, with the rain still coming and the jungle's sudden slide into darkness about to begin. He lay under his mat talking.

"I guess we ought to let one another know how the fuck we ended up in this situation," he said. "I was a special advisor to an ARVN command post at Pleiku working out of First Corps. There was one battalion of ARVNs. It wasn't raining or anything, it was a clear night, and we'd been out there on this hill, the ARVNs and me, for about two weeks. There were two American sergeants there as well, one black guy—three of us in all. The sergeants and I were inside the command bunker, playing cards and shooting the shit, when all hell broke loose.

"Every one of those goddamn gooks in that outpost threw down their weapons and ran. Before I knew what had happened the whole damn post had surrendered and the only thing we could think of was to try and hide in the trenches, but one of the ARVN officers, the commander of one of the companies, he showed the VC where we had been. They shot the black sergeant—just blew his head off 'cause he wouldn't get out of the hole—and then when they shot the black guy the other sergeant shot the ARVN officer, and they all opened up and killed him. I took off my cartridge belt, left my weapons in my hole, got out of the trench and surrendered. They tied me up and one of the first things they did was take my glasses. I'm standing there and they took my glasses and they strip the bodies of the two sergeants, and they push me off into the jungle, in a rush. It was in June or July.

"There's one thing I want to tell you, Bob, don't ever trust any of these fuckin' ARVNs," he said. "I've had much more experience with 'em. I've worked with 'em, I've lived with 'em. The only thing they care about is their own personal survival. They don't care about anything else. And they'll do anything and say anything that could benefit their survival. Stay away from them—have as little contact with them as you can. Don't tell them anything that you wouldn't tell the VC."

"There's a bunch of ARVNs here in the hooch down below," Garwood told him.

"How many of 'em are there?"

"I don't know exactly. About fifteen or twenty."

"Have you talked to any of them yet?"

"No," Garwood said. "It was prohibited, it was one of the first rules laid down to me when I arrived at the camp."

"Have they made an attempt to contact you?"

"Not that I know."

"Stay away from them."

Eisenbraun said this was his fourth camp. It sounded like he, too, had known the forced marches. But he had also been thoroughly interrogated and tortured. He told how bamboo sticks had been shoved up his rectum, causing bleeding and cramps. He had been shoved into a pit with land leeches. The torture was begun, he explained, because he would not answer some of the questions they'd asked him. He refused to answer in spite of the torture and the leeches. Later, he said, he did answer their questions, but not through torture. He'd had dysentery, malaria, hungry edema or beri-beri. After three weeks of forced marches they brought him to a hooch where he was face to face with the ARVN battalion commander, his deputy, and four company commanders from the unit that had fled at Pleiku.

"When I saw them I was real surprised," Eisenbraun said. "They still had their uniforms. They looked untouched. They were clean, they were well-fed, and they held a little party. It was like a mass interrogation, only the ARVN officers pointed to me and they told the VC everything they knew. I heard 'em 'cause I know Vietnamese. They told the VC everything. They told that I came from First Corps, how many units there were at First Corps, how many American advisors were there, as many names as they could remember, the command structures, the school I'd been to, that I was married, even how many times I'd been in 'Nam. It really surprised me, because I didn't think the ARVNs knew shit about me. Most of it was accurate."

Garwood told Eisenbraun how he was captured, and he told the younger man, "I can't believe your luck. A driver for division headquarters."

"Do you think they found my jeep?"

"I doubt it," Eisenbraun said, "knowing the Vietnamese as I do, they probably took your jeep apart piece by piece and used every damn part of it for one thing or another."

"What could they use it for?"

"They take the tires for shoes. They cut up the body of the jeep to make pots and cooking utensils. The engine, they take it out and hook it up to some kind of irrigation system. That engine's probably pumping water right now. I've seen them used for generating electricity in their machines, or just for parts. They got a use for everything. Never throw anything away. They use the lights, everything."

Garwood told him he had only had a few days before his R&R was to begin and the big man told him, "See, I told you. I can't believe your fuckin' luck."

"Do you know where we're at?" Garwood asked him.

"Exactly where, I don't. I know the general area. We're in central South Vietnam close to the Laotian border."

"How close you think we are to the nearest U.S. military base?"

"As the crow flies and stops to take a shit every now and then, about a hundred miles."

"So what do you think our chances for escape are?" Garwood asked.

"We can escape any time. Making it out of the jungle, that's one in ten thousand. But don't underestimate our intelligence operations," Eisenbraun said. "These gooks would do anything for a buck. I feel pretty sure that our intelligence knows where we are—or the approximate area. Sooner or later, there may be some attempt to get us out of here.

"Until then, when and if it does happen, we do whatever the VC tells us to do. Don't piss them off. Every one of those guards out there has had a family member killed by one side or the other, and they're itching for any kind of an excuse to blow your ass away."

Garwood was unsure, then, whether he should tell the senior man that he had signed a paper.

The guards brought the evening meal, and Garwood, alarmed by his companion's condition, gave him his half of the ration of rice. Ike refused, but took it when Garwood told him, "I got bad belly cramps. You can't keep any food. It's the rules they got here." Eisenbraun was obviously famished.

Garwood was secretly delighted to be eating with another American. The two of them sat on the long bed slats, mats draped around their shoulders, facing one another. They talked about home—it seemed a better mealtime conversation. Both men had chopsticks, and Garwood noticed that Eisenbraun was able to shovel his food with them exactly like a Vietnamese, a skill he had not learned yet. He resolved to try to be more like the older man, and to help him regain his strength.

"It must be snow on the ground back in Indianapolis?" Eisenbraun said.

"You know what date it is?"

"Yeah. It's about a week before Christmas."

Ike slept a lot. When he wasn't sleeping, he was talking. Eisenbraun loved to talk, and he loved to joke. He was wry and cynical, but cheerful. He had known a hatful of war—he had been an infantryman in Korea, a soldier when younger than Garwood. He'd hated Korea.

"Colder'n shit. Girls don't fuck worth a damn. Booze was flat," was Eisenbraun's assessment.

Garwood washed what was left of Ike's clothes, just black T-shirts. He brought water to wash his feet, which were swollen and badly infected by many small wounds. In two days there came a change in his appearance, and he grew more lively.

Then the camp commander came in and gave Eisenbraun pencil and paper and told him to use them.

"What you gonna write?" Garwood asked.

" 'M gonna write my autobiography," he said.

Garwood agreed. He had never seen the "autobiography" but knew that it was three or four sheets long. There had been no repercussions from the camp leaders, though Eisenbraun was frequently called up to the commander's hooch, presumably to translate. At one point after the "autobiography" incident, Garwood told Eisenbraun of the document he'd signed, the Fellow

Soldiers Appeal. Ike simply told him: "Don't worry about it. It did more good than it did harm."

"What do you mean by that?"

He explained that by signing that document he had helped the Viet Cong prepare leaflets that were to be dropped around U.S. bases. "And you can be sure that at least now they know you are alive, and that you have been captured, and this will give you hope that maybe some kind of rescue operation may get underway."

He asked, "Bob, if you had come across one of those leaflets before you were captured, what would you have thought of it?"

"I'd have probably picked it up and sent it back to the States for a souvenir. I don't know what I'd have done with it, I don't really know if I would have picked it up."

"Exactly. That's what I'm trying to tell you. There's nothing to worry you in that document. The only people're going to pay any attention to that document are going to be our intelligence units, who will use them to try to pinpoint our location."

It made sense to Garwood.

Garwood was amazed. But the man had amazed him before. Just a day before, Eisenbraun had noticed the ARVNs walking out to work, as he sat on the bed.

"Oh, shit . . . I don't believe this," he said.

"What's the matter?" Garwood asked.

"You see those guys out there?"

"You mean the ARVNs?"

"Yeah, those bastards are the reason I'm here. They're the ones I was telling you about."

"They're the ones who turned you in to the VC?"

"No, they just surrendered, threw down their weapons."

"I thought you said there was a whole battalion of them."

"There was. These are just the officers."

"Where are the enlisted?"

"They probably got them in some camp close by." The sight of the ARVNs regularly excited Eisenbraun. They looked at him, and he at them, but no words were passed. In private, he called them cowards, yellow, no-good bastards. "See that cocksucker over there," he would say, "I used to buy shit for him at the PX." They could be talking normally and conversation would stop if one of the ARVNs came by the hooch. It was hate made visible.

Garwood was astonished that Eisenbraun, the hard professional soldier who had been through torture, would simply sit down and write the facts about himself for the commander.

Garwood felt relief. Perhaps what he had done—no writing, just signing a document that he hadn't even contributed to, was not taboo, was not the unforgivable. The older man looked at him.

"I know what you're thinking, Bob. I've been here twice as long as you. Most of what you tell here," he gestured to his paper with the pencil, "they don't give a damn. They don't research it. They just want to play a little psychological warfare game and if you don't want to play, you end up the loser. What's real crazy is these damn people would blow you away just as soon's look at you. We mean nothing to them and are actually a pain in the ass to them 'cause they've got to feed us. I'm ashamed myself about some of the things I've said and done, but I'll probably keep on doing them as long as my survival depends on it. Ashamed and alive."

It was all new to Garwood, it was the last thing he had expected to hear from an officer, but it seemed to him that now survival would be the main goal. Simply to outlast, outtrick.

Eisenbraun wrote and talked. "Later on, one of us may decide to plan an escape, or try to do one. I won't tell you and I don't want you to tell me for the simple reason that if the one or the other is recaptured, he'll know nothing to tell." There was no more conversation between them about escape. Eisenbraun had tried to escape twice in previous camps. The first time he was recaptured within an hour, the second time freedom was even briefer. He had poor eyesight and was so shortsighted that anything over ten feet away was a blur.

After Eisenbraun had been there a week, the camp commander came down with a piece of fresh pork fat, tied with a bit of string. It looked to be about a half a pound. "Due to the lenient humanitarian policy of the National Front for Liberation, and today is the American Christmas, the camp has decided to give you this meat."

He left abruptly. After puzzling for a while, Ike had an idea. He asked a guard permission to go to the camp kitchen, and when it was granted, he went there and persuaded the cook to slice the pork into equal portions and then boil it. The two men sat, tearing off pieces of warm fat with their teeth. The guards came with a small wicker basket of cooked rice, more rice than they would normally see in three days' time. They ate the rice with the fat, and found it good. Delicious, in fact. The Christmas dinner was washed down with wild green tea, a drink that had the unpleasant quality of producing foul-smelling stomach gas, but to them, it seemed like a feast. They felt full for the first time. That night, they sat looking at the sky. It was a clear night and there were stars, and they sang a couple of Christmas carols and said a prayer. Garwood learned Eisenbraun was an unbaptized Protestant married to a Catholic; his attitude toward religion, like other things, was basic. If it works, use it. The Lord's Prayer seemed to be a common ground for the two men.

The day after Christmas, the commander came down and asked Eisenbraun if they were getting enough to eat. He immediately said no. "In that case, if you want to eat more, you have to do the daily work of some of the guards so that the guards may go and carry rice back here for you to eat."

Eisenbraun said he would talk to Garwood about it. "I'm not well enough to work, Bob," he said, and looking at his state of emaciation, Garwood agreed.

He asked if Garwood thought he would be able to do any work. "I don't know. But I'll try it if it means getting extra rations."

By this point Garwood had pretty much accepted Eisenbraun's survival doctrine. "What kind of work would I have to do?" Garwood asked, and Ike translated the question for him. "All you will do is cut and gather firewood every day for the kitchen."

Every morning now, Garwood went out for wood. He was given an oddly tipped knife, and on each trip he was accompanied by two guards. When he had two large bundles of dry wood, usually cut from the plentiful deadfall in the forest, the detail was over. But the guards puzzled him. Why had the commander said he was to work to lighten the load on the guards?

Both of them started feeling better almost immediately and Garwood even felt he was putting on a little weight. It was a luxurious thing, not to be hungry. And a bit at a time, Eisenbraun began to impart his knowledge of living on the edge.

Eisenbraun was not a good thief. He sometimes got caught. But he taught Garwood that stealing was one way of life for survivors. Garwood was instructed to steal as much food as possible when he went into the kitchen, and if he couldn't get food, keep a sharp eye for peppers, salt, anything.

The kitchen was a joke by Western standards; but it worked. It was like the other hooches, but in the middle of it were two carved mud mounds in which crude fireboxes were placed. It was there that Garwood's wood supply ended its journey. The cooks would cook the food on the twin fireboxes in two large vats, each with a top. Smoke was cleverly disposed of—it was somehow piped out of the camp in tunnels that ran up the hill and, in its long travel, cooled so it did not rise to signal U.S. planes. It would hang in the air and gradually dissipate.

Ike was a stern taskmaster to Garwood, insisting he learn ten Vietnamese words per day. Garwood never resisted, but he could not believe he would be able to master such a strange language. To hear the guards talking, it sounded like sibilant gibberish, as if someone said, "she saw sea shells" over and over.

"I'll never get the hang of this," he'd complain. There was no paper and the words had to be spoken, repeated, visualized, memorized.

"You gotta know the basic fundamentals of survival. The language is one of them. To beat the enemy you gotta be able to know him. You got to be able to speak to him, to know his habits, his likes and dislikes, that's the only way you're going to outmaneuver him." He explained that most Vietnamese had no more than a first- or second-grade education, and because of this it would be easy for them, with superior education and advanced culture, to outsmart them. So Ike said.

Some of the first Vietnamese words he learned were simple yes and no, then some simple verbs. The pronunciation was a nightmare, and Ike kept repeating: "The most difficult thing to learn is that this is a tonal language. It's like music. High pitch or low pitch will determine the meaning of a word."

But Garwood was to have no more than the normal problems with Vietnamese. He knew it was a peculiarity of his mind to be acutely attuned to the sound of words. English was his best subject in elementary school and he got straight A's. All his other grades were undistinguished. As an experiment, his Indianapolis elementary school offered Spanish to sixth-graders—it was an extra course, an elective that would add to English credits. He thought he would try it out; it sounded interesting. The twelve-year-old had never had any contact with a foreign language, but he found the course so easy it was boring.

In the camp, he found Vietnamese words coming to him. The accent was still a problem, but it seemed once the door opened a little bit with a language, it would continue to open easily. He soon passed through.

In his fourteen years as a prisoner, Garwood was to learn Vietnamese so perfectly that it became his first language, the one closest to his thoughts, and until he again became used to being surrounded by English speakers, he spoke Vietnamese when alarmed, frightened or put upon.

While learning, he began to know what the guards were telling him without really realizing it: "Get up, get wood, that's prohibited," and so on.

Ike also proved to be an encyclopedia of odd information about the jungle—like a Boy Scout's guide. Garwood learned about the properties of certain leaves—the banana, as common as paper for wrapping. The fresh shoots of the leaf were edible also, and a fresh leaf, rolled in the hands, made a kind of cleanser that served as well as soap for washing. The banana tree's soft inner core was also edible, and filled with water, it could be eaten raw, with a texture like a soggy apple. The green banana is good roasted or boiled.

Insects were also on Eisenbraun's menu. He taught his pupil, telling him, "This kind of bug just eats bamboo shoots." He held up a green beetle, pinched off its claws, feet and head and popped it into his mouth. "It's good," he said.

He taught Garwood that even if these insects were repellent, they should be eaten just once a day, for they were rich in protein. If bugs were not available, small frogs, snakes, snails, rats, grub worms, earthworms could be used.

"Just close your eyes, open your mouth, down the hatch," Ike would say, explaining that if the body did not have the things that the creatures had stored in their bodies, the resistance to disease of the underfed prisoner would simply go down. So malarial attacks, dysentery, loss of the will to survive would come.

He taught that most of the things a person needed were in fact at hand in a different, and sometimes totally unpleasant, form. There was a glossy, medium-sized leaf, similar to a citrus tree leaf, that could be chewed and swallowed for vitamin C—the best protection against colds and minor sicknesses, which, under the conditions the two were suffering, could lead to pneumonia and the end.

Then there was betel nut, the chewing gum of Asia. To the chewer, the bitter, chalky taste is soon forgotten, like the astringent effect on the mouth tissues, because of the gradual lift or rush—the warm sensation that starts from the stomach and flows into the blood. The betel makes one feel warm on the coldest mornings, makes a peaceful, shut-off place where time loses some of its closeness. There is no hunger, there is no tedium in the repetitious motions of marching or planting.

The guards disdained the nuts that fell from the betel clusters and said they were no good. Eisenbraun disregarded this advice, and told Garwood, who had found some of the nuts on the ground while gathering wood, "Fuckin' gooks don't know what's what."

Certain leaves, Garwood was to learn, could be steeped and made into medicinal teas for stomachache, nausea, dysentery. These things worked. The guards and the cooks were surprised to find the prisoners asking for hot water to steep the leaves and giggled and pointed, exclaiming the Americans were becoming "real Vietnamese."

But Eisenbraun was not so sure. "Gooks and slopeheads," were his English names for the captors, "slant-eyed bastards"—Garwood was glad that they knew no English besides a few rudimentary words of command, and the two men's Christian names, "Bop," which means corn in Vietnamese, and "Ech," for Ike, which produced much merriment. It means frog in Vietnamese.

The two prisoners were careful not to break the rules. They only nibbled with their stealing activities and pestered the cooks in a friendly way for little privileges.

The ARVNs were treated differently from the Americans, Garwood noticed. They were allowed to cook for themselves and had their own clay oven in their compound. They had flint lighters, and were allowed to go forage food. Details were sent out to do this, and returned with bundles of jungle vegetables and roots and occasionally meat in the form of snakes, birds, frogs. None of the foraged food came to the Americans, nor were they allowed to keep even a small fire in their hooch.

There was a month and a half of relative calm at Camp II. Eisenbraun's health continued to improve, and Garwood proved a likely pupil. To Garwood, the gaunt, bearded man of thirty-four, almost twice his age, seemed all things: comrade in arms, friend, leader, officer in charge, almost a father, almost the father he never had. "It seemed he knew everything," Garwood was to say. "He taught me everything I learned about the jungle." But there was frailty there, too, in spite of the better food, the normal routine. The mind was indeed willing, and the body was not exactly dying. But without Garwood to shift and do for him, Eisenbraun would have been helpless. He still suffered from dysentery, miserably dragging himself to the latrine six to ten times a day. His wounds remained unhealed a month later and then only very slowly scabbed solidly. His ankles remained swollen like those of starving men; he was never able to work at this camp. He could walk, but used a cane he had cut from bamboo, and his ankles pained him. He spent the day in the hooch, using what energy he had being the good housewife. The pair made a checkerboard from bamboo plaits, green and white, with bamboo rings for checkers. Ike would win the endless games without apparent enjoyment.

"What have you seen, Bobby?" he would ask when Garwood returned from his day's work. At first, Garwood would shrug, not knowing what he'd seen except some guards, some jungle, and some likely pieces of wood.

Then Eisenbraun would coax from him the shapes of certain leaves, trees, the names of guards, what kinds of weapons they carried—all the details that seemed to make so little difference to the younger man, the older one would hoard, until Garwood understood he was simply teaching him to notice his environment so that he could use it.

The Vietnamese New Year, called Tet, fell the first week in February, and Eisenbraun overheard the guards talking excitedly about it. The holiday, basically a New Year celebration, combines the importance of the Western world's Christmas and New Year. "The families get together, there's a lot of visiting, and no matter who they're fightin' they have a truce, sometimes a week of it," Eisenbraun said. He said the entire Vietnam War simply stopped while the enemy had this holiday. It was exactly as if someone had given a war and nobody came.

There was more activity in the camp. There were people coming in whom the two had not seen before, and a water buffalo was brought into the camp. Eisenbraun looked appreciatively at the calm placid monster. "They're gonna kill it," he said. "Kill it for the meat."

"You think we'll get any of it?" Garwood asked.

"If they go according to the Vietnamese customs, we sure will," he said, explaining that over Tet, everyone gained good luck by sharing and entering into the festivities.

It started the day before Tet, "Slopes' New Year's Eve," as Eisenbraun put it; the ARVNs got up at dawn and the U.S. prisoners felt complete isolation as the rest of the camp gathered banana leaves, wood, and pots and pans. Montagnards arrived, with their women, and some Vietnamese women also. To the newcomers, Garwood and Eisenbraun became the center of attention—each new arrival came to the hooch and boldy went inside. The two men were observed like museum displays or sideshow freaks. The women would giggle and laugh, the men would stare severely at the two. The Americans sat together, conspicuously doing nothing. "Smile when they smile," Ike said. "Don't do nothin' else."

The Montagnards at least offered tobacco leaves, which were gratefully accepted and seemed to be in large supply; but the Montagnards were amazed, amused, and offended by the two men's beards, and would try to touch them, or motion "No good," "Number ten," or would make motions of pulling the beards out. There were comments on Garwood's youth, translated by Eisenbraun.

Eisenbraun's intimation of the death penalty for the buffalo was borne out by a single shot. That night the Americans did not get fed at the usual time, but very late, with fires burning in the camp freely and openly. Two guards clomped down to the hooch carrying four bowls, rice and meat swimming in broth. It was like a feast for them. The meat was salted and tasted like beef, tough and chewy. It had been boiled and was the first real beef either man had eaten since captivity.

But Garwood was curious about the open fires, which would have brought all the guards rushing in other days. "Probably got a truce," was Eisenbraun's reply. Under the forest canopy the light from the fires cast shadows like spears and avenues into the darker space of the trees on the mountain. The guards had dressed in uniforms—just clean pajamas by the look of them—but it was obvious that each man had spruced up with a haircut and a cold-water bath. The figures moved enigmatically in the glancing firelight, a source of noise, smoke and snatches of songs and chants. There was no evidence of marijuana or alcohol, and the partymaking did not seem to crest until late in the night.

The camp supply officer, the man who had given them their mats and clothes, brought in two bamboo cups after the noon meal. Garwood took one not knowing what it was. "Ike, what is this?" Garwood asked.

"I dunno, I'll ask," he replied.

"It's buffalo blood," came the laconic reply.

Garwood looked at it. "What 'm I supposed to do with it?"

"Drink it."

"Ike, I'll eat rats, I'll eat bugs, I'll eat even the leaves off the trees, but I ain't drinking no blood."

"Try not to think of it as blood, but as some kind of wine," he replied. The supply officer stood expectantly, like the man who has given the party when the toastmaster rises. Or was it just a joke? There seemed to be a crowd gathering around the hooch, with eager eyes and grinning mouths.

Eisenbraun lifted the cup with majesty and drank down the potion. The Vietnamese clapped their hands at his gesture, and all eyes shifted to Garwood.

"Go ahead, it's good for your stomach," he was told.

"I feel like a cannibal," Garwood said.

"It isn't going to hurt you," he laughed. "If they give you something to eat or drink, just eat or drink it. Don't do anything to insult these people, especially on their New Year's holidays."

He closed his eyes, felt the wooden edge of the cut at his lip and threw the stuff into his mouth. It splashed over his mouth and ran into his beard. The taste was like a massive nosebleed. He swallowed hard.

"Tot . . . tot . . . tot," the crowd of onlookers said.

"Good," said Eisenbraun. Garwood never discovered whether the blood was a treat or a test. He never had it again. When it was over, he felt that he had been made to sit up and bark for these people one more time. He did it, and he would do it again.

About three days after Tet, Eisenbraun learned from a conversation with the guards that the ARVNs were about to be released in conjunction with the holiday. Garwood didn't understand why they would be released, but Eisenbraun was hopping mad. "Why would they release these people so they can go back to the army and fight *these* people again?"

"You don't know where they're releasing them to. Don't try to understand the Vietnamese. Their attitude, their ways of doing things change quicker than the climate." He was already angry with the ARVNs, but as long as they had been prisoners, he felt some release.

Now his hostility took on a chill hardness. "I don't give a damn where they go, long as they get out of my sight," he said.

When the release came, the camp commander came down to the hooch and told the two Americans, "Today you are going to witness the release of some of the Saigon puppet troops. When called, you will come up. The guard will show you where you sit. And one day, if you are progressive enough, maybe you will be the one released."

They were taken out of the hooch as the commandant had said, and about a hundred yards from the camp, sat down on the hillside. Garwood turned to Eisenbraun. "Ike," he said, "I've been through this before."

"What do you mean, before?"

Garwood told quickly about the Russian Roulette.

"Better them than us," the older man said tightly. "Bobby, there's so many things. Don't try so hard. Just be thankful it wasn't you. It could have been so easily." It was going through Garwood's mind that the two Americans would be just perfect for the game. Perhaps the ARVNs needed a little show before the release; there were close to twenty guards around the area, all with weapons.

But the tension was broken. The ARVNs, seated like the Americans on the hillside, but apart, broke into some "progressive" song offensive to the American ear—a dirge in dissonant key. But it clearly pleased the camp commander, who came out flanked by his staff. Everyone stood. He motioned them down, flourished papers. Garwood could only make out a few words; Ike said in aside, "Atrocities, U.S. aggression . . . four thousand years of fighting the enemy . . . U.S. doomed to ultimate failure . . . driven out from Vietnamese soil. . . ." The normally taciturn commander was turning into an orator.

He announced that the "decision of the SVNFL was that twenty former puppet troops of the Khanh regime will be released to return to their villages and families, and never to take up arms against their people and fatherland again."

Three of the ARVNs then rose, singly, and made speeches of ornate thanks and modesty. The whole thing lasted for about an hour and a half. Then, as suddenly as Vietnamese events habitually began, this one ended. The ARVNs, beaming, went back to their hooch, and that evening as the ARVNs marched to the main cookhouse to draw their supplies, Garwood crouched outside his own quarters, asked each man as he passed, "You speak English?"

One stopped. "Yes . . . little," he responded to the question.

"You go home tomorrow?" Garwood said.

"Yes."

"Where?"

"Saigon," said the man, beginning to look uncomfortable.

"You help me?"

"What can I do?"

Garwood handed him a dog tag. "Give it to anyone to get to my family. Tell them I am alive. That I'm a prisoner here in the jungle." The man hesitated, looking at the piece of pressed metal with words punched into it. He looked around, nervous in the dusk under the grass eaves.

"I will try," he said. He took the tag. He walked quickly away, murmuring, "I am sorry for you."

(That dog tag showed up in Da Nang in the spring of 1966 and an intelligence report on it is on file.)

The ARVNs left, plunging the Americans into a bitter gloom. There were no checker games, no survival lessons, no dreams of food that could combat the total helplessness both men felt. The commandant came to their hooch after the last of the ARVNs had left. Both men sat silently with their thoughts. He told them both: "You, too, can someday be set free if you show good, progressive ideology in working and thinking—and in begging the Vietnamese people and country pardon for the crimes you have committed. Beg for mercy and ask to rejoin your families, and vow never again to take arms against Vietnamese people. When we and my superiors are fully convinced you are sincere, then I'm sure you will be allowed to return."

Garwood said nothing. Ike made a response of some kind. He told Garwood, "I told him, 'Let me go back to the United States and I'll never return here to Vietnam.' "

Garwood said, "I don't see how they can expect us to be accountable for all the so-called crimes against the Vietnamese people."

The commander seemed to know a few of Garwood's words.

"With that kind of attitude," he told Eisenbraun sternly, "your friend will expect to be here for quite some time." Eisenbraun said nothing and told Garwood, "No more comments."

Then the commander dropped the bomb. "Gather all your belongings," he said grandly, as if the two had anything but a few rags, a coconut bowl, a bamboo cup, two mats, a tin can—not even a toothbrush. "You will be leaving tomorrow." The two men were astonished.

"Where are we going?" Garwood said over Ike's dark frown. The commandant seemed affronted by this question. "You will find out when you get there," he said slowly, leaving them alone again.

"Why d'ya think we're moving?" Garwood asked as soon as possible. "Seems like this camp is pretty well established."

"Probably security. ARVNs will return, get caught in the army again, they'll get debriefed, this place will be no secret no more." He still seemed angry over Garwood's out-of-turn words.

Bright and early the next morning the guards roused the pair, telling them to fold their mats. Each was given the ball of rice, the salt, and within a half hour, they were moving down the trail. Now Eisenbraun's disabilities became plain. He could hardly see and stumbled along with his cane. Garwood shouldered both men's gear, tied up with bamboo strips. They seemed to be moving off north and east, Ike calculated. But the pace was slow. The guards seemed to accept that the older man would slow the rate of march.

They were to travel three days and two nights, stopping for rest in Montagnard villages, with Eisenbraun growing weaker, and every time he stubbed his toe or slipped he would curse under his breath. Garwood massaged his feet during the stops, and somehow managed to maintain the pace, slow as it was.

On the evening of the third day the group walked up to a large camp, the largest so far. There were six hooches, four set into the side of a hill beside a stream. There was a large compound completely barricaded off with the now-familiar bamboo stakes and punji sticks, with two hooches inside it. The terrain was the same, but the jungle was thicker, vines hung everywhere like hawsers. To their practiced eye, the place seemed to have its advantages. The stream, both men noted, ran directly through the compound. That was to prove handy. It meant there would be no more begging the guard to be allowed to go and wash or get water. It was almost like indoor plumbing, Bob thought wryly.

They were to stay in this place for a year to the month, but neither of them could know that as they peered about the place. It was well established, if not old. Garwood could tell, because the bamboo was turning yellow on the low buildings. There were ARVNs too, perhaps fifteen or sixteen, milling about the camp kitchen, and all were taking note that two Americans were arriving.

6
Mr. Hum

A WEEK and a half into Camp III, a curious character arrived. Garwood first noticed him while he was sitting outside the hooch, sunning himself and picking at his body lice, particularly bothersome because of Garwood's hairiness. Through the gate a young man strode. An Oriental, baby-faced, plump, wearing a blue turtleneck sweater, plastic sandals, tailored trousers, a gold wrist watch; he was whistling and singing. The unlikely figure approached and Garwood realized what he was singing: "John Brown's Body Lies a-Moldering in the Grave . . ."

Garwood turned his head to the doorway and let out a hoot. "Ike," he shouted, "you ain't gonna believe this."

"What is it?"

"You'll see."

The man was as out of place in the remote jungle as a penguin. He looked like an American college boy, hair in place. He was a bit effeminate, Garwood noticed, and he half-trotted across the grass and dirt—the guards made way readily for him—and came up to Garwood and said "Hello." The accent was English. Garwood sat up and stared.

Garwood muttered, "Hello." He examined the new arrival. Unlike anyone else at the prison camp, he looked pleased and happy with himself, and Garwood realized how long it had been since he had seen that peculiar expression on a human face—the expression of normalcy.

"What are you doing?" the man chirped.

"I'm killing lice," Garwood said. He was both amazed and a little frightened by this character.

93

"Have you found any?" he asked in a voice that intimated that chase might be interesting and the kill a challenge. "How do you kill them?"

"I squish them," said Garwood, holding up his fingernails, stained brown from the spots of blood and carefully filed on rocks to make a kind of twin anvil for the creatures.

"I think it's better if you take off all your clothes and boil them. This would kill them all."

Where is this coming from, he thought, no pot, no place to boil, what's he got?

"If I did that, what would I have to do?" said Garwood, giving what he thought was a you-think-you're-smart-as-shit-but-you-are-dumber-than-hell look.

"I still think it would be better—to boil them," he repeated. "You must be Bob?"

"You're right." Garwood was no longer surprised by the twists of the Oriental mind. To him, everyone knew who he was, or seemed to.

"I was told you were so very young," the man said lightly, "but you are so very old. It's that beard. Why don't you shave?"

Garwood said to himself, This asshole is really right, you know. Why don't I just walk down to the PX and get a shave?

"I don't have anything to shave with," he said sourly. He imagined Ike looking out or overhearing. But the older man had not appeared. He was probably just enjoying it from inside.

"If you don't have a razor, I will see about getting you one," the visitor said. For the first time Garwood took hard notice. A razor. Here?

Garwood felt desires swimming in his brain. "Who are you?" he asked soberly.

"My name is Nonh (pronounced *Hum*). I have recently come from Hanoi to this camp to work. Where is Ike?"

"He's in the hooch."

"No, no, that's not a hooch. That's your house."

"It's a hooch."

"It's not. You live in there. Right? You sleep in there. Right?"

Garwood nodded. "Ike," he shouted, "there's someone here to see you." This was the time for jungle experience.

"Are you Ike's good friend?" Mr. Hum asked.

The gaunt frame of the older prisoner lurched through the door, trying to thread his toe into his flip-flops. "We are more than friends," Garwood puffed. "We're Americans."

"Hello," the man said, smiling at Eisenbraun.

"*Chao anh*," Eisenbraun said.

"Oh. You can speak Vietnamese?"

Ike said, "Yes."

"Where did you learn Vietnamese?" Mr. Hum said.

"I just picked it up," said Eisenbraun pleasantly.

94

"No," said the other. "I think you have been to school. You are Ike? You are captain?" He nodded to both questions.

"What rank are you?" he said to Garwood.

"I am a private, "Garwood said resignedly.

"Oh, how funny," said Hum. "A private and a captain living together." The two Americans looked at each other. This dude hasn't been indoctrinated yet, Garwood thought. We're Prisoner, Criminal, Imperialist—never Captain or Private.

The young man made other small talk. It was nothing. Questions about their health and complaints. He said, "Why don't you try to clean your bodies more often? Why don't you wash and shave?

"Well," he said, "I will be around here from day to day. We will have plenty of time to talk." He turned smartly and walked out the gate. Garwood noticed he was wearing a plastic brown belt. Garwood felt sure the man was homosexual. He asked Ike.

"Just be careful of him," said Eisenbraun.

The two prisoners sat down and began to pick lice together.

The razor did not appear until two weeks later. It was a plastic disposable made in Saigon in two parts—you screwed the parts together and a double-edged razor was between them. There was a blade also. The instrument, which must have cost a few cents to produce, became a precious item. They decided to shave with it once a month—almost as a celebration of getting through the sea of time.

Mister Hum visited from time to time. He was usually pleasant and trivial. Eisenbraun found out he was an interpreter, sent to the camp to interpret English into Vietnamese. This would allow visitors who came to see "the American prisoners" to have the importance of an official interpreter. Also, he would sometimes ask serious questions.

He asked one day, "What is the difference between the Marine Corps and the Army?" Eisenbraun answered, "They're the same."

It never ceased to amaze Garwood that the questions were so simple-minded. Hum asked Eisenbraun, "How many years have you been in the Army?"

"All my life," the man responded.

"No, how many years?"

"I didn't keep count," said Eisenbraun quietly.

"Oh, you are pulling my leg," he said with relish. "Bob, and how many years have you been in the Marine Corps?"

"How old do I look?" Garwood asked.

"You are younger than I am," said Hum.

"Only a few years," Garwood said. Eisenbraun later reprimanded him for even saying that.

Another visit, Hum asked both men where they were from. Both said "California," and the plump little face lit up. "Oh. You are from the same village?"

95

They decided not to enlighten him on the point and he went away with the air of one who has found the key to a problem that had others baffled.

And then Hum brought down a radio. It was Japanese, a Standard with three bands and two speakers. It had a brown leather case, and a long strap. The thing was playing American music. He marched into the hooch with a big grin.

It was the first time Garwood had heard such sounds since his capture. It was like a touch of civilization to him. The song didn't matter. Nor did it matter that the music ended with the voice of "Hanoi Hannah," who related the victories of the NFL, the number of aircraft shot down (1,000), ships sunk (100), and battalions of U.S. aggressors wiped out (20). Hum sat while the entire half-hour program went on. "This is the voice of Vietnam, broadcast from the capital city of Vietnam, Hanoi. To all American servicemen, fighting and dying in the quagmire jungles of South Vietnam. . . ."

The radio session was to become a regular afternoon event. They looked forward to it intensely. The voice of Hanoi Hannah allowed them to start their own calendar and gave them guideposts they could use to judge the time of day. Though the slant of the news never varied, it began to amuse the two to know that the whole U.S. military establishment had been wiped out—at least once every thirty days—by the efforts of the "heroic Vietnamese people."

The Americans noticed that the fastidious Hum never allowed himself to sit while in the hooch—for good reason, the body lice. They were never able to get one of the crablike creatures onto Hum's clothing, but they did gather numbers of them, take them to the bedding rolls of the ARVNs, and deposit them there. "Our gallant allies," Ike would say.

Garwood started to go out to work, separate from the ARVNs. He was given the kitchen wood detail again. The exercise agreed with him. Depending on the guard, he could forage a bit. He got a snake one day. He cooked it in the ARVNs' kitchen. The ARVNs never tried to get back at the Americans for the tricks that Eisenbraun initiated. They seemed frightened, distant and respect-ful, as if they knew the Americans had a political price on their heads and they themselves were so much dust of the war—ready to be blown away.

The monsoon went, the weather turned hotter. The annual assault of insects began and the night sounds of the jungle increased. Garwood realized that he was looking ahead at a full year in captivity. Eisenbraun's health varied. He could not stand weather changes, which brought on bouts of dysentery or malaria. But when things were at their nadir, perhaps on a rainy day when the wetness would continue for hour after hour and nothing rose to quell the wet length of time, he would crack jokes, tell stories of his life as a soldier.

As months passed, Garwood found his body was turning and changing—to a harder, much thinner man, his back bowed protectively, his eyes cautious and remote.

He had become hardened to the new life in a way he never was to the Marine Corps. Now, when he heard a bomb go off, it was natural. The thought that it might land on him was barely a blip on the screen. A snake was just a bit of food he might crush with his sandaled foot and roast later. The organized man's relationship to time, that great measure of music by which things fit and meet, simply evaporated in the jungle. There were no weeks, no days, no sense of what he might have been doing. Once death was the release and the escape but now, even that had disappeared into the days and the rice bowls and the coma of existence.

He often could not find the person he once knew as himself. There were so many others, and the jungle was endless, time was endless. He no longer felt he was an American, and asked himself, "What am I? Where am I? Why?"

There were no answers to the questions, because they did not await answers. The seed is planted, it grows, it is cut down or dies and another comes. There is no name, no memory of him, nor would there ever be. No one would know how Garwood had become an animal and then nothing.

He felt that if it had not been for Eisenbraun he would have gone totally under sometime in the first six months. Curious. For now Ike was clearly sinking, slowly, while he survived, in some sort of balance with nature that Eisenbraun's body could not achieve. It was the wrong mind in the wrong body. Eisenbraun had given him something to live for, so that he would set out into the forest and work himself into a numbness, chewing betel like one of the others. But he wasn't doing it for Eisenbraun. It seemed that the animal had taken over, that like a horse, it would work until it dropped, happy or numb to cause and effect. He would come back covered with scratches and find Eisenbraun concerned about his condition.

The absence of a future. He never tried to plan ahead now—that was always a mistake. The only thing was to be completely alert to what was happening in the compound. He was always hungry, always thinking about food—no longer the daydreams of meat and potatoes, but simply something to put in his gut. He would chew on leaves, pull up plants and sniff their roots. He would have liked to eat a chicken raw, simply to tear it apart and swallow it, get it down to where the void was, the ache that told him he wanted to live. Live, why? He didn't really know why his body clung to its hold on the revolting piece of packed dirt he stood on. It was as much use as picking off body lice; they were undefeatable, they were forever. But he picked at them each day. In the end it was some satisfaction to stop the itching for a little while. This was life—to buy an hour or two.

Yet events did intrude into the flow of his mindless days. June in the jungle is a greenhouse, muggy and damp; one is always aware that the other residents are attempting to devour one's body and turn it into the endless fertilizer of the forest. He had just made two wood runs, bringing faggots to the kitchen where the cooks sweated and fumed over the hot stoves. Ike was by the stream, sitting on a rock—a favorite place for him, for he could see the main path coming toward the compound. He was now a forward beggar of tobacco and would "hit up" any Montagnard he saw, sticking that huge right hand through the bamboo barricade and asking over and over again in Vietnamese "*Chao toi xin hut thuoc . . .*" which was "Please, tobacco." Smoking seemed to be his only occupation—his hands were oranged with the stains of it.

Garwood was resting, letting the sweat cool on his body in the shade of the hooch. He drifted off into a sleep. It was quiet except for the surly, far-off whines of the cooks. He saw the shadowy form of Ike cut off the light and he heard the older man's voice saying, "Bob, don't move."

Garwood was awake immediately. "What?"

"I said don't move. I mean it. Look right up above your head." Lying like a dark branch was a snake, seeming not to move but gracefully inching forward. It moved around the cross member of the rafter like a glistening metal cable. It seemed immensely long. It was the first time he had looked at an animal without thinking of eating it for some weeks. Now he felt a deep urgent pang of fear.

"Don't move," Eisenbraun said. "Python. They're color-blind and they won't see you if you stay still. *Bao Ve Vao Ve* (Guard, guard)," he shouted. The guard came hustling down shouting, "What is? What is?"

Eisenbraun pointed up to the snake, which for all its menace was lying still along the beam. "*Wo,*" said the guard, slowly lifting his rifle, clicking it off safety and onto single fire. He fired one shot, which to Garwood's horror was not aimed at the snake's head, but at its midsection. The snake arced up to the grass roof and shot out like a bending arrow—its backbone apparently not broken, it slid off the roof and onto the ground. The guards charged to the spot and began to beat it with sticks. They finally killed it. The snake was huge—it must have been over twelve feet long—and Garwood at once felt a pang of regret about the meat. The guards, laughing and smiling, were dragging it to the kitchen. It must have weighed close to a hundred pounds.

Mr. Hum chose that moment to arrive, looking like a graduate student, laughing at Garwood. "You almost got eaten by a Vietnamese snake, Bob," he said. "How lucky you are?"

Garwood glared dully at the little man.

"Bob, you should have seen your expression when you saw that snake," Eisenbraun said. "You turned white."

"I don't see nothing so funny about it. We should have killed it and got the meat." The guards skinned the snake, chopped it small and boiled it. A piece of it tasted not unlike chicken, though it smelled stronger that evening. The ARVNs roasted theirs, chirping like squirrels.

The camp commander told Garwood the next day, "You had nothing to fear from this snake. It eats only rodents and small chickens, it is not poisonous."

A month later, as Eisenbraun and Garwood lounged idly in the hooch, playing checkers, one of the ARVNs yelled from outside, "Ike—you have a new friend."

They tipped the checkerboard, got up, and walked slowly to the door. Outside the guard's kitchen was a white Caucasian in completely undamaged

98

condition. It was as if he had just stepped off a ship. The man was over six feet tall, dressed in jungle fatigues with boots—he looked healthy. Eisenbraun peered with dim eyes, "It's an American?"

"Yeah, Ike, I think it is," Garwood said. There was nothing to indicate the branch of service. It looked like a Marine uniform. He yelled across the compound, "Hey—Jarhead!"

The man stared. He said nothing. He was clean-shaven, with dun-colored hair, and Garwood could see he had a gold chain around his neck. The man stood, making no motion.

But the two veterans were babbling excitedly to each other.

"Hey, we'll find out about the war."

"About the States—news."

"Must'a been captured today—look at him. Not a mark."

Guards pushed the newcomer to the gate of the compound. His first words were "Holy shit!"

"Hi," said Eisenbraun.

"Hey, we're American, nothin' to be afraid of." The man kept staring as in disbelief. "Welcome to our humble abode," said Garwood.

A stiff introduction followed. It was clear the man was wary, afraid, and suspicious. What we must look like, Garwood thought.

"How long you guys been here?" he asked. He had told them his name: Corporal Russell Grissett, U.S. Marine Corps.

"About a year," Eisenbraun replied.

"Almost a year," said Garwood. The man looked like a giant compared to the two of them. Not in height, but in thickness. Grissett looked meaty. "You guys look terrible—what they do to you?"

"We don't feel that bad," Garwood said.

"You should have seen us six months ago," added Eisenbraun.

The two skeletons, almost jumping with joy, hustled their prize inside the hooch. They could not restrain themselves from touching the thick strong material of the fatigues he wore and staring at the boots. They were jungle combat boots with fabric sides. Garwood looked at them with naked lust.

Eisenbraun started firing questions at the man, asking what was going on "out there," was the war coming to an end, why was he here? Grissett hardly knew what to answer. Garwood sat, scratching his fleas and lice. Grissett said, "I don't know, I just don't know that stuff.

"What's the matter with you?" he asked Garwood.

"Damn lice won't leave me alone," he grumbled.

"You got LICE?" Grissett said. "You take a bath and burn them clothes."

Eisenbraun and Garwood looked at each other in mock shock. "Burn them clothes! You want me to walk around here ass naked?"

Russ Grissett wanted to know when he could write letters home, when did the Red Cross packages come? They looked at him as if he were crazy. Eisenbraun said, "I'm afraid you're gonna have a rude awakening."

"This is not the kind of prison camp you think it is," Garwood said.

99

Grissett told the two men that he was from a Recon unit, First Force Recon Battalion, Third Marine Division. He was on patrol, he said, near Quang Nam, mountain and jungle country, doing what took so much time and so many lives in Vietnam—trying to find somebody to fight. But part of the duty of Recon is to avoid contact with the enemy. Normally the group is twelve to fifteen men. It's called a squad or a patrol. Grissett said he had stopped by the side of the trail, "Just to take a shit. I tried to catch up with the patrol and got lost."

He made just one wrong turn, he said. Just one, when he could not have been more than one-eighth of a mile behind. But he didn't dare fire a shot or shout either.

For a full half day he quick-marched in growing panic, seeing the back of an American in his mind's eye around every corner, but never making it come real. Finally he found himself at the edge of a village. He watched, waited, walked into the open and found himself surrounded by people with guns. He didn't know who they were, they might have been friendly. But all he knew was that he had to throw down his M-14 and surrender. There was no point. "I realized immediately I was outnumbered and surrounded."

Grissett seemed a "regular guy" to Garwood. He was on his second enlistment, which made Garwood wonder about his sanity, but the world is made of all types, he thought. He was the same age as Garwood, and had roughly the same background—a Midwestern boy who dropped out of high school, bummed, finally was scooped up by the Marine Corps. Garwood liked having him there. It wasn't friendship, just a little more security—now it was like a little group.

Grissett was fit, well-fed, healthy. He had not been seriously terrified or tortured or starved. He had undergone a three-day march from the point of capture to the camp, but that was all. Blisters on his feet were the only marks on him. He hadn't been interrogated, he said.

He hadn't been in Vietnam more than five or six months, but at Da Nang, he said, he had heard about "the guy who disappeared at Marble Mountain." It was part of the Third Division's oral history now.

Grissett looked like a bouncer. He had a stocky, athletic body, big hands, long legs, thick neck. He was blue-eyed and his skin was very fair. He hardly had a beard. He was a handsome teenager who looked as if he could play games and take care of himself in a fight. He didn't look like a leader. He looked like a good grunt—that was all.

Grissett wasn't too bright. He wasn't streetwise, more like a suburban kid who hadn't scrapped his way through school. But in many ways he was smarter than Garwood. He knew more about history and geography, had a fine eye for detail. But he was not a realist. He thought about escaping a lot, just like some movie plot.

That first day the three spent talking together. It must have been a strain on Grissett, who was growing increasingly apprehensive with the hundreds of odd questions the two men were throwing at him. They wanted most to know what he knew least—about the troop buildup, who was winning, what the chances of the U.S. were. These questions made an angry question mark in his mind—what if these two haggard wraiths were informers?

Eisenbraun and Garwood were desperate for information. What they learned was reassuring: that the U.S. troop buildup had gone ahead—men were pouring into the country. If a full-scale war developed from the "police action," the veteran prisoners reasoned, there would be normal treatment of POWs—exchange of names of captured, inspections, medical help.

They saw that they were frightening Grissett. He looked around as if for the first time, to see the camp that might become his own home. He asked Garwood how much he had weighed at capture, and when Garwood told him 180, he swallowed hard and frowned in disbelief.

The commander of the camp, Duong, seemed as happy as a bridegroom about the new prisoner. He looked like a man who has just closed a bargain deal as he walked into the hooch at the end of a long afternoon of talk and told the senior men, "Tell your friend the rules and regulations of the camp."

But Grissett's first reaction to the camp was to plan early departure. "What are the chances of escaping this place?" he asked Eisenbraun.

Ike and Garwood eyed each other. "Escape to where?" the older soldier said.

"Back to the American lines."

"Where's the American lines?"

"Just follow the sun toward the coast, due east."

"Sounds like great odds," said Garwood sarcastically.

Grissett had a couple of habits that bothered the two veterans. He started sleeping a lot. He was overfastidious about cleanliness, taking a bath twice a day in the cold stream. The sleep, both men knew, lowered body resistance in the jungle. It was like succumbing to the fetid atmosphere, the diseases, the eventual malaria and dysentery. The baths were a reflection of Grissett's fear of becoming like the two others, yet they knew his health was not helped by the dips in the ice-cold water. He worked like a horse, lifting weights that neither Garwood nor Eisenbraun could possibly handle. It was waste, using the strength that they knew would eventually leave him. But all went well for two weeks.

Then they found him one morning moaning on his pad. He complained of chills, of fever. The others knew. The guards brought quinine, but the decline was visible. They told him to get up and move around as soon as a malaria attack eased—he wouldn't do this, and got worse as a result. He wouldn't eat, even though he had not yet contracted the on-and-off dysentery that both the other men suffered from. Unable to work, he lay all day in the hooch.

Ike tried to capture his attention with lessons about the jungle. But Grissett seemed to blank out on it. He was a victim of logic, not a follower of instinct.

"What's the use of learning Vietnamese?" he'd say, hollow-eyed. "There's three of us here, two already know the lingo. I'll never need the damn language when I get back to the States." He found some of Garwood's forage foods to be inedible. He'd eat only rice. The two older men just laughed—"You'll get used to it, Russ, just like we did."

He could be querulous with the veterans. He'd say to Garwood, "Haven't you got the bowls yet?"

"Why don't you get them? I've been out busting my ass all day—you lyin' there."

"Let him alone," Eisenbraun said.

Garwood grew frustrated. It seemed he had cripples on his hands, one physical, one mental. Eisenbraun told him to let time take its toll.

In August, Eisenbraun and Garwood conferred. The older man told him, "Bob, if we keep going this way, all our health is deteriorating, our bodies are dehydrating. Have you given any thought to takin' that one in a thousand?"

"Yeah," Garwood said. "I've thought about it, Ike. We're too weak. The odds are just too much. We've both tried it twice—both times we were in better shape than now. We couldn't make it. There's always something missing. I'd rather die of malnutrition or dehydration than at the hands of some damn torture instrument. Why do you ask me that?"

"I just wanted to know where your frame of mind is. It's nothing."

A month later a guard woke Garwood very early. Too early. "Where's Ike? Where's Russ?" he snapped, shining his lantern over the sleeping form. The other two mats were empty, their occupants gone. Garwood had not even noticed his bed partner's departure. They're probably down at the kitchen, he thought, remembering that the two men on cold nights would sometimes go down to the kitchen hooch to sit by the still-warm ovens and talk, half-asleep.

The guard snarled when he made the suggestion. "Not at kitchen." Garwood got up to his elbows. "You not get up," the guard said. "Stay." He roused the ARVNs with ruthless efficiency, kicking and yelling. The next on the scene was Hum, for once blowsy and disarranged. He stood in front of Garwood's bunk with hands on hips. Garwood took some satisfaction in noting the fear in his eyes. "Where is Ike and where is Russ?" he hissed tightly.

"I don't know," Garwood replied.

"You're lying! They would not go anywhere without telling you."

"I don't know where they are."

The camp commander, Duong, appeared, ripe with fury. "Stand up at attention," he shouted. He ordered the guards to tie him up. His hands were thrust behind his back and bound. He was taken up to the commander's hooch, flanked by sleepy guards. "How long have you been planning to escape?"

Duong's eyes sparkled with the possibilities of power. Garwood was still at attention, in the commander's hooch.

"I don't know anything about escape," he said.

"How can you be so ignorant as to expect us to believe that?" the interpreter hissed in his ear from behind.

Garwood was fighting a wave of panic that was almost nausea. He felt hurt and betrayed. He hadn't been included, though he was the strongest of the three. He thought ridiculously of being jilted by Eisenbraun. He felt a sting of hate toward Grissett. They'll both be killed and I'll be alone again, he thought helplessly. They'll never believe I wasn't in on it.

They grilled Garwood for three hours. Never once did they ask a question to which he had an answer. Their theory was clear. He, Garwood, the strongest, had volunteered to stay behind to fool the guards, who would carelessly think all were sleeping there together. This would give the escapers a long head start—then in the confusion when the escape was discovered, he would slip away himself and catch up. The plan included a precise direction and rendezvous, Garwood surmised from the questions.

There was nothing he could do. The bottom line was that he did not know— anything at all. It was to be a long day. They put him back in his hooch, untied but with two guards. Search parties had been noisily organized; and Garwood noted with disgust that the ARVNs were part of these groups, six of them with two guards.

"I can't believe you are going out on a search for Ike and Russ," he said to one of the ARVN prisoners. "They're prisoners, just like us. How can you do this?"

He responded, "If we find him first, they live. But if Montagnard or VC find him first, maybe they die."

Waiting. All day the guards fidgeted, Garwood sat silent. Near dusk there were two volleys of shots from a long distance. He blinked, tried not to think. Something was telling him that they had just executed the two. It was a fear like fog, blinding and everywhere. Things passed through his mind like a madman's slide show. He thought of snatching the gun of a guard. He was suddenly and totally convinced he could not survive by himself. It was as bad as when he was first captured and it enveloped him. Death, sleep, and the end. Why not just run until the bullets hit him? He knew it wouldn't take many. He thought too that it wouldn't even hurt. He had hardly felt the bullet that passed through his arm. He cried and cursed the war.

A guard's running feet pounded into the compound and in a breathless stream, he began to babble. Garwood caught only "Ike and Russ"—he didn't know the words, he couldn't be sure—a buzz of excitement started among the remaining guards. He reasoned there would have been silence if they were dead. His spirits rose.

It was an hour before he knew. It grew dark and he had not eaten. He heard the voice of Russ pleading, though he could see nothing. "Please don't hit me—" the voice said. He heard the rustle of feet. Russ's hands were tied behind his back, and behind him was Eisenbraun.

The two men were pushed to the ground beside the guard kitchen. He could not see their condition clearly. He could hear Hum, his high voice straining. "It was very foolish of you to think that you could ever escape. Very foolish. You will be punished severely." He saw the dim shapes hoisted to their feet and tied to trees that flanked the kitchen hooch.

Russ called out, "Bob—where are you?"

"I'm here. I'm all right," Garwood screamed back. "Are you okay?"

"Me and Ike are tied up. It's too tight, my arms are swelling."

"Are you wounded?"

"No."

The camp commander barked at the guards. "No talk," said one nearest Garwood, "No talk."

He yelled back, "They won't let me."

Ike's voice, slow and loud came through. "Fuck 'em. Don't pay any attention to 'em."

Grissett yelled: "Did you tell them anything?"

"No, what did I know to tell them?"

"They told us you told them," he yelled back.

"Russ, believe me, I did not tell them anything."

When Hum overheard these snatches of conversation, he said, voice high with excitement, "No talking or we will have to gag you." Garwood said nothing further.

Garwood felt overwhelmed by a feeling of guilt he had not known before. Why had he bitched about the work? How could they help their weakness?

He was sitting in the hooch while they, who had tried to do the impossible, were tied to a tree, suffering from who knows what minor injuries. He slept little. There was only silence from the trees.

The next morning he saw them clearly. They were like rags, heads lolling. They might have been dead.

Grissett's pants leg was torn, and both men were caked with mud up to their waists. Eisenbraun was the first to show signs of life. His head jerked up like a puppet's, and he shook it and looked around. He didn't seem to notice Garwood, peering from the hooch. The escape attempt was over—but would the three of them be allowed to stay together?

There was no more contact besides the shouting that day. While Grissett and Eisenbraun watched dully, four ARVNs and two guards set to work with chisels, saws and their bush knives to fashion a double set of foot stocks, staked firmly to the ground—they were similar to the stocks Garwood had in Camp I.

But there was an ominous addition after the foot portion was finished. He noticed their stakes were being driven at improbable distances, and became convinced that they were making more stocks for him. It was a real surprise when he saw two roofs and two rough floors of split bamboo taking shape. The stocks were going to be permanent!

That afternoon, so windy and cool that it reminded Garwood of September in Indiana, they took the two men, who had had no food or water since capture, and put them in the stocks, which were really just like doghouses, Garwood thought. Both men's swollen hands could be clearly seen.

The arrangement of the stocks was such that it was very difficult to sit up for more than a few seconds. Most of the time, you were on your back, staring at the sky or the leaves of the hooch roof. But at mealtimes, by twisting sideways, you could lie on one hip or the other, and propped on an elbow, eat with the free hand. The men were fed at last, but not the workers' ration. Grissett, who had cried for water during the afternoon, was given full measure of it.

Life in the stocks was not unlike life out of them, Garwood reflected, only it was infinitely more tedious and more difficult. You were completely at the mercy of the guards, mostly at the mercy of the insects, the cold, the functions of elimination. There was no release for body functions at first. The humiliation was nothing new to Eisenbraun. Garwood knew how it felt to lie on one's back in the same position for twenty-four hours. The pains would start in the small of your back. Your ankles, in contact with the stocks, grew sensitive to the touch of the bamboo, no matter how they were shifted they hurt—then finally went numb. Your legs and knee joints began to ache, and every effort to relieve one place cost in another. One of the worst things was the simple exposure of bare feet to the mosquitoes. Your foot, you found, was not used to this sort of treatment. It was a bizarre torture to long to itch in a place uniquely susceptible to itching, like the sole of the foot.

Eisenbraun accepted the conditions with the attitude of an old drayhorse. He neither grumbled nor moved much. He sang to himself. Once he had told Garwood, "You gotta try and dislocate your body from your mind. You sing a song, you make that song so strong it swells in your head and you don't hear anything else. And pain—it's no worse than the things you did when you were a kid. Skinning your knee, falling on a rock, cutting your hand badly."

But Grissett was new to it all. He shouted for the guards, he called for water, he complained that his legs were freezing cold. The guards clearly had orders to ignore completely any words from the young corporal.

It was Garwood's duty, he found, after two full days, to "clean up" after the two men. He was summoned to the camp commander's hooch. Hum was there, dolled up in sweater and slacks as usual. He had doused himself with some sort of scent. Hum, interpreting for the commander, said—as if it were an inexplicable but unpleasant result—that both of the "American prisoners under punishment" had become "very dirty—and they cannot clean up after themselves." He was told that an additional duty would be added to his work as bringer of wood to the kitchen. Now he must also bring water for them to wash and clean up defecation.

It wasn't that bad, he found. He was glad to get an opportunity to slip in a few words. He went equipped with his original T-shirt, the one he was captured in, and carried a big bamboo "tube" or bucket of water. He cut a supply of banana leaves so that they could use them to defecate into. He brought two smaller "tubes" for urinals. He also brought several stems of tufted grass long enough for the prisoners to swish flies and mosquitoes from their feet. He fashioned two wooden pillows out of deadfall, hacking a rough neckspace for each man.

He found that, not unexpectedly, the older man was in far better shape than the younger, at least mentally. Russ, whom he visited first, was lying on his back apparently dozing. He did not even respond when Garwood leaned over him to say, "How are ya feelin'?"

"How am I supposed to feel?" he answered at last, a touch of anger in his voice.

"I can't believe you at all," Garwood said. He found his own anger rising. Here he was cleaning up another man's shit, sure it was what he was told, but what about the bamboo things, the pillow, the leaves, the switches?

But he made no further comment. "How long you think they're gonna keep me in here, Bob?" Grissett asked as Garwood rocked back on his haunches and prepared to leave. Garwood shrugged. He didn't know.

Eisenbraun was awake, the sockets of his eyes deeper than ever, but the eyes alert. He saw the things Garwood brought and nodded, "I guess you do know what it feels like to be in this place," he whispered.

Garwood smiled, trying to be cheerful. But the man looked tired. More tired than ever before.

"Why did you do it, Ike? I'd 'a expected it out of Russ, but . . ."

"Well . . . I just had to give it the last try no matter how bad it seemed. I know you didn't know anything to tell them. Whatever Russ says, don't let it get to you. He's pissed at everybody. He's pissed at me, you, the whole world. Have you heard what they're gonna do with us yet?"

"They didn't say anything, just told me come down here and clean you guys up. If they were gonna do anything they'd have already done it. They didn't build these doghouses if they were . . ."

Eisenbraun cut in. "How'd they react when they found we were missing? How'd they treat you?"

"Other than tying me up and asking the same dumb questions all night, they didn't do anything."

"Bob, you're probably gonna hate me for telling you this, but if me and Russ had got clean away, they'd have probably killed you. They would have never believed that you don't know nothin' about this."

Garwood looked at him blankly. "You knew that when you escaped?"

"Yeah, I knew it. It was a possibility."

106

7
Trouble in the Wind

TEMPORARILY anchored in Indianapolis, the Garwood family was swelling. It was split more than one way. First there were the teenaged "boys," Bob and Donny. About Don, at this time little is said. He was restless, acquisitive, sometimes enough in trouble by his late teens to leave a juvenile record.

Bobby was becoming very much the older brother, the one who represented the split in the family, the one who was unaccepting of Helen Garwood—as she was of him. Helen had her own kids to worry about. The father was in the difficult position of being between his sons and their stepmother. A classic dilemma, and there is little evidence that Jack Garwood handled it with aplomb. Or that he handled it at all, except on a case-by-case basis.

Bobby was the tough, funny guy in school, the one who affected leather windbreakers, a shock of dark hair shining and swept back from his pug of a face, the creased jeans strapped on his hips and the black grease making a line under his fingernails. He was the joker, the wild one at parties, who quickly tried to win those above him and steadily pressed his will on those below.

His favorite at this point was Sharon, the first of the Helen Garwood brood, who was just approaching teen womanhood in a poor white neighborhood where girls suddenly started "going" with one boy or another, or belonging with a neighborhood group without knowing this might be a life decision.

Bobby was a student in trouble at Arsenal Technical High School. He knew the way to the principal's office and was sometimes brought there by police. But as he was dealt with, so he dealt with others, and kept a close eye on his little sister as she grew into her prettiness and form, for he knew well what was on the mind of the young tough boys he ran with.

There was one who was attracted to Sharon, one of the "wrong type," and Bobby, true to his version of what the good "big brother" should do in such cases, warned her off. But things weren't all that different from a play of Shakespeare's in East Indianapolis in the late fifties, and Sharon arranged a small time-honored subterfuge. She would go out on a double date with a boy of whom big brother approved, and the other couple, whose names need not be told to Bobby, were the exiled boy and another girl. Once together, the couples would simply switch partners. It never occurred to Bobby that his sister might like the forbidden boy. Women didn't know. He was the father figure.

But the night of Sharon's date, something caused Bobby and a group of his friends, who all belonged to a loose-knit gang called the Scorpions, to drive by and check at the drive-in, where his sister told him the date would take place. It was a warm Friday night and Garwood and his friends, who knew cars better than a mother knows her baby's toes, were able to see quickly that the car was not parked at the outdoor theater. Perhaps he meant only to chaperone or to give warning that no young suitor could force attentions on the young Sharon Garwood, but when he found no Sharon at the theater, he reacted as if she'd been kidnaped.

Garwood and two carloads of his young pals headed immediately to the place they would have headed for a "make-out" date. Out by the reservoir, reputations were made and broken. It's a measure both of the West Side Story quality of his youth and the figure he cut with his friends that Bobby was able to gather such a posse on a Friday night—perhaps five young men. At the reservoir, they found Sharon, the forbidden boy, the other couple. They were caught, it seemed, red-handed, for young Bobby Garwood's justice was swift and sure. He "beat the shit out of the guy and set his car on fire," he was to boast later.

Things were not smooth at school. They were not smooth at home, either, where Bobby was in violent arguments with his parents about staying out "running the streets," as his father put it. One memorable night Jack Garwood almost blew his son's head off with a 12-gauge shotgun as the seventeen-year-old scaled the side of the row house to get to the balcony that would let him into his room. The incident left the father shaking with rage, and the son perhaps even angrier. It was a culmination of the mutual insults and incidents of Garwood's teen years.

The father's usual response was to "ground" the son, a punishment that brought out all the self-righteousness that young Garwood was capable of. A student, he held part-time jobs, and claims that he also paid a room rent of thirty dollars per week to help out the family. He could afford to buy a used car, but his father forbade him, on the indifferent ground that the boy was a minor and if anything happened, "like killing someone," the father would be responsible.

In the summer of his sixteenth year, he ran away from his grandmother's home. It was not a glorious trip, but it had its moments.

Jack Garwood, Sr., had devised schemes to control his son to take the place of respect. One of these was to send him to Adams to visit the grandmother, which would accomplish two things at the same time. He would be out of Helen's hair—it was Bobby, not Don, who provided most of the friction—and he would also be away from the friends that the father disliked so much.

Another ploy that the father used was to report his recalcitrant children to the Juvenile Division of the Indianapolis Police Department. The father would declare that either Don or Bob was "uncontrollable" and on one occasion Don was made a ward of the court. It was a diabolical power, beyond the normal political push and shove of wills, and the older man used it.

But when Bobby was sixteen, it was a desperate time for another important reason. Garwood had discovered that his mother was not only alive, but living somewhere nearby. He does not remember how he discovered the single important equation, but it is probable that his grandmother told him, while he was staying with her at Adams.

He saw it as a holy grail, as the theme of a soap opera in which he was a hero. The more he learned about her, the more he looked at the few pictures the grandmother had, the more he became involved.

Garwood could not wait to make the contact. He phoned Ruth Macmillan, and found her voice "shaky and scared." It was as if he were meeting the first real thing in his transient life, and it was new to him, awesome. He found himself irresistibly drawn to a vision the opposite of the one his father had painted, that of the fatally pretty floozy, the hard-drinking party girl from the Midwest. He quickly found that his mother had married, and apparently happily, about a year after the divorce.

A meeting was arranged between the mother's husband and Bobby. They got along fine. It was decided to arrange a meeting at Adams in the little house there, and in a few days, a small woman arrived by car, while her husband waited outside. There could be no mention of this to Jack, the son and the two women agreed.

"When we met we just kind of looked at each other for a while, studied each other," Garwood said. "We both had difficulty finding words."

He found she was timid and quiet and had not found her tongue. It was the opposite of what he had been pictured. She was well dressed and "very well together . . . I was just relieved to know that she wasn't the person my father said she was."

It was in the late summer of 1962. Of course, Garwood could not keep such a coup to himself, and before long, he had bragged of his piece of social engineering to Don, who in turn dropped it on Jack, Sr., who went through the roof.

The father's reaction was to threaten to come down to Adams and take Garwood back to Indianapolis. It was a threat that must have made him smile, even under the circumstances. But the threats drifted off, the summer ended, and it was decided to enter Garwood in Greensburg High School rather than return him to Indianapolis. The rustication was to continue in spite of the contact he had made with his mother.

Garwood developed a friendship with Ruth Macmillan's husband, and that winter, he visited the couple at Christmas. The circumstances were another humiliation for Jack Garwood. Things had calmed down, as they usually did after the family blowups, and the father seemed to be taking a new, conciliatory tack with his son.

He decided to visit Adams, give presents to Grandmother Garwood and his son.

Unbeknownst to him, Garwood was taking the holiday with his mother. Helen and Jack arrived to find no son. Characteristically, the father became upset with both Bobby and Ruth and talked of taking Garwood back to Indianapolis.

Jack, Sr., would have been even more upset if he had known the new influences Garwood was coming under. As he visited his mother, another man in the holiday party introduced himself, another Buchanan, his mother's brother, who ran a business in California. With the effulgence of the season, he pressed an invitation on Bobby, telling him he must go to California, even hinting that he was welcome to stay, that a job might be found for him, and even more than that—it might be possible to start a new life for himself away from the difficult situation at home in Indianapolis. College, who knows. The future suddenly stopped gaping and seemed to smile to him. It was near Los Angeles, Bobby was told, and from the way his uncle was dressed and what he said, Bobby believed and it prompted him to do one of the most healthy things he ever did in his life—he ran away from home, determined to get to California and take up the offer of help.

He persuaded a friend to join him on the trip; he had to have a friend because he needed a car. Their plan included working their way, so a car proved invaluable. It was a 1955 Chevy, a year and model that fixed itself indelibly in Garwood's mind as a symbol of all things lovable about his youth and about his country.

Garwood was able to keep news of his trip quiet. He chose for an accomplice not one of the street bums from Indianapolis, but a boy he had met that previous summer in Kentucky while he had been picking tobacco there.

The car held up, but the wallets didn't. In three days or so, the money they had thought would carry them all the way to LA was gone. The country seemed larger than it did on a map, their bellies emptier. They were in Arizona near Phoenix, already out of the Midwest, determined to press on.

They found work, Garwood's friend at a laundry, and Garwood as a migrant laborer, picking cucumbers and cotton. He was put up by a family of Spanish-speaking laborers he befriended, and the friend moved in as well for a small rent. They worked steadily for over two months, until they made about two hundred dollars—enough, they were sure, to finish the trip.

Then another obstacle faced them. They heard on the grapevine at work that authorities at the Nevada-California border were checking all cars with out-of-state plates looking for runaways, who were streaming to California. It was said around Phoenix that unless you were with someone over 21 you were automatically suspect. The two boys, aged sixteen and seventeen, in their Kentucky Chevy, looked a good bet to be picked up. So the pair of them looked for an older man who would drive the car. They could scarcely have failed to find someone under the circumstances.

They loaned the man the car, and now the story begins to grow dim and odd. According to Garwood, he took it to a dance all three young men attended. At the dance, the driver borrowed the car and went to another party and, unknown to the two travelers, got into trouble there—enough trouble that the next day when the trio left Phoenix, there was already a bulletin out for the car, as well as the driver. They discovered later he had allegedly raped or molested a girl at the party.

They never made it to the state line. The state police stopped them on the outskirts of Phoenix and for the first time in his life, Garwood was in real trouble. All three young men were handcuffed and searched, television-style. They were told the charge was rape and that night they were put through a lineup. The lineup cleared them, though the police didn't believe their story; instead of calling Los Angeles for the uncle, the police called back to Indianapolis.

Jack Garwood told the police that his son was a runaway. He added that he didn't have enough money to come out there to get him, either. The other youth's father came out and got both son and impounded car, while Garwood waited in a juvenile detention lockup until an envelope arrived with a bus ticket in it.

Two months later, after Bobby Garwood's junior year in high school had begun (he was a year behind his age group because of frequent moves), he became involved in a really violent argument with Helen Garwood.

The scene was the end of an era, the distillation of the years of fear, frustration, and exhausting rancor between the two of them. Garwood moved out of the house on Takoma Avenue the same day.

But he did not move far. Down the block, in fact, to the home of a girlfriend, not really a lover, but a young woman whose parents he had befriended and who knew of the troubles he was having at home. Jack Garwood chased him down and brought him home in a scene that must have looked Dickensian.

But now Garwood was seventeen and he had threatened his stepmother, so Jack Garwood's reaction was to wash his hands of the problem. "For his sake and mine," the father said, he went to the Juvenile Delinquency Office of the Indianapolis Police Department. The police held a judicial hearing at which young Garwood was given two choices—either to go back home and live with his parents, or to remain in state custody until he was eighteen, which was about six months away.

Garwood told them, "Lock me up."

The father remembers, "He told the judge he wasn't going to stay at our house, so after he had stayed at the JD for about a week, he wasn't as big as he thought he was and he asked me to join the service. I said, 'Is this what you want to do?' and he said, 'Yeah.' "

Garwood recalls it differently. He said he was happy to be in the detention home and that before the judicial hearing a social worker interviewed him and told him that it was a waste of the taxpayers' money for him to be there. He had nothing on his juvenile record except that he had been charged as a runaway. The worker asked a Marine Corps recruiter to visit Garwood at the juvenile lockup.

It was September of 1963, two months before the assassination of John F. Kennedy. Two months before the murder of Vietnam President Ngo Dinh Diem. There were sixteen thousand U.S. advisors in Vietnam, and $400 million per year was being spent to support the pro-U.S. regime of South Vietnam. A few days before, the 250,000-person March on Washington had occurred, at which Reverend Martin Luther King, Jr., gave his "I Have a Dream" speech on the Mall.

8
An Enemy Offer

GARWOOD wondered long and hard why Eisenbraun had chosen Russ
Grissett, not him, to go with. What if Ike hadn't really wanted to go at all, and
Grissett pushed him into it with his persistent talk about escape? Garwood
knew that Eisenbraun would have been swayed by this and might have thought
it was his military duty to go along with an escape plan even against his better
judgment. Eisenbraun could easily do such a thing. He wasn't afraid of death.
He might even welcome it.

After Garwood's first visit, he went by the men every day, bringing fresh
water, leaves, and grass. After a week and a half, Grissett was let out and
rejoined Garwood in the hooch.

He was a changed man. When the camp commander came in, he snapped to
attention—a ludicrous effort in his state of physical disarray. But when the
guards appeared he made similar, desperate, jerky attempts, like an animal
wincing before the blow descends. He seemed to exist only on a physical level,
totally withdrawn, his eyes narrow, hooded, shifting. Before, he had refused
repeatedly to write any "autobiography" or sign statements. But the next day,
when Hum came down to the hooch, he brought both blank and printed
papers, and had Grissett write a complete history of himself, as well as what
Hum called "self-criticism," a paper blaming himself for the escape attempt,
statements that he was sorry and that the attempt had come about because of
homesickness. He promised never to try to escape again—and that if he did, he
would expect the ultimate punishment of death. He had changed completely,
Garwood thought. They had broken his will.

Eisenbraun remained in the stocks. Garwood told him of the change in their

113

companion. He had the same answer to everything now. "Don't let it get to you," he said.

"It isn't that he's writing it that bothers me so much," Garwood told him. "It's the whole change in attitude."

After Grissett's release, a barrier existed between the two unconfined prisoners. Small talk was reduced to almost nothing; though the two men worked together in the forest (Grissett had agreed to work), they had little to say. The young corporal seemed completely encased by his own personal demons. He prayed a lot. It was as if he had abandoned all the normal, bearable parts of prison life, as well as those unbearable things that had broken him. Wherever he was, he was no longer at the camp with Garwood.

When Garwood brought Eisenbraun his food one night he told him for the first time that there was real friction growing between him and Grissett. "Accusing, blaming—telling each other we're doin' shit," he said.

"You're doing just what they want you to," Eisenbraun said. "If we turn against each other now we're gonna be at their mercy. Bob, you're the stronger of the two. Try and keep some level head. Lots that you hear and see are gonna hurt and you're gonna feel helpless."

Two weeks later, the guards let Grissett and Garwood build a windbreak of leaves and bamboo around Eisenbraun's hooch. It resembled a tiny granary, but at least it kept the chill off. They cut the sleeves of the black shirts Grissett had been given and knotted the ends, making socks for his feet, a protection against both mosquitoes and the increasing cold. The camp commander apparently saw this latest move. He was not pleased, and sent word by Hum that "clothes are not to be destroyed in this way. When you were given clothes, you cried that it was too cold. Now you destroy the clothes you were given. These clothes are made from the blood and sweat of the Vietnamese people and are not easy to make. . . ."

They let Eisenbraun out after more than two and one half months in the stocks. He had boils on his back. He was weaker, but the swelling of his ankles had gone away. He could walk. His spirit remained untouched. He was happy, with the simple happiness of the very young or very old, just to be able to stay in the hooch and sit in the sun—he seemed pleased even to be able to pick lice again.

He made a point of trying to settle things between the two younger men, lecturing them about the impossibility of discord in a group as small as theirs. "We're gonna be here for quite some time, I think," he said. "We gotta hang together. Trust each other."

But Garwood and Grissett never really returned to the level of comradeship they had known in the first weeks of Grissett's capture. There was a permanent danger sign in Garwood's mind.

Then Ike was thrown in the stocks again. By the best calculation it was about two weeks before Christmas, 1966, Garwood's second in captivity. The Americans had been stealing whatever they could find of use—from the guards, from the ARVNs, from the cooks. The ARVNs had found a way to catch small fish, scarcely bigger than minnows, with their hands from the small streams. They would combine them with salt, pepper, and whatever herbs they could find and make their own fish sauce. Ike, who remained behind on work details, found three of the fish in a tin can in the ARVN kitchen and he ate them all—but he was seen by two ARVNs who were taking their turn at KP.

They confronted him. He stonewalled in Vietnamese, and the two would-be cooks started screaming for the guards. The guards rushed down from their quarters to find the two small men dancing like Rumpelstiltskins around the tall one. They accused him of stealing their "rations."

"Rations, bullshit," Eisenbraun roared. "They caught it in the stream. Three lousy minnows."

The ARVN prisoners held a group meeting to which they invited the camp commander. They accused Eisenbraun of stealing food, and the others of stealing food and tobacco. It was true, whenever possible it was true. Garwood could not believe these prisoners were holding a mock trial over three minnows.

The Americans decided to deny it, and with Eisenbraun thundering in Vietnamese, "It is totally untrue," he said. "We don't touch anything that belongs to them." The commander, acting as judge, was clearly pleased—he appointed the ARVNs jury, himself as judge. The ARVNs found Eisenbraun guilty and asked he be sentenced to two weeks in stocks. The charges against the younger men were dismissed: They had not been caught red-handed.

The camp commander approved the sentence, but reduced it to a single week. Garwood could not believe that for three minnows, Eisenbraun would be in stocks for a week. And it was their fellow prisoners who suggested the punishment.

Garwood thought of Eisenbraun's advice—how the Communists hoped that just such bickering would break out. Now it had, in a most unusual way. He noticed that only a couple of the ARVNs seemed the least unhappy at the sentence. Most seemed to approve it heartily.

Eisenbraun was led out to the stocks. "Don't trust 'em," he said. "See what I told you, don't trust these fuckin' gooks."

Whatever the effect on Eisenbraun, the sentencing had an electric effect on Grissett. For the first time since his own term in the stocks, he seemed to Garwood to be coming back to reality. He kept looking at Eisenbraun in the stocks as if the sight were something that would dissolve with enough examination. Since his "conversion" by stocks torture, Grissett, met by Garwood's hostility, had become openly chummy with two of the ARVNs. Now there was a fresh breakdown of whatever feeble social code had grown from familiarity or the signs of friendship customary to people in the same hole.

Garwood had never been more than distant with the ARVNs; now he went over to the cooks who had started the whole mess. Both were ARVN lieutenants. He knew one as Dang.

The cooks were in the kitchen roasting a manioc. They moved companionably over on their bamboo bench when the American approached. Garwood pulled the manioc out with the tips of his fingers, handling the hot root cautiously. He paid no attention to the cook's glances. He called to Russ, "Hey Russ . . ."

He broke the manioc in half—it looked like a roast potato, he thought, if only it could taste like one. He tossed half of the manioc to Russ. The ARVNs didn't say anything. "Where'd you get this at?" Russ asked.

"Our friends here gave it to us," he said heavily.

"*Do ma mi,*" muttered the thinner and younger cook, "Fuck your mother."

Garwood looked at him with the best hoodlum glare he could muster.

"You want to die, don't you?" he said.

Russ became instantly nervous. But he didn't move. Garwood stared straight at the little man, thinking lurid thoughts of cinematic violence—squeezing the man's throat, cutting off his balls, something horrible and grand.

"Damn," said Garwood, flourishing the manioc like a pistol, "This is about the size of ten minnows. And I haven't heard you call for the guard yet."

"Leave him alone, Bob. It ain't worth it," said Grissett. Garwood was chewing the well-cooked edges of the manioc. Grissett wasted no time but greedily ate the root as fast as he could. Garwood got slowly up, turned his back on the two Vietnamese and walked, with a dueler's dignity, to the stream.

Ike seemed to have conquered the stocks. When he emerged he looked little different. Perhaps it was because this time they kept him stocked up only at night. During the day it was hard labor, or as hard as the skeletal, half-blind soldier could perform. He was put to work splitting wood with a Vietnamese bush axe. He sat on the ground beside a growing mound of kindling, hacking slowly and steadily at it; his ration was not cut, and he was able to manage himself so that body functions were taken care of before the guards motioned him into the stocks.

When he returned to the hooch, he was without bitterness. Even his enmity toward the Vietnamese seemed to have softened. It was as if he had stood so much time in the stocks that he could face more with complete equanimity.

The trio of Americans didn't know it, but they were nearing the end of their time at the third South Vietnamese camp. It was nearly Christmas again. Grissett had been in the camp for about five months. He had taken on the same skin-and-bones look as the others, and his once-perfect boots had come to the point where he hardly dared wear them any longer. He would only get them out on wood-gathering trips, taking them off as soon as he arrived in the compound.

For Garwood's second Christmas in Vietnam, the guards produced a rooster the size of a bantam, a pound of rock candy, and a packet of Ruby Queen cigarettes. They doubled the normal rice ration. The trio was not allowed to cook the little rooster. Instead they were allowed to tell the cooks how to prepare it. Eisenbraun wanted it simply roasted over an open fire, but the other two decided they would rather have it fried. The argument came down to how much grease they could get out of the deal—and it was clear that there would be more grease with frying, while roasting, as one of them pointed out, "only burns the grease out of it."

The camp commander handed out perfumed cigarettes. But this time Garwood could understand a good deal of Vietnamese, and he came to realize how much was necessarily left out even of everyday speech in the process of interpretation.

"Due to the humanitarian and lenient policy of the South Vietnamese National Front for Liberation, the central committee of the NFL, as well as the Vietnamese people, has decided to increase your ration, so that you may enjoy the American Christmas," the commandant started. "We are limited in funds and materials, but we have received orders from our superiors to go out of our way to give you meat, candy, and cigarettes on Christmas Day. We have gone to great lengths, time and expense and labor to provide you with the bare necessities. It may not seem much, but understand that in order to bring you these things, our people are under constant threat and danger of death from U.S. bombs and shells."

Garwood went to the kitchen, just to see as much as he could of the preparation of the chicken. It was the first real chicken he had seen since captivity. Chicken, he had come to know, is a real delicacy in Vietnam, and even this particular rooster, which looked small, tough, and on the retirement list, made expectations rise. He told the cooks to fry the chicken, preferably in pork fat—but there was none. Instead they produced peanut oil, in a two-gallon tin with a pair of hands shaking on the front—a U.S. Aid gift to the South Vietnamese government. Garwood sighed in irony and anger.

For the celebration, a decidedly religious turn was taken. Grissett, with his strong Catholic faith, strung hardened berries into a rosary and made a bamboo cross and a rough altar. There was no work for two days, the three men sat around the hooch talking only of the past. Garwood and Grissett sang hymns, while Eisenbraun again recalled the colossal drunks of his earlier soldiering days.

It was not until Christmas night that the little rooster arrived, in a basket. The cooks had already divided it into three portions and the head was still attached. The three men cut it down further, making a little mound of chicken bits, and put it on a banana leaf, then sat, boardinghouse style, wielding chopsticks. It was a subdued gathering. Eisenbraun caught the tone of it when he made a wry toast: "If our luck keeps up," he said, "we'll be having Christmas next year in Hanoi."

The reason, the tall man explained, was that if Grissett was correct in his reports of increased manpower and activity by the U.S., the VC would soon find it too dangerous and costly to keep many prisoners in the south. "If there is more activity, there's gonna be more people captured," he said.

They ate silently, thankful only for the moment and for the tough little bird.

New Year's passed. There was no need to make resolutions. It seemed just like another day, another in the chain of muddy links that carried him to a great limbo. The cheerful talk and memories that such days inevitably brought seemed only depressing. The past, so dim yet so bright, was impossibly dear.

Yet suddenly from oblivion marched Bobby's old nemesis, Mr. Ho. The first English speaker Garwood had met in captivity reappeared a week after New Year's, 1967. "Oh, Bobby," he said, "long time, no see." The effect of this man, so doctrinaire and so calm, had its usual touch of unreality. "This is the guy I was telling you about," he told Eisenbraun.

"You must be Ike," Ho said, grinning at the blond skeleton.

"Yessir," said Eisenbraun, "Captain William F. Eisenbraun, sir."

At the word *captain,* Ho did a theatrical frown.

"And I believe they call you Russ," Ho said to Grissett.

"Yes, sir."

"That is a strange name. Is it a phonetic name?" Garwood, watching, could clearly see how Ho surprised and captured his opponents.

"Yessir," said Grissett, "it's short for Russell."

"Well. I have just come from my superior command," Ho said. "And they have asked me to come by here to check on your progress, attitude, and health."

The three grimy prisoners looked at each other with something approaching real amazement. Ike spoke, looking more like a walking death than an Army officer. "You've got to be shitting us," he said softly.

Grissett, once the healthiest of the trio, had begun to develop an annoying skin rash, which the other two dismissed as ringworm. It involved red splotches, scaling, peeling skin, and then a repetition of the process. His stomach was also taking on a bloated appearance.

Garwood had the lice, the beard, the lack of weight, the deep-sunk eyes, but he was now at least at equilibrium. He looked and felt as if he was in much better shape than the others. Together, it's unlikely that they topped 350 pounds.

Ho was a mystery. Garwood had not seen him in almost two years; the very thought of this length of time brought tears to his eyes. But the next day Ho brought the three for a private session in the commander's hooch, along with Hum. They were told politely to sit down on a bamboo bench—a minimal affair, more like sitting on a rail than on a seat. "Good morning, how are you today?" he asked.

"As well as can be expected, under the circumstances," Eisenbraun answered.

"I have called you here today to inform you that I'm going to hold a political re-education for your benefit, so that you may better understand the Vietnamese people in their struggle against U.S. aggression and its fight for peace and freedom."

The three men each inwardly groaned.

"So that you may know how and why United States is foolishly sinking in the quagmire, foolishly escalating its war of aggression against the Vietnamese people—but sinking ever deeper."

They suddenly perked up—Ho's words must be clues of tough new moves to finish the war successfully.

"But first of all. It has been reported to me about your progress and an attitude during the past year or so. I must say I am very disappointed in all of you, and hope by now that you have abolished your foolish and obstinate ways of thinking, and are seeking the progressive road to becoming a genuine American."

Ho seemed to want some gratitude to be shown for the fact that all three were still alive. As usual it was the "lenient and humanitarian policy" that allowed them to live on. He had a request: a joint "letter of appreciation" to the South Vietnamese Front for National Liberation, which was to be a self-criticism and praise for the NFL, and was to include mention of chicken for Christmas.

That was all. The trio's excitement was contagious. So Grissett had been right! More U.S. troops were coming in, and that meant more chance of rescue, or at least the war's end. How could these Vietnamese resist an all-out surge by thousands of well-equipped soldiers with air support, plenty of weapons?

The three of them decided to write the requested letter. The reasoning was that conditions would improve—they could scarcely get worse. Even if the letter was used as a propaganda document, it would be worded to give hints of their true plight and to hint that all was not as the words said.

When it was finished, any intelligence officer would read, not the thanks, but the fact that the men were badly undernourished and suffering from vitamin deficiencies. Not that the chicken was an example of humane treatment, but that it was the only meat in a year. Not that their treatment was excellent but that "Captain Eisenbraun had achieved a weight of 120 pounds for the first time under the diet provided."

They never knew where the letter went. Ho told them he was taking it back to the central committee as evidence of "gratitude and progressiveness." On one count, at least, Ho was well satisfied with the results of his visit. But he also gave the impression he was in a great hurry.

In the political classes, hyperbole had taken over completely. They did not believe his statements about "sweeping victories" over the U.S. foe, couched in much the same terms as those used by Hanoi Hannah on the radio; nor did they believe Ho's statements about "protests throughout the world, not only in the U.S., against imperialist aggression and murder."

Ho also spoke of a "great movement led by the prominent and famous baby doctor, Dr. Benjamin Spock, against U.S. presence in Southeast Asia. It is not just one class, but all professions, doctors and the lawyers, as well as workers and mothers with babies in their arms, raising up in protest."

There was so much about the protests. Names and what seemed to be small confirmatory facts. They dismissed it. Protest against war, Eisenbraun said, would always be alive in the U.S. "They'll always be the ten percent," he would say. But they thought the protestors were as much exaggerated as the battles Ho mentioned, or the planes being shot down, or the pilots captured. No pilots had been seen by the trio in three years.

Ho left, life resumed as it was. In February, with Tet approaching, the two camp veterans watched, not without relish, as a water buffalo came lumbering into the camp. Somewhere, the squeal of a pig. Another year of their lives; nothing had changed.

Garwood said, watching Eisenbraun, "Yeah, I know, Ike, I remember last year." The preparations. The sickening release of the ARVNs. It looked as if everything would be repeated to the letter. It always was in Vietnam, every rice bowl, every dipper of fish sauce, every speech from some hard-eyed camp commander, each dirty, lice-ridden day.

The Montagnards gathered as the year before. The ARVNs, looking hopeful and talking excitedly, entered into the preparations, singing in the evening, being overly polite to the guards and the cadre, even to the point that a disgusted Eisenbraun reported that one of the ARVNs had taken to calling himself "your humble servant" when addressing a guard.

The morning of the first of Tet's three days, while the slaughter of the animals was going on, a group of a totally different kind arrived. It brought movie equipment, a heavy, crude-looking gasoline generator, tins of petrol, boxes that seemed to hold film spools and others with contents that could not be discovered.

The things were set up in the largest building available, the main prisoner hooch. To the incredulous eyes of the Americans, it appeared that the Vietnamese were setting out to *show* movies, not to film them. They put up a nearly white sheet down at the end of the hooch normally occupied by the Americans. The three Americans found their excitement rising. A film. They had forgotten how much they missed simply going to a movie. They talked about films they had seen, actors they admired and women—Monroe, Hepburn, Terry Moore, Natalie Wood, Annette Funicello. . . .

But the camp commander first needed his own stage. "This is a Vietnamese holiday," he told them. "But we have decided to let you participate in the festivities in that your rations will be increased. And you will be allowed to view films that have been brought all the way from the Democratic Republic of Vietnam."

That evening, as the film was being shown, the light from the projector streamed out of the hooch like a beacon. They had not seen electric light in so long that it was unbearably bright.

"If the damn planes don't see this, they will never see us," said Eisenbraun, hooding his eyes with a hand. The trio, sitting where they usually slept, had front-row seats. "We're gonna get our ass bombed out of here tonight."

It took two hours to get the mechanics operating. When the black-and-white images finally came into focus, with Eisenbraun squinting and the other two gaping, Garwood recognized that the subject of the drama was a face he had seen before in camp pictures, usually behind a desk. Ho Chi Minh.

Even that proved fascinating in the prison camp. They would have been happy watching a man shoveling on a dung pile, if that was what the movie was

120

about. But the film was like a home movie. Ho Chi Minh with children, standing on a building's steps while they ran towards him with flowers. There was tuneless hollow music on the soundtrack, and even the music was clearly about the famous leader. The Americans simply watched. Ho, looking small and energetic, was wearing a white suit. He visited soldiers, he visited a boat, he visited villages. There was an incomprehensible narrative, and as abruptly as it started, it ended.

The hooch broke up in applause after the end. The Montagnards were delirious. One of them rushed to the screen and tried to touch one image, unable to understand that the sheet was not the clothing of the picture. Others hooted and laughed at the man, who was too amazed and delighted to take offense.

The second film showed people planting rice, digging foxholes, working with their water buffalo. It was clearly designed to show the bucolic life of North Vietnam; under any other circumstances it would have been as dull as a travelog about Iowa. The camera crew left the next morning. They had the look of superior beings about them as they went about their tasks, men of civilization giving savages a taste of honey.

But ARVNs were not released this time. Hopeful, they loitered chattering. The buffalo meat tasted good, but produced terrible intestinal upset. Everyone's breath stank for a day after that meat. And three days after Tet, the camp was bombed.

Whether the bombing had anything to do with the film was anyone's guess. Eisenbraun was sure his dire warning had come true. The prisoners heard no planes before the first bomb hit. It hit about half a mile from the camp—the first hostile action the camp had known since August, when an artillery spotter, tossing hand grenades into the velvet of the jungle, had managed to drop a couple nearby, without really guessing, to judge by his course and actions, that a community of half a hundred souls was under the high canopy of trees.

It was evening when the first bomb fell. Some soldiers know what kind of a bomb it is from the sound. Eisenbraun said, "Two hundred fifty pounds."

But quickly the sounds marched on the camp with an awful certainty. "Hit the deck," Eisenbraun said, and all three dove under the bamboo floor to the cool ground under the hooch. The air began to vibrate as the explosions came on top of one another, and the forest sounded with the tattering and whistling of fragments striking the trees and slicing the foliage. A bomb hit the camp, landing about a hundred yards from where the trio hid and prayed. They were jolted out of the ground as if they had been picked up and dumped down by a giant hand. The hooches went down like card houses—they simply fell over on their sides, the bamboo uprights unable to hold the thin walls. Limbs and rocks began to rain down from the sky and pattered on the bamboo floor, which still covered the Americans.

The silence fell in as quickly as it had been shoved aside by the monstrous noise. Whatever had produced the event had disappeared as silently and quickly as it had come, and left only the stink of cordite and the wide eyes of the Vietnamese. It was as if a hurricane had been compressed into ten seconds instead of ten hours. It was over quickly, yet for a few seconds while the tremor of the bomb gripped him, Garwood thought the whole earth would open and swallow him. It was his first time under aerial bombardment.

Eisenbraun, brushing dirt from his beard, commented wryly even before they had surveyed the damage, "That was a hell of a rescue attempt."

Shakily they examined themselves and found no damage. Their house was gone, and a new crater stank and let out wisps of smoke. They emerged to see others emerge, looking for life. The ARVNs had made for a bomb shelter, ironically one they had dug themselves. They came out like clowns from the tiny auto at the circus. The Americans could not believe how many little men were piled in there. One guard was seriously wounded by fragments, and the jungle around the point of impact had been vaporized, or so torn by thousands of steel fragments that there was nothing left but a green paste on neighboring trees. The high canopy had a hole in it about the size of a city block, and the sky stared into an unnaturally bright place where the camp was.

The chaos after the raid would have been the perfect time to escape, but none of the Americans even gave it a thought. It was as if they were adrift at sea, hanging on to any piece of timber. The guards, shock wearing off, scurried around to gather the prisoners. Actually there was little to do. The ARVNs sat quietly, like sheep, packed together in one place. The Americans formed their own clutch a few feet away. The wounded guard was carried past in a hammock. He was sedated, or at least seemed completely out of it.

The camp commander and the guards made a hurried assessment of the damage. But like the persistent noise that first intrudes into a dream, then joins it, and finally ends it, the sound of a light plane could be heard growing louder and louder.

Garwood recognized it as an L-19 spotter plane, not by sight but by logic. He knew that these light craft followed bombing raids to look into the craters and through the doors blown in the jungle. It was the only way to see through that hovering screen that hid the life of the ground.

"*Choi oui*," shouted an ARVN, "Oh, my God!"

Panic spread as the guards started shouting, "*L'muoi-chin tat ca xuong hom!*" "Bomb shelter—L-nineteen!" The ARVNs piled into their hole once more and to their dismay, the Americans were ordered in also. Garwood was near the top of the heap of bodies, but too high for the shelter to do him any good. He watched the guards hide themselves behind trees, their weapons at the ready—as if they were going to shoot down a plane flying at one thousand feet.

The plane made a single pass, banked sharply, slowing its engine, and made another run over their hole in the jungle. The guards did not shoot. The plane must have seen the remnants of the camp, or why the extra pass? The whole camp was soon in flight. The guards hurriedly gathered their meager belongings and the few tools they used. Dusk drew down quickly. The trio of Americans packed their two sets of clothing, their mats, their chopsticks, bowls. Garwood marveled at the baggage of his life, which now weighed only a few pounds. Grissett wanted to take his pillow, which he had labored over. Garwood said, "Leave it, I'll make you another, it's easy."

They marched all that night through hilly jungle terrain. Sometimes they seemed to cut through fresh jungle without any trail at all. It was a snake of stooped laboring men, winding through profound darkness, each man literally guided by the tail of the man ahead. The jungle night sounds filled the air, along with breathing and snatches of low urgent conversation or curses. On such a night Eisenbraun was nearly blind. The Americans were near the rear of the march, watched by the last two guards, and Eisenbraun was between Garwood and Grissett. He'd stub his toe or fall while crossing a shallow stream; he made a dreadful walking companion. But he responded to each reverse with resolute obscenities.

Dawn, and the march went on. The scouts searched for a new campsite, but the Americans took no part in this.

Eisenbraun learned the ARVNs were building the new camp, which was a source of amusement for him. He thought it a wonderful joke that they had been eagerly waiting for release at Tet and now, instead, were building the camp for the Americans. When it was finished, it took a day and a half to get there.

Camp IV, unlike the others, was on a hill. Close to the top was civilization of a kind—two Montagnard villages within hearing, and smelling, distance. The Montagnards traditionally chose hilltops for their village sites, which was a fine idea for security, but a problem for the one commodity the camps had never before lacked—water. Camp IV was the camp without a stream. Washing was about a quarter of a mile away in a clear stream, a rivulet really, which measured only about four feet across.

The camp seemed to be disguised as a Montagnard village itself, but without the striking and typical long communal hooch on low stilts. It was like being a suburb of a Montagnard town to live in Camp IV; the villagers passed freely through it and it became part of their community. The guards and camp organization were able to barter bullets, needles, cloth, and other manufactured articles for meat, labor, vegetables.

The Montagnards were a primitive and most effective security device. They were people who belonged to the hilly jungle, who were part of it, not visitors like the Viet Cong, or strangers like the Vietnamese and Americans. Thoughts of escape were impossible in this society, where the men could slip through the jungle like wraiths, virtually appearing and disappearing at will.

There was no high stockade, only a small bamboo fence less than waist high. Five small buildings—cooking, communal, guards, Americans, ARVNs, with a latrine shared by all prisoners—clustered together under the high triple jungle canopy.

The Montagnards spoke a dialect different from Vietnamese, so that communications with the guards were often strained and difficult. Both Garwood and Eisenbraun quickly tried to pick up the necessary vocabulary, the words for tobacco and banana. The tiny mountain men seemed to have a fascination for the white-skinned giants. They looked with pity at the hollow-eyed whites whose beards were as strange as their language. They would slip gifts of tobacco to them. This commodity was plentiful to the point where it would simply be given to the prisoners. It stank, but Garwood found himself getting used to it.

Eisenbraun taught him to roll the damply dry leaves tight between fingers and thumb and then seal them with spit. If they were rolled too tight, they had to be punched out with bamboo slivers. Ike was addicted to these pungent cheroots, and if there were any pleasures of that mountain life, it was the times when Garwood and Eisenbraun sat smoking their cigars after the evening meal, while the deep darkness of the jungle surrounded them and only voices drifted through the still air. The feeling that they were surrounded by other life, even if it was only the wild existence of the Montagnards, comforted them. In fact, the mountain people, with their curiosity and their ageless habits and superstitions, were the most calming and cheering element in their captivity. It was at these times that Eisenbraun, who seemed calmer and healthier than in past months, would reminisce about the past—an old man of thirty-six who had utterly changed, except in his mind.

He would talk about his wife, his daughter, and the days of a soldier's life. How he rose from the ranks. The duty stations. But the future had narrowed down to one impossible dream, his home in California and his wife; he planned to spend all his time with them. He had a mind for no more careers, and would retire forever.

It would start with food—steaks and barbecues and beer busts and picnics. He told Garwood of his experience as a cook, something he never thought he would be interested in. Now the memories of these simple meals filled his mind. As with so many memories, the things of little interest now were of most interest. The things that seemed so important before now meant little.

Garwood's mind would inevitably follow the flow—how strange it seemed to him, that ideal life that Eisenbraun painted. How unlike what he had known: fights with his father, resentment for his stepmother, the sneer of the tough kid who was not tough at all. Now he dreamed of making it over into what it could have been. The corniest family could not be corny enough for him.

In his life there had never been any future, only a succession of troubles he had to get out of. He was always, it seemed, running down some alley with an unnameable shape lumbering after him. He had always lived with the philosophy of just getting to the next corner. He had always been driven, and he had never been trusted, not by his school, his father, his officers. He had always been that little bit unclean, that little bit unworthy, that seeker of the way out.

Grissett's life experiences had not been unlike Garwood's. A broken home, a succession of places to live in Oklahoma and Colorado, little success at school, a dropout.

Grissett was deeply religious—whether it was something that had grown since captivity, or something he had always had, Garwood never knew. But in the jungle, it was something steady, stable and continuing, and connected with a history that was part of the outside world. Garwood saw for the first time how a candle on a piece of board could make a difference. But he had no such foundation in his own life. He had scoffed at it; liked it, but scoffed at it.

Life crept along for a month, then two. Mr. Ho returned to the camp and gave a quiet lecture to the three men. "I have orders from the central committee of the NFL to select one candidate for possible liberation," he told them all. The reaction was excitement, suspicion, disbelief.

Ho said that in accord with the "solidarity movement in the United States, and the progressive, peace-loving people, the SVNFL is seriously thinking about releasing one American prisoner to the solidarity committee headed by Dr. Benjamin Spock when they come to visit North Vietnam in the near future."

Ho said the decision would be made on the "progress, health and attitude in thinking and working of the individual person." It would not do, he said, to return someone of "incorrect attitude."

When he said health, both of the enlisted men thought immediately that Eisenbraun would be chosen. Without doubt his health was worst, and his problems with it did not seem to change. He was higher-ranking, had been in prison longer. Ike was silent. Ho continued for long minutes more, spieling along about imperialism, victories, U.S. isolation—none of which had the slightest hold on the listeners. They had long since learned to disregard the phrases that heralded news that the United States was losing the war, thousands of planes were being downed, and the rest.

Ho made it clear that all three were candidates. Then he dismissed his class in "progress," indicating that a decision would be made on the past records of the three.

They talked about it. The suspicion and wariness dissolved into fretful hopes. Both of the younger men deferred to Eisenbraun. After all, they figured, it would make more of a propaganda splash to have a Special Forces officer returned than a mere ranker.

Things moved fast, on the clock of the jungle. The rations for the trio were more than doubled—there was lunch for the first time in captivity and more manioc, more vegetables.

The ARVNs watched enviously as the extra food was taken to the Americans; the diners found the weight of those dark eyes on them disconcerting. They felt they were being fattened up for something, and the friendliness of the guards soured on them. Alone of the prisoners, Eisenbraun simply ate the extra food and said nothing to add to the speculation. He did not believe anyone would be released, he told Garwood. "It's just a scheme to check out our attitudes and reactions. Don't get your hopes built up."

Down deep, Garwood's secret hope was that it would be him. After all, he was practically a noncombatant. He hadn't wanted to come to Vietnam, certainly hadn't wanted to fight. His health was good, he had worked hard on details, and he had not joined in the last escape. Grissett's idea was that

125

everyone should stick together, and if one was to be released, all should be, and if not, all should refuse release. "That would be great," Eisenbraun commented dryly, with a gesture indicating that the outcome Grissett suggested was the least probable of all. Each man had his own thoughts—by this point in captivity there was no seniority among them; rather there was a mutual understanding of each man's hopes, each man's chances, each man's luck.

The extra food continued for three weeks. The difference, particularly in Eisenbraun, was immediate. He gained weight for the first time and the swelling of his ankles was reduced. He became positively jovial rather than laconic. Grissett looked better, complained less. Garwood gained about ten pounds in the three weeks and began to feel free for the first time from the constant fatigue. Everyone knew that the extra food was a finite thing, a thing to be taken advantage of, even if it was a simple, brutal manipulation.

In the first week in May, Mr. Hum and a guard came down to the American hooch where Grissett and Garwood were taking a noon break after wood detail. The guard stood there and Hum spoke. "Bop, get your belongings together, and come with me."

"Where 'm I going?"

"You are going to live somewhere else. You will not live here."

"Where's Bob going?" said Eisenbraun from inside the hooch.

"Don't worry," Hum said placatingly. "He will be here, in the camp. He can come to see you every day. If he wants to."

Why are they separating me? Garwood thought with that old familiar feeling he had known all his life, the feeling of the police siren, the dread. What have I done wrong?

He told Eisenbraun, "When I find out what's going on, I'll let you know." Their parting was astonishingly brief, partly because there was nothing to do but pick up a mat, a coconut shell, a toothbrush (the latest "gift" of the fattening-up), and a wooden pillow.

"Be careful," said Grissett with guarded eyes. Garwood didn't even bother to shake hands. He trudged obediently up to the guard and Hum with his arms full. It did not dawn on him that he might be the one selected for release.

They went to the small building between the commanders and the kitchen hooches, which had come to be known as the supply hooch. There was the store of rice, piles of manioc, square tins of fish sauce, and sacks of salt. But now there was nothing left but the faint smell of the foodstuffs that had lain there. The hooch was about half the size of his former quarters, and had shelves where the food had been stored. "This will be your new home for a while," Hum said. It was only fifty feet from where he had been before. His friends watched as he threw his mat inside and wrinkled his nose at the fishy, grocery-crate smell. Even Eisenbraun could still see him. There was no stockade. The mystery deepened.

"What's going on?" Garwood asked again.

"I cannot tell you that," said the placid Hum. "You will remain here until told otherwise—you will not leave the building without permission from the guard. Anywhere you go, you must tell the guard."

"Can I go down and see Ike and Russ?"

"Yes, but you must ask permission—both upon leaving and upon returning. You will continue your work for the camp with wood and leaves, but you will do it alone in the presence of a guard. You can at no time go anywhere outside this camp without the presence, knowledge, or permission of a guard."

In a way, it was as bad as the stocks. It was isolation, Garwood's yawning, screaming weak point. There was no one to talk to, not even a window. He had to break out pieces of bamboo to make spy holes.

He walked to the low door of his hooch and asked his guard to go out.

"Where you want to go?" the man asked.

"I just want to visit Ike and Russ."

"You cannot do that today." The man spoke sharply and simply in the words that Garwood knew in the language. "Maybe tomorrow."

"Hum said I could go with permission."

"I have my orders. Maybe tomorrow."

Garwood couldn't understand the conflicting statements. He couldn't understand a lie so blatant. Then at dinner, he got rice and meat—this was highly unusual. It was baiting and punishment at once. He almost didn't eat the food. His uneasiness was completely irrational.

He asked the guard to be allowed to go to the kitchen. He was refused.

Then when Ike and Russ came up to the kitchen to get their ration, Ike called out, "Find out anythin' yet, Bob?"

"Nah," said Garwood, standing by the low door of this new hooch.

"No talking," shouted the guard, turning to Eisenbraun and Grissett. "You return!" Eisenbraun looked at the Vietnamese with a bemused shrug.

He had trouble sleeping, and it was not only the fish sauce that penetrated everywhere with the night mist. He had left his tobacco at the other hooch. It was in Ike's keeping for the great lover of cheroots to divvy up. Now he missed it sorely. He could not think of any way to circumvent this simple and effective block to communications Hum had set up. He realized how much he had come to depend on their simplest chatter. He began to sing to himself without realizing why. "Sad Movies."

Hum came every day, with the camp supply officer and the camp commander; his was a new face, a man who later was known to other U.S. POWs as "Frenchie." Garwood, with his growing knowledge of the language, knew his name as Khoang. The supply officer he knew as Tum.

The short, stocky supply officer was a nervous man in his late forties. He looked like one who previously had not been rewarded by life. He handed Garwood a fistful of tobacco leaves, to the prisoner's relief. Garwood thanked him. Garwood, trying to please, stood at attention when the camp commander entered. Now he was told to sit down.

127

"On the orders of my superiors," Khoang said, "we have separated you from Ike and Russ. You will begin a class in re-education so you will have knowledge of the growing antiwar movement of the United States and the world over."

"Alone?" Garwood asked nervously. "Why not Ike and Russ, too?"

"I have my orders. Perhaps you can ask Mr. Ho, when he comes to see you after the course." Khoang was tall, taller than any Vietnamese Garwood had seen. His hair was gray and he was in his fifties, immaculately shaved and coiffured in short hair style. He wore Ho Chi Minh sandals and a gold wrist watch. He carried with him an exotic sidearm in a brown leather holster.

The next morning, Hum came down to the little, reeking hooch. He handed Garwood some pamphlets, clearly printed in North Vietnam, and some others more crudely made. "Read these. I will come back this afternoon and I want you to tell me what you think of them." The books were the size of U.S. comic books, and they had some pictures. The paper was cheap and thin. But the print was clear. They were all in English. One title was "Antiwar Demonstrations and Solidarity with Vietnam Grows in the United States." Another title: "U.S. Imperialists: No. 1 Enemy to Progressive, Peace-Loving Peoples Throughout the World." One pamphlet told of two U.S. servicemen who were released by the SVNFL in 1963 with "progressive attitudes." One's name was Smith—which immediately made Garwood think it was a phony, in spite of the picture of the man with his name tag visible.

The contents were what Garwood expected. It was the same sort of "news" they heard on the radio, which Hum played from time to time. All victories were glorious for the NFL, and U.S. forces were doomed wherever they appeared. He read that the antiwar movement was being joined by millions of people and was led by top intellectuals and university students. He was told that they had marched on the streets of many U.S. cities, and even to the White House in Washington, D.C.

This was not new to Garwood. He read rapidly through, trying to think how to answer Hum's questions without wrecking his chances, if they had ever existed. He decided there was never a plan that would work with these people. Take the questions as they came.

Hum came back, all smiles in the afternoon. "Well, have you finished, Bop?"

"Yes."

"Now. What is your impressions?"

Garwood looked at him. "I don't know," he said. He didn't know what he wanted him to say. Should he be enthused, frantic, what?

"Well, what do you think? Do you agree? What do you feel about the demonstrations in the U.S. and in the world supporting Vietnam?"

"I don't know what to think, really." Hum looked puzzled, perhaps a little hurt.

"Do you agree with the movement?"

"Yeah," Garwood said. "To an extent, I do."

"To what extent?"

"To where I agree we shouldn't be in Vietnam. But I don't agree with these things, like burning the American flag, this stuff about draft cards."

"Why don't you agree with this? Are you upset that they burn the American flag?"

Garwood knew he should be careful in his answers. "No," he said, "I just disagree."

Hum had set the pattern. He would talk about the same subjects—discontent in the U.S., students taking up the Vietnamese cause. He was pushing to make Garwood commit himself. Hum wanted Garwood simply to agree with the document. But he tried to ride the line, telling him that he agreed the country should not be at war, but stopping at the fact that he "disagreed" with U.S. policy. He went over the same questions and answers for three days. He grew quite sick of Hum, even if he was the only company. It was like the radio.

Very carefully, Garwood tried to keep his answers to "yes," "no," "I don't know," or his tie breaker, "I don't have any feelings one way or another."

"Mr. Ho will be coming here to see you in a few days' time," Hum said. "It is for your own good to be in a progressive state of mind."

Garwood, mightily weary of the game of fending off, asked if there would be more classes. He was told there would not. "Can I go down and talk to Ike and Russ?" he asked.

"I will go and report your request to the camp commander," Hum said, "and will let you know."

The next day when Garwood saw the camp commander, Khoang, walking by his hooch, he called out, "Sir, Camp Commander," he used his best Vietnamese, and stood at attention.

"Yes?"

"I beg your permission to go down to see Ike and Russ. It has been four days and I miss them very much." The commander looked at his watch.

"All right, but be back in your hooch before the noon meal."

Garwood almost ran down to the American hooch with only one guard who tried to stop him; he hurriedly told his permission and was let pass. Ike and Russ looked up at the figure hurrying in. Nothing had changed. They were sitting on the bamboo slats, picking lice. He grabbed Eisenbraun's hand, patted Russ on the back.

"What the hell took you so long?" Eisenbraun said in his best barroom manner.

9
The New Recruit

IT HAD not been a particularly stressful year for Marine Corps manpower in 1963, nor is it known why the decision was made, somewhere in the USMC recruiting command, to dip into the ranks of juvenile offenders for fresh men for the Corps. It was long before the era of the volunteer army; most young Americans were used to the idea of selective service, there was none of the panic and foreboding that later spread when the war began in earnest.

But the Marine Corps prided itself on never taking draftees (though this policy was abandoned later in the Vietnam War) and as a result had difficulties keeping enlistments up—except for cases where young men were faced with choices that made Marine boot camp look the lesser of two evils.

This was the case with many young men of that era who believed the Corps was a more elite, tougher, more rewarding way to do the duty years of military service. It was also the case for many who were faced with incarceration. In those days, the USMC stressed its rehabilitative image—that it was the service that could take roughnecks, misfits and rebellious youths, and make men of them. In many instances, they succeeded splendidly. The recruiting sergeant who found Garwood may have thought the sullen young man who chose jail rather than home was one of these energetic souls.

The first thing they did was to feed him compliments. Garwood was told he looked like "pretty good material for the Marine Corps," but at that point he felt he would rather spend his time in jail than join the military. Garwood and his friends were distinctly unmilitary types.

But it was boring in the juvenile home. "They came back to see me several times," Bobby said. "They thought I was a live wire, they showed me the pay scales, the branches, and they told me I would have a choice of duty stations. Other things went through my mind, too. I wanted to go to California to see the girl I'd been dating junior high through high school."

The recruiter told Garwood that it would be easy to arrange all this, that he would be out of the detention home, that he would be in California soon. How soon? "Next week," he was told.

Sometime after this discussion, Bobby Garwood made the most important decision of his life, sitting in the bare precincts of the Indianapolis juvenile tank. By the time he had thought it through, it seemed inevitable.

In the last week before he flew to California to begin boot camp, a chill came over the Garwood house. Bob submitted to sleeping there, but spent most of his time with his friends. His father drove him to the airport and he climbed on the airliner. "His look was like that was the last time he would see me," Garwood said. He explained that his father was often like that, a man who couldn't seem to accept what others were doing, no matter what it was.

Garwood was swept up immediately in the swirl of boot camp, and almost as quickly found he was not going to make a good soldier. A soldier that got by, a soldier who did his time, yes, but not a good Marine. His mates called him "scuzzy" because he carried the unwashed look of the gang into the barracks.

Garwood has often repeated that he neither swore nor drank before he joined the Marine Corps, but only afterward. The expression may simply be a way of contrasting amounts. He found boot camp onerous, exhausting, terrifying. He heard the stories and believed them—about how tough the drill instructors were, about young men committing suicide because of the toughness of the training. He failed to get through "boot" in the first three-week course because he caught pneumonia just short of graduation. His recollection is that he knew he was getting sicker and sicker but he wanted to pass through with his group and so told no one. Then, on parade, he passed out in the ranks and was hospitalized. Anyone who misses a week of the training is sent back through again.

In California, he was able to re-establish his relationship with Mary Speers, a girl he had known since early puberty and a longtime favorite of Garwood's—the one woman, he declares, whose purity has never concerned him. She was his "nice girl," the one he wanted to marry, and if their relationship proved the longest-lasting he was to know, it was also the most static.

As a second-time "boot" Garwood enjoyed some seniority, and took advantage of it to the full. He wrote to Mary. He began to enjoy the idea of being tough—not pasteboard tough, but tough the way soldiers are supposed to be: "We weren't pampered, we weren't given what we wanted, we weren't babies. You stand at attention and a DI (drill instructor) hits you in the gut and asks you how it feels and you say it feels good and you want another one, and he does it again." It was an accomplishment, perhaps Garwood's first to be marked with ceremony and reward.

131

Garwood came home on his first leave like a hero and confronted his father. But he did it in a new way, and from a new base. He traveled from Camp Pendleton to his mother's house and stayed with her and her husband, only visiting Indianapolis.

Jack Garwood was nothing if not flexible. No longer disapproving, he now chose to play the proud father. "He did a complete turnaround," Garwood said. "He took pictures, tape recorded my voice, he was real proud of me."

But Ruth Buchanan, who had only discovered her son that last summer, was apprehensive. She told Bobby her first husband had been killed in World War II, her brother taken prisoner in the Korean War and later reported dead in a Chinese prison camp.

Garwood was delighted with the results of his first political action and automatically took advantage of it. He looked grown up, at least in his dress uniform, though a picture of him in fatigues and helmet reveals a yeasty face with pouty lips. He felt grown up and talked to his father for the first time on the level.

He talked about the future, and glowing with affection for Mary Speers, planned what he was going to do after his four-year hitch was over: He was going to marry her and go into business.

For his part, the father waxed lyrical, offering to go into business with him as a printer. Garwood, feeling the shortness of time and the uncertainty of the future, embraced the idea, happier to be reconciled with his father than to be a future printer. He wanted to become a mechanic. He wanted to do things with his hands, repair machines that were broken.

This time it was his mother who took him to the airport to fly back to Pendleton.

Though Garwood had acted the tough Marine on leave, he was negative about being sent overseas, now that things seemed to be on a level plane at home. It seemed to him that as soon as something had been accomplished, it was taken away from him; he wished the Marine Corps had never happened to him, now that he had a California girl. He'd even had a job offer from his uncle, vague, but a talking point.

When orders came for Okinawa, Garwood was already out of step with his unit, which had shipped out ahead of him, because of his rerun through boot camp, and it was in the fall of 1964, the year Lyndon Johnson was elected president, when Garwood arrived at the Pacific home of the Third Marine Division.

Garwood's memories of that fall and winter are dim. He drank away his leisure time, racked up minor offenses and complained continually about vague medical problems. He said on reflection that he became "pretty much of an alcoholic" while on the island, but he may have been hoping to get sick enough to be sent back to the States, or may have just felt lonely. There were curious incidents, like the time he catapulted himself into a wall from a taxi while fleeing MPs, the rumors that he had such dreadful headaches he was forcibly restrained from pounding his head against a locker room wall, and a minor accident during which he had banged his head against the windshield of the truck he was driving.

In November, five U.S. "advisors" were killed and seventy-six wounded during a mortar attack on Bien Hoa, and after that came the first real steps America took toward full involvement, starting with the first air attack on North Vietnam, in February, swift manpower increases, and Lyndon Johnson's famous words, "We want no wider war. Whether or not this course can be maintained lies with the North Vietnamese aggressors."

Garwood started missing driving duty, and he did not hesitate to tell his comrades about his headache pains: "His complaints of headaches were common knowledge down in the motor pool," said a bunkmate. "We only had five or six drivers and when a man missed his turn at duty driver somebody else had to take it."

When the unit left for Vietnam, Garwood was left behind for a month and a half, while he was checked by eye doctors at Kue Army Hospital on the island; but they decided to push on to the war zone with the headachy driver in June, when the rest of the headquarters company of the Third Marine Division came to Da Nang.

Garwood and the men who were short, the men who had married Okinawan women, the men with legal problems, those in jail, were left in the original shipment to the war. Somehow Garwood's hopes of being sent back to the States, where he might have prolonged his treatment or found another military occupation speciality, did not work out, nor did a plan he made to switch assignments with a man who had been given duty in Hawaii, a far more congenial billet.

The trip from Okinawa by ship to Da Nang was a holiday for Garwood. He seemed able to invent ways to get into trouble where none might have existed. The good part of the voyage, he remembered, which took three days and two nights in a landing ship, was gambling with the sailors, using stolen Marine Corps cigarettes in the pot. The Marines thought it hilarious, since it was easy enough for them to break into the ship's stores and then hide the proceeds in the trucks in the hold of the ship.

"We anchored in Son Tay Bay," he said, "by Monkey Mountain. Off in the distance we saw flashes of mortar fire. And that's when it first hit us. We were curious and wanted to know where we were going.

"I didn't give a shit. I didn't care anything about it. The only thing I thought about was putting in my time and going home. I didn't know who the Vietnamese were, what we were fighting about and I really didn't care." He was in Da Nang, living in a tent, hotter than hell, no leave, days in a six-wheel truck, monotony.

Garwood was less than a small cog in a mighty machine. His duties were almost superfluous, in his telling. He was a taxi man for officers, part of the apparent excess that was the buildup. He saw it as complete chaos—units arriving with no place to stay and nothing to eat, officers shouting. Garwood

133

alone felt tight and organized, his headaches suddenly gone, knowing that he had five months to serve in the war zone, five months to the day, and a determination that nothing was going to happen to him to prevent his return to the U.S.

He soon learned to hate the place, hot, muggy, rainy, sticky, dirty, smelly as it was, the venomous glances of the churlish children who would beg and then spit, and the impossible anger that the soldiers felt towards them; and the feeling that grew in him that he didn't understand the war, and didn't want to have anything to do with it.

He did a stretch driving trucks, sometimes unloading ships, during which the Marines were able to steal whole truckloads of goods and sell them on side streets—practices that were widespread. He was beginning to like that part of it, making money on the side, when they assigned him to relocation duty, which meant he would go out into the "boonies" and stop at a village and simply load everything into a truck—scared civilians, furniture, food, animals, everything—while soldiers stood sniper guard with M-14s and shotguns. When the trucks got to their destination, the stuff would be unloaded, and if the people didn't move fast enough, it would simply be thrown off.

This was his introduction to the war: duty hours, beer, whores, sleeping in a tent, the dust of the thrown-together. He wrote letters to Mary, telling her nothing about his activities, for he thought that letters to home were supposed to be just that.

"Afterwards, I got the job of staff driver for headquarters. There were two sedans in Da Nang, and I had one of them, that made me a big shot, even though I was a private. The car was a '64 Dodge station wagon, on Sundays the general's staff went somewhere, and as a staff driver, you're on twenty-four-hour standby. I usually went to the USO to meet someone, 'cause I had one hometown buddy who I went to school with—he was in reconnaissance. I didn't even know he was in 'Nam, and I saw him in the PX.

"His name is David, and I used to go out and get him—that was a real trip 'cause the car had flags and stars all over it and all that crap on it, though 'course I kept them covered when the general wasn't in the vehicle. I kept the flags covered, but everyone knew who the vehicle belonged to, so I went to get David and take him to the USO. His unit was quite a distance, say three miles away. We had some beers, we'd compare notes.

"Every time I came into the recon area, this company snapped to attention because of the Dodge, and when I went to get him, everyone got into a panic. David's CO jumped on my case and he said, 'Who gives you the right to drive this vehicle where you want?' I said, 'The general.'

"He said, 'What are you doin' out here, where's the friggin' general?' he said. 'You care about us out here in recon?'

"I said, 'No, I just came to get a buddy of mine.' He said, 'Where are you goin'—to one of those whorehouses?' and I said, no, we were just going back to the USO. He said, 'Well, I don't want you to get my troops in trouble,' and I told him, nobody's gonna bother us. The recons act tough, and I got cocky after a while, and I was saying, 'The only person I answer to is the general.'

"It was the last week in August, and this incident was in the middle of August, where I'm talkin' to the CO. We went into Da Nang once in a while, it was called free time, and the last week in August and I went out to the recon to pick him up and they told me three days earlier they had shipped his body home. I tried to find out, and the only thing they said was he was on patrol, and he was running point and he keeled over and everyone else hit the ground and took up defensive positions. They checked him and he was dead."

There were other nasty surprises: He was standing perimeter duty and responded to stone-throwing children with missiles of his own made of bullet-heads he'd prised off their cases and thrown with a sling made of tire-tube rubber. The result was reduction in rank and a fine.

But there were also advantages: The food was good, for they ate with the headquarters mess, there was plenty of beer and new clothes, for the drivers of the top officers had to look good, and aside from the boredom and being constantly on call, he spent his time playing cards, listening to the radio, shooting the breeze, time getting shorter and shorter.

He wrote to Mary, the letters full of undying love. And he met General Lewis Walt, the Third Division's commanding officer, even drove the great man and stood by at parties he attended, liking him for his down-to-earth way with the troopers, a man who handed the enlisted a cold beer on a hot day.

Garwood was down to counting the days by the beginning of September, and though he had never fired a shot in anger, seen combat or faced any but the most accidental dangers, he was filled with anxiety.

The vibrations were extremely bad, like the slowly climbing casualty list. The year before, in 1964, there were 164 combat deaths, and this year the numbers had increased almost tenfold, rising to 1,365 dead and more than 5,300 wounded; 148 were missing or captured.

David's death shocked him. The man had been eighteen, just a boy. It was only a while since high school. He could see the members of David's family in his mind's eye, Indianapolis people, like his own, really. He did as little as possible from that point on, he took on the short timer's attitude.

It wasn't as if the older men or the lifers objected. They told Garwood to stay out of danger, and he shirked as much as possible, resurrecting his headaches; he sat as low as he could behind the wheel of the car he was driving. But he kept getting assignments that made eerie feelings come over him: a Catholic chaplain to a memorial service at a recon unit, and standing there with about a dozen men in a circle as the chaplain spoke, and only the rifle and helmet of the dead man in the middle, the body already bagged and started home. Things like that.

10
The Crossover

EVEN THOUGH Eisenbraun had meant to be wryly amusing, his words still rang in Garwood's ears: "What took you so long?"

"The bastards wouldn't let me come down," he said, and told as much as he could remember about the time in the hooch. It was clear that, though Ike and Russ were trying to be friendly, it was hollow. They were more sure than he was that the choice of the liberated prisoner was already made.

"Did ya find out what's going on?" Eisenbraun asked at length.

"Ike, the only thing I can figure, the way things are going, is one of two things. They're either gonna do this to each and every one of us separately, or I'm the one they selected to release."

"Don't get your hopes up," the older man kept repeating. He explained that the Communists frequently told one thing, did another. "They like to play with your mind. Don't believe anything until it actually happens."

Garwood asked Russ, "What do you think?"

Grissett said coldly, "Bob, you do what you want to do, but I still think we should all stick together."

"If you had been the one to be picked instead of me, would you still think so?" Garwood asked.

"Yes, I think so."

"Okay, you two," Garwood said, "just calm down. There's nothing happened yet. Nobody's got released yet."

"Well, they better fatten you up," Eisenbraun said. "They can't release you the way you are now." When they recounted the total ration, Garwood found he had been receiving slightly more meat than the others.

Garwood assured the other two that nothing had changed him and nothing would. "They'll use you. Any way they can, they'll use you," Eisenbraun said. "This is gonna be propaganda, Bob. You've got to promise me you'll draw the line to where it may harm another American. Other than that, do anything you have to do to get out of here and let somebody know we're alive."

He promised, and went up to the hooch. For the next week, he gathered wood and leaves for the guards. It was a mindless existence and he wanted to keep it that way.

Mr. Ho's arrival was announced by the killing of a chicken. Every fowl in camp was the subject of loving attention. They were allowed to run free through the camp. But they could not have been more taboo if they had been high religious objects. The guards owned some, the supply officer some and the commander about ten. But every guard knew whose chicken was whose—the Vietnamese, Garwood knew, thought the world of their hens and the killing of one was a culinary event of magnitude. When a guard boldly picked out one of the commander's fowls, snatched it up after a brief chase and carried it squawking to the cook shed, it was an event sensed and analyzed by all.

Garwood looked up to the commander's hooch and there was Ho. His reaction was a mixture of curiosity and dread. When one of the cooks came bustling by the hooch with a pot, he asked, "Who has come here?"

"It is Mr. Ho," was the answer.

Ho waited until the next day to appear, though the chicken met its fate in the pot the cook carried. The smell drifted through the camp agonizingly.

"Well hello, Bob. How are you?" Ho asked. After the greetings that had become a ritual were over, he asked, "Do you know why I have come here?"

"No."

"Where are you living now?"

"Here."

"Are you comfortable?"

"No."

"Why? What's wrong?" A very concerned expression crossed his face.

"It used to be a supply hooch. The smell of the fish sauce, the rotten vegetables. It has a very bad odor. I am also lonely by myself."

"It is your living quarters. It is not a hooch. Why don't you try to clean it up? My understanding of a hooch is it is like a chicken coop. We do not try to keep you in a chicken coop."

Garwood thought of several he would have much preferred to these living quarters.

"Any problems?"

"Living alone. I don't like it."

"You are going to have to overcome that and endure it for a short time longer."

"How long?"

"A couple of months, at the longest. Bob, I have some happy news for you.

137

Remember, the last time I was here, I told that it was a possibility that at some future date, when the occasion arose, we were considering releasing one prisoner to a delegation of the American Solidarity Movement which was coming to visit North Vietnam? We have decided that you are to be that prisoner."

Garwood's head swam. "What is your idea on that?" Ho asked, hardly heard now.

"Why was I chosen?" Garwood murmured.

"I have observed your progressive attitude in work and attitude. Your health seems to be the better of the three. You are not sick so often."

"I do as much as anybody else around here. I don't do any more or any less," Garwood said.

Ho laughed politely. "Don't worry about that. There will be plenty of Americans to take your place. Our victories are getting better and better. There will be new prisoners coming to this camp. I'm sure with a good attitude, Ike and Russ will soon follow you."

He told Ho he needed time to think about it. He did not dare to ask to see the others; Ho was too smart for that.

"That's perfectly all right," Ho said with dreadful soothing, "ponder it over very carefully." Garwood asked to be dismissed. It was done.

Alone in his hooch, Garwood could scarcely wait the ten or fifteen minutes for Ho to leave the area and be sure he would not return. He asked the guard if he could go down and see Ike and Russ. To his surprise, the guard said, "Duoc—di di." ("Okay, go.")

He must have seemed upset to the other two. Russ asked, "What the fuck's the matter with you?"

Garwood quickly explained the dilemma. "I wanted to talk it over with Ike," he said. He knew it would do no good to have Grissett there when he talked to Eisenbraun. The corporal showed hurt and resentment in his face. He was a one-level guy, Garwood thought.

But Grissett stayed. Garwood went through the whole scene with Ho, leaving nothing out. "What should I do, Ike?" he asked.

"I understand your bein' worried," Eisenbraun said. "It's legitimate. It goes with what I first told you, Bob. Before they ever release you, if they are gonna release you, they're gonna get as much propaganda value out of you as they can."

"There's something I can't understand, Ike, why they would choose me?"

"For the first reason that I can think of, it is your age and your health. Your age coincides with the age group of this antiwar movement in the United States.

"Health is important. If they're gonna release you from North Vietnam, they're gonna march you up there. That trip itself could take a couple of months. Another thing. From their way of thinking, you're young and inexperienced and they're probably thinking because of this you could be more easily swayed than I could."

Russ spoke in a voice thick with hurt. "Well, I'm the same age as Bob. I'm in the Marine Corps."

"That's true, except for two things," Ike said. "Bob's been a prisoner longer than you; he was younger when he was captured, his health is better'n yours, and he can speak Vietnamese, which you can't. Which makes three.

"By speaking Vietnamese on the journey to North Vietnam, it means they would not have to send an interpreter along." Russ said nothing.

Basically his advice was difficult. "Let your conscience be your guide. Remember what I told you. We are in a drastic situation here. No one knows whether we're alive or dead, or how we're being treated. We're all at the full mercy of these bastards. It's important that one of us get out—any way he can. Draw the line only if by your judgment, you think it will harm another American. Forget about the gooks. Only another American. That should be your only concern."

Garwood was not encouraged. The decision was still his and he saw no path. He'd hoped that Eisenbraun would have made it simple, black and white. Garwood would have followed that, no sweat. If Eisenbraun had only said, "Fuck it, don't do it." That would have been okay. He just wanted to hear something hard, an order, anything. He'd never felt so immature, so insecure, so unable to make a decision as important as this one.

Over and over the cloudy thoughts rolled, keeping him awake on the reeking mat. He grew unhappy, with one guilt toppling on top of another.

Alone in the hooch, now not even wanting to see the others, he wrestled for three nights with the problem. On the fourth, he discovered by observation that Ho had been talking with Eisenbraun and Grissett.

This was a fresh worry. He knew Eisenbraun would be as steady as some mossy rock stuck deep in the ground. But what would Grissett say? He kept a lot hidden—and he showed a lot in his one-dimensional way. Garwood feared somehow that Grissett would tell Ho that Eisenbraun had advised Garwood and that Garwood had resolved to follow his advice.

One of the first prescriptions the captors had laid down was that there was to be no leadership, no giving and taking of orders. In his tortured state, he felt sure that the subtle Ho could interpret Eisenbraun's giving advice as disobeying this order.

Ho left Garwood alone. Then, about four days after the question had been put to him, a guard came into the hooch, telling him to report to Ho. He walked up the incline to the commandant's hooch looking around him like a man who wanted to remember before he was changed.

"Well, Bobby. Have you come to a decision yet?"

Mr. Ho sat at a table flanked by the camp commander and Mr. Hum. They liked this formality. Or perhaps he liked it.

"Yes, I have," Garwood said quietly.

"Good," Ho beamed. "I hope it is a favorable one?"

Garwood nodded.

In the morning, his waking was hastened by the usual Oriental bustle preceding a ceremony. The supply officer, Mr. Tum, came into Garwood's hooch with a pair of trousers and a shirt. Both were blue and looked like American work clothes. Putting them on, he found the trouser bottoms came above his ankles, and the waistband would not reach around his shrunken waist. The trousers were about three sizes too small. Tum looked on approvingly. The shirt was similarly small, and in them Garwood, gaunt as he was, looked strangely like a man popping out of clothes. "Cut off your legs," Tum advised with an odious smile.

They walked out together to where the guards were busily rounding up the prisoners. At the kitchen hooch, the tables were covered with plastic sheets; they had been hauled outside and paper posters were sewn roughly to other plastic strips hung from the trees. The slogans read: "Down With U.S. Imperialism—SVNFL," "Long Live SVNFL."

He saw the ARVNs assembled, the two Americans apart from them. Hum led him toward the tables. The camp commander began to speak. It was the usual speech about the victories, the defeats, the inevitability. He approached from Garwood's side and handed him a piece of white paper, a single sheet. "You will read this in English," he said. "Hum will interpret it in Vietnamese."

Instead of joining Grissett and Eisenbraun, he was taken to one side with Hum, where he stood, looking like an underdressed camp official. He could see Ike and Russ looking curiously at him. Their eyes were guarded, cloudy. He had a chance to glance at the speech. It only took a glance to see its role.

The speech was a speech of thanks for "showing me the light to the way to becoming a progressive, peace-loving American, and a promise never to take up arms against the Vietnamese people again." There was the usual "humanitarian and lenient policy of the NFL." In all, it was only about three paragraphs.

Ho turned elaborately and with hands extended, said, "I would like Bob to come up and give his impressions as a candidate."

He walked up. He did not know who had put the tape recorder on the table. He just saw it and noted that its plastic reels were not turning, and he saw it and he felt afraid. He stood behind the table. He heard a man shift, heard a soft smooth snap and saw the wheels turning surely. "Mr. Ho," Garwood read, "Camp Commander, guards, fellow prisoners." Then he read the paragraphs in a normal voice. He looked up only to Ike and Russ, trying to get across that these were not his words.

The tape recorder rolled on quietly in the silence. He went on: "I thank the SVNFL for their consideration," he said quickly, shocking himself by deviating from the text he had been given, "but I feel that I am not worthy of their consideration and decision and wish to decline in accepting the selection. I feel that I should work harder and study more about the Vietnamese culture." He blurted several more phrases, excusing himself from the choice on the grounds he was not qualified.

Eisenbraun and Grissett stared in disbelief. Somehow he could see it all clearly, as if he was separate from what was happening. "They can't believe I'm refusing release," he thought.

Ho seemed to be the only man who clearly understood Garwood's hurried speech. He, too, looked incredulous.

Garwood was suspicious but pleased to be allowed to visit his companions the next day. Grissett was in a state close to shock. "What the hell you think you're doing? You blew the only chance we've had!" Ike was calm, calm and slow as usual. "Lay off, Russ," he said. "He did what he felt he had to do."

The reunion was tense and unpleasant. There were too many fresh and gaping possibilities. "What are you gonna do now?" Eisenbraun asked.

"I'll wait and see what they do," Garwood said.

"They're full of tricks, Bob. If they can't use you, they'll dispose of you."

"Ike, what would have prevented them? If I went along with their bullshit at the meeting yesterday, and they could take me away from this camp, blow my ass away, or stick me in another camp, and leave you believing that I'd been released."

"Anything's possible in the jungle, Bob. It's just the chance we've got to take."

"Ike, I'm sorry, I just couldn't bring myself to do it. One part of me said to take the chance, another told me not to. But when I got up there, and saw you and Russ, the part that told me not to take the chance won.

"Russ is right, I'm beginning to think. If we walk out of here we walk all three of us."

Ike's eyes slowly rolled up from where he lay slouched on his mat, "Yeah," he said, "and then we may never walk."

Grissett, fidgeting, started to say something. Ike cut him off. "Enough!" he said. "What's happened, happened."

Garwood told them he was going to ask if he could be allowed to rejoin them. "Don't count on it," said the older man. "When they get an idea in their heads, it sticks. You fucked up Ho's plans. I'm sure he didn't take kindly to that. I'm sure he'll have an alternate plan for you and I don't think it will be you coming back to live with us. The main thing now, whatever, is don't worry about it. It's past, that part of it, just hang in there. Don't do or say anything that will piss them off more."

"Try to make Russ understand," Garwood said. "Talk to him."

"Yah, okay. Don't worry about it."

Garwood had started to leave when the familiar voice slowed him. "Bob, don't let this get you down. We've come too far to quit."

The three men parted without so much as a handshake. But from that point, sometime in June of 1967, the three were never together again as they had been. It soon developed that there was a new plan; the camp officials had come to the decision that they had been too lenient. There was a small hooch erected about fifty feet from the hooch the three had first lived in at Camp IV. It took the chattering ARVNs only a day to put it up—scarcely larger than a stocks shelter. The day after, Eisenbraun was taken to it. It was obvious that he, like Garwood, was to live the life of a student from now on. He could see the lanky figure, characteristically sitting in the doorway with his legs folded in front of him. It was ludicrous. All three Americans, for Russ had been left at the original hooch, sat in their doorways like three old neighbor women; except that they were unable to leave without permission.

Visits were daylight only, and seldom were all three allowed to be together at once. The most common event where all three men were allowed to converse was at "radio time," the evening playing of Radio Hanoi's "Hanoi Hannah," a daily diet of "news" about how all U.S. forces had been "wiped out," all ships sunk, all planes shot down. It was difficult to understand how even the most hardened cadre member could suppress cynical winks about these reports. During "radio time" everyone gathered. It was enjoyable, in spite of the static noise. Garwood looked forward to the evening breaks. The guards warned that they were "instructed to listen . . . silence . . . strict attention." But between the propaganda chunks, two songs were usually played, inevitably American hit parade songs. The thought, of course, was to get U.S. servicemen to tune in. The songs were the high point of the day—they were the only real news. Especially when a new song came out, the three would dissect it for any message at all. Sometimes there were tones in the words of these minstrels that showed what was happening. Sometimes the radio would play what seemed familiar melodies with new, antiwar lyrics. Yet these were American songs. Bob Dylan, Joan Baez, and a few others became recognizable. Pete Seeger also.

There was a simple feeling of puzzlement at some of the sentiments expressed, rather than anger or resentment. After all, these were American songs, American singers: That was most important, not the words.

Garwood could tell from the comings and goings that both of his companions were getting the same sort of "instruction" as he had. Clearly, there was a three-way threat working. Garwood was no longer an exclusive candidate, and it might be expected that each man would work against the others in the circumstances; but it was not so. Grissett, who had been most upset that he was not selected, simply felt bereft of Eisenbraun. Garwood could sympathize completely with the young corporal. Eisenbraun had become his own pillar of sanity and reality long before.

The new separation went on for about ten days, apparently a repetition of the pattern they had used on him. All three men felt the pressure of an impending decision. By now, they were getting to know the strangely ponderous and lightning-swift movements of Oriental logic. Like tigers, they could wait and wait, and then spring. Rumors came through the guards to Eisenbraun and thence to the others that other Americans would be coming to the camp. There was a specific tale of a single American prisoner who was at a Montagnard village, "very big, very strong," a man whom they were having trouble with, and who had been at the village for a couple of weeks.

Garwood's own "education" had slid into a daily repetition. Hum seemed to have lost much of his interest and friendly manner. He would occasionally appear to ask Garwood the meaning of certain English words. Once he asked Garwood if he could speak Spanish.

"I only know a few words," Garwood told him, glad of the conversation. "Not enough to make up a sentence or nothin'—why?"

"I am just curious," Hum said in his boyish way.

Garwood knew there was no idle curiosity in the Vietnamese mind, so he was not totally stunned to see a man, not so clearly an American as a Puerto Rican or Mexican, come into camp. He was short and wide, and Garwood thought immediately of a wrestler. He looked freshly captured, still wearing army fatigues, topped by a cone-shaped "sampan" hat. His boots were standard jungle issue, as Grissett's had been, months before, and not in bad condition. The man wore a full beard that made him look like a caricature Castro, and thick black hair. His arms and chest were large, his thighs solid. He was whistling, and it seemed strange to Garwood. He looked curious. He looked with amazement at the other Americans—his eyes swung to them immediately, as a child's will to other children.

He was not tied. He was accompanied by only one guard and one Montagnard with an ancient rifle, a cap single-shot musket, steel bright as silver. The new prisoner stood closest to Garwood's hooch when he first appeared, standing quietly in the shadows of the jungle, looking fit and rested.

Garwood hailed him across twenty-five feet of compound, "Hey there . . ."

Hum, who was examining his new American with relish, yelled back sharply, "Bob, no talking."

The man did not respond to Garwood's hail. He was walked up to the camp commander's hooch. The others, consumed with curiosity, waited expectantly by their doorways. In twenty or twenty-five minutes he reappeared with the guard and Hum, and walked blankly past Garwood's hooch.

"Bob," said Garwood, pointing to his chest.

"Ortiz," said the man in a calm voice—he was clearly a Spanish speaker from the accent. "Ike," Garwood heard his companion shout.

"Ortiz," said the newcomer again.

He was put in with Russ. Garwood's reaction was puzzlement and jealousy. He knew—or did not really know—that Grissett could not speak any more Spanish than he could. There were so many things he wanted to ask the new man, so many things he had to know—but mainly there was the longing to fill the huge gaps of reality that yawned in each man's past. It had been almost a full year since Grissett came into the last camp.

Garwood waited, never so eagerly, for radio hour.

The three Americans met at the usual spot before the program began.

Grissett brought the new man out, introducing him. "This is Ortiz-Rivera," he said. The man smiled, nodded, shook hands. Garwood spoke first.

"How are you?"

"Okay," the man said with a smile.

"He don't speak English so good, Bob. Just a few words," Russ said. Garwood thought: "Bullshit. How's this guy get into the U.S. Army if he can't speak English?"

Hum asked all three: "Can *anybody* speak Spanish?"

Eisenbraun said, "I know a little."

The older man asked Ortiz-Rivera where he was from and he said, "Puerto Rico." The radio came on, temporarily halting public conversation. Russ whispered loudly to the new man, "D'ya understand the radio?"

"*No comprendo,*" he said. "*Poco Anglo.*"

From the beginning, Garwood found suspicions about Ortiz-Rivera coming unbidden to his mind. It seemed after a few days that the man had either been entranced in some strange way by the shock of his capture, or that he was playing a very long game, pretending he could not understand the language, making the interrogation process virtually impossible.

He seemed to live in his own mental stockade, whistling and singing to himself, smiling with his big white teeth, going uncomplainingly about all the tasks assigned to him. He held stilted conversations with Grissett. He soon became a favorite with the guards, and he behaved for all the world to everyone like a large and intelligent dog.

He did not seem to mind the diet. He never complained, eating whatever was given to him, except that once, grinning and laughing, he gave Grissett to believe that he knew fish sauce. He pointed to it and said, "*Culo . . . culo.*"

When Grissett told Eisenbraun about this, the older man howled with laughter. "He means the damn fish sauce smells like a woman's pussy," he told Grissett.

Grissett might as well have remained in isolation, except for two things: Both men were Catholics, and they shared the Latin words each could remember from the Mass and prayers. Ortiz-Rivera was regularly, simply, profoundly religious. With his strong hands he was able to fashion things out of bamboo, using only his wood-gathering knife. The first thing he made was a cross—not a simple thing out of bamboo, but cunningly jointed, made of the forest deadfall and squared and faired. He could make almost anything. He made baskets out of bamboo strips he split with his wood knife—the guards soon allowed him to keep the weapon all day, seeing there was no harm, and before long he was making baskets and bowls every day when he was not working. He seemed in the same relation to nature as the Montagnards in his easy acceptance of what existed, and his utter lack of intellectual curiosity.

Tortuously, they learned he was a PFC, U.S. Army, that he had been drafted; and that he was captured when his position was overrun. He was surrounded and captured. He seemed to bear no malice toward his captors. They were part of his life, like the jungle, like the lice, the plain food.

He had a sweetheart in Puerto Rico, and was about twenty-two. He had been a common laborer. His first visit to the States was when he was inducted into the Army.

Hum and the guards soon regarded him as a favorite. But for Hum he was much more. The translator called the Puerto Rican, "A true example of the peace-loving and progressive proletariat. Ortiz-Rivera is a prime example of another one of the United States imperialist atrocious exploitation of the masses into the U.S. war machine to be used as cannon fodder against Vietnam."

Ortiz-Rivera showed no understanding of his role as the good example, and no desire to find out. He was pleased enough that Hum, a man clearly of some importance, looked kindly at him.

"It's his way," reasoned Eisenbraun. "He's blocking out the rest of the world." Garwood was less kind. Ortiz-Rivera would agree with everything his captors said to him, whether or not he understood it, he would nod and grin and say, "Bueno, bueno, number one okay. Muchas gracias." This formula got him past reefs and shoals that the others had foundered on. But Ortiz-Rivera would say the same things to his American companions. They found this disconcerting. Ortiz-Rivera was tolerated and ignored. He himself preferred it that way.

Things ran this way for a month. July and August were hot, humid, sometimes rainy. Life in the camp was simply round, self-beginning, self-finishing. It seemed like the time could flow forever this way.

There was no rumor, no notice when the fifth American arrived. A thin, jungle-worn, weak-looking man in black pajamas, he stood dejected beside the guard who brought him. He looked like a very old boy, clearly of Spanish-American descent. He looked, to Grissett, Garwood, and Eisenbraun, like one of them.

The new man was Agostos Santos, twenty-three, USMC lance corporal. He was in one of the grunt units in an outpost at Quang Nam Province, First Corps, when his unit was overrun. He was wounded in the stomach and back and left for dead. Most of his unit was wiped out. The VC were going through the bodies of the dead, collecting rings, ammunition, money, sidearms. Santos, they found, was still breathing. He was put into a hammock and lugged off. SVNFL at that time was offering a reward of a transistor radio for the capture of a live American prisoner. The VC unit that picked him up took the chance that he would live until they collected.

According to Santos, he was taken, slung like a dead deer, to a first aid station, was operated upon, and cared for in a cave for about a month. He was well treated. "I owe my life to the VC," he said. "If I'd been left there, I'd'a died of loss of blood if nothing else."

He was brought in the usual way, taken to the camp commander's hooch and then put in with Ortiz-Rivera and Grissett. Ortiz-Rivera was overjoyed, because Santos was a fellow Puerto Rican, and the two fell immediately into a Spanish huddle. Santos knew English very well, too.

145

He brought news to the three veterans that the war was at a phase of intense buildup—over one hundred thousand Marine Corps troops, whereas, when Garwood was captured, all forces amounted to only about sixty thousand—there had been many major battles, not all victories for the U.S., but Santos said confidently there was a ratio of about ten VC killed to each American fatality. He was on "search and destroy" when they were caught in an ambush, apparently well set up. As far as he knew, he was the only prisoner taken from the action.

He had been in the U.S. within the year. He said the antiwar protesters were mainly students who did not want to get drafted. He dismissed the subject.

Santos' character was a puzzle. He said he had been drafted into the Marine Corps, a fact that Garwood could not accept. He told Santos angrily, "You're full of shit. The Marines don't draft people."

Santos retorted, "Let's put it this way: I was drafted and I selected the Marine Corps." It was more than a decade before Garwood was to learn that the Marines did, indeed, draft men during the height of the Vietnam manpower squeeze.

He was friendly, but reserved, as if he held some suspicion of the men who had been there longest, the Anglos, Garwood, Grissett, and Eisenbraun. He was clearly in awe of Eisenbraun, particularly after learning of his rank. With Ortiz-Rivera he was most friendly, a constant companion—but Ortiz-Rivera, for the first time, showed signs of displeasure. The reason was to be read in the broad smiles of Hum. Heaven had brought him a translator of Spanish, and now he could interrogate Ortiz-Rivera!

The amiable ex-laborer's attitude changed abruptly when he found that his countryman would act as interpreter for the Vietnamese translator. With the two-tiered approach, Hum was tied up for hours on end with his "information."

The others could not have cared less about the interrogation, which gave Hum most of his visible pleasure. They figured there was so little inside Ortiz-Rivera's head that if they got it all out in their double-translation, it wouldn't amount to much more than name, rank, serial number.

But the two of them were asked by Hum, and later assented to writing an "open letter to all Hispanic servicemen in Southeast Asia."

Eisenbraun asked Santos what was in the letter. The Latin's face fell. "Nothin'," he said, "just some propaganda." Garwood, who had already written a propaganda letter, made a tape recording and starred in a movie for the Vietnamese propaganda machine, felt he had no room to criticize. Eisenbraun restrained his criticism to asking about the contents. They proved to be the usual propaganda lies.

Of the Anglos, Santos seemed most friendly to Grissett. The two Hispanics and Grissett lived together, so it was natural. But Garwood felt some caution and reservation towards him. Why did he keep saying the VC had "saved my life"? Santos seemed to feel he owed them a debt of gratitude. If Ortiz-Rivera behaved like a Labrador retriever to the guard and officials, Santos was like a humble employee. Like the ARVNs, he would snap to attention when a guard approached. He would smile; Ortiz-Rivera would smile, too. The Anglos rarely did smile and kept their comings to attention in the resentful mode.

The Puerto Ricans were treated better—they were not harassed in little ways. They were never yelled at or served the noisy and empty threats that certain guards liked to shower on Garwood, Eisenbraun, and Grissett. The guards liked to lecture the Anglos on the "suppression of the Puerto Ricans, such a small minority."

"The Puerto Ricans simply want to work and be left alone," Hum told the downcast gringo trio, "but it is the scheme of the United States to make the country of Puerto Rico into another state, and thus take peaceful people from their villages and families and make of them fodder for the war machine. How can you Americans do such things?"

"Puerto Ricans are the same as the blacks in the United States, a minority, an oppressed people," he said. "One day these minorities will unite into one and the U.S. capitalists will suffer a crushing defeat."

Santos, still, seemed to accept everything. His health improved at Camp IV.

There were five "candidates" now. Garwood and Eisenbraun, still isolated, began to lose whatever expectation they had of a decision. The meeting and the announcement of "candidates for release" was history—probably, both men thought, rewritten by this time. And a subtle but significant change was noted. Santos, Ortiz-Rivera, and Grissett were given permission to cook for themselves. They built, with some help from the guards, one of the clay and stone cookers and were given pots and pans. The two others still went to the cook shed for their food, or had it delivered by guards.

A sixth American, Robert Sherman, a Marine Corps corporal, was marched into camp in late August. It was the same day, or near to it, that Ortiz-Rivera, out gathering wood, stepped on a punji stick. It missed his foot, went through the calf of his leg and caused a bad wound. He was able to pull it out himself and hobble back to camp—for once without his happy smile or a tune on his lips. Sherman simply appeared with a couple of guards that same morning. He looked like he had lost his last friend. He was of average height and build, still had Marine fatigues on, was unwounded, and barefoot. His boots were slung over his shoulder, and he was walking barefoot to spare his blistered feet. He seemed defeated and dazed, incurious, half-asleep. When the other Americans introduced themselves, he seemed to look right through them. "Hello," he said, as if remembering. The only question he asked was, "How long you guys been here?"

When the long timers told him, he looked shocked, but he said nothing.

He told them he was captured while on picket duty at an outpost with some ARVNs—it was simply an observation post, he said—when he decided to walk into the nearby village, hoping to get laid. He acted as if this were perfectly normal. A girl in the village approached him. "Fuckee, Suckee?" she said, and on this brief introduction, he followed her for about two miles. It was daytime, nothing had been going on in the area or had been for days.

They finally got to a hooch. Inside, there were two more women and a man.

147

All of them had weapons and they were pointing at him. They told him to put his hands up. Sherman proved to be a passive character. He was put with the Ortiz-Rivera-Grissett-Santos group. Russ reported that he was "slow." He came from Idaho and had enlisted in the Marine Corps. He was young, about the same age as Garwood. Garwood hardly got to know him because of the isolation policy. Sherman was a fatalist. "If they're gonna kill me, they're gonna kill me," he told Grissett. He slept a lot and he was very homesick.

Meanwhile Garwood and Eisenbraun were sinking into a new kind of despair as the camp grew around them; before Santos and Sherman arrived, an ARVN had been executed.

They would never have known his name. The camp officials had been in the habit of using the ARVNs as virtual pack animals, taking ten or twelve out of the fifteen or so there on trips, which sometimes lasted as long as five days. They would return laden with sacks of rice, fish sauce, salt, tools, ammunition, cloth, and trading goods for barter with the Montagnards.

On one trip near the first of July, three ARVNs made an escape attempt. According to the charges brought against them and read to the whole camp, they formed a plan and one night while on the march all three set out in different directions, hoping that not enough guards could be spared from shepherding the normally placid ARVNs to chase them all.

But all were captured. The organizer, Captain Nghia, an ARVN battalion commander in the artillery, captured in Pleiku in 1966, was betrayed by his two co-escapers, who fingered him as the leader.

All three men were badly beaten—that was when the rest of the camp first knew that something out of the ordinary had happened with the trip. Their arms were tied tight, their arms and hands swollen. Their clothes were torn and their faces dark with bruises and cuts. The guards immediately began to build stocks, three pairs. The Americans could piece together what had happened. Eisenbraun was as surprised as anyone that the ARVNs had made a break for it. "I pity those poor bastards," he said. "They don't have a prayer in hell." The guards had said they were sure there would be *thu hinh*—execution.

The three were put into stocks. But they were treated far worse than the Americans had ever been. Guards would urinate on them, curse and spit on them, and take bamboo sticks and hit the soles of their feet. Two would cry out, begging for mercy, but not Captain Nghia, who would only grunt, "Death to Communists" or some such phrase, which would bring on a flurry of frantic blows.

Heated sticks from the fire, put to his feet, could not produce the desired result from the tough Nghia, who seemed to get stronger as he abandoned himself to fate. The effect on the new American prisoners was remarkable. While the three weeks of torture and stocks went on for the escapers, the new prisoners became models of alacrity, volunteering for work, carrying extra-large bundles of wood, springing to attention. Garwood, Eisenbraun, and

Grissett simply lay low and obeyed all the rules. It was clear that the guards were determined to completely destroy the three men. When the cries and screams went on for more than half an hour, the camp commander would order them to stop. He seemed to be disturbed by the excess of fury the guards showed.

One guard explained to Eisenbraun that if one of the puppet troops had escaped successfully, the camp would have been bombed, and it was necessary to discourage the escape plans of the ARVNs completely. Most probably knew how to find the camp again, and all could easily have melted into the countryside. Garwood began to see why they were so docile and obliging in camp. "It would have been very dangerous for you also," one guard told Eisenbraun, "for we have orders to shoot all prisoners if there is any type of rescue attempt by U.S. forces."

But the brave or insane Captain Nghia's time was drawing to a close.

The guards took it as a matter of simple justice, that the ARVNs knew how the game was played and could expect no better.

"Puppet troops are unlike American prisoners," a guard explained. "When they escape, or break the rules of the camp, they fall under the laws of treason, for they are Vietnamese. The only reason that they are prisoners and are not dead is because of the lenient and humanitarian policy . . ."

Garwood was surprised to find two young Vietnamese boys walking freely into the camp one day after the escapers had been under torture for about three weeks. They were beautifully dressed in native attire, but it was clear the fabric was nylon. They both wore nicely cut nylon pajamas, one black, one powder-blue. It was clear they had a special role. They could walk where they wished, and seemed oblivious to the guards. Even the Montagnards who owned the jungle were not so trusted—they had to get permission from the guards to make gifts of tobacco to the Americans, for instance.

The two children visited Garwood. He saw they were about twelve to fourteen, and he was told they were both related to important camp officials, the older boy the son of the camp commander, and the younger, the son of supply officer Tum. They had come to the camp at their fathers' invitation, they said, to "observe the executions."

The boys, sweet-faced, called the doomed ARVNs "cruel agents of the Saigon administration." Garwood was dumbfounded that any father would allow a young child to see something as dreadful as the end of these suffering lives. But the boys were polite, pleasant, and curious.

The morning of the fourth day, a meeting was announced. The Americans were almost glad for the miserable three that it was nearly over, as they were sure it soon would be.

Garwood and Eisenbraun sat together. It did not seem a time for conversation. The ARVNs, barely able to stand, were brought before the whole camp, and the guard commander, who had administered some of the most brutal beatings to the three, read the order. The camp commander, it seemed, was removed somehow from participation and set apart, a mere observer with his son.

The guard commander read the autobiographies of all three men. The two lesser officers were both well educated. Both were in college, both were conscripted. But Captain Nghia was a career man, with the "Saigon puppet army" for almost twenty years, as an enlisted soldier and later, up through the ranks, as an officer.

"Many years a cruel lackey and slave of the Saigon regime, he has the deaths of many patriots on his hands," the guard commander read of Nghia. The subject of this essay stood straight-faced, showing no emotion.

"Proven to be very stubborn and obstinate and determined to fight against his own people and country, there is no other recourse left but to order the most severe punishment," effective such and such a date. . . .

But the condemnation seemed to include all three men, though clearly, by the texts, the two younger men were painted as mild villains compared with the career soldier.

The three unhappy men were led away, out of sight of the camp, linked arm to arm by stout ropes. After half an hour, as everyone in the camp sat still, waiting, the guard commander again appeared. Everyone was ordered to attention, and guards pushed the prisoners into two rows; in front the ARVNs, behind the Americans. The column, flanked by guards was marched off in the direction the three condemned had gone. Ortiz-Rivera asked and pleaded to be excused, and he was allowed to return to the American hooch.

A hundred yards from the camp, the three condemned were lined up, backs to the creek. Eight guards stood in squadron in front of them, each man armed with an AK-47. "Attention!" called the guard commander. The machine-gun squad snapped to, and with a flourish, the commander of the guard pulled a knife from a sheath on his belt and walked to the three ARVNs. He cut the ropes holding the three men together. The two younger men he ordered away and they limped back, behind the squad, their faces masks of terror. Nghai stood alone.

"Communist dogs will suffer ultimate defeat!" the condemned captain shouted. "Down with Communism." He spat angrily.

"What's goin' on?" Eisenbraun asked, screwing up his dim eyes.

"Let the two young ones go," Garwood said. "They still got Nghia standin' there. I think they're going to shoot the poor bastard."

"He's better off dead than the shit they've been putting him through," Eisenbraun replied.

The weapons were leveled on the guard commander's order, the two end men kneeling; and in an instant, it became clear that Nghia was bolting. He turned his back and started across the stream, arms still tied behind him. The commander shouted, *"Ban . . . ban"* ("Fire! Fire!").

All eight weapons opened up on automatic fire, but miraculously Nghia did not fall. Bullets poured at him and he started to stumble. Slowly he fell and bullets continued to flow with a noise like the roar of monstrous traffic. They tore his body to tatters in thirty seconds.

"The poor bastard must've had sixty rounds in him before he hit the floor," Garwood told Eisenbraun.

The guard commander, when the burst was finished, moved to the corpse. He pulled his pistol and fired two more rounds into the man's head. Guards dragged the body to a shallow grave.

"You see," Eisenbraun whispered as the column returned to camp, "they think they're so damn smart, huh? The logical thing would have been, just walk up and put a bullet in his head. He would have been just as dead and saved a lot of ammunition."

11
The Saddest Loss

THE EXECUTION of the brave Captain Nghia had an effect like that of a low virus. It spread a kind of sickness, not exactly hatred, more like despair, among those who had seen it. The veteran U.S. prisoners, the original three, were used to the Viet Cong, knew their faces and their ways, knew which guard liked more pepper on his rice and which was troubled with gas, and had even learned a little about their families and their lives away from war.

But after the shooting ceased over Nghia's body, the guards gave a wild shout of joy, a sound that tore. They walked back to camp chattering happily—one mimicked the dead man stumbling and the guards near to him doubled up with laughter. The Americans were disgusted—both at the guards and at themselves for their weak wishfulness.

The guards, the camp, the VC were able to execute a brave man like squashing a bug. It was done dirty, with hatred, malice and no release.

Garwood and Eisenbraun had almost forgotten that these men who watched them every day were actually guards and soldiers—and not what the Americans might wish or imagine: men with families, men with moral baggage, doubts, fears, laughter, children.

Garwood and Eisenbraun were shocked, but would not show it. They had gone soft, they had let down their guard, they had made up their own soap opera in which they were figures, not mere bugs to be squashed. Grissett, who had not seen an execution before, was even more affected. His reaction was one of pure fear, the effect the VC may have wanted it to have. It made him into a cringing, terrified prisoner who could not face even the memory of the bullets

152

slamming into the running ARVN captain. He would not just fall silent when the subject came up, he would demand that the talk stop.

Grissett adopted a nervous hopeless attitude of servility to the guards. He tried to be the same with Eisenbraun and Garwood but he could not. He clung to the new friends, Ortiz-Rivera and Santos, who was not in the camp when it happened.

So it came that Grissett was appointed "leader of the Americans" for his new attitude. The camp commander announced that because of his helpfulness to the new prisoners, Grissett would be given authority over Ortiz-Rivera, Santos, and Sherman. Those three did not seem to resent the move. Grissett, in his new role, got the others their rations and tools for work detail and was responsible for bringing the tools back. So the Americans were neatly split.

Eisenbraun and Garwood remained in their separate hooches. They worried and fretted about this. Then it became clear that the segregation was for one main purpose—to keep the Vietnamese speakers and nonspeakers apart.

While all the Americans were together, the two senior men, Garwood and Eisenbraun, were constantly translating for the others. In the endless hours of the camp, the guards inevitably talked—and they talked a lot. They were curious, as curious as the Americans, and before long, both the Vietnamese-speaking Americans knew a good deal about many of the guards. The camp authorities did not like this.

"Bob," Eisenbraun said one day at radio hour, "something just occurred to me. They're never gonna release us. We know too much about 'em. If they release anybody, they'll release someone who doesn't know Vietnamese. Hell, we know names, dates, places, we know too much."

There was no going back. "We gotta learn Vietnamese better," Eisenbraun told him. "We gotta learn everything we can about the language, the culture, the habits, everything—then we can use our intelligence and outmaneuver them. It's the only way to make anything out of this spot we're in."

Garwood could always tell when Eisenbraun was upset about something. He was usually pretty open and would take hours sometimes, telling Garwood how and why things were happening. He made the young man study his own life. To Garwood, the man was more than human. He was the father he'd wished he had, he was the man who seemed to know everything, the one who always remained calm in each crisis, who combined stoicism with reality and daring.

But there was a deep disparity between them. It was always Garwood who came to Eisenbraun with his problems and worries, not the other way around. A frequent feeling of Garwood's was that of a little boy at the knee of a kindly but companionable teacher. He never really knew what Eisenbraun was thinking outside of the roles that each had created for the other.

Garwood fully trusted Eisenbraun. He would have had no problem with any decision the older man made for the both of them. But the other way, there was simply a gap. Eisenbraun was reserved and guarded, the tough old soldier who is used to loss and change. He made Garwood feel that he never really trusted him, though he was very interested in the young man.

Now that the two of them were isolated, the dependency increased. Garwood forgot completely, as a day-to-day matter, about the other men in the camp. The only thing that mattered was the talks with Ike—sometimes the guards would let the two men visit as in the old days, and they would sit in a shaft of sunlight and pick at their lice and talk. Eisenbraun had noticed Garwood's growing worshipfulness. "You gotta try to find ways to help the others, Bob," he said one day, "but don't tell them. I don't want them to be in the role that they have to depend on you. If they start making demands, it'll never end. If you steal one cup of rice, they'll want two. Because you speak Vietnamese, they're gonna think you're not taking chances. Because you know the guards, they're gonna say you've got it easy. Don't let this happen."

The tone puzzled Garwood. His idol was a complete skeptic, a man who lived day to day, and he was giving, more and more, advice for the long haul.

But there was something that Eisenbraun wasn't explaining, and that was why he was giving the advice as if Garwood was to go it alone. Garwood sensed some unknowable sadness, as if he could look at the sky and see thousands of miles. He asked Eisenbraun what was wrong, not really expecting to get an answer. It was not the master's place to open his heart to the student. All he would say was, "Don't worry about it. You got enough to worry about."

Eisenbraun was a champion at hiding his feelings, but after so long Garwood knew the signals, and he knew, too, that Eisenbraun didn't want him to know about it.

"Why'd you say that, Ike?" Garwood asked the older man. The two of them sat comfortably on the bare dirt in the Oriental position, arms crossed, chin to one side. They were chasing a spot of sun which moved slowly across the jungle floor. Eisenbraun had made the statement. It was: "Don't trust Russ. Do anything you can to help him, but don't trust him."

It was a mid-September day. "Russ has never trusted you. I thought I owed you that much, to tell you. Russ still believes, from the day of our escape attempt, that you told the bastards one thing or another that got us recaptured."

"Ike, that's bullshit."

"Russ doesn't know. Or he won't know. He found it hard to accept defeat. That's the way he is. He had to put the blame on somebody and you were the only person available. All he could see was himself in the stocks and you still in the hooch."

He explained that the situation was perfect for discord, perfect for self-destruction, suspicion, hatred. "These bastards would love nothing more than to see you two go at it like spiders in a jar. You would both lose . . ."

A guard sauntered down: "Bop, *di ve nha*" ("return to your house").

"See you tomorrow," Garwood said.

"That's all we got to look forward to."

"Hey, I'm the one's supposed to be saying that."

They both laughed. Garwood trudged back to the shadowy hooch beneath the funereal layers of leaves that never fell.

He noticed nothing the next morning. In the dawn the guards would blow a whistle, and he knew that from the time of the whistle, he had another fifteen minutes in bed. It was still half dark, but the routine, which ground on without meaning and without end, had already started.

He pulled himself to a sitting position. He wore the same clothes day after day, night after night until they stank too much to stand. These were still half good. It was cold, and he sat like an urban bag lady in the uncertain light, his stiff rug a tepee around him. Shivering slightly, he looked out the door. Had to take a piss. He got slowly up, like an old and fragile man, mat still around his shoulders, and slipped into his sandals. He straggled outside. The jungle air smelled fresh and clean, moist. A light mist, like floating dew, was in the air, the exhalation of millions of trees and bushes. He walked out the back door of his hooch to a bamboo clump. He always pissed in the same spot. He noticed the bamboo seemed to grow better there, though the grass died. He walked back, picked up his cloth washrag from the bamboo stick on which he hung things to dry, walked out the front, stood at attention. He asked the guard if he could go down to the well to get some water to wash. The guard sternly said "No."

Garwood, who had already started to move, came fully awake like one stung. He froze, turned back to his hooch, asked again in Vietnamese, "I beg the guard that I may go to the well to wash my face."

"No," the guard repeated threateningly. "Return to your house."

Garwood stepped inside and sat down. He quickly kneeled on the sleeping shelf and pushed his finger into the crack he had made in the wall through which he could peer, more or less unobserved, at the area between Eisenbraun's hooch, the "Americans'" hooch, and his own. The guard's outhouse sat in the middle like a traffic kiosk. He saw nothing, shifted to the other wall's spy hole. What's so important about going to the well? he thought. Looking toward it he saw a small group—five men, ARVNs and guards—washing up and brushing their teeth. He noticed it was too cold for the men to strip. All normal there. He walked casually to the front door and asked the guard, "Why cannot I go to the well?"

"I have orders from the camp commander that you are to remain in your house until he talks to you."

He saw Hum heading towards the well, a fine flowered washcloth and a bar of soap in his hand. Garwood looked at the translator. The young man was nonplussed under the stare. "What's the matter?" he said petulantly.

"I asked permission to go wash my face; the guard said no," Garwood said.

Hum looked at the guard, he looked at Garwood. "Go down and wash your face," he barked.

Garwood started quickly. The guard yelled a second later, "Return to your house!" He sounded demanding.

Hum turned to the guard. "Let him go," he said.

155

"But the commander said . . ."

"I will take responsibility."

Garwood got to the well ahead of Hum and dipped his cloth in the bamboo pipe of water. "How are you feeling this morning?" chirped Hum.

"I feel all right," he said nervously, totally at a loss.

Out from the guard kitchen came Yen, the camp's female cook. She walked to the well, and as Garwood stood washing his face with the vinegar-smelling cloth, he noticed the cook, a skinny, cross-eyed woman, was waiting for the men to finish before filling a metal pot with water. Rice. Like every morning.

While waiting deferentially she said to Hum, "Too bad about Ike."

The tone was like train conversation between strangers; the translator said to her quietly: "Shut up."

Garwood's eyes registered her look of surprise and hurt. He turned his glance to Hum and found the dark eyes merely curious, wary, searching his own face. He was going very cold inside as if there were someone in ambush behind him.

He kept staring at Hum, trying to make the man lower his eyes. "What is the matter with Ike?" he asked flatly.

Hum said nothing. It was Garwood who looked away at a sudden motion. The female cook bowed her head and backed quickly away. He saw she had not fetched her water after all. He felt a chill breath; the ARVNs stopped their washing. Their eyes went to Garwood.

Garwood looked over his shoulder to Eisenbraun's hooch. Everything looked the same as yesterday. "Ike . . . Ike," he crooned across the space of seventy yards. Nothing. He called again, louder.

Russ yelled, startling him, "My God, Bob. Ike's dead."

It was not the voice that he had expected, and this startled him, a voice from another hooch and not the familiar sound. The words seemed to make no sense.

He stood for a moment and thought, and the word *dead* hit him. "He's not dead," he thought hurriedly. "I was just with him yesterday. He's all right." He looked at Hum. Hum looked down this time, folding his cloth around the soap bar. Garwood ran.

"Please let it not be true," he thought as his feet pounded up the compound, sandals slapping. "He can't be dead, can't be dead, can't . . ."

He stopped in front of the hooch. To his relief, there was no change. He called "Ike." He called several times, not daring to go inside. He decided he would not go inside, he was too scared. He listened for the voice that would say, "What the fuck you want, Garwood? Can't you let a guy sleep?"

There was nothing, no rustling, no breathing. He stepped inside. There was nothing. The mat was there, and Eisenbraun's hammock hung across the corner of the hooch. It looked deflated.

In the background he could hear the guard angrily arguing with another voice he did not recognize. He came out of the doorway, looked toward the "Americans' hooch" and there was Grissett, standing outside with his arms at his side and his shoulders drooping. "He's here, Bob," Grissett said. "Ike's here."

Russ simply stayed there. Garwood walked slowly to the hooch. The other three Americans were sitting on their long bed, hands in their laps, eyes intent on the man coming in from the light.

Beyond them in the gloom, lying on the long bed and away from the door, Ike lay on his back, his feet looking huge and obscenely naked. He was wrapped and tied with crushed bamboo, and looked as if he had been rolled up in a porch window shade. Garwood could only see the thinning hair and the enormous feet, not his face, nor his hands. But it could be no one else. He looked at the body, turned to Russ. Grabbed him.

"What did you do to Ike," Garwood snarled. Russ made no motion with his hands, only looked straight into Garwood's face. "Bob. Ike is dead. Nobody did anything. He died last night."

Garwood looked back at Eisenbraun's body. He walked over to him, and started to undo the bamboo strips that tied the bamboo poles surrounding his body. The things were like knives, they cut his hands, and he could not get them undone.

He felt Russ's hands grabbing him from behind. "For God's sake, let him rest in peace," he said.

"No, no," Garwood said calmly, "he's not dead."

He pulled his arms away and continued to tug at the bamboo. Russ hit him in the face with his fist, and for a moment Garwood saw white light. The blow landed on the side of his face and seemed to disappear almost immediately. He grabbed Garwood's shoulders and said, "Let him rest."

Patiently, Garwood pulled Grissett's arms off his shoulders, knelt down by Eisenbraun's head and touched his hair. It was blond, straight, no gray in it. He prayed silently. He did not know how long he stayed there, praying and sometimes yelling, "It's not fair! Ike fought for so long . . . so hard . . . he did so much good for so many people. It isn't fair." Santos and Grissett tried to pull him away, gently at first, then more insistently. But he was easily able to shrug off their hands. "Leave me alone . . ."

Santos said to Russ, "He's sick. He's crazy."

Grissett was saying, "No. You don't understand, you don't know Ike."

Garwood thought bitterly, "Now he defends me, now he shows compassion." He stayed until the ARVNs came in.

He found himself quailing before so many foreign eyes. He got to his feet. It was clear they intended to do something. He faced them, threatening, and pushed the first one away. Ike had hated them, he thought, and now they're going to take him. It was because of them he was dead. They went out and returned with a guard. "Get up. Leave!" the guard shouted, holding his gun across his chest.

He got off his knees again. The guard's eyes shifted uneasily, his muzzle lowered an inch. Grissett got up, Sherman got up. Ortiz-Rivera and Santos got up. The five Americans stared at the guard.

Hum's feet slapped the dirt outside, and the little man swung around the entrance pole. He motioned Grissett aside and talked to him quietly.

"Would you like to dig Ike's grave?" the translator asked. "We have puppet troops here ready to dig it for you if you need. It is too bad about Ike."

"No," said Garwood. "We will dig it."

"We'll dig it," Russ said automatically.

The four were given hoes and two shovels. They found a place, far from ideal, for there were many roots, under a tree within the boundaries of the camp. It was a place that the three, Eisenbraun, Grissett, and Garwood, had often used as a rendezvous before the segregation was enforced. Now they went back to it and broke the ground with their tools. They worked slowly and carefully, fashioning a long, deep grave, estimating it to the proper depth. It was a job that took all day and left them filthy and exhausted by late afternoon.

They went back to the hooch and held a service. Grissett acted as the priest. A few prayers were said there and all four men carried the body out. It was terribly light, easy to carry after the heavy work of digging, and quickly they placed him in the grave with his mat, his bowl, his tobacco, lowering the bundle with pieces of rope. They said the Lord's Prayer and Grissett threw in the first handful of reddish-black dirt. Garwood threw some in, the others followed suit. Ortiz-Rivera, Sherman, Santos. The Catholics crossed themselves, the Protestants bowed. They started shoving back the dirt with their hands.

It was nearly dark by the time they finished. Ortiz-Rivera started to fashion a cross out of wood before darkness fell.

Garwood, in the compound, could not believe the events of the day. He had seen, but he had not accepted.

They spent a week making a stone for the grave, and during that time Garwood was in a state of shock. He was glad to have the slow chipping and shaping to do, and with a broken knife they pounded a rough engraving onto the face of it. They didn't know Eisenbraun's date of birth. They put his name, the date of his death: September 17, 1967.

For what seemed a long time, the death was not mentioned. Garwood, already isolated, was glad of it. He avoided the others at radio time, sought no permission to go to the others' hooch. He ate listlessly, looked at the place where the two of them had sat and talked. Garwood tried to remember everything Eisenbraun had said and found already it was slipping from his mind. He ceased believing, every morning, that Eisenbraun would come limping out of his hooch. But the little building remained empty, as if the Vietnamese had no use for it, and sooner than he had thought possible, it began to take the appearance of neglect.

The Vietnamese are superstitious people, especially about the dead. He thought they were scared of him. They looked at the grieving figure, wrapped in its aloofness, and stayed away from it. They would not reprimand him when he walked to the gravesite. Hum suddenly became solicitous, asking almost every day, "Bob, would you like to go down and visit with the Americans?"

"Leave me alone," Garwood would reply. For once the little man did not giggle and flounce.

Grissett came to Garwood's hooch twice. He tried to talk, but Garwood soon found that unless he was willing to take the lead in conversation, the visit would falter and then peter out. He kept saying the same thing.

"If you keep this way, you'll be lying right beside Ike," he said.

"Russ, Ike loved you," Garwood said. "Why can't you have any feelings?"

"Ike is dead. You are alive," Grissett said. "Ike is free now. We are not. We have to keep fighting."

Garwood suppressed a bitter smile. Here Grissett was telling him that we had to keep fighting; it was almost as if Ike had to die to convince Grissett of what he had been saying for all these months: Keep on fighting.

For two weeks after the little ceremony in the jungle, Garwood found himself in a state of paralysis. The process had started all over again, and he was as lost, ignorant, stupid, and frightened as he had been in the thirty-six hours after his capture, when he first lived in animal fear.

He had relied too much, and decided he would never rely again. He had not learned many things because he felt he could simply ask Eisenbraun. Now it was all gone forever, the whole net of knowledge and ideas, fragile but wonderfully durable. He wept sentimental and heroic tears, wishing only to change places w 'th Eisenbraun—let him lie in that sodden gray dirt, away from the light. He flirted with suicide, had thoughts of unutterable melancholy.

Two weeks later, with time to think and rest, he knew, somehow, that he was recovering when he had the idea of finding out the truth about Eisenbraun's death.

For the first time, he went to Russ. Russ told him a bare and simple story. In the middle of the night, two guards and the camp nurse brought Eisenbraun to the "American" hooch—Grissett assumed it was from his own. They laid him down on the bench. He was still alive.

Eisenbraun was moaning, semiconscious, unable to communicate. Grissett and the other three tried to talk to him; he could not recognize them, or their voices. They pulled down his clothes, looking for wounds, but found only some bruises on his rib cage, on the front of his chest. Eisenbraun moved restlessly, as if struggling with a shroud, but his movements were weak, like those of an old man. He called out the names of his wife, his daughter.

Grissett tried to talk to the nurse. But she spoke no English. Impassive, she stood and watched the man by the light of the tiny kerosene lamps the guards brought. Grissett told the nurse to get Garwood, but the nurse, when she relayed the message to the guards, was emphatically told no. The guards stood stiffly, intent on their duties.

Hum appeared about a half hour later. It was very late in the night, an unusual time for the dapper translator to be up. Grissett said Hum did not explain why he had come to the hooch, but he interpreted from the nurse the following story.

Eisenbraun, the nurse said, "had fallen out of his hammock onto the ground and broke some ribs, there had been punctures, there was internal bleeding. Because of the facilities, there is nothing to be done."

Eisenbraun sometimes did sleep in the hammock he had fashioned, but the idea of him falling out of it seemed ridiculous. Garwood had fallen out of beds. Never had he even been bruised.

"Do you believe that?" Garwood asked Grissett.

"I don't know what to believe," the other man answered. "Whatever he died of, there's nothin' we can do now. Just forget it." Garwood felt he wanted no more questions on the subject.

Grissett said Eisenbraun's condition never changed. Then, after an hour, he seemed to quiet and to rest. The others thought he was sleeping. He stopped moaning and moving his soft movements. He was dead when one of them leaned over to check.

Grissett said he tried artificial respiration, but it took only a few minutes to realize it was useless. He felt no broken ribs. The only evidence he could find was a thin rim of dried blood on the edge of his lips and nostrils—no great amount, just a line of it.

The Americans covered him with his mat until the morning, when the ARVNs came in carrying freshly cut bamboo, smashed into a stiff packing. They laid it down, rolled Eisenbraun onto it, and bound him in it in a sort of package.

Garwood left Grissett satisfied that he had told all he knew. He interviewed the guards casually. They were nervous about the details of the death, and said they were not sure how it happened, but that it was "Too bad."

The nurse told him, "Ike was really sick," and refused to answer the questions Garwood posed—what had caused his death, who found him and when. Why were the unlikely bruises on the chest the result of a tiny fall from a hammock slung in a hooch? She grew antagonistic to the questions, "He was sick and he died," she said. "That is all I know. I am not a doctor."

Was he himself guilty of Eisenbraun's death at one remove by refusing to take on the liberation part? Had Eisenbraun been tortured, or interrogated, and then "got rid of" because they found he was the source of the problems with the other prisoners? With Eisenbraun removed, there might be more success with the new men. The new prisoners would never know how to catch a rat, eat grasshoppers, learn the language. He became convinced that Eisenbraun had not simply died, but had been murdered in one way or another, and that the camp regime had tried to make it look like an accident.

It kept going over and over in his mind that Ike was fine, just the day before. Ike had been cooking along as ever, picking his lice. A man like that didn't fall out of a hammock, and if he did, he didn't die of it.

If what Garwood was thinking were true, then he was partly responsible for his friend's death, and his own guilt grew.

"Was I, or am I ever, to be released?" he asked Hum one day.

"I don't know if you were to be released for sure," Hum said uneasily. "But I do know now that you are not going to be. Because of your attitude. We feel that you have been lying to us. You are not who you say you are. You have not been truthful with us. We know everything about you. Don't think we are so stupid."

"What do you mean?" said Garwood, alarmed thoroughly by the newness of this. "What haven't I been truthful about?"

"You are very intelligent, but you are very stupid," Hum said. "You cannot make me believe. Take myself. I went to the University of Hanoi for four years to learn to speak English. And I cannot even compare my English ability to your Vietnamese ability. It is a known fact throughout the world that the Vietnamese language is the most difficult language to learn. And you expect us to believe that you have never had any schooling. You must have gone through a special school to be able to learn."

"What are you getting at?"

"You have never been truthful with us. A normal American soldier, as Russ—they are normal soldiers, you can see. It is very difficult for them to adapt to the language, the culture, the environment. Much more than you. This is too much suspicion for us to believe you are a normal solider."

"These fuckers still think I'm with the CIA," Garwood thought dully.

He was totally bewildered. Two and a half years after his capture, what use could anything he had known be now?

"You must think it over very carefully," Hum said.

So the end of his investigation of Eisenbraun's death was a bamboo wall—the only thing he knew was that the Vietnamese would never release him. They had never believed him, and he had told them the truth. They had killed Ike and would not admit it. And he had been, no matter how obscurely, to blame for the death.

Later he asked Hum to see the camp commander. He proposed simply that he be allowed to spend his days with his countrymen.

"No. You cannot," the commander said stubbornly. "You are feeling bitter about Ike's death. You don't understand, won't understand, and probably blame us for his death. That kind of thinking will poison the other prisoners' progressive way of thinking. You must first prove to us that you are sincere and that you have truly adopted a progressive way of thinking.

"What do I got to do?"

"You don't know?"

"No."

"Well, you go back and think about it," the commander said. "When you have figured it out, or think you know, ask the guard to come and see me, and I'll arrange a time when we can discuss this further. The importance is that you must see your mistakes—that they are wrong and unprogressive. . . ."

"Can I still go down and visit the other Americans?" he asked.

161

"Yes, you may go down in the evening, when Hum takes the radio. You may go with Hum. But you cannot stay without Mr. Hum."

The interview was clearly at an end. Garwood hoped that he would be spared the usual speech about the "humanitarian and lenient policy."

He realized that he was in a dangerous position as a suspected Vietnamese-speaking provocateur who could stir up resistance among the other prisoners—even if it were as little as learning to live off the land and eke out their rations with what they could find in the forest. The policy of the camp was to keep the prisoners in a state of total dependency.

But there was a far more important effect. Garwood felt, for the first time since Eisenbraun's death, that there was a challenge, and something to aim toward. The challenge would be to gain the confidence of someone on the camp staff. He would have to be a good actor. He would have to learn lies so good and so true that they would be easy to believe, because there could be no other way. He would have to turn off his feelings, hide his emotions, and he had to learn to know the enemy, study how they thought, how they acted, learn so much about them that he could anticipate what they were going to do before they did it, or knew they were going to do it.

It gave him the excited feeling of being alone and on a mission, nobody to help, nobody to share. It was a feeling he had never really recognized before. He also had to establish some kind of communication system for private conversation with the other Americans. For this he had no idea, no solution.

It was more than a week into October when, for no reason he could decipher, Garwood was moved to another camp.

He had had no chance to put his new resolve into practice. He had gone back to work, causing the guards' faces to split into broad smiles. "Not bad," they said, pretending to know some English. He practiced being alone, ignoring the chance to talk—and be spied upon by Hum—during radio hour. He tried to be friendly. Grissett had told him, to confirm his suspicions, that Hum was asking steadily what Garwood was saying. They replied that he had said nothing beyond the briefest courtesies.

He left without saying good-bye, on orders from a guard, with his mat on his shoulder and his other poor things. He asked where he was going, and the taciturn guard said only "about two days from here . . . you must go and meet some people."

The second morning out, he was surprised to find himself in the throes of a malaria attack so bad he thought he would not be able to move. As it was, he was too weak and dizzy to travel for two or three hours. The trio of guards, clucking at the familiar symptoms, did not push too hard.

It took a week to march to the camp, not the two days the guard had estimated. The malaria made it a hazy, miserable voyage. He was not tied, but surrounded; he could not have escaped if he had wanted to.

It was an old camp. There was only one inmates' building, a big hooch, and the usual kitchen hooch, guards' hooch, command hooch. The whole place looked run-down, as if it had been allowed to succumb to the ruinous climate. It was a prison, he found, with no prisoners except him. There was a camp commander, several guards and Garwood, alone in a long house. It was two months before other prisoners came.

An unusual place. There was no welcoming speech from a commander, no work detail; his day consisted of meals of manioc and rice and isolation. He could sleep all day if he wanted to. There was a stream nearby, and a rocky outcropping under the triple canopy. There was the distant sound of shelling almost every evening. Even the shells seemed to ignore him, like everything else. He spent his time recovering from malaria and tasting the complete silence of the place. The guards would not talk to him and he soon gave up trying.

Then in November, two South Korean prisoners appeared. One spoke English. He asked Garwood how long he had been in prison. When he was told since September 1965, the man was clearly shocked. The new arrivals had been captured, they said, during a battle for Que San. They talked of a new kind of war, with fierce battles, bitterness, and ambushes. It was hard, they said, to tell the enemy from the civilians, and they had been told, when coming into a village, to shoot anyone who ran. Garwood was oddly unexcited by their arrival; he found he was uninterested in them and their attitude.

"It was a great disgrace for us to be captured," one of them said. Garwood was unsurprised. Disgrace took on some varied forms, he had found. The ARVNs who had betrayed Eisenbraun had also felt it was a disgrace to be captured.

But he was hustled out of their presence shortly after the Koreans arrived. "We have our orders," he was told when he made mild protests. He was taken from the large hooch to another, outside a bamboo and punji-stake enclosure. It was as decrepit as the rest of the camp and the roof leaked. He was only about fifty feet from the other men and could see them moving about through the gaps in the bamboo. One of the Koreans went on a hunger strike—in line with his "disgrace" idea. This idealist said he wished to die, asked the guards to shoot him, and announced he would starve himself to death "to die with honor rather than return in disgrace," as Garwood overheard two guards putting it. Several weeks later he made it. Garwood saw them carrying his body out.

The remaining Korean, suffering from malaria, continued to eat and exist. There was no communication, for Garwood. A week before Christmas, while Garwood sat stuperous in his hooch, another American walked into camp.

Earl Clyde Weatherman, PFC, USMC, was tall and heavy, with blond hair and blue eyes. He had lived in San Francisco, had dropped out of high school and joined the Marine Corps with trouble behind him. He had wanted adventure, he told Garwood, but he found he hated being given orders. They made him into a not-very-good rifleman.

He arrived in the evening, and Garwood noted immediately that he could speak Vietnamese—a few words at least. He was talking with the guards who had brought him. And he was friendly with the guards in a manner Garwood had not seen. He imagined that the young man had not seen guards do the things he had seen.

Weatherman wore pajamas—but they were made of nylon material, and he had his Marine Corps fatigues and sandals. He did not seem to notice Garwood, and was taken to a small hooch, more like a shed, where he talked and laughed loudly with the guards for several minutes. He wanted to know when he could see his wife and child and after a minute or two, Garwood realized the man was talking about a family in Vietnam. He slept in intense curiosity.

In the morning, the two men met by the stream and Weatherman seemed surprised and somewhat abashed that another American was there. Garwood looked with envy on the other man's well-filled frame and shaved face. He wore a wedding band.

Garwood looked at him. "Hi," the other man said tentatively.

Garwood offered a greeting. Something kept them from shaking hands, and Weatherman said, "How long you been here?"

"I was captured on September 28, 1965."

"Jesus Christ! All that time?"

"Not in this camp, in several different camps," Garwood replied.

"Where you captured at?"

"Other side of Marble Mountain near Da Nang."

"What's your name?" the newcomer asked.

Garwood told him. "I'm Marine Corps, too," the other said. "I'm a private, or I was."

"Where were you captured at?" Garwood asked. Weatherman paid no attention to the question. Later he provided an answer.

"To make a long story short, they had me in the Third MAF Brig at Da Nang (Marine Amphibious Force) and I escaped. I was headin' to Saigon to see my wife and kid and I got picked up by the National Front."

Garwood couldn't believe that a Marine would use these terms.

"Are you a prisoner, or what?"

"Well, I don't know if they consider me a prisoner or not, but they've treated me fairly good since I come in contact with them. They give me a lot to eat, and enough clothes. I got a mosquito net, a mat, a hammock."

"What are you doin' here?"

"They told me they were bringing me here to meet with my wife and kid," he said cheerfully. The camp commander shouted down for Garwood to go back to his hooch. It was as far as they could get acquainted. The man told Garwood quickly, "M' name's Earl Clyde Weatherman."

Long stories have a way of coming out in prison, and when the two men were thrown together (as a concession, on Christmas Eve) Weatherman told him all about the brig at Da Nang.

His story was that he'd asked his company commander for permission to go to Saigon to start the complex paperwork necessary to bring a serviceman's foreign wife to the U.S. The practice of marrying a foreign national while

164

overseas is frowned on by the Marine Corps; but it is a civil liberty that the Corps has had to accept. It has done so with bad grace.

Weatherman had married in a Vietnamese ceremony—this was not officially recognized by his commander—his bride came from a merchant family and they'd met outside Saigon, where the woman had her own fruit stand.

The commander refused permission. The company was what Garwood knew as a "grunt unit"—a combat unit with such duties as guard duty, perimeter duty, night patrol, reconnaissance, search and destroy, the dirty work of the war. Weatherman's skills were needed, he was told, the papers would have to wait.

But Weatherman told Garwood, "My wife and kid were more important to me than the fuckin' Corps. If I couldn't get the papers to get her to the United States, I'd damn well go somewhere else."

He had one aim, he said, that was to get them out of the fighting zone and out of Saigon. He was from California and had chosen the Marine Corps rather than be drafted into the Army. His long-range plan was to plant his family in some peaceful place—he had heard Bangkok, the R&R dream, was the best place. Later, when time permitted, he would get her home.

Garwood found Weatherman was what his companions would call "dufas" or ignorant, or dumb as shit, or crazed. The kind of guy who would pull some stunt with no chance of success—the opposite of GT, or "smarts."

"How could he think he was gonna get away with it?" Garwood told himself as he heard the sad little tale unwinding itself like a cheap clock.

Weatherman told how he tried to get six hundred miles to Saigon, on foot, and was picked up at a checkpoint. He'd had bad luck, getting no good rides except two Vietnamese who carried him short distances on their motorbikes. He was nailed with no papers. Alone. No weapon. A phone call, and he was shipped back to his unit in handcuffs. Unauthorized absence. Same thing as desertion in time of war.

They put him in what they called the "holding tank" at Da Nang, waiting for a ship for the U.S. It was too fast. They'd ignored his excuse. "Excuses are like assholes," he told Garwood, "everyone's got one." The facts were, they told him, he'd left his post.

He said it was pretty easy to escape from the holding tank. But it was a major step. He could be placed in deserter status. He could have been court-martialed and shot. In deep shit. But he decided he'd try it anyhow.

Weatherman simply walked away from a work detail one day, he said. He found himself near Da Nang. He went to a Vietnamese he knew. He had nothing, for when they throw you into the brig, they take everything—money, ring, watch. Somehow, the Vietnamese agreed to help him, and for a week he waited in the cellar of a home in Da Nang, eating meager fare and hoping, while the man tried to make contact with the wife's family.

The man brought him clothes—to his disgust they were a woman's and too small—and on the back of a Moped he putted slowly out of Da Nang City, feeling a complete fool, but unnoticed. He was dropped in the countryside and walked again on the long trip to Saigon. He changed back into his fatigues and started to hitch. Tired and fed up, he relied only on his ability to bullshit to get himself past any outpost. But there was no military outpost. He came to a village and found the people there friendly. But they turned him over to the Viet Cong and next thing he knew, he saw Garwood's haggard, bearded face staring at him from behind bamboo. It was not Saigon, after all.

Garwood wasn't really sure why he had been told this story. Either Weatherman was the world's dumbest shit, or . . .

Garwood knew that those who tried to use the VC inevitably got used by them. Weatherman seemed both dumb and unlucky.

That Christmas Eve was Garwood's real exposure to the man. They were housed separately and never again met at the stream in the morning, though whether this was the guards' doing or chance, he could not decipher.

It was Garwood's third Christmas. The camp took little notice of it except that the camp commander told him, "We are going to allow you to celebrate the holiday of your people with your fellow American." There was an extra ration and the second chicken he had eaten in prison was cooked and served to the two men. They got rice noodles and each man got a glass of rice wine. "At this rate," Garwood thought, "I'll be getting turkey with trimmings in five more years."

The men were given a deck of playing cards, used. They were American cards, with a complex blue design on the back.

Weatherman said he looked on himself as an "adventurer" who wanted to go places and see things, and who couldn't stand taking orders.

"I've got no views on politics," he said. "I'm not pro-Communist and I'm not pro-anything-else. I'm on my own goals and ideas." He said he had not wanted to go into the military and felt no particular obligation, since he had been forced to go. "Now if they was invading California, that's different," he said. "Then, I'd fight." He said he was antiwar, not anti-American.

Garwood simply did not know what to make of these views, and found himself thankful that Weatherman spoke so much.

"Lots of things have changed since you left the United States," Weatherman said darkly. "The American people, especially the kids and students, are refusing to accept the policy of the United States and the war over here."

Garwood only thought of getting his hands on the radio.

"The simple reason is they do not want to end up in a body bag or in the situation you're in right now. For what?"

"Weatherman, I don't know if you're gonna ever understand this, but you are in the same damn situation as I'm in. They could take you out, blow your shit away, bury you in the jungle, and you'd still be a big secret."

That was Christmas of 1967. By the end of the month, Weatherman was gone. As far as Garwood knew, the young Californian really believed the Viet Cong were going to help him with his family.

For the next three weeks, Garwood and the Korean occupied the camp alone, in silence. He found to his surprise that he had become able to deal better with time. Or, at least, he no longer worried about the periods he spent half-asleep, devouring his imprisonment half-awake, half-interested. It was, he guessed, the human version of hibernation, and felt himself lucky to have discovered its secrets.

Fred Burns, a Marine Corps private, broke the stuporous monotony. Garwood first became aware that the Weatherman hooch was occupied again, and then, that a Caucasian was inside it. When finally he heard it, Garwood shook his head at his story. Burns was very young, eighteen, and he was from New York City, new to the field and the jungle when he was sent on patrol from Da Nang. He dropped a grenade, and went back to find it, terrified he would not be able to account for it after the patrol. He never found the grenade, he never found his patrol. The Viet Cong found him, though at the time he thought he was still in supposedly friendly territory. The women who led him to a village were friendly, but the men there were firm. He threw his gun away, thinking that no one would shoot an unarmed man.

"You went back for a damn grenade?" Garwood asked incredulously.

"Yeah," he said. "You have to account for everything now. Ammo, grenades. They think you sold it."

They had marched Burns for a week and he looked it. Garwood looked at the young man, baby-faced with his light brown hair matted up, his eyes innocent and anxious. "Could this have been me?" Garwood thought.

12
A Growing Community

IN THE early weeks and months of 1968 a momentous military event convulsed the war. Battles erupted throughout South Vietnam, the U.S. embassy was raided; but to the prisoners, it was only voices on the camp commander's radio. Garwood first heard of the Tet Offensive from Hanoi Hannah, who excitedly talked of "The whole country rising as one, devouring battalion after battalion of the aggressors, delivering crushing blows." It was one-sided, but it was more one-sided than ever before, and by that measure, Garwood knew something was happening in the outside world he had left so long ago.

About the second week of February he got some proof. Mr. Ho, whom Garwood fervently hoped never to see again, came into the nearly deserted camp. He met privately with Burns, to what end he did not overhear, and then he found to his annoyance that the little interrogator was greeting him like an old friend.

"Well hello, Bobby, how are you?" he said.

He grinned from ear to ear. "Haven't you heard about our great victories?" he asked. Garwood said nothing.

Whatever confusion Burns had caused by his quixotic capture was apparently at an end, for the young prisoner was ushered up to meet with Mr. Ho, and in marathon sessions, underwent three days of interrogation.

Garwood's turn was next. Guards, taking on an official severity, marched him to Ho's interrogation hooch. Garwood steeled himself for another game of verbal dodge with the familiar little man. There was no smile this time.

"Stand at attention," Ho demanded. "Sit down."

A guard stood menacingly at the door, and Garwood wondered what new element Ho would add. He told the guard to come over and told the man to bring "the prisoner" a cup of green tea and a cigarette.

Garwood asked him for a light. "Go ahead," Ho said. For a moment it passed through Garwood's mind that this was not unlike a meeting with the insurance man, or some other person normal to a normal life—only it was here. He could almost forget his fragile mortality in the comfortable little ritual.

He sucked in the factory-made smoke eagerly. "Well, Bobby, quite some time has elapsed since our last long talk, and I have received some very discouraging reports about your behavior and attitude. It seems you have taken a turn for the worse. This has surprised me. I understand that Ike's death upset you," he said, motioning with his hands, looking briefly away, past Garwood and out the door. "So what else is troubling you? Why have you changed?"

Garwood, without a clear line to follow, said nothing. He kept his eyes on the walls behind Ho's head.

Two minutes of silence passed as both men smoked elaborately. "Well, if you have no answer, I must draw from that that the reports I receive are true. And if they are true, then we will have to take some steps, shall I say, to help you to correct them." Ho's dignity of speech was always a danger sign to Garwood. Bad news in a good suit. It was when he was telling what was to come, not what might come.

"Bobby," Ho said, "do you remember what I first told you when we first met, how it is easy to die here in the jungle and how hard it is to survive? To put out a fire, would one normally use water or gasoline?"

"Water."

"So far, you have been using gasoline. If the flame gets bigger, then we will have no recourse but to put it out."

It had come across crystal clear that he was teetering on the edge of some final abyss. They were frustrated with him. It sometimes appeared to him that he must come across as worse than a mere prisoner because of his attitude. He was no longer the innocent, scared Marine teenager he once was. He knew the jungle and had survived it, likewise he knew the propaganda. They almost had to destroy him. He had to develop a new response, a new idea. He had tempted them into thinking he was a possibility for "progress."

He went back to his hooch that night with foreboding he had not known in months; Ho had told him: "I hope for your sake you make the right decision. If you don't, it will be out of my hands."

From then on, Garwood saw Burns every day. Burns reacted very badly to the camp regimen. From bewilderment, he became demanding, refused to eat the food, kept demanding to see the camp commander and get his rights under the Geneva agreements. He asked for materials and postage to write letters home, and even demanded toothpaste. The guards, at first only annoyed by this, became belligerent, and one of them threatened to shoot him unless he kept his mouth shut.

Garwood admired his "balls." When they met at the washing place, Burns asked Garwood, "Do you think they would really shoot me?"

Garwood looked at him. "Yeah. I know they would. I'm gonna give you a little piece of advice. Something that took a long time for me to learn—they care as much about you as they do stepping on an ant. These guards here, they do not like carrying food for you, having to cook your meal and standing guard twenty-four hours over you. A bullet through you would relieve them of all of those duties."

For a little over a week, Burns kept it up. Ho left, apparently unable to make progress with this hard case. Then without warning, Burns gave up the strike. Garwood learned that Burns had chucked it in when the Korean finally overcame the language barrier and told him what had happened to his hunger-striking colleague.

Mid-February passed. Two more Americans appeared. Garwood's heart no longer leaped when he saw a new face, however. The options he had were slimming ominously. The two were accompanied by a full half-dozen guards, all armed with AK-47s. The two Americans were tied fast, shoulder-bound. Both wore their battle-dress camouflage fatigues, and appeared unwounded.

They seemed to be a pair, Joseph Zawtocki and Dennis Hammond, both Caucasians, both corporals, USMC, friends. They were about the same age, twenty-two or twenty-three, but they looked very different. Zawtocki was of Polish extraction, big-headed, fair-skinned, stocky, powerful. Hammond, part American Indian, was tall, lean, dark.

He found they had both been captured in a Tet Offensive battle. They were holding defensive positions at an outpost when they were overrun by large numbers of Viet Cong and regular North Vietnamese Army troops. They had run out of bullets for their M-16s. They were stationed about one hundred feet apart when the final assault threatened, and their line was a shambles of dead and wounded. They knew there were too many for hand-to-hand combat, so in a lull, they crawled toward each other, and smeared each other with blood from the wounds of nearby corpses. Then they lay down in their holes and waited. The assault swept through unopposed, and when the enemy stopped to strip the bodies of watches and valuables, they were seen to be alive, and were kicked to their feet. They were roughly bound, shoved on to the trail and marched for four days and nights. They said they were the only American prisoners, though there were an estimated one hundred ARVN prisoners seen by the pair on the trail to the camp.

The pair were still tied, and sitting on the ground outside Garwood's hooch, only minutes after their arrival at the camp, when Hammond caught sight of Garwood in the door. "Holy shit!" he said to Zawtocki, "A white gook!"

Garwood looked at the man. "You spend as much time as I have in this jungle, you'll look like a gook, too." It was weak, but it was all he had. The exclamation had hit home.

The camp commander, making his inspection of the two new prisoners, called Garwood out. He told the guards to take the ropes off the two bound Marines.

The commander handed Garwood a piece of paper and told him to translate

170

it to the pair as best he could. It was titled "The Lenient and Humanitarian Policy Toward American Prisoners to Be Carried Out by All Officers, Cadre and Militia Serving Under the Banner of the South Vietnam National Front for Liberation."

Garwood started to read the text haltingly and said, "Listen, Marines, you guys play it cool, you will have no fears of being tortured or anything else. If you piss them off, anything can happen. Look at me. I've been here almost three years and I'm not dead yet."

The camp commander looked pleased at the attentive expressions on the faces of the new men.

He returned to the text, reading the usual prohibitions. He ended it, "You are not the only Americans, there are more at a bigger camp. Don't give up, try to keep your strength."

The two Marines made no sign of recognition. They were led off to the prisoners' compound, where Garwood saw the guards erecting a partition to keep the new men away from Burns and the Korean. Garwood was always amazed by the Oriental mind. Didn't they know the Americans would talk through the bamboo screen?

Garwood saw them daily. The two men seemed to get along well, if surviving was well. They even seemed to like the fish sauce, which astonished Garwood, and neither got dysentery in the disabling, crippling way he had remembered.

"How can you guys eat that shit they put on the rice?" Garwood asked.

"When you're on an outpost with the ARVNs, you gotta try it or you'd go crazy. We thought it was better than eating C-Rats," Zawtocki said.

In Hammond's face, Garwood could see the reaction he had feared. The man thought it could not be as simple as Garwood made it. What must I look like? he thought. He looked down at his stained pajamas, his filthy hands, his feet that looked like the feet of some scaly animal, with only the nails white.

"How'd you learn the lingo?" Hammond said.

"Just picked it up," he said. "It's been a long time I've been with these gooks."

For at this point again, Garwood was truly at sea. Different from the new men, who thought of themselves as prisoners. He knew he was not simply a prisoner, he was some kind of Oriental experiment that was failing to jell. He was the waste of war, even less valuable to the enemy than men from whom they hoped to win some propaganda advantage. What was the reason the Viet Cong took prisoners at all? Surely they were not doing it for good will—they did not believe in the Western conventions of war, the duty of prisoners to make escapes, the rights of prisoners. The only reason that kept coming back was that in the total war they waged, a war that lasted decades, lifetimes, the Viet Cong would use the prisoners for something. They used everything, the carcasses of tires and the sheet metal of a wreck. They would use the prisoners as bargaining chips, they would use them to demoralize the enemy, they would use them to clear minefields. The bottom line, he knew, was that if they were of no more use, they would be—"returned to the soil of Vietnam."

171

Garwood had to make a decision; he knew he was flirting with death. The men coming in, like these two, were hopelessly inadequate to the task awaiting them. There had been no training in this kind of survival, the code of conduct was a sheet of paper that a man like Hammond would die mouthing, that Burns would die shouting about.

Garwood had opted for survival. He could catch a rat with his hand and kill it and eat it, he could make marginal soap out of banana leaf, and he could make tea from leaves and he knew the magic of the betel, but all these things paled beside his real gift—which was the language. It had somehow seeped into his brain after the first initial effort under Eisenbraun and he felt quite at home with it. He did not see how he had gotten along without it.

This new decision was simple, the making of it was hard. He would have to say yes more often to the Communists' demands, or seem to. This would split him off even further from his fellow Americans, but without seeming to acquiesce, he would be completely isolated. He had to pretend to play along, be the interpreter, be useful to the Communists rather than be useless and dead.

He had, he found, achieved some independence of mind. He had fallen on Eisenbraun's neck like a child, but now he watched coolly as the Americans moved around the compound. Clearly the arrivals did not feel the same about him. He saw himself in them, but without the solitude that had oppressed his spirit. They had each other, and as he knew, two was enough.

Quite by chance, while he was in limbo, the camp commander accidentally pushed him in a new direction. In the jungle, he had noticed, mechanical things took on the nature of art objects—the guards treasured their weapons, sometimes wore three or four watches. Aluminum was made into jewelry, its soft silvery glow so pure and clean. Knives were always kept bright. So when the camp commander's personal transistor radio, a small green Sony portable with three bands powered by three flashlight batteries and sporting a broken antenna, broke down, it was regarded as far worse than an attack of malaria.

Garwood knew nothing of this, except that the daily broadcasts the prisoners heard were missing. He first suspected there had been only bad news from the battlefield, and the commander had censored the broadcast. Then he was summoned to the commander's hooch.

He came in. The radio was lying on a piece of black cloth, its back off, dials beside it. Garwood stood at the door. "Come on. Come on in here," the commander said, with a wave of his hand dismissing the guard and the normal formalities; he anxiously offered Garwood a cigarette and motioned him toward a chair.

"Do you know anything about radios?" the commander asked directly, settling himself. Garwood nodded, not too eagerly. At Arsenal Technical High in Indianapolis he had taken courses in the electrical shop. He took it as an extra course, for no particular reason except an interest in "hot-wiring" cars.

There, instead of the things he wished to know, he got a rudimentary grounding in the mysteries of 110 house current and its application.

He got a basic understanding that if you were able to follow a circuit all the way around, chances are you would find the break, and fixing the break, the thing would work again.

"Yes, a little," he said.

"Would you look at my radio, please."

Garwood was shocked out of his Ho Chi Minh sandals. "Please"—it was the first time since he had been captured that one of the Vietnamese had treated him as anything but an object to be manipulated, or an animal to be herded and threatened. The man must be desperate, he concluded.

He pulled his chair over and looked at the radio, and asked for a screwdriver, and a pair of pliers. The commander had neither one. Garwood asked for a nail. The commander didn't have even a nail. He got, at last, a pair of tweezers and the clip off the commander's ballpoint pen. He took the clip and broke it off—planning to use it as a miniature screwdriver. The commander looked goggle-eyed, snatched back the pen—a cheap plastic type—and stared ruefully at the break. "Why did you do this?" he said. Garwood explained.

He looked over the radio, examined the circuit as best he could, and found it seemed intact. Garwood asked for the safety pin he had seen the commander using. He straightened the safety pin out, while the commander watched, aghast, and stuck it through the hot wire into the ground post near the battery pack. A tiny spark snapped, and he knew the power source was okay. He then stuck the pin through the ground wire, up the line a little, and when he touched it to the hot post, nothing happened. He knew the ground was not properly connected to the post. With the tweezers, he jiggled the tiny ground wire where it was soldered onto the post—it was not loose. The wire must be broken up the line. Boldly, he jerked the ground wire out of the radio with a flourish. The commander's hands fluttered off the desk in despair. Garwood had seen that the antenna wire was far too long; he clipped it with a knife, cut it in half and used it for a new ground, wrapping one end to the battery pack, the other he placed under a screw at the metal base—the radio surged on with a blast of sound even without the antenna wire. He hooked it up—the sound improved. Garwood looked up.

The commander was grinning widely. "Very intelligent," he said, "wonderful."

Garwood started putting the radio back together, leaving it tuned to Radio Hanoi. The commander went over to his pack and fished out a pack of Ruby Queen cigarettes. "They are yours," he said.

"What are the chances of getting a bar of soap?" Garwood asked pleasantly. "I have not had soap in so long. I would rather have soap than I would cigarettes."

"Soap is very hard to come by. I will see. The cigarettes are yours."

There was little doubt that from what he had seen the radio would break down in the humid climate again. His repairs were not soldered, and he noticed that battery acid had seeped out and corroded the metal case in which the batteries were kept. That evening, he found an extra ration of rice in his hooch.

Ho's appearance was always heralded by extra personnel. Garwood found that the man's vanity demanded attendants, and whenever new officials appeared at the camp, the little interrogator was not far behind.

Garwood, for the first time, knew what he wanted to do with Ho. He wanted to convince him that he was no threat to the other prisoners, and that he would be an asset, at least as a translator, in the camp.

Ho interviewed Zawtocki and Hammond first; Garwood could see him lecturing them in his queerly perfect English as they sat on a bamboo bench before him. He smiled at his memories of these sessions, and could almost hear the phrases falling from Ho's lips.

Then Ho came to Garwood. He seemed content—but he was usually smiling at the beginning of a session. "I am happy to hear about the good report from the camp commander," he said. "That is very good for you, Bob. I had many doubts as to whether or not you would come to the right decision."

Garwood weathered the interpretation—it was as important to him as to the commander to have the radio going. It was the only source of news and entertainment in the camp; without the radio, the guards got edgy and bitchy. If Ho thought that the repaired radio boosted camp morale, and therefore he had made the "right decision," so be it.

He made no answer. Ho inquired gently, "Now, do you have any ideas what you can do to show me you have taken on a truly progressive attitude?"

Garwood suggested to Ho that he be allowed to return to the American's joint hooch, and he told him that he would help the other American prisoners to "understand the importance of appreciating the lenient, humanitarian policy of the SVNFL."

Ho at first looked suspicious. He's wonderin' what the fuck I'm up to, Garwood thought.

When he told Ho this, he didn't know how the interrogator would react. If Ho did let him go back to the other Americans and he didn't try to do what he'd just said—could that be his last chance? Ho would take it as double-dealing and treachery. A perfect excuse for an execution or a disappearance. He said to himself, You have just stepped into some deep shit.

He was thinking of an exit, but Ho cut in. "I will give you a test, Bob, to see how sincere you really are." He set to work with ballpoint and paper and wrote a little speech, which he was to deliver to the three Americans in the camp the next morning. There would be no assembly, no official formalities, just Garwood and Zawtocki and Hammond, and Burns—and Ho.

The paper was familiar propaganda, but in the first person. "I find it very difficult as an American with American ideals to think of children in the United States playing, going to school, joyfully eating ice cream cones while Vietnamese boys and girls are having to suffer the barrage of U.S. bombs and shells

174

twenty-four hours a day." Ho had outdone himself, Garwood thought dolefully. "I wonder if he's ever seen an ice cream cone."

It went on, "I have committed many atrocious crimes against the Vietnamese people, of which I have had personal involvement. My hands are stained with the blood of the Vietnamese, which can never be washed away. But still, the Vietnamese have shown compassion to me as a misguided young soldier, and have sought, under the lenient, humanitarian policy of the SVNFL, to give me the chance and opportunity to beg forgiveness and repent, and they have done so. I have lived now, here in the jungles with the heroic Vietnamese people still waiting for the day I may rejoin my family.

"I thank the Vietnamese people and deeply appreciate the policy of the front and humanitarian gestures in feeding, housing, and helping me to survive so that I might one day return to my country as a new person."

Garwood read it, Ho watched. Both were silent. It was as if a deal had been struck.

In the morning, Garwood, blank-faced, read the document in the Americans' compound. He tried to read it in a straight way, without emotion, and he was reminded of reading a book report in school. He read in a monotone, and carefully watched the eyes of the Americans between phrases, when he could lift his eyes. Burns acted as if he could not even hear it—Hammond glared and grimaced in disgust, Zawtocki looked on with the sympathy that is half relief. "Better you than me," his eyes seemed to say.

The reading done, Ho asked Garwood to stay in front of the other three. Ho asked: "What is your impression?" Garwood swallowed hard. "Shit . . . here it comes," he thought as he scanned the faces. No one said a word. Ho picked one man out—Burns.

He thought a moment. "Have you really been in the jungle for three years?" he asked. Garwood nodded. "What do you think about the demonstrations back in the United States?"

Garwood would have gladly strangled the man. He squirmed, answered, "When I left the United States, to my knowledge there was no such demonstrations. Because of that I really don't have any knowledge of how big or who is demonstrating against what. I maintain a neutral attitude until I find out more about it."

Ho fired the same back at Burns, "What is your impression?"

"I think they're a bunch of cowards," he answered. "All they are is a bunch of hippies using the war to get recognition."

"What is a 'hippie'?" Ho asked.

"A deadbeat," said Burns, "you know, someone who doesn't work; they bum. Vagrants. Jobless, penniless, all they do is sit around."

"Aha," said Ho. "You are speaking of the people who have refused to be exploited by the U.S. capitalists."

"No, no, these people are no benefit to society. They are like leeches, they live off other people."

"What is your father's profession?" asked Ho.

175

"President of a bank in New York."

"So," said Ho, "you don't really have any idea of the sufferings of the proletariat class in the United States, do you? When the exploiter cannot exploit, they automatically brand them as hippies, gangsters . . . you have never known the meaning of poverty, so how can you even try to say that you understand why or for what the working class is protesting, and the foundation of their struggle against the capitalists of United States.

"You yourself grew up in a capitalist household," Ho finished triumphantly. Burns looked confused to have produced so much with so little.

"We will talk more about that in future times," Ho said. He turned to Hammond with the same question: "Impressions?"

"Well," Hammond started, "in any war it is always the civilians that are the victims, from both sides. Civilians are caught in the middle of a battle."

Ho said, "Yes, but these civilians are Vietnamese, half a world away from the United States. It was United States that invaded Vietnam, not Vietnam invading. It would be like your home—if a robber came into your home, you, of course, want to defend your wife and family. You Americans have come into my home, you have no right to be here. This is my home. I have the right to defend my home."

"But we were invited here, to help the South Vietnamese drive the Communists out of South Vietnam," Hammond put in.

Ho looked very upset. "The Vietnamese people did *not* invite you. There were only a handful who call themselves Vietnamese wearing the cloak of representatives of the Vietnamese people, their pockets bulging with U.S. dollars, their Swiss bank accounts overflowing with U.S. gold, who bend to the U.S. capitalists' every whim."

Hammond looked at Ho with resignation. Joe Zawtocki was next.

"I thought it was very good," Joe said with a big smile.

Ho smiled back, but with a chill. "I'm glad," he said. "Maybe you can relay your feelings to your fellow Americans so that they may understand as you do." He turned his olive eyes. "Bob, you may return to your house." Garwood left, hearing Ho continue with the other three—more "education."

It was noon the next day before Ho called a worried Garwood up the hill. "Bob," he said, "against my better judgment and only because I have been called away on an urgent matter, I am allowing you to travel with the other Americans to return to your last camp."

This was happy news to him. Ho told him, "It is a long journey, and we do not have anyone who can speak English and Vietnamese who can travel, and that is why I have based my decision on letting you return to the camp, so that it would make it easier for the guards to communicate their instructions and orders to the new prisoners. I advise you that you should tell the new prisoners that I have given orders that if there is any hint of any attempt to escape, that they are to be immediately executed, on the spot."

Ho knew his man, Garwood thought. He remembered the two executions he'd already seen. "You will leave tomorrow, when the sun rises," Ho said. He went on to warn Garwood that he was under trial. "How well you do on this trip will bear greatly on any decisions I make," he said. "Have a good journey, and I will see you sometime in the near future."

Ho left him, as usual, in turmoil. But events intervened, choking off introspection. That afternoon about fifteen ARVN prisoners were marched in. Garwood recognized them immediately—they were the ARNVs that Eisenbraun had despised, who had lived with Garwood and Grissett for almost a year, and who had expected to be released at Tet.

Garwood noticed that the men were dressed in white clothing, and they had cheerful expressions, playing and laughing among themselves. Each wore plastic shower shoes, flip flops. Several waved at Garwood. "Hello," they shouted. The man that Garwood had assaulted seemed to have forgotten the past. "I think you are dead by now," he said cheerily. "Very surprised to see you."

"Would you like for me to carry letter to your family?" one of them asked.

"How the hell you gonna do that?" Garwood asked. "You goin' to the United States?"

"Oh. We are being liberated at last. I will see my family, I can take letter for you, put it in the post for your family."

"Yeah, I'd like that," Garwood said, scarcely believing what he was hearing. "Do you have any paper?"

"No," the man said happily. Garwood's hopes fell quickly.

"Remember my name," he said. "Bob Garwood. U.S. Marine Corps. POW. That's all you have to put in the envelope. Write to my family saying how you met me and explaining that I am still alive and well. Can you remember that?"

"Yeah, I can remember for you," the man said. "I am so sorry you have to stay here in the jungle. I wish you could come with us. I hope that some day they will let you go home too."

Garwood had the distinct impression the man was practicing his English. But maybe . . . maybe he would write what he said he would. Later the white-clad group of ARVNs, escorted by about ten guards, moved off down the mountain to the plain and freedom. "Good luck," some shouted. "Hope you home soon."

It seemed totally unfair. We came to help them. Now they were released and he was to stay. He had never understood the war, and now less than ever. He turned back to his hooch.

The journey took ten days. No one was bound. There were eight guards and the pace was slow as the new men developed foot problems. The three Americans were cold and suspicious to Garwood, only coming to him as a last resort. Not one of them had leveled with him about the "speech" Ho had made him give. He was not really bothered by this. He knew that time would make a difference. Time, he hoped, they would have. At least he could see the looks of respect they had for his hard-won physical prowess. Garwood shouldered the rice ration as well as his own gear, offered them betel, kept up a steady, silent pace.

At one rest stop Hammond said to Garwood, "You been here so long you're turned into a gook. You don't sit, you squat, you chew that red shit, you dress, eat, walk, carry things like one of them. The only thing left is when your skin starts turning yellow." He said it without bitterness.

"Lay off him, Dennis," Zawtocki said. "Poor fucker's out here three years."

The incidents that marked the march were simple. One of the guards had a malaria attack so bad that he had to rest frequently, and his load had to be shifted to other men; there were frequent bombing raids nearby, and on the fifth day they were persistent. Garwood overheard conversations between the guards that indicated they were fearful a landing zone was being established so that U.S. troops, perhaps a patrol-in-force, could land. Garwood thought it was only the incredible unloading of ordnance that the U.S. did in the early years of the war—bombs thrown willy-nilly into the jungle.

Because of their fears, the guards shoved the prisoners ahead. Garwood was sent out as lead man. The guards took the sick man's AK-47, took the magazine and firing pin out and thrust it at him, telling him to hang it over his neck. Garwood refused. "No," he said, "I'll go first, but I won't take a weapon."

The guard told him to set his pack down. He did so, and the guard tied the heavy weapon on top of the pack and told him to go. He shouldered the pack and moved out. He knew why they did this. As the point man, he would be the first shot, a sacrificial warning to the rest. If he were recognized as an American, and no shots were fired, it would confuse the ambushers and give the guards time to make a flank maneuver or retreat. He was the decoy. But that was not the only thing that scared him about the proposition—what scared him also was coming up from the other direction on an NVA force that would see him as an American, shooting first and asking questions later on the jungle trails.

He told the guards of his fears, but they put them aside, saying there were passwords, and they would yell them in time. "No fear," one guard said.

There he was, a white Caucasian, AK strapped to his pack, black pajamas, sandals, beard—and behind him three men in U.S. fatigues. He thought wearily he looked the worst of a hippy, a grunt, and a gook, all rolled up in one.

They had been marching for about an hour in the cool of the day, when from the side two black soldiers escorted by four Vietnamese guards appeared. They were in the distance—whether the groups had seen each other was hard to tell. The guards halted everyone. At first, Garwood thought the guards were suspicious of the others, but then as the groups confidently approached, he noticed the two black men had no weapons. They were dressed in Army fatigues, both apparently unwounded, and they approached on a converging course. He could see that the two black men were prisoners—both of them staring wide-eyed at Garwood. They passed, not close enough to talk, and moved on ahead.

"What do you think they're thinkin'?" Garwood asked Zawtocki, who seemed to notice the preoccupation of the blacks.

"They probably think you're a Russian—or a white Vietnamese," he said.

The guards of the two groups talked for a minute, and the prisoners in Garwood's group were told to wait. They took off their packs and sat by the trail. "He can speak Vietnamese?" one of the guards asked.

"Very well," said another.

"That's wonderful," said the first. "We have trouble talking with the black American prisoners, they do not speak Vietnamese, we don't speak English. We need someone to tell them it is only a short distance more to the camp—to keep on moving, they can make it," the stranger guard said.

"You will go over and tell them," Garwood's guard ordered. "Tell them they cannot rest before it gets dark. The camp is very near. But you are not to tell them anything more about where we are going, where we come from."

Garwood walked over to them. "By order of the guard, you are to keep moving because the camp is very near. Upon arrival, you will have plenty of time to rest."

"Who are you?" one of the blacks said.

"You will find out soon enough," Garwood told him. The blacks both complained of blistered, bloody feet, and Garwood translated to the guard.

Garwood was devastated to see that the new camp was totally unfamiliar. His eyes kept trying to move things to the pattern he knew, and then his mind began to question his memory. It was stranger still, when he saw a Caucasian, unmistakably Russ Grissett, in the compound. Then he realized that it was not the same camp, the whole thing had relocated.

Grissett waved and yelled, "Bob, Bob . . ." He seemed okay, Garwood thought. It was almost like coming home again, he found himself thinking, then brought himself up with a jerk. Had there ever been anything else but this jungle, the dirt, the smells? He began to see other Caucasian faces, men he did not recognize.

Zawtocki, Hammond, and Burns started toward Grissett but when Garwood started after them, guards half politely said, "No, stay here. Camp commander wants to speak to you." One of the guards shook his hand, "Glad you are back." Garwood mused that even for the VC, a human face that is familiar has its charms.

He was taken to a separate hooch and the old cycle of separation seemed to be starting. Garwood steeled himself for the tightrope. Duong, his tall thin figure instantly recognizable, walked up, "Hello," he said with a thin smile, and asked about the trip. He stood beside Garwood. "I suppose you have heard of our great many victories throughout South Vietnam?"

"Yes," said Garwood. "I've heard about it."

"This is good news for my people and my country," the camp commander said, "and of course it is bad news for the U.S. imperialists." There was to be no second chapter in this conversation, Garwood thought. He stood there uneasy in Duong's presence, glancing over to the compound, where there seemed to be about ten Americans milling around. One stared fixedly at Garwood, a man he had never seen before, clearly an older man, small and thin, wearing black pajamas.

"To my understanding, you know the reason you have returned to this camp," Duong said. Garwood was unsure if it was a question or not.

"Yes. I have been given another chance by the SVNFL," he answered, playing it safe.

"But also," Duong added, "there are some circumstances that warrant your returning here . . . but you are right, yes. That is the main priority, remember that. Due to the big victories, the whole people had to participate in the uprisings throughout South Vietnam, and to achieve victories, of course, there are many sacrifices. I am very sad to have to tell you that Mr. Hum has been sacrificed."

Garwood was surprised, totally. The last place he would have imagined the little faggoty guy was in some kind of military action. "How'd he die?" he asked.

"The Tet Offensive was at its peak. Hum went to the American post with many hundreds of Vietnamese. Hum participated because of his knowledge of English. During the demonstration the puppet troops fired into the demonstration to disperse it. Many were killed and wounded, many civilians. Hum was one of the first to be sacrificed. He was shouting for the Americans to go home, for them to lay down their weapons."

Then it clicked in his brain—Why did they bring me back to this camp . . . because Hum is dead . . . now they're gonna make me be the translator for all these guys, holy shit. . . .

You always had to read the message and then read between the lines when anything was told to you; plenty of prisoners, no interpreter, Ho is too big a deal. It was like the perfect trap: You learn the language to survive, the language is the thing that keeps you alive, and in the end the language makes you into the white God. . . .

But back at the day-at-a-time level, his main worry was how to walk the path between the prisoners, who had only Grissett to tell them he wasn't collaborating but only surviving, and the camp, which needed him and couldn't be fooled, not now, about his knowledge of the language.

He had a quick dark thought that whatever he did, he was already marked. His first impression on the guys over there, only a hundred feet away, was that he was different, cut out from them, talking to the camp commander, shaking hands with the guards, and those black guys had seen him toting that gun on the trail. He just hoped that the Americans would understand. He hoped that Grissett would translate a difference much more important than language.

The voice of Duong roused him. "It is very important that you continue to practice your Vietnamese," he said sweetly, "there are still some words that it is difficult to understand—it is for your well-being as well as for the other Americans' well-being."

He led Garwood to a small hooch—one of the smallest he'd ever seen, more like an enlarged doghouse or a big bathtub, with barely room to lie down on a bamboo shelf.

It was then he saw Weatherman, walking down to the creek. He had a sort of bouncy, aggravating walk. Even at a distance, the blond hair marked him out. Garwood couldn't figure out where Weatherman had come from and why he hadn't been visible with the other Americans. He spotted Garwood, stopped and waved. Garwood shuddered, and it occurred to him that Weatherman was not *with* the Americans but with the ARVNs.

He saw the thin, older American still watching him, seemingly fascinated.

Duong waved Weatherman on down to the creek. "Tell him to go on," he ordered Garwood.

"I'll talk to you later," he shouted at Weatherman.

"You know him?" Duong asked. Garwood nodded. "He is reckless and stubborn," he added dryly. Garwood was totally muddled. He'd expected a good minute of praise for Weatherman's "progressive" ways. Duong continued: "Altogether there are ten Americans in the camp. We have a communication problem. A lot of them are sick, and we are unable to understand clearly what their illness and their symptoms are. We now have two nurses in the camp, of which neither can speak your language. Besides yourself, there is but one Vietnamese who can speak English, not very well. His name is Quy, but I have received orders from my superiors that I am not to use him. He is not to be trusted. It is my feeling that you yourself, being an American, can have more compassion for your fellow Americans and you would do your best in trying to translate as correctly as you can so we can find some way of treating them."

They would never give in to Garwood's requests to join the others—this much he'd learned by Eisenbraun's death. He was like a hard-core prisoner, an old con, the last person the warden wanted loose among the fresh charges. His lessons of self-sufficiency, retreat, seeming compliance would be learned by some.

He was never to be trusted, then. Already he could imagine the rumors and the talk among the just-captured. Could imagine how Russ Grissett, at first defensive, would probably have to agree to avoid being tarred by the same brush.

He decided to do the translating. He decided right on the spot, with Duong's face before him as deep in color as yellow osage orangewood, that he would do the minimum and depend on daily contact with the prisoners to work in his favor. They would see that he was helping them—he could slip messages into the translation and they would see that he was not what he seemed.

Why him? he thought with new sadness, out of two hundred million Americans, to be put into this situation by a process with so many twists and turns that it defied logic, and even recall. How can it end? There were times he thought he was going crazy—these were times he could remember not only acting like an animal, but thinking like one.

He could not remember, from time to time, what an American house looked like, or what a car motor sounded like. He tried to bring these things up on the screen of his mind and found them only fuzzy, like animated cartoons, only the simplest lines. He could not remember what Mary Speers looked like, he could

181

not recall her voice. Sometimes, a flash of thought would come behind his eyes when he was seeing something else, and there he would have captured, for an instant, the past. He found the names of his brothers and sisters slipping away, the numbers of the familiar houses on his street in Indianapolis, all sliding from him into some furry, dusky dark, and in their place, today's ration, a clump of rice, not clean, in a bamboo container. Eating with his hands—now natural. He would hear a toad or a frog and register it as possible food immediately; the same was true of mice or rats, even insects—everything seemed worthy of putting in one's mouth. Other people, no longer of any interest, save as they were dangerous or not. Suspicious of all—all of them eating up the food that was available, all of them capable of harm.

About a week after his return, he was given the duty of carrying the camp radio down to the American compound for the daily dose of Radio Hanoi. They always knew, he was to find out, whether he tuned the radio correctly, because at the beginning and the end of the half-hour program, the SVNFL anthem would play, a tinny, up-and-down melody, and the words:

> To liberate the South
> We are determined to march forward
> Kill the American imperialist aggressor
> Avenging the fatherland
> So much blood has been spilled. . . .

It was a standard Japanese battery radio with separate speakers. His job was to carry the radio into the compound, a guard at his side. The guard would call the Americans outside of the hooch. Attention was not insisted upon. They could sit or squat or stand as they liked. He would tune to Hanoi Hannah. The guard, very curious, would ask at intervals, "What do they say?" in Vietnamese, as if doubtful whether the same news came over the native-language news station.

But on the first visit, the camp commander came too. He introduced Garwood to the other Americans—and to his humiliation, he had to translate. "Bob is a progressive American," he barked.

"*My name is Bob Garwood, I am an American*," Garwood translated. "*I was captured September 28, 1965. I was a member of the United States Marine Corps stationed in Da Nang.*"

"Did you translate it?" the commander asked. When Garwood nodded, he continued, "Bob has come here from another camp and we have given him the duty of interpreting and bringing the radio for you to listen once a day so that you may be able to understand the American aggressors' defeat."

"*I have been ordered here,*" Garwood said, "*from another prison camp to join you here, and I have been instructed by the camp commander that amongst other work required of me I must bring the radio for you to listen to once a day.*"

182

"This is the voice of Vietnam, broadcasting to all American servicemen fighting and dying in the battlefields throughout South Vietnam . . ." began the saucy voice of Hannah.

Garwood watched carefully the reaction of his countrymen. He could decipher nothing from the stares. Grissett and Sherman gave no clues. He could not find Ortiz-Rivera or Santos—he saw the two black soldiers, and the small thin man who had stared so hard at him the first day.

"For those of you who are not aware, I am the camp director," Duong said, after a daily accounting of VC triumph and corresponding U.S. disaster ended with Hannah's juicy tones.

"I am the camp commander," Garwood translated.

"There are certain rules and regulations that have been set forth, which each of you must obey. For those who do not obey, there will be severe consequences." Garwood translated verbatim.

"You must try to help each other, for there are many hardships and sacrifices you will have to make in this harsh jungle environment. We are Vietnamese and even for us, it is a great hardship. It will be much worse for you. We understand this, but due to the circumstances, after all it was the United States that put us all here."

He turned to Garwood meaningfully: *"The camp commander said that you're gonna face many hardships here, and things will be difficult and that you'll have to stick together and help each other so that you'll be able to survive in this cruel environment here in the jungle."*

"I want to stress that it is very easy to give up and die here," the commander continued, "but if you do so, we have a lot of jungle here in Vietnam in which you can be buried. To survive the hardships here, you must work hard, sleep a little, and obey the rules and regulations. Any thoughts of escape will be dealt with by severest punishment. The guards have orders that if any prisoner creates the situation where it might threaten his safety, he may shoot to kill to preserve his own life."

"To put it bluntly," Garwood told his listeners, *"the camp commander just said that if you do anything to piss off the guards, like trying to escape or something, he's given them the order to shoot to kill."*

"Bob is here solely for the purpose of relaying to you. What Bob tells you is not Bob speaking, it is me. And that is only because I cannot speak English. Anything that Bob tells you is by my order and direction."

Garwood translated: *"The camp commander can't speak English, so he's usin' me to interpret for him. You must realize that anything I interpret is coming directly from him. I am only interpreting from Vietnamese to English."*

"Does anyone have any questions?" Duong asked.

Grissett was the questioner. "Glad to see you back, Bob," he said.

"Thanks," Garwood said, "but you better ask somethin' or the camp commander's gonna ask *me* somethin'!"

"Ask him," Grissett said, "that 'cause there are so many Americans here, we need some kind of organization, someone to represent us for gripes and bitches and to tell who is sick and so forth."

"You want me to ask him that?" Garwood said. Grissett nodded.

Duong's reaction to the question was quick. "I have been thinking about this. Russ, because you have been here longer than anyone else except Bob, you will be responsible for reporting to me once a day the situation and condition of the Americans here."

"You're not gonna like this, Russ," Garwood said. "The camp commander has made you the chief of the Americans and you're gonna have to report to him once a day on everyone's situation."

"I don't want that," Grissett said. "We just want someone to bitch about the food or the medicine from time to time."

"I know what you meant. The camp commander said, 'Russ, you be head of the American prisoners.'" The order was to stick. The commander would not retreat. Grissett wore a hunted look.

In subsequent visits, Garwood was able to make rudimentary contact with the new prisoners. Grissett was ordered to make a list, which included full name, rank, branch of service; Garwood noted that there were two officers among the arrivals, and one was a doctor—Captain Floyd Harold Kushner, MD, an Army officer, and Warrant Officer Frank G. Anton. Kushner was the short, thin man who had stared so intently at him.

Next in rank was a wounded first sergeant, "Top" Williams.

As the days fell into a string, things loosened somewhat at "Radio House," and Garwood was able to make some contacts. Several men were completely closed off to him. "Why are you out there and we're in here?" typified their reaction. His response to these hostile questions was short. "Just be glad you're not in my shoes. It isn't what it looks to be."

He grew anxious to find what the others thought of him. Grissett told him: "Be careful. It's a different situation now. Most all of 'em don't believe you and don't trust you."

Garwood thought of turning to the senior officer, Kushner, in hopes he might have some of the understanding Eisenbraun had had. He sat next to the obviously curious doctor at Radio House.

"How did you get captured?" Kushner asked. Garwood told him of the ambush in the boondocks near Marble Mountain.

"How come you're not in here with the rest of us?" Kushner asked after several minutes of silence. Hanoi Hannah was still going strong over their heads.

"At one time, I was," Garwood told him, "then I made a decision that fucked up everything, and I just got in deeper."

"Yeah, Russ told me a little about that," Kushner nodded. "What's your status now in the camp?"

"As far as I know, they brought me here for the sole purpose of bein' interpreter, so as to prevent clashes between the prisoners and the guards."

"That's a hell of a spot," Kushner said.

"Yeah. Guards don't trust me. Prisoners don't trust me." Kushner looked deeply at him.

"Guards don't trust you?" he said at length.

"Nah, they don't."

Between the two forces, he withdrew further from each side. He could not help it—Kushner did not encourage openness, and he had his own annoying traits; unlike other officers Garwood had known, Garwood saw him as lazy. He had status as a doctor, and he used it. He seemed well at dinnertime, sick at work detail. He was the ranking officer at the camp, yet he never took command, allowing Private Grissett to take over what functions there were as the lead official among the Americans. Grissett warned Garwood about him in cryptic terms.

Besides radio hour, Garwood was instructed to interpret work party orders, telling the Americans that one day they should gather wood, the next they would forage for certain types of wild vegetables. He would make these announcements to Russ, spared the humiliation of making public announcements. Three weeks after his arrival at the camp, a Vietnamese named Hung arrived at the camp, ostensibly to be interpreter, but Garwood soon found his English was rudimentary at best.

The other prisoners scarcely entered Garwood's consciousness. He would greet them in the morning, or when he crossed paths with them. The conversations simply never developed. They seemed to be almost totally incurious—except for Kushner—and wary to a degree he could not remember from his own experience.

Hung, the new interpreter, tried to take over the functions of interpreter, radio announcer, and bearer of orders. Garwood was relieved, both of the duties and in his mind. But Hung had problems of his own. He could not begin to fathom American slang—without which his translations could become positively dangerous.

He would get words and phrases famously, hopelessly wrong, and every time, the translation would come down on the American prisoners. Hung was near the compound when he heard an American say, "What a fuckin' beautiful day," since the sun was shining and it was warm. Hung hustled away dark-faced, went to Garwood and asked him, "Bob, it is very bad, the Americans are cursing Vietnam . . ."

"What's the matter?" Garwood asked.

He explained.

"What was said?" Garwood asked. "Can you remember every word?"

"They curse the people and Vietnam and they think we do not understand. But I do."

"Who said it?" Garwood asked, unbelieving. "I think you misinterpreted."

Hung grew even angrier—hotter because his knowledge of the language had been questioned.

Garwood was soon put back to work, not in the mental sphere, but in the physical. He was given tough laboring assignments, sometimes with ARVNs, more likely alone or with two or three guards, all of whom worked. There were week-long farming trips, during which a group would clear small fields out of the jungle to be planted in corn or manioc. They cut the foliage, let it dry in the sun, then burned it. The rubble, ashes, and roots were then pulled to the side, so that the tiny field was surrounded with what looked like barriers of burnt stuff. Sometimes, it would be planted immediately, in other circumstances they would wait for the first rain. Tillage was minimal—planting would be done with a pointed stick.

More prisoners came in. One of them, a man known to Garwood only as Cannon, had been shot with an incendiary round and was brought in in very bad shape, two wounds on his back. Among the others wounded, the Army sergeant Williams had a hand wound and Private Lewis, a slight shoulder wound.

The camp commander had forbidden Kushner to practice his art on his fellow Americans. "You are a prisoner, you may show no sign of rank here. You can have no title, not that of doctor. All are equal, with no distinctions."

Garwood noted that Kushner had been forbidden to help the wounded men. He never saw the man make any effort to help the others, though prisoners told him that Kushner had indeed helped them, unnoticed by the guards.

Cannon was clearly in a fight for his life. He lay on his stomach or his side in his bad periods, and would sometimes sleep sitting up, which seemed to ease his back wounds. His wounds got infected. The guards gave him aspirin and novocaine, but nothing that could reverse the effects of a deep wound on a weakened body.

He lasted nine months before he died. He would travel in waves, to death and then away from it. His wounds would heal and then would burst open. It was almost a miracle that he lasted as he did.

Others died more easily. When they started dying, Garwood was not really sure, partly because it was so surprising to him, even after Eisenbraun's death, that men could simply give up and go away. With the new additions, some of whom he never really knew except as faces, the camp had close to seventeen Americans, including Garwood, in the spring of 1968.

He noticed that many of the American prisoners were suffering from hunger edema, swelling of the joints and ankles. It was progressive from ankle to leg, until the whole trunk would appear bloated with water, skin tight. The victims could not work, had no energy whatever, grew cold very easily, and liked to sit in the sun. They craved salt, which probably hurt their condition, and they would just fade away like old, old men until they simply stopped all activities.

Whether a man got this disease was the luck of the draw. Garwood had a mild case, Eisenbraun had suffered constantly from it, but not fatally. Williams, who survived his hand wound, died of it while Garwood was out of the camp. It was said he died of the edema, blood poisoning and a possible heart attack. Garwood's first notice of the death was a grave below the camp with a wooden cross. It was a carelessly made thing, and Garwood later took rocks from the stream and with a broken field knife, scratched the name and the date of death on one of them for some kind of record.

He did not know why he wanted to do this, except that he thought that everyone should have a tombstone, no matter how crude. The soft rock, he knew, would not last forever.

The little graveyard gradually grew, and the red humps subsided over the buried, so that they could tell with some accuracy who had gone when. They could also tell, from the activities of the living, when someone was heading for the area below the camp. They would grow tired, they would stay tired, no matter how much they slept. But the first real sign was the loss of appetite; they would prefer to sleep rather than eat, and in some cases, they would reject their food, vomiting it up. But a man only vomited once; after that effort, he would be wary of eating again. Their minds would wander aimlessly, like spaced-out kids, but in fact they were concentrating, departing, gathering in their last days of the light.

Their days would be spent in lassitude and hallucinations, from weak cries in the night to silence, disorientation, unconsciousness and finally a sleep too deep to break. Kushner tried to revive the victims after breathing ceased, but to no avail. It was all he could do. He had become very weak himself.

Rations were pitiful. Before the Tet Offensive, each American would get three cans full of uncooked rice per day—the cans were the little half-sized ones used for condensed milk—plus manioc and fish sauce and salt. After Tet it was reduced to one can per prisoner per day—and the manioc and salt ration was similarly cut to one third.

The malnutrition alone brought the camp to its knees; the guards and camp commander seemed to notice this only as a minor matter. The guards themselves complained of short rations. Garwood told the camp commander that the prisoners were slowly starving to death—though in his own case, his jungle knowledge partially made up the difference; he could not seem to teach the new Americans to eat insects or rats.

The camp commander told him, "It is impossible to increase the ration because of the defoliant that the United States is dropping on the jungles. We are unable to grow rice or vegetables, and therefore have to rely completely on supplies from the north." Garwood had heard of the chemicals that could kill whole forests, but he never imagined that their effect could be anything but local. The guards often spoke of them.

One guard claimed the chemicals simply killed all plant and animal life in an area and prevented replanting—nothing would grow in a place sprayed. The Montagnards in the area were famous for their rice, so famous it was said they had so much they could feed rice to their pigs. Now they claimed they had to go through the jungle far away to get to fields that had not yet been touched by the defoliants to get even their simple staples of jungle vegetables. They claimed the trees and undergrowth that had been sprayed could not be eaten for fear of poisoning.

When Garwood told the Americans how he'd trapped rats, and eaten insects and wild herbs and roots, they were as dubious as ever. Not only were they paranoid about picking up any fresh diseases, but they also had not seen Garwood catch, skin, boil, and eat a rat. He ate at the guards' kitchen, not with them, and the Americans believed, with tenacious prejudice, that the guards got far better rations than they. Sometimes they did, but Garwood did not. He was never able to convince the other prisoners that he had maintained his life on vermin and insects and a bit of foraging.

It was another low point for Garwood. He found there was nothing he could do for his erstwhile colleagues, who were forfeiting their lives in a remote jungle camp—perhaps in perfect accordance with the code of conduct. If they had only known what he knew, they might have survived. But after the first death, their attitudes became harder. The inevitability of death did not seem to open their minds; rather, the contrary was true. The compound prisoners took an even more hostile view of Garwood, who was free to move with the guards, whose health seemed good, who did not run to the latrine fifteen times a day, and whose legs were not swollen.

The other prisoners simply stopped talking to him. But the body language was savage. The looks he got were silent stares. In his guilty mind, he saw what the eyes were saying. No matter what he said to the others, it was not believed.

At radio hour, talking with Kushner, Garwood noticed the doctor did not come out and say it but he felt it too. Garwood, like a comic with a rocky audience, was babbling about his youth, his school in Indianapolis, how he came to join the Marine Corps, how he got captured. All he wanted was some kind of reaction from the other man, something to get the ball rolling, but Kushner would never react strongly to what he said.

But at least he did react. Worst was the complete shutout practiced by some of the other Americans, who had determined that Garwood was an enemy agent and simply ignored him. Some literally turned their backs on him. He would not be saying anything, and someone close to him would turn his back and move away. Others would not respond to casual conversational openers. Others would have sarcasm ready. They treated the guards and the camp commander with more respect, he thought bitterly.

He'd say, "Good morning."

The response, "What's so fuckin' good about it?"

He'd ask, "How're you doing?" and the response:

"You got eyes, Garwood, how do you think I'm doin'?"

At first he would try to explain, telling them that the food was no better for him, that the arrangements were no more comfortable, that he would have preferred to be in the compound with them.

"The Communists put you in the compound," he exploded at one of the Americans at last. "You had no choice. It's the same for me. You think I like it living up there?"

"Sure, Garwood, you're eating at the guards' kitchen, and you don't see none of the guards starvin' to death, who are you tryin' to shit? We got eyes," one of them would say.

"I eat where they tell me to eat," he said. "I sleep where they tell me to sleep, I work when and where they tell me to work—same as you do," he said.

"Sure, Garwood, you can make all the excuses you want."

He took the insults and the sarcasm, because he knew that if the situation were reversed, he would probably be reacting the same way. He couldn't get angry. The issue was larger—like an animal that wants to mate, he had to take what he found. It was hard to be rejected by one's own people, but that too, he could stand, if he could avoid the separation, the loneliness. He felt he was now descending to a place he had not been before, a place far worse than that of a prisoner.

Words had failed and time had failed by the fall following the Tet Offensive, when the food dried up and the Americans in the camp were beginning to die without help, and so he grew away from the Americans, meeting their conduct with hostile conduct of his own. He no longer made small talk, no longer tried to get what he wanted from them, the companionship he knew he must have. He put himself on hold.

13
Another Escape

"BOB, THERE is a very progressive American who partook in many demonstrations in the United States," Hung told him that fall of 1968. "And because of his participation against the war in Vietnam, the U.S. government drafted him and sent him to Vietnam to be used as cannon fodder and to die on the battlefields," Hung said feverishly.

Hung said the man's name was Be, which means small.

A week later Garwood was to meet the man. For all the days of that week, it was thrown up to him by Hung and the guards that Be was the ideal prisoner, that he was a man who had technical skills, and that he had helped repair radios. "He refused to serve as cannon fodder," Hung said.

Hung told him to go to the production house on the order of the camp commander. He was told to take rice seeds with him. He toted a forty-pound bag of seed rice on his back, as did two guards, and the trio took off. After two and one half hours, they arrived without incident. Garwood did not see the man when he walked into the hooch. But he noticed him later, repairing a transistor radio. Garwood's first impression was that he was very young, about nineteen he guessed, but that he had on the VC pajamas rather than fatigues, and the clothes were new. Something made the man look up, and seeing Garwood, he enthusiastically jumped to his feet. "Hi, my name's Gus. What's yours?" asked this long-haired individual, whom Garwood guessed had not been in the jungle long. The two shook hands, but Garwood did not say his name.

"What are you doin'?" Garwood asked.

"Just lookin' at a radio for one of these guys," the young man said, with a total lack of the nervousness and the testing atmosphere that was inevitable to most meetings between new arrivals.

"You repair radios?" Garwood asked, feeling like an idiot, not knowing how to proceed. The young man said he was not really good at the job. "Why're you doin' it then?"

"Back in the States, I use to tinker with them. You want to take a look at it?" Garwood's first impression was that here was a person not yet touched or wounded by the jungle. He looked at the radio. The man's full name was Gustav Mehrer, Army private.

The two men were to spend a few days together in the production house and during that time, Garwood found out why Hung was so enthused about Mehrer. The young man said he had been simply caught up in antiwar demonstrations back home—but he must have been an enthusiast, for he told how he had been in jail twice, had his head broken by a policeman on another occasion, and had burned his draft card.

After a chase with the local draft board on his heels, he was arrested, he said, and given the choice of going to Army boot camp or jail. He chose boot camp. Mehrer called the Army a "drag" because it took him away from his main avocation, women. Garwood found him using words he had never heard before, like "Pot," "Weed," "Grass."

"Man, I can't believe you don't know what grass is," Mehrer laughed. "Everyone knows what grass is."

"Hell, I know what grass is, I grew up on a farm," Garwood retorted.

"Way out . . . I don't believe this," Mehrer said. He shook his head.

Mehrer claimed German descent, which he was very proud of. Either he was born in Germany, or his mother was pregnant when she came over, something like that. He was undecipherable to Garwood, every other phrase being "you know," or "hey man"—Garwood did not know.

"What is *your* scene, anyway, man?" he asked after a few preliminaries, and after a biographical sketch Garwood thought confusing and too complete. He was astonished to learn of the length of Garwood's sojourn in the jungle, and that he could speak the language.

"Man, if they knew about this back in the States, they'd proclaim you a national hero, just from the fact you're still alive after four years in the jungle," Mehrer said in the false glow of a first meeting. "What have you got to do to get some pot and some women around here?"

Mehrer seemed to have traveled to college campuses to demonstrate; he told Garwood that you didn't have to be a "college boy" to take part in the action. "There's free love," he told the unbelieving Garwood. "You know how it used to be how the guys would go after the girls? Well, now it's the girls after the guys, and free love is the in thing." He spoke of miniskirts, parties that turned into orgies, music that had changed entirely, and a whole new attitude of devil-may-care commitment to a few ill-defined principles. The war was simply something to be fought. At home his friends thought he was a fool to go to boot camp. "Not that I had no choice," he said.

Mehrer was trying to survive, like Garwood, but he had none of the framework. He was drifting free, and he drifted into prison in Southeast Asia. They were thrown together for about four days and nights; it came across to Garwood in that time that his main role was to cheer up the new arrival. Garwood knew this because he was asked almost hourly by the cadre what Mehrer had said and done. He resented being sent in to Mehrer like a tame sheep on the ramp, the Judas sheep. It would have been easier if the two men had been able to strike some sort of connection, some sort of recognition in conversation, some sort of pattern wherein they both could converse without danger. But it was not to be, the bridge between the old and new was never made.

The guards roused Garwood just before dawn of the fourth day while his countryman slept, and told him that "On orders" he was to return from the production house to the main camp. Mehrer woke as Garwood rolled up his mat and gathered his few belongings in the pearl half-light and the cold. "Where ya goin'?"

"By the order of the commander," Garwood said with maximum safety, finding the words a comfort. "I have to return to the camp of which I came from."

"Where is it?" Mehrer asked, and Garwood told him it was only a couple of hours' march from where they had been staying. "Can I come to visit you?" he asked with an air of pathos.

The two shook hands. Mehrer was in the grips of a newfound fear of isolation—Garwood could see it closing around him like a wet glove. He asked again if he could visit, which made Garwood bitterly reflect that the kid must still think this was some kind of a tea party.

In four days the other Americans had become a world apart. Just four days of some milk, some sharing of rations with Mehrer had taken him out of the world these other men were suffering through. He saw them and he knew that the bottom line was not counsel, was not hope, was not a leader, but was merely food. He felt he had been a traitor to them, that he had broken every bond, that the excuse of survival and self-preservation was not enough. He could not escape, but had the terrible feeling of insincerity in his own sin, as if he had not enjoyed even that which he had betrayed to do. He had not had the joy of his time with Mehrer, and would have liked to forget him, but like the albatross, Mehrer hung around his neck, damning. Automatically, he decided to break all laws a bit further. He began to steal.

The things to steal were few enough. He knew where the rice was, in the rice bin hooch, and he knew that it was closely guarded. A cadre officer slept in the little building, and rice was counted out in "milk cans," one for each man. There were no locks, only wood pegs, but the hooch was out in the open, visible to all. He calculated risks as an old soldier would. If there was a ten-percent risk against him, he would usually do it, more, he would not. One chance in ten, he figured, was presentable odds—the sort of thing he would not do was expose himself to the point where, if caught, he could give no explanation whatsoever. Always, there had to be a reason for him to be where he was—a strong stand to lie from.

But if they caught him in the rice bin, with rice in his pocket, there could be no explanation, only the simple fact. He started thinking of grabbing handfuls of it, as fast as he could, trying to reduce the time element. He found there were places where a hand could be thrust through from outside of the building and he developed a system of grabbing almost on the run once he had established where he could stick his hand. The bamboo was tied only with strips, there was always slack.

For once, he was glad of his anomalous position, not a prisoner, not a guard. He was less watched than anyone in the camp, so he took the chance. He would empty his pockets, hardly swelled with booty, into Grissett's waiting hands; he always found an excuse to visit them. It was lucky the amounts were small. His trips to the Americans must have seemed small and harmless, and very quick, no longer than it took to pull a handful and pass it to Grissett.

"You're taking quite a chance," Grissett told him. It was a hanging offense, but Garwood never thought of getting caught, only of his guilt and the collective damnation of the others. Still, it was noticed in the supply room. They thought it was the rats. The number of kilos of rice had been apportioned so finely that even the handfuls he took showed up in the tally. Garwood no longer cared.

The rice stealing eased some of his guilt. It was almost like a religious exercise, he thought to himself, like doing a rosary, and perhaps just as useless in this circumstance. Then he had the idea of stealing an egg.

The camp chickens were regarded with the same jealous pride of possession that a Texas rancher might feel for a prize steer. The eggs were not eaten, but were used only to produce more chickens. The eating of an egg would be considered almost a sacrilege. But the preservation of the eggs from their fertilized state to a live chick was a perilous journey in the camp. There were rats and weasels, both of which would raid the helpless chickens and kill chicks and steal eggs, in spite of the best efforts of the guards to protect their livestock. The guards laid traps, mostly unsuccessful, and the idea of poisoning was out of the question also, because of the pigs and chickens—and the fear of tainting the food. When the guards managed to catch a rat—these were not jungle giants, but rats the size of a beer can only—they would take it straight away to the cookhouse to be prepared. But Garwood knew that the activities of the rats and of the weasels made it impossible to maintain an accurate count of the eggs.

But the major problem was how to get close to a chicken. Ironically, it was the guards who taught him how. He saw a guard slip his hand under a hen and with a single swift movement, lift the bird for a couple of seconds while he took a good look at the egg production. "I am surprised you Americans are not so smart that you don't know this," the guard told him with a grin. "Every Vietnamese knows that." And the man did it again for good measure.

193

The chickens were roosted in a henhouse—or rather there were two of the little bamboo structures of stilts, one for each side of the camp, three to four feet off the ground and sheltered with a grass roof. There, the chickens roosted and laid, and during the day they were free to wander about pecking at the dirt floor of the camp, on which, to Garwood's knowledge, not a single grain of rice could fall undetected. He never knew what they subsisted on.

It turned out to be simple; Garwood discovered the guards' enormous paranoia about their chickens. After dusk, he would simply throw stones to create a furor among the chickens of one henhouse. As soon as they grew alarmed, every guard on duty would rush to the henhouse—Garwood, meanwhile, would be stealing toward the other one, and it was too simple to pick up a chicken and take one egg at a time. A rat, he reasoned, could only take one egg at a time. The dangerous part was getting back to his hooch with the egg undetected. He had no permission to be out after dark and one of the henhouses was much closer to him than the other. But he came to count upon the preoccupation of the guards. They were blind to all except the clucking of their charges.

Of course he couldn't cook the egg. This would be too dangerous. He tried all ways of eating the eggs—shells and all, sucking out the contents, breaking the shells. The eggshells themselves were dangerous and had to be buried. Sometimes he was able to get an egg to the Americans' compound. He believed Grissett boiled one of them. He didn't really care what became of them, he only wanted to deliver the little spheres of protein for his own sake.

The egg stealing proved so simple and easy once he got the hang of it that he may have become careless. Or perhaps the chickens grew resentful. All he knew was that one night the wrong chicken squawked, and squawked loudly, and with the lightning reaction of the hunted, he simply crushed its head as hard as he could and stuffed the flopping, silent body under his pajamas. He fled back to his hooch unseen, praying that there were no feathers floating behind him.

For the rest of the evening he sat with the cooling corpse of one of the camp commander's favorite fowls. There was no alarm, no notice that the hen was missing. It was raining, a fact he counted as a blessing. The camp was sodden, silent, waiting for the night to pass, when Garwood heard an American telling the guard, "Cannon's awful bad, go get the nurse, guard, get the nurse, the man's in a coma."

The guard, of course, did not understand, except that the translator was needed. The guard called for Hung, but got no response—either the man was fast asleep or elsewhere. "Bop, Bop," the guard called, "come down to find out what he wants."

Garwood went down, having carefully brushed off his pajamas. The chicken he carefully secreted outside his hooch under cover of darkness, hidden under leaves so that he might not have its death pointing any fingers at him. Grissett was up when he got there, and the translating was simple and short. One of the men seemed to be failing fast, now he was in the stage of unconsciousness, and

194

when Garwood made this clear to the guard, the man went nodding up to the hooch of the camp commander, presumably to get the nurse.

"Russ, I've got a chicken," Garwood said in the silence. "D'ya have any way of cookin' it?"

"Oh, shit," Russ responded.

"Maybe I'll just throw it away or bury it, or tell them that a weasel got it?"

"No," Grissett said. "Meat's too scarce. Try to bring it down here. I'll find some way to cook it."

Glancing up to the camp commander's hooch, he saw no movement. He ran lightly back to his hooch in the darkness, easily found the damp chicken and returned as fast as he could with the thing lumping wetly against his belly and sending up the comfortable smell of feathers. He thrust it at Grissett, who turned and disappeared not a second too soon, for the guard returned instantly, to find Garwood alone standing stupidly and staring into the darkness. With the guard came the nurse, walking like a woman going to the bus stop, with a piece of plastic protecting her head against the rain.

"What is the matter?" the nurse asked him, and when he told her she walked down toward the hooches where the sick man lay. He noted with dismay that as usual she had no medical kit with her. It was just a visit to a dying American. "You stay here," she told him when he started after her.

He lingered, feeling no need to hurry as she walked off. "What did you do with it?" he whispered to Grissett's ghostly form as it appeared.

"Don't worry about it, Bob. It's taken care of," Grissett said. The two men stood together, talking about the chance they were taking, not only with the chicken but with the rice. "They don't want to take no chances," Grissett told him, speaking of the other Americans. "But they all want their share."

Garwood only shrugged. "Well, Bob," Grissett said, "we have a system down here, what we call the 'lion's share'—that is, whoever takes the risk gets an extra share of the booty. I'm gonna keep the two legs of the hen for you."

Garwood walked away. The rain was running down his neck now, and though it was not really cold, he could tell it would be several hours before he could get dry. He thought of towels and how simple and beautiful they were.

It was not until the next morning that the hue and cry began; Garwood kept a straight face as he heard the voices of blame and outrage. The hen, he noted, was now eulogized as the commander's "prize hen," and the guards were arguing about who had seen the hen last, and it was pointed out that the commotion in the henhouse the evening before came from the other house, not from the one where the victim lived. "It is too big a hen for any weasel to drag off," the camp commander could be heard saying. Eventually a guard asked Garwood if he had seen the chicken, or heard anything out of the ordinary. He shook his head solemnly, his stomach in turmoil. What if they had left feathers about? Or if someone smelled the aroma of it cooking? He hoped they would boil it deep in the pot.

Feathers, bone, anything left of it would point the finger directly at him. He felt the other Americans would betray him gladly. After all, it would have been almost impossible to steal out of the compound and back in. Only Garwood was in a position to do something like this theft. And Weatherman, who was stationed now with the ARVN POWs.

He stayed at his hooch. The weather, he noted, was breaking slowly, with some drizzle. There would be no footmarks. Finally, at radio time, he got down next to Grissett. "You take care of it?" he asked.

"Everything's fine. I cooked it and divvied it last night. Skinned it and boiled it, put the feathers and skin 'n all down the shitter." Grissett boldly passed a banana-leaf package to Garwood. He knew immediately what it was. It was right under Hung's eyes, but he noticed nothing.

He took it. He could feel the drumstick in his hand through the thin leaf and he thrust it into his waistband, rolling it in the cloth so he could stand without holding it. He took it back to his hooch and ate it quickly, swallowing madly, chewing up the bone until the hard parts, taking what was left with the greasy banana leaf and carefully depositing the remnants in the latrine hole.

But he had not heard the last of the chicken. The next day he began to hear the comments. "Enjoy your leg?" one man asked, eyes hard. Kushner said nothing, his eyes on Garwood.

He learned that the camp opinion was that he had deliberately endangered the rest of them by "dumping" the chicken on them when he had no other place to stash it. Thus, if the chicken were discovered he would go scot-free and they would share the blame. He could not believe the ingratitude. Yet he kept stealing and kept delivering. He could not really explain it except that it was for his own conscience. It was not to prove anything, unless it was to Grissett and Zawtocki, the only men who did not openly despise him. The weight of hatred hung heavy on him.

A day later Garwood was ordered to the production house, and after two weeks of intermittent hard labor, he was ordered back to the camp. To his surprise, Mehrer was with the other Americans.

Hung told him. "It was not to be discussed. It is a decision of the superiors. Be (Mehrer's Vietnamese name) is now a prisoner."

Garwood wondered how the flaky Mehrer could get on with the starving, angry, suspicious Americans. He talked to Grissett, who told him that Mehrer had a new story. "He said you lied to him, and that you tried to get him to cross over and to write leaflets, and that you tried to get him to join the liberation forces as *you had done*. And he said that you were a VC and that you had interrogated him, and had ordered the guards to torture him."

This was quite a load.

"What do you think about it, Russ?" Garwood asked. "Did it look like he'd been tortured or anything?"

Grissett said no. But his eyes were full of reproach and suspicion. "Does it look like he's been underfed? Well, I'll tell you Russ, you know me, you know me longer 'n anybody here, and if I was you, I wouldn't trust him. Be careful of him. He's gonna try and turn it all around to make everything to fit so everyone's to blame but him. They made him do everything. It's his way of justifying, of saying 'they made me, I didn't want to.' "

The Americans were in a sorry state. With each death, the morale of the survivors plummeted. He found that suggestion was a force that could almost be felt, almost smelled, like the heavy, cruddy stench of the latrine, a medicine that brought numbness and despair. The grim reaper who could touch men through their eyes and make them weaken seemed very real.

Three or four had died already. In the single year of 1968 he was to see seven to nine die. At the time, there was such an inevitability about it that the deaths lost their ability to shock him. He found himself judging the survivors on their ability to get through the starvation, the hunger edema, the dysentery. Ability to adjust to the jungle environment seemed to count for most. He believed the blacks had the easiest time—none of them died, and they seemed less afflicted with the gut-related hardships.

The poorer the individual and the worse the background the better the survival rate, he thought. Kushner was a case apart. He was definitely weakening with the rest, and Garwood thought he was doomed. But he survived. Work was important, too. He found that no matter what the job was—something like sweeping up the hooch, or carting wood, or chopping and digging—it made a difference. It made prisoners willing to eat anything, and in his experience one of the most "survivalist" tendencies in a person was the ability to stuff anything that crawled, flew, or grew into their gut.

The human stomach, he found, was an amazing muscle, once it got past dysentery. The only thing he found inedible within the greatly expanded world of the hungry prisoner was anything dead over three days. He found that anything that could be forced down—that is, chewed and wet with saliva and swallowed— would ease the hunger pangs at least enough to get to sleep. Even if a mouthful of grass had only one calorie or one vitamin, he was determined to get it. The tragedy was that some of the Americans rejected the available food while they were able to digest it. Later they became so weak that they could not reverse the process of dissolution even when they became desperately famished. In the jungle you could not gain weight. The struggle was to retain what you had.

It was about midsummer of 1968 when the camp was segregated. The four or five black POWs—William Watkins, James Daly, Isaiah McMillan, one man Garwood knew only as Lewis, perhaps another—were now taken out of the American compound and placed elsewhere. The reason, according to a statement read by the camp officers, was that the "black Americans" were "the most oppressed minority in the United States, that they have been enslaved by the white Americans, in spite of the fact that they are the most progressive people in the United States. So they should be allowed to live and work free of any decision from the white Americans—the lenient and humanitarian policy," and so on.

This at first caused consternation hard to imagine among the other Americans. But there were few prerogatives for these new "progressive Americans" that meant anything; there was no difference in the rations. When news of black-oriented issues or demonstrations in the States found its way through Radio Hanoi, the blacks were called on to comment on the news. It was then that Garwood first heard the names of Angela Davis, Bobby Seale and others— all of whom were painted by the radio and the camp officials as the heroes of the black race in America. For their part the black prisoners glumly went along with the show, showing as little enthusiasm as they dared.

Though there was an element in the whole idea meant to sow discord among the two groups of prisoners, only a little was harvested, though some of the white Americans felt the blacks could have demanded that everyone be allowed to stay together. Yet they did not. Watkins became the acknowledged leader of the black camp. But the blacks continued to help the whole camp; mainly because their health was so much better than that of the whites, they contributed much more in the way of work, cooking, and other duties.

Almost a year later, Watkins was released, though Garwood never knew exactly why.

Garwood would never have picked Earl Clyde Weatherman as an escaper. As Garwood pieced the story together, from the conversations of guards he overheard and from the American prisoners, who heard it from Dennis Hammond (who shared with Weatherman the distinction of having tried this escape, though unlike the Californian he did not lose his life at it), there were five of them.

They were sent out on a manioc run. Weatherman, who was penned up with the ARVNs, simply begged his way onto the run, which was why Garwood decided the whole caper was not so much planned as thrown together with the chaos the jungle bred.

It was Hammond, Zawtocki, Sherman and another man, perhaps Daly (Garwood never got it clear in the two versions that were told), who set out from camp on this manioc foray, with one guard. This seemed unusual, but was less so considering the state of the prisoners.

The manioc was in a Montagnard field about two and a half hours away.

There are usually four edible tubers—shaped like a sweet potato, with red skin and white meat—per manioc plant, so that the actual harvest is relatively quick and easy compared with the toting of the roots. Laden with as many as each man could carry, the groups of prisoners would stagger back home over the trails.

It was a cruel contest, because there usually was one manioc run per week, or at the most two, and the rule of the guards was each man would carry as much as he could. Naturally, the strongest carried most, and the men's return was watched jealously by every eye in the compound—for each load had to be split equally among all members of the camp. The reward for the run was the chance to stuff your belly with raw manioc in the field. Filthy, spongy, or so hard that it had to be gnawed, it was still a dish men relished.

The departure of the little troop was unexceptional. But shortly after noon, a greatly excited Montagnard came running into the camp. "All the Americans have escaped, and they have killed the guard," was the message he got across in his dialect, and "they have the guard's CKC" (a Chinese-made assault rifle).

The guards were assembled with a blast of a whistle, which sounded exactly like those used by football umpires. The guard on the perimeter of the camp was doubled, armed Montagnards hurriedly brought in from nearby villages. Prisoners were told to stay in their hooches. Garwood, having been turned back by a guard after trying to get down to the American compound, was able to watch what happened from his hooch door.

A Montagnard of importance, apparently a chief, came into the camp. He was a man with a huge voice, whose comments were louder than the radio and whose bearing was medieval. "The American prisoners," he said, "are a threat to my people, to their safety and well-being. I have given orders to my people that they are to kill the Americans on sight and take no prisoners."

It was a day of silence and downcast faces. No one in the camp could believe the escapers had a chance. It was a day the men did not like to look at each other. The only version anyone would learn of this escape, Garwood thought, was the official version.

At about dusk two or three men—he could not immediately see in the gloom—were shoved into the jungle clearing, bound together, everything about them spelling defeat. Hung was with them. When they were tied to the trees, he could see that two of them were Zawtocki and Sherman. The returning guards were telling another version of the escape, in which the guard was not killed or even wounded but knocked down by Weatherman, who got the only gun and ran off into the jungle with Hammond, leaving the others behind.

The men who were left behind, this version said, walked quietly to a nearby Montagnard village and gave themselves up. They were bound by the Montagnards, they found the guard, hardly the worse for his experience, and then were escorted back to camp.

The guards seemed to know what direction Weatherman and Hammond were headed and that there was little chance of them escaping a net of Montagnard and Vietnamese men watching for them. They would be shot on sight.

The restless night saw shadowy forms constantly moving in and out of the camp as the Montagnard force established its own rhythms with its own whispery language. The two returned prisoners said nothing. Garwood lay on his back, trying to see through his ears.

But there was nothing more until the morning, when Garwood woke to the sound of shots being fired. Single fire, he thought, coming instantly to a state of wary readiness like a careful animal. He sensed an excitement among the guards. One man had been killed, they were saying. One had been wounded, captured, and was still alive. The shots were a signal to draw other members of the dragnet to tell them the manhunt was over.

The excitement gave way to relaxation. Garwood was allowed to go to the stream. He found Kushner and two other Americans there. "Good morning, Bob," Kushner said, as he busied himself washing his face. "Have you heard anything?"

"This ain't straight scoop," he said, "but according to what the guards are sayin', it's one killed, one wounded, and they've called off the manhunt."

Late that afternoon, with the two prisoners who had done nothing, but were still tied to the tree, drooping into unconsciousness, the guards brought one of the escapers back into the camp. It was Hammond. Alive.

Hammond was still on his feet, but was a mess. He had been shot in the ankle and walking must have been worse than a torture, even with a rough bandage on it. They tied him down near the ARVN troops, and unlike the other two, who remained tied, he cried out all that night in pain, begging the guards to loosen the ropes, though none could understand his words, begging for water.

The stocks were begun the next day and Garwood knew what was to come, or thought he did. Two sets were made. But there were three men tied to trees. Hammond was taken and put in the stocks as soon as they were finished, the other two, Sherman and Zawtocki, were led off to the camp commander to be interrogated—and they were soon released back into the compound with the other Americans, to find themselves bombarded by questions from the others.

Garwood did not find out how sick Hammond was. The end of his ordeal was out of sight, behind the American compound and near the ARVN hooch. The other prisoners brought him food and water under instructions. Garwood was able to talk to him once.

His wound turned out to be to his leg above the ankle, apparently not resulting in a bone fracture. Garwood had made an excuse to visit the ARVNs, a difficult feat, for he was unable to pose as the translator for them. On the way he stopped by the stocks, roofed over, as was the custom, with a leaf shanty. Hammond had been in the stocks about a week. The excitement of the escape and the ordeal had worn off. He was a man who had tried and lost and now could expect nothing further from a life that was too close to death. He was actually glad to see Garwood, as if the name-calling and bitterness directed at Garwood had never existed. He wanted to know what the Communists were going to do with him.

"Stupid thing I did, huh?" Hammond said sympathetically.

"Well, Dennis, if it's any comfort to you, I did it twice and I'm still alive to tell about it, so don't give up hope."

"They murdered Weatherman. I bet they didn't say that."

Garwood was surprised at the word. "What you mean, murdered?" Earlier he had heard guards talking. They said Weatherman had been killed in a miniature firefight with a Montagnard. Weatherman had fired, missed, the

Montagnard had fired, killing Weatherman, and then turned his gun on Hammond, wounding him.

But according to Hammond, when they went on the manioc run, the pair had no intention of making an escape, no plan. Weatherman may have wanted to get on the expedition for that reason, but no one knew it. It was a spur-of-the-moment decision that came on the way to the fields. Weatherman had spoken boldly, not afraid of translation into Vietnamese.

The others put down the idea of a breakout, counting the risks, saying it was hopeless, and the young man dropped his talk about cutting through the jungle to find a U.S. position.

But when they got to the manioc, Weatherman brought it up again. He stressed the point that there was only one guard, and he spoke of it as the best chance yet for success. He said he would jump the guard, grab his gun, knock him out, and they would escape. The only man who was interested was Hammond—he said Weatherman told him he knew the way out of the jungle, and Hammond figured if anyone knew it, he did. He said there was a fifty-fifty chance of making it. No chance if they stayed.

Weatherman simply went up to the guard to ask for a drink of water, and when the man took his canteen to give it to him, he turned slightly. Weatherman swarmed him, knocked him over and went for the gun, then started beating and kicking the still prostrate guard. Weatherman put down the gun and even started to strangle the guard. He wanted to kill him to make more time, but Hammond tried to stop him, saying, "If we're recaptured, our chances are zilch."

This argument prevailed and the pair tied the guard after beating him almost unconscious. They tried to get the other men to join, but they refused, saying they were too weak, that numbers were no benefit, but made it suicide. There was no anger that the others felt they could not come along. They took off down a creek bed, pockets stuffed with manioc. The theory was that if you follow a creek, you find a river, and so on.

They found a hiding place, waited for dark, but they found the going very difficult among the stones in the blackness, and the stream bed seemed to branch in a bewildering fashion. When light came, they hid out under heavy bushes. When a Montagnard came into view, they figured they were surrounded, came out with hands up, leaving both bayonet and rifle in the bush.

But the Montagnard merely lifted his rifle and shot Weatherman through the chest. Hammond only knew that the shot could not have missed, and heard Weatherman's short scream followed by a slap to his foot and a fall. Before he knew it he was in captivity and the volley was being fired by the triumphant Montagnards, who were eagerly handling the guard's gun.

Under the weight of the failed escape, some gave up. Those who did almost always died. Those who hung on suffered large changes. There was no need for torture, the life did all the softening up without such effort. The two superior officers, Frank Anton and Harold Kushner, took little part in camp activities.

Kushner maintained his ironic reserve, Anton simply retreated, spending whole days wrapped up in his blanket, coming out only for meals. When Garwood ribbed Kushner one day about how the two officers were behaving, he snapped back defensively. "You're the highest-ranking man here," Garwood told him one day, referring to the fact that Grissett, a Marine Corps corporal, was the acknowledged leader of the Americans.

"I'm a doctor, not a commander," Kushner said. The tone was sarcastic, just as Garwood's had been. He reflected that it was the first time he had gotten anything but an arch and mannered reply from the doctor.

Once when he talked to Anton about the same subject, he got a sterner rebuke. "Garwood," Anton said from his makeshift bunk, "if you'd learned how to control your own actions instead of worrying about others, you'd be in better shape."

But both men had been changed profoundly by the camp, and it was the lower social echelon that had stepped in.

After the aborted escape, Hammond stayed in the stocks for about a month. He bore the regime cheerfully, but his health declined. The others took turns tending to his needs. There was a deep change in him, too—no longer was he the strong-willed and determined man who had come into the camp. He was now complacent and flexible. His good humor appeared less frequently, and he seemed to be stripped of any decorations to his character; he was profoundly upset by the way he had been treated by his own colleagues on his return. Hammond had tried to escape, and he expected respect as a result. He had lived by the code of conduct, and almost died by it. But the other prisoners only told him how lucky he had been to get out of it with his life. It seemed that all fury had been washed out of them, as it had from the Vietnamese as well— they punished him in a half-hearted way. Then there was the matter of Zawtocki; Hammond and he had been captured together, but when the crisis of the escape came, Zawtocki had not risen. It was never again the way it had been before between the two.

In the cooling of the friendship between Hammond and Zawtocki, Garwood got the benefit; Zawtocki began to show signs of a new interest in him, waiting for him at the stream to make conversation, showing concern for him. This was a painful wrench to Garwood, who had become used to being completely alone and rebuffed. He had longed for another friendship, or at least a civil conversation without the sarcasm and the patterned chill.

"How are you, Bob?" Zawtocki said one day. Garwood could have cried. It had been so long, no one had asked such a thing of him, and he thought no one could know what it was to move and live completely enshrouded by bad opinion—a pariah.

14
War Crimes

GARWOOD DIDN'T understand Zawtocki's new overtures. The old effusiveness had been dried out of him by countless withering glances and cutting remarks. But he welcomed Zawtocki, this grubby, bearded Polack from New York, a man of about the same age, but a wildly different background—he came from a close-knit immigrant's family, which centered around a single neighborhood and a single set of friends. He loved to talk about his father, how hard he had worked, building a small retail business from nothing.

The pair would meet at the stream or at Radio House and sit picking their lice, and eventually Garwood got in the habit of strolling to the Americans' stockade to chat with him. He would tell Zawtocki about his own youth, but he never broached the delicate subjects of his strange role at the camp or the accusations against him. There seemed no need to add any unpleasantness to what already existed. They talked of food. Garwood of steaks and potatoes, barbecue, grilled chickens, ribs, hamburgers; Zawtocki of his mother's home-cooked stews, dumplings, sauces, corned beef.

There was some hostility from the others when Zawtocki began to take up with the camp's black sheep. Conversation would slip out of its easy gear when another prisoner came close to the two; Zawtocki put on a different attitude then, much more in line with the general coldness. Garwood accepted this, thankful for the attention and affection even under these whorish circumstances.

In his mind, Garwood knew what Joe was going through—he knew it double, for he had to walk the line with both the camp officials and the Americans. Zawtocki only had to pretend with one set. It was nice to be able to talk to another American, that sufficed.

203

For about two weeks, they got along in easy friendliness. It was a period of lull in the camp, almost relaxation, during which the guards allowed visits to go on. It was like high summer, a time of stability.

He didn't know who brought it up. But the two men decided to exchange rings. More than that, they made a compact. They would trade their rings back again if both survived. If only one, the other would return the ring to the other's family. If neither—well, nothing lost. Garwood had an emerald stone set in silver or white gold, which he'd haggled for in Da Nang—it had cost about sixty dollars, enough for him to be assured the stone was real. It was too tight to get off, though that had been tried. It was still one of his proudest possessions.

Zawtocki's ring was also white gold, with a star sapphire set into it. He'd acquired it in Bangkok. Inside it had a small engraving with his name. The exchange was not easy. Garwood had great difficulty getting his ring off, eventually working it over the knuckle with saliva and water. He put Joe Zawtocki's ring, much larger, on his middle finger, while Zawtocki slid his on a little finger. The deal was sealed, and with it, Garwood felt for the first time in many months that he was not completely isolated.

Then something changed. Garwood was sent off to the production hooch for a week, and when he returned he noticed that Joe no longer wore the emerald. Zawtocki didn't want to talk much about it. He told Garwood he had lost it at the washing place and when he had tried to scour the area had been ordered back to camp by the guard on duty. Garwood was devastated, not so much by the loss of the ring, but by the uncomfortable way that his friend spoke of it. He didn't come across like he was sorry, just said that it had happened. Garwood said nothing. He offered the other ring back but Zawtocki refused. "It's all right," he said, "you keep it, but I'd appreciate it if you wouldn't wear it, okay?"

Garwood acceded. But during radio hour that night, Kushner, with that cold and scientific curiosity of his, asked, "Where's Joe's ring?"

"I lost it," Garwood said, looking straight at the man. Kushner asked how and where he had lost it. "Not the same place Joe lost mine," Garwood retorted. That was all that was said, but Garwood felt resentment growing like nausea in his stomach. It was clear to him that the other members of the camp had pressured Zawtocki about the ring. Though he did not know, he imagined the others demanding to see the ring, saw in his mind's eye one of them taking it, throwing it into the jungle. This was the only way Zawtocki could have lost such a thing, a ring that fitted tightly on his finger and had lasted Garwood through years of peril. He made it a point never to mention the ring again, to see if the subject came up. It didn't.

It always seemed an event of consequence when Mr. Ho came into camp. He would arrive and usually something unpleasant would follow. There was something about him that reeked of authority, rigidity, and threat. He could not really be put off with excuses and evasions, and by this time, almost four years after Garwood's capture, Ho had got to know his man very well. Garwood was unsure how much Ho actually knew, after all that. He never seemed to budge from the belief that underlay much of what he said and the maneuvers he tried, that Garwood was an intelligence operative.

But the negatives were mixed with curiosity at the latest arrival of the eminence. He had to face the fact that he almost enjoyed tangling with the little man. The central secret was that Garwood knew nothing about intelligence, and no amount of trickery could budge him from this stronghold. Ho kept biting and chewing on him but could never draw closer to the middle because there simply was none.

This time his approach was authority. Ho came into camp with two others— they were clearly underlings, who deferred to him almost like servants, Garwood thought. They brought him water, tended to his clothes, cooked his meals and delivered them—this was not what cadre would do. Garwood figured it was only a matter of time before the inevitable visit began. He wondered, hopelessly, whether there was some way to gain some security in this world of balances and hairbreadth escapes.

Ho was in camp almost three days before he talked to Garwood. In the meantime he interviewed Kushner, Anton, Williams, Daly, Hammond, Zawtocki, Pfister (a late arrival) and several others (Strickland, Tinsley, Lewis, McMillan, Burns). In fact there were few he did not interview, calling each man individually.

Then he called Garwood. The greetings were the usual exquisite platitudes. Garwood answered his questions by saying, "Well, I'm still alive and kicking."

"And how are you getting along with the other Americans?" he asked sweetly.

"Not very good."

"Why?"

"It's pretty evident, isn't it? They're in there and I'm out here."

"Why should that make a difference?"

"I can't be accepted as part of them," Garwood said patiently, "when they see me living outside the compound, eating from the guards' kitchen, cleaning and repairing guards' weapons on occasion. Plus my speaking Vietnamese with the guards, it's just an impossible situation."

"How can we rectify this?" Ho asked with a look of worry on his smooth face.

"I think it's too late now," Garwood said wearily. "If I went back in the camp now, they'd probably think I was a spy. Anything that I tell them and certainly anything you tell them, they wouldn't accept that as the truth—if it was."

"I'm sorry to see it. But you see, Bobby, that is one of the reasons why I am here. I am going to hold a re-education course here for you Americans. And after the re-education course, I'm sure that if it has been any value to them, they will not treat you so harshly."

"What will be my participation in this re-education?" Garwood said, feeling the inevitable clamps on his stomach.

"You will attend, as will everyone else."

"Can I sit with the other Americans?"

"I have not thought about that yet," Ho said. "But because of the dissension against you, it might be better if you didn't. I think it is better for you to sit separately." It was the first time Garwood could remember Ho's being unsure of himself. But this was no good news. Ho would do as he pleased, screw the American prisoner in front of him.

"How long is the course going to be?" When Ho answered it would last a week, Garwood's heart sank. The impression could be made of his total betrayal.

In the morning it was announced by Hung that the re-education course would start that day and all prisoners, of course, would attend. There were to be no exceptions, even for the sick. The guards threw together some bamboo benches, and three tables in front of them. It was a fresh-air classroom, and when Garwood went down, he decided to sit on the first bench in the front row. The other Americans filed to other benches. A couple of them snickered, one saying, "Garwood! You've got to attend this thing, too? We thought you knew this shit frontwards and backwards by now."

"I know more than you do, but not as much as you think I do," Garwood told them evenly. They came back lamely.

"Sure, Garwood, sure."

Hung marched down, every inch of the bearer of knowledge. He sat at one table. An unknown Vietnamese sat at another. Guards stood at all four corners of this class and when all was prepared, even to the placing of cigarettes and a pot of green tea on the table, Ho came down. Attention all hands. He looked regally around, adjusted his glasses, glanced down at some papers. Garwood had a feeling of unreality. Class in the jungle. Without looking up, he said, "Bobby?" A murmur was felt more than heard.

"Yes, sir," Garwood answered.

"You will sit at the table to my left."

Weakly, he got up and moved to the table. What was the use. . . .

He looked at the other Americans, now looking at him with eyes of hate. He felt the friction in the air, making it hot, making his armpits seep cold. Ho disregarded him completetey, turning to the prisoners at large. "Is everyone here?" he said loudly. Ho looked closely at Kushner. "What do you think is going to happen this time?"

Kushner grinned and shrugged ingratiatingly. "We are all hoping that you will liberate us."

"That decision is not made by me. I do not have that power. The decision can only be made by the Front committee." He went on to tell that there would be a political education course on Vietnamese history. It would take four or five days and during that time the schedule would be rigidly adhered to.

"Your rations will be increased during the week of the course. In the morning, we will hold group discussions on Vietnamese history, politics, and current events. In the afternoon, we will divide up into three groups, each will hold their own discussion as to what took place that morning."

Garwood asked, "Will I be required to participate with the other Americans?" He wanted a public explanation of why he had been cut out from the prisoners and sat down apart.

"Yes," said Ho. "You will, unless otherwise directed by me." He went on to explain that there were four bilingual persons; besides himself, Hung, and Garwood, there was Trieu, who had come with him on this visit. The name translated to "a million."

"Quite unfortunately, the documents that I have are in Vietnamese. Therefore," Mr. Ho said to Garwood, "you will be required to sit with one of the groups and read the document from Vietnamese to English to the other Americans. Hung and Trieu will do the same with other groups."

"I do not read Vietnamese well enough to be able to translate the documents accurately," Garwood said.

"That's quite all right. I will be coming around to check on any mistakes you may make and to answer any questions you may have." Garwood looked plaintively at the other Americans. "Get your ass out of that one, Garwood," was all he could sense from the hard looks.

The second day of the course Sergeant "Top" Williams, his wounded hand still ghastly, was stood up while Ho was talking along the lines of the "lackeys and puppets of U.S. militarism carrying out the policy of destruction in South Vietnam." It was close to question period. Williams was asked if he had been following the thread.

In his response, Williams repeatedly used the word ARVN. Ho reacted as if stung every time the word was spoken. He reprimanded Williams. "I prohibit the use of the word ARVN. The ARVN stands for the Army of the Republic of Vietnam. It is in fact a puppet and lackey army bought and paid for by the United States and is not in fact an army of the people of Vietnam." He said the only true army of the people, and the "only true and correct administration," was the NFL.

When he returned to Williams for another question, the sergeant used the word again. Williams explained he was used to the word. Everyone used it, while "puppet troops" was new to him; it was just what came first to his mind.

But Ho did not accept this excuse. He slammed down his hand on the table, and shouted at Williams that he was "unprogressive . . . obstinate . . . trying to sabotage the class and trying to jeopardize everyone else's progress, and to threaten the morale and ideology of everyone. . . ."

Williams strongly proclaimed he had no intention of doing so. He said he felt sure he had not hurt anyone's morale or ideology. Ho would not accept this. "You, Williams, have a long record of serving the favors of U.S. capitalism. You waged war against the Korean people; your hands are stained with the blood. Your life has flourished with the blood money you have received from the U.S.

capitalists, from your atrocities you committed against the Korean people, and you have come to Vietnam to reap the same benefits by committing the same atrocities against the Vietnamese people, but quite to your despair, your plans were foiled and you were captured by the Liberation Front, putting to an end your hideous acts. That is why you refer to the puppet troops as ARVNs, because in your mind, you are still dedicated to the U.S. imperialist, capitalist." Williams denied this, shaking his head. It was a single gesture in a gale of invective. Ho became incensed. He declared the class a "disaster," and told Williams, "You are a saboteur." He dismissed the group until further word from him. Williams was to remain behind.

Garwood trudged to his hooch in bewilderment. He could still hear Ho's agitated voice speaking in Vietnamese and English, accusing Williams. "Remember that you are a prisoner of the National Front for Liberation," he shouted. "They have full control of you. Your destiny lies in their hands, not in yours."

Ho told the man that if he ever wanted to see his home and family again, he would be "advised to change your ways promptly and sincerely."

Williams, a forty-eight-year-old Army lifer, had seen action in World War II. He was on his second or third tour in the country. He had held up under the treatment in camp and had been unhappy that Kushner and Anton had not taken the leadership role, and had tried to do it himself. But there was something about him that they would not accept as a leader; they rejected his bid and he grew frustrated. Now he stood before Ho, sullen and defiant.

He was the type of man who was set completely in his ways, a professional soldier who knew only one way to do things. He followed rules with habit that had become belief. Rules were his rosary. He was stronger in his following of the code of conduct than anyone else there. He was the type who believed in name, rank, and serial number only. His attitude toward Garwood was a combination of scorn and horror. He couldn't believe that any American could do the things Garwood did daily. But he told Garwood he understood, somewhat, because of Garwood's youth and inexperience. The men he could not excuse were Anton and Kushner, men of higher education who had failed. Garwood was brainwashed, Williams thought.

"You're fucked up, Bob," he said. "You're young, you're immature, you don't know the seriousness of the trouble you could get into. One day if you survive, Bob, you're gonna be back. It's gonna tear you up and you're gonna regret it for the rest of your life."

But that day, Top Williams took the brunt of Ho's wrath on his balding head. Ho took him up to the hooch. There were self-criticism papers, which took several rewritings to get to Ho's standard. Garwood never knew what sort of pressure the little man exerted on this old soldier, but he seemed confused and distressed and listless after the sessions. And he stopped using the term ARVN, even among his mates. It was one of the strangenesses of the strangest world to hear Williams call them "puppet troops."

The course stubbed its toe, limped on under Ho's wrath. He got everyone back to the classroom, proclaiming that every American "will criticize Williams openly." Williams was made to come to the front of the class, looking like some shaggy, baited bear standing at attention while Ho called, at random, on every American, not only to criticize the use of the forbidden word but also to suggest punishment for trying to "sabotage the class."

Suggested punishment from the prisoners ranged from having Williams apologize to the whole class and promise he would never use the word ARVN again, to a half-cut in rations for three days, to a week in the stocks. When it came to Garwood, he criticized Williams. "He should carefully think before speaking so that he would not jeopardize sabotaging the class, and at the same time risking the release of the other Americans." His suggested punishment: "He has been punished enough by having to go through with this public criticism."

Ho then criticized Williams himself, leaning with both hands on the table and telling them that Williams had committed too many atrocities "against all Asian peoples . . . he is a hardened mercenary of the U.S. and its lackeys, having carried out policies of aggression against all of Asia for many years."

Ho turned to Garwood.

"Do you disagree?"

He looked at Williams and back to the other prisoners. Williams had gone through hell already. If he had said yes, he would have gone through more. He said, "No." It was, he thought, the way to get it over with.

Ho looked up with the satisfaction of revenge on his face. He dismissed the class. Later Williams told Garwood, "I can't believe an American can act in the way you did."

Garwood's group was made up of five. His role was to read the questions in English—then they were to discuss the questions and appropriate answers. It was like a round-table debate.

"Question one," Garwood read haltingly, "U.S. imperialist aggression in Vietnam is doomed to ultimate defeat."

The four men looked up at Garwood, their faces masks of disbelief, curiosity and hostility. "Keep talking," Garwood said, "or start talking. When Ho comes around, start saying something about U.S. imperialism and how it fucked up your life. Otherwise just keep talking."

This went on for two days. There was a lecture by Ho, punctuated as before by Ho's method of close questioning of a single "student." Everyone had become far more cautious in their replies, however.

At night, the Americans talked of the baffling "re-education course" and its possible outcome. Garwood heard of the discussions from his group, when Ho was not near. Grissett was convinced that the course would end with the release of some of the prisoners. He made it no secret that he was hopeful that he would be selected himself.

Garwood thought it was a good possibility that someone would be released. It fitted in with their stick-and-carrot method of "indoctrination," which was crude and clumsy but worked because it was backed with sheer terror. He put out of his mind that he might be the one. If they were going to release him at all, they would have done so by now. But he had become too useful for that. He had become Vietnamese to survive in order to go home again, but the circle was perfect. By surviving in the only way he knew how, he had made it impossible to grasp the reward of survival.

There seemed no climax to the course, and no graduation. It lasted about a week, just as Mr. Ho had said. One day he simply announced that it was coming to an end, and in fact had ended. He said he was satisfied and that he would report to his superiors that "the course has been a success."

Grissett looked like a hound on point, watching Ho's every move, but the man took no notice. He was inscrutable. Kushner asked a question, "Is anyone gonna be liberated?"

The question froze the moment, as a loud report can stun a crowd. There were seconds of dead silence in which the jungle sounds filtered in like a summer zephyr.

"That is not my decision," Ho said politely. "Everyone is eligible. But this will depend on your progress, sincerity, attitude."

Ho's passages were always like a frontal system and it took several days for things in the camp to settle, for men to readjust to their lost hopes or to the kind of resignation that Garwood was coming to know as his single most durable mood. But in such a prison society the tiniest bit of news or the littlest break in the routine can become the size of a fresh thunderhead. So it was with the bomb-shelter project.

Bomb shelters were required in every camp, not because there were raids on every camp, but as one of the guards put it, because "a man does not wait until bombs are falling to get into his hole."

But when the camp commander, about two weeks after Ho left, announced that there was to be a bomb shelter "for the Americans," he added that the men who would build it were "Kushner, Anton, Harker."

This was extraordinary. Anton and Kushner were the ranking men in camp, though they had not acted in their military roles. David Harker, Army private, a man little known to Garwood, was the third. All three were in bad condition. Kushner was extremely emaciated. Anton seemed to live in his own withdrawn world and besides the ills the others suffered had had little exercise since coming to the camp. Harker was a skeleton, albeit a hard worker, who looked like he could hardly lift a shovel. The fittest people in the camp besides the blacks were Garwood, Pfister, Strickland, Tinsley, Grissett, Mehrer, and Zawtocki.

The bomb shelters Garwood had seen were deep holes with logs on the top and sod and dirt piled over all. Each hole had to be big enough to shelter six to eight men and had to be over six feet deep. The logs had to be cut fresh from the jungle. It was tough work for fit men in the best of times. The three were given one shovel, one hoe, one basket, and were shown, by means of bamboo stakes driven into the ground, where they were to dig. It looked an impossible task—the tools themselves seemed stronger and stouter than these insubstantial men.

Kushner protested to the camp commander. When the trio of unfortunates was shown the side of the hole, the doctor could be heard telling Hung, "We're all too weak, Anton's got malaria, Harker's too weak to do this."

Hung told them, "You are very lazy and dirty. You want everyone to work for you." He was clearly angry, an anger, Garwood felt, that was on order from the camp commander. In two cases, that of Kushner and Anton, Garwood felt the slurs were justified. Harker was just too weak to work. Hung was unrelenting. He pushed the tools into their hands. They started making ineffectual moves at breaking the ground. Kushner still found the energy to bellyache. He turned to Hung and told him, "The Japanese never treated their prisoners this bad . . ." Hung flared, walked quickly off to the camp commander's hooch. The men kept scratching at the packed dirt, taking turns with the shovel and hoe while the basket man rested.

The camp commander came into Garwood's hooch, clearly agitated. His hands clasped and unclasped. He formed a torrent of words, telling Garwood, "The Americans are digging a bomb shelter for their own protection, not for the protection of the guards or the cadre. You come with me," he said.

They marched to the site of the hole. Seeing a break in the work, the laboring three snapped to attention—slumped to attention would be more accurate— and listened as the commander told them, through Hung, that the bomb shelter was being built for their protection "against U.S. bombs and shells, not Vietnamese bombs and shells. And as far as the Geneva Accords are concerned, these do not and will never apply to you. . . ."

Kushner and Anton turned stares of hatred at Garwood. It was clear they thought Garwood had told the camp commander what they were saying. He did nothing. He just stood there trying to show no expression at all. Anton spoke: "Garwood, you're gonna get yours one day. You worry about yourself and let us worry about ourselves. We don't need your damn help. Mind your own business."

Garwood kept silence. The same to you, he thought. He didn't need them either.

Cannon was the next to go. Wounded in the back and never healed, his body reached a state of stability, but that could not last. Gradually and almost unnoticed it slipped into the gloom of failure. He fought all the way, coming back from sinking spells all the others thought must be the last. He swam to the surface each time and somehow hauled himself up to a sitting posture, which eased his wounds. Then one day he did not swim back. There was a small service, another grave in the little yard one hundred yards below the American compound.

Williams seemed to have flown apart, like a doll whose stuffing has leaked from one spot. The whole thing becomes soft and flabby, with only the single

211

tear. Williams never recovered from his experience on the first day of the Mr. Ho lectures. He had found himself alone, he had discovered that his comrades were only a frightened rabble of separate voices, and it poisoned him as surely as something in his veins. Perhaps it was his age—no one who was twenty-two looked under thirty-five, and Williams looked sixty.

Even his robust health gave way. His wound, caused by a bullet that ripped across the back of his hand, had scarcely bothered him until now, but it became infected—and it stayed that way, leaking poison, aggravating with constant pain and pressure. It was like watching the denouement of a movie, the part where the forces, fully in motion, move swiftly to the end.

He came to Garwood one day. He was seeking some kind of help. He wanted Garwood to talk to the camp commander—to strike some kind of a deal.

"I need to get out of Vietnam," the older man said.

Garwood was squatting under a tree near his hooch when Williams approached. They were out of hearing of the others. The guard was bored and inattentive. "Why did you come to me?" Garwood asked.

"I can't trust Hung to interpret what I say to the camp commander."

"What makes you think you can trust me?"

"I'm hopin' you as an American will sympathize with me more. I'm old, I can't make it no more out here. I'm gonna die here if I can't do somethin'."

"Do any of the others know what you want to do?"

"No."

Garwood asked him why he hadn't talked it all out with them. He had been no friend to Garwood, had never shown sympathy to him.

"All those guys think about is themselves. They never listen to anything I say. I thought you could understand my reasons more."

"I understand you," Garwood said warily. "I don't think I can help you."

"Why not?" the older man asked, not pleading, half-angry.

"First of all, if I went up to the camp commander with you and told him what you just told me, if he didn't laugh at you, he'd probably lock us up. Top, you're a professional soldier, you've been in the Army over thirty years. They know that. My opinion of what I know of these guys, there's no way in hell they're gonna listen to your requests or even give a second thought to granting them. You'll just be creating more trouble for yourself."

The anger faded in his face and was replaced with downcast eyes. "I just thought I would ask . . ."

Garwood discovered later that Williams had gone to Hung after seeing him and Hung and the camp commander had made Williams write a paper. Garwood told Grissett about it. Grissett seemed merely curious, but he told the other Americans about Williams' bid for freedom. The camp immediately turned on him; in their paranoia, they saw Williams as a threat who was reporting to the camp commander on their activities to make himself look better. They isolated him completely. Their action completed Williams' dissolution. He took to sitting in the sun by himself when he could, and picking lice.

He was like a very old child, and a strange one at that. He developed hunger edema for no particular reason. His health failed and not until he was actually in the phase of weakness that many knew to be part of dying did their attitude toward him change. They started taking care of him, cleaning him, helping him to the latrine. He had trouble walking. But Williams seemed unconscious of the new solicitous attitude of his comrades. He seemed to be walking surely and quietly toward death and toward his escape, as if he had planned it. All he would speak of was his wife and how much she had always reminded him of Elizabeth Taylor. "I only want to see her one more time," he told one of the Americans.

They told him to stop talking like that but he assumed an extraordinary sweetness. Nothing made a difference to him, there was no bitterness toward those who hadn't stood by him during his psychological testing. It was clear he wanted to be off. He died a week later. Garwood heard it from Kushner, who said he thought he'd had a heart attack. Whatever it was, he could not be revived.

Every American death discouraged those left behind. But the deaths also had a disturbing effect on the camp structure.

Before Williams' death Hung told Garwood, "That is such a waste for the American prisoners to die. The liberation forces have to sacrifice many lives in order to capture one American. We go through great pains, time and expense to build a camp and try to keep the Americans alive. But it is so hard when the American culture is so high. It's hard for me, a Vietnamese, to live in the jungle."

"All we need is a little meat, maybe some medicine," Garwood told him.

"In North Vietnam, that is possible. They have all of that. But here in the south we have to get most of our food and medicine through the American-controlled areas—and that is little enough and too far. Whatever food and medicine we do get is reserved for the revolution."

"He's on the verge of death. Why don't you release him back to U.S. forces? This would be a great humanitarian gesture on your part."

"That is not my decision," Hung said, like a parrot of his commander. "I do not question the wisdom of my superiors, I only follow their orders."

"Well, in the meantime, the Americans are gonna keep on dying," Garwood told him.

Burns simply went downhill. There was no turning with him. He got dysentery, but everyone got that. Hunger edema too. But for Burns these things carried him right out of the world. He simply sank. In a delirium for two days he cried for his mother and even his father. Then he just stopped breathing and it was over. His decline had lasted only about two weeks.

Bob Sherman's turn was next. He was the same age as Garwood, and they had been together since the summer of '67 when he came in with the Puerto

Ricans, but the two had never been close. Though he was not talkative, he smiled at everyone, kept to himself, never made much of an impression, it seemed. He got one of the worst cases of hunger edema, compounded with malaria. Garwood was not in camp when he died. He had been sent off to the manioc field, leaving when Sherman was in bad shape. There was no way of telling. Guys like Anton and Harker seemed in much worse shape but they hung on. When he came back, Sherman, corporal of Marines, was another mound in the graveyard.

The four deaths were quite close—within a month and a half. The effect on the camp command and the guards was unique. The guards seemed actually scared, almost deferential to the Americans who were able to die with such rapidity and to decline so surely. They were suddenly treated as if they were carriers of some plague. It looked to Garwood as if everyone was going to die; only he was immune. He would be bothered by an occasional malaria attack but nothing like the attacks he had known when the disease was new to him. Four had died in succession and four others—even one of the blacks, Lewis— seemed in bad shape. Hammond was still weak from the stocks and his foot wound and was near the edge where the long and sure slope began.

It looked as if nothing could stop it. Things were going a certain way and all they had to do was keep going. He lay in the gloom of his hooch at dusk while the air closed down. There was an unusually loud commotion that clunked into his reverie. He saw Hung running past his hooch door like a dark orange shadow-man, heard the shouts of the guard, angry and confused. "What's going on," he shouted after the fleeing Hung.

"Stay in your hooch," the man replied. At the door, he could see Hung with the Americans. He ordered them all out of their hooch. "Get out, get out and be in line," he shouted. They were lined up, shuffling, and it seemed that he could hardly wait to begin. "You have committed a cruel and criminal act!" he cried, standing in front of them with his arms by his sides, his hands clenched, shaking his fists downward. Garwood wondered where the camp commander was and what Hung was talking about. The fury was real, not political.

The guards were cold with malice, too. They were talking and acting violently—he had not seen the same tone since the execution of the unfortunate Nghia by the stream. He stood carefully half-in, half-out of his hooch. "Who has killed the cat?" Hung shouted.

Garwood sighed with relief. It was only a cat after all. The only cat he knew of was a yellow tomcat that appeared frequently and tended to hang out in the guard kitchen. He thought it belonged to one of the guards and he sometimes saw it gnawing the heads off rats. Garwood had sometimes taken rats from it, but only if he could move very fast. The cat had grown wary of him but Garwood had tried to regain its favor by bringing it pieces of inedible cooked rat, like the tail. The ruse seemed to work.

No big deal, he thought. There was no response from the prisoners, nor was there any sign. But Garwood could tell that some at least knew what was going on. There was defiance on some faces.

The guard commander was stalking with rage. Hung was facing the Americans one by one, asking each: "Did you?"

When he came to Kushner, the doctor cracked a grin and said in his clear voice, "Not me. I don't know a thing about it." The guard commander didn't speak English but he knew that grin. He pulled the stunned Kushner out of formation, slapped him hard alongside the face just once and ordered a guard to tie him up. He pushed the American into the guard's arms like a broom.

Garwood suddenly became very quiet and very worried. He couldn't believe the way the guards were acting. He moved out of his hooch to get a better view. Kushner was tied to a pole, hands in front of him. A red splotch marked his pale, dirty face and his eyes were only hollows in the bosky dusk. Hung came to Grissett. "This is no laugh. This matter is a serious situation," he said.

"Did you?" he asked.

The prisoners who did not look at Grissett were far more obvious than the ones who did. Hung knew, Garwood thought, he had to.

Hung told Grissett to remain at attention. The guard commander ordered the others back into their hooch. Grissett, silent, was pulled out of the compound. The guard commander hit him in the stomach with a fist. Then he hit him on the back. Grissett fell to the ground as if the wind was knocked out by the sudden blows. The guard commander started kicking him. Garwood, furious, couldn't believe what his fellow prisoners had done. Grissett was the scapegoat. They had as good as pointed a finger at him with their looks—or lack of them! And Kushner, the stupidity of that superior laugh! Garwood ran past the guards, into the compound, up to the hooch. Harker was in the doorway. Garwood shoved him aside with a backward slap. "You call yourselves Americans," Garwood hissed. "You let Russ out there take all the blame? If you stuck together, nothing would have happened."

"Garwood, we don't want to hear your shit—get the fuck out of here!" someone yelled from a corner. There were growls of approval. "You don't know a goddamn thing. Just get out of here. Now!" They demanded that he leave in the sullen voices of accusation. Angry and frustrated, he turned and left.

They'd tied Grissett to a bamboo pole about fifteen or twenty feet from Kushner, and he was to stay there all night. Guards were posted. Garwood walked back to his hooch. He stared through the thickening nightfall at the place where the two men were tied.

Cat. The only thing he could come up with was the whole rotten camp situation. The food was the main problem. There was not enough food, because the defoliant had destroyed the crops. The air war had increased and the guards were filled with the hatred for airplanes that can only be known by those who have found themselves under attack by those fast, roaring monsters of flying dirt and noise and chance and death. It wouldn't have taken much for a guard to simply flip his safety to full automatic and spray the whole camp.

Grissett and Kushner were released next day but Garwood noticed Grissett did not appear outside the hooch.

215

Garwood asked someone, "How's Russ?" The man replied that he was not too good. He couldn't get out of his bunk. He had been kicked in the head, had spent some time unconscious.

Grissett did not appear for radio hour for the next two days, and on the third, Hung and Garwood went to the Americans' hooch. They saw Grissett lying on his mat. He had bruises on his face and his breathing was shallow but near enough to normal. He seemed half asleep.

"What can I do, Russ?" Garwood asked.

"Nothing . . . nothin', Bob." The voice seemed distant and drugged. "Stay away from 'em, Bob. Stay away."

"Stay away from who?" Garwood said.

"Other Americans," Grissett whispered. Garwood explained that his advice was going to be hard to follow.

"I'm tellin' you if you ever come down here, don't ever come down alone."

Garwood was sent to the production fields, where he cleared weeds from manioc for a week. When he returned, he asked one of the guards, "How's Russ?"

"Russ is very sick," the man replied. Garwood asked how was he so sick and the man replied that he did not know. The guard stared at him. "Russ is the only friend you have left."

Garwood made no reply. He walked to the stream with a bundle of clothes, dirty with the mud of the fields. Kushner arrived to do his own laundry. "Where you been, Garwood?" Kushner asked, without looking at him.

"Workin' my ass off. How's Russ?"

Kushner scowled. "I'd give him a couple of more days."

"For what?" Garwood asked, annoyed and alarmed by the man's tone.

"Well, if you'd stayed in camp instead of tromping all over the countryside you'd know. Russ is in a coma. He's delirious. He won't eat. He's dying."

Garwood's eyes widened. "Is there anything you can do for him?"

"In a hospital, yes," Kushner said. "Here, no. There's nothing I can do for him." Garwood asked him if there was anything he could do himself. "Well, if you haven't give up being a Christian, you can pray."

"Kushner, I haven't given up bein' a Christian any more than you've given up bein' Jewish," Garwood snapped. The other man stood up, very angry. "You can say anything you want about me but don't you ever say anything about me being a Jew. There's a lot of shit I'll take from you, Garwood, that's one thing I won't."

"Drop it. Forget I said it," Garwood said. He walked away with half-wet clothes. That evening, Garwood went to the compound. He approached the guard directly for permission to see Grissett. The guard, for once, did not need the usual excuse or story. Inside the hooch, Kushner was sitting with Grissett, his head in his lap. The sick man had no shirt on and lay only in dirty shorts. Garwood asked the doctor where the shirt was, where his clothes were.

"He only had one set of clothes—he's shit his pants, he's vomited on his shirt.

They're both drying now." Kushner seemed resigned and tired. Garwood couldn't believe that one of the others could not give Grissett another shirt at least, or a pair of trousers. He took off his own shirt and he heard a voice behind him say, "If you want to give it away, why don't 'cha give it to me. He's gonna die anyway, it's just a waste."

He did not even turn, but disregarded the comment. He helped Kushner put it on the unconscious Grissett. "Thanks," Kushner said.

"It must be nice, t'have so many clothes you can just give 'em away," came another mocking voice from behind.

"Yeah. Everybody's hurtin' but Garwood," came another.

Garwood thought to himself. "You're right. I've got three sets of clothes." He made no response, trying to focus on Grissett. He could not. Grissett looked so normal, like he was asleep. But his chest was bulging with bone; the change had been violent over the week. Garwood left the hooch slowly, his eyes never searching out the owners of the barbed voices.

Kushner sat up all night with Grissett, but in the morning and without regaining consciousness or showing any sign of trouble or pain, Grissett stopped breathing and disappeared from the camp and life on this earth for good.

Now they were all gone and the gulf was complete. Once it was Eisenbraun, Grissett, and Garwood. Now the links had been broken and no one would know who he was, what he was, what he had gone through. There would only be the accusation and the hatred, the "facts" that were close enough to a kind of truth, but still very far from it.

He was the last of the original three.

15
War Crimes II

FROM THEN on there was a new segregation in the camp, one imposed by Garwood himself. He illogically blamed the others for Grissett's death, and he no longer had the link of the other man to soften his feelings. He returned their hatred and scorn in full measure.

Grissett had told Garwood how the others had kept on about his apparent complacency with "the turncoat" and had harassed him about it. But he had kept up a thin string of presents—perhaps they were guilt gifts, at least they were proofs that he was pledging some sort of loyalty to the other Americans.

The gifts now stopped and there was no reason to visit. Joe Zawtocki went sheeplike along with the scorn of the rest. Garwood only went down to the compound when ordered. When he stole, he kept it himself. He occupied his hours working for the guards. He became almost their servant, mending their clothes, washing them, cleaning their weapons. In exchange, they gave him cigarettes, sugar, bananas. The guards were delighted, they thrived on it; people who had never given orders in their lives were now waited on by one of the feared enemy.

One guard, Quang, claimed to be a former college student at Hue who had joined the revolution because his sister had been raped and molested by American troops, resulting in her suicide. He wanted to learn English. Garwood found himself spending more and more time with the man, and in return for English lessons Garwood got a pair of nail clippers and other small favors, like a piece of soap.

It took a week or two for things to return to their old ways. The season of summer had passed and the autumn of 1968 approached, hardly noticed in the eternal jungle. Gradually the camp bumped back to normal—that is, to starvation on one side, frustration on the other, stagnation overall. It had been so long since a new prisoner had arrived Garwood was not sure what was going on in the war. Hanoi Hannah had switched from the theme of victories and was now daily drumming in a new theme: the "criminal atrocities" of the "U.S. Nazis" in dropping chemicals on "three-quarters of the country of Vietnam, killing thousands of women and children."

The effects of the defoliants, he knew, were to make the rice ration smaller. Sometimes the food they did get brought on unpleasant effects, cramps of the stomach and nausea. Garwood had seen the areas where the defoliant had been used. The effect was weird and dramatic, because instead of dying from the inside of the tree, as in the fall season back home, the greenery died from the outside. Leaves simply shriveled, turning brown while the stems remained green. Then the stems would rot. Once in the manioc field he saw three propeller-driven cargo planes flying in V formation near where he stood staring up. They looked like the crop dusters he had sometimes seen in Indiana, billowing brooms of vapor. It drifted toward them, dropping like a mist. It did not stink and its touch was light—less than the mist of a dewy summer evening. A Vietnamese he was with, weeding the field, died later of mysterious internal bleeding. Garwood, as soon as he saw the stuff drifting down, ran for the nearest stream, wet a piece of cloth and put it over his nose and mouth. The work party fled away from the direction of the drift. Still, Garwood got cramps and vomited. There were spots of blood in his feces and blood in his urine later.

It was with shock that he learned secondhand that the ubiquitous Mr. Ho had heard of Garwood's illness and had raged at the camp commander, saying, "You will be personally responsible if Garwood dies."

It was Hung who told him of Zawtocki's end. Garwood, recovering, asked the translator for details. "Hunger sickness," was the response.

Garwood had no energy to react any longer. He had his own hunger sickness. He could not eat many of the foods he had eaten with ease before the defoliant poisoning. Everything seemed to bring on fresh bouts of dysentery, and his body was flattened and weakened. The weakness allowed his malaria to mount more serious attacks. Everything seemed primed for a serious decline.

Garwood had dragged himself down to the stream to wash his vile clothes when he had the first contact in weeks with another American. "Where have you been?" said Kushner, looking skinny but fairly fit.

"I've been in the hospital," Garwood muttered, not liking the doctor's tone. It was clear that this was not an acceptable answer. Kushner gave him a withering look.

"You get sick, you go to the hospital. We get sick, we die," Kushner said.

The obvious reference to Zawtocki amazed him. "I didn't walk to the hospital. They carried me there," he parried.

"Yeah," said Kushner, "we had to carry Joe to put him in the grave, too."

Garwood hurried through the motions of washing on the greasy rocks and chill water and crawled back to his hooch to collapse, weak as a child. "What the fuck did I do wrong when I had no choice?" he thought, tormented by Kushner's reference to Zawtocki, the closest thing he had to a friend in the new group. It seemed to him then that his merely being alive was some kind of an affront to whatever code they were working under down there.

He waited and tried to gain strength against his rebellious body and bowels. Two days later, he made his way to the camp commander to make one final plea about his position in the camp. "I am not going down to the American compound anymore," he told the man. "I would appreciate it if you would not order me to do so under any circumstances." The commander looked puzzled.

"Why—you have asked before to be with your friends?"

"There is too much friction between me and the others. I just want to avoid trouble."

"What has brought this on?" the commander asked, bemused.

"My living outside the camp—they don't know what I eat or who I eat with or what my living conditions are, what my rations are. They see me come and go from the camp, not knowing where. They see, when I get sick and I'm taken to the hospital and when they get sick the best thing they can expect to receive is a few aspirins or maybe a can of condensed milk. If I was in their position, I'd feel the same way."

"Where you live, what you eat, where you go—these are my decisions."

"Hell will freeze over before you're gonna make those other Americans believe that!" Garwood said.

"I am sorry for your problems," said the commander with narrowing eyes and a dismissive flick of one finger, "but I don't have to explain anything to anybody. Have any of the Americans threatened you?" Garwood shook his head hopelessly. "I will make sure that they don't: From this day on, you will have a Vietnamese name—Dau" ("freedom fighter").

Then to Garwood's dismay, the commander took him down to the American compound, motioning Hung to join the party. The three stepped across the dirt of the compound, picking up guards as they went. There was no need to tell the prisoners to gather. They did that automatically.

"From this day forward, Bob will be known as Mr. Dau to you." He looked right and left at the faces.

"Dau is a Vietnamese name. And because it is a Vietnamese name given to Bob by me, I will consider any threats or discourtesies as threats or discourtesies toward me." He smiled. Garwood was floored. He decided that he would continue to ignore the other Americans. Stay away from them. He would simply survive.

Once again the camp was moved. But not before Hammond died. After his health came back, Garwood was less in camp than before, but he heard it was dysentery and hunger edema. He didn't go down to talk to the Americans, preferring to get the news from Hung.

There were several reasons for the move of camps. It was partly psychologi-cal, or superstitious to put the right name on it, Garwood presumed. If something bad happened, it was Vietnamese logic to abandon the place where it happened. If something good happened, they would build a temple on the spot or leave food there. They moved.

There were seven graves in the yard, and for all seven, Garwood had scratched names in the soft river stone. No one knew where Weatherman's body lay. When they made a move, Garwood would always marvel at the simplicity and economy of the people who coped with this wild and inhospita-ble environment.

They could carry the camp on their backs, as it consisted only of an idea, some sacks of rice, the AK-47s of the guards, assorted utensils and some mats to sleep on.

The camp commander went on foot, leaving before the others, and like them, he toted his own gear—in fact, since he owned more things his pack was heavier. He left alone. Hung carried the radio. It was a full day's march to the new site with the weaker Americans, Kushner, Anton, Harker, and Lewis, lagging behind, nagged on by the guards.

Garwood walked near the head of the line of march, a guard between him and the other Americans, carrying his personal gear and mat plus his share of the cooking utensils from the guards' kitchen where he ate. The guards had the heaviest loads, the rice they toted in sacks and the square oil and sauce tins tied by vines and supported by cloth tump straps around their foreheads. Garwood could never fathom how the slight Vietnamese could carry such heavy weights, even with betel to jazz them up, for so long. Quang carried a huge sack of rice, his AK, his pack. He looked like a loaded donkey.

The new camp was like the old one—just a collection of hooches with more to be built, each hooch simply made and furnished with the now-familiar sleeping benches. The water was better, however—a stream twice as big as that in the last camp, and there were rocks Garwood could see would be handy for drying clothes. The Montagnards abounded also, a good sign for trading tobacco, food, betel, and other things the guards had missed. Garwood found it positively pleasant. About four days after their arrival, Garwood looked up from his morning ablutions to see a mountain goat, a large animal with longish horns, a gray coat, and a beard. It stood on a rocky outcropping, clearly curious about the creatures clumsily dipping and leaning below.

As he looked, the new guard commander, a robust NVA lieutenant, gave muttered orders from behind him with a voice full of tension. A guard fled back to the hooch and brought out a rifle, which the lieutenant raised and took careful aim, the barrel rested against a tree, Scottish style. It was a CKC, a Chinese assault rifle, open sights, and the man drew a bead on the fearless goat and toppled it with one shot. The guards whooped and sped like goats themselves to the site, soon returning with the handsome creature.

There was meat that night, both for Garwood and the guards and for the

Americans. After Grissett's death, James Daly, a black Army PFC, cooked for both black and white Americans. The other blacks, McMillan, Watkins, and Lewis, were still given separate sleeping quarters.

There was Christmas that year, 1968, but because of the move, because of the segregation, Garwood took no part in it. The Americans were given half of a small pig and a couple of chickens. He got a pullet for himself, but little cheer. He could smell their cooking, hear talk and snatches of song. He had seldom felt so miserable or so immersed in regret.

In February, Tet. Watkins, Tinsley, and Strickland were released, for no reason he could discern, except that they were probably in the best of health of the lot. The three were tape-recorded, announcing that they would join the demonstrations in the U.S. and work hard to make the war end. They promised to denounce the U.S. atrocities and war crimes and to work hard to make the release of other Americans possible. Then they were released to U.S. forces, dressed in NVA khakis and sandals and red sashes. They were taken to within a mile or so of a U.S. outpost and set loose, supplied with documents and handbills. Only years later he learned that all had been safely returned to the United States.

Garwood broke his silence to beg Watkins: "If you get home, tell my family that I'm alive and well." Watkins never made the contact. (He said later that if Garwood had been living with the other Americans, he would have acceded to his request, but as Garwood lived with the guards, he regarded him as a Communist.)

The liberation saddened the other Americans more than Garwood. He had been through it all before, in fact it was all he really knew of the tactics of the Communists, a roller coaster of rising and dashed hopes, and if you chose to get off it, you simply withdrew to where no other people were.

Before the liberation, Garwood was called in by the camp commander to make his comment on whom he thought "most progressive" of the Americans. Garwood put Watkins on the top of the list for the reason that he sympathized with the tough, hard-working black Army private. He had been "selected" head man of the black contingent by no fault of his own and had received a lot of abuse from the others because of it.

Chief among their complaints was that Watkins was under order to report daily to the camp commander on the health, attitude, and other particulars of all the American prisoners.

Watkins was black, of course, and that may have made a difference. When hopes for the liberation of some of the prisoners fanned around the camp, the assumption was that all those to be liberated would be black. The blacks kept their health better and shouldered most of the heavy tasks as a result. They did not have the annoying (from the camp commandant's point of view) habit of dropping dead after using large quantities of medicine.

Then it was thought that there would be two blacks and one white. In the end it was one black and two whites. The guards were puzzled and so was Garwood.

They were only a few months in the "new camp," the camp of the liberation of Watkins, Tinsley, and Strickland. Tet seemed to signal a need to move. Garwood was told by Quang that it was a simple security measure. They did not really believe the released prisoners would do what they were told, and there was some chance that a raid would be organized with their assistance.

Once again, the little train of Americans, led by the Vietnamese officers and mingled with the guards, all sweating under heavy loads, plunged off into the jungle. They marched a full day. Every place in these mountains seemed to look the same to him. One Montagnard village was quite like another and on the trail, one soon stopped looking up, but concentrated on the heels of the man ahead and the burden on one's back.

The next new camp they came to was tiny. The camp commander's hooch— usually a two-room affair to give the top man private sleeping quarters—was not finished. The commander stayed in the guard hooch with the guards, and Hung and Garwood built a lean-to for themselves.

The eight Americans had the other hooch. Garwood had inherited a hammock from a guard, a thing made of bamboo strips. He hung it in the lean-to, covered himself with mosquito net and had an uncomfortable night of it. The mosquitoes could work through the hammock, and then the netting only kept them in.

The next few days were for building. They didn't bother to build a stockade. It seemed pretentious, since the Americans long ago had had all thought of escape starved out of them. Spring in the jungle was an oddly unsettling time. It grew gradually warmer, but it had not been exactly cold. The bamboo shoots sprung light green from the edge of the forest and some flowers emerged—but to a Westerner, it was a shabby sort of affair, not the sudden wrenching of the March and April days in the Midwest.

Spring brought clearing of the fields—the guards were busy laboring, the Montagnards trudged through the camp on the way to their fields and back again in the evening. Garwood was not always sent out to the fields, perhaps because there were now so few prisoners. He had acquired a pack of cards, so dirty and worn that the little familiar symbols on them could hardly be seen. He often sat in the pleasing spring weather, playing seven-card solitaire, a game he'd learned from his grandmother. One day when Hung had been gone two days (a blessed relief—except that he had left the radio with the guard commander, who was as strict in his interpretation of the rules as he had been accurate as a rifle shot), he was playing just so.

The camp commander had him summoned from his cards. "You will go with the guard commander to a Montagnard village about one hour from here. There will be four new prisoners there. They are weak and tired. Without Hung, we have no one else in the camp who can speak English and Vietnamese. You will go with the guard commander and tell the prisoners that the camp is very close and they must try to get here before it gets dark."

"What's the problem?" Garwood asked him.

"When they arrived at this village, they sat down, refusing to march further," he replied. "They are scared and tired. You are to tell them then no harm will come to them. They must continue their journey."

Garwood thought they were probably as terrified as he had been of the wild Montagnards and their crude ways. With the NVA lieutenant and two of his guards, they set off. It was a hot day. They swung along a mountain trail, up a stream to the village, which they knew was atop a certain hill. It seemed uphill all the way, one ridge giving way to another. No wonder the prisoners had not wanted to move on, he thought.

They marched into the village to the stares of women, the usual bright-eyed children and the old people, the music of pigs, the clucking of children. The lieutenant told Garwood to wait on the edge of the village clearing. He went to a hooch and two NVA regulars emerged, armed to the teeth. They were in full battle dress, green from head to toe, bayonets dangling, grenades, plenty of rounds of ammunition, forage caps with stars on them. They looked like tough men—they wore watches with linked metal bands—tough, unsmiling soldiers with automatic weapons.

Garwood could not overhear their palaver. The guard commander came back. "You speak German?"

Garwood shook his head. There must be some mistake. "You won't be much help then," he added.

"Why," joked Garwood, "are these guys Germans?" The commander nodded.

He walked to the other side of the village, to find that sitting under a tree was a woman, a European woman in skirts. A young woman. And two men dressed in jeans and shirts and city shoes. The sight was more than a surprise, it was shocking, wrong, terrible. It was unbelievable.

The women was tall, thin, shapely, dark-haired. Her face was smudged with fear and fatigue, her hair clotted. She was past the point of caring how she looked. She sat in a guarded position, uncomfortable and weary.

The woman's eyes widened at Garwood's bearded, shrouded face. "Hello," he said, "can anyone speak English?"

"A little," one of the males said.

The two men had gone completely unnoticed by him in his fascination with the woman. He could not stop staring and had to jerk his eyes to the man who was addressing him. He was young but older than a student. He had almost blonde brown hair and blue eyes. He was well-built and unmarked, smooth-skinned, and he spoke with a marked accent. The other man was older, perhaps in his early thirties, with a small beard like a decoration on his chin. The guards, Garwood noticed, were carrying equipment out in a bamboo basket—a movie camera, some still cameras, wallets, watches, small bits of jewelry. The articles sat on the bamboo like jewels on a background of straw. They were being checked against a list of some kind that one of the NVAs had.

"I'm American. There's no reason to be frightened."

224

"If you are American, why you are with these?" He tilted his head to the group gathered around the basket, gabbling excitedly and peering at the items. They looked afraid to touch the things.

"I've just come from a prisoner-of-war camp where there are other Americans."

The German said, "You are a prisoner?"

"I'm not here on a jungle safari," Garwood said with as wide a grin as he could manage.

"I'm sorry," the German said. "I have no mood for the joke. We are very tired."

"How many days have you been traveling?"

"Six days—I think."

"The camp where you will stay is only about an hour from here. It is downhill, down the mountain," Garwood said. "There is food and shelter and some medicine. Please try to make it. There are no accommodations here in this village."

"Okay," the German's eyes swept downward in submission. Garwood told the guard commander they would go on, but slowly. He asked the man his name and was told it was Bernhard Deihl.

"This is George, this is Rika," he said. "There are two other girls of our party."

"Where are they?" Garwood said.

"One has got very malade, the other stays with her," Bernhard said.

"They say there are two more?" Garwood turned to the guard commander, who nodded and affirmed Bernhard's story. He said they would follow when the sick girl was well enough to travel.

"They will come when they are well."

The three Germans struggled to their feet and the party set off painfully down the mountain. It took almost three hours of slow, stumbling, sore-footed progress to get to the camp. They complained of the distance. "It is not as you say, one hour," Bernhard said. Garwood pointed to the girl's leather sandals and her raw and blistered feet. "You are slow."

At the last part of the trip, Bernhard said to Garwood's back, "I do not understand why they capture us. We are only nurses. We are international volunteers with this protection. We come to help."

"I don't know," Garwood threw the words over his shoulder. "Where were you captured?"

"Quang Nam Province."

Garwood wanted to know how.

"We were on a field trip—seeing sights, to visit the peasants of the country to take photos. In a village we visit, from the forest, really from nothing, men come with guns. They ordered us to put hands high, they take the cameras and the equipment, even my watch and the girls' jewelry from our hands. They have hold us prisoners six days."

225

The guard commander grunted, "What are you talking about?"

"They are only nurses," Garwood told him swiftly in Vietnamese. "They are not Army or anything. Why were they captured?"

"They are spies working for the U.S. government," the guard commander said. "They work to bribe the peasants and plains people into their villages under the so-called pacification program. Therefore they are worse than American soldiers. These people have been trained in psychological warfare by the United States."

When Garwood had told Bernhard the judgment that had been made, the man was aghast. "What you just told me," Garwood said, "stick to it. Don't change your story. You are tagged as spies."

"That's ridiculous," the German sputtered, though winded. Garwood explained that they would find the truth didn't really count.

"It may be true but it will be as hard as hell to convince them of it."

"What will happen to us?" Garwood shrugged. "How long have you been here?" Garwood told him. "You have lived here in the jungle for four years?" Garwood nodded. "How come you are still alive?"

Garwood could not give an answer. He shrugged again. "I sometimes ask myself," he said.

"How much longer will you remain here?" Bernhard persisted.

"Your guess is as good as mine," Garwood told him.

"Surely they would not keep the women here in the jungle?"

"I wouldn't bet on it."

"Enough talking!" the guard commander barked in Vietnamese.

As they approached the camp, the party crossed the camp water supply, a shallow stream. Pfister and Mehrer were using it to wash. Pfister's mouth hung open. "Holy shit, I'm dreaming!" he yelled.

"What are they?" Mehrer asked.

"You're gonna love this, Mehrer," Garwood said. "They're German."

He asked excitedly if they could speak English. Garwood motioned so-so. "How's your German?" he yelled at Mehrer.

"A little rusty, but it's comin' back fast," he said.

"Be careful, Mehrer, you're playin' with dynamite," Garwood said.

"S'matter, Garwood, you jealous already?"

"Unfortunately, I can't speak German."

"Well, I can," he said with a grin.

Rika stopped at the creek, dabbling her sore feet in the water, cupping up water to her face and neck. It was the camp commander's time for surprise. "A female?"

Garwood imagined how Rika must have felt with all the staring and obvious comment. Bernhard said, "Please, Bob, tell them not to stare so at her, she is frightened."

Garwood told the commander of the request, asking that she be allowed to go somewhere in privacy. The camp commander nodded briskly. He ordered the

guards to their hooch, Mehrer and Pfister back to theirs. He motioned
Garwood to follow him back to his own hooch.

Deihl, George, Rika, and one guard stayed at the stream, washing away
some of the dirt and cooling their sore feet.

Meanwhile the guard commander lugged in the basket of cameras and
jewelry and other things. "There are two more still on the trail due in a couple
of days."

"Two more women," Garwood corrected.

The camp commander seemed upset. "I have nothing for women here," he
complained.

"Why don't you let them go?" Garwood said evenly. Both Vietnamese looked
at Garwood in stony disbelief.

"You will speak only when spoken to," he told Garwood sternly.

To the complete envy of the rest of the camp, the Germans were housed in
the hooch that the guards had just completed, which was meant for general
purposes, including interrogation.

Rika wasn't exactly beautiful but after four qualifying words, she was as
interesting as a creature from another planet. That she was a woman, there
could never be a doubt. Her body announced the fact with every step she
took—she was well-proportioned, twenty-seven, and when captured was wearing a blue blouse and a dark skirt to the knee. The sandals on her feet
accentuated her legs, and her short page-boy hair, which retained its stylish cut
for many days, shone against pale, pale skin, which was marked with the welts
left by mosquitoes and leeches. She had a sharp, longish nose, Garwood
thought, but what of that! He realized that he had not even thought of the other
sex for as long as he could remember. But the thoughts of sexuality had been
too far repressed to return. Garwood felt only pity for her.

She was fragile, like a fruit, like something that could not maintain itself, that
had to rot and fall away. He looked sadly at her, trying to remember everything, her hands, her body, the outline of her underclothes, her fingernails,
and her manner of restraint, her shyness and fright, knowing that the jungle
would surely grind her into a shapeless skeleton. He tried to imagine how she
must feel, with fifteen to twenty pair of male eyes on her every time she
moved. The Vietnamese, though more reserved, stared with animal interest
that was so frank it was shocking.

She looked on the verge of a breakdown anyway. She seemed always
nervous, she was afraid to eat, afraid to look around for fear of meeting a pair of
the questing hollow eyes of the men. The two Germans did their best. They
stayed with her, waited on her, talked to her. It was clear from their tone that
they were soothing her, trying to make her eat.

The camp did its best, too. She was given two sets of new pajamas, a towel, a
thin blanket made out of some sort of raw cotton. When she persisted in
refusing her portion of rice with fish sauce, she was given condensed milk. The

guards brought bananas and sugar cane, though it was clear that they did these things from a desire to get another look at her more than from concern.

The guards said, "Big, very big." They were fascinated and somewhat repelled. They said she looked too white, not healthy, and was too large. She would take much food and it seemed to them that she had no muscles.

They thought she would not survive for long. Garwood asked Quang, "What are you gonna do with the Germans?"

"We are waiting orders; they will be transported to North Vietnam. They are civilians." He took a sympathetic view of Rika, though he condemned the men as spies. He thought that a woman like her, the same shape as those he had seen in Western dress in Hue and at the movies, was only "the girlfriend that is used by these men."

Two days later, another woman arrived. Garwood found out her name was Monika. She was short, dark-haired and plump—not a beauty, but he found a beauty in her fatness. He was sick of thin people, sick of the sight of muscle that looked like rope under the skin and against the bone. This woman had a blanket of softness and smoothness that appealed to him.

She looked stronger and healthier than Rika, more like the plain and bountiful farm girl than the statuesque pale-skinned woman. Monika brought bad news. The third nurse, whose name Garwood never remembered, had died. When Monika came into camp the two women fell into each other's arms, as Garwood had with Isenbraun, Bernhard was crying, they were all crying and speaking very fast in German. George did not cry, however, nor did he say much. Garwood asked about the third girl who had been reported.

The guard seemed subdued and sad. He did not respond, simply turned to his weapon with a rag, wiping the dust and mud from the action. The camp guards had come out, all were watching the spectacle of the Germans greeting one another.

Garwood called Quang over. "What happened to the other girl? I asked another guard, he wouldn't tell me."

"They say she came down with malaria. She went into chronic malaria. Within two and one half days she was dead. She couldn't stand the fever."

Garwood said nothing. It was clear to him that these European women could not stay here and live. No American had died of malaria. It took two, maybe three diseases to kill even the weakest.

When Garwood was able to speak again to Deihl, the man treated him as a translator, not a fellow in misery. He spoke only in speeches, telling Garwood that they should never have been captured, that their organization was known all over the world as a neutral force, interested only in mercy.

He obviously intended for Garwood to make his case to the camp commander and treated Garwood as if he were himself a member of the camp organization. "Why?" he asked, making the usual inquiry about Garwood's accommodations in the guard hooch.

"The same as you are—different reasons, but similar to you."

He told the man he had been promised release and later denied it. "To make a long story short, they didn't keep their promise. Over a period of time this led to complications between myself and the other Americans, and them understanding me. When I asked to rejoin the Americans, I was refused."

He told Deihl that he had been reduced to attempting to survive the best way he could—day by day.

"You must be very lonely?" Deihl said. Garwood nodded. "But there's nothing I can do about it." Deihl asked how many other Americans were in the compound. "Including myself, there are eight." He went on to tell the German that nine others had died in previous camps—one shot while trying to escape, eight of different diseases.

"What has the International Red Cross and its organization done to help you?"

"Nothing. They don't even know if we're alive." Deihl asked why.

"The way the Communists explained it, they do not recognize the Geneva agreements dealing with prisoners of war."

"They must do this. It is under international law," Deihl protested.

"They've made up their own rules and regulations in Vietnam."

Deihl was shaken. "No," he said, "I think you are wrong in this." Garwood merely raised his eyebrows; experience would teach him.

The presence of the German women was a full-time occupation for the camp commander, and some others in his command structure. Six men, identified as cadre from their dress, arrived at camp. Two of them carried bullhorns strapped to their packs as they hiked into the area.

He never knew exactly why there was such a summit meeting, he suspected it was because of the "German problem." But the guards told him that one of the bullhorns was broken. He had a premonition that he would be asked to fix it while the men remained at the camp. And so it was.

Garwood told them he didn't know anything about bullhorns. The thing was battery-operated, self-contained. But he was coaxed to open the back of it and as soon as he did he noticed the battery connections were corroded, just as they had been in his first repair "miracle" for camp commander Duong. It was the same disease. He took the batteries out, asked for a pocket knife and scraped away the rust and white crud. It worked. The thing was loud. He said, "Testing, one . . . two . . . three."

"Garwood," someone yelled from the U.S. compound, "what are you doing with that?"

He turned it on them. "Can't you see I'm calling U.S. troops?" he boomed.

The Vietnamese who was with the bullhorn grinned happily. He pulled a pack of Ruby Queens out of his pajamas and thrust them at Garwood. "Thank you," he said, taking the instrument and clicking it on and off with pleasure.

The same day in the guardhouse with Quang, Garwood gave an English lesson. The guard had to leave, perhaps for the latrine, and when he did he left his weapon, a CKC assault rifle, propped up against the wall. He had said he would be right back. Quang was so used to Garwood's presence the whole thing seemed natural. He sometimes handled the weapons and cleaned them for the guards.

As he sat there Daly came in. Facetiously, he asked permission to go to the latrine, speaking as if Garwood were a guard. Garwood thought he didn't even recognize him. "The guard isn't here, just go ahead," Garwood told him.

"Garwood! What are you doin' here?"

"Never mind—just go on," he told the lanky black.

"Garwood on guard duty! That takes the fuckin' cake," Daly snarled.

He saw the rifle, he saw the scene, he knew it was no use to remonstrate. Quang returned; he grew angry to learn that Garwood had given the permission to Daly. "You can't do that," he said. "I'll get in a lot of trouble if it gets back to the camp commander."

"Not half as much trouble as if the camp commander found out you left me here with a loaded gun," he snapped.

"Forget it," he said sullenly.

The gun got Garwood in trouble again the next day. He was sent out to portage manioc for the guards and the Germans, who had been eating from the guard kitchen—though Garwood got precious little conversation out of them. He was sent out with Quang and two other guards, and Lewis and McMillan.

While on the trail, Quang stopped, sat down and hugged himself, in the throes of a malaria attack. It passed, he got up and moved on. They arrived at the manioc field, quickly filled their baskets. Quang, without a word, came to Garwood, took the clip out of the AK-47 and handed it silently to Garwood. "I am too tired," he said. "I cannot carry this." He shouldered a basket full of leaf vegetables, shivering and sweating at the same time. "You will carry this for me back to camp."

"Is that thing *loaded?*" one of the Americans asked as they trooped along. Garwood had it slung over his shoulder. He looked back annoyed and pulled back the bolt.

"No," he said.

"Garwood, you keep carrying guns for *them,* you're gonna get your shit blowed away one day," the prisoner said.

As they entered camp, one of the perspiring guards took the AK from his shoulder. When the camp commander found that Quang had given the weapon to a prisoner, he was reprimanded before the whole guard force. It never happened again and never again was he allowed to clean the guns. It was a job he had rather enjoyed.

Garwood's health continued to recover that spring and he was sent with regularity to the manioc fields. He would go out with a few ARVNs, the guards, and they would stay working for as long as two weeks at a time. By this time the ARVNs were used as almost full-time field hands and construction crews—they spent little time in camp; but no American other than Garwood was used for the manioc planting. He was a good farmer and he didn't mind the repetitious, mind-numbing work.

But he began to be alarmed on his periodic returns to the camp by the stories that were circulating among the Americans. He tried to ignore his countrymen as much as possible, and ignore the glares and insults. Then after one trip to the manioc fields and back, Pfister sought him out and confronted him.

"What is this shit I hear about you going down to the American lines?" the Army private asked angrily. He had come up behind Garwood as he knelt with a bundle of clothes at the washing place by the stream.

Garwood looked up. "Wish I had. You wouldn't see me back here then, Pfister."

"Hung's been tellin' us about your 'adventures,'" he said, making the word seem like a dirty secret in a soap opera.

"What has he been tellin' you?"

"Oh, just about how you've been down there calling to American troops for them to come over to the front on your little bullhorn."

"Pfister, if nothing else, use your common sense. He could tell the Germans that and I can understand the Germans maybe believing it. Maybe. But you . . . just how long do you think I would last if I went down to some U.S. post and shouted, 'Hey you guys, throw down your guns and come out'?"

"I don't know," Pfister said, wind slightly down in his sails, "it's what we hear. You don't ever tell us where you're goin'."

"You guys never gave a shit what happened to me before, so I don't want to hear any of this bull about how I don't tell you where I'm goin' or what I'm doin'. And if I did tell you, you know you wouldn't believe me anyway. You take care of Pfister, I'll take care of myself."

"Okay, okay, let's drop it."

Pfister left, Garwood proceeded with his washing, took off his shirt and began to bathe. He hardly noticed the raw marks on his shoulders where he had packed seventy-five pounds of corn into camp. Anton wandered by. "What you been carryin', Garwood?" he asked.

"What else—ammo," Garwood retorted with as much sarcasm as he could manage. "All at once these guys are all concerned," he thought. He was becoming angry with the hypocrisy of it. Anton said nothing else. Silence fell like a cold fog between them.

After his next prolonged trip to the fields, about two weeks later, he was given a day off from work and he rested. He went down to check on the Germans, knowing that Quang was on guard duty and there would be no problem with a quick visit. Bernhard sat outside the hooch. "Hi, Bob," he said, in a friendly way that surprised Garwood.

"I have not seen you in some time," he said.

"I know. I have been out of the camp," Garwood told him. "How is Rika?" Bernhard gave him a queer look.

"You make joke?" Garwood looked puzzled and said no.

"Rika has died," Bernhard said. Garwood could hardly believe this. Only two weeks before, he had caught a glimpse of her and she seemed fine—thin but fairly healthy. "Soon after Rika died, George died, too. He had a heart attack, it seemed."

"How did Rika die?" Garwood said.

"The hunger sickness, as they call it. Now there are only the two of us left. What will happen to us?" Garwood did not know how to answer the question.

Radio hour had resumed after several weeks' delay while a new radio, a Dutch Philips, was brought into camp. The time gave him contact, if not conversation, with the Americans. Most of it was uncomfortable, but Garwood was still drawn to the gatherings. Only one man in the American group had deigned to continue to converse with him—Kushner, who from the beginning had maintained his neutral, sardonic observer's detachment about Garwood.

Recent conversations with the doctor had taken on an existential aura. They scarcely mentioned the fact that they were both squatting in a filthy prison camp in the godforsaken jungle, or that one of them had been reviled and rejected as a traitor. They were simply two sojourners in a miserable life on the only inhabited planet.

Somehow, the conversation got onto the intelligence level of the Vietnamese and the Americans. It was like the argument at the bar over whether a lion could beat a tiger. Kushner's view was obscure, as usual: It seemed he only wanted to draw Garwood out.

"What do you suppose is the rank of the good camp commander?" he asked.

"I'm not sure," Garwood said. "I think he's about the same as a major."

Kushner wanted to know how much education the man had had. How was Garwood to know? He guessed that the man had been past the fifth or sixth grade.

"What's Hung's rank?" the doctor said.

"To my knowledge, he doesn't have any rank. But I'd say he's the equivalent of a lieutenant." Kushner wanted to know details about his education. This time Garwood had an answer. Hung had told him, whether truthfully or not, that he had only gone as far as the second grade—it may have only been a way to demonstrate the egalitarianism of the great democracy of the Front.

"What about you, Bob?" Garwood told him he had quit school at tenth grade. "Well, then, if you were in the NVA Army you'd probably be at about the rank of a colonel then?"

Garwood said, "No, not really. About the only thing I know how to do is languages. I guess I wouldn't be any higher than Hung is, a lieutenant or something. That's about all Hung does, is interpret. And that's about all I could do.

"You'd probably be a general, on the other hand," Garwood continued.

Kushner glared at Garwood. "What?"

"You got twelve years of school and seven years of college don't 'cha?" You might find one out of a million Vietnamese who have the same education you do."

"You don't like Hung, do you?" Kushner pumped.

"That's pretty obvious."

"You know Hung's been telling us quite a bit about you," Kushner said. "Any of it true?" Garwood looked at the man's cold eyes.

"I doubt you'd believe me if I said no."

Two days later, Hung came stomping into his hooch, mad as a hornet. Here in the jungle there was always a surprise. "Do you know you can be shot for impersonating an officer of the Liberation Front," Hung shouted.

He looked at the translator in honest bewilderment. Hung shook his head with disgust.

"The Americans tell me that you told them you were a lieutenant in the NVA," Hung stormed. Garwood recoiled.

"Who told you *that?*" he asked, not expecting a reply.

"Never mind. Is it true?" Hung waggled a fist. "Did you tell them you were a lieutenant in the North Vietnamese Army?" Garwood shook his head repeatedly.

He scowled. "I have been fighting with the revolution for over eight years. And I am only a sergeant!" Garwood could barely suppress a grin. Hung went on to explain that it was very difficult to become an officer, and might take several generations of revolutionary activity.

"And as for you! No matter what you did, you have fought against the Vietnamese people! You have killed the Vietnamese people! You can never even be considered as the lowest private in the Vietnamese Army! Not the lowest!"

Hung, when he calmed himself a bit, told the real reason. He, Hung, had been shamed that Garwood had even suggested that he might be equivalent to some rank in the glorious, privileged, heroic, specially chosen Vietnamese Army.

"Your attitude is growing worse and worse and something is going to be done with it and about it," Hung said.

Garwood scarcely heard the tirade. All he wanted to know was, Who? But Hung would not tell him.

But all this was swept away by a truly monumental event in the history of Vietnam. Ho Chi Minh died. The word came only on the radio. The first clue that the camp got was the simple sentence, "The Vietnamese people all over the country, radio of the voice of Vietnam, radio of the Democratic Republic of Vietnam, is very sad to have to announce the news of the immortal President Ho Chi Minh's death last evening . . ."

It wasn't even radio hour. The camp commander, alone in his hooch, listening to the morning broadcast, heard it first. He ran out—most unusual for this man of protocol and correctness. He strode to the guard commander's hooch and whispered briefly in his ear. Immediately, the whole camp was turned out in formation. The guards and cadre assembled. But the Americans and the Germans were left to their own devices, as was Garwood.

The camp commander simply repeated what he remembered of the announcement. All three radios in camp were brought solemnly out, placed on a table before the commander's hooch. It would have been a perfect time for a breakout or merely to walk away. Women began to cry. The guards started to silently blubber. A Montagnard from the perimeter force shouted, "What do we do now? We have no president!"

An American voice rang out clear: "Hey Garwood, what the fuck's goin' on?"

"Ho Chi Minh is dead," he shouted. "They just announced it over the radio." He eyed the guards fearfully. With the emotionalism he knew they struggled with, he thought they might very well slaughter every American in the camp. They were crying like school girls at a basketball game.

The radio said Ho had died after a long illness. "The most qualified doctors in Vietnam attended him," a funereal voice was heard to say, "yet his heart stopped beating."

The broadcast asked for calm and renewed dedication. Premier Pham Van Dong would make an announcement later to the "entire people and the armed forces."

The radio was left on for three full days. The camp commander declared a state of mourning, in accordance with a national period of mourning. There was to be no working, no playing, no laughter, no shots fired for three days. The war simply ceased for three days because of one old man's termination.

In the camp, the mourning activities were strictly zero. Nobody did anything except the cooks. The guards sat by the radios, which poured out endless ballads about Ho Chi Minh, letters that had been sent from various dignitaries read in full, including one from Gus Hall, identified as an "important voice in American politics," and the leader of the growing U.S. Communist movement. The letters were uniform in their praise of Ho for his struggle for the national destiny of a united Vietnam. Garwood simply laid up in his hooch, sat in the sun when he could, avoided Hung.

The translator took a radio down for the Americans to benefit from. They appeared to take little interest. For the Germans, who had never had to work, the days were like the others, except there was more radio and less activity.

On the second day, the radio told that Ho's body would not be buried, but that a mausoleum would be built in the center of Hanoi so that he could be laid to rest in a glass coffin and future generations would be able to view the "father of Vietnam."

Mourning over, things returned to normal. There was no halfway stage for these people. It was either weep or work, Garwood reflected. And then the Germans simply disappeared.

There could be no other way to describe it. One day they were there, Monika only a shadowy form who stayed in the hooch most of the day, waiting for dark to use the latrine made for her. Bernhard and Mehrer were often seen together talking in German. Then nothing. The hooch empty, the guards uncommunicative. Mehrer knew nothing.

Garwood asked Quang. The guard grew surly. He said he did not know in a way that discouraged pursuit. Garwood let it drop. He imagined either they had been released in the wake of the Ho Chi Minh hiatus, or they had been taken to North Vietnam. There were two guards missing and the others were silent about their whereabouts.

There were usually signs when a camp was about to break up. There was no formal notice, nothing seemed to change on the surface. The guards knew, but they didn't tell. A camp seemed to have an age, though it was never the same. It could be triggered by the release of the prisoners—then a camp was doomed. Or a chance spotting by a probing American plane. Or some other reason. But this had been a quiet camp, no artillery activity, no bombing. It seemed in its middle age, except for the loss of the Germans and the death of the man who was most responsible, in Garwood's mind, for the war's continuance—a tiny wisp of a human, now almost a god.

There were no signs the day it happened. The first light of dawn was usually announced by the Montagnards, slipping like shadows through the clearing on their way to hunt or work on their fields. Then the crowing of the roosters, almost simultaneous, the inevitable whistle from the guard commander, which sometimes fooled the cocks and sometimes did not, and the whole slow slide of the jungle from its somnambulant state into the pattern of thousands of tiny and large lives that was its day.

He knew it was something different for him when the camp commander, usually privileged to take his time in rising, called Garwood while the air was still gray, before the sun had started its stare over the mountain in the east. Two guards, one a Montagnard, the other a Vietnamese, accompanied him to the hooch.

The camp commander was fully dressed. He looked as if he had just risen. He had not lit his first Ruby Queen and his glasses were still folded on the table, making him look naked and disarmed. But he put on his sternest tone and told Garwood he must without delay pack all his belongings and prepare to go with the guards—where, it was not made clear.

Garwood, expecting only a manioc expedition, casually asked where.

"You'll know when you get there," was his dismissive comment.

They were to hit the trail early. There were to be no good-byes. He asked if he would return, feeling that there was something different about the trip. "I don't know," the guard said.

He hurried back to his hooch to get his stuff. The whistle had sounded, and Garwood crossed paths with Kushner, who was walking to the stream. "What's wrong?" he asked, noticing the concentrated worry on Garwood's face.

"They're moving my ass out of here and I don't know where to."

"Well, Bob, you can only play two ends against the middle for so long." Garwood felt he had never hated before. "Do you have any idea where they might be taking you?" the doctor asked.

"It might be to North Vietnam. They might liberate me. They might shoot me. Or they might take me to another camp." Garwood tried to keep his voice slow and even. "Kushner, would you do me a favor?"

He said, "I'm not sure. What is it?"

"Just try forgetting the past a little and if by some chance you get out of here alive, could you find it somehow, if from nothing else out of decency, to let my folks know that I was alive and well the last time you saw me?"

"Wow," Kushner said, apparently amused. "It must be really serious, huh?"

"It doesn't look too good. I've a feeling I'll never see you guys again."

"Yah sure. Okay," Kushner said. "If I get out of here."

"Thanks and take care of yourself," Garwood said.

They walked down the trail out of the camp until the jungle hid them from sight and the forest closed out the sky. Early, it was still almost dark there in the jungle.

16
The Last Years

ALTHOUGH GARWOOD had no certain way of knowing it, he was in fact never to see their last jungle camp again, nor the Americans in it, until he faced them at his court-martial a decade later. His premonitions ended during the all-day walk. With him were two guards—there was nothing unusual in that. They chose a line that seemed directly opposite from the route to the manioc fields. But Garwood knew the system of agriculture they used, a primitive slash and burn and move on, depended only on finding fresh ground to plant.

The terrain was similar to what he had seen in the mountain camps, but they saw more and more soldiers. They were regulars of some sort, probably NVA, and they were bivouacked on the creek banks wherever there was a level space. In a twelve-hour march, he must have passed hundreds of men—he reckoned almost two battalions strung out along the trail.

At midday, the jungle track debouched onto a much wider and better-surfaced road. It was about ten feet wide, and the guards referred to it as a transport route; on it was a continual traffic—the vehicles were bicycles, and the Vietnamese had loaded them with everything from ammunition to rice sacks. The bicycles were pushed, not ridden. Two poles were added to the little machines, he noticed, and the seats removed. One pole was shoved into the seat socket, so the "driver" could push with his shoulder, while the other pole extended from the left handlebar so the machine could be steered by the man on foot. The bikes were loaded up like metal burros, with bags, guns, boxes—whatever was to be transported—strapped to the central frame. Garwood had no doubt that somewhere in the load was the seat as well, so that the heavily laden freighter of the foot-trails could return to a normal bicycle in a few minutes.

There were hundreds of the bicycles, going in both directions. The drivers were soldiers of some sort, probably NVA, some in uniform; much of the freight was clearly war material. He had not imagined that so much was openly done: They must be very far from the American lines, he thought, noting the difference in the attitude. He was amazed by the traffic, like an endless stream of walking men and bicycles. Cheap, slow, and effective.

The rubbernecking that went on reminded Garwood of the scene at a traffic accident at home, when the cars slow and the blank faces of the passersby turn as if by machinery to the wrecked cars and the blinking lights, all with the same expression . . . yet these stares were all for him.

At dusk, they returned again to the cow paths of the jungle. The traffic of laden bikes had never stopped during that time. Darkness fell in the familiar vastness of the jungle forest. He followed the guards as they clinked and padded along, until ahead through the shifting vantage of the black trees, tiny lights shone and grew. They came into a camp—in large shadows, with more lighting than he was used to, the place seemed old but very well kept. It had an air of permanence to it that he had not seen in years. He was taken to a small hooch slightly separated from the other main buildings—two large hooches with his between them. They fed him. He was supplied with his own kerosene lamp, an unheard-of luxury.

When he awoke, he heard the noise of the day already well started. Peering from his doorway, past a large and unfriendly guard, he could see that this was the largest camp he had been in. There were over a hundred ARVNs, he estimated, most of them enlisted, grouped neatly in squads of ten or a dozen, clearly doing separate tasks. It was easy to see why the camp was so clean and well maintained.

There were no Americans, no explanations, no communication. It was almost a week before he knew why. He was kept incommunicado, refused access to the washing stream until all the other prisoners had finished their morning toilet. The food was okay, the routine almost luxurious but overhung with boredom.

Finally, he was taken to what he recognized as an interrogation hooch. It looked almost like a classroom—benches, a central table, which they faced. The little one-room school of bamboo. Garwood found himself facing four men—clearly cadre from their holstered pistols and satchels.

They seemed to be trying to get at one thing. What and who led the organization of the American POWs? They seemed to know the names of all his former colleagues—Kushner, Anton, and the other survivors. Of course Garwood's answers were vague. "As far as I know, there is no organization," he told them, reiterating what he had told his former camp commander many times, that the living arrangements imposed on him had made it impossible for him to coexist with his countrymen as friends. They read from papers before them. "Who are you?" asked the lead questioner, with a serious stare of several seconds.

Garwood felt floored. After four years! His answer was, "You know who I am. I have been in your prison camps for four years."

238

They had two autobiographies written by Garwood, one written while he was a novice prisoner. One told that his family was rich, the other that they were very poor and he was an orphan. The differences were pointed out. He told them he had been confused and scared and didn't know what his captors had wanted and that he had lied to protect his family.

As the interrogation proceeded, Garwood had a feeling he was up against a new type of adversary. He was like a lawyer or a judge. He did not forget the slightest detail. He never moved his hands, but maintained perfect cold discipline.

"We have proof beyond a reasonable doubt that the only thing you have told us that is true—is your name." He said this with perfect calm in a reasonable tone, which made it the more chilling. "You have been trying to hoodwink us and pull the wool over our eyes. But you must realize that through resistance to the Chinese, French, and Japanese we have become experts, not only in intelligence but in psychological warfare. Your pattern, and the reports we have received over the years about you, strengthens and confirms our suspicions.

Garwood was at sea. He remembered Mr. Ho's early circling questions about Garwood's intelligence activities. He thought, with a droopy certainty, that they were in the room of the CIA and the walls were closing in.

"May I have permission to ask just one question before we go on any further?" The man nodded.

"What category am I in?"

But the questioner was relentlessly circular. "What category do you think you are in?" he asked maddeningly. Garwood answered that he considered himself a POW.

"There are no prisoners of war in Vietnam," the man said. Garwood groaned inwardly.

"Am I a prisoner?" he asked. The man nodded, eyes glittering. He asked what category of prisoner.

"A special category," the questioner said with satisfaction. Garwood slumped in his chair, he heard the man begin to tick off the points. "First, your capture is very strange in itself, as you will have to admit. You were captured on an isolated beach area, by yourself, as you claim, in a division commander's jeep, wearing a pistol, in new clothes—alone." He stressed the last word with Oriental irony. "Is this not strange?" Garwood shook his head.

"Look at the other American prisoners. Has one, just one, been captured in such a way as you?" Garwood shook his head sadly.

"You say you were a private and an enlisted man. Yet you were driving the division commander's jeep, your weapon was not a rifle, your clothes were not soiled as a soldier's are, but were new. And you expect us to believe that you are a simple soldier, lost. We were not born yesterday!

"Second. Of all the American prisoners that you have met, is there one other American that can speak Vietnamese? Not only speak. But one who knows the culture and the customs? Survival techniques of the jungle?"

"Yeah," Garwood said. "There was one, but he's dead, and his name was

Captain Eisenbraun." The man grinned briefly for the first time and Garwood had a pang of dread.

"Exactly. Only one other. Mr. Eisenbraun."

"I am Marine Corps. I was not Special Forces. I was not an advisor," Garwood complained.

"You will note that some of the other American prisoners that have been in the jungles for two or three years have not acquired the skills that you are reported to have a mere two or three months after your capture. How can you explain this? Not only you have knowledge of the Vietnamese language, but also of the Montagnard language dialect, which few know."

He took out another piece of paper. "Now here we have summarized your activities over the past years." He recounted petty thefts in one camp, thefts he had thought undetected in another. He had also been accused of stealing things he had not stolen. He had sometimes stolen one thing from a guard, and for a subterfuge, hidden a portion of it in another guard's clothing, or near his bowl. This, he found, was interpreted as deliberate provocation of unrest.

"What will happen to me now?" Garwood asked. The man fell back on the old formula—reports, decisions by others. Garwood would stay, live alone, food would be brought to him. He would work as directed.

In the following days he consistently asked what lay ahead, and his questions were always palmed off on others, the "superiors." From October of 1969 until May of the next year he lived in the twilight—eating, working, sleeping. His isolation was more organized than ever, and more complete. Guards were told not to converse with him. The days melted. Tet that year came and went. He was not allowed to join the celebration. There was no Christmas for the lone American, no more interrogation, just the silence. There was no torture, no starvation. The food came twice a day, the work was simple and familiar, but done always alone, with the disciplined pair of guards.

Then in May, as Garwood lay on his back in the darkness of night, half asleep, listening to a radio that he could hardly hear, thinking that if only that noise were less loud, or if it were more loud—one or the other—he could either sleep with it or listen to it, but it happened to be on the edge between, so that all he got was a word now and then and an annoying jumpy kind of wakefulness.

There was no warning. The world suddenly shattered in a cataract of sound. He knew it had to be a dream, a sudden nightmare, but something took his body and accelerated it out of the hooch and before he knew it, he was on his knees and the hooch nowhere, and he was wondering where the hooch was, and where to go, when there was another crash, which brought light into the darkness, a brightness and a full push backwards, very fast and then nothing.

He woke up in the darkness, alone inside his mind. He could still hear the noise, loudly roaring but constant, like a machine running full blast very close by, and he couldn't see, but that made sense because it was the middle of the night. And then his body began to tell the brain that it was hurt, and it told him he had better lie still. The wounds were bad, he could tell, the kind that you don't want to know about, but maybe, he thought, if he just lay still it wouldn't get any worse. Opening his eyes, he could see nothing, just a dark blurriness that reminded him of the face of a dead television set.

Gradually sensation returned. He felt he was lying on bamboo. He hurt whenever he moved, in a general way. He could not hear anything above the roaring. Then he felt hands on him. His right hand he could move, and his left was numb and still. His back hurt. The pain was becoming specific, and his head hurt.

He could feel something binding his neck, and as he became more and more aware, he felt that his chest was also bound with something and his left arm might have been mobile but it was pinned fast to the rest of his body.

There was a sheet over him. His toes and legs responded to tentative movements without pain.

The first thing to come back was blurred sight. They gave him injections, terrible surprises he had to try to fight in his silent but roaring world, where he could hear no voice and see no shape. But the injections, which seemed to be right into the eye, hurt with an almost refreshing pain, sharp and new and specific. He could talk, but he could barely hear himself say the words. After a while he gave it up.

The eyes responded very slowly. First the light got brighter, then shadows with definite edges began to take shape. He saw movement but no color. But it was always noisy. Then he saw the shapes take definite form, but always out of focus—so badly that he made mistakes. A hand in front of his face would not resolve. It would remain a blob with fingers. But there was improvement until color returned and he began to see familiar objects within a range of about five feet.

He realized he was in a hospital. There were people in white. There were women, talking silently. A sheet. He was helped to excrete his waste, he was fed with a spoon. Soup. He localized the pains. He had a cut on his head, on his shoulder, his elbow was completely stiff.

His only relief from the noise was sleep, when the roaring became like white sound, sheets of water hurtling over a dam. The doctors began to write him notes, simple questions; he would try to answer over the roaring. He would scrawl notes, wave his head about.

He learned to sit up, then to walk on the dirt floor. It was not a hospital after all, but simply a large hooch. There were many other men there, all soldiers. Wounds, burns, malaria. He never found out why the camp had exploded: Logic suggested it must have been a bombing. There would have been some warning for an artillery walk-up. So it was a bombing—a big plane, probably a B-52. He never saw another survivor of the raid.

Normalcy came back slowly, almost unnoticed. He gradually realized that he could hear other noises above the roaring. Or had it receded? But he couldn't hear voices. The blindness lasted for two and a half weeks; for a month, the roaring blotted things out. After a month he was on the mend. He could walk at two weeks, and by the end of the first month, he could read. He spent his days lying on the bunk. The other patients resented him bitterly. He could not hear, but from their eyes, he knew they hated him—more than any Vietnamese he'd known.

He was fed rice, soup, fruit, condensed milk. They injected him with vitamins and sulfa drugs, he guessed. Then they took him away, still deaf.

Two guards came, and Garwood was examined by a doctor. They tried his ears with a tuning fork—then held it to his forehead. Garwood had known terror of blindness. But the deafness was almost worse. It was like being muffled completely. The doctor wrote on a piece of paper, "You will go with these two men to North Vietnam." The doctor wrote that the journey would be long, arduous, and dangerous.

The guards looked to Garwood like tough and battle-hardened veterans. They were soldiers with their own ways. Compared to them, the guerrillas looked like peasants with guns. These two men wore green khakis and pith helmets, and carried AK-47s, large packs that looked like overstuffed pillowcases or duffel bags. They also carried rice in surprising amounts. Nghia was one. Tum the other. They treated Garwood like a child. He could not carry anything, they took it all; he remembered the alarm of being separated from his only worldly possessions, his bowl, his hammock, his mat. They were all lost in the wreck of the camp.

Garwood was watched jealously by the two men. Every three days, they took time to attend to Garwood's remaining physical complaints, cleaning out his ears, checking the bandages on wounds on his back and elbow. The elbow remained stiff. It made Garwood feel like an old man to be in such disrepair.

He was given a new set of pajamas. The only thing he had from the past was his shoes, the faithful rubber sandals. The road north was busy and wound along beside a larger road with marks of having been used by trucks and other equipment; they traveled day and night, walking about ten to twelve hours every twenty-four hours.

Guards cannot resist talking to their prisoners. It is an exercise in the pleasure of power. But these men were abrupt and minimal with their comments, and it was only when they seemed to have forgotten Garwood's ability to speak their language that he learned more about them.

He found that he was their ticket home, and their solicitous care of him was motivated largely by a fear that he might die and they be sent back south into the fighting. They were surprisingly young and did not mention rank. Instead, they had papers indicating they were junior men, and they had to produce the documents at frequent intervals—though mostly because of the curiosity Garwood aroused. Because he had been almost deaf at the beginning of the march, the guards paid little verbal attention to him.

Again, Garwood was amazed by the mighty movement of slow traffic along the trails. Bicycles, carts, trucks. It was clear that the larger road, where vehicles could pass, had received plenty of attention from the enemy. It was bombed on both sides, there were detours where the repairers had found it easier to reroute the road, most of the foliage had gone, blasted or defoliated.

But there were no trucks on the wide road, and the traffic on the smaller trail avoided it completely. There was a swarm of life on the foot trail and emptiness on the main road.

Garwood's health grew better, as it usually did in periods of exercise. The guards gave him salt meat—it was almost jerky—and there was plenty of rice to go with it. Sleeping arrangements were crude—hammocks slung wherever convenient. There were only two of the hammocks, one used in turn by the guards, the second for Garwood alone.

The harassment from the air was intermittent but terrifying. It became clear that the main road, barely used, was a chief target while the smaller trail received less attention. But at least there was some warning from the noise of the jets. The guards would simply plod on, barely looking up. There was no taking cover from this bombing. From the first sound of the jet to the delivery of the bomb, you could move perhaps twenty feet. He began to realize it wasn't worth it. The guards first allowed him to crouch when bombs fell near, but later as he became accustomed, they pressed on, motioning him to "Di . . . Di" with their hands.

The human traffic stared, and once or twice made hostile gestures. Once, he was knocked down by a blow from a soldier he was passing. It may have been an unintentional blow, like a collision in foot traffic, but the guards dealt ruthlessly with the soldier, angrily shoving and striking at him with their gun butts. It was a strange world.

Somehow, Garwood conceived a wish to get to North Vietnam—it was perhaps the only way he could communicate with the silent, urgent guards. But he was sick of the bombs, the hostility, the hours on the road. He also felt that if he was going to sit out the rest of the war, it must be better to do it in North Vietnam rather than the south.

The trail seemed endless. It never crossed a village, pagoda, depot, cache. The only life was on the trail itself, always in motion. At night it went on, blacked out against attack from the air, with the angry whispers of men hurrying, the low stink of effort, the rasp of breaths, the pounding of feet.

The road north took three months to complete, but Garwood never knew the length of it. Like a child in a car on a weekend drive, he would ask plaintively— how long? As his hearing came back, they told him: "Long way. Don't worry."

They crossed a strip of Laos after ninety days on the trail. The terrain was tending more to pines than jungle trees. There were no border guards and he wouldn't even have noticed except that the guards told him. They thought it very clever to be able to pass in and out of the country at their wish. Garwood saw it only as more mountains, rather drier and hotter. But the guards told him, "After this, North Vietnam."

Garwood saw his first motorized vehicle a week after the little party had gained the border of North Vietnam. Again, there was nothing—no signs, no cities—only a slight lessening of the altitude, as if gradually they were coming down from the mountains into more rolling terrain. It was warm and dry. The guards' steps lightened. Nothing really changed, however. The food on the trip had been surprisingly good, much better than camp fare. How they got it was an ill-kept secret. There were towns and villages, all right, but not for Garwood. One of the men would stay with him and the other would disappear on a side trail. The man always brought back plenty of goodies. There were cigarettes, candies, even some canned goods after these hauls. Now, it seemed, there was food in plenty.

After they crossed into North Vietnam, the food was even better. Powdered eggs appeared, fruit disappeared. But still no peasants or civilians, only the endless movements of the military. He saw the vehicle the day after he saw his first electric light.

It was a day of changes, like coming out of a movie house in the afternoon. The first surprise was a real road, not paved, but wide and equipped with signs—not traffic or directions, but slogans about the war. On the road were armored troop carriers, trucks, real "6-by" trucks like those he had once driven, most of the traffic heading south. Garwood marveled at the sight, reveled in the choking dust and smelled the welcome flower of exhaust fumes. Here was an end of jungles, the beginning of a new world where everyone was not continually thankful for a canopy of jungle overhead or the darkness. It seemed the war was behind at last, and the back-of-the-mind fear that for all the other dangers, one was going to be killed by a bomb released by someone miles away who was simply dumping ordnance—this was gone.

That evening, he sat in a hooch with an electric light. He couldn't stop staring at it. Food was brought on a tray: canned chicken, vegetables, rice, tea. There was a camp nearby, clearly a military base of some kind. Garwood was kept away from that, not allowed to walk around, but it was clear that they had finally got *some*place. The guards simply would not field questions like this. To them, it was sufficient that he knew he was in North Vietnam, that their troubles were over, and that he would be moved on in a few more days. The two men, with whom he had gone through an amazing journey, were almost unknown to him. It was clear that they were overjoyed to be back in their homeland, however, for they talked excitedly.

They had rested by the base for a day and a half when, on no particular signal, a Chinese-made jeep pulled up at the hooch. There was a cadre member in the passenger seat, an officer with insignia who said nothing. On his lapel were three stars and a red slash. Garwood was given the back seat, a guard on each side, and the jeep drove into the night. There was no talk in the car and the guards were unusually uncommunicative. They drove the road, which a day before had seemed so smooth to foot—now it was hellish with bumps, Garwood found himself uncomfortable with the violent lurching and banging. The jeep drove on tiny blackout lights, which made terrifyingly little impression on the flying blackness. Big trucks would whoosh past, so close that a crash seemed inevitable. They drove down, down to a place where the road became more level, gears were changed less often, and Garwood guessed they were on some kind of plain.

At daylight, he found himself speeding at about thirty-five miles per hour through a flattish landscape, which his fuzzy vision could not really take in. At midmorning they hit blacktop, an unbelievable luxury. Its smell was like some rare perfume, its smoothness and the song of the tires a melody. He yearned for the life he had known, of smooth surfaces and intriguing machines, lights, gadgets, plastic, metal, glass.

The road was littered with other vehicles. There were civilians of all ages and descriptions using this marvelous road, some in ox-carts, some on bicycles, most walking, carrying vegetables, poles, jugs, sacks. It was a colorful, lively, civilized sight. The motor vehicles all appeared to be military—big trucks, jeeps, buses, all painted green or camouflage. The vehicles looked both old and new, as if older trucks were made new. It was clear there were no private passenger vehicles, as he knew them, in this country.

The cadre in the front seat pulled himself around as if examining Garwood for the first time. He started to speak. Garwood yelled in Vietnamese, "Talk louder. I can't hear what you're saying." He pointed to his ears.

The officer told him: "We have shot down over one hundred U.S. planes here and captured alive over fifty pilots; this is the most heroic bridge in all of North Vietnam. Garwood could barely make out the bridge and the water below. He could see it was made of stone, but he could not see gun emplacements or craters, or other sign of military activity.

"On your right is the ocean over there about five kilometers." The man turned again, seeming satisfied that this cryptic information was what Garwood most wanted.

He could not see the ocean, only the vague dun and green of fields.

The last leg of the trip took two hours. They came to a city called Ninh Binh, where he was told there was a famous church, "the biggest Catholic church in all of Southeast Asia, all of stone."

Garwood's impression was of a midsized market town, a big main street, a dusty place overcrowded with traffic that throttled it and crept past in a stream of machines, pigs, cows, oxen. The proliferation of tiny shops amazed him. Every shop sold one thing—watch shop, shoe shop, shirt shop, hat shop, and so on. No one had heard of a general store or a department store or a supermarket.

They were still near the downtown shopping area when the jeep pulled up next to a pair of lofty iron gates in decorative style, painted green and attached to stone pillars. They must have been relics from the days of the French colonial regime. The gates swung open, a guard standing by. The jeep rolled through and the gate closed efficiently behind. On the inside, Garwood was faced with a most peculiar sight: It reminded him of nothing so much as a hacienda, or a Spanish building in a Western movie: whitewash, heavy walls of stone, balconies.

Garwood was left with the guards in the jeep while the cadre officer walked briskly inside. He came out, accompanied by a man who looked like an Oriental surgeon. Wearing glasses, he was clad completely in white topped by a white skullcap.

The white figure walked up to the jeep, introduced himself. "My name is Doctor Am," he said in accented English. "I will be your doctor. You are to stay here until your health is better." He turned to the cadre and began talking in Vietnamese. "He can speak Vietnamese," one of the guards warned. The doctor shot a curious look at Garwood. "Very good!" he said. "This will make it very much easier for my nurses."

He was led to a peculiar room on the second story of the large, low building. Patients were playing cards. A group of them were practicing music; they stared as he walked past; others peered out of their private rooms.

"This will be your room," the doctor said in Vietnamese with a nod of his head. "You will not leave this room unescorted under any circumstances." But Garwood saw no guard.

The doctor told him further rules—and that a nurse would be assigned to him, a female. "Anything you want or need you will tell her and she will tell me. If we have it available and I see the need, it will be supplied to you. You will make no demands. You may make requests. You will not go into the other patients' rooms, and you will not talk to them, even if they try to talk to you. I want to impress upon you that only a few selected people here know that you are an American.

"For your own safety, I must strongly advise you that you do not answer to anyone about your nationality while you are here. Most of the people here are soldiers who have returned from the battlefield with severe wounds—and hatred for the Americans."

In two and a half months at the hospital, Garwood's sight and hearing improved. He was told that he had suffered a severe concussion and a temporary blindness not unlike snowblindness. His ear problem was caused by the concussion of the bomb. "It is remarkable that you are even alive," the doctor told him early in the treatment. "I think your health must have been miraculous. According to this report, you were wounded by two bombs—one fifty meters from you, the other only seven. The only reason that I can see that you are alive right now is that you were under the cone of the explosion and were not hit by fragments."

He was well fed—bananas and tea or rice cookies for breakfast, a noon luncheon of soup, rice bread, tea; dinner was pork or chicken or beef, boiled or stewed, rice, a vegetable and green tea. He also was given ten cigarettes a day, and a tiny kerosene lamp to light them with.

Just before Christmas, Garwood was nearly back to normal. The roaring was almost gone, his eyesight could compare with what he remembered before. The doctors told him he was ready for discharge, and would be taken to another place, a camp, as it was described.

He was taken in a closed truck to Son Tay Prison Camp.

After what he calculated was four hours, or a morning's drive, he was let out of the back doors in the countryside. There were few trees on the lowlands, and hills and mountains in the distance. It was a far different vista than he had known, with endless rice paddies stretching through a valley like the scales of a snake. In front of him was a small bamboo gate with a low fence stretching on either side. It looked like something for domestic animals, not for men. Beyond were two hooches, as different from the ones he had known as an Irish cottage was from a teepee. The roofs were densely thatched with rice stalks, the walls mud and straw—giving an appearance of solidity. The buildings were white-washed. Only the dirt floors reminded him of his former homes in the past five years. It was February of 1971. He had missed both Christmas and Tet, he thought.

He was shown to the largest mud-and-whitewash hooch. Two rooms divided the interior space. His was about eight feet square with a bamboo bed, a bamboo chair, two windows. His glance took in the sleeping mat, wooden pillow, blanket of thin material, mosquito net, rubber sandals, washcloth, towel, toothpaste, toothbrush, and a bar of soap. There was a deck of playing cards, a paper pad, a pencil, two pairs of pajamas, a pair of socks, a bowl, sticks, a metal spoon. Christmas after all.

As he became accustomed to his new surroundings, he found that he was again the only inmate in a prison establishment. Not even ARVNs were there, only four guards and no camp commander. The place was an offshoot of Son Tay, one of many cells in which men were kept in complete isolation from other prisoners.

He asked the new guard where he was. "You can speak Vietnamese? . . . the camp commander will be here to talk to you, then you will learn what you are to know." The speaker seemed another tightly disciplined northerner. As in the Marines, he was "A J squared away," as one said. The commander's name was Minh, a captain of about thirty-five. He came across as the iciest of men, concerned only with the maintenance of a perfect reserve. He showed neither hatred, bitterness nor sympathy, but seemed like a robot. He wore full-dress uniform, including well-worn and polished boots, green dress uniform with sidearm, a pith helmet of green with a star in the middle. On the collars, which lay like those on a dress shirt buttoned at the throat, were four silver stars and a slash, sitting on a red patch.

"First of all," Minh said, "you are in Son Tay Province. This is a prison camp composed of both American and Vietnamese prisoners. You have been sepa-rated from the other prisoners by order of the higher command. The reason is not known to me. What is expected of you is that you follow the rules and regulations of this camp to the letter."

He told Garwood that four guards would be assigned to the hooch, and told him the guards' duties were "as much to make sure that you stay here, as to keep civilians, intruders and others out of here. You shall tell no one that you are an American. If anyone should ask you, you should always ignore them and turn a deaf ear. This is mainly for your own safety and security. There are many peasants in this district who have lost their sons and daughters at the hands of the U.S. imperialists. It would be dangerous if they found out.

"There will be a radio assigned, for which the guards will be responsible. As you can understand the language, they can tune to Hanoi radio for your enjoyment. Under no circumstances are you to adjust or turn on the radio yourself. At no time may you leave this area without the escort of the guard or one of the camp officers.

"Daily work will comprise work in the paddies, digging fish ponds, cutting or planting trees, planting vegetables, manioc. There will be two or three meals per day—this is your decision. Your daily ration will be given to the guard, who will cook for you. Later, if you prefer to cook for yourself, you may request to do so. Settle in! This will be your home for quite some time.

"If you have any questions, you may tell the guard, who will inform me, and when I have time, I will tend to them."

"I have one question now," Garwood said. "Will I be allowed to write my family? You've given me paper and a pencil."

"You have been given these things for your use. Whether you may write to your family is a matter for discussion with my superiors. But it is unlikely that we can send mail to the U.S. as we have no ties with them."

"What about reading material? Are there any newspapers or books?"

"Can you *read* Vietnamese?" Captain Minh asked quickly. Garwood said he could, a little, but not as well as he could speak. "Very well. There will be books."

He added: "It may get cold here. We are in higher latitudes. If you wish, you may have a fire to keep yourself warm, but we cannot supply wood for you."

The life was easier than that in the south—no doubt of that. Garwood asked the guards to allow him to plant banana trees in a kind of garden around his hooch at Son Tay. He found the four men were local lads who went home in their off hours, who lived with their families.

As he grew accustomed to the life and work, he noted that there were no civilians in the area, and understood by overhearing the guards chat that the Son Tay was a military zone where permission was needed.

The guards were true provincials. They had never been to the battle zone, there was none of the seething hatred that could be sensed in war-torn South Vietnam. They were young peasants who were glad enough to fulfill their military obligation close to home in the relative comfort, if total boredom, of domestic guard duty. So light were their duties that he often found time to play cards with them.

They showed a strong interest in all things American, but it was based only on a movie-and-propaganda knowledge of the country. They knew that the U.S. was the wealthiest country in the world, and believed it had become so by invading small countries, robbing the wealth of each and turning the people into slaves.

"An example of this," said Dang, one of the young men, "is the black

American." He told Garwood how these people had been invaded, kidnaped, stolen away, and led into slavery. Garwood could find little argument to raise against the example. He bogged down in the Civil War, trying to explain how at the end of the Civil War the blacks were freed, given independence from their former masters, and in many cases, free land.

"We do not think so," Dang replied, "or why do the black Americans still demonstrate and protest against oppression in the U.S.?"

Garwood had noticed that Angela Davis' name was frequently mentioned on the radio in terms of high praise. She and Jane Fonda seemed to be the women Vietnamese admired the most. Garwood had never heard of Davis, whom the guards regarded as a well-known American hero.

The other strong example for imperialist aggression was the "white Americans' invasion of America," early in the country's history, an invasion of unparalleled ferocity in which the invaders "took all the lands, put the people in concentration camps, and over the next hundred of years, contrived to kill them all off. Only a few survive."

"You are not a real American," Garwood was told, "any more than if I was in Thailand; I would not be a Thai, but a Vietnamese. No. The only real American is the oppressed red American who is now in concentration camps."

The views of the young men, so uncomplicated and bearing one aspect of the truth, were hard to counter. He always found himself making lame explanations in defense. All he could do was to stress that the country was run by the people.

He would think of this period later only as a sort of hibernation. He was not uncomfortable, he was not hungry. His health was as normal as he could remember. The radio was the biggest thing in life, the only connection to a world outside the paddies, the fields, the other work, the meals, his garden.

The permission to write never came. He wrote letters, they were taken by the guards, and he never got anything in return. The camp commander, when he appeared, seemed satisfied with Garwood's conduct. Months passed dully and he learned to write Vietnamese in order to read the materials he was given. He got newspapers, magazines—they all had the same "line" about the country, the history, the war.

The radio seemed to indicate the war must be drawing to a close. In 1972 the broadcasts spoke of peace talks. When he first heard of them, he was working planting groves of trees for eventual harvest as pulpwood in the uplands. He dug and planted over ten thousand of them, he recorded.

In the first year, he was given a stupendous task of manual labor—he was provided a shovel and told that he would dig a pond to raise fish in. It seemed just like the logic of the Orient to him—a shovel to build a fish pond. How many strokes would it take, how many clods of earth? He was instructed each day on how to proceed with the work. He first dug a pit about ten by ten feet and six feet deep; then he was told he should widen the pit to a size he estimated at fifty meters by one hundred meters. Each second day he would widen the pit, the days between he would carry the dirt in baskets to the eventual bank of the pool. At first, he simply could not believe the work. He had never done anything like this in his life. A bulldozer might have done it in a few hours, but with a shovel it seemed impossible. But once he got into the swing of it, it was not too hard. He spent two months cutting blocks out of the ground and widening the pit. Then they brought water from a nearby paddy into the pond and over a few days, with the help of two rainstorms, the pond filled. Fish were brought in in buckets, carried on bicycles from a hatchery. There were thousands of them—they were fed grass cuttings, slops, whatever could be spared.

One day the radio announced that there was, in their possession, a letter from a "Valerie Kushner," the wife of a prisoner, Harold Kushner, an Army captain. Garwood's ears pricked up. But the letter was surely made up. In the letter Kushner's wife seemed to be condemning the U.S. government, urging U.S. troops to stop fighting and asking that the U.S. withdraw all forces from Vietnam.

Kushner himself had been on the radio more than once by this time in 1971. They were tape recordings of his voice, and there was no indication where he actually was. Garwood recognized the familiar voice of the doctor, reading the leaden syllables of a propaganda blast. To Kushner's credit, the tone was monotonous and unconvincing—like the voice of a robot.

As the peace talks droned on, Garwood's fish were growing. By then, there were several generations of fish who had lived their lives in the pond. He often wondered if there was one that had survived all the way from the original tin pails of fry. Some of the fish were close to a pound in weight when the Vietnamese harvested them, with large square seine nets hung from poles, dropped to the bottom and lifted.

He ate the fish, found them good but bony, roasted over a wood fire with the guards. You could peel the skins off them and almost nibble the skeleton bare with your lips. Once a month the seiners would come with a truck to harvest the fish, which were taken to the other camps around Hanoi, he was told.

They set him to work growing pumpkins and a large crop developed in the area near his hooch. He used human dung mixed with wood ashes to fertilize the clay soil. In 1972 he was to fill most of a large truck with the results of his efforts.

First, he dug a hole the size of a washtub in the clay soil and lined it with topsoil, urine, human feces, fire ashes. In thirty days, he planted two or three seeds in each "hill." The yield was very good—as many as two hundred such plantings produced thousands of pumpkins. It amused him to hear via the guards of the complaints about the pumpkin soup, and pumpkins mashed, fried and prepared every imaginable way, which the whole camp had to eat. He wasn't exactly the happy farmer, but the soothing feeling of caring for the plants and the fish and banana trees made him feel more peaceful.

He began to enjoy cooking and eating his own vegetables and forage, and thus developed the Garwood Cookbook. Every day during the growing season he would weed the pumpkins in rotation. It amazed him what could be produced with a little water. He found frogs at the fish pond, removed them to a special pit and fattened them with pumpkin rind, rice, and other refuse. When they were fat, he ate them eagerly.

He took the frog, while still alive, held it by the head, cut off the nose and mouth, skinned it, gutted it, and washed it in salt, then rinsed it in cold water, cut it up into small pieces, and added it to soup. With a few pumpkin slices, a little fish sauce, and a dash of salt, simmered for a couple of hours, the taste was acceptable.

Snake basically came out like eel and might be caught in a number of ways, but usually by watching the edges of the pond and then drowning the snake with a stick or by hand. Land snakes could be found sunning at the edge of the woods. When sighted he killed them with a rock to the midsection. Cooking was the same. The skinned corpse could be broiled over the open fire or boiled. Flavor: slightly like beef, sometimes tough.

Another method: Chop, bones and all, as fine as energy permits. Wrap in banana leaves, boil.

Turtles were frequent in the summer. He split the animals out of their shells after bleeding them and saving the blood. He drank the blood, which tasted rusty but was said to be a tonic for the lungs and throat and protection against colds. The skinned body of the turtle, cut in sections, was boiled for stew. Turtle produced its own fat, which was good for seasoning other dishes.

The rat recipe was basically the same as used in South Vietnam—skin and boil—but was little used after he began to feed mice and rats to his pet snake, which he dubbed Blackie. The snake lived in the rafters in the hooch, crawling gracefully out into the sun when it was cold and under the eaves when it was too hot.

He was instructed how to grow a spinachlike vegetable, a sweet potato and a hard pea, a dandelionlike lettuce, hot peppers, cabbage, kohlrabi. He thought wryly that his family would laugh at him now he had become a farmer—they had always rather prized the image that the Garwoods were mechanical rather than agricultural.

Within two years, he had become a full-time agricultural worker. He had his own shovel and hoe. His health was greatly improved. The seasons of North Vietnam he found to be much different than those of the south and much more like those of his own Midwest home. There were days of light frost in the winter from December to March. Spring and summer weather could vary violently— long dry spells and steady, soaking rains that could last a week. But the growing season was so long that mistakes could be made over. A first planting in February could be harvested in July, the second planting to be harvested in November.

He came to know the Vietnamese fall, the good eating of the harvest, the fresh winds blowing down from the mountains, the smoke from hundreds of fires taking on fresh smell and meaning, the rice standing yellowish-green in watery fields, the men and women working late in ragged rows across them, sometimes singing:

> How many years have passed
> Our country, our land has known no peace,
> Oh, mother country, your face, your body is scarred.
> Nevertheless, you endure and flourish.

17
The War Returns

NORTH VIETNAM suited him. He blended in with this calm country, became a part of it. The war seemed to recede. Then in 1972 in the summer the war and his anomalous place in it came back to him with a shock. The Hanoi air raids had supposedly ended. He was working the fields near his hooch when the anti-aircraft weapons opened up at midday with no warning. The targets, high and tiny, looked too small to hit, the reverberations of their engines varied like a rolling thunder, far away. From the land, the flak batteries pumped shells into the sky: They must have been waiting in absolute boredom for all this time, he found himself thinking. The antiaircraft shells exploded in black puffs and a delicious, long-delayed noise.

He couldn't tell what the planes were doing. They were in a formation of three, coming from the direction of Hanoi. Then a new sound and sight. First a noise like an earthquake, followed by one exactly similar, and a rocket rose and accelerated, with the deadly direction of a stone destined to hit its target, toward the tiny planes.

Missiles, he thought. There had been no indication of a missile site beyond the hill he had often marked, though the radio spoke of U.S. planes being destroyed almost daily. Now the pair of projectiles, with their fiery tails like a kids' sparkler, seemed to be converging with the tiny planes, with the sun. He lost them in the sun and them glimpsed an added silent light, a delayed explosion. One of the aircraft seemed to be falling and on fire and four parachutes were floating, with black ants underneath them. The parachutes seemed to be floating close, then drifting beyond him. He could not be sure whether the things beneath the orange and red and white parachutes were still

253

or moving. The plane fell far away, so far he could hear nothing, the parachutes disappeared behind the foothills of the Ba Vi Mountains.

When the sky was empty, he could hear cheers in the silence. He was suddenly aware of his guards' presence, both of them standing on the edge of the paddy, looking up at the sky and smiling.

"It seems we have more guests for the Hanoi Hilton," said the one named Dang.

"It looks like you got four new boarders," Garwood said. But Luong, the other guard, said no, there would be only two. The other parachutes, he explained, were diversionary—fakes. In this country, even if they landed in the forest, there would be no way to escape. There were too many peasants, too many eyes watching eagerly, too much light.

The radio claimed three planes shot down that afternoon—it added a claim that two pilots had been captured, and gave their names, both Air Force officers. One man, according to the guards after the broadcast, was badly burned and had broken bones. He died in the hospital, leaving only one survivor.

The raid had brought Garwood dark thoughts. He had seen that the "firepower" of North Vietnam was not a simple propaganda boast. The flak had been like black popcorn filling the sky suddenly. These peaceful mountains were alive with posts and guns.

His valley and Son Tay quieted down again. The guards had a new god besides Ho Chi Minh, however—the Russian missiles. "Twice as fast as U.S. jet," the guards would say. "Missiles that can follow the heat of the plane's exhaust, just like a dog."

It was mid-December. The radio was blaring about the Paris peace talks and "stubborn and obstinate demands by the U.S. government that cannot be tolerated by the Democratic Republic of North Vietnam . . . Vietnam has sat in on the negotiations as a good will gesture, but if it takes the last Vietnamese and the last drop of blood, we will not give in or surrender to the U.S. imperialists."

Garwood paid little attention to the broadcast. Its sound was a constant part of life. The story was repeated each day. Then the talks were broken off, and the "peace representative" of the DRVN went home. It was December 22.

During the cold season, Garwood's farm activities were in hibernation. He was working on his personal woodpile, plus his job of providing a load of wood a week for some destination in Hanoi. He would use an axe to cut each tree, usually one a week. It was hardwood and split easily, but the lack of a saw made the job laborious. He would cut and split and stack all day, pausing for a cold lunch of a ball of rice or a boiled manioc.

It was like other days when the dusk came early and smoke from heating fires joined that of the cookstoves. Back near his hooch he took a brief bath with the well water, splashing himself. His body was wiry and muscular with the work. His hands were hardened to a shine from the axe, his shoulders had bruises and pads from carrying wood. A bearded, long-haired hermit, a man growing old, growing wrinkles, growing to be part of this soil.

Shivering, he'd go back into his hooch, dancing with the cold. As soon as he could, he lit the fire, which sat on the dirt floor and spread its smoke up past the blackened rafters and out into the evening.

At least the hooch had doors. He lit his lamp, noting the level of kerosene, and he sat by his fire, warming first one side, his hair, then the other. He might make some tea, or bring his venerable soup pot to the fire and place it on the triangle of rocks there. It was a pleasant time of day. It was possible even to read. The guards would come in at the beginning of the night and often the three men would share hours of conversation.

But this night the guards were still out, sitting on the rude furniture they had made for the winter to avoid sitting on the ground, and Garwood at first did not catch on when one of them half whispered, "They're bombing Hanoi!"

He didn't make much of it. So what, he thought. Hope they blow it off the fuckin' map, he thought to himself. Then he heard the first of the noise. It was bombing, big bombing, but it was like the rain, or a fireworks display at its end when all the salutes pile up like grapes. The sharp detonations were heaped onto one another in a bouquet of sound.

"B-52!" shouted one of the guards.

Shit, said Garwood to himself, there's nothin' but prison camps around Hanoi.

He got up and went out the door and on the northern horizon against the blackness of the sky there was a wild activity of light. Sound traveled from the distant battle. It all seemed about ten or twenty miles away and strangely beautiful. There were no searchlights. Instead, he could see the flaming tails of missiles like shooting stars going the wrong way.

"How can the U.S. be so cruel," said one of the guards, "as to bomb a populated city like Hanoi?" They seemed to be panicked. There were relatives, friends, and of course no telephone.

The guards clearly wanted to leave and get to some command post with communications. The radio was silent. On the frequency reserved for Radio Hanoi there was only static, blankness. The guards thumbed around the dial, picking up Chinese radio and a Russian station. Nothing.

The attacking aircraft were invisible, high above the light of the antiaircraft. There were pauses in the pattern of bomb explosions, then a renewal of the steady, overlapping concussions. "For every Vietnamese civilian killed in Hanoi," said a guard in a strangled voice, "there should be one American." Oddly, the man looked at Garwood for approval of this comment. He watched the excitable and frantic men carefully as they stood silently watching the raid ebb and the huge sounds of the planes fade slowly.

The guards continued to wait by the radio. After about an hour of strained silence, a weak signal could be picked up, apparently from Hanoi. The voice spoke confidently about the number of B-52 "air pirates" that had been shot down and roundly condemned the raid, which had done little military damage. They compared the U.S. regime with Hitler's mass extermination of the Jews, however, which made Garwood wonder how light the damage had been.

"Bombs fell on the hospital and on the most populated section of Hanoi, Kham Thien Street . . . there were bombs on two other hospitals completely demolishing them, several pagodas and churches, four elementary schools, and the entire thoroughfare of Kham Thien for approximately two kilometers . . . estimated civilian casualties on this street alone close to five thousand dead and wounded . . . most of them old men and women and small children . . . the young men and women were in factories and not at their homes."

On January 15 Garwood was abruptly put on a bus loaded with ARVN officers, more than twenty men from a captured battalion, and they were all taken, with five guards, to Hanoi. The bus seemed to be going on a tour of the bomb sites.

Garwood saw what they said was the hospital. "People's Hospital," read the broken sign. It looked like a French colonial building, painted white. But the skeleton was all that remained of the central structure, and the hospital complex, at least a city block, was dotted with craters. A huge poster was the first effort the city had apparently made to restore things. Flying from the main gate, it read "People's Hospital—Bach Mai," with a list of about forty names below it. "Our people who were maliciously murdered by U.S. air pirates, December 22, 1972, while undergoing treatment at this hospital."

The bus ground on through the streets with frequent barricades to another hospital, said to be the city children's hospital. The hospital was damaged, but parts were still intact. There was another list of names and the usual sloganeering.

At Kham Thien Street, Garwood could see the full effect of direct hits by bombs stacked on top of bombs. The buildings were totally demolished, whatever they had been. The street was deep in rubble, as far as one could see. The stench of lighting gas, rotting food, and plaster dust, and the strange smells of the cellars of houses, were in the air. The prisoners were let out and told to walk the street, where hundreds of Vietnamese were hard at work, individuals as well as organized teams, searching through the rubble. Decomposed bodies, many of them clearly children, were laid together in rows. A guard told the prisoners that the children had not died from the blast but were buried alive in collapsed houses.

After the bombing, the peace talk in Paris was the only thing going. The radio no longer counted glorious victories and planes downed. The communiques continued to report the U.S. as "stubborn, obstinate, hysterical, warmongering." The Vietnamese would continue fighting to the last man. It was planting season again, the digging and setting out of seeds took up his attention. It was either late February or early March, he couldn't remember exactly, that the radio announced that a "protocol" between the U.S. and Vietnam had been signed.

Garwood didn't know what the word meant. But it was big news in Vietnam. The guards' attitude changed completely; they laughed and smiled at him. One said: "Bob, the day when you will be allowed to rejoin your family is coming closer and closer."

The whole air of the broadcasts seemed different. The "protocol" seemed to mean that the war was ending—but not yet. But there were still the usual encouragements and warnings and propaganda.

Garwood was not just cynical about the future in Vietnam, he was completely dubious. But after almost eight years the thought of really going home had to be kept at bay at all costs. It was too good to be true. In Vietnam if you heard something good was coming you relished the hope and didn't expect anything to change. It was the same with the "protocol."

All he cared about was getting out. If the U.S. was getting out, why so would the prisoners! All he could think about was what he would do when he got back to the States. "I might be going home," he thought. The idea, first pushed aside as it had been many times before, began to grow as more broadcasts outlined plans to withdraw U.S. troops from Vietnam.

The broadcasts announced there would be three immediate releases of prisoners—"all prisoners to be released," the broadcast said. The guards, however, still knew nothing. He simply assumed his name would be on that list. He saw himself being escorted out of the camp, being taken to an airport, meeting other prisoners, taken away to Saigon or Da Nang.

The first mention of the release of prisoners came in early May. The first release, however, came in February 1973. He was anxious, and his work lost its appeal. He had something to care about besides his pumpkins and the thought that the endlessness was itself ending cheered him. On dry days he would look down the valley for the dust of a jeep or truck. Even the guards began to share the anticipation of release.

Then in late January the names of the first group of prisoners to be released was read out on the radio. There were almost two hundred names, most of them Air Force officers. They gave a man's name, rank, his plane, the year he was shot down. It seemed to go on for hours. He listened patiently. He knew, with his luck, he would not be there, and when he found that those whose names were read over the air had already been released, his interest dropped further.

The first group went, picked up by two U.S. C-130 transports, taking off from Hanoi. Still, he went out to his prison pumpkin patch. He wondered whom all his marvelous pumpkins would feed as the first crop set its fruit and began to vine out in the bare fields. The guards didn't know. The camp commander never told him anything but propaganda on his infrequent visits.

He waited through the second release, and the third. With one bunch of released was the "Group of Eight" described as Americans who had begged and pleaded to be allowed to remain in Vietnam, but were repatriated anyway. He dimly recognized a couple of the names.

Then the last release had passed. Still he sat in his hooch, worked in the fields. The names had all been read, and his was not among them. But they would release more. The guards had another version: "Vietnam is not so stupid as to release all prisoners," one of them said. "What would prevent the U.S. from coming back and bombing Hanoi again?"

They chattered on happily about how the genius of Vietnam was always to have an ace up the sleeve. Never lay all the cards on the table at one time. Play them one by one.

The fall harvest arrived without news of other releases. The radio spoke of the U.S. trying to "hoodwink" the Front by taking its soldiers and putting them in plain clothes and returning them to fight in secret. There was also the theme of the weapons—how the U.S. was withdrawing and leaving its weapons there: They would be used by "reactionary puppets" in the south to continue to strike at the people. They laid heavy condemnation on the minefields the U.S. had strewn in the entrances to Haiphong harbor and in the Gulf of Tonkin ports.

Who was going to use the pumpkins? He could see that the Caucasians he had occasionally seen in distant fields were now gone—but the other farms like his were still being cultivated by new people. The truck came and took his pumpkins, as usual.

The guards inadvertently told him that in the mountains just behind him was a very large dairy farm, that this farm had been supplying milk to Hanoi for years, and that it had been and still was operated by the remaining French prisoners captured during the years of counter-revolutionary war with the Viet Minh.

Garwood was aghast at the implication: "French prisoners?" he said.

The guards looked at each other nervously. "Why are they still here? Why is Vietnam keeping them so long?"

"Because most of them are crazy," Luong said. "Sick in the head."

"How come you don't release them?"

"We don't know," he said defensively. "They do well on the farm. They have plenty to eat."

"Are they allowed to correspond with their families?" he asked.

The guard did not know. "They can speak Vietnamese very well. There are some black, some white, some brown."

He wanted to know how many there were on this farm just out of sight beyond the shoulder of the hill. "At one time, there were over two hundred," he said. "I don't know how many there are now." He added that they were members of the French Legion force, made up of Spaniards, Moroccans, Algerians, expatriate Germans and others. They claimed that some of them had married Vietnamese women who, like them, were outcasts, prostitutes under the French who had been declared pariahs by their own people.

A new and dreadful dawn was breaking in Garwood's mind. The French were still here. He could end up spending the rest of his days in the country running a vegetable farm. No one would be the wiser.

Curious, Garwood thought. The lowest on the totem pole of American soldiery regarded himself as infinitely superior to the Vietnamese, yet accepted that all types and races of people were properly "American." The Vietnamese, pure, ancient, primitive, felt only superiority to everyone else in the world. To them, Americans were simply mongrels, animals, monsters.

He had spent the last five years living with one mental basic: that he could outlive the war, that his reported denial of death and his ability to survive would overcome the desires of his captors. He had seen the Vietnamese as wanting to use him to help to win the war, and that was a respectable, if not comforting, motive. Now the war was over. Or shortly would be, for without the American presence, everyone knew that the north would be irresistible as a starved dog that fights a fat and tame one.

The basic idea was dribbling away, leaking sadly like a wound that cannot be stopped. He had outlived one of the longest wars in modern history and now there was no use in keeping him. Yet they did. He was like a hamster, or a vegetable.

The camp commander was to tell him, "I would think if you could learn to eat, think, do everything as a Vietnamese, it would be very easy for you to live here." He checked himself. "In fact, I think you can now do these things."

He realized then that he had begun to dream, to think, to calculate in the Vietnamese language. He tried to think of the U.S., and found to his horror that he could only see certain things—the face of a cartoon, the shape of a car—only superficial things; all the subtlety was gone. He could not remember his father's face—it was easier for him to remember a photograph of him than the real thing. And he could not bring up the faces of his brothers, his sisters. He decided that his mind had starved away to half of itself, and that the memories had been the part that was lost.

That same year, after Christmas, an NVA lieutenant came into the camp, and to his quarters. His name was Cuong, an English speaker with a large scar—wrinkled and shiny like a burn—on the lefthand side of his face. He observed Garwood with a cocky air; he was tall and thin, and his bright eyes relished the prisoner. He told Garwood that he had worked at the city prison called "Hanoi Hilton" with American prisoners, as a translator, and now worked at Son Tay. Garwood cast caution to the winds, asked him if there were still other Americans in the camp.

"This is not your concern," he said with pleasure, "your only concern is you."

He complimented Garwood, who had answered Cuong's English questions in Vietnamese. "I see you have mastered our language—perhaps it is better than any other I have seen." But when Garwood started to talk in English, he found it heavy and hard—particularly to find the right word.

"You speak English like a high school student," Cuong laughed. This reflection frightened Garwood. It seemed like a sentence of mental retardation to him, an illness he could not cure or even fight. "You are an American only in appearance, nothing more. You do everything but think like one. You have everything but the dedication that a Vietnamese has. Your life here can be as easy or as hard as you make it."

The same line over and over. Maybe it was the fact that the Vietnamese themselves did not know what they wanted of a prisoner. Or more likely they were telling him with the maddening indirection of the East that they simply did not owe him an explanation.

Since he had been in North Vietnam he had not been asked to *do* anything to gain his release, but now, Cuong seemed to indicate that some change of attitude would make a difference. "Dedication." What did that mean? Friend of the Vietnamese?

Life was the broadcasts, the fields, now in the winter slowdown, the newspapers and Russian and Cuban magazines in the Vietnamese language. He read every word, finding some news in them: Two Russian astronauts had died, a city named Watts had exploded in riots in California, much to the obvious pleasure of the editors and writers, and a scandal seemed to surround the U.S. president, Richard Nixon. This last, it was said, "Proves the corruption of the U.S. administration, caught red-handed and red-faced in lies and deceits . . . like every president, he had indulged in these practices, but he is unlike every other in that he is caught. . . ."

The biggest thing that happened in his first four years in the valley—which was without a town—was the installation of electricity.

The job was done entirely by the military. In two days they brought a line and poles in from the road—about seven hundred yards—and strung a single double wire into his hooch with a socket in the end of it and an off-on switch. With a string. There was no fuse box, no meter box, no nothing.

The guards were excited by this vision of the future. They told Garwood that all their lives as peasants, they had only known kerosene lamps; some elders had known even a time before that, of the cruder fat lamps and open fires and darkness at night. The war had won culture, in the form of electric light, even for a prisoner.

The bulb was strung in the center of the room that Garwood lived in. It hung from the rafters and spread its yellowish glow—the glass was clear—around the room in harsh shadows. One result was that the guards began to spend the night hours inside the well-lit hooch, playing cards and talking.

The pumpkins of the first crop were in vine and fruiting out when a new officer, Ky, arrived. About thirty-one years old, small, handsome, thin, he looked like a whippet, but without a whippet's hang-dog look. He had the wire and the pluck, and something else. He had the air of a fighter who knows limitations, and, as Garwood came to know, his body was covered with scars. He was a man who lived on his luck, a man who claimed "over two hundred battles" to account for the marks on his body.

He said he had killed more than sixty Americans, but he said it in such a way that Garwood felt only fear and no fury. Most of his career had been in the south—he wore a ribbon on his tunic that read *Dung Si Giac My*, or "Heroic American Killer."

He was only a first lieutenant, but the guards, corporals, looked up to him as

260

if he were a general. Like a general, he filled the space around him and he made demands with a natural sound in his voice. It was the order of things that Ky should criticize the guards, run his finger around the action of their weapons and hold it up in disgust until one of them gave him a rag so he would not dirty his own perfectly smooth handkerchief that rested folded and pressed at his breast. He asked that they be better soldiers, and the card games stopped. He seemed to be able to give them something to fight for when there was no fighting going on.

The visits were irregular, unscheduled. Sometimes he talked about his wife, the beautiful Hoa. They were an odd couple for Vietnamese. He was in his early thirties and she about eight years younger. But the couple had no children, because both were so involved in and committed to the Front. Iron discipline had been required. Separation was a fact of everyday life.

Hoa, Garwood found, was stationed in the south, and was involved in the most dangerous type of intelligence.

He dwelt on her beauty and intellect; they had come from the same village; like admirers from afar, they had known of each other, but had thought the age difference was too great. Then the families met and made a match. They had been married for eight years, comrades in the revolution who had made the world of ideas their life.

She was a sergeant, he a lieutenant. But there could be no question of their spending this recreation period together while she was still on duty in the south. Ky told Garwood, "She's coming to North Vietnam . . . it's been two or three years, sometimes I can't remember which." Because of poor communications between Hanoi and Saigon and the south, he could not be sure of the date.

Garwood's curiosity was piqued by the stories of the perfect couple's reverses. He thought of them often during that summer of 1974, for though he had only known Ky since April, he felt, in the void that existed around him, that the family Ky was his society. So, one hot day in August, when he saw a small figure in black slacks and a white blouse walking determinedly up the dirt road toward his hooch, hers was the only name he could think of.

The woman only seemed tiny. Closer, she was tall for a Vietnamese, without the short-legged look, though she had enhanced her natural height with black high-heeled leather pumps of what looked to be excellent make.

There was dust on the shoes and a fringe of dust on the slacks, and rings of sweat had stained her blouse. But it was hot, and these small humanities were the only blemish to a picture of perfection. Her black hair was not lank, but lifted as it fell into a kind of wave. She wore jewelry, a gold ring, a gold bracelet, gold watch, gold necklace, gold earrings, she carried a shoulder purse. The guards stared like moviegoers as she approached, picking her way along the dirt road.

It was as if she had dropped from the sky. Where was the car? This was the first thought Garwood had. This is like Rockefeller livin' in a slum, he thought then. She seemed to know which house to go to, for she glanced at the guards and at Garwood and made ready to go on. It was clear she had not found whom she sought, that she might have already come too far, that she was annoyed.

She looked hard at Garwood. He stared back, a dozen thoughts running through his mind. She glanced away, found the guard's eyes. "Where is Lieutenant Ky, comrade," she asked, with that delicious formality of a woman who is sure of her rank.

"He is not here," the guard mumbled, clearly confused as to the title he should use to this personage. Garwood began to take in the details. She wore no makeup and her skin was unusually pale for a Vietnamese. No peasant, not a mannish militia-woman either. Her hands and feet were small and clean, and even her eyes seemed larger and clearer than those of most Vietnamese women. She did not look down, but held her ground.

"Do you know where he is then?" she said, politeness edged with irritation. The guard was still a bit confused.

"He could be in any one of the compounds," he said, "but he has not been to this one today."

"How many compounds are there? Must I walk to the mountains?"

"Who are you?" the guard said, worried by the tone of the guest.

"I am the wife of your good lieutenant, and I have come from South Vietnam," she said, choosing to take the easy route of smile and banter with this guard. "I wanted to surprise him."

Garwood had edged closer, walking slowly to the well as if performing some routine task. He picked up a mass of soggy clothes that were soaking in a pan, and laboriously, slowly, began to wash them, carefully positioning himself so he could watch with apparently inadvertent glances. But he saw that he was an object of a much less covert curiosity. She spoke low to the guard. "Is he an American?"

"I can't answer that!" the guard said with some shock.

Garwood, wiping his hands, sidled up to the guard's side. "Do you want me to boil some green tea?" he asked. The woman's eyes widened. They were always surprised, so surprised, and the look was always the same. "He can speak Vietnamese?" she exclaimed.

"Quite well," the guard rolled his eyes toward Garwood. "Yes. Go ahead, boil some tea."

When the tea was well boiled, he took out two tin cups and went out with pot in one hand, cups in the other. He gave both to the guard, and turned to go back, making the humble servant in every downcast motion.

"Please . . . have tea with us," she said in slow and over-pronounced Vietnamese. Garwood glanced toward the guard like a spaniel, and the man shook his head yes. Garwood went in and got the third cup and another chair, and quietly placed it beside the guard, careful that he was further from her than the other man.

She pulled a packet of cigarettes from her purse—Dien Bien brand, he noted—and placed the packet on the table, offering it to the men with her hand. She plucked out a gold cigarette lighter—Garwood's eyes popped as he noticed it was a Zippo. The guard, with a flurry of politesse, made an elaborate display of offering her a cigarette, which she accepted, giving one to Garwood and taking one herself.

Garwood was transfixed by the gold Zippo in the thin-veined hand. She lit her own cigarette expertly, inhaling gratefully, and set the shiny little machine down. The guard fumbled with it, lit his cigarette almost to a bonfire, and put it down. Garwood reached for the object, savoring its heavy smoothness, the smell of the rich fuel, the click of the lid. It was cased in what appeared to be pure gold and on the bottom, Zippo—Made in USA.

The cigarettes were perfumed. "It's an American," she said, clearly indicating that the tone was no longer to be official.

"It is very nice," Garwood ventured.

The guard, searching for a lead in this obscure game, asked, gesturing, "Is this real gold?" she nodded.

"It is a gift for my husband," she said.

"He's very lucky . . . in more than one way," Garwood said in a low voice. He looked at her gratefully while the guard frowned.

"I will take this as a compliment," she said, with a light two-note laugh.

"My intentions were that of a compliment, nothing more," Garwood said as smoothly as he knew how. Silence fell, and grateful shade hung like a bower against the iron day.

"How long have you been in my country?" she asked, tilting her head.

"Going on ten years," Garwood answered, keeping his eyes down.

"Were you very young when you came, then?" She looked at him with fresh interest. "Why are you still in Vietnam?"

"Vietnam has not released me to go home," he said, glancing at the glaring guard.

"Why not?"

"I wish I knew . . ." The guard cut in with a loud noise like a cough.

There was a strangled, distant cry and on the road, perhaps one-eighth of a mile away, was Ky, pedaling on a high-handled bicycle as fast as he could. He raised a hand, then returned it to the bars as the bike jounced over the stones and lumps of the ill-traveled road. She remained where she was, composing herself, and then gave herself to his hungry embrace, as the sometimes reserved Ky threw himself, buried his face in her hair and hugged her with little grunts of joy. They talked in the sun for a few minutes, happy in the light, and then he drew her into the shade of the hooch.

"Bob, do we have any tea?" he asked, for once the normal, emotional man in front of the guard.

"I just made some for your wife," Garwood said. Ky smiled and nodded.

They left. That night, Ky returned, walking with his bicycle. He carried a long flashlight, it looked as if it would hold four cells, and a Vietnamese *num*, a kind of frog trap built like a basket, which is clopped down on top of the prey from above.

She was not with him. He came to the hooch happily, asking the guard to join him in a hunt for some fresh fish in the paddy irrigation ditch. He told the guard to take the light and go ahead, shining it in the water. Then when the fish swam under the beam, Ky would pop the trap over it. They went off into the darkness, returning about two hours later to where Garwood sat alone with the remaining guard, staring at the skies in the hot night. They had captured some good medium-sized carp and a few frogs, which Ky gave to Garwood on a string.

"This is for your courtesy to my wife today," he said. Garwood knew they wouldn't keep long. He thanked the man and started to clean them for the pot, leaving them in cool water with a wet rag over the bowl.

On his creaking mat, Garwood was assailed by memories he had not known for years. He thought, not so much about the woman, but about the couple and the strong contrast between them. She seemed to be so unlike any other Vietnamese woman he had seen. Like a society beauty, it was in her manner that she did not expect to live like others. She seemed to have been on easy street, with her jewels and her saucy questions, her lack of fear of men, her playful plan to surprise her husband.

Nothing happened for two days in a hooch now enlivened by the first woman in almost a decade. Then the couple returned, to repeat the fishing venture. She stayed behind with Garwood and Luong, while Ky and the other guard of the shift made off into the shadows.

The two men left behind were as delighted as cottagers hosting the princess. The guard hastened to make tea, Garwood adjusted the chair by the table. Again, she had worn trousers, made of some sort of khaki material. But no one in Vietnam, where all women wore either the native wraparound or the light trousers, could wear them with quite the style of Hoa. Above the trousers, and overlapping at the waist, was a flowered blouse in blue. On her feet, the black pumps, no stockings. The effect was exotic, Oriental, controlled, and fresh. Her hair was clean—that would have been enough, and it hung in glossy curtains around her face.

The evening was sultry and conversation was slow. No one had any idea how long the hunters would be away. It suddenly struck Garwood that this was the most civilized thing he had ever done in his rough, sometimes gruesome, and often absurd life—entertaining a high-born lady at the edge of the hunt. Tea was brought in silence. The guard was busy with the pot and cups.

This time, she seemed to have no interest in the military. She wanted to know about American women, about their customs, and those of their men. "What do you like in a woman?" she asked delicately.

The question unmanned Garwood, who could not even think if he had ever formulated such a thing. "Beauty and intelligence . . ." he said. She asked him quietly about the Vietnamese women he had seen. Did they fill the requirements?

"Every woman has her own beauty," Garwood said, with satisfaction at his own profundity.

"Are you married?" she asked. He shook his head with appropriate sadness indicated by a drop of his eyes. "If you were in the U.S. and had not been captured, you would be married now?"

Garwood said he could not know. He had come to Vietnam as a boy, he told her, unsure of what he wanted and very restless. Through the years of captivity, he told her, he had matured very quickly.

Hoa blazed with boldness: "Have you ever had a Vietnamese woman?"

"No," Garwood lied. He had had whores in Da Nang.

She looked at him coldly. "That's hard to believe, especially if you were with the Marine Corps."

The guard appeared with the tea, breaking the hold of that conversation. They began to talk of other things. She asked a thousand curious questions. Clothes, religious observance, houses, cars, freeways. "You were very young when you were captured," she said. "You have been in prison camps all over the country for so long. It must be very hard for you. Do you ever think about American women?"

"Sometimes," Garwood said. But, he thought, not as often as you would think. He told her of his romance with Mary Speers, their engagement, and the simple ending of everything with his capture.

Hoa looked impressed. "Why didn't you marry her before you came to Vietnam?" she asked.

He tried to clear away the cobwebs from his memory, tried to reconstruct the image of her face, could not. He remembered with silly regret that he had been so virtuous with Mary, he had never tried to put the make on her. They had so many luxurious principles then, he thought mournfully, saving "it" for marriage.

Sometime during the tea drinking, Garwood felt his foot touch hers. In sandals, his toe felt as if it had been shocked. He jerked his foot away as imperceptibly as possible. Hoa giggled with a short, light noise, and asked, "What's wrong?"

"Nothing," Garwood said, burying his eyes in the tea.

"You're embarrassed, aren't you?" she said.

He was scared. He thought the foot had been an accident, now he feared it might be a trap. He was frightened by what had happened; she was not.

18
A Brief Pleasure/A Final Victory

GARWOOD WAS returned to his solitary life for the next two days. It was nothing new, yet he felt somehow deprived. He tried to put the visit out of his mind, but he often found himself returning to it. Most of the women he had seen chewed betel and were pock-marked and let their sagging breasts flap freely. Their hair looked like black hemp, their expressions were blank or docile, or fearful when the men appeared. Hoa had seemed like a movie star beside the others—and particularly he remembered her feisty argument, and her style of defiance, both to him and to her husband.

The fields needed water and weeding, the rice dikes had to be tended. It was not bad work, but it went on forever. He banished the incident as just another bizarre piece of Vietnam.

After two days he asked the guard what had happened. The man said Ky had "taken his wife to Hanoi city to take in the sights." Garwood had not asked about the wife, so was gratified to get more of an explanation than he had bargained for.

The next time he saw the couple it was a summer evening with the clouds as heavy and gray as the dark sea. He was resting after dinner when he saw them walking up the road, their legs moving swiftly as they turned their faces to the darkening sky. Hoa, he saw, was almost trotting to keep up, her hand on her husband's elbow.

She wore black, baggy trousers, made either of silk or nylon, a cream blouse and her pumps. Her hair was wet and hung down black as coal. She looked as if she had just washed it.

266

Ky was bursting with energy. He said that he planned to fish heavily that night, since any freshet of rain brings the fish upstream to the source of the water that is gathering and flowing. This way, they could be caught in greater numbers, even in the muddy water. Ky spoke excitedly about kilos of fish and asked for the guard. "Where is the other guard?" he said, seeing only Kien on duty.

"He's gone off to a guard's meeting at command," Kien said.

Ky said, "I need one of you to come with me to the river—there will be plenty to catch with this rain."

"He ought to be back before too long," Kien said. Ky seemed to pay personal attention to Garwood for the first time. He put his heavy four-cell flashlight on the table and looked at him.

"How are you, Bob?" he said quietly. He sat down at the little bamboo table. The rain began to rustle the thatch and run on the mud outside.

She sat beside her husband, looking out to the rain, watching it march over the dry ground, but demonstrating less enthusiasm about it than he. Ky began to strip off his shirt. "Come on, Kien, let's get going and get ahead of them. As soon as the water starts to flow, that will be the time."

It was getting dark and Kien looked uncomfortable. He peered out the door in vain for his colleague. "I don't think I can, Captain, not without the other man here," he said. "The order specifies that one is to be on duty at all times."

"It's all right. Hoa is a good guard," he said, laughing. "The other will be along."

Kien grumbled about the guard commander. But the rain made a safeguard against any lightning inspection tour.

Kien stripped off his shirt and pajamas, standing in undershorts as Ky did the same. The two men took the fish basket and the flashlight and made for the fields. Before he left the house, Kien carefully stripped out the shells in the chamber of his AK-47, unclipped the magazine, slipped it into his belt, and leaned the gun against the wall close to Hoa with a smile.

Garwood and Hoa watched the men walk into the gathering gloom. "Good luck!" she shouted. Ky did not turn, but only lifted his right hand in a gesture of salute with the basket.

Only the drumming, rustling rain filled the silence when the slim figures slipped from sight, leaving the two sitting under the eaves. The flashlight dimmed to a yellow point, then winked out. The voices faded to murmurs and fell under the tone of the rain. "I'm cold," she said, shivering suddenly and violently. "Let's go inside."

Inside, the kerosene lamp was barely enough to show the shapes of things: the rack bed of bamboo mat against the wall, the jerry-built table, the bamboo chair. The mosquito net and a thin blanket lay in a jumble on the bed. Outside was the gray of dusk before the extinction of the light, but inside it was quite dark, with the rain softly whispering on the roof.

"Is this where you sleep?" she said. Garwood nodded in assent. She was looking away, not at him. "Do you mind if I sit down here?" she asked.

267

She sat herself on the bed, settling her back against the wall and bringing her feet up under her, knees under her chin.

Garwood, sitting uneasily in the chair close to the door, could see every line of her legs where they joined her body. The roundness seemed a shock.

Garwood could not take too much of the sight of the beautiful woman, curled comfortably in the flickering of the oil lamp. He looked continually to the window, expecting at any minute the dripping fishermen or the guard.

"What are you looking at?" she asked. He shrugged.

"To see if Luong is coming from his meeting."

"Why worry about the other guard? I'm in charge," she said with a smile, giving special emphasis to the words. She was looking straight at him with a curious hardness in her eyes. "You must spend too much time here," she said. "It must be very lonely."

Garwood murmured something. "I've got used to it after the years."

"This isn't true," she said carefully. "You never get used to loneliness. Do you miss your country?"

"Especially on nights like tonight. Raining."

"I feel the same, even though my village is much closer than yours," she said. "I'm unfamiliar with North Vietnam. It's so different from the south—don't you feel that? I have found it difficult to fit in here."

"That's hard for me to see," Garwood said. "North Vietnam, South Vietnam, the customs seemed the same."

"In almost all ways. But the people of the north treat southerners as southerners, which is to say they think we're simple people, peasants almost, not serious like them."

"At least you have Ky," Garwood said.

"I have thought so. But he is changing. Has changed so much." Garwood looked puzzled. "When I first married him, he was always eager, energetic, and happy. Always joking and smiling. Now the war has done something to him. He talks very little, makes demands as if I were one of his soldiers, and would rather go and catch fish then spend the evening with me."

"But he fishes for you," Garwood said.

"True. But the idea of going excites him. This is not something he has to do, it is something he wants to do." She looked as sad as a puppy, head tilted on her knees, eyes glistening in the light that wobbled off the wick of the lamp. "Bob, do you think I'm a beautiful woman?"

"Yes," Garwood said.

"If you had seen me at eighteen or nineteen, you would think differently of how I look now. I was queen of my village then."

Garwood was feeling helpless. He simply listened as she told a little about her early life, the village, her admirers. The knowledge she had, even as a girl, that she was to belong to Ky. The families had arranged that. He was almost an unknown to her, but had been another village legend, the boy who had run off to join the revolution at the age of fourteen. At first there was disapproval, but later, he was treated like a hero. They married when they hardly knew one another, during a brief visit. He was a young soldier, dark and quick, his weapons stacked in the corner of their house on the wedding night.

"How strange for a Vietnamese woman to sleep with someone she hardly knew," Garwood said absently.

She laughed musically. "You are right. Very frightening."

"What do you do when you are frightened?" he asked.

"I made every excuse I could think of not to go to bed. I waited until I thought he was asleep. I lay down quickly with my back to him. But he wasn't asleep. He turned around and grabbed me," she said softly.

"Were you dressed?" Garwood asked.

"Yes," she said. "Why?"

"Did you resist him?" Garwood asked. It was his turn to be coy and arch.

"No. The woman is taught to lie there, to let him do what he will. I was a virgin when I married Ky."

"Have you slept with other men but Ky?" Garwood asked.

She looked at the floor. He knew his answer.

"You have then," he said.

"It was no fault of mine," she said angrily. "It was my duty to the revolution."

"You had to do what? What duty?"

"My work for the revolution in South Vietnam was to get information any way I could. Your officers are very tempted."

"From Americans?" Garwood asked. She nodded. "Does Ky know?"

"No," she said. Garwood asked her what would happen if he found out. "I don't know. I'm afraid even to think."

Tears suddenly came to her eyes. "It's not the same as being unfaithful," she said in a weak choking voice.

"Don't let it get you," Garwood counseled. "Ky has the same problem with nightmares—about the Americans he has killed. He killed to stay alive and you did what one must to stay alive also. There is no difference."

She looked at Garwood. Then she simply uncurled herself, moved swiftly across the dirt floor, and the next thing Garwood knew she was there in his lap, hugging him fiercely. He didn't know what to do. His arms were frozen to his sides. "Thank you," she said. "If only Ky could understand. I'm so afraid of what will happen if he ever finds out."

Garwood felt an instant kinship with the woman, tormented by a guilt she couldn't discharge. She could not even tell another Vietnamese because of the social code. Even her closest friend would discard her as a whore. Garwood, as a nonperson, a prisoner and an American, was the one safe person she could speak to.

She untangled herself quickly and stepped back, sitting again on the bed. "Come here," she said.

Garwood looked out the window. There was nothing but the blackness that was now complete, and the rain glinting by the door in the feeble lamplight. He sat down on the bed, but a distance from her. She took her purse, fumbled through it and pulled out a pair of fingernail clippers.

"Give me your hand," she ordered. Garwood did so, placing the cracked and toil-hardened claw in her small soft one.

"That's all right, I can do it," he protested needlessly.

"Are you afraid of me?" she asked with the old mocking.

"Yes, I am," Garwood said. She asked him not to be afraid.

"I don't like people to be afraid of me," she told him, busily leaning over his hand, which she held by her fingertips, palm down. She crossed her legs Indian fashion, so that one of her thighs rested on his leg, and drew the hand close and began with the clipper to cut his nails. She finished one hand, put it down on her leg and took the other. His hand rested on the warm leg.

She finished the second hand and turned away from him. "Now," she said, "would you please rub my back?"

"I don't think I should do this," Garwood said. He felt the nagging fear of something ominous.

"It's all right," she said. "Don't worry." He pushed the heavy mass of hair, still damp inside, over her shoulders, and began to gently rub her shoulder blades.

"Is that right?" he asked. By way of answer she turned, slipping her hand deftly under his arm. Her face was close. He leaned forward, fell into a kiss. She seemed to melt into his mouth, strange and new.

Garwood's world was quickly dissolving. "This is what you Americans like," she said with a tight giggle. She took one hand and placed it on her belly where the flimsy, slippery pajamas stretched over her hips. Not knowing what to do, he kissed her again, felt her guiding his hand down. She quickly darted her tongue against his, breathing out with what seemed to be fire and spice; he felt her hand leave his and saw her loosen the top of the pants. He brought his hand up, felt the elastic waistband, and slipped his fingers inside it, feeling the silk of the skin, hearing her, hearing her mouth against his teeth.

Garwood shut his mind to caution. His free hand encircled her back, drawing her to him. "No," she said, pushing him away. But she was smiling, he saw. She unfolded her legs from their crossed position and leaned back on the bed. "This is better," she said. "I think the Americans like this too."

Garwood leaned toward her, disengaged. He slid beside her, gathering her in his arms, wondering how badly he smelled, feeling the size of her svelte slippery body, trying to remember nights at high school, slipping down to her waist with his hand and clumsily plucking at the thin material of her pants. She mumbled against his mouth when he had the garments to her knees. "No," she hissed. "We must be ready to dress. I will show you." She held his hand where he was fumbling at the waist of his own filthy pajamas, and quickly rubbing him through the cloth found how she could draw him clear outside.

She traced the shape of his manhood. Holding it gently, she spread her knees and guided him as he adjusted his limbs nervously toward her. Stroking the back of his neck, she calmly placed him where she wanted him with a little sigh, such as a teacher might make when a student finally understands the problem.

Garwood was beside himself with quivering excitement. He felt his consciousness slipping away and an uncontrollable wave, all wrong, swept past him, leaving him panting and cursing and out of control and empty. She went suddenly hard. "Did you . . ." she asked.

"No," he said weakly, "more like I exploded." He felt the wetness, the hollowness of rushing thoughts, all of them foreboding, the fear, the ruin of the moment. She struggled against his weight, pushing now without the smile. She sat up quickly, drew up her pants and without a word or glance ran quickly outside in the rain. Garwood frenziedly adjusted his own pajamas, rubbing at the evidence of passion.

He turned to the lamp and lifted it. Dimly, he could hear her washing at the well. She returned, but not to the bed where he sat. She called to him in a voice of friendship. "Bob. Come out."

He came out with the lamp. She sat, legs crossed, combing her hair, a slight smile playing about her lips. "How you feel?" she said, still with the friendly tone, like a girl you would meet in school. "I have never seen anybody come so fast," she said flippantly. "Ky takes forever." She smiled the whore's smile. Garwood was silent. "I just hope I don't get pregnant. We will both be in trouble."

She explained that she had hoped her quick washing would prove effective. Garwood said little. He felt nervous, scared. He had affronted her in some way he didn't understand. He wished only that she would be gone.

Whether she felt the tension or not, she never showed it. "Pull yourself together," she said with perfect coolness. "Try to act normal. He is a jealous man and we are still in some danger."

"Think nothing of this," she said, pulling her comb from underneath through the end of the hank of hair she held. She was acting as if it had never happened, he thought to himself.

The next time Garwood saw Ky, he brought other news. He was returning to the war. He had been transferred to a different post in South Vietnam. He spoke of it as the last push before the final victory.

About a hundred yards away, dressed in her usual slacks and blouse, stood Hoa, looking bored, resentful, and a bit downcast. She stood with a small flight bag hung in her hands in front of her, and a hat on her head, looking like a precious girl bound for the train. "Is your wife going with you this time?" Garwood asked Ky.

"No," said the captain. "She has some duties here, and will follow me later."

Garwood felt the regret of war like a cup, filling too fast. "Will I ever see you two again?"

"I doubt it. No. After our country is completely liberated, you will be returning to your own home." The news was too stunning for Garwood to fully stomach. He did not pursue it. Liberated, he thought. That could be tomorrow, that could be ten years from now!

The last sight he had of Hoa was of her waiting for her husband as he walked back to her. She gave a straightened little wave of the hand and turned to follow

271

him. It seemed to Garwood that she had even slightly exaggerated the motions of following, almost tottering like a wooden doll. It seemed to him like a blessing and a relief. She would be the master of all situations, he was sure.

Summer passed, the crops ripening, the afternoons announcing the demise of another season. Garwood passed his days like the toiler in a medieval woodcut: Hoe in hand, he bent to the plants, he waited for them, and one day he knew it was right to gather them in. It must have been late, for the pumpkins had to be carefully picked over to separate the usable from those already rotted.

Saigon fell. It was the spring of 1975 and Garwood had been hearing excited reports on the radio—filled with names instead of invective—reports that Hue, Da Nang, the cities to the north of Saigon were threatened, had fallen—Saigon was surrounded.

When Saigon fell, the sky of North Vietnam opened up. He thought sourly that if there were a bird flying, it wouldn't have a chance. Bullets flew everywhere in a country where bullets were a standard item of commerce. The antiaircraft emplacements poomed into the sky, everyone with a rifle shot it at the stars. When the news came over the radio loudspeakers, the guards with Garwood hugged one another, smiling at Garwood, cheering, shooting, stamping on the ground.

Garwood was at last justified. He had endured it all and he knew at last that the north had won—completely and utterly won. There could be no more negotiation, no more bargaining chips. He realized there was no more reason for his existence. Like a hangover, he was simply there.

A feeling of hope filled him, for whatever reason. He thought that any day, someone would come for him to announce that he could simply pick up his mat and leave. He imagined walking out—to Thailand, to Laos, somewhere where he could get to a phone, write a letter, tell the Marine Corps that he was still alive.

The guards became like old friends. Discipline relaxed—for one thing, they had no more bullets for their weapons and no more were issued to them. If Garwood had the desperation or desire, he could have walked out with four angry guards chasing him. They still were uncommunicative about their instructions from cadre, but their actions spoke louder. "As soon as the U.S. recognizes the government of Vietnam there will be negotiations for your return to the U.S.," one of them said.

The planting was forgotten. He spent his days waiting and lounging. Even the card games seemed too much to do. He walked aimlessly around his little plantation with the melancholy thoughts of one whose future is completely in the hands of others.

19
Uprooted

TWO WEEKS after the announcement of the fall of Saigon, he was sleeping, it was close to midnight, when in his recurrent dream about the road, he heard the jeep. In this dream, a truck or some vehicle is seen on the road down the valley. It hesitates, but eventually it comes closer, turning at last to his hooch. The dream always faded. Now he knew, in the dream, that it was not a truck but a jeep and the jeep stayed there, its lights shining, the dust swirling in front of the radiator, the engine idling.

He woke fully and the sound of the motor followed him out of his sleep. He got up, tottering stiffly and half awake, as if to go to the latrine. The jeep was still there, burbling softly in the night, scenting the air with the delicious perfume of burnt gasoline.

In its light, a short man, fatter than anyone Garwood had seen in years, approached him, his eyes glistening, as black as ripe olives, and as impure. "Were you asleep yet?" the man asked confidently. Garwood, peering into the poor light, saw he wore a Western-style trenchcoat. It was Army green.

The guard put the lantern on the table. The visitor motioned to Garwood to sit. He took out cigarettes, a lighter, and put them down. Inside the trenchcoat was a uniform, also green, and Garwood got a glimpse of the lapels—two bars, three stars: lieutenant colonel, by his calculation.

The man kept a fixed smile on his shiny, sensuous face, a face without a wrinkle. "You don't know me," he said. "But I know all about you. I have been very impressed by the reports of your work and progress over the years," he added. He spoke for a few minutes about current events—the fall of Saigon, the fulfillment of the triumph of arms. "Have you been kept up with the news?" he asked eagerly, as if Garwood had the *Washington Post* delivered to his hooch doorstep.

"The loudspeakers," Garwood said. "They blared the news over and over throughout the valley."

"Because Vietnam is now one country again, there are many changes in the political situation," he said. "There have to be many adjustments made. You are included in these adjustments. You will prepare your things and come with me now."

The guard seemed overly bright-eyed. "Will he be coming back, sir?" he asked obsequiously. The colonel shook his head.

Garwood's mind raced in circles, not daring to center on the main thought. He could suddenly see no other reason for the night visit. He simply went to get his clothes, saw the familiar walls, the mat, the tools still shiny with use. "Don't take anything that belongs to the camp," the guard warned. "Only the things that have been issued to you."

It took him ten minutes. The farmer who owns nothing, he mused. He thought of the little place, truly almost his, and of the fields he had known season after season, first hating them, then indifferent and now not without a measure of love. He said good-bye to the guard. The man, not knowing how to do this particular ceremony, told him good luck. Kien looked at him, told him, "I hope your dreams will come true."

He climbed into the jeep. In the front seat he could barely see the driver in the gloom and the tiny light of the dash. He had the curious but obvious thought about the man—here was himself ten years ago, driving a jeep for the brass. The jeep made a simple turn, heading toward the tar road and toward, he knew, Hanoi.

Tension filled Garwood's body, making him silent and prayerful. He wanted no interruptions, dreading every stop as they whizzed along in the dark. Along the road, people in hundreds and thousands were out. They were walking, waving at the clearly military jeep, their black eyes glazing silver in the light of the headlamps. In Hanoi, it was midday at midnight, the city was ablaze. Whether it was the end of the war or simply the activity before market day, he did not know. Carts, produce, bicycles—he remembered how it had been two years before when he went there for the bombing "atrocities." There was no longer any sign of the damage.

The trip ended before the iron gates of what seemed to be a large warehouse complex. In the first light of dawn, he could see buildings, they could have been barracks, stretching before him. The street sign read Ly Nam De, the name, Garwood knew, of an ancient Vietnamese ruler who was said to have driven the Chinese back to China.

They seemed to be expected. The gate was opened by a uniformed man who didn't need any papers. The colonel, silent as he had been throughout the trip, merely lifted his gloved wrist an inch or two. In front of an unimposing building, the colonel got out.

Garwood was told to wait. The driver, too, remained in the jeep, the hot metal ticking as it cooled, the young man's unmarked face impassive, only his eyes, curiously darting to the rearview mirror, showing his interest.

Garwood saw a huge brick wall, topped with barbed wire stretched on iron standards, which seemed to match the whole perimeter. The buildings, all brick, looked distinctly industrial. He was puzzled by the place, by its lack of human inhabitants. Ten minutes passed. A fully dressed soldier, rifle, shiny boots, and creases in his green tunic, came to the jeep. He crammed himself into the back of the jeep.

Garwood marveled. Was he being taken to China? They drove north through daybreak and for most of the day.

It stood in a valley amid the woody hills, a very large place. It was the prison in which the captured French of Dien Bien Phu had languished for years. The Red River was on one side, barring escape. They were very close to China. This collection of buildings was known as Prison Camp Number Five. Bamboo buildings, all similar, were scattered widely on the little plain. There were no water buffalo, no kids, no garden patches, no wagons, no baskets or churns or rice trays.

The command post was in the middle of a half-moon of buildings set impressively on a small decorative lake, clearly manmade. A tiny causeway was the only access. Beyond the undulating valley floor, which was mostly clear of trees, a tea plantation could be seen. Rice paddies had been crafted out of the gullies in the valley floor, their shape following the contours of the land.

Garwood soon found out that the camp was unlike any he had ever seen. A sawmill, a brick kiln, widespread tea culture, a coal mine—all these were run by the prisoners. The whole place seemed to be in a state of ferment and expansion. Garwood was taken to a hooch near the decorative lake—a one-man affair with three windows, bed, bench, dirt floor, no fireplace.

He found that he was isolated again, and most completely this time.

He was to have some freedom in the camp, including the "privilege" of living in the solitary hooch without guard, excuse from work with the ARVNs, and the freedom to fish in the decorative pond and plant his own garden. But to keep these privileges, he must obey one primary rule: He was to have no contact whatsoever with anyone at the camp—not the guards, not the ARVNs.

He was allowed to go to the kitchen anytime he chose during the day, and food would be his for the asking.

It took Garwood almost a year to fully comprehend the extent of Camp Five. During that year, he saw the place turn into a major concentration camp that housed close to forty thousand Oriental men. They were shipped from South Vietnam wholesale in truck convoys, many of them apparently civilians. It was clear they were not prisoners of war in the ordinary sense, but political prisoners.

He arrived there in the summer of 1975, and for the first few months he simply existed in his hooch, his mind a blank, his will a void. He walked through the days, sometimes fishing for hours in the pool. The food was adequate, endlessly boring. The camp grew its own tobacco, which was available. He saw, on one of his walks about the camp, the underground solitary confinement cells that were being built. They were about the size of an icebox.

The ARVNs, he saw, did everything—they tended the tea plantation in the hills, they cut trees in the mountain and skidded them to the sawmill with the help of buffalo and elephant to make planks for the continuing expansion of the camp, they worked in the paddies, raised stock, chickens, ducks, fish. The camp was a food and material factory, where labor was plentiful. The ARVNs worked with a good will, though they were under indeterminate sentence.

They were there for "re-education," a process that could take years of hard labor. But no one was released in that first year.

The camp commander, Major Thuc, broke the cycle of idleness in September.

Friendly and apparently concerned, he started with pleasantries about Garwood's fishing activities. "We have received orders from Hanoi concerning you," the thickset major said. "I would like to talk to you about them." He was ordered to appear in the command post that afternoon.

Garwood was motioned in by a uniformed guard in pressed utilities. Thuc sat in a plain but comfortable office, with cushioned chairs, photo-posters of Uncle Ho, Lenin, and Stalin livening up the walls.

Garwood found the luxury of a cushioned chair an odd sensation as Thuc told him to sit down. He raised his eyebrows as a guard came carrying a lacquer tray on which was a plate of sweet rice cookies, a pot of coffee, and a packet of Russian cigarettes. These were placed in front of Garwood.

"You have been here over three months now, and we have not required much of you. Rest is important, to better your health. We have an important project which may require your immediate assistance. This is something of importance to the well-being of the whole camp. If this project is accomplished successfully, this would naturally be counted as a very progressive attitude of mind—and would be rewarded. But if it is a failure or destroyed, it would be considered an act of sabotage to be dealt with accordingly—with the severest penalty."

Garwood felt the familiar churn of fear in his stomach. What in hell do I know about that can help the camp, he thought.

"I have read in the reports since your capture and in your military record, and too, about your change of attitude since you arrived in North Vietnam almost six years ago." He smiled. "The high command was impressed with your work record and after reviewing your work as a truck driver and one with mechanical knowledge, wishes to try your skills. This will give you a chance to prove that you are who you say you are—if you show that you have these mechanical skills. You can drive a truck—you can also repair them."

Garwood tried to protest, but Thuc shook his head. "No," he said gently. "In Vietnam truck drivers have knowledge of repairs."

"It has been a long time with no practice—over ten years," Garwood said.

"Once a person learns these things, it is like the power to swim—never forgotten. As you may have noticed, we do not have electricity here. I see in your progress reports that you have experience of repair of radios, so you have electrical as well as mechanical knowledge." Garwood shuddered, inwardly thinking of his jery-rigged "repairs" on small transistor radios. "Before the U.S. withdrew from Vietnam, before the fall of Saigon, hundreds of thousands of jeeps, cars, trucks, and buses were requisitioned by the liberating army. They are all U.S. made. Unfortunately as yet we have very few mechanics that know about U.S.-made machines. Our mechanics are trained to work with socialist machines. There are many of the puppet troops here who are mechanically inclined, but we will not use them because they have only recently been captured and the threat of their sabotaging this equipment is too great.

"We are trusting that after your many years in captivity you do not have these tendencies. I have been ordered by high command to set up a motor pool, a repair shop. You will act as the foreman of this repair shop." Garwood was stunned.

"You will not be given authority, other than to see that the shop is run without mistakes that could be damaging to the machinery. We are not mechanically inclined, but we can tell if something is not running properly. Trucks, jeeps, other machinery are considered to be weapons. If a vehicle is repaired incorrectly, you will personally be held responsible.

"The biggest project, however, is what I brought you here for," Thuc said. "We are expecting to receive an electrical generator—brand new, still in its crate from the factory. It must be assembled. You will take charge of the assembly of this generator. Vietnam had to buy this generator at a cost equal to twenty thousand dollars—unfortunately the machine directions and instructions are written in four languages only, Russian, Czech, Hungarian, and English. With your knowledge of English, there should be no difficulty. While you work, your rations will be increased as you wish. Ten packets of cigarettes per month will be yours, five tins of condensed milk, one kilo of meat, all the rice you can eat, one-half kilo of sugar a month. This is even more than I receive. I'm sure you can see the importance of this project. We need the electricity to run the sawmill, for the dispensary, the kitchen, and for general light of the camp. So you see, it is of great importance. Any malfunction from your own negligence—though as I have said, we do not foresee this—will be beyond my hands. It will not be tolerated by my superiors."

"Do I have a choice in this?" Garwood asked.

Thuc smiled blandly. "No."

"At least will I have the opportunity to study diagrams or plans of assembly before starting the project?"

"You may take as much time as you wish, but the deadline by which the machine must be operable and in working order is the first day of our Tet."

"Am I the only worker in this project?" Garwood asked plaintively.

"No. Hand-picked puppet prisoners with specialties in mechanics will do the work. You are required to make sure the work is done correctly."

Thuc, with a beneficent smile, then handed Garwood his "tools" for the job—perhaps fifty sheets of unlined paper and some pencils. "First, draw up the plans for a shop for the motor vehicles just as the Americans would have. Leave room for the installation of the generator and for the house that will protect it."

Garwood had never faced a task even remotely like this in his life. As he sat numbly in the office, as the voice of the commandant rolled on, describing the facilities for engine repair, electric shop, and so on, he tried desperately to remember the setup for the motor pool at Da Nang. There had been a complete shop there with lathes, welders, machine tools of every variety. But here, there was not even going to be electricity for the first phase.

Thoughts swirled through his mind. There seemed no end to his captivity. The war was over, yet they kept him on. The situation was changed completely. He decided that he might as well make the best of things as he found them. Left in Vietnam by a country that apparently didn't care about him—at least not enough to make some effort to get him back—he thought that if he could get into a position of trust so that he could be regarded as a useful cog in their machine . . . then he might be able to manipulate a way out. He would never get anywhere staying by the lake.

Garwood remembered the occasional stories in North Vietnam about the former French prisoners who had worked in shops, farms, and prison factories after the fall of their regime. Some, it was said, were still working there. The huge grounds of the camp had been built by others, by hand over the years—years after their war was bitter history. Somehow, most of them had won their freedom in the end. It was as if the Vietnamese demanded war reparations of their prisoners. It was as if he had been in a ten-year coma of hopes.

The first step was to make a rough sketch of what he remembered of the motor pool at Da Nang. It had been under canvas, with generators supplying electricity to the motor pool as well as to the other divisional activities.

He could only dimly remember where the various shops—transmission, main motor, and such—were placed in the tents. The whole place took up the space of a city block. He marked off the parking area where vehicles were to be parked and stored. He left a big blank space for the generator in one corner of the drawing, as far as possible from the shop. The noise and exhaust fumes of the diesel he wanted out of the way.

The whole was to be in a one-story building made of bamboo. It would have to be a dirt floor, he decided. Work benches would run down both sides of the shed. The sides would be more or less open.

The site for the shops had been predetermined, and the whole plant was to be completely fenced for security. The site was a drained paddy, the largest, flattest area available that was close to the entrance road.

Boxcars full of parts and tools, with every indication that they were straight out of the U.S. expeditionary force's stores, started arriving at the station at Yen

Bai. Vehicles started to pour in until the parking area, with room for about fifty vehicles, was close to full.

Many of the vehicles had been purposely damaged by the U.S. before they were abandoned to the advancing enemy. Some of the mechanics' most serious problems were engines that had been "burnt up" by running without oil, sand in the crankcases, smashed carburetors, battery acid in the crankcase, and just plain mechanical damage done with hammer blows to fragile parts. It was the small parts that caused the problems—generators, gaskets, belts, nuts, and bolts. Sometimes long hours would be spent patching together fuel pumps, carburetors, distributors, improvising or making home-built replacements where necessary.

The generator arrived in December, a vast machine on a wooden sled that had to be eased off its flatbed truck by close to one hundred ARVNs, all straining in unison. They first dug a hole in the ground, shallow and long, into which they backed the flatbed. By this method they got the wooden skids of the sled at the same level as the ground, and with greased planks they skidded it off.

While Garwood was studying the plans and diagrams, the ARVNs built a concrete base for the generator, rolled it to the place on wooden logs, and lifted it bodily onto the new base.

The assembly diagrams and instructions were easier than he had imagined—clearly this type of machine was designed for export to Third-World countries. He had to arrange for a fuel supply—in this case a fifty-five-gallon drum of diesel. The pickup ran directly to the fuel pump, and all that had to be done was to shift fifty-five-gallon drums of fuel.

ARVN electricians did the wiring to the shops and the general lighting. It was a proud moment when, using a truck battery, the diesel was started up for the first time. It rumbled into life with a healthy knocking sound and, according to the manual, was run-in for twelve hours. Garwood had to watch the entire process, reading the oil pressure and water gauges. The commandant sent him the reward of toil—his first North Vietnamese beer, which tasted bitter and unpleasant but made him almost immediately high, a boiled chicken in a bowl, and a pack of Dien Bien cigarettes. "Compliments of the camp commander," read the note.

In March of 1976, he got his first break. It had to do with a tank on a diesel "6-by" truck, a vehicle he knew well. The driver complained that the engine would start and then stop, as if the fuel pump were faulty or there were air in the feed. The mechanics checked fuel line and pump and found them to be in order.

In spite of the work done, the truck was checked out and came back twice with the same complaint. It was always all right when Garwood gave it its test, but then later would revert to the old symptoms. The camp commander told Garwood that "this time, check the work yourself, not only the results."

Garwood had no idea. But he checked the pump and the screen, taking off the fuel line where it entered the tank through a sizable plate. Then he reached his hand down into the tank to feel to the end of the feed tube.

His hand felt something soft and feathery and grasped it. It was a plastic bag, quite heavy. He drew his dripping hand to the surface. Emerging from the tank plate was a zip-loc plastic bag about the size of a shoe box. He pulled it gingerly past the opening and saw the glint of yellow metal.

No one else was nearby. It was midafternoon and the other mechanics were busy with jobs of their own. Shielding the bag with his body, he opened it, peered at the contents: twenty gold rings loose in the bag, and close to a dozen watches, diver's style, stainless cases. Expensive watches with luminous dials and date holes and sweep second hands. He was astonished. The watches shone like liquid mercury, like jewels in the dirt. Each watch was in its separate bag.

Watches like these were worth a lot of money, he knew. Soldiers who had served in the south boasted of them, sometimes wearing more than one, sometimes wearing them on chains around their necks. They loved gold. He wondered where this group of bands had come from, whether there had been fingers in them, fingers no longer of any use to their owners.

It was bright in the shed. He let his eyes pass slowly over each item, turning the watches in their tiny bags in his oily hand. The bag had floated into the fill in the tank, the thing had inevitably blocked it—yet when they blew it out, it yielded easily. Clever.

His mind moved like lightning. It was too big. If he showed up with a watch and a ring, there was only one way he could have got such a thing, and that was by stealing it. He thought of a time when he might have taken the things, hidden them for later use. But now, as a sign of how much he had changed, all he wanted to do was disassociate himself from the stuff. He couldn't just put it back into the tank, he thought muddily, because the feed would block again. He put the package on the seat, wiping it with his service rag, and busily reassembled the plate, the fuel line. He tested the truck's engine, sitting beside the package, barely noticing it gleaming and heavy beside him. He felt free of it.

The truck worked fine. He scribbled his OK on the windshield for the third, and he knew final, time. If they had only wrapped the package tighter!

The truck rolled off the work floor to the parking area. The routine was for the drivers to wait until the repairs were finished, then pick up their vehicles and go on. The driver sauntered over to the truck as Garwood swung down to the oil-stained ground. "Fix the trouble?" he asked, apparently unaware of the prohibition on talking to Garwood.

"Yeah," Garwood said under his breath to the man, now quite close to him. "I got your trouble, I found it." He pulled open the cab. "Here it is," he said evenly.

The driver moved like a man under sniper fire. He dove into the seat, his head swiveling, snatched the plastic bag and shoved it under the seat. "Has anyone else worked on the truck?" he asked, as he tried to resume the casual appearance of a driver getting ready to carry on with his routine duties. Garwood shook his head.

"No one's seen it," Garwood said.

The driver looked with relief that was almost hysterical at Garwood. He started a long explanation: "These were just some souvenirs I brought home from South Vietnam for my family . . ."

What the drivers had been doing, Garwood surmised, was confiscating watches and rings from ARVN troops, citizens, and anyone they could find to rob during their trips south to gather prisoners for the camps of the north. These were the "souvenirs."

Garwood said as little as possible. The man, at first defensive, later confidential, gradually grew less nervous as he talked and saw Garwood's neutral reaction. "There are opportunities to help you in this," he said, "but the authorities can't understand. Of course if something like this is reported, I must deny all knowledge. As far as I know, the things were on the seat when I returned after the truck had been repaired."

"No problem," Garwood said.

"I will be back tomorrow on the way south," the man said. "I will have a little something to better your health."

The next day, the man returned, leaving his truck outside the motor pool. He called Garwood over. Both men walked into the generator room. Shouting over the roar of the diesel he said, "That was a good job on the truck—we want to thank you for fixing the persistent problem. He pulled out a carton of English cigarettes in gold foil cartons, boxes of smooth cardboard, "555" brand. There were ten packs in the untouched carton. He also pulled out a Zippo lighter, brand new, a bag of nougat candy, five cans of condensed milk, a kilo of sugar. "Put this someplace safe."

Garwood knew that what the driver had just done was a worse offense by far than stripping prisoners who were, after all, the enemies of the "Democratic Republic." He was collaborating with the enemy by bringing food and presents into the prison camp and into Garwood's waiting hands.

Garwood, on the other hand, would be expected to take the articles, it was just in the nature of a prisoner to hanker after such things. He would be reprimanded, but if he turned on the generous driver, he would escape even a light punishment. "Why didn't the idiot leave well enough alone?" Garwood thought.

The driver left, with false smiles. Garwood split up the loot, stuffing some of it into the thatched roof, scattering the cigarettes, the milk cans and the sugar. He was one of the few men allowed near the generator, he knew, and he knew also that most of the guards were terrified of the noisy place, the warning signs in foreign languages, the great unknown of electric charges.

The lighter, on the other hand, he dutifully took to the camp commander's hooch, reporting that he had found it in a box of parts sent from South Vietnam. He piously noted that "the lighter was not a part for any vehicle. I thought I should report it." He handed the thing, which he had been sure to smear with grease and clay, toward Thuc. He waved it away.

"You may have it," he said.

He started doing his routine final checks with a good deal more care. He took out door panels, looked under the dash fascia, took the plates out of tanks. He always left the packages he would occasionally find, but he always managed to let the driver know what he knew. "I checked your door panel and it was loose," he'd tell a driver. "There was something stuck beind there, but I was able to adjust it."

He began to have a problem in storing the boots, tennis shoes, thermal underwear, C-rations (amazingly regarded as a gourmet treat), tins of fruit and meat, toothpaste, toothbrushes, razor blades, blankets. He was even offered American-published porno paperbacks. But he never got greedy. He only wanted enough extra food to vary the diet, enough clothes to keep warm. It took considerable ingenuity to "launder" some items.

He took two blankets that had been given to him new and trampled them in mud. He then reported that they had been used as packing for a box of used parts from the south. Could he have them to use? The request was granted. Garwood was never able to get all the stains out, but what the hell, he figured. For once, his solitude was working in his favor.

He began another enterprise—radio repair—in the wake of a request from the camp commander. He soon found that many of the guards had their own radios, some in disrepair. When Garwood began repairing the guards' radios, he began to get gifts of eggs, cigarettes, bananas. Even when the repairs failed, the guards were so grateful they gave presents.

It took months to gain the confidence of a wide circle of drivers. But at the same time, he had gained the confidence of the camp commander, partly because of his luck in getting the generator together, partly because of his carefully orchestrated "confessions" of trivial items of contraband.

He got a freer range of responsibility at the engine shop, and was soon told that he could instruct the mechanics as to which jobs got "priority." This was a rich source of new influence. Drivers with tight schedules would pay well for his cooperative directions to the crew of mechanics, and the mechanics themselves were drawn slowly in as Garwood distributed the "thanks" he got to the men who had worked hard and quickly on the "priority" jobs. But always, it was his aim to become more and more necessary to the various elements in his part of the camp, rather than trying, as others were, to increase his wealth. Money meant nothing to him.

By 1976, though the order had never been officially lifted, no one enforced the regulation forbidding conversations with Garwood. He could talk freely with the guards, the drivers, some of the cadre. Rather, they talked to him, as they found how quickly and well he fitted in with the operation of the machine shop.

20
A Slim Chance

IN DECEMBER of that year, Garwood was given a pair of blue corduroy pants and a white shirt, and was told he was going to Hanoi with the camp commander. "In appreciation for your determination and progress since arriving at Camp Five," he was told, he would have the honor of accompanying Thuc to the capital city.

They drove in a jeep with a guard without a weapon. It was a long, mostly silent ride.

"Circumstances should be made favorable for you to have your first Christmas in unified Vietnam," Thuc told him. Garwood could not believe that he had forgotten Christmas altogether—it was December 24.

They went to what appeared to be a large house where they were expected, but entered through the back door. There was a dining room set up for the members of the party, the camp commander, and two or three civilians whom Garwood did not know. The guest of honor was Colonel Thai, the security chief of the Democratic Republic of Vietnam, a member of the Central Committee of the Communist Party of Vietnam.

It was a peculiar dinner altogether. The food was brought by young female attendants in traditional Vietnamese garb, the graceful combination of long white pants with a dress over them, long hair tied carefully behind their ears.

There was a fish dish, two meats, four vegetables, two huge common dishes of rice, soup. But no wines. Garwood was given a single beer, which he sucked down lustily. The other guests took their lead from the ranking men, leaving curiosity behind and carrying on in a manner that was so correct it became complicated, except that all knew exactly how to perform.

Cigarettes were brought out when appetites were finally sated. Garwood asked if he could visit the lavatory. Thuc looked worried, as much that he might leave some dainty behind as that he might lose his exotic prisoner.

He was given strict instructions where to go, and told to talk to no one. He went down a corridor, through a door and suddenly found himself in what seemed to be the lobby of a large hotel. The carpet felt soft under his unaccustomed feet, there was a smell of cigarettes in the air. But what amazed him was that though the room he had dined in was neatly painted and complete and comfortable, this room was another world. Oil paintings hung on the paneled walls, ornate European furniture stood in patterned disarray, the clink and noise of a bar could be heard—it was suddenly the real world, not the Orient. The corridor between the small dining room and the lobby was like a space warp for him.

He moved as slowly as he could toward the lavatory described to him. He saw faces, white faces, Europeans or Americans, he wasn't sure, sitting in the lounge chairs, standing by the bar. He could catch no sound of English. The men were dressed in suits and ties, the women in dresses. He could hardly tear his eyes away from these creatures.

He reluctantly went to the bathroom and got another shock. There were urinals, rich porcelain with crystals which made perfume from the sour smell of urine. Behind wooden partitions there were toilets, so dear and lost and familiar. Lovingly he flushed both of them, listening to the roar of the water. He went to the sink to wash his hands and felt that someone was watching him. He looked up.

Chrome strips held the large mirrors in place, and his eye first went to them, and then he had a moment of confusion as the forty-year-old man, apparently in the next unit of this large lavatory, stared at him. But the old man didn't go away. Thin and pale, eyes sunken, it was a nightmare image of the Garwood he knew himself to be. His hair was thin at the top, and there were white straggles. His eyes were surrounded by patches of sallow purple, wrinkles stood out on his forehead; he started in shame, putting a hand to his own face.

For several minutes he stood there, staring at his image, trying to meet himself. It was no good. He was gone and in his place was a stranger. He noted later that it was practically the only public bathroom he had ever been in without graffiti scrawled on the walls.

He tried to compose himself on his way back to the corridor. At least he had struck it rich in his uncontrollable urge to see everything there. In the trash basket there had been a cheap plastic comb, with only a couple of the large teeth broken. He stuffed it quickly into a pocket, feeling much better.

When he arrived back at the dining room, Thuc and the guard were the only men waiting. They faced the seven-hour drive back to the north in adverse conditions. The only favorable element was the night, which kept people off the street. But the visibility was bad and the tar slick, the air cold. The three passengers gradually fell into a state of near-comatose shivering, stopping only twice for tea at roadhouses.

He had trouble getting back into the little world he had built after that trip to Hanoi. His mind kept coming back to the picture of comfortable luxury, the well-dressed businessmen at the bar, the way that they looked at him. And the face he saw in the lavatory, which he still could not connect with his own. But he knew.

He went back to his usual routine of work, extracting small favors, distributing bribes. Everywhere he saw the camp changing, growing larger and more permanent. The brick kiln was in operation, there seemed no end of fresh prisoners from the south to join the camp. In this place, instead of moving the prisoners through, they moved the walls out, made more barracks, built more roads.

The motor pool no longer provided the comfort he had known before. He had blended into the camp lifestyle, he had worked his way up from prisoner to unpaid manager. His body had accepted the routine, and his mind had been quiescent. But the trip to Hanoi had split that wide open. The shock of the hotel. He had been thinking, working, sleeping exactly like one of them, hoping only to continue the flow of little gifts, comforts, penny-ante bribes. But the hotel!

He knew he would be tired after the trip, but not as tired as he found himself. There were sudden flashbacks to scenes of America, fresh fears at what he had seen in the mirror. "What's gonna happen to you?" that face he would never forget asked him. "Are you gonna spend the rest of your life runnin' generators in a prison?" The thoughts that had flooded his mind before the war ended were carted back, more grisly and doomed then ever. The seventeen-year-old punk who went into the Marine Corps and was spewed out into Da Nang was now thirty and looked forty-five. His whole life had been taken from him, and the frightening part of it was he could scarcely see how it had happened and where the years had gone. But they were all taken away forever. His mind now worked in Vietnamese and he saw things "their" way. When he saw a dog or a cat, he would see it as food. A bird to him, no matter how beautiful, brought on the thought of killing, of crunching the morsels of food between the teeth. Not now, but he *had* eaten rats with relish. One night, a few weeks later, he became ill.

At first he didn't register the feeling, but when pain stabbed at his stomach, he was caught by the ache and doubled up on his bunk. He felt his face growing hot and heavy, red swimming behind his eyes. He vomited hard, until it seemed that a muscular hand was pulling out his stomach mercilessly. Only yellow froth appeared, and the bitter taste.

He was like a man with great seasickness, the kind that leads to death because the body cannot take in any water. He felt very weak, tired of struggling with his stomach, and asked only for the periods of calm between the frightful spasms of retching. He lost the ability to measure time.

The first thing he noticed was that the walls were white, and he felt calm with the feeling that he was no longer in the camp. He was weak, but his stomach

285

felt like a friend, not the enemy, at least. He was content. There was a thin rubber tube firmly bound to the side of the bed he was in and the tube led into a metal needle, which was taped to his arm.

In three days he was walking around, wondering what had happened. It was a hospital with a tile floor with designs, polished and waxed, and the walls were white distemper. There were men in other beds, four to a room, with two men who looked like Caucasians and one who was a black. At first these amazing messages brought by his eyes were incomprehensible to his brain.

The whites must have been Cuban, for he knew it was Spanish they were speaking. The black spoke it also. His knowledge of Spanish was both limited and scatalogical—nor did he care to speak to these men. He was simply feeling his body return to life.

There was a Vietnamese doctor, another undifferentiated Oriental face like a thousand others, who spoke English. He seemed uninterested in Garwood's case, if that was what it was, because he seemed mainly concerned that Garwood was an American prisoner. Garwood learned this was Hanoi's Army Hospital 354, the same place he had been when he arrived so ingloriously from the south years before. He had no plan at all, spent his days sleeping, eating, staring at the ceiling, and trying to remember—what, he was not sure of.

Garwood's treatment was a mystery. Injections twice a day and medicine to drink. Every other day, a doctor would probe his stomach. It dawned on him that either they didn't know what they were doing, or they didn't care. After a week of this, and light meals of potatoes, minced beef in soup, real bread, and other new things, he was feeling better, physically at least. He began to explore his surroundings.

He noticed that the other patients were a silent lot; there were no Vietnamese there at all in the small ward he was in with about ten other rooms like his. There were Laotians, whites who by their looks might have been Russians, Cubans, Somalians (like one of his room-companions), or others.

There was a pecking order, but little cameraderie among his fellows. They seemed to take Garwood for granted, and kept their comments to the doctors and nurses.

But the silence was broken one day, to his surprise, by a man whom he had taken to be a Cuban, one of his own room-companions. Sitting on the terrace on the second story, where patients were encouraged to hang their washing to dry, the man broke the ice, saying hello in Spanish, making some comment about the afternoon. "No comprende!" Garwood answered.

"You speak English?" he said with surprise and pleasure. Garwood nodded. "I'm from Cuba, but I know a little. Call me Juan." He asked the usual things—how he was feeling, his malady, and so on. Garwood found that Juan's problem was persistent headaches. "Why are you sitting in the sun?" the Cuban asked, and when Garwood replied that he liked the feel of it, he asked curiously about Garwood's time in Vietnam.

Garwood did not want to let on that he was an American. He didn't know how they would react, these men who were all clearly Communists, all clearly allied troops. How had he ended up in a ward with these types? He gave evasive answers and found that questions about his background were not pursued.

Juan was clearly curious. For one thing, many of the other patients there had visits from officials, sometimes from embassy personnel of their own country. Garwood had none. Juan was fascinated by Garwood's mastery of Vietnamese, a language he considered totally impossible, in spite of his attendance at a North Vietnamese training school. The man was young and lighthearted, and when his headaches were not on him, filled with energy.

One night, about three weeks into his stay, he heard Juan's cheerful voice say, "*Eh, hombre!*"

Garwood walked out on the terrace to find the Cuban leaning against the side of the building eyeing him. "You can speak the lingo pretty good, eh?"

When Garwood nodded, he said, "You know any Vietnamese girl?" Garwood shook his head. Juan asked him lightly if he was married, then lifted his eyebrows. "You want to go have a beer with me?" he asked. Garwood said that he had no money. The man smiled, flashing strong teeth. "No problem. I have the money—you have the lingo."

"Where we gonna go in this place for beer?" Garwood said.

"To the hotel, of course!"

"I don't know the way to this hotel." Juan said this was no difficulty. Garwood mentioned the guards. He looked at him again with a queer look. "Guards never stop me," he whispered, "what reason the guards stop me?"

"Okay, okay," Garwood said, "I never tried it. But all I have is hospital clothes, I got no good clothes." Juan shrugged this off, speaking of his suitcase where he could "borrow" Garwood some clothes.

Garwood decided he would go. What are they gonna do? Shoot me? he thought.

He was dressed in tennis shoes, too-short trousers, and a sports shirt. Together, they walked out a side gate, watching a sleepy guard nod to them genially. There was not even a show of cards or papers.

They walked down busy streets. Juan kept his eyes ahead, ignoring the inevitable Oriental stares. Within about four blocks, the pair of patients walked up the steps of a building clearly marked "Tourist Hotel" in several languages. The place was ground-level, clearly not posh. Inside, the lobby was a single large room with tables, a bar, and the hotel restaurant. Garwood noted a great number of incurious Asian faces, Laotians, a couple of Europeans, and Vietnamese serving people. The Laotians were in military uniforms, apparently of their own country, or at least, to Garwood's eye, different from the NVA uniforms he had become accustomed to.

They sat down at a table, Garwood trying to keep cool, collected and nonchalant.

Juan was behaving as if he owned the place, greeting the waiter, who gave not a second glance to the American. He ordered four cans of Asahi beer.

Juan gulped one beer, sucked greedily at a second, and while Garwood sipped politely at his, reached for the third. He grew mobile and active, asking the waitresses to come over, then finding himself unable to talk to them, clumsily asking Garwood to translate, then throwing up his hands as the girls, thinking the foreigner was only asking for some rare drink, continued to ask questions to which Garwood was loath to respond with the coarse answers his mentor supplied.

He went to the bar to pay his bill. Garwood told him he had to go; after some argument, Juan agreed. "I'm in a different situation at the hospital than you," Garwood said. Juan seemed well flush with cash. He bought two cartons of cigarettes, a couple of pounds of candy. Grandly, he gave Garwood one of the cartons.

Juan ogled every female he could find on the way back. Garwood could not get used to the idea that the man was acting more than normal in this foreign city of black-eyed watchers—he was actually acting as if he were on the prowl.

"Hey, don't you know it's dangerous to make advances to a Vietnamese girl?" he asked.

Juan looked unconcerned, shrugged, and frowned as if to say that Garwood had reacted too strongly. There was no further incident, and they both clattered up the stairwell and into their room, where their return was greeted with a welcome indifference. There was no aftermath. It was too easy.

The night on the town made Garwood into a man who thought again.

In the heart of Hanoi the eyes had checked and glanced on. Two guest soldiers, the eyes said. He talked again with Juan. There were no papers, no IDs. All he had to do was keep being a guest soldier—a Cuban, Palestinian, Russian. He had the best identification of all—he was a European, not an Asian. Whenever the subject of nationality came up, he avoided it. He would simply smile, and the mysteriousness was greeted with respect. The others may well have thought Garwood was an American or that his mission was such that it must be kept secret. This kind of thing they could understand.

He decided he could not become a better "buddy" to Juan, whose libidinous desires kept him asking this Vietnamese speaking friend if he wanted to share another evening of waitresses and beer. He began to wonder how much longer this little paradise could continue, and then it ended.

He learned later that someone had blundered—either a guard or an official at the camp—and he was not supposed to occupy quarters with other nationals. They were clearly quite upset when the matter came to light. A member of the camp cadre, sent to check on his health, quickly had him switched to a private room in another building.

It was only a few days after that his cure was considered complete. He once again made the long, cold trip north in a jeep, feeling bed-weak and pasty in his thin coat as they bounced up the long road.

He resumed his old duties, but he found he could cope once again. The hospital visit had set the stage for a new series of mental dramas with which he filled his mind as he went through the day at the motor pool. There was a glimmer, a crack in the blackness, a vague shape out there somewhere, which he tried to bring into focus. If he could only get into Hanoi at the same time as an American delegation—he knew they were visiting. But it would have to be blind luck. He would have to try to get into Hanoi frequently; as frequently as possible.

He saw hope in the trucks. The trucks ran constantly back and forth, the drivers brought supplies, and especially parts, from the railhead at Hanoi. He already had the trust of the drivers, or at least their acquiescence.

But there was no way he could demand a quid pro quo. The Oriental mind did not work so straight. There had to be diplomacy, there had to be indirection, there had to be an offer, sympathy.

The first thing he had to do was to consolidate his position in the motor pool. He began to make noises and moves to improve the efficiency of the motor pool. He reported to the camp commander that all was not exactly well with the organization. Often, he said, a job would have to be delayed because parts had not been available from their own salvage yard, and drivers sent to Hanoi to pick up a distributor would come back with a generator. There were problems with the quality of the parts, also. The drivers, many of them just country people, couldn't tell a piston that was worn to the point of uselessness. The drivers agreed, not wishing to make the mistakes they couldn't help.

Garwood proposed he should go to the city, where large stocks of parts were warehoused—no mistakes, no delays. There would be savings, he told the commander, there would be efficiency.

Yet the camp commander was reluctant. He was totally responsible for Garwood, he said. "This trust is placed by the commander himself, security chief of all Vietnam," he complained. "What if something happens?" It became clear that the man had no fear that Garwood would escape, but that he would not have total control over the prisoner for a day or more.

Surprisingly, the drivers took his case up vigorously. "This is a good idea," one driver told the commander. "We are saved time, gasoline," which was strictly rationed. The commander shrugged his shoulders uneasily. "I need time to think this over," he said.

It took longer than a couple of days, but when the backlog of needed parts including tires, starters, generators, and piston parts reached truckload dimensions, he told Garwood to be in charge of the requisition in Hanoi.

"Stick close to your driver and the guard I am sending with you. If you wander off by yourself, the security police may think you are a spy. The dangers from this are extreme."

It was a happy day for Garwood when he made that first trip under his own power into Hanoi in a "6-by" truck. The mission was to get the parts and return immediately. They took off at dawn, the truck driven by one of the regular drivers, a man known by Garwood to be active in the business of "bringing north" valuables. He was a relaxed man, as was the guard, whom Garwood did not know, but who seemed not very bright but well furnished with patience. The truck could only make an average of thirty-five to forty miles per hour because of the clogged road. But in the warm cabin of the big truck, the three men became quite conversational.

The guard was a Hanoi man who complained he had not been home for six months. He and the driver worked out a little "liberty" scheme whereby the guard would get home for two or three hours while the driver took the papers, loaded the truck, and picked him back up. It seemed like a bad deal for the driver, but Garwood did not question that.

The driver agreed and after passing through the outskirts of the city, they dropped the guard off. They bumped past railroad tracks and gray warehouse buildings, pulling up next to a yard with three buildings. There was little trouble filling the order and stowing the items in the back—it took a little over an hour, leaving about two hours to kill before the time agreed upon for the return trip.

Garwood, sitting in the cab for a smoke after loading, told the driver casually about his stay at the Army hospital and how surprised he had been that he could simply walk out onto the street and into a hotel where they sold, and clearly were in the habit of selling, cartons of foreign cigarettes, bottles of whisky and other items that "a man would give an arm and a leg for with the restrictions as they are."

The driver could never go into these "Tourist Hotels"; only foreigners were allowed. Garwood had a suggestion.

"If I had some clothes, I could get in and out of one of those hotels—no problem at all, I did it before," Garwood suggested bluntly. "They'd think I was a Russian or something.

"I'd just walk in, and if I had some money, I'd just buy the stuff—candy, cigarettes, liquor—and walk out."

The guard finally seemed to be thinking, the wheels turning like an ancient waterpump run by peasants' bare feet in a paddy field.

"You could," he said, "you could do it. What do you say when a Russian or a Cuban comes up to you and asks what you're doing?"

"Unless it was official, I'd tell them nothing. That it was none of their business. Unless I did something really suspicious or out of place, I'm sure no one would really ask me for anything. People go there to drink and have fun."

They had wasted about forty-five minutes in conversation, with Garwood gently trying to tempt this reluctant smuggler whose door panels he knew often carried jewelry, sugar, electronics.

"But what are *you* doing it for?" the man asked.

"I thought that if I helped you, you might let me have a pack of cigarettes, or a beer."

"You really miss that, eh?" the driver looked curiously at him.

"If you know anything about Americans at all, yes, I do."

Garwood was wearing his blue work clothes, stained with oil and rust and grimy at knee and wrist. "I would find it hard to get clothes for you," he ventured. But he turned, and poking with his hand behind the seat in the V-shaped storage place, he pulled out his pack and produced a pair of blue jeans, a T-shirt of bright orange, and a pair of flip-flops. "Try these on."

The man said no more, but drove through what looked like the Oriental version of a suburb—a continuous series of villages, clumped up and close to one another. They came to a largish lake, dominated by a sprawling, modern, and luxurious-looking place called "Hotel Victory."

The driver stopped the truck on the main route, about three hundred yards from the gate that led to the hotel. Garwood could see Caucasian faces, men, women, and children even, and sedans driving up to the front of the place. Feeling as conspicuous as a gaping wound, he walked "casually" up to the hotel. He noticed to his discomfort that the place had a complement of guards or police in tan uniforms, some with automatic weapons.

In his pocket he had one hundred dongs in ten-dong notes, which had been pressed on him by the driver, who had whispered "get anything—the main thing is cigarettes, wine, whisky, any canned goods." He motioned him to hurry.

Garwood was imagining wildly how this caper was ever going to be explained—how an American had got through the security into one of the tourist hotels, how he had bought whisky and then been arrested.

But no one took a bit of notice, as if the outlandishly dressed foreigner must *not* be stared at. One of the security guards nodded politely. He walked in, and found quickly that one side of the lobby was taken up with what looked like a snack bar, and on the other side was the front desk with slots for keys in a wooden counter. The style was the amazing thing—not Oriental, it was really like nothing he had ever seen before, flowers and curtains and decorative elements, even a television set in the lounge.

Garwood walked slowly toward the snack bar, a half-formed plan in his head. Stay in the hotel as long as possible. Try and overhear conversations, try to get close to people who look Caucasion without raising their suspicions—and get the goodies for the driver.

He sat carefully down at a small table in the snack bar. He couldn't tell what nationality the other customers were, but he did not get the feeling that they were English-speaking. He didn't dare use English himself. He occupied himself with the menu that was posted behind the bar, many brands of liquors, cigarettes, tinned hams, chocolates, other imported items, with foreign currencies, dollars, francs, lira, marks—and dongs. He ordered two cartons of Vietnamese cigarettes, Tu Do brand, Russian sherry, which seemed the best price; the money was soon spent. He looked for a newspaper and saw none. With his purchases they gave him a shopping bag of synthetic material; he had never seen one before, but the bag reassured him, like having his own papers. He wandered into the lounge, sat on one of the couches. Listen as he would, he could hear no English spoken. The time passed too fast. He rose to leave and walked out of the entrance reluctantly. From over fifty yards away he could see the driver's nervous face. Garwood smiled the first genuine smile in months.

291

The driver didn't even notice what had been purchased. He just wanted to get away, and it wasn't until they were on their way to pick up the guard that he peered into the bag at a traffic stop. His face lit up as he saw the heavy bottles in their flimsy wrapping of tissue, the cigarettes in their cardboard. He flipped open one carton, shoving a packet across the seat.

"Keep them out of sight of the guard," he told Garwood. The guard was like a child after a visit to Santa. He had a box of rice cookies that his wife had given him and he chattered happily about his family. He didn't even ask where the others had been.

When he finally assessed the mission, Garwood was surprised to find that the camp commander was more pleased than any of the participants with the trip to Hanoi. For the usually stiff and reserved man to show the relief he did was unusual. Something perhaps that Garwood could use, too.

He was able to travel to Hanoi under the same regime a week later. The same guard came along. He had put in for the duty and was pleased to get it. The driver was the same man as well.

After they let the guard off for his "liberty" they went to another hotel, parking on a side street in downtown Hanoi. Garwood walked a few blocks as directed, and found himself in front of "Hotel Independence," obviously a structure from the French period—terrazzo floors, high ceilings, fans stilled by the winter chill. He wore the same ludicrous orange shirt and blue jeans but found he got glances of admiration rather than oddity. It must be the jeans, he figured. Though they were not as thick a material as he remembered, they were the same shade. This time be bought two hundred dongs' worth of goods and was standing at the cashier's end of the counter when a Caucasian in slacks and loafers and a short-sleeved shirt began joking with one of the waitresses. At first he didn't believe it, but he heard the words as if from an old-time record. The man had said just a few words, but he was sure it was English. The waitress responded in English.

He just stood there at the counter while the chance that he had dreamed about stood beside him. The Caucasian ordered a drink, clearly in a cheery mood. "Hello," he said companionably. Garwood murmured something. He introduced himself as Paul, said he was New Zealander, a journalist.

"My name is Roberto," Garwood said in a flash of inspiration.

The man smiled knowingly. "Cubano, I presume?"

Garwood just smiled back. "Are you in a hurry?" the man asked. Garwood shook his head expectantly. "Well then, have one with me. Not many speak English here."

"Sure," Garwood said, trying to think how to speak in Spanish accent in a language he could hardly remember without stumbling.

Paul quickly told how he had come to Vietnam after covering the China-Vietnam border conflict. "Been up to the border y'self, mate?"

Garwood shook his head. "New Zealand is a neutral country?"

Paul nodded brightly. Garwood was poring over the hundreds of thoughts

292

swarming in his head. Take a chance? But a journalist! He sat while the conversation lagged from Garwood's side. He knew nothing to say, and Paul thought he was a Cuban. He wanted to tell him he was an American, but years of caution were yelling silently at him. He said nothing, merely tried to nod along with the flow of talk. Paul was telling him how he planned to drive up to the border with a film crew the next day. Garwood asked him, "Do you have your notebook?"

The man nodded, pulling out a spiral pad. "If you let me borrow it, I'll put in something you will find very interesting," Garwood said slowly.

The man handed over pad and pencil with a shrug. "You won't read this until you are in your room?" Garwood asked.

"Okay," Paul responded.

"My name is Robert Russell Garwood," he wrote in his stiff but clear handwriting. "I am a member of the United States Marine Corps, captured September 1965 in South Vietnam. #2069669. I request that you please give this letter to any U.S. embassy, military establishment, or simply mail it to the U.S. Post Office." He wrote: "Father, Jack Russell Garwood, 430 N. Takoma Avenue, Indianapolis, Indiana."

Garwood stood up, shook the other man's hand, and trying to show all the urgency he could in his eyes, left decorously with his bag of contraband. He walked slowly out the hotel door and down the street, steeled for the scuffle of fast feet or the shout that never came.

Tension filled the next few days. Garwood kept a wary eye on the camp commander and the comings and goings near his hooch. One thing out of the ordinary would have spooked him—not that he could have done anything about it.

He would take whatever they dished out. What excuse was there for a note in his handwriting?

Day by day the tension eased. He continued to work at the motor pool with the same feeling that one has with a bad cold—the cold in the foreground, the job something to be weathered while the cold lasts.

Garwood figured that he would set two weeks as the limit that he could expect something to happen. The note proved that there was an American still in the prisons of North Vietnam five years after the war was over; that Vietnam had lied.

But the days passed, and kept passing, and the men in the motor pool were wondering why Garwood was so silent and stand-offish, preoccupied, not his normal self.

With an added wariness but no other outward sign, he began to return to his old manner. Morning meal, off to the shop, the mechanical work, the occasional passing of contraband. The guard and the driver did not discuss another voyage. Cigarettes and candy were what he got—the usual—and at no time in his life in prison had he ever been more thankful for the usual.

He had passed the note to Paul in the fall of 1977. The fall and early winter dragged by cold and windy—he almost longed for the monsoon with its sensual fury, rather than this iron season with feet always wet in the mud and the tools rusting, fires blowing smoke as the mechanics tried to remain comfortable.

In the spring, a new type of prisoner appeared, to be put to work in the rice paddies. They were considered "suspected Chinese sympathizers," according to what he could cull from the broadcasts. They were called the Woa people, and for all he could discover, they suffered the same fate as the Japanese internees in California in World War II—they were gathered and incarcerated for the crime of having Chinese ancestry and living in Vietnam. They had no sentences. The radio spoke only of the "fleeing from Vietnam to China of the Chinese people." But there was no explanation. Garwood heard that "Chinese infiltrators" had tried to contact indigenous Chinese in the country and told them of a "coming invasion" by which they would be endangered.

Garwood noticed them only by their slightly rounder, flatter faces. Otherwise they were simply other bodies, clad always in the monotonous pajamas, tending to the endless duties of rice cultivation on the hillside terraces.

The Woa were considered political prisoners, and were allowed to have their families with them. Their guards were government police, not military, considered harsher than the military guards.

Time churned out its allotment of same days; none of them brought relief to Garwood's increasingly intense belief that the device he had used to attract attention was the only practical one to consider trying again.

Every time he had made another trip to Hanoi for parts—on average, twice a month—he merely went to the hotels as with blinkers. He didn't want anyone to get used to his face, so he varied the hotels he visited.

The new element in the scheme was a new driver—and he was eager to join in their little scam to get hold of the cigarettes and the liquor. The original driver was only mildly annoyed that a new man had come into the scheme. But unlike Western black marketeers, they cooperated, pooling their money to make larger purchases. This changed Garwood's operation slightly, for with the extra cash he found it convenient and safe to visit more than one hotel, where he could buy without attracting the attention that always comes to a big spender.

The radio was reporting daily on a war between China and Vietnam over the border of the two countries. It was amusing to hear Hanoi Hannah in her new role as defender of the Republic against a Communist rather than an American invader. She laid heavy stress on the fact that Vietnam followed the precepts of the Russian Communism—the "right path"—while the Chinese were "adventurers . . . expansionists who scheme world conquest."

"Socialist invaders" was as close as she came to calling the Chinese Communists.

The workload in the motor pool did not change much, but the smuggling business was slowed down because gasoline was rationed to the extent that only the most urgent needs would justify a trip. When Garwood did visit the capital

294

during the period of war hysteria, he saw it thronged with soldiers and bristling with weapons, slogans everywhere on buildings condemned China and urged the people to "unite to throw out the old enemy."

But nothing had happened with the note. Nothing at all, and Garwood remained inert, unable to make his move.

21
Freedom!

IN DECEMBER, Garwood almost expected some sort of ceremonial trip to Hanoi, as he had enjoyed in the past. He wondered as Christmas Day passed. Instead, he was given a chicken, a couple of bottles of beer, and some cigarettes. He had acquired a pet monkey by this time and the two of them made a solitary kind of party, because he hadn't really expected to be there. They boiled the chicken, Garwood talking to his pet in Vietnamese. The monkey was intensely interested in the chicken, and helped him to pluck it, but he was disturbed by blood. Garwood had to calm him when he saw the entrails.

Later, they gave Garwood an explanation. The camp commander told him, "It is the intensity of the situation. Even foreign visitors have been told to restrict their activities in the city."

In January, things seemed to have eased. The threat of Chinese invasion seemed to evaporate, with the radio claiming a victory, stating that the Vietnamese had "driven the invader back into his lair," and that negotiations were at hand.

In the first week in January, Garwood was taken out of the hooch that had been his home for three and a half years. He was simply told to move. He was appalled, like an old pensioner who finds his favorite park bench is gone. He had fitted the little building out with blinds of a sort against the sun, a hammock, some furniture, including a chair much like the cane chairs with fanlike backs that are now popular imports, his fishing poles and nets, two cooking pots, cups and bowls that he had fashioned out of oil pans, oil filter casings and other bits from the motor pool. It was all junk, but somehow precious.

The move was to a compound area, where he found himself sharing a hooch with a Thai pilot who had been captured as he flew innocently into Vietnam airspace in a monsoon rainstorm, had engine trouble and bailed out. The man spoke English, at least some, and claimed he had got training "in the Texas airfield."

Garwood was puzzled, not alarmed. It had been almost a year and a half since he had passed the note to the man "Paul," and nothing had happened.

The hooch was further from the motor pool, causing him to walk half a mile to the job. There were guards on the gate of the compound. Their living space was enclosed by a stockade. The pilot, Son, was an older man, in his forties, who had been knocking around North Vietnamese prisons since 1963. He had half of the hooch and Garwood the other half, with a communal table in the middle. He was a silent and morose man who seemed half-mad, assuring Garwood that he could not give his real name. He had been accused of spying for the United States, a country he hated as much as that of his captors. He could never forget the injustice of this accusation, and his conversation centered around his total innocence, when on a routine mission he wandered into Vietnamese airspace. He did not like Garwood's monkey.

Garwood always kept a small lamp burning in the hooch to light his cigarettes and show the way to the latrine at night. He made another one for Son and presented it to him. But the older man came into Garwood's section of the hooch one night to relight his lamp, and the monkey attacked him like a watchdog, nipping his hand. It was a chill to the relationship.

It was two days before Tet, January 29, when the camp commander announced that both he and Son would be allowed to go to Hanoi. "You will be allowed to see a film and visit the museums and attend a Tet dinner. You will be able to see the fireworks planned by the city celebrating the victory over the Chinese," he told the two men. Son seemed completely indifferent to the news; but Garwood eagerly prepared for the trip. No plan of escape or note-passing was in his head, but it would be good to get away from the camp, not on a hasty illicit side trip, but as a holiday.

He dressed in a yellowed white shirt issued to him three years before, blue pants, a pair of sneakers that were the fruits of a deal with one of the drivers. He shaved and washed for the trip, turned up early at the appointed place to find Son, a guard, a driver, and a Vietnamese lieutenant he had seen around the camp. Five in a jeep for six and a half hours! It was not the best way to contemplate a holiday.

The trip was far longer than those he remembered from the trucking days. There were several checkpoints, presumably hangovers from the latest war emergency, so that it was a late winter nightfall when the cargo of men, road-weary, chilled, and agonizingly stiff in the joints, rolled into the outskirts of Hanoi, past the warehouses to a sort of freight yard in the warehousing section. The men were showed to rough accommodations in part of a warehouse, and were given a skimpy supper of vegetables, rice with fish sauce, and tea.

They had readied themselves for sleep on bamboo cots when two officials arrived. The men were in military uniforms but without rank, though it was clear they were officers, not enlisted. The visitors were genial, and told the pair of prisoners that they would be getting new clothes in the morning and would be escorted to the Hanoi Museum. In all, they were told, they would be in the city five days, and they would have a "program" each day. They were not to wander off, as without identification they might be arrested by security forces.

Early in the morning, in the dim and chilly warehouse, a man brought two boxes of clothes—for Garwood, blue pants, blue shirt, leather sandals, and a blue jacket made of poplin with a zipper front. In spite of poor fit, Garwood felt a new man in the new clothes. "Do we keep these?" asked Garwood as the bemused guard watched the scrawny American slip them on. He nodded.

They were taken into the center of the city, to the "museum," which turned out to be a museum of the war against the "American aggressors." There were uniforms, weapons, every sort of military hardware, bits of B-52 bombers claimed shot down—and a text that drove home a single point: The Americans had been beaten by an invincible foe.

Garwood silently watched and listened to the guide who took them on a tour. The place seemed popular with the natives—school classes and citizens thronged the halls, gazing at the exhibits, but not taking the slightest notice of the pale Caucasian who followed the guide. There were other Caucasians, too, Garwood noticed, but he could not spot their nationalities. The only difference he could note was that most of the men he saw from the West wore suits and ties.

He spent most of the day there with Son, and returned to the warehouse at dusk. The next two days, the pair visited a lifetime's worth of Democratic Republic of Vietnam sights: another museum celebrating the war with the French, amazingly similar to the "historical museum" of the day before, except in the age of the artifacts; the mausoleum of Ho Chi Minh, a vast floodlit building decked in flags, fronted by a park, planted with flowers. Guards in dress uniform, all white, with perfectly maintained carbines, and, for once, boots, stood to attention outside.

But it was not permitted for the visitors to enter, as the guide acidly explained, "Only patriots may view the remains of President Ho Chi Minh."

The fourth day began the same. This time the museum was a complete history of the country, starting four thousand years ago when the country was ruled by kings. This Garwood found the most interesting of the displays. They had bodies of kings, lying in caskets of state, there were displays of dress, tools, household utensils. Garwood was amazed to see that in many ways, the items of everyday use were the same as those that he had seen being used in the jungles and villages. The same tools, the same rude plows, the same agriculture, architecture and customs.

Part of this museum illustrated the life of Ho Chi Minh from birth to death. One interesting sidelight was a placard telling of the visit of Henry Kissinger, U.S. secretary of state, to the museum in 1973.

The day dragged after that, and in the evening they returned, weary as only reluctant museum wanderers can be. But at the warehouse was a new arrival, one of the drivers from Camp 776, the younger man who had been with Garwood in many a profitable Hanoi trip before the Chinese border war heated up.

The younger man had been assigned to them for the last day of the holiday. It was the eve of Tet, and Garwood and Son found themselves with the driver in the empty warehouse. The guards had simply disappeared.

The driver made a slight motion to Garwood and the two men sauntered toward the door. Outside, the mist was gathering and the lights of the city glowed like a luminous fuzz on one horizon. On the other, blackness without a star. "What is your plan for the evening?" the driver said eagerly. "Let's go to Hanoi." The man's eyes were bright with the chance. It had been a long dry spell for the smugglers.

"You think it's safe?" Garwood asked, knowing that this man was both young and incautious.

"It's no problem, because everyone has gone home for Tet," he said.

"What about the other man?" Garwood asked. He could not trust a man whom he hardly knew and who he expected was mentally unbalanced to boot.

"I will tell him you were called away to repair a vehicle," the young man improvised. Garwood shrugged. He had nothing to lose, and the young man was taking the greater chance. He could simply say he had done what the driver, a Vietnamese soldier, had told him in the absence of others to give orders.

The driver was brief in his instructions to Son, and in a few minutes the two men were speeding down side streets toward the Victoria Hotel, the one with the lake, about a mile from the city center.

"There will be a lot of people here tonight—many foreigners. You will not even be noticed." But they parked a fair distance from the entrance and Garwood walked into the pool of light armed with his blue poplin windbreaker jacket with about a thousand dongs bulging in his pocket. The driver told him not to worry about spending such a large sum, but to say that he was making preparations for a party.

In the hotel, music flowed from a band—it was a kind of jerky fidgety style of dance tune, definitely Western in origin, and people flowed, smoking, puff-faced, many of them rosy with drink, billowing with it.

He headed for the snack bar where he had successfully bought before, and saw a table with four relatively quiet people sitting there. The place seemed empty except for the four. Everyone seemed to be out with the band and the merrymakers in a large room off the lobby. The noise was like waves in the distance. The two women attendants saw his face at the counter and shouted out that they were having a bite—he should wait a minute or two.

Garwood picked the table closest to the counter, where he could watch the door and the two couples. He noted, almost without thought, that they were speaking English. The men wore business suits, the women dresses. All were middle-aged.

One of the men with his back to Garwood said something about "Washington . . . next week," and Garwood's entire sensory apparatus froze like a setter dog on point. He stayed quiet, trying to catch another sound, straining for it. He thought of other Washingtons, wondered why he had been so inattentive in his classes as a youth; but he could think of no other Washington besides Washington, D.C.

He didn't really think. He saw in front of him and to the side the smooth surface of the counter with a ballpoint pen on it, ready to write up receipts, and he found himself at the counter picking up the pen. He slowly took out the envelope the driver had given him with the money in it and laid it on the counter and his fingers, seemingly acting on their own, gently separated the flap from the rest of the paper pocket, which he stuffed away. He was left with a triangle of paper.

He quickly wrote on the bit of paper "I AM AN AMERICAN IN VIETNAM. ARE YOU INTERESTED?"

He rolled the paper as small as he could make it, got up, went over to the table like a zombie with the rolled-up paper in his right hand. He bent over the one he knew only as "Washington" and asked slowly and carefully, "Do you have a cigarette?"

Garwood saw a thin, lined face turn towards him, a pair of cautious eyes, a clean-shaven face. There was surprise in it. He picked a pack of cigarettes up off the table and offered Garwood one. He took out a lighter, a heavy metal object that hissed as the flint ignited it, and held the flame up to Garwood's cigarette. He quickly half-tossed, half-flicked the rolled-up note into the man's lap, and he could see that the toss registered. The man clipped the lighter shut and looked down, then screwed his eyes up in surprise.

"Thank you," Garwood said slowly again, looking at the face. He turned and went back to his own table and sat down.

He wasn't thinking about the contraband he was supposed to be buying or the weight of money, crinkling behind a paper envelope in his pocket. He sat at the table where he was, drawing deeply on the cigarette. Garwood looked ahead, and from the side he saw the man unrolling the note. The others were interested too, looking at the scrap of paper, but the man shook his head as if there were nothing to it. He turned his face toward Garwood, rising at the same time, and came over and sat at Garwood's table. Garwood, seeing the counter attendants, casually rose and walked to a table out of their line of vision. The man, getting the game, ambled after him. He sat, he said nothing.

"Are you interested?"

"Yeah," the stranger said.

With surprising difficulty, Garwood answered, "I'm interested. I was captured September 28, 1965, in South Vietnam," Garwood babbled, "and right at this moment I'm being held at a concentration camp about a hundred forty kilometers north of Hanoi." He was speaking quickly but was strangely uneasy with his words.

"What are you doing in Hanoi?" the man said cautiously, evenly.

Garwood tried to place the accent, could not, could not even tell what his own accent sounded like. "They brought me to Hanoi on occasion of Tet, the holiday," he said, his voice thick as a drunk's.

The man looked coolly. He raked the room with his eyes. "You alone?"

"No. Guard outside," said Garwood, unable to control his hotch-potch diction.

"Why are you here?" the man asked. Garwood felt he was not being believed. All his life he had not been believed. He felt a sharp pang of despair.

"That is not important. We don't have that much time to talk."

"What do you want me to do?" he asked Garwood.

Garwood's nervous energy rose quickly. He asked for the note back, and on it he wrote his name, rank, serial number, and U.S. Marine Corps. "I want you to take this and give it to any U.S. authorities and tell them that I'm alive, and want by any means possible to come home."

"What you're doing . . . aren't you afraid?" the man asked stupidly.

"Yeah, I'm afraid. But probably not as afraid as you are."

"I don't think I should be sitting here with you," the man said quickly, retreating palpably into a shell of nervousness. "How do you know me?"

"I don't. I heard you say something about Washington."

"Yeah?" said the other. "What do you do at this camp?"

"It's a forced labor camp north of Hanoi, several thousand prisoners." He could see one of the women looking half-curiously at him. "You've got to go now."

He started to get up. "How many others are there, like you too?" he asked.

"Fifteen others," Garwood said unblinkingly, hoping this lie would be believed, would make it more than just a single man's message on a torn bit of paper. The man nodded his head and walked slowly back to his table with the note.

Garwood walked quickly to the counter. He started ordering liquor and cigarettes. "Why are you ordering so much?" she asked coyly.

"Party," he said nonchalantly.

"If you want to buy so many things, you had better go to the desk outside in the main lobby and they will get cases for you." Garwood turned and left. He could see, from the side of his eye, the man's eyes following his face.

Outside he gathered a boxful of whisky, wine, candy, cigarettes, as much as he could carry, and stepped out into the night. He had not been able to spend all the money. He had to make an excuse to the driver about that.

"Anybody ask you?" the young man said in the gloom of the jeep.

"No . . . seemed everybody was drunk on their ass in there."

The driver gave Garwood a bottle of wine, a box of cookies, and some cigarettes, counted the change, and they headed straight back toward the warehouse with the loot. Garwood got out of the jeep with his share and watched as the driver disappeared with the rest. Where it was to end up he neither knew nor cared. Son was still up. With the goodies, Garwood approached him. "Happy New Year," Garwood said with the largest smile he could manage. The two shared the things. It was an odd party, Garwood trying his best to be merry on top of a feeling of intense nerves and Son growing sentimental with the wine and cookies.

One week from the day he came back from Hanoi he knew something had happened. Son was told to move, Garwood was left alone in the double hooch, and he was informed that he would not be going to the motor pool that day. Two guards were placed beside his hooch, and he was no longer allowed to make cooking fires.

Three days later, wordless, they bustled him into a jeep and drove him to Hanoi under heavy guard. He asked the guards what was going on. It was not punishment, it was not at all what he had imagined in his nervous imaginings. But the guards were chillier, and the motions had a purpose to them that was not favorable; he was told that he was going into the hospital for "a health checkup."

He was taken once more to Army Hospital 354.

The first day, it was as the guards had said.

The doctors pored over him, checking his heart rate, making blood pressure tests and other things. Then, on the second day, he was taken to a different room and laid down on what looked like an operating table. His pajama pants and sleeves were rolled up, his hands and feet were securely strapped.

It was at this point, as the gentle but completely masterful pressure of the wide straps were snugged down, that he began to worry and asked a nurse; she told him that the hospital had a new type of Russian machine, very sophisticated, which was used for checking the human nervous system.

"There's nothing wrong with my nervous system," Garwood protested.

"No one has said there was anything wrong," a voice responded out of his sight. "This is just to check your nervous system."

The machine was wheeled in. It was the size of a large typewriter, with an array of controls and gauges. From his back, he could see the wires of its complicated innards, different colors. The nurse began to rub some sort of salve on points of his body—forehead, neck, chest, arms, stomach. The stuff was put around his thighs, down to his ankles, it had little smell and glistened like Vaseline. Leather bands were placed around his head, his chest, arms, wrists, following the area that had been smeared. Wires were attached to the bands, which Garwood could see were themselves wired.

The machine was then turned on. It felt at first as if tiny needles, harmless but incredibly sharp, were shooting at will through his body. He was asked if he felt anything. He described the feeling.

"Move your feet," a voice commanded. He moved them. The same command was repeated for the other extremities. The machine was adjusted. The sensation went from needles to heat, very quickly. He felt like a radiator, as if

302

his blood was actually heated. Nausea swayed in the bottom of his stomach, and his vision began to dim and slip.

Garwood saw his arm move without control. He could not fight the muscles that were jerking his limbs around. He felt as if his limbs were aching, as if he had slept on them, numbing and paralyzing them. The last thing he remembered was a loss of discomfort and a slate-colored blackness descending on his helpless body.

When he awoke, the bands were gone, the nurses were wiping and washing the salve off his limbs. His body felt prickly, numb, as when blood returns at last to the arm that has been slept on.

A doctor leaned over him, solicitous about his feelings. "It will come back to you," he told Garwood, who was complaining about the sensation of numbness. "That's all for today, but we're going to have to run some tests on you." The doctor politely asked Garwood his name.

He had to stop and think for a minute. Then he remembered and told the man.

He was asked where he was, and felt the same separation and delay before answering. He could not remember the name of the hospital. To this and subsequent simple questions, he had similar trouble making an adequate response. He wondered, but without alarm, whether his memory had gone, and thought that this might not be a bad idea.

For a day he drifted, resting, taking three draughts of a chalkly liquid not unlike what he remembered being given as Milk of Magnesia. For nine or ten days he stayed in a state of drugged suspension, feebly fighting the waves of forgetfulness that seemed to close in each time his mind would take a channel into the past. They would ask questions, the simplest, and he could not answer. The doctors seemed neither pleased or upset about his loss of memory. They showed polite interest and persistence. Then at last, he was taken back to the camp, to his hooch, where he sat, ate, slept, and defecated for two days before he realized his monkey was gone. This upset him far more than the loss of memory. He angrily asked the guard to explain where the monkey was.

"He ran away," the guard said, looking like a man trying hard to look truthful. Garwood did not believe him. "The monkey heard others calling from the woods."

Garwood knew this was a lie, because the monkey was actually scared of the woods. It was a full week before he learned that the guards, thinking Garwood was gone for good, killed and ate the monkey.

He stayed under guard for over a week, not working, but mourning in some way for what he had lost, quiet and reserved, cautious, while the food was poured at him. There was more meat than rice, he got a can of condensed milk a day, the soup was thick.

He was left in his hooch for a miserable two and one half weeks, being given incongruous amounts of food, no company, no explanations. The cloud of speculation in his mind had not cleared. Whatever had happened with the note, he concluded, it had got to someone's hands and eyes.

In the second week of March a jeep came. The guard ordered him into it and they set off for Hanoi. He was told to leave everything. He asked if he would return, and was roughly rebuked. He was crammed into the vehicle with driver, guards, and officers.

They drove straight to the center of the city. It was useless, now, to even try to start a conversation. And no one at 776 had bid him adieu. That was typical of this world. You were in it, and you were out of it, and there was nothing left of your passage, not a mark, not a wake, not a memory.

They arrived at one of the most heavily traveled streets of Hanoi, a street he had never seen before, and on one side there was a large military establishment, where they stopped. Garwood was taken through a ground-floor room with two beds in it. He noticed that the beds were made of wood, the first such he had seen in many years. There was a table and four chairs, and the number of chairs was an ominous sign.

Above him, directly over his room, there was a guard's room—he could hear them talking through the floorboards. He was taken there, given one of four beds. Being on the second floor was a strange feeling for one who had been on the ground floor for fourteen years, with a few days' exception. The food was nothing special, but there was plenty of it, rice with pork steamed into it, condensed milk, and bananas.

He could barely see out of the shuttered windows, through which filtered the sounds of a busy city street, a sound he couldn't get used to.

The next day, awakened, he was taken to a tailor shop on the street and told he was to have two suits made. He wanted to cry with joy, but something held him back. He couldn't really digest what these suits meant. One might have meant a pretty corpse, a bribe never to be delivered, a blind trap, an attempt to get him to reveal whom he gave the note to, but two—that could only mean future.

The suits were made of some dark worsted material, and he was outfitted with two white shirts. He went to a shoe store and was bought a pair of black leather shoes, the first real shoes, besides pilfered sneakers and sandals of tire tread, that he had worn in thirteen years.

Underwear, socks, one tie followed. Then back to his room where a full complement of guards seemed always on duty.

On the third day, the clothes were brought to him at midday. He was told to put one suit on, which brought a smile even to the sour faces of the guards. He tried to get a look at himself in the faint mirror that the window glass afforded, but all he could see was a dim shape. He was told to shave, and did so. Nobody had told him a thing.

Nothing happened through that long afternoon as he sat in the chairs or on the edge of his bunk waiting. He took off the suit eventually and folded it neatly on one of the chairs, and went to bed miserably as the guards sat at the table playing cards in a pool of light from a lamp. Even their radio gave no clue.

But bright and early a new figure appeared, wearing the rank of captain on a full-dress uniform. "Put on clothes," the man said, as if there were nothing at all out of the ordinary about sitting in a cell-like room for several days with nothing to do. "We are going to take some pictures." He dressed in the suit, which was too big, and the shoes, which he could tell would soon blister one of his heels, and wobbled out after the man to a jeep. It was a Russian vehicle, from the lettering on the instruction plate on the dash. Heavily guarded, he was driven to a green outdoor park, pleasant with flowers.

Citizens walked the paths—or he assumed they were the city folk of Hanoi, and Garwood and his party of military men seemed to garner no unusual glances. They walked deeper into the green space, to a water fountain. There the officer told him, "Stand here." Not ungently, he positioned Garwood in front of the fountain and, pulling a small camera from his pocket, shot some film. He then posed Garwood on a stone bridge nearby. He did not ask Garwood to smile, and Garwood didn't really feel like smiling in any case. The captain, in the manner of all amateur photographers, asked two passing children to pose with him, one on either side. They obeyed happily.

He shot a whole roll, and with the guards, they proceeded out of the park to a market area, where produce of every sort was displayed on both sides of a narrow street in a bedlam of activity. He was told to walk up and down the street between the stalls while the shutter clicked. They walked on to a hospital, an Army facility. More pictures.

Inside, he was taken to what appeared to be an empty dental clinic, and while the camera played about them, a "dentist" pretended to check Garwood's teeth. In another area, pictures were taken of a doctor pretending to give him an examination. On his way back to his room, more pictures were shot outside the building housing him. Garwood noticed that the guards, who wore their AK-47s like comfortable trenchcoats on a sunny day, were always out of the field of focus.

He was given a meal and photographed eating. Then bathing. Then shaving, while Garwood's spirits rose. There was always the knowledge that all these poses were leading nowhere. Yet it was good that they were doing these things, it boded well, to his thinking.

He slept easier that night.

Next morning he was told by a lieutenant colonel and the photo-taking captain that there were "some people who want to meet you." He was told that they were not Vietnamese, and he was told that "Vietnam has granted that you should meet with them."

Good, getting better, Garwood thought. Even if it was all phony, it was phony for a reason, and the reason could not be execution. The senior man told him in Vietnamese, "They will be speaking English. They are with a newspaper. We realize that your English is not very good, so any questions having to do with Vietnam or politics, we will help you to answer."

Garwood had figured that much. In the jeep again, he was sped to a hotel. He saw that it was the Victory, where he had passed the note, and all the positive signs dissolved in acid fear. That fucker was KGB, he thought wildly.

But in the hotel, there was no sign of the traveling "Washington" man. There

305

were four new guards, however, dressed in outlandish gear reminiscent of a gangster movie, black suits, white shirts, black ties, and black shoes. They carried no long weapons, only pistols, and the combination of cowboy and business thug was ridiculous.

They were ushered into the lobby, where foreigners could be seen, walking the lobby on whatever errands. But near the door were a Caucasian man, a Hispanic man, and an Oriental woman, all expectant in look and posture. The small group moved past and sat down on lounge chairs. The lieutenant colonel elaborately pulled out a packet of Salem cigarettes as a waiter sidled up to take orders for drinks. It was still only midmorning. The lieutenant colonel ordered coffee for the whole party. He had made no sign toward the little group at the door.

When the coffee arrived, almost simultaneously a Vietnamese woman in her thirties arrived. She seemed to be known to the lieutenant colonel, as the pair separated themselves and could be seen talking in a corner of the lobby. Garwood was mystified.

"We will retire to a room," the lieutenant colonel announced, and the group filed into a long room resembling a dining room, dominated by a long table, set with place settings, with couches lining the walls. A Vietnamese arrived, asked the colonel, "Will you meet the delegation, sir?"

"Just a minute," the lieutenant colonel said in a calm way. "I want to brief Bob."

He sat next to where Garwood had been placed on one of the sofas. "Do you know why you are here?" he asked gently.

"I was told for an interview," Garwood said. The soldier nodded.

"These are American newspeople," he said seriously, "who have found out about your presence here, and who have requested to interview you. The interview will be held now. We will help you with the questions, so your English should not be a problem to you. It is most important for you that you need our advice in how to answer these questions. Don't be afraid. There is no harm to come to you in this—but newspapermen are very tricky and may try to trap you into saying something you don't want to say."

Garwood nodded his head. "It's no problem," he said. When the colonel said American newspapermen, he knew. He knew at last that the note had gotten out. But there was now no elation, only more tension.

The first one through the door was the Caucasian. He might have been an American, but this young man was wearing Ho Chi Minh sandals, blue jeans, a pullover shirt with a picture of Ho Chi Minh on a tin button, which many wore, and he addressed the lieutenant colonel as "comrade."

Garwood was shocked. He had never heard anyone calling a Vietnamese "comrade" unless they were, too, a member of the Communist party. The term had come to have a special meaning, almost a signal of cadre membership to him.

The man was strong-looking, well-fed—but he just didn't look like an

306

American. His hair was medium length and he was clean-shaven. He looked at Garwood with a big grin that Garwood was suddenly afraid to return. The man's eyes seemed to be devouring him.

"Hi, my name is John Albert. I'm freelancing for NBC out of New York." His accent rang dimly in Garwood's memory. A California looseness? He wasn't sure. "You must be Mr. Garwood."

Garwood nodded. Behind him entered the woman, loaded with camera equipment, a movie camera in her hands. "This is my wife," he said. The woman nodded, "Hello," she said.

She was dressed in sneakers, jeans, and a turtleneck, and was either Japanese or Vietnamese; the third of the party had batteries strapped around his waist, a heavy box hanging from his neck, and earphones draped around his collarbones. He was introduced as Victor Sanchez.

Albert eased into conversation while his crew was unloading. "D'you know what this interview is about? What it's for?" he asked. He looked surprised when Garwood shook his head in the negative.

"You do know your note got out, don't you? And that it was hand-delivered to the State Department?" Garwood's eyes simply widened. He shook his head again. "Well, believe me, it did," he said. "I don't know if you know or not, but you stirred up a lot of shit, not only in Vietnam, but in the United States."

"I don't know what you mean," Garwood said.

"Well, you do know that there aren't supposed to be any more Americans in Vietnam?"

"As you can see, I am not Vietnamese," Garwood answered. There was something in the tone Garwood could not fathom, an edge to it.

"Are you serious? This is the first you've heard of it?" he said. Garwood nodded warily.

"Did you know you were having this interview with us today?" Albert said.

"Not until this morning," Garwood answered. Albert continued to remain in the mode of disbelief.

"Evidently, no one had told you. I have some very good news for you. You are going home." Garwood just stared.

"What do you mean, I'm going home?" he said, fighting disbelief, watching for the catch.

"You are probably the biggest news story going back in the U.S.," Albert bubbled on. "I can't believe it."

Garwood noticed the crew had not yet begun to film or record, nor Albert to take notes. "How long has it been since you've talked to an American?" he asked.

"About ten, eleven years," Garwood said.

"You are thin. How were you eating?"

"I'm eating all right," Garwood said.

"Are you being well treated?"

"Yes."

"We want to take pictures while I ask questions," Albert said, signaling with his hand to the crew. The woman put the camera to her shoulder, the other man quickly flipped on lights he had busily assembled on portable poles. Garwood was suddenly bathed in hot, white glare.

"I don't like the lighting in here," Albert said. "Let's go outside by the pool." Albert talked to the colonel's Vietnamese friend. It would be arranged.

The crew moved to the pool, and Garwood with it. The lieutenant colonel stopped him and told the camerawoman, "He'll be out in a couple of minutes."

The lieutenant colonel told him, "Now you know why you are here. After this interview, you will be interviewed once more by the chief of security of Vietnam, General Colonel Thai. Answer the questions very carefully, and with no malice toward Vietnam. You are not out of Vietnam yet."

"I understand," Garwood said. He was meant to tell these people how loving the Vietnamese are, how wonderful Vietnam is. Very well.

"Wait a minute more, the lieutenant colonel said. "This is something I forgot to tell you. Nothing is to be said about the camp; your key to freedom is your statement that you have complete freedom." The colonel quickly let Garwood understand he was to avoid mentioning that he had been a prisoner—this was the "key."

Garwood nodded and kept nodding. Outside, they were waiting. Albert asked him to walk around the pool. He was posed looking over the lake, sitting down.

The questions began, the camera whizzed busily. "I have something to show you, it's a newspaper clipping," Albert said, in a voice that had suddenly swelled into an orchestra. "I want to show it to you now, so I can get it on film, your expression as you read it."

Garwood was handed a clipping: "U.S. MARINE WANTS TO COME HOME AFTER 14 YEARS," it read.

Garwood saw only the headline.

"You know, when you return to the United States you are going to be a very rich man," the resonant voice enunciated.

"How do you mean?" Garwood said.

"The U.S. Government owes you about a hundred and fifty thousand dollars," the voice continued. "What do you think about that?"

"If you divide that up into fourteen years, that don't mean nothin'," Garwood found himself saying.

"Then money isn't important to you?"

"Nah," said Garwood, "only my freedom."

"Are you against the U.S. government?" the rich voice trilled.

"No."

"I would think you might feel pretty bitter. You've had to spend fourteen years of your life in Vietnam," he asked, suddenly mild and worried.

Many other questions followed—Albert seemed to want to try every question in a way that would make Garwood accuse the U.S. government of having abandoned him.

The interview ended. He was taken back to his room, but before, Albert asked if he could film in Garwood's quarters. The lieutenant colonel quickly sidestepped, saying "perhaps later this afternoon."

More shots were taken with waitresses, who paraded on either side of Garwood around the pool.

Back at the room, things were happening fast. The guards were rushing out the three beds, replacing them with an armchair, putting on a tablecloth, a radio, a case of beer, a nightstand with a box of cookies. Posters of Vietnamese girls were hung on the walls as Garwood watched, and the floor was mopped. By the time Albert arrived, the place was a fair approximation of a hotel room—with beer and cookies.

They filmed shots of Garwood entering and leaving, walking up the stairs, until they had it just right. They walked him up and down the street, they took him to a hat store nearby where Albert got one of the "NVA" hats, looking like a pith helmet, and put it on Garwood's head for a shot. They took more shots of Garwood staring at market stalls.

At the end of the interview, Albert asked if he wanted to say a few words to his family. "Dad, Mom," he said, "what you see here and what you have heard—please don't make any decisions one way or the other until after you have talked to me. I'll explain everything when I see you."

Sanchez, the equipment sound man, told Garwood, "Here's my name and address. Look me up if you get to New York." They left. The beer left also, and the cookies too.

There were more surprises. He was awakened in the morning, urged to dress, given a breakfast of rice cookies and hot tea, and taken by jeep to a building that was emblazoned "International Red Cross Headquarters."

Garwood could feel the tension, even in the guards. The officers with him chain-smoked, checked each detail of the guards' equipment, yelling harshly at any flaws. They checked the weapons individually to be sure there were no rounds chambered. As they drove, Garwood asked one of the guards in Vietnamese, "What's the gun for, you think I'm gonna escape now?" The guard sat stiffly through the clumsy jest.

At the Red Cross, the party walked inside like a burial guard. Garwood, in his fresh suit, was in the middle. There had apparently been warning given. News cameras started flashing and the shouts of the pressmen were heard loudly.

There were tables set out, in the shape of a T, and Garwood was put at the long table, facing a Vietnamese. At the other table, the head of the T, there were officials of the Red Cross, in business suits. The press, at bay, seemed only able to film and issue strangled shouts.

Garwood let events carry him. Still skeptical, this was one time he was willing to simply observe himself. "Until I get on that plane," he thought, "until I get on that plane . . . out . . . of . . . Vietnam."

The Red Cross officials asked him polite questions: "Mr. Garwood," he was addressed. It confused him. They wanted to know the simplest things—his name, his nationality, his membership in the United States Armed Forces. A representative from the Red Cross and one from Vietnam signed a paper. He was told by the Red Cross official, "You have been signed over into my custody. I am to escort you to Bangkok, where there will be an American delegation waiting to pick you up. There, you will board an aircraft to fly you to the United States. You will leave with me tomorrow to Saigon at 6:00 A.M. There we will board an Air France 747, which will transport us to Bangkok. Are you ready, Mr. Garwood?"

Garwood thought he was going with the man. He nodded eagerly. "Yes, I am ready," he said, feeling wild emotions surging through the fear.

Then he heard the grating voice of the Vietnamese behind him. "As Mr. Garwood has been in Vietnam fourteen years, we feel it only appropriate that we should give a little farewell party for him," the voice said. The Red Cross official shot a glance of puzzlement at Garwood, who stood mute.

In a second, the Red Cross official had swept up his books and papers and was only a disappearing back. Garwood sat, wondering what happened. He knew of no party—for fourteen years . . . a party?

The press conference followed fast on the heels of the Red Cross representatives. Garwood was asked by one reporter, "What was your status here in Vietnam?"

"I was captured on September 28, 1965, in South Vietnam. I am an American citizen. Not a Vietnamese. I am a member of the United States Marine Corps. After fourteen years, I have finally secured my release to return to my own country."

"How did you secure this release?"

"No comment," Garwood said.

Bitterness?

"No."

"There have been people who have made accusations against you in the U.S. What are your feelings towards these people?"

"This is the least of my worries at this time."

"What is the first thing you are going to do when you arrive back in the United States?"

"Spend as much time as I can with my family, try to get to know them again."

He knew that there was no such thing as a good-bye party planned for him. Outside, a jeep pulled up, and Garwood and his escort departed; it took him a full half hour in the silent fury of that jeep to realize they were not going back to his room or to any place in Hanoi, but back to Camp 776. It was getting dark when they caught the ferry across the Red River. But there was to be no sleep for him.

Half an hour after his arrival back at the camp, he was taken to the headquarters building, still in his suit, and put in a room with a long table. At least he was fed. Forty-five minutes passed before the door opened and, one by one, some faces familiar and some not, the camp's top brass and other officials filed in and sat down, some of them carrying papers or files.

Coffee and cigarettes were passed in silence. There was no feeling of night; the time might have been morning in that well-lit room, for the attitude of the men there was not of fatigue, but iron discipline and concentration.

The singular presence in the room was that of a man called Colonel Thai, the security chief. Not an impressive-looking man, he became impressive through the deference of others—he did not seem to enjoy it, or revel in it. It was as natural to him as flicking the ash off one of the cigarettes he smoked so delicately.

The colonel turned his olive eyes to Garwood and looked with the cold regret of a man who had been cheated at cards. "Tomorrow you are returning to your country," he said. "What must you be thinking of us?" The question, if it was one, did not really need a question mark as much as an exclamation point.

Garwood vacillated. Was the man now going to be magnanimous? "I haven't really thought about it," he said. "The only thing I wanted to do was to go home. I never hated anyone."

The Communists told him simply that there had been an investigation, and that they knew exactly how he had got to the hotel and passed the note. Garwood knew the technique well. "They will tell you something," he thought, "and then will ask you the same thing and explain that they are asking simply to find out if you are telling the truth."

Garwood told them nothing. When direct questions came, Garwood simply looked at the questioner. They were furious, but they kept it in check. He could see the steel of bayonets and the dull gleam of bullet-heads in their eyes.

They wanted to know everything: whom he had talked to, how he had entered the hotels, what other hotels? How many times? Who was the guard on duty? Who received the note and who set up the meeting? He knew that if he had told the whole truth—namely that luck was sixty percent of the mechanism—he would not have been believed. So he kept silence.

They questioned him for three hours, never threatening, only asking in the tone of men who are reasonable because reason is what's left when force is spent and pleading won't work. They told him that no matter how far he traveled from Vietnam, he would be kept under close watch.

Thai let the others ask most of the questions. He sat and smoked after the beginning. "It is a very foolish thing that you have done," he told Garwood near the end. "You have been thinking only of your own life and well-being. You could have jeopardized the lives of many others. But Vietnam always learns from experience and never makes the same mistake twice."

Ashen-faced, the camp commander sat through the whole interview like a scarecrow. It was clear that his professional life had suffered. Aides would write questions, hand them to Thai, and find out, from a slight nod or a frown, whether the question was thought to be appropriate by the head man.

"You are going to have a hard time convincing the U.S. government that you were a prisoner here," said one of Thai's aides with a smile of portent. "Because Vietnam has made statements that there are no more prisoners here."

They gave him coffee and cookies after the meeting, and he was put back into the jeep. This was a bad moment, a moment from a nightmare, but like a nightmare it ended, when the little vehicle turned south and headed down the long highway back toward Hanoi. The night was losing its grip when they finally arrived at the now-familiar city; while barrow men stirred about, beginning to pull the dirty cloths off their tiny shops, and the first people showed on the streets, wobbling off on their bicycles to their work, the jeep rolled into an airport.

They put him in the deserted lounge, with his road-weary escort, but he was too tired now to sleep. The eyes stared, wide open, and he could feel their rims, like the latest of late-night drunks; his head was extraordinarily clear. He saw hurdle after hurdle behind him. He seemed to be moving almost effortlessly now toward a finish line.

The Red Cross official appeared, busy and punctual, about ten minutes before the plane was due to take off, while the airport was filling with new people, leaving the small crowd of Garwood and his attendants feeling old and fragile. They were merely travelers. Garwood felt seamy in his too-new suit, too much worn and soon dirty from the road.

His last moments in North Vietnam were prosaic. There were no tickets, only the walk out of the building. It was a propeller plane. The motors on the wings were running with the biting sound of the air over the hearty roar. Garwood mounted the steps, noticing that the whole delegation was mounting as well. There was no stewardess to greet him as he stepped into the relatively silent, gently shaking fuselage, and he had no knowledge of when he actually left the country behind. The Red Cross official, cool and friendly, settled down beside him for the flight.

The flight south was without event. About two hours, a bit bumpy. The Red Cross representative warned Garwood not to talk. "Not safe," he said in accented English.

There was a layover of more than an hour at Ton Son Nhut Airport, Saigon, which was now called "Ho Chi Minh City." The airport was big and modern but amorphous. He sat, he rose for the bus to another plane.

Garwood had never been to France and his French was at the "parley voo" level, but he knew immediately he was on another continent when he stepped through the hydraulic door onto the 747. The plane seemed huge, new, luxurious. He was led into the bow section, up a tiny stairway to a lounge, and there was no one else in the compartment with its few rows of brocade couches. On one side he could see the cockpit, crammed with dials and winking lights, and men in neat uniforms. He was clearly the center of a lot of very warm attention, at first unnerving. The ship's captain seized Garwood by both arms, pushed him away slightly with a smile and then drew him into a hug. The man kissed Garwood on both cheeks, which gave him a helpless feeling. Then he was given the same treatment by at least three stewardesses. The blouses of white silk gave off intoxicating perfume in the warm air; one of the perfectly made-up women took off her blood-red carnation and pinned it to the lapel of his suit.

Garwood was stunned by this reception. He hadn't expected anything different than would be afforded by a ticket collector. He had never been treated by anyone in his whole life in this way. The eyes of the people were glowing. They fastened on him like magnets, coaxing him to smile, which he found difficult. He felt stiff and out of place. He couldn't say anything to the warm expressions of welcome, and when he ventured a tiny grin, the effect on those watching him was electric. He was being treated like some kind of movie star. Other pilots, or perhaps they were navigators, shook his hand and imitated the kissing process.

He was shown to a seat, he was almost forced into it with attention, and his strap was tenderly fastened. He kept craning his neck to get the view out the window. He wasn't sure what he was looking for, but the stewardess suddenly had tears in her eyes. "There's nothing more for you to worry about," she said. "You are now on the territory of France."

Garwood had trouble adjusting his face to meet those of the over-emotional people. He felt hopelessly behind in some race, as if he wasn't reacting in the appropriate manner, like an actor whose lines are suddenly forgotten and the only ones he can now remember are from another play.

The plane began to tremble silently. It was unlike any feeling he knew, this vast machine, and its takeoff was like an elevator's ascent. From his vantage he looked out at the mountains fleeing beneath, paddies, roads becoming bits of string, buildings tiny cubes, people—nothing.

It was not a long flight to Bangkok, but the French crammed it with a week's work of attention. The first thing they did was to announce, "We are out of Vietnam airspace." Something clicked in Garwood's mind, but he wasn't sure what. The captain, resplendent in his uniform, swept back, busily carrying a bottle of champagne. He peeled the foil back with a strong white fingernail and said, "This is to your freedom . . . you are now really free."

Garwood didn't know what to do, so he cried wordlessly. The stewardess was crying too. He tried to kneel to pray, but the strap was still on, so he sent up a jumbled prayer of thanks. He must have seemed to be struggling, the steward- ess put her hand on his shoulder, and said, "Everything is okay, it will be okay."

They were pressing food on him, asking him to eat it, but he didn't feel hungry, and they, seeming to interpret this differently, began to feed him by hand. Garwood's tears seemed to have brought tears from the other steward- esses, now trying to push fingersful of caviar past his lips. He tasted the champagne, and found it strange. The caviar was too much like fish sauce.

In no time at all, the huge craft landed gently. Bangkok, the city he had planned to visit on his R&R fourteen years before. Now, March 22, 1979, he was finally there. When the plane came to rest, officials told him he was not to

313

leave it. But after a ten or fifteen minute delay, the United States ambassador to Thailand came into the cabin. He was tall and thin and reserved and spoke like a senior schoolmaster. Garwood was told there were hundreds of press around the plane and was asked if he wanted to speak to them. "No," Garwood said.

"Good," he replied, "we have taken the necessary steps."

They walked swiftly to a limousine, the first he had ever ridden in, and drove to customs. He had nothing to declare, no papers, no passport. The ambassador left and an interminable hour passed while officials made up some documents for him to fly with. They drove to another part of the airport.

They parked beside a military transport plane, a big four-engined craft in muddy green. He was ushered into the plane by the ambassador, who wheeled and left without a word. An American officer greeted him. There was no handshake, just a correctness: "You are Private Robert Russell Garwood?" the man said.

"Yes."

"Before you say anything, I am Major G——, U.S. Marine Corps. This is Gunnery Sergeant Langlois, and this is Captain Joseph Composto, military counsel assigned to you."

"Don't say anything. Shut up. Don't say anything to anybody about anything," Captain Composto said. Garwood had not said a word. He looked at the men. They were Marines, the Marines he remembered. They looked at him as if he were some sort of prize cargo that their jobs were on the line to protect. He felt like freight, and slightly uneasy.

The next thing Garwood heard was the gunnery sergeant reading, in that peculiar voice that is used on texts committed to memory without being understood, the "rights": "You have a right to remain silent . . ."

Garwood found it very difficult to pay attention. He had no idea what they were doing or why. He knew they were not as friendly as the French had been, but they were probably scared. He was back under U.S. control. That was all he cared about, and if they had taken his suit off and made him sit on the bare, barnlike aluminum bones of the cargo plane, he wouldn't have cared. Somehow that aircraft was connected, with threads and wires, and maybe electric currents, by men duty-bound, by orders and bits of paper, to the continental United States.

Besides, the engines of the plane made so much noise that the crew handed out earplugs. Garwood said no word during the next ten hours. When he was awake, he wandered around the barnlike interior of the plane. He couldn't sleep, even though he had been up for almost four nights before this.

His mind stayed in neutral, wishing the time would pass. After a while he turned to the stern-faced major. "Did anybody ever find my jeep?" he asked. The question was met by icy silence.

22
Homecoming

THE COLONEL on the Air Force transport had told Garwood something that was to ring in his memory later, not then during the blank flight filled with the noise of the four engines and the warnings, but later when he had some idle time. The man had told him, not unkindly, that he would find out when he returned to the U.S. that he would not receive the welcome he might have imagined.

Perhaps the man had scented the champagne on his breath, or perhaps he was aware of Garwood's singular position to the policy makers. There were plenty of other things too, like Joe Composto telling him to watch out because there were security men taking pictures of him on the plane. And they had tape recorders.

The U.S. government can act oddly at times, and this was certainly one such time. They had told him his rights, they had supplied a lawyer, and in the world of guilt and innocence, Garwood was no fool.

He had some Vietnamese money in his pockets that he had been given by his captors at the last, during the time he was on display—he supposed it was for cigarettes. He offered it to the crew as souvenirs and found that they took it eagerly, like a prize.

He, in turn, was given a packet from his family. The gunnery sergeant told him, "We've got some articles that your family sent to you and I've been instructed not to give them to you until you arrive at Okinawa. But if you want them I'll give them to you."

Garwood nodded, and was told that the things were from his immediate family only, and there was no written material from anyone outside it. That, he found out later, was a formula worked out by the government. They wanted him to know what his people looked like, whether they were living or dead, and they gave him a photo album with color pictures of his half-brothers and his brother and his half-sisters, his father and stepmother.

Garwood fastened his eyes on these things, feeling shaky and upset, but not crying. And he noticed that he was being filmed while he was looking at the things. His father's clumsy letter said he'd hired a lawyer and it repeated one thing over and over: "Don't say anything."

"I know you've got a lot of questions," Composto told him, "but wait until we get to Okinawa."

The young military lawyer didn't brief him, didn't tell him what he would be facing or the possibilities. The plane landed after the eight-and-one-half-hour flight at Okinawa in rain. There were bright lights everywhere around the darkened airfield and the press was clearly on the scene as well. Two military police vehicles had arrived and he was immediately under escort when he walked out of the plane. He was beginning to wonder what was going on, but not with foreboding, just excited. He did not think there was a case against him, in fact that was the last thing on his mind. He was trying to remember how the U.S. military behaved, and having his memory shoved around by what was happening to him now. He found they were acting perfectly normally.

What followed was normal, too, to his mind. The escort avoided the media by going into the back of the hospital rather than the front. While the reporters chafed and the photographers clattered around, the MPs quickly led him through ranks of security people to a room that was like a suite. They left him alone there.

Garwood felt like Alice in Wonderland, not because he didn't know what a television looked like, or a sofa, or a bed, or for that matter a tailor, who was his first visitor to fit him with a new suit of clothes. He knew what these things were, but he did not believe he was seeing them. Everything was completely new, like the model years of cars he had never seen. He sat with a little remote control device in his hand, flipping from channel to channel, watching the faces, the ads, the colors.

His hair was cut, his face shaved. People shoved things at him, clothes and food. He sat with the television and the remote control, content in the indifferent warmth of "medical care," content to be stared at by doctors, nurses and interns.

After a cursory examination, they decided he should sleep. They gave him pills and put him to bed, but instead of lying down, he insisted on sitting up on the sofa and as the chemicals took hold he slept that way, the remote control still in his hand. He said later he was afraid to lie down, the bed was too strange to him.

He spent a week in the suite, the first suite he had ever occupied, and an unworldly time it was. They kept his coffee table loaded with food and drinks, and he wasn't sure whether he was supposed to talk to anyone, so he didn't. He spent a week with the color TV in a kind of wasteland, between awareness and illusion. He watched the programs, remembering none of them, except that they were in color, and he looked at an assortment of magazines, all of which had been scanned and censored for news of him. He might have only felt a mild curiosity to know what journalists and their editors were saying of him. He looked at the cars and tried to remember how they had looked the last time he had seen them, fourteen years before, in the era of fins and chrome. He said it was just like being born, and trying to take a lot in, but he formulated that thought later. Then, it was simply a live picture show.

He felt no restlessness, no anxiety, no wish for exercise or for anything beyond the moving colored pictures and the static pictures of the magazines. Meals came regularly, and he was to have anything he wanted. He hardly knew what to order, so he ordered steaks and ice cream, over and over, and called for cigarettes and tried to smoke as many as possible. He asked for Jello, he asked for Winstons.

He didn't know what the doctors were doing in their brief visits to his room. They would examine him as he had been examined as a child, testing his reflexes with a little rubber hammer, peering into his eyes and ears, taking his temperature, giving him shots, taking blood and urine. They asked no questions about his mental state, gave no explanations, and he felt no need for any. He felt in friendly hands, taken care of and secure for the first time in years. Always, when there were medical visitors, the military lawyer, Joseph Composto, would appear.

After about seven days, the stay at Okinawa ended. He was put on a commercial jet liner with Composto on one side and an officer on the other. He was told the aircraft was bound for Chicago.

Perhaps the government had thought that with enough silence, ice cream and cigarettes and doctors, Garwood would be so thankful that a great number of their puzzles would be solved. For among the military a nagging feeling about Garwood was growing, a feeling that he was a nasty problem that would not go away; the worst of it was that the Garwood they had in hand, the skinny man with the smudged eyes who kept asking for ice cream and Winstons, was nothing like the Garwood they had heard of.

In the way that a minor character can easily assume a large, if one-dimensional, image without facts to deflate it, Garwood's name had become associated with one of the barracks-room myths of the Vietnam War, the man called "Super Charlie," or the "White Cong," a figure of prodigious strength and even greater cunning, but more than these qualities, a depth of evil bordering on insanity.

In a war in which each side completely misunderstood the other, the figure was that of a soldier, either crazed by battle, brainwashed, or simply perverse, who had abandoned the U.S. forces and joined the Viet Cong and combined technology with jungle cunning. The central outrage was that the soldier had abandoned not only his country and his ideology, but also his hemisphere and his race.

In the triple-canopy jungle where trails were spiked with bamboo spears poisoned with feces and so sharp they felt only like a nudge when it was already too late, the legend stalked in his tire-made sandals, dressed in loose pajamas. He spoke in an American accent through a bullhorn telling the troops to lay down their arms because, like the jungle, the foe could not be overcome.

If there was some foundation in truth to the figure with the AK-47 and the American voice, there were plenty of reasons for its existence. Like all soldiers in defeat, whether at Waterloo or Happy Valley, many grunts thought they had been betrayed in the jungles, and the turncoat who understood their minds and their manner of operating was the obvious culprit, if only to explain some of the unusual successes of the enemy. The turncoat took on an almost religious significance as a scapegoat whereby all the losses and effort wasted, the cries and hopeless blood could be made right and fair.

But on another level, the personal level, Garwood had become a name that, after 1973, took up its own space in the filing cabinets at the Pentagon.

This was because of the remarkable chain of events that followed the release of American prisoners of war in February and March of 1973, events that followed on the heels of the signing of the peace agreements between the U.S. and the Democratic Republic of North Vietnam on January 27, 1973.

There were 591 of them, an abnormally high proportion of the number were Air Force, Navy, and Marine fliers who had been shot down during the air war against North Vietnam. There were relatively few ground troops imprisoned, for the simple reason that few prisoners were taken on either side in the ordinary course of operations.

This often-overlooked fact was to result in much confusion and ethical and moral conflict among the top rank of politicians and soldiers who had to decide how to regard the 591 returnees in 1973, and the small number of others who had been granted early release from captivity.

Some had accused the returnees of wrongdoing. Though the public saw them as a band of brothers, many had kept themselves alive just to see "justice" done to comrades in arms who had committed offenses against the code of conduct, which basically limits a prisoner to "name, rank, and serial number" when questioned by the captor, and forbids any activity injurious to another American prisoner or disloyal to the service to which the individual belongs.

The code was already outmoded and useless in World War II, at least in the Asian theater, because it was not accepted by the Japanese. A measure of the uselessness of that code is found in the tiny number of escapees in Asia compared with the large number in Europe during that war and the tiny number of prisoner-returnees compared with those listed as taken prisoner or missing in action.

But the Japanese made more of an effort to live up to the dictates of the Geneva Convention than the North Vietnamese or the Viet Cong, both of whom denied the validity of the convention, or the code itself.

The fact that the code proved useless to those who were tortured and forced to give information made no difference to the men who after release wanted to bring charges against their fellow prisoners. One such was Air Force Lieutenant Colonel Ted Guy, who filed charges against eight returnees when he was released himself, only to be confronted with letters of confession, apology, and "solidarity" with the Vietnam Veterans Against the War that he had written under duress in early 1972.

Guy's charges were that the eight POWs had aided the enemy, been disrespectful to a superior, disobeyed a superior, had conspired, and had carried out a conspiracy. The charges were dropped after one of the accused, Abel Larry Kavanaugh, a Marine, committed suicide in July 1973. The then secretary of the army, Howard "Bo" Calloway, dismissed the charges against the five Army men, and the secretary of the Navy, John Warner (now a Republican senator from Virginia), dismissed the charges against the two other Marines.

The reasons given to the press were lack of evidence against the men. Charges against the only two commissioned officer POWs accused of misconduct were dropped by the secretary of the Navy in September 1973. One of these men, a Marine Corps lieutenant colonel, was censured; the other, a Navy captain, was given no official punishment, and later retired.

There was political pressure against pressing charges against the returnees, who were lumped together in the public mind as suffering heroes in the thankless work of war. But it is known that the Marine Corps, at least, wished to prosecute every individual who was guilty of breaking the code or behaving in such a way that unfavorable notice was taken by a fellow prisoner. Without a public prosecutor in the situation, charges against prisoners of war have traditionally been brought by fellow prisoners.

The fact was that almost every prisoner to whom the North Vietnamese applied pressure for long responded by breaking the code of conduct, either by signing "confessions" or by making statements for propaganda use. Among the prisoners themselves, hard reality replaced the code of boot camp with another code that was at least useful, a sliding scale of resistance that was based on the fact that no prisoner could outlast Asian torturers. The leading POWs, men like Jeremiah Denton, now a senator, and Air Force ace Robinson Risner, both of whom were tortured (and both of whom produced confessions and other documents under extreme pressure), decided that resistance was limited to the edges of sanity, to permanent disabling injury or death.

By the end of 1973 charges against all of the returnees had been wiped out, in spite of efforts by a friend of Guy's to renew action against the flagrant violators of the code of conduct.

More than five years later, the Pentagon got the news that Garwood had been sighted in North Vietnam. Military experts believed the last of the POWs had been returned, as did a congressional committee that had traveled to North Vietnam to gather information.

By the time Garwood had been picked up as a major news story, his file had already been closed and put away, except for one important part of it. His back pay and his GI insurance had never been paid out, a firm indication that the Marine Corps was convinced he was still alive, though nothing had been heard of him from the returnees that was very recent.

The file was reviewed by the top echelon of the Marine Corps with a growing sense of alarm as Garwood's flights sent him with his curious escort first to Great Lakes and then to Camp Lejeune, North Carolina. Further files revealed that numerous '73 returnees had seen and known him in the southern camps, but none in the north; that the stories told by the prisoners to their debriefing officers were first-person observations, vehement and detailed. Many of the incidents told by different POWs dovetailed and echoed perfectly. And there was another element. The accusations of malfeasance that came out of the debriefing tapes did not all come from hard-core officers, but from foot soldiers, a warrant officer, a doctor—from blacks, whites, from Hispanic soldiers. From Monika Schwinn, the German nurse who was unceremoniously dumped into one of the camps where Garwood was installed, came corroboration, even, from a woman. All the voices were unified in one point: Garwood had chosen to give his allegiance to the enemy, and in this he was alone, separate from the other prisoners.

Bob Garwood came only gradually to know that his past had been exhumed and examined, gradually to know that the doctors' attentiveness was not all positive, and it was not, as Joe Composto first told him, standard operating procedure to read the rights of the accused to him.

It was only when he saw the eyes of his family and heard their apologetic voices, the half-hearted attempts to cheer him and pretend that everything was in hand, when he heard his father reaffirm that a New York lawyer named Dermot Foley had been engaged, that he began to know that his trouble had not gone away.

But this had not presented itself to him at Okinawa. He left for Chicago, dressed in the fresh Marine Corps uniform the tailor had made for him. He was given no choice in the matter of clothes, so they put him in the crisp olive worsted and the too-shiny shoes, and they gave him the left breast decorations that he had won fourteen years before, including his marksmanship badge, the only soldierly thing he had really won as a Marine, and they sent him to another set of doctors at the Great Lakes Naval Training Center, where his parents were allowed to see him—a painful interview, for it was clear that they were all as shocked by his appearance as he was by theirs. His stepmother, Helen, had blossomed to a large girth, his stepbrothers and sisters were unremembering, and his brother Don was now an ex-convict and a balding, limping middle-aged man of thirty-three. His real mother was dead.

Then he had thirty days of home leave, too long and too short, at Greensburg, where there was no escape from reporters or the crowded trailer, or his family's happy-go-lucky poverty. He saw some old friends in Indianapolis and spent evenings trying to catch up, evenings of too much beer to cover up that everyone else had moved on and Bob—well, as Ken Banholzer, who is the most faithful of his friends, put it, "Bob is just the same as he's always been."

But it was not good after the first time, for the cloud over Garwood was just as sure to produce the same isolation he had known in Vietnam. He would be with other people, and he would fall too easily into their ways, and he would say something that would make them realize that it wasn't true, that he was telling it only to impress, out of some terrible feeling of need. It was not good.

Other people found themselves arguing about him, and saying "at least he didn't go to Canada." Bob, meanwhile, said nothing as he was told, and he moodily drifted through Adams, waiting for the government to do something to him, borrowing his brothers' cars and going to the American Legion Post at Greensburg, a place with a rusting howitzer and a bar in the cellar. He was looking for memories and they seemed to be rejecting him, as if he were cut off from them in some peculiar way.

The time of the home furlough ran out, and the Marine Corps still had not made its decision to charge him with desertion and aiding the enemy, charges serious enough for the death penalty. Garwood was ordered back to Great Lakes in the middle of May, where he was examined again, and changed into civilian clothes, flown down to Camp Lejeune, at Jacksonville, North Carolina.

This time, the hunt was up and reporters were with him on the plane during its eight-hour flight from Chicago via Atlanta. Garwood told them nothing, withdrawing behind the mirror-faced sunglasses he had bought in Indianapolis. It was a pouty, showery spring day in Jacksonville, and the press had gathered to mark the next turning of the story.

Garwood had been silent as a Buddha on the plane. On the ground he was downcast and grim, murmuring negatives to the crowd. It would have been a typical celebrity arrival, with all of the empty activity and sudden ending of such things, if it had not been for a local woman who pushed up to Garwood's escort, military lawyer Captain Dale Miller, and gave him a garish red carnation, flaming against the drab waiting room. Miller had been appointed the same day and seemed confused. "You give it to him," she said. "He should be welcomed home like any other prisoner of war."

Garwood looked at the half-pretty face without registering. But the holder of the flower was Donna Long, who was at that point perhaps Garwood's only fan in the steamy Marine Corps town of Jacksonville. She had already written two letters to the local paper about his case, the first one in a white heat at the first news of Garwood's impending release from the north in March; "A fact that was not so widely publicized was that when Garwood passed his letter he also told the foreigner 'I know of fifteen others,' " she wrote the *Raleigh News & Observer*.

It's unlikely that it would have deterred Donna Long had she known that Garwood mentioned "others" he had seen in North Vietnam because he knew that was a sure way of getting attention when he passed the note: She had already found in him a dream come true, the embodiment of an idea.

By 1979 Donna Long was a well-known figure in Jacksonville. She had forced the military to revise its dress code for dependents (to allow women to wear pants at a convenience store on base), she had forced the city to renovate the dog pound, and she had staged a one-woman march on the state capitol in 1969 to oppose the antiwar moratorium, and she had become an important spokeswoman for the POW/MIA organization then fighting to prove that there were more than a thousand men still unaccounted for and distributing the distinctive copper POW bracelets with the names of Vietnam missing and POWs on them.

She remembers that Garwood looked somehow both vulnerable and tough that day, a boy trying to look good, a boy trying to look okay behind his shades. But more than that, he was her current cause. She told herself, "Here I go again."

23
Bobby's Girl

JACKSONVILLE, NORTH CAROLINA, is entered from the east by a coastal road that drives like a silver needle through endless pine forests. They are truly a sea, these Carolina pines, whose semiregular waves are shaken only once in twenty to thirty years when crews of foresters clearcut them for pulp, for poles, or for timber.

But before their trunks, scaly barked and reddish and heavily fragrant, are chained and dragged off, other crews are preparing to plant the ground again with fresh thousands of pine slips, to be thrust into the sandy clay as carelessly as rice shoots, the planter walking behind a man who bayonets a hole for them.

The modern settlements in these plantation lands are always along the roads, seldom if ever out in the "company lands" of the pines, and the little clearings in the forest are called coves, just as a weary sailor would term them.

Here, where all is brand new, most of the houses appear to have been built as quickly as possible, and as cheaply. Most of the houses that are not "mobile homes" are ranch style, built on top of a concrete pad or on a shallow cinderblock foundation, one story high with the low sloping roofs that can only exist south of the snowbelt.

It's not likely that Bob Garwood cared much about the local architecture when he arrived at Jacksonville in the fall of 1979 to face his accusers at court-martial and to begin almost two years of limbo in the Carolina lowlands. He was a man with more on his head than trailers and bricks, a man without even a home, whom the United States Marine Corps doubtless sincerely wished was dead.

But Jacksonville, home of the sprawling Marine Corps base, Camp Lejeune,

323

was what he first really saw of this country after fourteen years away, the first place he spent any time outside of the military. And the first person he saw besides his military guardians and his lawyer—the first person he saw for a social reason—was the little woman named Donna Long who had given him the flower at the airport.

Donna's own house is brick, a place with a tiny drive, a carport, and full wall-to-wall carpets over the flooring, and the kind of paneling that taverns use because it looks perfectly okay in the dim light and if someone puts a fist through you can always put up another bit.

Attached to the square one-storied house is an addition, also in brick, of which she is inordinately proud. It is one room, with a pool table in it and a wall dominated by a two-shelf mantle on which are dozens of silvery motorcycle-racing trophies.

The room is dedicated to motorcycle racing with the singlemindedness with which a millionaire "sportsman" would dedicate his to horse racing. Most of the trophies have been won by her husband, Dale, but a few are the work of her older son, Butch, her younger son, B.J., and herself.

Dale and Donna Long became Bob Garwood's best friends on earth until Dale's death in a motorcycle accident later in 1979.

Donna—bright, tough, unschooled, hyperactively sentimental and like a horse full of oats ready to run for fame—became Bobby Garwood's lover even before her husband died, but there is little reason to think that Dale Long liked Bobby less for that, or that Donna felt that she had put the horns on her man's head.

That brick addition belongs to Dale and motorcycling. The rest of the house, though, with its eclectic furniture and look of haste and make-do, is dedicated to Garwood.

An odd couple, Garwood and Donna met as he stepped down from the military plane carrying him to what amounted to house arrest in Camp Lejeune.

It was Donna's plan—in fact it could be argued she "laid up for him" just as a deer hunter waits for the prey to come into the clearing—for she was a principal activist in Vietnam veterans' affairs, particularly the affairs of the missing in action (MIAs) and the prisoners of war (POWs).

That meeting was eye contact only, but Garwood told her later that she was the only smiling face in the entire crowd of military shepherds, Nikon-clicking pressmen and onlookers that greeted him there. One smile—which just about tells the story of Garwood's welcome to North Carolina itself.

Donna was certainly the most important person with whom Garwood had contact in his life as a suspect. Important does not mean famous, though Donna at her apogee was certainly that. In this case it means full or weighty, for Donna was a woman of ideas, principles, and activity, a person who did not just talk, but who did, and was often a citizen in the old-fashioned sense of the word, one who made her weight felt in her community.

324

But with the same intensity that Donna Long built up the relationship, she also pulled it down, as her story will tell. With her and Garwood, it was a parody of the boy-meets-girl, boy-loses-girl theme. In her case, Garwood's mere existence as a POW still in Vietnam was more important than if he had been rich, handsome, and all for her. It was the answer to a dream, the dream of a person unmercifully unstrung by Vietnam, in a way that many Americans were unstrung by that war.

Donna was stubborn in a cause. Few were like her in her intensity in pursuing the unpopular subject of the prisoners of war in Jacksonville, which is in the pocket of the military, and she had the quality, so necessary in publicizing causes, of being certain what is black and what is white, and also certain that all things must be one or the other. She never got beyond the labels in Vietnam, and that was enough.

She may not have wanted to see beyond the labels, for there is a strong streak in her that simply likes a fight, and likes it even more if she is the underdog. If she were a college girl, she would be accepted as a nonconformist. As a roughneck and a redneck, though from auspicious beginnings, she was simply an eccentric woman with the charm of quickness of mind and some beauty, and an ability, almost uncanny, to do and say things that fit in exactly with the preconceptions of the city editors and newsmen who decide what is a good story and what is not.

It is decidedly a good story when the wife of a decorated Vietnam veteran takes up the cudgels against the war protesters. And the story could hardly have a better stage than Jacksonville, where the reigning opinion is that the enemies of democracy always deserve to have their hearts cut out, but do not always get what they deserve.

Donna Long provided a good story to a city that is the Marine Corps capital of the world when the rest of the media were going bananas in a direction completely opposite. Mind you, she did her thing long before she met Bobby Garwood. But it was necessary for her to have done it in order for her to have met him. Things do not come from the void, particularly in North Carolina. There is a route, there is the continual awful question of continuity, whereby if one's father is crazy, one may be as sane as Konrad Lorenz and still be regarded as daft, "just like his daddy."

Donna does not come from Onslow County, but neither does most anyone else there. The credentials were with her helicopter-crew-chief husband, Dale. Dale Long, who remains on this earth only as a color photo and a hero image in the minds of his two sons, and as a queer mixture of love, regret, and anger in the mind of Donna Long, was a good, tall, strong-looking Southern boy. He did not belong to the group in high school that was headed for college, but he was a leader among those who were not.

Dale Long was, by all accounts, a different and ancient model. A man who would have done well on the Scottish borders, a journeyman of the hard-handed variety who could be counted upon to do the tasks, all nasty, all totally necessary, that lead up to the main actors' being led onto the stage and saying their piece. The Dale Longs of the world get nothing for simply doing what they were trained to do; and when the worst has happened and the line is overrun and the few holdouts are shot or bayonetted in their lonely holes, then the officers and the officials say they are good fellows, or if they have all fled, that nothing else could have been expected of such men. . . .

That was Dale Long's type, like Donna, but unlike her, a person stilled and kept quiet by lack of education. Not a poor boy, not deprived, but simply led down paths by his own nature and the forces of his neighborhood and his friends and his society that he might not have succumbed to if he had read the wisdom of the ages. What, for example, could lead such a man to become a U.S. Marine? On this, Donna at last is silent, because she, among about ten million others, accepts the reasons that are offered to excuse, accept, and even love the Marine Corps.

Just as it is often the lowest soldier who turns the tide of battle when he stubbornly keeps firing his weapon, perhaps out of fury, perhaps out of fear, perhaps for no reason at all, just so it was left to Dale Long to revolt against the war in Vietnam. But his was the revolt of the foot soldier, the gunner who couldn't stand being shot at without shooting back. From that point on, Dale was out of the war.

Until he met Bob Garwood and found two things. First that his wife, whom he loved and sometimes hated passionately, was on Bobby's case like a hound. She was literally on point from the moment she heard of Garwood's existence, even more when she heard he was coming to her part of the country. Donna's frustration was like Dale's—that everything had been bungled, that the government had betrayed its own people, and now in some way, Garwood was the sunken-eyed proof. There were few things about him that could seem attractive to Dale. Though both were Marines, Dale was the epitome of the gung-ho combat trooper, the door gunner who could repair chopper engines under fire, who once took off from a hot drop zone holding to the rails of one skid while a wounded Marine hung on to him. These are the things Donna tells of him. Less readily, she'll admit that he was not the steadiest of husbands and that he had ways of going after girls. But the second thing Dale found was that Bobby Garwood was that uniquely adaptable type of character who finds it easy and comfortable to mold himself to a leader.

Not that Garwood was a good soldier: There is little evidence that he was anything but a semireliable time server, but he was and is above all a companionable man. Garwood in his way worshiped Dale, the same way he had worshiped Ike.

For Long was a competent person. Longing after competence is one of the strongest unexpressed desires of Bobby Garwood. He lusts to be good at something—to have a good car, to be looked up to. This is in direct contrast to his family and background—the aimless, drifting Garwoods who are not so much driven across the flat landscape of Michigan and Indiana as they are chased by fortune. In Dale Long, Garwood found his Ike reborn, the man his half-child mind wished still he could become.

Dale Long was a motorcycle racer, whose avocation was a quest to become one of the top drivers in the country. Garwood, on the other hand, was one of the worst drivers his intimates have ever known, combining the feckless recklessness of the fifties' "Neckers' Knob" style of wheeling with an inability to find his way.

The few pictures that remain of Dale Long, Bobby Garwood's only real male friend since his return, show a man of medium height with a large narrow head and blonde hair, holding himself in that stiff and unusual studio manner, as wrong as plastic flowers. Whatever Dale Long's thoughts, he did not write them down, but he told everything to Donna, and much to Bobby Garwood when the two men went out drinking, almost like father and son, or at least older and younger brothers—a role that must have been a relief to Garwood—though there are those, and Donna is one, who say that Garwood simply shifts from one overlord to the next, from the juvenile officer, to the recruiting officer, to his sergeant, to his captors, on and on. It is better to take things as they appear on the surface, however, roll them about and see the shapes they take.

But it is clear that at one point, for several months, Dale Long and Bob Garwood became alter egos, the dark-eyed aimless seeker and the intense disillusioned soldier. It was partly Donna's doing. She was simply *too* much, she simply couldn't stop with her POW/MIA business when both men were losing interest, getting back from the war, from the Marine Corps. In both Dale Long and Garwood is a strong tendency to desist in impossible situations, a parallel form of survivor's wisdom. Instead of flying missions and taking fire without returning it, Dale simply quit flying. In the end he said the hell with the Marine Corps after fourteen years. In a way, both men were in similar straits, as Bobby Garwood says it, "Torn up by the war."

Donna, on the other hand, was not torn up by it. She was excited, invigorated, educated, made passionate. While Vietnam took everything from men, it gave an identity to her.

This is her story.

"I got hold of every book I could on Vietnam, on the Vietnam War all the way back through history. I figured if my husband could possibly die, I want to know what it is for. I became very familiar; I was against any antiwar movement and for winning the war.

"The Red Cross had special meetings once a month. And at a dinner one night, the speaker was someone from the university.

"This guy stood up and started speaking and he teed me off. He started saying things like making fun of LBJ, and building up Ho Chi Minh into some kind of hero. And I got angry and stood up at dinner table. All of a sudden the microphone came to me and I told him that I did not appreciate what he was saying because my husband was in Vietnam. That it was not wrong for us to be in that war. It was not a civil war. That once Vietnam started going into

Cambodia and into Laos, it was the domino theory. I figured my role was, my husband was fighting in Vietnam, I was going to fight in the U.S. Understand. Shoulder to shoulder.

"Dale was writing me. I was getting letters telling me he wasn't doing anything but working on airplanes. He told me nothing about his flying. He did not want to worry me. Then he got the Navy commendation medal for changing an engine under fire, bullets flying everywhere, on a downed plane. I found out that he had gone in and picked up people, risked his life, but he did not want to worry me."

But, she said, Dale was still a soldier who loved to fight. It was a free-fire zone in '66 and '67. Then in '69 when he went back a second time, he took sixty rounds inside his helicopter and could not get permission to shoot back. He shot back anyway.

"He said he'd never fly again. Because they had a new order out by '69 and '70. It was not even a war anymore, he was very disillusioned. You had to sign a piece of paper that you wouldn't fire until you had been fired at first. You got permission to fire back. So he quit flying completely. He just worked on the planes.

"We had one year together between 1966 and 1967. We called it . . . our joke was one year of loving, one year of fighting, and one year of separation. That is what kept us together, he'd be gone and we would realize what we had. I worshiped Dale. He was my hero. He was fighting the battle in Vietnam and I was fighting the battle here at home. My enemy was Jane Fonda. The SDS, anyone who was in that left-wing moratorium group."

Donna did not expect the marriage to continue in peacetime. She somehow felt the separations were necessary, that the fighting, which she hurries to explain was fighting between Dale and herself and not against the Viet Cong, was also somehow necessary. In an archaic sense, their relationship was a most primitive and fierce one, violent and vivid. Being called "Donna Long's husband" did not sit well with a boy from the South. They fought, they made love, they fought again.

But the change that came over Dale Long swam slowly into focus. Donna and her husband were not introspective, but this was too large and too steady a change of course. Dale was getting wasted by the year.

"He said the Marine Corps was going to hell, and that it wasn't what it was supposed to be, and that we were going to lose the war over there, because we weren't proud enough to win it. People were dying . . . and he hated the antiwar people because he said they were causing it. The politicians were running the war, gotta let the soldiers win it . . . he'd been there and he knew what it was. He was hostile toward me, he would not talk to me."

Dale had signed off Donna. The Corps, he felt, had been unfaithful to him, and he was now unfaithful to her. What was worse, she had become, in her own right, a sort of intellectual soldier of the right, a voice that couldn't stop criticizing and nagging, and he found himself the audience. He came home to a wife who was far more into the war in Vietnam than he was.

"This time when he got home, I reminded him of the war, because I was fighting my own battle, and he wanted to forget it.

"Here's what had happened while Dale was away. My sister and I were sitting there watching TV and there was this blonde-haired, horrible-looking guy getting national coverage, talking about how they were going to close down the capitol in every state. It was their moratorium, mobilization, and it was called the antiwar moratorium. I was thinking of putting my foot through the TV. I said, 'I've got to do something.' My sister said, 'Now what are you going to do?'

"I said, 'This Sunday, I'm walking to Raleigh.' She said, 'You gonna do what?' It was 125 miles, some people say 150. Some say 130, I don't know, I just know I got out and started walking. I made Kinston the first day. I pushed it. I tried to make three miles an hour and rest. And I pushed it so far that my legs cramped up, my younger sister had to come up with her fiancé. I remember them taking horse linament and doing my legs. People at first didn't know what I was doing. They offered me rides, I don't know how the newspapers found out, but they got it on the wires. People were flying in from CBS, NBC, and I was gettin' mad at them, because they were wearing me down. I'll never forget one woman, CBS I believe it was, she was walking around in her high heels, complaining about how she had to fly into some cow pasture, and I said I don't care."

Donna finished her march and threw herself actively into supporting war causes. She became involved in the following years in the POW issue, more especially in the missing in action cause. There were some two thousand men still carried as missing when the North Vietnamese finally returned the American flyers, and there was a big debate on whether to declare them dead, so the government could stop paying their salaries to their families, or keep them listed as missing until further proof was found. In March 1978, when it became known that Bobby Garwood was alive and wanted to come home, Donna was ecstatic.

"I was sitting at the kitchen table, and I opened the newspaper and there it says, 'Marine Wants Out of Vietnam.'

"I said, 'GOD!' Dale asked 'What?' "

"I said, 'It has come true! Look!'

"I used to pray to God, if there was anyone alive over there, it would take a miracle, but please help him out. I went bananas. Shortly after that there was a station that showed Bobby in Vietnam surrounded by Vietnamese. He was thanking them but I couldn't understand what else he was saying 'cause his accent was so bad. I could tell it was posed, I could tell by the way he chose his words. They were not falling into line. I told Dale I would wait until he got on free ground and heard what he had to say. And I would make up my mind then.

"The next time I saw him was a Japanese TV interview. I listened to him. I remember the things he said. Things that stood out in my mind most of all (I fell in love with Bobby right then and there), someone said to him, 'Don't you feel cheated not to get a hero's welcome?' Bobby looked at the guy and said,

329

'Vietnam was not a hero's war.'

"I picked up the phone, called the florist. I said I want red, white, and blue flowers with a 'Welcome Home.' The only thing I had from the newspaper was his church, so I sent it to him there."

Donna found out from the press that a civilian lawyer from New York, Dermot Foley, was going to handle Bobby's case, so she phoned him.

"I told him I heard Bobby was coming down here, that he would need a friend, a place to get away. I know how this town is. He was going to need somebody. 'So you tell him,' I told Dermot, 'if he needs me, my family, our home is open to him, if he wants to get off that base.'

"Bobby got here on May 15, 1979. I went to the airport. I started to get flowers like I always did when a POW came to welcome him home. I decided no, I did not want to make a show of it. There was a heavy guard there, all the news media; so what I took was one simple red carnation. Just to welcome him home—I had to welcome him home. Dale said he would stay home with the kids. He said, 'You go on.'

"Dale was mad. He said that what they should have done when he got off that plane was to welcome him home, hand him his money, give him three women and send him to Las Vegas. 'And if I go,' he said, 'with the reporters or somebody, I'm liable to punch someone.'

"When Bobby came off the plane, he had on glasses. He looked gaunt, he was wearing civilian clothes. I stood back and looked at him. Cameras stuck in his face, he was trying to turn away. Finally he took his glasses off. He looked up, I smiled at him, and he smiled back. And I found out later that the reason he smiled at me was I was the first smile he had seen.

"I wrote him a letter at the base. I told him who I was and offered our place this weekend. I gave him my telephone number, and so on.

"Friday Bobby called.

"I could not understand him. He was speaking with a thick accent. He was thinking in Vietnamese and interpreting into English, searching for words.

"He was afraid of the antiwar groups. They were all trying to solicit him at this time; they thought they had a big hero.

"That night I went over and picked him up and he and Dale and I sat around the kitchen table and talked, literally, all night long until eight o'clock the next morning until the kids woke up. Now when I say talked, Dale said nothing, Dale sat and listened. Bobby and I talked. Dale was visibly trying to judge what man this was, whether you should believe him or not.

"Bobby and I were trying to carry on a conversation, but it was very hard. He was very upset, he was scared. He was slipping into Vietnamese and out of Vietnamese and he was stopping and searching for a word and then he would repeat himself, so it was a very tedious conversation. It was emotional. He was shaking. He was scared.

"He kept going over and over and over it. The main thing he kept saying over and over was that he didn't understand what was going on—he didn't understand what was happening. I was trying to tell him, 'Bobby, of course you don't understand, but let me try to explain to you in the simplest terms I can: Bobby, you are an embarrassment, you are not only an embarrassment to the Vietnamese government, Bobby, you are an embarrassment to this country because you are not supposed to be alive. You are not supposed to have come home.' All night he talked about Ike Isenbraun and was very emotional, he talked about Russ Grissett. He spent that weekend with us, and later we went to a motorcycle race.

"That night when Bobby went back, Dale said, 'They ought to leave the kid alone. You know,' he said, 'Donna, he is close to a breakdown. Why don't they let him go to a psychiatrist, he needs help?'

"Well, as the weeks progressed Bobby would come over. A friend would pick him up, he would come over, sometimes stay at night, always stay on the weekend. Plus he'd make some friends at the base, and he would always go to church on Sunday, unless we were out on account of a race. And he was very religious. He said God got him out of Vietnam, and I said, 'Yeah, I know.'

"Along about the end of May, first of June, we went to a road race.

"It was the first time Bobby really lost his cool. We were having a wonderful time, and a friend of mine named Moriko, I don't know if she pronounces it that way, it's Japanese, came up to us and Bobby flashed back, Dale had to literally restrain him. He saw an Oriental face and he flashed back. I didn't know what was going on and neither did Moriko, and Dale just took Bobby away. He wasn't the same the whole rest of the day and coming back he started crying. He started talking about Ike and about Russ, the Vietnamese, how much he hated them, how much he hated all Orientals, and how they turned him into an animal. He started talking Vietnamese again.

"Out at Lejeune they were hassling him. Someone broke a window in his barracks, they had him across from the enlisted men's club—the kids would go get drunk.

"Dale said, 'Pack your bag, you're moving in.'

"We fixed up that back bedroom for him. He started dating a girl, and then another girl. After a while I found out he had a problem. He told me he could not—how can I say this without sounding gross?—he could not keep an erection long enough to reach a climax. And masturbation was about the only way he could go.

"He was convinced that he would never be normal. I told him that it was all in his mind. I had had POW wives, friends who had had husbands come back from Vietnam after eight or nine years who had gone through the same thing.

"Here's something that nobody knows but me and Bobby. And probably Dale. I decided I knew what Bobby needed, and I knew how to do it. I chose my time, and I chose my opportunity, and when things were just right, I seduced him, and I did it in a way that completely surprised him, that completely took him off guard, without a word, and he reached a climax.

"I did it with no guilt, with no feeling of anything except that I loved him like a baby. Like some lonesome child. I knew what he needed—I'll never forget the words he said—he just smiled, he got tears in his eyes and he said, 'I beat them again.'

"Afterward Bobby got cooler and cooler to me. He was polite but it was like he didn't trust me anymore.

"I don't know whether he was telling me the truth or not, but he felt guilty. He didn't want it to go any further, he said he loved Dale more than he loved me and he trusted Dale more than he trusted me. He was still suspicious of me during that whole time. My motives, my reasons.

"He said he hadn't met anyone he had been completely honest with and told things and had done things the way I had done. And he said he wasn't used to that. And he was very suspicious of it. He didn't understand it. One night they came in and they had their arms around each other and both of them had been crying. It was the third time in my life I saw my husband cry. They had been drinking. I loved both of them so much—in different ways, and Dale looked at me and said, 'You know I love this kid.' "

24
The Court-Martial

"I THINK that's quite clear. The charges come out of a very short period of time, essentially the witnesses can only testify between 1966 and 1967. Bobby was in Vietnam for fourteen years. The severity of the crimes he is charged with from a moral point of view isn't very high. These aren't heinous deeds, at least not pulling out fingernails or cutting off hands or killing people or whipping people, or even pointing a weapon at anybody. There's no charge of anything like that. So we're dealing with a very small quantum of misconduct but nevertheless it's considered misconduct by the letter of the law, which is what the Marine Corps is completely adhering to in the trial. That's why I say this is a one-issue case. It's a psychiatric case because the evidence is overwhelming that Bobby did . . ."

Vaughn Taylor, Garwood's young lawyer (in conversation with a psychiatrist he hoped to sway to his way of thinking), did not complete the sentence but he has said often enough the thrust of it: that Garwood did some of what he is charged with in the jungles of Vietnam; but he did not deliberately desert.

The high and youthful voice of Taylor, careful but apparently artless, is at one with the man's character. Small and trim, he has slightly protuberant eyes and his hands and hair look soft, so that in his U.S. Army uniform, he looks an enigma.

Taylor, fresh out of the Army himself, intensely ambitious but also scholarly, had himself written the instructions for military judges in insanity cases. They then had called him the "genius of the JAG (Judge Advocate General's) School"

333

and had deferred to him. He was the kind of young lawyer the Army wishes they had more of—clear-thinking, specific, intense, and a specialist in an age of specialization.

Taylor took immediate notice of the Garwood case, but like a man in the wrong place at the right time, he could only wish that it might fall to him. It happens so seldom in the Army that a case with huge publicity comes along, a case that seems to capture the essence of a whole chapter of history, a case involving the military, a case that could certainly have a psychological defense.

Taylor's yearning, from his station as a JAG assistant professor at the Army's legal headquarters at the University of Virginia, Charlottesville, must have been almost audible.

But Garwood was already in the hands of several attorneys. Two, Captain Dale Miller and Lieutenant Joseph Composto, had been appointed by the Marine Corps as a matter of course. The third, Dermot Foley, had contacted Garwood's father and told him of his interest.

So Bobby Garwood first heard about Taylor when he was already lawyer-bound. Always shackled, always unarmed, Garwood can no more escape entanglements than fly to the moon. They follow him, stick to him like monstrous flies drawn to some scent. His choice is usually abominable, but in the case of Taylor, someone else made the choice for him.

That was Miller, the mustachioed beaver of a man who was one of the first military lawyers on the case. But Miller, in his humility, suspected he would not be the man to see the case through.

Not that there were no immense attractions in the case, and in the notoriety of conducting the defense of the only Vietnam War veteran to be tried after the release and official pardoning of nearly six hundred POWs in 1973.

Miller and Composto were simply cogs in the Marine Corps' legal machinery. What Taylor saw as opportunity, they could only see as a legal case far too complicated, far too scrutinized, far too out of the ordinary.

They were to learn this the hard way, struggling through a preliminary hearing in which they came to rely on their more experienced civilian counterpart, Foley, only to find that though they were expected to defer to Foley, he rarely would to them, only to find that Foley's method of running the defense was too much oriented toward the media to mesh well with the strict and codified procedures in which they had been trained. The situation, by the end of the Article 32, or grand jury proceeding, had become impossible. It was clear by then that the case was not simply going to be a question of identity, witnesses. It was clear that a defense would have to be something quite different from a denial of the evidence.

Though he did not know it, Bobby Garwood was a marked man in his home country long before he returned. As early as 1967 he had been marked, reported on and set up for possible criminal action if he survived prison camp.

Sometime in 1967 the commandant of the Marine Corps had heard enough about his alleged activities to administratively order that he be frozen in rank—an action that would also freeze his pay at the lowest scale in the Corps. This paper money continued to accumulate and the Corps would send status accounts to his father. He was already labeled.

At that point, the Marine Corps was still behaving in what could be called its traditional mode. It was actively seeking the names of men who had committed offenses prejudicial to good discipline with the hope of prosecuting them later. When the mass of POWs were released in 1973, of course, the mood of the country was different. The word came then from Washington that indictments against any of the six hundred men who had suffered so sorely would be out of tune. "Operation Homecoming" couldn't coexist with prosecutions, unless there were very few. And there weren't many. In fact, there were few surviving POWs from either south or north who had not collaborated with the enemy in some way, most usually by signing statements or making propaganda messages. It was such a frequent thing in the camps it had lost all horror, and was almost routine. The prisoners had armed themselves against the guilt involved—and some of the most patriotic officers had "broken" under direct torture.

But 1979 was years later and the Marine Corps memory was long, longer than the tenure in office of officials like President Richard Nixon, Secretary of the Navy John Warner, or Secretary of the Army Howard "Bo" Calloway, who had made it unwritten policy to drop charges against the returnees.

Hodding Carter III, spokesman of the State Department, was the man who set the ball rolling that was to take Garwood to one of the longest and most expensive court-martials in military history, though Carter's part in the action was small, simply the release of the bizarre story that Garwood was alive.

It was not long before Jack Garwood, Sr., already weary of phone calls from the press, or affecting weariness amid the effort of trying to believe that the son that he had thought was dead, or all but dead, was still alive, walked to the phone in the dingy trailer at Adams and heard on the other end the excited voice of Dermot Foley.

By that point Foley almost certainly knew a lot more about POWs than the father of the Garwoods but it was not with the object of offering his services that Foley had tracked Jack Garwood, Sr., and gotten him on the line.

The lawyer had been deep in veterans' affairs ever since his brother Brendan, a pilot, was shot down over North Vietnam in 1967. His obvious reason for calling the elder man was to secure an audience with the son and to find out from someone who knew, he hoped, more than anyone else alive, what had happened to his brother and the rest. Whatever happened in the "Garwood case," he had a double interest in the man.

Jack Garwood, Sr., remembers the call because he hired Foley to become Garwood's civilian lawyer. The father says he asked for no money and if he undertook major work in the case, only payment for his "expenses," when it became "available."

That conversation must have put the fear of jail or worse strongly in the

335

father's mind, for there survives that short and strange letter that he wrote to his son, included in the "orientation" packet that Gunnery Sergeant Langlois gave Garwood on the flight to Okinawa, in which he repeats over and over his advice to remain silent—clearly Foley's work.

By the time Garwood had been through a medical "debriefing" at the Great Lakes Naval Training Center and a three-day reunion at Adams and Indianapolis, Foley was installed as his lawyer and on the military side Miller had been appointed by the Marine Corps.

He was already well aware that the heaviest weights were coming down on him.

Garwood was told, almost as soon as he stepped off the plane at Great Lakes, of charges accusing him of deserting in time of war, urging U.S. soldiers to lay down their arms and unlawfully communicating with the enemy. The worst of the charges, desertion, was punishable with the firing squad.

Perhaps even more foreboding were the words of a congressman, Representative G. V. "Sonny" Montgomery, a Mississippi Democrat, who urged members of a House Veterans' Affairs committee, "Let's not make a hero out of him. . . . He should be put in jail, he should be tried."

Foley started immediately to advise Garwood to fight back, telling his client to reveal nothing about the period of his captivity and attacking on the strongest point in Garwood's favor—the almost certain assumption that he never "deserted" in time of war.

Garwood's capture story quickly leaked to the press: that he was in uniform, that he was on a legitimate military errand, that he was surprised and taken but not before he had drawn his weapon and attempted to resist, killing at least one Vietnamese, and that he was tied up, stripped, and taken away from the place of capture.

The day after his first reunion with his father, Garwood was expanding on this story, adding the memorable statement, "I've read in the newspapers that the maximum punishment for me is execution. That's what the Vietnamese told me all those years. At least I'll be buried on American soil."

This approach suited Garwood well. In the first place, it was the way he saw himself. He had always been accused of doing the wrong thing and always, to him, the accusations had nothing to do with his own reality. The second, most important charge against him, desertion, was simply impossible. For all the unsavory incidents of his career as a soldier he had never wavered in his desire to return to the one home he knew. When, in a moment of forgetfulness, he described himself as a "simple American street bum," he made a statement that precluded desertion.

Whoever in the Corps decided that desertion should be among the charges made up for Garwood must have reflected the venom that the officers who make up the Marine mentality felt about the whole shabby "Operation Homecoming" business. Plus an additional jolt that Garwood was a Marine, that the last POW was a Marine.

There is an argument that if Foley had not made himself accessible to the media as he did, and the press had not forced the trial by rubbing the Marine Corps' nose in the case, there would have been no court-martial, and the Marine Corps would have been satisfied with some lesser punishment. Garwood believes this now but when he was Foley's client he could think of nothing but to rebut and Foley seemed to be doing well.

Miller, the Marine-appointed lawyer, saw that his client was in desperate trouble and in truth not such a bad fellow, perhaps miscast as a soldier and certainly miscast as a stolid prisoner of the death-before-dishonor variety—and that he, himself, had only a smattering of the knowledge required to do the defense of a case like this justice.

Miller, however, knew of Vaughn Taylor, who had practically written the book on psychiatric defense in military cases and was the author of jury instructions so good they had been adopted by the military courts.

Miller later knew another thing, and that was that Taylor, while teaching at the Judge Advocate General's School, where the Army's young lawyers are given their training, had taught a student named Werner Hellmer. That young man, capable, tight, nervous, was about to prosecute the biggest case of his career, one involving the last POW to return from Vietnam.

Just as chance found Taylor frustrated at the JAG school, it also threw Hellmer into the case; he was an understudy, hauled in to take the place of the original prosecutor, Major R. J. Marien, who left the military. Hellmer and his colleague, Lieutenant Theresa T. Wright, were replacements, brought in in the middle of things. Hellmer and Wright knew nothing about the case until it had reached the Article 32, or grand jury, stage. They were both fledglings—Hellmer got his law degree in 1976 and Wright, a former school teacher, had even less experience.

The Marine Corps moved with such a stifled, muffled pace, taking four months to hold an "investigation" of the charges against Garwood and another two months for a preliminary hearing, that the internal argument may be seen as having been fierce. From May 16, 1979, to November, they probed what Garwood had allegedly done, doubtless going over the dozens of "debriefing" examinations from 1973 from returning POWs who mentioned his name and studying especially carefully those debriefings which gave specifics, names and dates, of the various acts of misconduct he might be charged with.

The prosecutors were never part of the investigation, not Marien, and much less Hellmer and Wright. When Garwood stepped off the plane at Camp Lejeune, a voluminous file, which has never been made public and probably never will be, was sent from Marine Corps headquarters. Defense inquiries revealed later that the file was approximately two and one half feet high.

Marien was ordered to study the file and report periodically to Lejeune's deputy staff judge advocate Major Neal Rountree. The summer passed and then on November 26, Foley made his first move, filing a writ of habeas corpus with the Court of Military Appeals. Habeas corpus, one of the simplest actions a lawyer can take, asks simply that the accused be brought before a court and that some announcement of the intentions of the prosecuting authority be made.

In this case, Foley wanted more than a simple statement of intent to justify the long delay in the case. Foley needed money for the defense. His method was to include in his writ arguments asking the higher court to dismiss the charges against Garwood, which were not formal charges, but merely a notification of pending charges; he filed a deposition from Garwood himself, which said he was virtually imprisoned by poverty and circumstance.

The petition to the court said that he could not get medical and psychological help because under military law whatever he told doctors could be used against him; that the Corps had not taken a single step to move the case ahead, and that the Corps was withholding over $145,000 in back pay that had accrued during his imprisonment, making it impossible for him to prepare his defense.

Foley's strongest case was for the back pay, since a similar case had been decided in favor of a returning turncoat after the Korean War; but another point, which must have caused some consternation, was the undeniable fact that the Marine Corps had extended his enlistment without his permission, a step which was not taken with the 193 returnees, all of whom were separately interviewed about their wishes.

Of course without Garwood in the Marines, the military would have no jurisdiction; he would walk free.

Both sides seemed to be waiting passively; the Marines were unclear about policy and Foley had little knowledge of what specifics he would have to contend with. Things happened fast enough when the papers were filed in Washington, however.

The next day, charges were lodged against Garwood. According to Rountree, the coincidence of time had nothing to do with Foley's writ. The investigation had simply come to an end.

Ahead lay the first public part of the legal process of assessment of blame; the Marine Corps scheduled the Article 32 hearing to determine whether Garwood should be tried for the charges against him. Foley, infuriated, called it "retaliation." But he was pleased by one thing—some of the original charges had been dropped or changed. Garwood was now accused of having deserted in 1967, not 1965. The period between September 1965 and March 1979 was designated by a new charge, "unauthorized absence."

Two charges—that he had caused the tortures of Eisenbraun and Grissett— were also dropped but another charge, that of maltreatment of a prisoner named Harker during the cat incident, was added, as was a charge that he maltreated "Top" Williams verbally by shouting at him, "I spit on you, and all people like you disgust me," while participating in a "criticism" session under the guns of Viet Cong guards.

As the allegations boiled down, they included five charges: that Garwood deserted in time of war when he disappeared in the September dusk in 1965 outside Da Nang; that he solicited American combat forces to throw down their arms and refuse to fight, allegedly slipping close to U.S. lines with a bullhorn in 1967 and 1968; that he unlawfully held conversations with the enemy, a vague catchall of a charge; that he maltreated two other prisoners of war; and that he acted as an enemy interrogator, interpreter, and guard against his fellow prisoners.

Though these charges sounded heavy from the prosecution's side, there were plenty of problems. In the first case, the idea of taking Garwood to court was not a full-blooded thought, but a limp defensive obligatory kind of thing. There had been rumors for years about Vietnam turncoats, and debriefings from 1969 when three POWs, including Jim Strickland of Dunn, North Carolina, and William Watkins of Sumter, South Carolina, were released as a propaganda gesture to coincide with the massive moratorium on the war that November. Both men had lived with Garwood in the jungle camps and knew him, and both thought that Garwood had simply disappeared in 1969, perhaps to North Vietnam, perhaps to another camp. The Marine Corps' wish was that he remain forever out of sight. A year before, a patrol had spotted a Caucasian with Viet Cong or North Vietnamese regulars west of Da Nang; they had fired a burst of bullets at the strange figure, who was said to be wearing a red diagonal sash. The man fell, shouting for help in English, and later four troopers identified Garwood's face from file photographs. That encounter was on July 15 but POWs at camps said Garwood was there with them at the time.

The trouble was that the issue of Garwood was becoming close to hysterical. He was the turncoat personified, the White Cong. Even though the Marines had cut his raises in pay and automatic promotions in 1967, they were enigmatic in a letter to his father in December 1969, telling Garwood Sr. that three recently "released U.S. Army prisoners of war reported conversing with your son on October 24, 1969, the day before they were released. Your son made no specific requests; however, he did state that he would like for you to know he is okay. The three returnees reported that they saw your son in the prisoner of war compound frequently and that he appeared in good health."

This of course was not half or a quarter of what the Naval Intelligence Service, the investigatory arm of the Marine Corps, thought they had on Garwood.

The Marine Corps thought it had most of its case laid out but much of it was only vague rumors. It is perhaps because of the age-old love of rumors, and their ability to take every conceivable form in the minds of soldiers—who have been lied to by commanders throughout history, and never more so than in the Vietnam War—that the military system of justice is far more rigorous than the civilian system in the matter of hearsay, and in other ways. Thus, tactically, the situation did not look bad as the winter drifted down on the North Carolina lowlands. In the life of any case, only the defendant sees it as a whole, a developing drama with a beginning, middle, and end. To the lawyers, it is a group of pressure points, or stages, between which other cases and other matters must be dealt with. The case simply disappears from life for long periods of time.

One of the most peculiar facets of Garwood's existence was its complete lack of underpinnings, its vagueness, its quality of being without the guideposts of experience or learning. His past was nothing but a jumbled nightmare, his education a dim and useless memory, his knowledge confined to the innards of internal combustion engines, his moral sense only that of a boy who has been senselessly burned by the flame. He knew how to cook rats, how to cozen guards, how to avoid punishment to a degree. What did he know of lawyers, tactics, military law? Foley . . . was he a good lawyer or a bad one?

His problem was far more serious than simple ignorance, for he did not know which of the voices to believe.

So from his point of view, it was a lucky thing that he was to be examined under the legal system of the military: paternalistic, class-oriented, and inflexible, but in some ways more equitable than the civilian courts.

In a court-martial, the person being tried is not the defendant but the "accused," a difference symbolic of the whole tilt toward burden of proof. In court-martial the prosecutor has a greater responsibility to make the case beyond reasonable doubt.

The makeup of the jury is one of the most important distinctions; they are not called jurors, but "members"—indicating their identification with the court rather than the public. They are not peers but, in Garwood's case, they were officers or senior NCOs selected for their length of service and "judicial temperament," a far cry from the ideal of civilian lawyers in criminal cases. Their number can vary but there must be more than five. The selected panel may be challenged, with no limit on the challenges for cause, but only one per side may be excused for no reason, peremptorily. Every verdict is automatically appealed, adding some little pressure on prosecutors to build a fault-free record.

Another large difference lies in the judges, who are always lawyers, and are chosen not by ballot, but by the Judge Advocate General, from among recommendations from a battery of military lawyers. Most military judges attend special schools, and they are accountable only to the Advocates General of their services, not to the commanders of their bases.

The judge in the Garwood case, Colonel R. E. Switzer, was a fifty-year-old Korean War veteran from Buffalo, New York, who quit the Marine Corps for twelve years between wars and rejoined at the outbreak of the Vietnam War. He looked like a Norman Rockwell dentist or druggist, kindly but easy to affront and a little self-conscious, with his balding head, creased eyes and moustache. He was one of only two Marine Corps judges in North Carolina qualified to try general courts-martial.

It is interesting to speculate what would have been the outcome if Garwood had returned with the 1973 bunch. There would almost certainly have been some move to prosecute him, and almost as certainly the decision not to would have been made. Among those returnees were men who had performed far worse violations of the code of conduct, including a group who are alleged to have formed a peace committee in the Hanoi prisoner of war system and among whose deeds is counted the manufacture of model planes, replicas of those flying against the north, so that identification by Hanoi's gunners would be easier. What would have happened to this group, numbering eight enlisted men and two officers, if they had been detained instead of Garwood and returned in 1979?

The politics that guided the Defense Department will only be known when the pertinent memoranda are unclassified and published. What surfaced at Camp Lejeune was an agonizingly long period of investigation and a military preliminary hearing or an "Article 32 investigation" that was an anticlimax.

Garwood, in the meantime, was going through a series of changes more drastic than anything since that September day in 1965.

Within a short space he had returned home, appeared like a ghost to his stunned and slightly wary family, and found that he was no hero, nor was he a nobody. He was, instead, notorious. He was famous the wrong way and he found out the hard way, from hostile, poisonous letters and the obscene shouting and ranting of the youth of the Marine Corps.

He stepped out of a hospital almost into the arms of Donna Long, and when he arrived at his "duty station" at Camp Lejeune, where the Marine Corps decided to stash him while they decided what to do with his still-breathing remains, he fell almost immediately into the Longs' orbit.

At first he withdrew completely. He was given a job sorting mail, with other clerical duties added to it. It was on the base in an office away from the mainstream of life, away from the process of training and toughening young men to be soldiers and to kill. In the early days of his time at Lejeune, he went to his job at 8:00 A.M., worked until after four, returned to his barracks room and never left it.

Those who saw him in this period said he was fearful, crippled, a wreck. He walked hunched over, shuffled his feet, spoke with a Vietnamese accent, was completely passive.

His first home was one of a few three-man rooms on the base, room 210. White-walled, standard military, with the minimum ninety square feet of living space per man. The space was no problem. Garwood owned literally nothing. He was as clean in that respect as a baby; he was returned to Lejeune on March 25 and declared fit for duty on the fourteenth of April, 1979.

The hate the Marine Corps instills in its trainees didn't take long to find its way to Garwood in glances, gestures, letters. In an almost bravura note of callousness, Garwood's bedroom window opened on the parking lot feeding the enlisted men's club, a place where the most noisy outrages can be heard. The window was soon broken.

If it had not been for the Longs he would have had reason to go mad—still a boy, in his own mind, balding, with no education or family guide, no past and certainly no future, and carrying dreadful secrets, in the country where every seventeen-year-old punk is a hero and a killer of "gooks."

So he sat in his barracks room alone, flicking his butane lighter, one of the first purchases he had made, and watching television endlessly while the military legal process walked heavily down its own jungle trails.

Dale and Donna Long may have saved him from madness. Certainly no psychiatrist, psychologist, or therapist could have in that early period, because under military law, anything he told a doctor could be used against him. He could not leave the Corps, because if he did, the authority of the military courts would cease—and the crimes of which he was accused were not even on the lawbooks of any other U.S. court. It was a proper sort of limbo, for once with no hyperbole.

With Garwood under their noses the military made no attempt to question him or those with whom he associated—the casual friends he made on the base or the Longs. Take this for kindness, stupidity, or simply fear of legal problems later, there was a certain correctness in everything the Marine Corps did, an air of playing the game fair. Hard but fair.

There is little doubt that somewhere, possibly in the office of the President, in the corridors of the Pentagon, on the rich carpets, there was a consensus that the "rot had to stop." It was bad enough to let the collaborators in the Hanoi camps off, to let the draft dodgers and deserters dribble back to the U.S. unhounded, if not unpunished. The thing that made Garwood different was that it was alleged that he had joined the enemy. Not simply deserted, not simply broken down and used as a gofer by the enemy, but actively joined them. The key in the military minds was that Garwood had allegedly refused repatriation in 1973, when everyone was allowed to come back. He had cast his lot with North Vietnam; he had made his bed and then been unable to sleep in it.

To Garwood, it seemed but a continuation of the cloud of trouble in his life. He took advantage of what was offered to him in this year of limbo between the awkward homecoming, with the one flower from Donna, and the repeated warnings and the beginning of his trial on May 22.

He was offered friendship as well as enmity, and he took it; he was offered another man's wife, and he cannot be blamed for taking that. He lived a miniature lifetime in that year, all in the weekends and evenings. He was given a car, he was given a place at the motorcycle repair shop operated by Dale Long, taught to ride a motorcycle. It was the pleasantest time of his life, in spite of the trial hanging over him. In a way it was the only life he had in all his years.

Garwood was thirty-three when he met the Longs, but really about nineteen. Nothing that he had learned in Vietnam was useful to him, except to make him a spectacle, and a curious sense of shame kept him from exploiting that. He waited, and watched, and attached himself to other people. It was not difficult.

He went to the Longs from his bare room out of curiosity, out of an unnatural sense of refuge. He went to them because they wanted him, or at least Donna Long wanted him to fulfill her work on the missing in action and the POWs. She was hoping to make something out of him, something of the cause. But he was impenetrable, passive, and emotional. He had retreated so far into himself that every effort they made was just to bring him out. It was as if they were training a retarded child who made large progress but was still far behind. In this, he was captivating, and at length both Donna and Dale Long centered their lives and their troublesome marriage around this large and passive child who seemed so vulnerable and needy.

To Garwood, the year was a waterfall of bounty. He was used to being in prison, under suspicion or far worse, so that hostility and legal action had little effect. He was fond of saying that if someone had put a gun to his head he would have laughed at them. But he was also fond of looking at his red '56 Chevrolet, which Donna Long gave him, and saying that it was the first real "thing" he had ever owned in his life.

The car had more than a garage existence. It is still the first citizen of Garwood's emotional republic in 1982. He drove home to Indianapolis with it like the farm boy showing off his city style, but the engine blew up. To Garwood, everything about the car, from its stifled fins to its whalelike maw and its roaring hoodlum V-8 engine, was "better than they make now."

Garwood's only mark of activity in the preparations for his trial was to drive the car to the court sessions. He devoted his time off to it, spending all his salary on parts, and with the help of friends, repairing the damage done by driving with the old engine, installing a new engine and several special fittings that gave it the air of a resurrected hot rod, a car somehow mashed into life, as if a grandfather were given a heavy dose of speed.

It was the third of December when the Article 32 proceeding began in a tiny military courtroom on the base, but the week was taken up with procedural matters; it was announced that fifteen witnesses would be called by the government to testify against him. Foley said he was undecided about witnesses.

In fact, there were no witnesses Garwood could call. Foley asked for a postponement until January, arguing that since the hearing did not have subpoena powers, witnesses would be reluctant to testify on a mere request and would substitute statements, which could not be cross-examined by counsel for the accused. The appeal for delay was rejected.

Six days before Christmas, Frank Anton, the helicopter pilot who was shot down in Happy Valley in 1968, looking jaded and slightly plump, testified before the presiding officer, Major T. B. Hamilton, Jr. Anton made the first serious assault for the prosecution.

He said Garwood lived apart from the other prisoners, with camp interpreters, not in the compound where the Americans were kept, that he appeared to act as a guard on missions to gather food, that he carried a picture of Ho Chi Minh, and that he carried a rifle on more than one occasion. He described a Garwood who was eager to explain that he was working for the Communists because he had been promised his freedom.

Anton also confirmed two other stories, which were to become staples of the prosecution case: that Garwood had stolen a chicken and given it to the others, telling them to cook it and leave aside the two legs for him. The chicken was to have served a dozen starving POWs, Anton related; at least six later died of malnutrition and wounds in the camp where Anton and Garwood were together.

The other story crucial to the prosecution was that Garwood had struck David Harker after the Americans tried to hide a camp cat they had killed and skinned and were preparing to eat. Garwood and the guards rushed down when the cat was discovered and Garwood was apparently infuriated that one prisoner, Russ Grissett, had been allowed to take the entire blame.

Anton set the tone that others followed, elaborating the theme with incidents, adding accounts of conversations they personally heard, details that differed, yet were the same in kind. The prosecution's witnesses repeated over and over that Garwood was the different one, that he "went the whole hog" in cooperation with the enemy, while they, though they cooperated also when under threat, did as little as possible.

The essence of the POW testimony, and more important, the impetus behind the testimony, the reason why the ex-POWs were willing to testify against Garwood after so many years had passed, was that they hated him while they were in the camps, but their hatred only kindled anew when they heard that Garwood was denying all the allegations against him.

Anton wrote to the authors long after the trial, an angry letter full of denunciation, ending with a milder, almost sorrowful note. "A lot of mistakes were made by the POWs in Vietnam," he wrote. "None of us, however, except Bob Garwood, crossed over to the side of the enemy, in spite of the hardships. Garwood certainly spent a long and miserable fifteen years in Vietnam . . . The amazing thing to me is that if Garwood had come home admitting his mistake and professing a sorrow for his actions, some of us, myself included, would not have testified against him at all."

The first four witnesses to state the government's case against Garwood were all enlisted men, like him. But there were other factors which linked some of them together, and to the case.

Anton and the three men who followed him to the stand to testify, Sergeant Isaiah McMillan, Sergeant William Watkins, and Sergeant Robert Lewis, were still in the military. The subsequent witnesses, Gustav Mehrer, Luis Ortiz-Rivera and David Harker, were all civilians by then. There was balance, after the military lead, and there was diversity—the white, the black, the Hispanic.

It was a world of time away and another universe from the hot paddy land where the other prisoners of the Viet Cong/NVA first knew their strange captivity, to the courtroom at Camp Lejeune; all they had to link them with that past, now twelve years in memory, was "the accused."

Garwood sat as usual—taciturn, motionless, his eyes neither guilty with interest nor bored. He claimed to have fallen asleep several times during the preliminary phase of the trial, and had no particular feelings of shock to see his former prison mates, Anton, Lewis, McMillan, Watkins, Harker, and Ortiz-Rivera, testify against him. Garwood's explanation of their actions was equivalent to his own.

The explanation, which never came out in court because Garwood never took the stand, was that he had been picked as a kind of "scapegoat" by the others, particularly the group who testified against him. Because of his seniority in captivity, his adaptation to jungle life, his tutelage under Isenbraun, he immediately offended the new prisoners, who saw him as a "white gook." His efforts to be friendly with them first got him into trouble, for it is his way to exaggerate his advantages, to try to make others envy and look up to him. This explains the extraordinary admissions he is said to have made, such as disclosing that he broadcast messages to U.S. troops with a bullhorn—things that were described at the trial in the kind of fine detail that lends credibility to them as bravura gestures.

Whether Garwood did these things is a question that each individual interested in his case must decide. But there is little doubt that he talked about it.

There may have been other reasons the rookie prisoners turned against him. He turned against them, as well, resenting their dependence, as one who has solved a problem may resent the struggles of the ignorant.

"They kept asking for more and more," Garwood remembers.

The recollection of Anton, at least on the subject of the first sighting of Garwood, has a certain precision to it because of the events of Happy Valley. He, Lewis, Pfister, Harker—all met Garwood at the same time. All of them spoke of the same things—that Garwood had a weapon, that he seemed to be "with" the guards, that he was obscurely in charge of some part of camp life, that he was allowed the freedom of the camp, that he assisted with interrogations.

There could have been little doubt, after Anton's testimony was corroborated by the others, that Hearing Officer Major Thomas B. Hamilton would recommend that Garwood be court-martialed. The versions told by Anton, Lewis, McMillan and Gustav Mehrer all converged. Except for one thing, it would have been repetitive.

During the third day of testimony, Watkins almost casually let out that prisoners had "signed statements" against the war under duress. The information seemed to electrify Foley, who had expended much of his energy on arguments that the defense be allowed to review unedited tape recordings of NIS interviews of the ex-POWs who were testifying against his client.

Under Foley's questioning, Watkins told the hearing that it was simply impossible to resist when the camp leaders and guards decided to force the submission of a prisoner. Foley also made the discovery that witnesses would backtrack on their testimony under cross-examination pressure—not such an important point in a hearing where the outcome is not a judgment of guilt or innocence but merely a decision to put the question to a jury. But a development more hopeful at the early stages than Foley's tactics outside the hearing room, where he continued to spread the word that Garwood was suffering from several severe diseases, and mental problems as well.

Christmas intervened in what was to be the only relatively swift part of Garwood's ordeal, and after it, the prosecution put on the most interesting witness of the pretrial hearing. He couldn't even really speak English, the burly, gray-tinged Puerto Rican the others had called only "Ortiz."

Luis Ortiz-Rivera was the cavalryman with the least time in prison of any of Garwood's contemporaries. He had been released by the Viet Cong only thirteen months later in a "good will" ceremony with another Spanish-speaking GI, Agostos Santos.

It was clear within a few minutes that Ortiz-Rivera's sole purpose from the government's point of view was to establish that Garwood had become a deserter. Since it took only a little investigative prowess to discover that there was no way to disprove his story about the Mighty-Mite, the trip to Marble Mountain, and the terrifying materialization of twenty to thirty of the enemy at dusk, there had to be a way to justify the most serious of the charges. Now Ortiz-Rivera supplied it.

Through an interpreter he told the hearing that at the time of his release he simply signed statements that were put before him by his captors. He had to be told of his "liberation" by Santos, who knew enough English to interpret into Spanish what the Vietnamese interpreter said to him.

In Ortiz-Rivera's eyes, there was no reason for his good fortune. He and Santos were both picked out, as Garwood had been six months before. They were given red sashes, there was a ceremony, a special meal. Meat made it a feast, Ortiz-Rivera said. But after the ceremony, only he and Santos were released.

From the point of view of the defense, this "desertion" charge must have seemed as slim as rice paper. And as to collaboration, Garwood seemed to have done no more than the others.

Harker was the last POW witness. There had been talk of a Vietnamese ex-POW, Le Dinh Quy, but that was not to be at this stage. Harker, a probation officer in Lynchburg, Virginia, was articulate and forceful, and unlike Anton, Lewis, McMillan, he was not still military. He came to the hearing as a volunteer, not a military volunteer. Harker was tough and respected by the other POWs as a hard worker and a resister. He pictured Garwood as a man with special privileges, a man to whom the guards pointed as a "progressive" prisoner, a man who greeted his captors with hugs and smiles.

Harker was the subject of one of the worst counts in Garwood's charge sheet. "That, during the period from about June 1969 until December 1969, in the Democratic People's Republic of Vietnam, PFC Garwood maltreated PFC David M. Harker, U.S. Army, a prisoner held by the enemy, by striking him in the ribs with his hand.

"That the act occurred while PFC Garwood was in the hands of the enemy in time of war;

"That PFC Garwood held a position of authority over PFC David M. Harker; and

"That the act was without justifiable cause."

The "maltreatment" was glossed over by Harker, as if he was a little ashamed of being the cause of such a heavy matter as a possible death penalty: It was the cat incident, and Harker said, "PFC Garwood struck me with the back of his fist in about the middle of the rib cage and said something to the effect that, 'someone's going to have to pay for Russ being punished like this.' "

Harker's strongest points, like those made by Anton, who was recalled to drum them in, were that Garwood was completely different from the others. The difference, as put by Anton, was that "the few things he did to help us were outweighed. Simply, that's the difference. We were prisoners."

Harker: "PFC Garwood at no time indicated to me that he was being forced to do those things by his captors. PFC Garwood accepted favors by living with the Vietnamese. He had a different status from us. He had free access to the place, to come and go as he pleased. He seemed to enjoy his work. He greeted his captors with hugs and smiles when he came back into camp. He was emotional; they would welcome him with open arms."

Fortunately for him, Garwood did not stand accused of smiles, enjoyment, or hugs. With Harker's testimony, and that of three non-POWs, two of whom testified that there was no evidence Garwood had an authorized duty errand the night he went missing, and the third that he had personally heard English-language messages broadcast to his troops while on patrol near the estimated location of the 1968 POW camps—the hearing ended with a jerk.

Foley was baffled by the sudden finale; he had been told of a parade of witnesses, and since his method was to pick away at detail, he almost welcomed more material with which to weave a contrary record. "I wish to hell I knew what's going on," he told reporters, his red face beaming sincerity, "I'm getting more confused than anybody."

Though Foley had contented himself with lawyerly doubt-seeding, his counter-move was on a different tack. After the prosecution finished its case for a court-martial, Foley decided to edge toward some sort of a mental-incapacity defense. He discovered that, putting together Garwood's medical record, recurrent headaches and head injuries were mentioned more frequently than anything else. He called it "classic symptoms of a very severe brain concussion," and told reporters it had occurred before Garwood was sent to Vietnam in 1965.

It was not very much, even when backed by the testimony of a contemporary from Garwood's Okinawa days, who said he had once witnessed a serious head injury that Garwood suffered.

Foley's strategy was to go to court-martial and win a complete exoneration rather than reveal his full defense at the outset.

347

A day later, on February 1, 1980, Major Hamilton recommended that Garwood be court-martialed. He did not need to review the testimony. Composto argued that the government's case was too vague, but Hamilton was not listening to a well-made point. "No one had any free will," the young military lawyer told the court. "There was no free choice." He said Garwood should be tried in a special court-martial, the military equivalent of a misdemeanor court.

Hamilton grew stentorian: "If believed, the evidence clearly supports the inference that the accused engaged in the conduct alleged for the express purpose of escaping the fate of all the others, who for one reason or another, found themselves in the hands of the enemy," he said. "Clearly, their fate ranged from eventual release to death. It is my opinion that the accused should now, if convicted, be placed at the risk of the same spectrum of fate endured by those from whom he freely disassociated himself over a decade ago."

But in spite of Hamilton's doom-tinged verbiage, he recommended dropping two of the original charges: that Garwood was on unauthorized absence during his years in Vietnam, and that he tried to cause insubordination and disloyalty among other POWs.

Nevertheless, the charges remained desertion, soliciting American troops to throw down their arms, collaborating with the enemy by accepting a position in the North Vietnamese Army, acting as a guard, interpreter, and so on, "maltreating" Harker, "maltreating" another POW verbally.

Foley said he was pleased that the two charges had been dropped and hinted to reporters that he had plenty of ammunition—he simply had not wanted to use it.

25
A Question of Sanity

LESS THAN a week later, Garwood was arrested for what they call DUI in Jacksonville. His blood alcohol registered one hundredth of a percentage point over the legal limit for intoxication. The charge was later reduced to reckless driving, to which he pleaded guilty and got a thirty-day sentence (suspended) and a fifty-dollar fine. He had been stopped on a Thursday night. One of the taillights on the gaudy but aging red '56 Chevy was out and the driver smelled of beer. A few days later, the commanding general at Camp Lejeune, Brigadier General David B. Barker, ordered Garwood's court-martial, to the surprise of no one; what was a surprise was that Barker rejected Major Hamilton's larded "same spectrum of fate" argument and excluded the death penalty.

Once again, Bobby Garwood floated free, now more quickly drifting toward the final judgment of his behavior. He returned to his mail-sorting job, with the important difference that he was now a man in process, one who could not evade his future. He had the dignity of the condemned, and few who had followed the Article 32 proceeding could think that he was anything but guilty of the substance of the charges against him.

His private life somehow echoed this sinking. Dale Long had died in a motorcycle accident, a dreadful blow, an unaccountable stab by fate. Garwood was already Donna's lover, and remained so after Dale Long's death. He interested himself in the children, spending hours with them, dabbling with his car. She took the quick mind's interest in the trial proceedings, trying to get information out of Foley. Garwood asked his sister East to be company for Donna—that ended in a squalid disaster and recriminations; there were too many temptations in Jacksonville, and Linda Garwood was exposed to most of them.

To avoid contumely, Garwood moved out of Donna's home and with her help (he was still almost helpless in practical terms) rented a trailer, mainly to give himself an address off the base. He made desultory efforts to date other women. There was curiosity about his notoriety and no repetition of his sexual problems, but Donna was too sympathetic, too available, too strong a presence. He succumbed slowly to her guardianship.

After the Article 32 hearing, with a court date two weeks away, the defense was like a football team that was down 35–0 after the first quarter. They needed a radical change to get on the scoreboard. The first thought, held by both Foley and Miller, was to somehow get Vaughn Taylor on the defense team. There were problems, not the least of which were that Taylor was an Army man, not a Marine, and that Garwood had military attorneys already.

These problems were cut through in a manner so swift and abrupt that it hardly seems credible that Garwood, who was unable to manage even getting his rambunctious and party-loving sister out of town, could have pulled it off.

First Foley, Miller, and Composto asked the judge assigned to the case, Colonel Switzer, for an additional lawyer—Taylor. With this request, Foley submitted a blizzard of motions; the obligatory moves to dismiss for delay of speedy trial, prejudicial news reporting, selective prosecution, and the inability of the accused to use the approximately $150,000 in back pay for his defense. Foley asked also for a change of venue, complained that the military jury system was unconstitutional, asked that Garwood be granted a protected session with a military psychiatrist, and asked that the defense team be allowed to visit Vietnam to gather evidence. He also asked a delay of a month to prepare these motions for argument.

Switzer granted immediately that Garwood be allowed confidentiality with a psychiatrist, and that a delay, though less than Foley had asked, be granted. On March 28, with a day or two of deliberation, Switzer denied all remaining motions relating to the charges.

As a result of all the publicity generated by the case, a trickle of letters had begun to flow into the camp's postal system addressed to "Bobby" Garwood, as the public became aware that one of the country's favorite spectator sports, a large-scale public trial, was waiting to burst forth in the media.

Behind the scenes, some tense maneuvering was going on. Foley is silent about what was passing through his mind at this stage, but it is possible that the prosecution made some sort of sign—some sort of offer, perhaps, to close the case with a plea. Garwood returned from a session deeply troubled, telling Donna that the decision he had to make was the most difficult of his life.

Garwood has said that the only decision was to drop Miller and Composto. They had delivered an ultimatum—either Foley went or they did. Foley had his own way of doing things, which from their point of view completely unmilitary. The only consistent ideas the team had come up with were these: to present Garwood as a lifelong survivor from a deprived background, imprisoned longer than any other U.S. soldier, a man who had simply done what he had to stay alive; and to intensify the evidence about Garwood's headaches and head injuries. He was to be presented as a man who did no more than other, pardoned POWs from Operation Homecoming in 1973, a man who had been singled out for prosecution *"pour encourager les autres."*

But there was doubtless another consideration that night of decision: Either the military lawyers had argued hard for a plea bargain and Garwood had rejected their arguments, forcing them to offer to resign, or Garwood simply preferred Foley's way of doing things. In any case, Miller and Composto left the case and for a while, Foley was alone as Garwood's defender, until the name of a Marine Corps lawyer, Captain Lewis Olshin was put forward.

Garwood and Foley went into conference over the notion of a plea bargain. Afterward, he gave Donna brave words when he returned that night: "I have decided that no matter what happens I am not going to take anything except the trial because I am innocent," he told her.

Foley was well pleased. Now he only needed Vaughn Taylor, who was eager to get in on the case, to add a completely new dimension to the defense. Taylor, he was told, felt strongly that there should be a "coercive persuasion" argument made, proofs shown that Garwood was not only forced by long torture and fear to do the things that he was repeatedly accused of having done, but also had fallen into a mental state wherein he was no longer responsible for his actions.

Switzer had ruled that Garwood could choose either a military or a civilian lawyer but not both—and because of Foley's presence, he had chosen a civilian. Therefore, the argument ran, he could not also have a military lawyer—he would have to stick with what he had.

Taylor was equal even to this. He had already contacted John Lowe, of Lowe and Gordon, an ambitious and rising Charlottesville lawyer whose ambition was only whetted by the fact that he had come to his profession late in life. He had already started a military career and was at the rank of captain when, in a funk about the future, he took an aptitude test used to screen students bound for law school. He scored brilliantly and decided then and there to follow his bent.

Lowe's Army background suited Taylor, who wanted to develop his own little acres of the legal garden and envisioned a military practice centered on the use of his own specialty—legal defenses of insanity of a distinctly fresh, scholarly and thorough nature.

Taylor, the younger man, had applied to the firm for a job when he was thinking of leaving his interesting but unremunerative job teaching young military lawyers. Lowe, silver-haired, socially adept, financially alert, made it clear that Taylor was bound to the firm.

Taylor, as firm as granite under his curly locks and boyish brows, made

351

"arrangements" with John Lowe, his boss. He left the U.S. Army one early spring day and the next day simultaneously joined the firm of Lowe and Gordon and was hired by Bobby Garwood as civilian counsel to aid Foley.

The trial was set to begin on April 21. On April 6 Miller and Composto were relieved and the twenty-nine-year-old Olshin installed. Olshin asked for, and got, a month's delay to familiarize himself with the case. April 11, Garwood checked into a civilian hospital in Jacksonville with an initial diagnosis of a bleeding ulcer, malaria, and mental stress.

He left the hospital after eleven days. Meanwhile, Lowe and Taylor came to terms with Foley and Olshin. Since Taylor had joined Lowe and Gordon, they hired the entire firm, as is customary. So Lowe entered the case, quickly taking a leading role.

Lowe had thirteen years of law behind him when he entered the case. His most notorious case was that of Robert Robideau, an American Indian accused of murdering two FBI agents in Cedar Rapids, Iowa. Robideau was acquitted by a jury. Lowe had wide experience in defending clients in drug cases and had lectured law students on defense tactics in criminal trials.

He is a man of sudden decision and swift action, lightning calculation and the tunnel vision so important to a defense lawyer. But he also has a thirst for the things that money can bring. He married a wealthy woman from a socially prominent family, installed a Jacuzzi in his beautifully restored Charlottesville home, drove a Jaguar with personalized plates and sometimes gets mentioned in the kind of local magazines that cater to the peculiar set of society farmers and well-heeled retirees that make up America's exurban gentry.

The first move the team made, on May 15, was to insist that Garwood see civilian psychiatrists; the attempt, couched in a motion to Judge Switzer, to ask the military to pay for private examination of their client, was a disaster for the defense.

Switzer not only denied the money but ordered instead that Garwood be examined by a panel of military psychiatrists. In the effort, however, Garwood took the witness stand for the first (and almost the last) time in the conduct of his silent defense. He told the judge he no longer trusted military psychiatrists after his experience at Great Lakes, where the main thrust of questions put to him shortly after his return from Hanoi seemed to be to get information that could be used against him at the court-martial.

Lowe denied to Switzer that the defense had decided to raise questions about Garwood's sanity during their part of the case; of course, this was precisely what they *were* hoping to be able to do, but Lowe ingeniously argued that there could be no determination about his sanity under military law until a "substantial basis" had been laid—by psychiatric evaluation.

Between that hearing and June 9, Foley, who was ostensibly the lead lawyer of the defense team, was forced out of the case by Lowe and Garwood, who had been swept off his feet by the new man.

After reviewing the case for a few days, Lowe made a startling move. He decided to persuade Garwood to fire Foley, in whom he had no confidence. And he had a *casus belli*, a *Playboy* magazine interview with Garwood that Foley had permitted and Lowe felt might be damaging to the case. Needless to say, he persuaded Garwood.

He also accepted Donna Long's offer to go ahead with a casual proposal she had made—to throw forty thousand dollars she had in survivors' insurance from Dale Long's death into the defense kitty. Lowe signed a note for it and took the money. "I have received from Donna Long $40,000. I agree to repay Donna Long, or in the event of her death her surviving children, 40 percent of all payments received towards the fee to which I am entitled for the defense of Robert R. Garwood until said $40,000 is fully repaid."

The date was June 4, five days before the dismissal of Foley.

Garwood's rejected attorney could only fume. It is one of the few times in the dance of the law when the power is truly out of the lawyer's hands, and Foley did not take it kindly. Sometime that month, he decided that he would withhold many of the files he had assembled on the case. After all, as he explained, what else,other than these pieces of paper, did he have to show for the legal fees he already estimated at $130,000?

Shortly before her contribution of all her remaining funds, Donna was made paralegal to the team.

Lowe, now in charge through his deft maneuvers, kept up the momentum with a blizzard of new motions, raising the question of wiretaps on Garwood's phone; asking for a study of the use of the herbicide Agent Orange in Vietnam, a defoliant by which Garwood had almost certainly been poisoned, however slightly; and asking for a twelve-member jury to hear the case. This was the civilian touch, and an announcement that a new lawyer was on the scene. Lowe started another flurry of publicity, which spread his name quickly among the local military, by seeking to haul the Camp Lejeune commanding officer, Brigadier General Barker, to the stand, to probe whether he had any knowledge of the details of Garwood's case before he simply put his signature on the official charges that led to the court-martial.

In particular, Lowe was convinced that Barker had not known that Garwood had only ten days to serve in his overseas assignment when he disappeared. It was a good point—another hole in the flimsy case the government was forced to make on the desertion charge.

Lowe knew that there were more important things than getting Judge Switzer to go along with his barrage of motions—though he did manage to get one specification of one charge changed and made such an impression that Switzer told the local newspaper, "I am intrigued with the novelty of defense proposals." He knew that almost every man on the base, and particularly the officers, would be reading about the case. The jury, whatever its numbers, would certainly be picked from men who knew about the case, about Lowe's motions.

Garwood was also to be examined by both military and civilian psychiatrists.

The defense was clearly in a different gear; and a new theory of what may really have happened to Garwood was evolving in the resourceful, relentless mind of Lowe, who was in the game for one thing—to win.

Taylor, for his part, was like a precocious violinist presented with a perfect Stradivarius for the first time. This was his case, his specialty, and in all ways it was apt. The defendant was pliable, the action distant, the witnesses few. Symptoms had already been seen in others with parallel experience. Besides this, Garwood was a symbol of more than mental illness, he was a symbol of the whole tragedy of America in Vietnam—part war, part collapse, part a disturbing mental sickness that leaves everyone uncertain, including any thinking jury.

The final mix of the medical facts of Garwood's mental condition and the evidentiary facts of the imprisonment had surprising roundness. It was like a Catch-22 working, for once, in favor of the enlisted man faced with war. Garwood had to be crazy, or he wouldn't have become the "White Vietnamese." If he was crazy, then he wasn't responsible for what he had done.

It would be Taylor's job to submit Garwood to psychological testing in such a way that it could be shown he had been subject to coercive persuasion—the kind that had already forced even the most diehard prisoners of the North Vietnamese, tough aviators like U.S. Senator Jeremiah Denton, or celebrated jet ace Robinson Risner, to "crack" under severe torture.

It would be up to Lowe to perform a less dramatic but much tougher job: to use every part of the law available to screen testimony, challenge the representation of the two younger and less experienced prosecution attorneys, Hellmer and Wright, and keep out of the case as much evidence as possible.

Nothing unfair about this last tactic—rather it is the essence of the system of advocacy that has made U.S. civil and military courts an example of fairness for over one hundred years. But it made John Lowe's task an essentially negative one. He took the role of the quibbler, the objection raiser. This role had every chance of backfiring, but was helped immeasurably by a device in military law that removes the jury from the courtroom during argument.

During Garwood's long trial, almost as much testimony was recorded in these nonjury sessions, called 39-A sessions, as was heard before the jury; in a great majority of the nonjury sessions, the voice of Lowe, pleading, cajoling, insisting, demanding, refining, fills the entire stage of the courtroom, empty now except for the huddle of attorneys, the judge, and the reporters. It was Lowe's quality that he would not let the smallest point get past. His patience was infinite, though at the same time, he complained bitterly of the delays. Complained at the prosecution, that is.

Lowe's objective was always the same, to limit the material the jury would hear. He would argue for a definition of the time at which Garwood was alleged to have, for instance, used a bullhorn on American troops, and further argue that allegations of the use of a bullhorn outside these perimeters could not be brought in. Only what was exactly relevant to the charges Garwood faced, he repeatedly told the court, could be admitted as evidence against his client. And most of these things happened thirteen years before.

Day after day, the court was filled with the booming voice. And the court bent slowly with the verbal surf, and the prosecution, in its rigid way, could do little against it.

Taylor, armed always with his innocent pale face and a tape recorder, insisted on his right to interview prosecution witnesses, particularly those whose expertise bore on his vision of the psychiatric defense. His view was that the case would be won or lost on the mental issue—whether the jury was convinced that Garwood was suffering a mental disease that affected his mind, emotions and behavior.

Taylor was thorough, as careful as a man working on his own creation, which it was. A conversation he held with one of the prosecution's psychiatrists, Captain Benjamin R. Ogburn, illustrates the dimensions of the defense better than any explanation.

Ogburn was a member of the psychiatrist's panel that examined Garwood, termed a 121 board—three qualified psychiatrists who examined the accused individually and then combined to decide whether, in their view, he was competent and responsible to stand trial.

The board was also asked to answer five questions about him: (1) whether he had sufficient mental capacity to understand the proceedings, (2) whether he had a mental disease or defect at the time of the alleged criminal conduct, (3) what, at the time of the examination, was the psychiatric diagnosis of the accused, (4) whether or not at the time of the alleged conduct, he had the capacity to appreciate the criminality of the conduct, and (5) whether or not he was able to "conform his conduct to the requirements of the law" at the time of the alleged conduct.

The panel found nothing wrong with Garwood; they found he had a personality disorder reaching back to his stingy, gritty childhood—a tendency to avoid situations that threatened him. More damning, the board found that some of the tests Garwood submitted to resulted in scores that showed he tended to feign mental illness.

But under the solidity of the board's findings, the individual psychiatrists had serious doubts, as Taylor was to discover when he reviewed the tape he had made of their interview.

TAYLOR: I've read the report now and realize that you did not find any mental disease or defect in Bobby during the period of time he was in Vietnam, and not at this time either, for that matter. What is your definition for a mental disease? How do you arrive at what is and isn't a mental disease?

OGBURN: I would arrive at it by an examination and by consideration of the history and consideration of how he appears to me and how, what his mental state was at that time.

TAYLOR: What kind of definition of a mental disease would you turn to?

355

OGBURN: I would say a mental disease is an emotional condition that substantially impairs a person in his everyday life and in his relating to other people. That's about it.

TAYLOR: The legal definition that we use in the military is *any abnormal condition* of the mind that substantially affects mental and emotional processes and substantially impairs behavior controls. You found no evidence of that in Bobby?

OGBURN: No, I don't think that's what our report said. I think we did find a defect in the sense that he's got a personality disorder.

TAYLOR: Okay. I guess I'm using terms from the legal sphere that may be too restrictive. You found a dysthymic disorder.

OGBURN: I feel he does have a personality disorder. I also feel at this time he's clinically depressed, and the current nomenclature for that is the dysthymic disorder: the old *depressive neurosis*.

TAYLOR: I understand your assessment of his degree of depression was probably more in tune with what our psychiatrists have told us—that it was very low and that his suicide potential was high, which concerns us for his safety. Is that correct?

OGBURN: Well, I'd say he's depressed; I don't think he's severely depressed. I would say he's moderately depressed, if you want to put it in categories of mild, moderate, or severe. And, I think too, that the suicide potential is there but I don't think that he's actively suicidal at this time or when I saw him.

TAYLOR: Why is it that you don't feel that there was any relationship between what Bobby's charged with doing and the dysthymic disorder?

OGBURN: I don't think the disorder was that disabling or rendered him not able to understand what he was doing, whether to realize the consequences.

TAYLOR: Do you think that he felt that the things that he was doing were wrong?

OGBURN: I felt in his understanding of his situation that he felt that he was doing the best he could, he was trying to survive.

TAYLOR: When he did tell you about it, did he seem to be credible?

OGBURN: Yes.

TAYLOR: Of course, the other prisoners didn't feel that it was appropriate, at least by the time they saw him. They both can't be right, therefore . . .

OGBURN: Yes, they *can* both be right.

TAYLOR: They can? How's that?

OGBURN: Well, I think, you know, his perception of what he was doing is seen from his own eyes and you can take any two people who have seen an event and they will see it differently because of their own experience and their own backgrounds.

TAYLOR: That seems to tie in to Bobby's ability to appreciate the criminality of his conduct. I gather from what you are saying to me that Bobby's perception of what he was doing was that it was not criminal.

OGBURN: Yes, I don't think he felt like he was acting in a criminal manner.

TAYLOR: What was it that kept him from appreciating the criminality of his conduct? I think all the other prisoners felt it was criminal. Society now has taken the point of view it's criminal.

OGBURN: I don't think he was dealing with whether something was criminal or not. He was dealing with himself as a person who was in an extremely harsh environment and he was trying to survive in that.

TAYLOR: Is that saying that if he had stopped to think about it he would realize that it was criminal, but just didn't think about it?

OGBURN: I don't think it's that. I don't think he thought it was that important. But the kind of rules that ordinarily guide us were not pertinent to his situation.

TAYLOR: Well, I don't want to put words in your mouth—and believe me, I'm not trying in any way to change your thoughts on this at all, I'm just trying to understand it—but we have psychiatrists and psychologists working independently for the defense, some in the military, some not, who have come to a conclusion different than the one that the three of you doctors here came to. They found that Bobby did misperceive and the reason he misperceived was because of a mental disease. I'm not sure whether you're saying he misperceived or he just didn't perceive, or he understood that what he was doing was wrong and decided that those laws didn't apply over there because of the prison camp situation or what?

OGBURN: I think he found himself in an entirely alien environment in which his primary goal was to survive and I don't feel that he felt that the ordinary rules that apply were applicable to that situation.

TAYLOR: Okay. But that had nothing to do with a thought disorder or anything like that?

OGBURN: No, I didn't think so.

TAYLOR: What made Bobby's thinking different from the rest of the prisoners?

OGBURN: I don't know if he was that much different because, as I understand it, many others committed similar type actions. And the authorities did not pursue conviction.

TAYLOR: When you speak of the dysthymic disorder that you discovered in Bobby is I guess best described in layman's terms as being an acute depression, isn't it?

OGBURN: Yeah. I won't call it acute. I think he's depressed and has been depressed for some time.

TAYLOR: Before captivity he was depressed as well?

OGBURN: I think he's always had a core of maybe a depression which is reactivated by a particular event.

TAYLOR: Do you think that that experience in childhood and early adolescence was something that made him more susceptible to influence by the Vietnamese? I mean more susceptible than the average person would be.

OGBURN: Probably.

357

TAYLOR: Did you find that Bobby ever adopted their ideology or was he simply playing the role in order to survive?

OGBURN: I never got any indication that he had adopted the ideology.

TAYLOR: There was testimony last week by a man by the name of Gustav Mehrer who was in prison with Bobby, and Mehrer described Bobby's physical actions as those of a "white Vietnamese" in that Bobby had taken on a lot of the mannerisms of the Vietnamese as his own. His way of walking, his way of bowing, his way of squatting. Do you have any thoughts as to why?

OGBURN: I can speculate. He could have been trying to curry favor with them for one thing. The other is that it could be a way of identifying with them. And those *could* be both on a conscious or unconscious level.

TAYLOR: Did you think that the version that Bobby told you of his being tortured in the early months so extensively was credible? Did he show you, for example, his scar in his forearm where he says the bullet went through, and from your medical experience did that seem to be a corroborating scar?

OGBURN: Yes.

TAYLOR: What changes in Bobby's personality do you think that that torture created?

OGBURN: It certainly provoked significant fear in him, bewilderment, not knowing what was going to happen, he was confused, he didn't know what would happen from one day to the next.

TAYLOR: Did he ever attain any stability during his captivity?

OGBURN: I don't know. I would suppose he became more stable after the initial period. I think he was always fearful of what was going to happen.

TAYLOR: I'm wondering if Bobby has certain beliefs about what happened that are not correct, but he honestly believes them. Because to not believe them would be requiring him to label himself as a traitor. In other words, a defense mechanism type thing where he's altered his own perception of the past in order to live with himself and to live with the present and hopefully in the future.

OGBURN: I didn't think he was doing that.

TAYLOR: Has he engaged in overrationalization of his conduct?

OGBURN: He certainly rationalizes, I don't know if you'd call it overrationalization. He's trying to explain his conduct.

TAYLOR: What did you think about his relationship with Ike Isenbraun? An Army captain in captivity.

OGBURN: I thought it was an extremely significant relationship. Probably the closest relationship he's ever had with anyone.

TAYLOR: It's fair to say a fatherlike figure in Bobby's mind?

OGBURN: Very much so.

TAYLOR: And what effect did Ike's death have on Bobby?

OGBURN: He certainly became depressed after his death. I'm sure he wanted to know what was going to happen to him. I think both Ike's death and Grissett's death were very significant.

TAYLOR: So he said, this is a bad situation and he was a coward enough to say I'm going to do whatever I need to do to keep myself from being tortured? It's incredible that the government has a case where they have spent this much money and this much time and have evidence of moral misconduct that is so paltry. He hasn't killed anybody, or hurt anybody.

26
On Trial

THERE WERE two things about the defense that the psychiatrist Ogburn did not know when he began the interview with the sympathetic little lawyer, Vaughn Taylor. One was that Taylor's brother was himself a psychiatrist. The other was that John Lowe would manage to have Ogburn's rebuttal testimony heard out of the presence of the jury.

At worst, Taylor was fighting for a standoff between psychiatrists, and he was to get it.

The psychiatrists discovered Garwood to be predictable. The military psychiatrists found that there was nothing wrong with him, but their first examination, which had to be redone after one Navy psychiatrist collapsed in an alcoholic stupor in a Jacksonville bar and had to be disciplined, was perfunctory. Ogburn's state of indecision was not what showed on the record.

The difference for the defense was felt by Hellmer and Wright, not like a challenge, but an affront. As good prosecutors must, both lawyers had become strongly emotional, entrenched in their position. Garwood represented not the tragedy of the Vietnam War, but the cure—cauterize the Garwoods and restore the purity of the Marine Corps. To the military mind, the efforts of Lowe and Taylor were unsoldierly and oblique. Hellmer's constant complaint was that the defense was trying to have things both ways—that they wanted both an insanity plea and an argument of reasonable doubt on the evidence.

Lowe spent the summer making motions. He was like a verbal artillery battery with an enormous target, and he threw his ammunition everywhere. After the wiretaps motion, he asked the court to specify who, when, and where Garwood had subjected to indoctrination; he asked a revision of the collaboration charge, arguing it was too vague. He argued that deserted-in-war was not a proper charge since the Vietnam War was never declared by Congress. By July, the motion machine was rolling even faster, and over sixty motions had been filed—over thirty of them asked changes or reductions in the charges. Lowe came up with a highly publicized "mystery witness" when he claimed that Garwood had recognized a masked Oriental man testifying before a congressional committee as the former director of North Vietnam's secret police, whom Garwood said he had met three times in North Vietnam.

In mid-July, Lowe, arguing that Garwood had been singled out for prosecution while nearly six hundred participants in Operation Homecoming had been exonerated of any blame for making propaganda statements, asked for testimony from Richard Nixon.

That seemed to snap some long-buried cord in Judge Switzer. He gave Lowe and Taylor a chewing out, accusing them of making no progress. "Two months later, and we're almost no further ahead than we were when the motion was filed," he said, referring to an initial filing for Nixon-administration information. "We've got to get on with the court's business . . . we're not playing games anymore and we've got to get down to the business at hand here."

Later, he told the defense they would be permitted to see the relevant Nixon papers. Not unexpectedly, there was no written policy outlining who should be pardoned and who not in the wake of Operation Homecoming. In any event, Nixon's lawyers refused.

The pretrial hearings were in their eighth month when Garwood was sent to be interviewed and treated by Dr. Robert Showalter at UVA Medical School, Charlottesville, for "stabilizing" psychotherapy. The trial was already considered by experts as one of the longest in military history.

The psychiatric treatment proved a vital element in another trauma, which was to erode Garwood's reputation even further. Showalter had arranged to meet Garwood on August 8, and Garwood left Camp Lejeune on August 7 at about 4:00 P.M. to make the long trip to Charlottesville, to stay at the apartment of a colleague of Taylor and Lowe's.

It was a fortunate thing that he made the trip; it later proved a perfect alibi against the charge that he had molested a seven-year-old girl that same August 7 afternoon. That indictment drew headlines. The *Philadelphia Journal*, for instance, a tabloid with 110,000 circulation, said it all after the charges were filed: "Traitor Garwood Sexually Attacks Girl, 7." A lesser front-page headline said, "Church Child Ravaged—Pg. 3." Inside, there was nothing but a few paragraphs from a wire service story about the charges. Similar stories appeared in the *New York Post* and other tabloids, but all were damaging.

The main effect of the molestation charge was to lower Garwood even further in the general gossip that, wrapped together into a cloud of sentiment, makes up the public's general opinion about a public individual. For those who were inclined to believe Garwood was being made a scapegoat, and those who sympathized with him for the suffering he must have endured in Vietnam, the sex charges brought doubts of his sanity. But in practical terms, the charges ended any thought of starting a Garwood defense fund that would solicit public contributions.

There was financial strain from another quarter. Foley, still fighting to retain what he called "work product" from his months of representing Garwood, had submitted a bill for $130,000. He had been subpoenaed to come to Jacksonville to explain why he would not allow the defense to have all the materials relating to his case. The matter was never satisfactorily resolved, because Switzer, by now in the habit of giving way in part to the persistent demands of the defense lawyers, had ruled on July 16 that Foley was to turn over any materials that were prepared for the case with Garwood's help, but that he could keep those he had prepared himself. In open court, Lowe blasted Foley as "incompetent and unethical because no contract had been agreed upon" (about fees for Foley's work), but the judge called that "a cheap shot."

On the first of August, the announcement was made that Garwood would plead insanity. By this time, the defense knew that they had at least three highly competent psychiatrists who agreed with Taylor's reading of the legal standards for the insanity defense: that Garwood had been sick enough due to isolation and torture to be classified as not responsible for his acts, and that the way he behaved, according to the prosecution witnesses, pointed this out.

That seemed to be the last hurdle, when Lowe, jogging as was his wont, suffered a rare accident, a separation in an important neck artery, resulting in a serious reduction of blood flow to part of his head and brain. It affected his eyesight: He was out of action for six weeks.

The defense announced it would go forward without its main courtroom gun, and Taylor, whose style was relatively mild and tuned to the etiquette of the military, in contrast with Lowe's booming contentiousness, found that he had to ask continuance after continuance to keep the trial from slipping up on them while the defense was undermanned.

In the end, the defense had exhausted every avenue available to dilute the charges, raise collateral issues like amnesty, and perfect the basis for the psychological defense. They could only wait for the jury and do the hardest part of a criminal trial, sitting through the prosecution case. The jury was seated September 4, with Lowe still recuperating after minor but delicate surgery; six members and four alternates were selected with a minimum of opposition. There was only one man on the panel below the rank of major, and the senior officer was a full colonel.

Each of the jury members was a Vietnam veteran, and each, during the selection process, was questioned by Lowe about what he would do if captured and forced at pistol-point to sign a statement, even an innocuous one, something like "All Americans are imperialists." Some of the jurors told Garwood's lawyers that they would refuse and ask for death. And they were split on the question of whether they believed a Marine could be "broken."

Under military law, the verdict need not be unanimous, as it is in a civilian criminal case. Only four of the members need to vote guilty for a conviction.

The jury was to have more than two months to wait before hearing a shred of evidence. Lowe was slow to heal, and it was not until November 14 that he made his opening statement.

If Lowe was peaked with recuperation, his opposing counsel, Captain Werner Hellmer, looked wrecked by the long duration of the case. Hellmer had been with the case longer than anyone except Garwood himself. He alone of all the lawyers had been there from the beginning. He had seen his colleague, Major Richard Marien, resign from the service, pushing him forward from an assistant's position, and had been assigned a former schoolteacher to help him; Captain Theresa Wright was one of the few female Marine officers and even fewer female lawyers.

He looked as if burned away by his own intensity, and admitted to losing over twenty pounds since December 1979 after almost a year of waiting and maneuvering. As described by Ken Englade, a local reporter, at the time the trial began, "He has a desperate look in his eye. He seldom smiles, and when he does, it is with the facial muscles only; there is no humor behind the grin. His dark green military trousers bag in the rear, and his belt has been pulled so tight that the pants bunch at the waist. His cheeks are hollow, and his arms look like toothpicks. His face is drawn. A stranger walking into the courtroom would think Hellmer, not Garwood, is the returned prisoner of war."

It was Hellmer's first major case as a prosecutor. Wright, his assistant, seemed separated from him by an icy wall, and it was suspected that he meant her duties to be minor. A man of tense nerves and almost visible anger, Hellmer seemed borne down by his burdens, yet unwilling to let any part of them go.

Not surprisingly, neither Lowe nor Hellmer was at his best for opening statements on November 13. After Hellmer's opening salvo, Lowe told the jury that Garwood was not responsible for anything that happened to him after 1965, and forecast that half a dozen medical experts would explain the mental illness that led him to behave in ways that brought this prosecution. Then he gave the first details of Garwood's version of the hidden years—the capture, the subsequent imprisonment, marches, cages, torture, the "Russian roulette" in one camp. He pointed out that Garwood, unlike the other returnees, was alone with the enemy for an extremely long period before he met his first prison companion, Captain Eisenbraun.

Lowe brought up Garwood's past, the less than adequate kid, the shuttle childhood, the reform school threat, his stumbling progress as a Marine. The history of Garwood's life was so short—almost shorter, it seemed, than the preparations for his trial.

Hellmer had painted no pictures. He relied on military deference, and asked the jurors only to pay strict attention to the witnesses the government would present. "Gentlemen, they were there," he intoned. The prosecutor simply outlined the case. He told the jury that Garwood had been absent without a reason from September 1965 until March 1979. The government would show, he said, that he stayed voluntarily and cooperated with his captors.

Suddenly the trial was moving with a pace of its own, and at least during the presentation of the prosecution's side, it could not be slowed down. The prosecution led with the same witnesses that had appeared for the Article 32 session, leading with Frank Anton.

But it was a different Anton from the casually dressed, bushy-haired man who could have passed for a young father on his day off at the earlier Article 32 investigation. Anton was crisp in his Army uniform and decorations, armed with the symbols of a veteran, and armed, one supposed, against cross-examination, which he would face for the first time.

Anton had little to add: He said he had seen Garwood with a rifle several times, but not with any other weapon; he said Garwood guarded prisoners at least twice in his observation, and he said he was told by the camp commander to treat the young Marine in the same way as the camp guards were to be treated. He said that Garwood could, in his opinion, have returned to the U.S. during the years they were together in the camps.

Lowe's first cross-examination of the trial was an unqualified success. He had Anton state he had never seen Garwood with insignia of rank, or a weapon other than the rifle (and that unloaded). He had Anton state that prisoners other than Garwood had struck one another, and that Garwood had never "espoused or advocated Communism."

But for all that, the questioning was brief, somehow an anticlimax after the unreeling of months that had led to the little courtroom, now crammed and airless with attentive people.

Anton's waist gunner, Sergeant Robert Lewis, followed suit, just as he had in the trial's preliminary session, the Tuesday after the trial's opening Friday. Over that long weekend both sides had granted minor interviews, with Hellmer pointing out the upcoming battle of the doctors. "It will make the Patty Hearst case look like nothing," Hellmer said.

Lowe seconded the notion, but from a different angle. "What these people [the POWs testifying for the prosecution] saw has never really been an issue in the case."

Lewis added a pistol to Garwood's observed armament in the jungle camp, and made it clear that his quarters, unlike those of the other Americans, were with the guards. He added that the Vietnamese had given Garwood a name, translating to "Brave Liberation Fighter" in the custom of their country, and added that Garwood wore a Ho Chi Minh enameled button on his pajama uniform.

Somehow the facts that the jury heard were far less damaging to the defense than they had seemed at the Article 32 phase of the proceedings. It turned out that Garwood's weapon carrying was witnessed only once by Anton, and that he could not know whether the weapon was loaded, though he observed what appeared to be an ammunition clip, and said he had seen Garwood remove it from the weapon.

He also testified that Garwood had guarded prisoners, but only on two occasions that he could specify, and that he sat with the guards and the camp commander during the "indoctrination" sessions that were a repeated part of the camp routine. Instructors at one of the sessions told the Americans in the camp that they should treat Garwood with the same deference shown to the guards; yet Garwood, Anton testified, neither asked for the special treatment, nor received it from the prisoners.

But the cross-examination of Anton showed that Lowe was heading in a new direction, as when he approached Anton like a stalking hunter on the subject of Garwood's alleged "informing" on other prisoners.

LOWE: Now, you were asked about instances which might have related to how information got to the camp commander from conversations that took place among the prisoners. I am correct, am I not, that you have only the barest suspicion that you can attribute to Bobby Garwood reporting any of those things? You have no personal knowledge of ever hearing him tell anybody anything that would be informing, am I correct?

ANTON: Of course not, sir.

LOWE: All right. And in fact if a prisoner, any prisoner, wanted to report something to the camp commander he could have called an interpreter or could have called the camp commander and had the interpreter be present, and they could have communicated. There was no bar to other prisoners talking to the camp commander, was there?

ANTON: No, sir, I guess not.

LOWE: Or in fact if there were any ARVN prisoners . . . who overheard conversations, you cannot preclude the possibility that they might have told somebody something.

ANTON: No, sir, I couldn't.

LOWE: You were asked about PFC Garwood making any comments about his opportunity for release. And you related at least one occasion where he said that he wouldn't go home—something about while Vietnamese children were being killed and so forth. In fact you never took him seriously about the fact that he wouldn't go home, did you?

ANTON: No, I believed all along that if they offered him to go home on any one day he'd—he probably would have went, yes.

LOWE: And in fact within hours, or certainly within a day, of him making this very dramatic statement about not going home while Vietnamese children were being killed—within hours he was talking to other people about how he couldn't wait to go home and eat pizza in the United States. Isn't that correct?

ANTON: I don't know about the "within hours," sir.

LOWE: I mean a short period of time.

ANTON: I would say yes. You know every time he came down and talked to us it—whatever the conversation was started—it degenerated—that's a good word—into talking about home and food, yes.

LOWE: And talking about driving his car and other things?

ANTON: Yes, sir.

LOWE: There was never any doubt in your mind that he longed to go home just as much as any of the other prisoners. Isn't that true?

ANTON: No, I wouldn't say there was never any doubt, no, sir.

Next came Sergeant Isaiah McMillan, who testified to a consistent picture of Garwood as a translator—sometimes an unseemly toady of the camp cadre to whom his will was bent, but always as a tool, rather than a participant in the working of the camp. Perhaps because Hellmer thought McMillan would be a secondary, backup witness, he allowed Theresa Wright to question him. This might have been safe in normal court practice, but this was anything but a normal case for the defense—and Lowe attacked with the full force of his experience, frequently humiliating Wright with repeated successful objections, to the point that she asked for a closed session with the judge to go over coming testimony to avoid the hail of Lowe's objections. But then, Lowe objected again—to the recesses the prosecution kept asking for to discuss his bewildering objections. Taylor, working the other side of the line of Lowe's aggressiveness, seemed sorrowed, like a lecturer who has been misunderstood by a promising student.

And when Lowe had a chance to cross-examine, he took full advantage of the fact that McMillan, more than the other prosecution witnesses, seemed to be truly neutral to the defendant:

LOWE: Now, turning the clock back to the POW camp, I would be correct, wouldn't I, in saying that the guards did not really trust Bobby Garwood completely, even though he did a lot of things with them?

MCMILLAN: I cannot answer that, sir. I don't know what those guards' feelings—

LOWE: All right. Your camp was situated in an area with some sort of fence around it, wasn't it?

MCMILLAN: Our compound was.

LOWE: And then the camp itself was also circled by a jungle type of growth?

MCMILLAN: Right, sir.

LOWE: As a practical matter, was there any question of a realistic possibility of escape for any of the prisoners?

MCMILLAN: For any person?

LOWE: Yes. For you.

MCMILLAN: Including PFC Garwood?

LOWE: For you.

MCMILLAN: It was possible, but it was highly improbable for me to escape.

LOWE:	You were aware, were you not, I think you mentioned earlier that there was something like probably a couple of hundred Montagnards in the general area around your camp.
MCMILLAN:	Right, sir.
LOWE:	Were you familiar with the fact that these Montagnards didn't think very kindly of escaping prisoners, and that they would be hostile to you if you tried to escape?
MCMILLAN:	Right, sir.
LOWE:	I think I may have omitted asking you before, in addition to never seeing him with a pistol, you never saw him with any kind of live ammunition that you can actually say personally you saw the ammunition, am I correct?
MCMILLAN:	Right, sir.
LOWE:	And you have no way of knowing whether any of the rifles that you saw him with were actually operable; that is, either that they would work or they had a firing pin or anything. You would have to speculate in order to guess that, wouldn't you?
MCMILLAN:	Right, sir.

But McMillan stuck to one important point: He insisted throughout Lowe's close questioning that Garwood himself had used the term "crossover" to describe his position with the camp cadre. The word has a specific meaning since Korea; Lowe could wring no ambiguity from it, and instead, he added another damaging word:

LOWE:	Now you used the term "crossover." Isn't it true that the first time you actually heard those particular words used to mean somebody who switched sides was actually after your release? These were not words that Bobby Garwood himself used, are they? He used some other word like "cooperate" or something, didn't he?
MCMILLAN:	No, sir.
LOWE:	He didn't. He used the word "crossover"?
MCMILLAN:	Crossover, yes sir.
LOWE:	You remember that specifically from twelve years ago as you sit here?
MCMILLAN:	Crossover or liberated.
LOWE:	Or liberated?
MCMILLAN:	Right.
LOWE:	It might have been one or the other?
MCMILLAN:	Those two words were used frequently.

Luis Ortiz-Rivera was a good witness for the prosecution. He had an interpreter, as he spoke bad English—no one was likely to press such a witness, so he was free to give the simple answers that lawyers hate to see in the record of a trial. The damage was done very neatly, showing that Theresa Wright could get on the scoreboard; the point she wished to make was simply that Garwood had made a deliberate choice, according to Ortiz-Rivera's testimony:

WRIGHT: What, if any, conversation did you ever have with the accused later regarding his choice to return to the United States?

ORTIZ-RIVERA: One time after he was liberated, one of the times that he returned to the compound, because he would come and go, we were talking and I asked him why hadn't he gone and he said that he couldn't. I asked him then, "Why don't you go to another country if not the United States?" And he didn't say anything.

WRIGHT: What, if anything, did the accused ever tell you about why he could not return home?

ORTIZ-RIVERA: That same time he told me that he felt better with them, with the Viet Cong, and they treated him better than the U.S. Army.

For these few sentences, the government flew Ortiz-Rivera back and forth from Puerto Rico four times.

Thanksgiving was drawing close. It was November 21. The government's witness, Gustav Mehrer, was due to testify. The defense knew Mehrer to be a dangerous man: He intended to say that Garwood, in addition to the kinds of things already alleged, had done soldierly duties for the enemy, and had carried ammunition, for instance; that he had told his POW friends that he was engaged to a Vietnamese girl. Moreover, Lowe had been apprised of an old antipathy between Garwood and Mehrer, and thought that unless strictly limited by the court, Mehrer might "blurt out something without realizing he's not supposed to say it."

Mehrer was a draftee, a man who now lists his occupation as "unemployed disabled veteran." He had suffered in homecoming since his return to the States in 1973 and was regarded by the defense as unstable, emotional, and wrecked by the war.

It went badly from the first. Mehrer opened up by saying that the first time he ever met Garwood in the camps, "primarily he wanted to know about the peace movement, the antiwar movement. He wanted to know about the symbols that surrounded that, such as the peace symbol itself. He wanted to know the numbers of people in demonstrations . . ."

There was worse to come:

Hellmer: "At this first meeting, what, if anything, did the accused show you?"

Mehrer: "During the course of our conversation, he invited me to cross over, or asked me if I had crossed over and then invited me to work with him."

Lowe could do nothing against such testimony, but he did do what he could to stop it, calling for a recess to discuss the extraordinary admissions of Mehrer out of the presence of the jury, a tactic he used throughout the trial. It was a way to see what was coming, to limit and disarm it. "Maybe the witness ought to be asked what his testimony is," Lowe asked Judge Switzer after the panel had filed out of the room.

Mehrer then gave some of the most damaging evidence of the court-martial—at first in the hearing of the lawyers and judge only, and a few minutes later, to the jury, as Lowe stood helplessly by.

"He had a satchel," Mehrer said (answering Hellmer's question—the planned blockbuster, "What, if anything, did the accused show you?") "He said it contained leaflets."

Near the satchel, Mehrer said, was a megaphone, at least the funnel-shaped part of one. This is what the jury heard, and it hurt in its detail and precision, and the picture it inevitably conjured. Lowe argued that having the papers, and even the megaphone, was not proof or an "admission" of having made any broadcasts—which was what Garwood was charged with.

Mehrer plunged on into the swamp. He told how Garwood had lectured him about the history of the Vietnamese people, how he taught him some Vietnamese phrases, how Garwood explained to him that he was the equivalent of a first lieutenant in the enemy's forces.

And Mehrer told the court that Garwood had in his possession a picture of a woman, a Vietnamese ID card filled out with his name and particulars, some money, a watch, and other things. He said that he had been deluged with pressures to join Garwood in his work, was billeted with him, and then eventually thrown out, back into the pen with the other Americans, when he said he would not cooperate any further.

Mehrer told the court of a Garwood story—Garwood told him that he had encountered friendly troops, American GIs, while out on a mission for his new masters, and at one point was within a few feet of the Americans, but could not signal them. A Viet Cong was with him, armed and on the alert.

The direct examination of Mehrer was ended simply with the identification of the accused.

Lowe's response to Mehrer's extremely damaging time on the stand was thin. He took him through Vietnamese torture techniques in great detail, intimating that Mehrer's mind had been twisted by his harsh experiences, and gained the admission that Mehrer had learned to "block out" his perceptions of the most painful periods of torture. Lowe indicated his entire memory of Garwood might have been altered, too.

At the end of an extensive cross-examination, redirect, recross, a member of the jury asked a question, as is permissible to do under the rules of courts-martial—though the judge actually asked the question, as is the protocol. The juror, Major Frederickson, wanted to know if Mehrer at one point had promised to cross over and later had refused. Mehrer said this was correct.

"So you did not actually cross over?" asked Frederickson.

"No, no, not as I understand the meaning, no I did not. When I said I would, it was only to stop the torture."

Mehrer explained that before he ultimately refused, he was given such special treatment as bananas, tobacco, and sugar, and afterwards, nothing. The impression left was that Garwood had succumbed to such blandishments.

Theresa Wright examined William A. Watkins, the POW who by all accounts was the leader of the American contingent in the camp that produced most of the witnesses who testified in Garwood's trial. A big man from Sumter, South Carolina, he was a former Golden Gloves boxer, a self-confident twenty-year-old who had been trapped in an ambush at the notorious Happy Valley disaster in January of 1968.

He was one of the early releases, also. Those who were with him in camp described him as mercilessly tough and a man who unwittingly helped, rather than hindered, the cadre in keeping order. His early release was won partly by his cooperation, as was Strickland's. The two had a reputation for toeing the line of the camp's rules and working hard at their assigned duties.

If anything, Watkins survived with his hard skin intact and his countryman's wisdom unshaken; this made him difficult to disbelieve and Lowe chose to take the tack of limiting the damage he could do by insisting he testify only about matters that directly concerned the charges against Garwood.

What Watkins added to the government's case was corroboration of what others had said, a sense of simplicity and practicality after Mehrer's emotional tales of torture, and answers. He said that Garwood had informed on the American prisoners on one occasion by relaying to the camp commander a comment made by an American POW to the effect that he would like to strangle a guard.

Trial spectators found David Harker cute or handsome. The volubility and articulateness of the young former soldier, another victim of the Happy Valley battle, had made him memorable in the Article 32. Now, in the real trial, his unburdening was tinged somehow with regret, as if he had needed only to get off his chest the draining end of the war and his long imprisonment, the vows he had made to dead comrades and a long, slow infection of dislike for Garwood.

But it was Harker who had called the Garwood family with a sympathetic message when news of the "last prisoner" seeped out to the country in 1979, and it was he who told reporters before the Article 32 hearing, "He shouldn't be prosecuted if nobody else was."

Harker was a man who explained things, and in his explanations came some of the clearest views of what it really meant to be there, some of the most defaming for Garwood, but level-headed too, not exactly what one might expect from a man who later became a probation officer in Lynchburg, Virginia.

WRIGHT: Can you describe his physical movements?
HARKER: Yes. He, as far as getting around, he was not disabled in any way. He moved just normally. He appeared to be coherent. He was always lucid, knew right from wrong. . . .
WRIGHT: Do you ever recall seeing him carry a weapon?

HARKER: Yes.

WRIGHT: If you know, what kind of weapon was it?

HARKER: As I recall, it was an AK-47 assault rifle.

WRIGHT: Do you recall the occasion on which you saw [Garwood] carrying it?

HARKER: He would go out on runs, sometimes we'd go gather rice, we'd go and pick up rice. Usually we'd go get the manioc, the root, and we'd carry that back into camp. That was the bulk of our diet. On this particular occasion, some men had been designated the night before to go under armed guard to pick up some salt; Willie Watkins, Thomas Davis, and Pfister—Jim Pfister, I believe, was one of the ones that went. It seemed like maybe Robert Lewis went; but anyway, I know Willie and Dave went. We fell out for formation in the morning, we'd eat our rice and then they would come down, the armed guards that were going to escort us would come down and then we would go out with them. On this particular occasion, Bob came down and he had a rifle with the other two—well, they usually had one armed guard per person: Two or three people came down armed, two or three of our captors. And Bob was with them. . . .

WRIGHT: Mr. Harker, do you recall an incident concerning the camp commander's pet cat?

HARKER: Yes, I recall.

WRIGHT: Would you please explain the circumstances of that incident?

HARKER: Well, the setting was mountainous jungles of South Vietnam; nineteen people were starving. We'd already buried two men, in fact, my first sergeant and PFC Cannon that were captured with me, we buried them in September. We'd gone—we'd endured a terrible rainy season. We weren't used to living like Vietnamese and we didn't know you were supposed to put wood inside to keep it dry because it rained just continuously; and for sixty days it rained. It rained hard or it rained easy but it rained continuously; and the mud, the slime . . . and we were depressed. We were depressed because, not just because we were captive and we didn't know what our fate would be, and we didn't have much to eat, and we had people dying. We had disease, and we had malaria, and dysentery; we had to walk through defecation because men couldn't make it to the latrine. And the stench—I mean—that's enough; you get the picture. Okay, we were desperate. And desperate also for meat; we didn't have any protein in our diet; and whenever an opportunity presented itself or we took advantage of an opportunity, we would swipe their chickens. And on this particular occasion, they had brought a cat in just weeks before; and we hadn't seen a cat, we didn't see one afterwards. They did have pigs walking around and one time there was a plot to spear a pig and make it look like a punji stake, [that] he had fallen on a punji stake, and that never did materialize. On this particular occasion, it was the camp's cat. And Joe Zawtocki thought it would make a nice

371

morsel and we all agreed. And we killed him and skinned him down, and disemboweled him and threw away the intestines; didn't cut the feet off. But we were desperate and so we killed the cat for some protein in our diet.

WRIGHT: Then what happened after you killed it?

HARKER: We were caught. We had some people standing watch but they got in, one of the guards was attracted by unusual activity. We were always in bed at dark, generally, we didn't have any lights, didn't have any kerosene lanterns like they had. So at dusk, we were—we had to get on a bamboo bed. And we were detected, you know, so much commotion, we really drew attention to ourselves, not realizing it. You know, we were trying to be quiet and do it without detection. They found out, and then they fell us out, the six of us, seemed like it was about six of us.

WRIGHT: Once they fell you out, then what happened?

HARKER: We had to stand in columns of two; they all came down and we realized the seriousness of what we had done.

WRIGHT: Was the accused present?

HARKER: He came down, yes.

WRIGHT: What if anything did he do?

HARKER: I believe Mr. Hum interpreted. I don't believe Bob interpreted. He walked into the compound just after they'd taken Russ out and were punishing him, kicking him, tying him up. And that's when he passed by me and hit me with the back of his hand, struck a blow to my right side.

WRIGHT: Will you explain in more specific terms the type blow that he struck, how he did it and exactly where he hit you.

HARKER: As I recall, he hit me with the back of his hand, I don't know whether it was in a fist or whether it was open hand that he hit me, in the rib. I remember he had a disgusted look on his face: I turned and looked at him, I guess it was a normal reaction, when he hit me. And he made the statement, I don't think it was addressed specifically to me, but made the statement, something to the effect that "you're gonna have to pay for what happened to Russ"; which I found rather ironic.

WRIGHT: Did it hurt you when he hit you?

HARKER: I was more afraid of what my captors were going to do; I don't . . . you know, hurt? It probably offended me more than anything, that one of my fellow Americans would strike me.

Harker was twenty-two when he went to the camps, a slim, narrow-faced boy; the man who testified against Garwood was not so much a criminal trial witness as a dutiful voice, an echo of events that burned in memory. To Lowe, the less said by such a man the better; cross-examination was respectful and short, the trial broke for Thanksgiving.

In a way, the testimony of Harker was the end of the prosecution's case, except for Dr. Harold Kushner. There remained the embittered Vietnamese, Le Dinh Quy, a man who clearly hated Garwood. He had been in prison since

372

1966, a Vietnamese Marine with a phobia for Communism, and had escaped Southeast Asia to Palestine and later to the U.S. His effectiveness as a witness was diminished by his anger, which seemed to stem partly from the fact that he had received fewer marks of favor from his captors than Garwood had, even though he was the camp leader of the Vietnamese captives in the jungle. Lowe took advantage of Quy's animosity and Switzer's fear of mistrial to severely limit the areas of questioning by successfully pleading that the witness could not be counted on to confine his testimony to the areas relating to the charges—this argument, of course, took place out of hearing of court members.

Two Marines, John A. Studds, a lieutenant colonel at the time of the trial, and in 1965 Garwood's company commander, and Charles Buchta, Garwood's battalion motor transport officer the day he disappeared, were put on the stand to support the charge that Garwood's absence from the base at Da Nang was unauthorized. It was one of the weakest charges the government had.

Lowe fought hard for every inch of reasonable doubt, and was later rewarded when the charges were rejected.

Floyd Harold Kushner was an anomaly among Vietnam POWs. A doctor, closer to the characters of *M*A*S*H* than to the desperately convinced officers who led fighting men, he was still a captain and the highest-ranking man by far in Garwood's prison world who survived. And his wife, Valerie, had become a public figure in the antiwar movement in her own right.

Kushner was one of the few noncombatants captured; it was after all an accident of war that the helicopter carrying the young flight surgeon of First Air Cavalry Division from Chu Lai to the division's forward area at Bong Kong went down on a rainy night. The Viet Cong would claim the craft had been shot down. Kushner felt it had crashed because of the foul weather.

When he appeared at the trial on the eighth of December in a dark blue pin-striped suit, it was clear to observers that he was the witness the jury would listen to. Who would blame them? He was an officer and so were they. He was white, he was an MD. These things, which aren't supposed to sway juries, are most important. And he was quick to state his bona fides as a competent and accurate witness, right from the point of that fateful afternoon when he'd left Chu Lai after an afternoon of lecturing pilots on the dangers of flying at night. Lecture over, he took off into the dark himself.

HELLMER:	Dr. Kushner, could you explain to the court members when it was—when was the first time you saw Bobby Garwood?
KUSHNER:	Yes, sir, it was in March 1968.
HELLMER:	What were the circumstances?
KUSHNER:	Garwood escorted some prisoners into the camp, five prisoners, I believe.
HELLMER:	Now, what do you mean by "escorted"?
KUSHNER:	I mean he brought them to the camp with another or several Vietnamese guards.

HELLMER:	Okay. The first time you saw PFC Garwood, was he armed?
KUSHNER:	No. The first time I saw him he was not armed.
HELLMER:	Just to put this in scope, sir, when is the last time that you saw PFC Garwood?
KUSHNER:	In the fall of 1969; November of 1969.
HELLMER:	This is going to be a general question and I'll narrow it down for you if you would like—could you explain to the court what the general living arrangements were in Camp Number Two? This is the one you spent the most time in, I believe, in South Vietnam, 1968 to 1969.
KUSHNER:	Yes, in general the living conditions were unspeakable.
HELLMER:	What—how would you describe the general appearance of yourself and other prisoners? Your clothing.
KUSHNER:	It was quite tattered, if that's what you mean.
HELLMER:	How was the accused dressed?
KUSHNER:	The accused, Mr. Garwood, had better clothes than the prisoners. He had khaki twill clothes and I think he also had black pajamas, too. He had one of these little hats that the Viet Cong called "liberation hats." He had a parachute that he wore as a scarf around his neck and in the camp the parachute was a type of status symbol almost. It was only the cadre had parachutes. They slept in them. They had them outrigged as hammocks and they enveloped the sleeper like a cocoon. They must have had elastic in them and they functioned as a mosquito net and a hammock. He had sandals. He had a wallet and he had a watch, he had fingernail clippers, he had—you know, he had some things.
HELLMER:	Did he ever show you any of these personal contents?
KUSHNER:	When I first saw him, he showed me his wallet, and I recall this very well, that he—I was captured in December of '67, early December, '67. He opened his wallet and showed me some air mail stamps, American stamps that were ten-cent stamps and I was surprised because the last air mail stamp I had seen had been a seven-cent stamp or an eight-cent stamp.

Kushner was the first witness to address Garwood as "Mister," and the effect of that name on a man who was almost universally dubbed "Bobby" was as sinister as the minute detail that Kushner remembered from fourteen years back, from the days in the jungle. Together they were effectively convincing; if Kushner had witnessed Garwood in some spectacular wrong the outcome of the trial might have been different. But he hadn't.

HELLMER:	What, if any, weapons did you ever see the accused carry?
KUSHNER:	In the course of my contact with him, which covered from

March of '68 till November of '69, and was intermittent, I saw him carry rifles, and I saw him carry hand grenades. I don't know much about weapons, but I came to learn something about weapons—

HELLMER: Dr. Kushner, what time, if any, did you ever observe the accused acting as a guard for prisoners?

KUSHNER: On many occasions. Not one, not two, but many occasions he functioned as a guard in that he carried a weapon and he went with the prisoners on forays outside the camp to get food or this vegetable, this tuberous plant that we called manioc.

HELLMER: Were there any other guards with him?

KUSHNER: Yes. As far as I can recollect, there was always another guard with him. I never saw him or never remember seeing him going out alone. . . .

HELLMER: Did you ever personally see PFC Garwood interrogate prisoners of war?

KUSHNER: I saw him assist in translating, in talking to prisoners of war. I saw him assist in translating and speaking to prisoners of war.

HELLMER: I'd like to direct your attention specifically to the area of informing. Did PFC Garwood ever inform on you to the camp cadre?

KUSHNER: Yes, sir.

HELLMER: Would you please explain the circumstances?

KUSHNER: Yes, sir. In the fall of 1969, and we were in Camp C, Camp Charlie, I was detailed to dig a bomb shelter with several other prisoners, one of whom was Harker. And during the course of digging the bomb shelter the other prisoners were asking me about the comparison of the Vietnamese treatment of American prisoners of war with the Japanese treatment of American prisoners of war in the Philippines. And I remarked that the Vietnamese was as good or better than that rendered by the Japanese to the American prisoners in Camp O'Donnell or in other camps in the Philippines, and we had a, just a conversation, a relaxed conversation about this. PFC Garwood was asleep or feigning sleep nearby. The next day, a special meeting was convened by the camp commander at which I was accused of making inflammatory statements about the Vietnamese treatment of American prisoners of war. And to the best of my knowledge, the camp commander identified PFC Garwood as the informant.

HELLMER: What did you do as a result of this accusation?

KUSHNER: I said that PFC Garwood was lying and actually called him a liar in front of the camp commander.

HELLMER: What response or reaction, if any, did PFC Garwood have?

KUSHNER:	He made no verbal response; he only smiled at me.
HELLMER:	Sir, getting to another area now, what, if anything, did the accused ever tell you concerning rank that he held?
KUSHNER:	He told me that he was a first lieutenant in the NVA Army.
HELLMER:	Can you recall the circumstances behind this at all?
KUSHNER:	No.
HELLMER:	Sir, what, if anything, did the accused ever relate to you concerning broadcasts to American troops?
KUSHNER:	There was a time in the fall of 1968 when he said he was going to be leaving to go down to the plains to make announcements, broadcasts to American troops.
HELLMER:	Did he tell you what the nature of the broadcasts were to be?
KUSHNER:	They were to be propaganda broadcasts. He didn't specifically go into what he was going to say.
HELLMER:	Another area, sir, I'd like to cover at this point are indoctrination classes, political courses if you will. Did you ever receive any indoctrination courses or political courses?
KUSHNER:	Yes, sir.
HELLMER:	Could you describe the circumstances?
KUSHNER:	Yes, sir. In the early summer, in May or June of 1968, a man named Mr. Ho—we were told that his name was Mr. Ho—came to our camp. We were told he held equivalent to general officer rank. He spoke excellent English. And the purpose of his coming to our camp was to have a political course—I'm using the words that they used—a political course. And they cleared an area and built a classroom and hung slogans out in the jungle painted on cloth and we had a fourteen-day course.
HELLMER:	Now, Dr. Kushner, this may sound like an innocuous question, but were these classes voluntary or mandatory?
KUSHNER:	No. They were mandatory.
HELLMER:	Now, did you see the accused during these political courses?
KUSHNER:	Yes, sir.
HELLMER:	What role, if any, did he play during these courses?
KUSHNER:	He functioned sort of as an instructor. He helped to lead one of the groups and he sat in the front of the classroom with the cadre and with Mr. Ho, whereas the prisoners sat on these bamboo benches.
HELLMER:	Do you have any personal knowledge of an incident involving PFC Garwood and First Sergeant Williams?
KUSHNER:	Yes, sir.
HELLMER:	Can you explain to the court what the circumstances were that you observed and overheard?
KUSHNER:	Yes. This was during the same political course. It was in a morning session and Mr. Ho asked First Sergeant Wil-

liams to describe or to answer a question. And in the
course of First Sergeant Williams' answer, he used the
term "ARVN," the acronym for the Army of the Republic
of Vietnam, and Mr. Ho became enraged and he said that
they were not the Army of the Republic of Vietnam, that
they were puppet troops. I was not with First Sergeant
Williams while he was in the camp commander's house. I
can testify that he went to the house and came back.

HELLMER: Thank you, Dr. Kushner. You should have been in law
school.

KUSHNER: And upon coming back, he was in bad shape. He was not
physically injured, but he was very tired and had been up
there the better part of the night.

HELLMER: What, if any, involvement did the accused have in this
incident?

KUSHNER: The next day, or a couple of days thereafter, the camp
commander decreed that there would be a criticizing—
with quotation marks around that—meeting in which all
of the American prisoners would stand and criticize Williams for the things that he had done, the bad things that
he had done, and he would defend each of these criticisms
one by one. And these were terrible days. These were
horrible, unspeakable days. First Sergeant Williams was
very ill, he was bald-headed with a gray beard. He was
suffering from malnutrition and I recall this very vividly.
He stood in front of the American prisoners and each
prisoner criticized him and then he responded to their
criticism. During this time, PFC Garwood also criticized
him more savagely than the others.

HELLMER: What did PFC Garwood say?

KUSHNER: He said that Williams was a mercenary and had the blood
of the Vietnamese people on his hands and he spit on him.

LOWE: Objection. Your Honor, I think it should be clarified that
he *said* that he spit on, he didn't actually spit.

KUSHNER: Right. Correct.

HELLMER: Dr. Kushner, do you ever recall an incident concerning
the camp cat? If so, would you please relate that to the
court?

KUSHNER: Yes, sir. That happened in November of 1969—'68, I'm
sorry—November of 1968, fall of 1968. Again, these were
probably the hardest, harshest conditions that we endured during that time.

HELLMER: What were the conditions like during that time period,
sir?

KUSHNER: Well, from September until January six men died, most of
them in my arms, and we—our ration was very low. We
were eating approximately three coffee cups of vermin-
infested rice per day, with some fish sauce. We had a
terrible skin disease that was keeping people up all night.

377

It was itching. It was causing a lot of psychological anguish as well as physical anguish. We were horribly malnourished. People had malaria and dysentery, so that they were perhaps defecating many, many times a day, fifty or sixty times a day, could not make it to the latrine so that the prison yard was littered with human excrement. It was the rainy season. It was cold and miserable, and in general just a very horrible—I don't know the words that can describe how bad these times were. This, coupled with these men dying like dominoes, one right after the other, had a tremendous effect on those remaining prisoners of war, the effect of making us feel helpless and hopeless and depressed—and I don't use that in the pathological sense but just sad, very sad, and desperate.

The camp commander had a pet cat that weighed about two and a half pounds, I guess, and one of the prisoners, I think it was either Strickland, it may have been me, decided that it would be a good idea to kill this animal for the meat that it would provide. And we waited until late at night and the cat came down to our compound and Russ Grissett and myself killed this cat, and then we had a razor blade and we dressed the cat out. And we were cooking the cat and we were apprehended by one of the guards. He was a Montagnard. He came down and he saw the animal dressed out, butchered, and he said, "What's this?" And we said it was a squirrel or something that we hit with a rock, and then he saw one of the paws and being a woodsman he recognized that that was no squirrel, it was a cat. And the whole camp went into an uproar. The camp commander strapped on his pistol and came down and the guards and cadre came down. We were marched to the fence and asked to admit who did it, and for a while nobody admitted who did it and then Grissett came forward and said that he had killed the cat, and Grissett and I were singled out and beaten. Grissett was knocked down and kicked and beaten, and I was standing up and I was told to remove my glasses—which were Fred Burns' glasses—and I took the glasses off and held them behind me and I was hit with a closed fist several times. Then Grissett and I were tied up. During the course of this, David Harker, who was one of our group, was, as I recall it, elbowed in the side or in the ribs by PFC Garwood, who was on the other side of the fence, who came down with the guards and the cadre when we were apprehended in this cat incident. . . .

HELLMER: What, if any, discussions did you ever have with PFC Garwood concerning his opportunity to be released?

KUSHNER: Well, I talked to PFC Garwood hundreds of times during

	my contact with him, and on several of these occasions he had told me about his release.
HELLMER:	What did he tell you about his release?
KUSHNER:	He told me two versions. Version number one was that he had struck a deal with the Vietnamese and that they had agreed to release him and in return he would work with them for several months or for a short period of time, at the end of which he would be repatriated home. Okay, version number two—oh, and they had not kept their bargain and that after he had worked for them for this short period of time he was not repatriated and he was just continuing to work for them. But version number two was that he was morally and philosophically opposed to the war in Vietnam and he wanted to stay and help the cause.
HELLMER:	What, if any, aid did PFC Garwood ever give to the prisoners, American prisoners of war?
KUSHNER:	He gave material things to the prisoners from time to time. He always had tobacco, when most of the time American prisoners did not have tobacco, and he was generous in sharing his tobacco with the American prisoners. I remember one occasion when he brought a chicken to the American prisoners that he had stolen from the cadre.
HELLMER:	Can you explain that?
KUSHNER:	He took the drumsticks and gave the rest of the body for the remaining thirteen American prisoners.
HELLMER:	Do you recall what his demeanor was like during that time period when he brought the chicken?
KUSHNER:	It was normal for that circumstance. I'm not sure I understand what you are asking.
HELLMER:	Did PFC Garwood ever bring you or the other American prisoners medicine?
KUSHNER:	I don't recall him ever bringing me any medicine.
HELLMER:	Dr. Kushner, were you allowed to practice medicine?
KUSHNER:	Certainly not as you might understand it. The Vietnamese, early on, wanted to break down any semblance of respect or rank structure between—among the prisoners, and one of the effective ways of doing this was to prohibit me from being a doctor. Usually a physician of some respect in that circumstance—and the prisoners were forbidden to call me "Doc," which was the name they had adopted early on, and I was not allowed to practice medicine formally, and in fact was made the latrine orderly of the prison compound. I did practice the rudiments of medicine as best I could by hoarding medicine. We would have prisoners fake attacks of malaria and hoard quinine, and hoard Mercurochrome and things like that.

379

	There was not a lot of medicine available, but I was not allowed to practice medicine.
HELLMER:	What instruments, if any, were you allowed to use?
KUSHNER:	The instruments that we could garner, like rusty razor blades and things like that.
HELLMER:	Did you ever have an opportunity to give medical assistance to the accused?
KUSHNER:	Yes.
HELLMER:	What were those circumstances?
KUSHNER:	He came down, saying that he had an ingrown toenail, which indeed he did, and I removed his toenail.
HELLMER:	At the time that you removed the accused's toenail, did you have an opportunity to observe the rest of his physical appearance?
KUSHNER:	Yes. It was relatively normal for that circumstance. He was in better shape than the American prisoners.
HELLMER:	Did PFC Garwood develop any close friendship among the American prisoners of war?
KUSHNER:	I certainly wouldn't describe it as friendship. He was closer to some than to others.
HELLMER:	Who was he the closest to?
KUSHNER:	I would venture Zawtocki, Joseph Zawtocki.
HELLMER:	Now, you indicated earlier—
KUSHNER:	That's an assessment, let me just—seeing the—but it was not—I want to emphasize here that there was not a great deal of difference between his relationship with Zawtocki and the other individual prisoners of war, a shade, a little bit.
HELLMER:	What, if any, reaction did you ever observe PFC Garwood have as a result of Grissett's death?
KUSHNER:	Grissett died on the night of 2 December 1968 in my arms and Garwood shortly or immediately came down after he had died and appeared to be deeply moved by the event of Grissett's death and said, "I told Grissett to follow me and he followed Eisenbraun. I told him if he followed me, he would live. He followed Eisenbraun."
HELLMER:	Dr. Kushner, did PFC Garwood at any time ever tell you that he was forced to do these things, like guarding American prisoners?
KUSHNER:	I don't recall him ever telling me that.
HELLMER:	Dr. Kushner, do you recall any incidents with the camp radio, concerning PFC Garwood?
KUSHNER:	Garwood had access to the camp radio from time to time and he would bring the radio down to the American hooch. I want to preface this by telling you what a great thing it was to listen to *non*propaganda-type news—he would bring the radio down and sometimes dial in the Voice of America or some other station that was not a propaganda station. But to the best of my knowledge he

	never let us listen to anything of significance and it was only for seconds, brief seconds. We would just hear snatches of the news.
HELLMER:	Did you ever, at any time, indicate to him that what he was doing shouldn't be done?
KUSHNER:	No.
HELLMER:	Why not, sir?
KUSHNER:	I would have been afraid that I would have been punished.
HELLMER:	Directing your attention to the conversations you had with PFC Garwood, what mannerisms, if any, did he portray when he spoke to you? Was there anything abnormal about the mannerisms?
KUSHNER:	No.
HELLMER:	Could he carry on a coherent and intelligent conversation with you?
KUSHNER:	Yes.
HELLMER:	Do you recall an incident concerning PFC Garwood when Ho Chi Minh died?
KUSHNER:	Well, when Ho Chi Minh died the camp went into a mourning period, and PFC Garwood, along with the other camp guards and cadre, wore some badge of mourning. I believe it was a black ribbon.
HELLMER:	Where did he wear that, do you know, sir?
KUSHNER:	On his breast, on his lapel or his breast.
HELLMER:	No further questions.

Lowe could sense that the trial was drawing to its central, if not final, phase of danger to his client; yet there was little way he could see to challenge the bite and sharp detail of the doctor's answers. He took another route, leading directly to the essence of the defense case.

LOWE:	Dr. Kushner, during the time that you saw PFC Garwood in captivity he always appeared to you to be escorted when he would be going in and out of the camp, didn't he?
KUSHNER:	Yes, sir.
LOWE:	And on occasions when PFC Garwood served in a role which you thought was a guard, that is carrying a weapon and so forth, he was always escorted by other Vietnamese guards on those occasions, was he not?
KUSHNER:	He was never alone as a guard as I recall.
LOWE:	All right. The living arrangements during the period of March 1968 to November 1969 when you were in the same camp facilities with Robert Garwood were fairly close living, weren't they? All the facilities were within visual line of sight for the most part?
KUSHNER:	Almost.

LOWE:	And if things took place within the life of the camp it would be commonplace for a lot of people to see it and for things to become common knowledge, if they were remarkable. Isn't that true?
KUSHNER:	Unless they took place behind the wall of a house or out of our sight.
LOWE:	During the time that you knew Bobby Garwood in prison camp do you ever remember seeing him wearing a pistol or a pistol holster?
KUSHNER:	I never saw him carrying a pistol.
LOWE:	During all the time that you say PFC Garwood was acting as a guard or otherwise carrying weapons you never saw him point a weapon at any American POW, did you?
KUSHNER:	I don't recall him ever pointing a weapon at a POW.
LOWE:	You never saw him fire a weapon, did you?
KUSHNER:	No.
LOWE:	You never saw him display live ammunition for a weapon, did you?
KUSHNER:	No.
LOWE:	In fact if you get right down to it you have no way of knowing whether any of the weapons he was seen carrying had firing pins or were otherwise operable, do you? Personally.
KUSHNER:	No, nor do I know if the guards' weapons had firing pins. . . .
LOWE:	As to overt signs, there were some prisoners of war, a number of them, who had overt signs of psychosis, particularly in their final days before they passed away, isn't that true?
KUSHNER:	Yes, sir.
LOWE:	And it's true for example that some who survived, such as Chief Warrant Officer Anton, exhibited overt signs of serious mental illness, even though they later did survive, perhaps pull out of it, isn't that true?
KUSHNER:	Yes, sir.
LOWE:	And in the case of CWO Anton, I believe you told us, that for many months he would literally pull a blanket over his head in order to shut out the outside world, and would stay under the blanket?
KUSHNER:	Yes, sir.
LOWE:	I believe you said in his case it went on for a period of two or three years, isn't that true?
KUSHNER:	Two years, I think.
LOWE:	And in the case of Sherman, who was another prisoner of war, Sherman manifested very serious signs of psychosis, did he not?
KUSHNER:	Yes, sir. Sherman carried a psychiatric diagnosis apparently before he even came to Vietnam.
LOWE:	And Cannon had organic brain syndrome, which gave

some very bizarre symptoms that you could see obviously, isn't that true?

KUSHNER: I think he did, according to me. I think he had—

LOWE: The symptoms were very obvious?

KUSHNER: Yes, sir.

LOWE: That Grissett manifested mental symptoms, which were characterized by withdrawal and aggression?

KUSHNER: Regression—regression.

LOWE: Regression. All right. And isn't it true that Grissett was also obviously disoriented at times in regard to space, time, and person?

KUSHNER: Space and time, for sure.

LOWE: And a prisoner named Burns manifested bizarre mental symptoms such as sucking his thumb, lying in a fetal position, isn't that true?

KUSHNER: Yes, sir.

LOWE: And the prisoner Cannon—

HELLMER: Your honor, again we're going to object. The government fails to see the relevance of this.

LOWE: Well, I think Your Honor knows the relevance.

MIL. JUDGE: I'll allow it. The witness—objection overruled.

LOWE: Now, prisoner Cannon—there was a period of a month or two when he did not know where he was or who he was, isn't that true?

KUSHNER: Intermittently. I don't mean to imply that for the whole month he didn't know who he was.

LOWE: That's right. But he would drift in and out of knowing who he was and where he was, and not knowing?

KUSHNER: Yes, sir.

LOWE: Isn't it true that much of this was brought on by the protein problems and the terror that was imposed by the camp and other things that were obvious to everybody there?

KUSHNER: That's my assessment.

LOWE: And is it not true that at one time or another almost all of the prisoners would demonstrate an overt lack of insight, that is a real misperception of the whole situation, from time to time, overtly?

KUSHNER: Could you be more specific about that?

LOWE: Well, I'm picking—weren't there times when virtually every prisoner at one time or another would have misperceptions about what was really going on in his life, how he related to the prison situation?

KUSHNER: No, I can't say that's true of every prisoner, sir.

LOWE: Many of them?

KUSHNER: Yes, sir.

LOWE: And in fact, Dr. Kushner, the stress and the other problems did not escape you personally in this regard, did it?

KUSHNER: No, sir.

LOWE: And at times—excuse me a moment (*going through documents*)—isn't it true that you made in your—at the time of your debriefing when your memory was fresh, a statement substantially to the effect—which you had a chance to review recently: "At this time I felt like I was right on the edge of insanity. All of those people died in my arms and I was just helpless. I knew what to do for these people, but was unable to do it. I wasn't supplied with anything to do it with. And the way it worked was when these guys died—when they were dying and moribund, within an hour or half hour from their deaths, the nurse or medic would come down with all the medicine in the camp and say, 'Okay. Now you're the doctor. You take care of them.' This was done every time and I just couldn't handle myself. I blew up at the camp commander several times, was threatened, but nothing was ever done to me for my lack of respect. It was just at times I know I didn't advance good rational judgment. This was in November, December, January of '68 and '69, and I was really insane. I was on the edge of insanity and I, you know, couldn't control myself, you know." That's an accurate paraphrasing at least of things that you said, and those were true, weren't they?

KUSHNER: Yes, sir.

LOWE: Now, excuse me a moment (*defense, counsel conferred*). Now, you've described an incident with First Sergeant Williams in which there was criticism. We've had other witnesses who of course testified about that too; it is true, is it not, that all of the American prisoners not only participated in the criticisms but essentially told Sergeant Williams that he had blood on his hands and was a cruel, brutal agent of Yankee imperialism. That is the sum and substance of what each American said to him in turn, is it not?

KUSHNER: He was criticized. The plan was for all Americans to criticize him. I'm not sure of the wording that was used. I can't tell you what words were used.

LOWE: A while ago you listened to the tape recording of what you told the DIA agents in 1973 in your debriefing.

KUSHNER: Correct.

LOWE: And at that time you told them that the Americans all said Sergeant Williams had blood on his hands and he was a cruel and brutal agent of Yankee imperialism. Isn't that true? You heard that, didn't you?

KUSHNER: That's what it said.

LOWE: And I believe you also said, and is it not true, that at that point in the life of the American POWs in camp resistance had totally broken down?

KUSHNER: Yes, sir.

384

LOWE:	In fact, you saw the fact that you would all have said this to Sergeant Williams as showing how far these guys had gone and how far you, the American POWs, had gone with your part of it too. Isn't that correct?
KUSHNER:	Yes, sir.
LOWE:	And you related that that was due in part to the lack of leadership of the officers, such as yourself, isn't that correct?
KUSHNER:	*(Nodded affirmatively.)*
LOWE:	You'll have to answer because the court reporter—
KUSHNER:	Yes, sir.
LOWE:	And you also attribute it in part to the lack of training and ideological preparation, that people weren't prepared to deal with that type of thing?
KUSHNER:	Yes, sir.
LOWE:	And also in part to the terror tactics of the camp personnel?
KUSHNER:	Yes, sir.
LOWE:	And in your debriefing . . . interview . . . which you have just listened to—at no point did you mention Bobby Garwood a single time as separate from the Americans in general, did you?
KUSHNER:	No, sir.
LOWE:	And, Dr. Kushner, as a result of the terror tactics and all of the other factors that you have described in detail here this morning, there came a time in prison camp in South Vietnam when you capitulated and signed statements, propaganda statements, not only for yourself, but wrote them for other American prisoners to sign, isn't that true?
KUSHNER:	I wrote the statements that others signed, yes, sir.
LOWE:	And you also made broadcasts, didn't you?
KUSHNER:	Yes, sir.
LOWE:	And it would be fair to say that this was as a result of the coercive atmosphere and the life-threatening situation you were existing in, wouldn't it?
KUSHNER:	The totality of that, yes, sir.
LOWE:	That's right. No further questions.

Perhaps most interesting was Kushner's admission that he had not mentioned Garwood's name once as separate from the other Americans during the long debriefing that followed Operation Homecoming. It is certain that Kushner's debriefing would have been particularly thorough: He was the only doctor to be captured and later returned from the Vietnam War.

Kushner told reporters, after his return in 1973, "I am the only man captured prior to 1968 who survived the camp at Quang Nam [in South Vietnam]. The only one. All the rest are dead." Kushner was sure Garwood had not survived, somehow. But he was wrong.

Lowe announced that the defense was about to get into high gear.

What Lowe meant, however, was that the defense was getting into the only gear it had—psychiatric testimony from experts that Garwood had been a victim of coercive persuasion from the moment he fell under the control of his captors, soon after his ill-fated adventure with the Mighty-Mite, to the time he made his escape (and particularly throughout the rather narrow two-year span to which the defense had assiduously narrowed Garwood's legal jeopardy).

As the war of the psychiatrists took over center stage and dominated the last part of the trial, the dozing jury members were faced with a relatively simple choice: whether to believe the doctors of the defense, or the doctors of the prosecution.

But to counter the particularly serious charge that Garwood had deserted or gone AWOL, the defense cleverly brought on a human being, not another analyzing machine. He was Billy Ray Conley, of Detroit, a Marine from Garwood's service company in Vietnam, another driver for the motor pool.

He told the story of how the last "run" or assignment came down that day in September 1965, and how it was a "gravy" run with time for side trips and how "after I heard the call from the dispatcher, I ran up to the dispatcher office to try to get the run, and at that time Garwood and I was racing and we got there about the same time. And the dispatcher gave the run to Garwood. . . ."

The next time he saw Garwood was on television, in 1979. He recalled the last run so clearly, he said, ". . . for the fact that he was chosen for the run and I wasn't and he never came back from it. I always felt that it could have been me. It was just my lucky day."

The other witnesses were weak candles who could shed no light on the case; the testimony of Mary Speers Crabtree, Bobby's old girlfriend, was simply to confirm that Garwood had been engaged to a girl in the States. Donna Long's testimony, that she hoped to make a life for Garwood with her two sons, had been obvious to the court since the first day she had appeared on the defense side of the courtroom, her face a neon sign of approval of Garwood and hatred for his enemies, her shining simplicity causing one reporter to note in his private diary:

"Donna Long takes the stand. She had been there every day, without fail. She was short and hard. Her face was scarred. She was embarrassed the few times she had had to rush to court in less than what she thought was proper attire. She took Garwood's side down to the tiniest detail. She was an active advocate. She made sure—buttonholed journalists—made sure they had heard all that was in his favor and the many faults of all that was not. She made a quick and absolute judgment of the news stories that appeared. It would be good, I thought often, that almost every criminal defendant could have or be assigned one so devoted fan/friend."

But no facts. No facts, for the POWs themselves had had them all, those lifeless memories of Garwood in the jungle that had burned on, changing lives even when the time was dead and eventually even wearing themselves out, until they no longer mattered, and the reasons for revenge, the reasons for caring any longer, were exhausted. Even hate could lose its soul.

27
The Verdict

THERE IS a point in long trials when the weight of the structure that has been erected by the adversary system simply tops out. The feeling is that there is no place to go, no more to say, no more people to bring to court to tell their tiny part of the whole picture.

By January 24, 1980, after a year of pretrial maneuvering and two months of testimony, the Garwood trial had reached that point. To those following it, it was as if the participants continued to wade, like soldiers in a deep swamp, through an endless mass of contradictory words. But in review, it was really quite simple at the end, in fact, for the whole trial.

There had been twenty-eight days of testimony. In that mass of words and opinions, there were eight defense witnesses and eighteen for the prosecution and a complete silence from Garwood, the one man who knew the story as a whole web, the only man who knew about huge stretches of time, stretches unmentioned in the court-martial, during which he said he was a Caucasian alone in North Vietnam. Garwood remained silent, quietly staring.

The prosecution had depicted him as a weak opportunist, a man who simply cut the best deal he could, notwithstanding his friends. The defense erected a picture of a man with an explanation for every misdeed he was charged with, and a man whose emotional disturbances made these misdeeds, even if they could be proved, blameless.

Ten ex-POWs told the jury members Garwood appeared to them to be one of the enemy, living apart from the POWs, serving as guard and interpreter. Garwood was silent during this portion of the trial—the logical place for him to explain, in carefully led and specific direct testimony, why he did what he did, what they said he did, and how.

But instead the defense relied on four psychological experts who from different angles approached their subject as an example of the peculiar wastage of Vietnam—a man who because of inhuman conditions became a creature of the enemy's own creation, a zombie, a brainwash.

Not unnaturally, the prosecution followed with four military psychological specialists who found Garwood, when they examined him after his return, to be perfectly capable of understanding the law. The psychological witnesses battled back and forth through rebuttal and surrebuttal, when each side is given the chance in an ever-narrowing scope, to refute the arguments of the other. It had become one of the longest and most complicated courts-martial in military history.

Then on the twenty-seventh John Lowe made a motion, a long-winded affair that reviewed the entire case, and he asked that all charges be dismissed. "Your Honor," he said at the outset of a long speech, "we have here a one-issue case. At opening statements, I pointed out that we essentially had a two-issue case; one was mental responsibility after the time of capture for all these charges that were alleged. And the other was the precapture desertion charge. The reason I say this is a one-issue case is that I don't think anyone seriously thinks that Bobby Garwood deserted on September twenty-eighth, 1965, particularly in the light of Billy Ray Conley's testimony, and of the absence of any testimony that some way he was unauthorized absent or had intention of doing anything improper."

Somehow, the impassioned Lowe must have known it was his day, for shortly after 1:00 P.M., Judge Switzer made the most important statement he was to make in the trial: "It is my determination, first that Charge I and the specification thereunder be dismissed; second, that Charge II and the specification thereunder be dismissed; and finally, third, that the second specification of Charge IV be dismissed."

Switzer also told the quiet room, "I would also say that I have expressed, even publicly on occasion, that I do have a great deal of sympathy for the accused and in fact have some empathy for him."

It was the high point of the case, from the defense point of view, and totally unexpected. In a few seconds Garwood was relieved of the charges that he deserted, solicited other U.S. soldiers to throw down their weapons, or verbally mistreated another POW (Williams, in the propaganda class incident). The charges that remained were led by collaboration with the enemy and the physical mistreatment of Harker.

Switzer explained that a lack of evidence had led him to dismiss the charges. Garwood was left still facing a life sentence, but with the label "deserter" gone. Gone, too, was the ugly "bullhorn" charge.

"Justice is happening," a happy Vaughn Taylor told the press. But beneath the elation, the defense was curious and wary. They noted that the motion had succeeded completely apart from their efforts with the psychiatric defense.

Switzer was in fact blaming the prosecution for not backing up its charges with witnesses and evidence. It was a case of a weak prosecution, not a strong defense.

Garwood sat with his fingers to his forehead and appeared close to tears as the charges were dismissed. Captain Wright congratulated Lowe on his courtroom forensic display, apparently forgetting that nothing Lowe said in his long review of the case had much to do with the reasons for dismissal that Switzer gave.

Further motions to dismiss the rest of the charges, quickly pressed by Lowe in the wake of success, were rejected.

The two sides sat down and girded for the last procedure, their individual summations of the case to the jury members. Meanwhile, the defense sought unsuccessfully to erode the government's case by asking that the wording of several charges be changed in the charge to the jury, particularly that the "maltreatment" charge in the Harker specification be reduced to a charge of assault. Switzer had given all he was going to, however.

At 10:45 on the second of February, Hellmer took a drink of courtroom water, stood up and moved to the podium. In his dress greens, he still looked much older than he should. He was clever and popularizing for once. He used a projector and pictures of Garwood as a little boy of ten, then a progression of photos, to show what the case was "not about." It was an effective tactic, and forestalled Lowe doing something similar—which he had planned to do, until he saw that Hellmer had stolen his idea, and used it on him. Lowe, for dramatics, spoke of a "scale of justice" weighted with round steel balls to dramatize his contention that the government's psychiatrists and psychologists were only seventy-seven percent sure of their conclusions about Garwood. It was a metaphor that would come back on him later.

Hellmer's argument was symbolized by another dramatic motion. He approached a blackboard, which revealed the words "insanity defense," and with a piece of chalk, angrily and elaborately scribbled over the word. "Smokescreen," he told the jury heavily.

He later did the same thing with the words "coercive persuasion." Hellmer spoke for four hours and bragged later that he could have talked for "two days— just the facts and no bullshit," and he characterized Garwood as a simple manipulator who had used his own comrades as pawns for his own survival.

"Gentlemen, the entire insanity business has been orchestrated. It's a smokescreen. You can see through that smokescreen. . . ."

Hellmer hit the defense psychiatrists hard in his summation, saying they had been captured by Garwood's story, which fit perfectly with their own professional creation of the state they called coercive persuasion. He covered the case adequately—but that had been done by now so many times that there was no electricity left for the listeners. Hellmer made one slip during his performance, calling Garwood "PFC Accused." It seemed to fit the subject.

With considerable strategic cunning, Hellmer turned the floor over to Lowe at 3:10, a time of day when there is both too much and too little time to deal with. Lowe rose to the task.

The tall, silvery Virginian with his owl-like eyes told them, "I've waited nine months for this." He then repeated three times that Garwood was not guilty.

"A finding of not guilty would not make Bobby Garwood a hero," Lowe crooned, "he'd still be a sick man. There'd be no tickertape parade for Bobby Garwood . . . no medals from the President . . . no vindication." Lowe told the members, rather, "A not guilty verdict would simply give him a toehold in the face of the cliff he will have to climb in search of some measure of mental health and humanity."

Lowe did not dispute the testimony of the POWs. Instead he returned to the balance theme, repeating prosecution testimony by their doctors that Garwood, in their opinion, was between fifty and eighty-five percent able to appreciate the criminality of his actions. It was Lowe, during cross-examination, who had repeatedly asked the doctors to quantify their judgments.

"Would you get on a plane without hesitation if there was one chance in four the engine would fall off?" he paraded to the jury members, "or jump out of a plane if there was one chance in four the rigger said the parachute might not open?" It got a grin from the usually stern-faced Marines sitting in judgment.

Lowe held that Garwood remained suicidal and still suffered from his deprived childhood, and said, "You might ask 'Was he credible when he told the psychiatrists [about his time in prison]?' They said he was credible.

"If what he told them was candid from his perspective, that's a complete defense . . . it means that when he was in Vietnam, he didn't know what he was doing on a conscious level. If you'd asked why he was carrying a rifle for the enemy, he'd have said 'I'm not carrying it,' but if you'd said 'What about that rifle over your shoulder?' he'd have rationalized it."

Lowe, in his closing arguments, struck again and again with the testimony of the defense psychiatrists: that Garwood had been subjected to "coercive persuasion," and because of this and other mental derangements, he had not been capable of making rational decisions. Lowe conceded, in fact, that Garwood had "held conversations with the enemy," but argued that he was not mentally responsible during the period of his captivity from which the charges against him arose.

"Please remember," Lowe told them near the end of his time the next day, "we don't have to prove he is mentally ill beyond a reasonable doubt, but we did it." He reminded them that it was the prosecution's duty to prove Garwood sane. If the prosecution could not meet that standard, "you have to find Bobby Garwood not guilty. That's the law."

Garwood's eyes were nearly closed, either from fatigue or gratitude as he heard Lowe tell them that yes, perhaps now, Garwood understood that he did what the POWs said he did, and perhaps now he knows that it was wrong. The day ended, Switzer instructed the jury, and it was over.

Almost.

The jury deliberated over two days, starting at 9:30 A.M. on February fourth.

They used the now-empty courtroom, simply gathering their government-issue chairs around the prosecution table, now bare of papers. The sum total of experience on courts-martial for the five men was forty cases. The jury foreman was Lieutenant Colonel A. L. Valese, a balding manager of the Lejeune base's service clubs, a cushy job to say the least. At 4:45 P.M. on February fifth he announced that the jury had decided on a verdict.

The courtroom filled, Garwood stood to attention. It was all very quick.

Garwood was found guilty on all five specifications under the two remaining charges: that he served as interpreter during indoctrination classes. That he informed the enemy about complaints and feelings of fellow captives. That he interrogated POWs about military matters, including escape plans. That he had indoctrinated POWs as part of a political course and suggested that they cross over to the enemy (in this charge the jury deleted an accusation that Garwood had termed his fellow Americans "mercenaries"). Also, that he served as a guard. Second, he was found guilty of simple assault—hitting Harker with the back of his hand.

Garwood blinked. Switzer seemed to be quaking as the decision was asked for. Valese read from two prepared forms—only "guilty" had to be read into the blanks. Donna Long, who had kept her vigil, first as spectator, then as Garwood's court-recess defender to the press, and lastly as a paralegal gofer on the defense team, wept openly, a believer.

Garwood was let out of the courtroom by a side entrance, a kindness to him in the face of the mob of journalists who waited for him to appear. Five days later, Switzer, with smiles of relief on his face, denied defense motions to set aside the verdict. Already, Garwood was unnoticed again.

The sentence still waited.

Among those who pleaded for mercy for Garwood after the verdict but before the sentence, Donna Long and Garwood himself were the unique voices.

Donna, true to the end, looked small and tough on the stand. Her scars, from a motorcycle accident, marred her face and were made harsher by her unsmiling demeanor. She told how Garwood had become a second father to her two sons after Dale Long's death and described him as a gentle and compassionate man. She told the jury members that she had seen Garwood beside her husband's coffin after his death in the motorcycle accident, "crying and talking to him in Vietnamese."

"I think he shouldn't go to jail because, for one thing, I love him," Donna Long said. She spoke of the hope she held that he should get the mental care he needed and that "he and I can make a life together for our two sons."

Garwood's own plea, not subject to cross-examination, not read by himself but by Lewis Olshin, claimed that Garwood had been already tortured by his ordeal in Vietnam, and was punished again on his return to the U.S. "In many ways the two years since freedom have been a punishment," Olshin read with clarity and dignity. "He himself cannot explain to himself what occurred. He believes he would never knowingly violate the law."

Others to ask for Garwood's freedom were Donna's son, D. J., in a bit of

Disney melodrama; Harker, in a written statement asking for leniency on the assault charge; and Dallas psychiatrist David Hubbard, who recapped Garwood's unhappy career and childhood and was "surprised and puzzled" by his apparent devotion to the Marine Corps. "He has yet to knock a corporal . . . or a general," Hubbard said. "What I find is an intense sense of devotion."

The government, of course, had its chance to rebut.

When Captain Theresa Wright watched the jury go out to deliberate the verdict, she leaned toward Garwood and patted his shoulder and wished him good luck. But with the guilty verdict, her attitude changed. Hellmer assigned her the duty of closing argument. Under the circumstances, the job consisted of attacking mercy.

She brought the imaginary scales back on Lowe for real, lugging a foot-high balance to the government table and a clear dish like that secretaries use for their clips and odds and ends. It was filled instead with small brass-colored balls like a boy's BB shot.

She railed tirelessly against Garwood with hackneyed phrases and tired literary references. All the while an "arty" (artillery) exercise was going on somewhere in the prespring outside, rattling the windows with ominous booms.

Wright placed the BBs in the dish with each of Garwood's reiterated offenses, and by the time she got to the cat incident, they were already starting to bounce on the floor.

In a few minutes more, they were on the tray of the scale, and then skittering from dish to floor as she asked how the jury thought it felt for POWs to watch a brother American turn on them. "O Death, where is thy sting?" she asked at the end, with the little balls falling. It made no sense at all at the time.

Still, Lowe had to rebut, and he did. He raised again the haunting question of why none of the several hundred returning POWs in Operation Homecoming had been prosecuted when in fact quite a few of them had violated the Code of Conduct. Why had they been given amnesty and Garwood not? But he placed greatest emphasis on the suffering Garwood had already endured during fourteen years in Vietnamese prison camps. Then the judge gave instructions to the jurors.

The jury this time took less than one hour. They came back with a minor verdict, a verdict that was indifferent; a slap in the face compared with death, life imprisonment, or even a stiff brig sentence.

The jury ordered Garwood reduced to the lowest rank, a dishonorable discharge, forfeiture of pay and allowances. But the forfeiture applied only to the week between sentencing and conviction, and not, it was thought first, to some $147,000 due him by computation of his lost pay while in prison.

That sum is the subject of a suit still pending in the U.S. Court of Claims. The Marine Corps, in an administrative hearing, denied that he was due the money in June of 1982, leaving the ultimate decision to the civilian court.

Donna Long whispered loudly, "No jail! No jail!" and embraced and kissed her son. Garwood turned slightly and smiled at her. He then closed his eyes for a few seconds, wearily got up and made his way to the exit the court officials had prepared for him, away from the press. "It's been a long time . . ." Garwood said to one reporter who got to him.

It was over. And it was not over, or never would be.

Judge Switzer seemed almost anxious to talk about the case afterwards. Sympathetic to Garwood, the thought that he was against the defendant soon dissolved during an interview. He sat at his desk, smoking his pipe and shelling peanuts.

"I wish we had gotten the truth," Switzer said. "We never heard the Bobby Garwood Story."

Navigators know that there is always a slight difference between magnetic north, the direction the compass points, and true north. Though this error may be slight over the short haul, there can be serious problems in the long run unless it is considered and compensated for. So it is, in a way, with the truth of the Garwood story, which Judge Switzer so plaintively wished to know. Garwood sees it all now clearly. He has a reason and he has an explanation for everything: When he is charged with carrying enemy guns, he says yes, but only a few times, and besides, they made him do it. When he is charged with striking a fellow prisoner, he says yes, but he just hit him with the back of his hand, and that only to save his friend Russ Grissett further torture. And so on.

The other prisoners have their varying views. The events occurred more than a decade ago. Memories are fading. The one thing sure is that Garwood was different from the other surviving inmates, and that in fact he did some, if not most, of the things he was accused of. The question boils down to why.

In the Marine Corps you cannot plead "guilty with an explanation." First you must plead guilty and then, once guilt is established, you can give your explanation and throw yourself on the mercy of the court at sentencing time.

Convinced they could win an important acquittal, Lowe and Taylor opted for an insanity defense. As the verdict showed, the court did not buy it, but Garwood's punishment of dishonorable discharge and forfeiture of pay seemed quite mild compared with the years at hard labor he might have received.

Still, the question lingers and nags: Was Garwood insane when he performed those acts in the little prison camp in the jungle during 1968 and 1969? By the standards humans use to judge one another, probably not. He did not rave, drool, babble, see ghosts, or insist that he was the king of Spain. The ideas of "diminished capacity" and "coercive persuasion" seem plausible enough, given the situation all of them were in. But how "diminished" was his capacity and how "persuasive" was the enemy?

The simple fact that he spent some months in terrified, lone captivity in the animal-like jungle cage—wasted by malaria and dysentery and push-pulled by the ubiquitous Mr. Ho—before he ever saw his first fellow American, had to have taken its toll. That he was not a hardened combat veteran or a career-minded officer, but a nineteen-year-old kid one step ahead of the juvenile authorities, certainly made a difference with respect to his appreciation of the code of conduct.

None of his accusers even knew him when it was only Ike, Russ, and himself in that isolated camp. Did he actually cross over to the enemy? It doesn't seem logical, except as it could have led to a way out. After all, weren't Santos and Ortiz-Rivera and Watkins and Strickland released? But why then were they, and not he? After all, he was the one who had been there longest. He carried the enemy's guns and translated for them and acted as go-between with the other prisoners. Had he simply hoisted himself on his own petard by learning the Vietnamese language, so that his captors decided he was useful to have around?

Can anyone ever really know the whole of it? It is not likely. Probably even Garwood himself can't. What he remembers is clouded by time and resistance to memory and his own shadings of events, possibly because he is embarrassed at a few of his actions, or at least not proud of them. For this last, his lawyers have concocted a convenient euphemism, declaring that there is "the historical truth," and there is "Bobby's truth." An example might be taken from the occasion of Mr. Ho's propaganda session, where several witnesses testified they heard Garwood say to Sergeant "Top" Williams, "I spit on you . . ." or some such thing. But in Bobby's version he claims that particular statement was made by Mr. Ho and he merely agreed with it by answering "yes" when Ho looked to him for concurrence. Slight differences, perhaps, like that between true north and magnetic north, but significant nonetheless.

And so what is Garwood? A traitor? A patriot? A hero? Or simply an unfortunate, trying to make the best of a horrible and impossible situation? After all, the crimes with which he was charged—even the one carrying the death penalty—are not even on the books in any civilian court in America.

The only thing for certain is that Bobby Garwood was a survivor. He probably sums it up best himself. Once when he was asked if he thought he was a traitor, he shook his head "no," but then added, "I think now that I could have done more for the others. I regret that." And a moment later when he was asked if he had done the things he was accused of he looked the questioner in the eye. "Well," he said, "there were fifteen or sixteen guys in that camp and twelve of them are dead now. I did the best I could."

28
More Trials, Dishonor

HOT WITH the heat of the Carolina lowlands, the wet heat that comes from the sea with the southwest wind, Onslow County and Camp Lejeune and Jacksonville, North Carolina, waited for the summer. In May, the sun has not yet become the enemy, and there is some storage yet of the cool piny cellar air. At the county courthouse the brick holds the night and seems to push it out into the open with a welcome draft, scented with dry wood, linoleum, paper, and the Pine-Sol the cleanup crew uses.

The courthouse was unusually busy, for it was the first day of the sex trial of Robert Garwood, a personage already of some note in Onslow County. It was not only a trial, but a celebrity trial with the charges to match. In fact it seemed made for a seamy novel or daytime television; Bobby Garwood, the nation's last prisoner in Vietnam, having just cleared the hurdle of a court-martial for desertion and treason, stood accused of molesting a small child.

The child was (by then) an eight-year-old girl with a white mother of bad reputation and a black father of unknown address. The charges had been brought by the child's adoptive parents, one of whom had agreed to provide sworn character testimony for Garwood in his court-martial, and the prosecutor had spread rumors that there was more than one instance of the offense.

The state's position was that on a bright day in August 1980, Garwood lured the little girl into his distinctive red '56 Chevrolet by means of an offer of an ice cream cone and drove her to a deserted sand-dirt road in the midst of the ever-present pine trees and asked her to "do things." It seemed that Garwood, just out of the frying pan, was now in the fire.

But first Jacksonville, his first American experience after Asia, his first taste of freedom, his first taste of an American home, and an American woman, an American relationship. The Marine Corps camp on the lowlands, Jacksonville is like a cancer grown to its full size, having already swallowed the remnants of a quiet Southern town on the banks of the New River. It is a hideously ugly place to live, caught between the tawdry barracks of the base, the depressing housing provided for noncoms and officers off base, and the virulent slabs of commerce alongside the road. There are more nude dancers, peep shows, macho bars, pawnshops, used car dealerships and fast food establishments than in Washington, D.C., and as one local reporter put it, "there are 36,000 Marines in Camp Lejeune, and 37,000 whores in Jacksonville."

The place has the unmistakable air of the collapse, while fairly new, of all things meant to be permanent. There is a restlessness, a continual skinning over of a wound, which will only partly heal before breaking out again.

It is the lowland South, the sand hills, the endless pine forest, the salt marsh, which seems to creep in from the low banks of the New River and permeates everything with decay, rot, and new luxuriant growth in a repeated cycle. Sea wind, heat, moisture, a sun that beats down unceasingly, as if from the mouth of some molten cannon. It has its effect on the people. Surely an old man in court in tennis shoes and suspenders and work shirt and net-sided hat—his face a combination of deep creases, wisdom, and animal idiocy—is molded by this climate. It is a climate that forces retreats.

Except for the young Marines who forge out, careless of gas consumption, driving the kinds of cars that used to be seen in the fifties. Jacked-up rear-ends, chrome wheels, flat undercoater and fat tires that look like bursting donuts. They wear mirror glasses and stare with half-hostile arrogance at any female. They are in another world from the land they're in. They are not comfortable at peace and, trained to kill, they do or try to so often that one of Jacksonville's streets is crammed with lawyers' offices manned by men who make a living from the energy of Marine fists, knives, and guns.

This was the place Garwood came home to. He looked older, with his thinning hair and his ghost eyes, and his spectral smile, and his ability to sit still, without moving a muscle, for hours on end, his ability to hold everything back forever, or for as long as it took.

At thirty-four, Robert Russell Garwood is a stranger in his own country; but his alienation is far more profound than that of any other Vietnam War returnee. He doesn't properly know who he is. Like Dorian Gray in reverse, there is an eighteen-year-old punk of a boy behind the eyes of the thirty-four-year-old man.

Garwood's physical type is not one that weathers well. His black hair is shot with white and it is falling out in combfuls. There is a wide bald patch in the back, which threatens to move forward, and his long-trunked body, held up by short, almost bandy legs, is beginning to swell into a sway-backed paunch.

But the most haunting and noticeable feature of Garwood's appearance is the eyes, surrounded with charcoal smudges of darkened skin on all sides. They are not deep-set so much as set in pools of darkness. Brown eyes that stare warily at the world, and wearily. The boy who has all his life been in one kind of serious trouble or another is in it again. Up to his neck, the worst kind of trouble—a sex crime.

Garwood is not at Onslow County Court as part of his court-martial this sweltering June 12. That section of the troubles of his life is behind him, docketed in sheaves of paper at the judge advocate's office of the Marine Corps, which has already ordered him dishonorably discharged for disloyal activities.

Yet he is at the mercy of others again here, as if he cannot escape the jail that has been his life, and having escaped, rushes to be jailed again.

The three men come into the courtroom chatting and amiable, as if these devastating and wretched charges were no more trouble than a dispute with the milkman: Garwood, cupid-mouthed and bull-nosed, with shadow eyes and an odd blankness about his face, a lack of cohesion; his lawyer, Vaughn Taylor, who looks for all the world like a pert young fox; and his local lawyer, Ed Bailey, a man who aggressively tries to look like Abe Lincoln and is a Civil War buff and such a large local personality that it's difficult to seat a jury without including someone who has been his client or his friend, or who has worked or is about to work on his fine new house.

What is charged is that Garwood, who had befriended the girl while he was staying at a sort of halfway house run by a retired Marine colonel named J.W. Rider, took her for a ride one day in his spangly 1956 Chevrolet, the red hot rod given him as a bizarre present of remembrance by Donna Long, and during this ride, down one of the nameless dirt roads of Onslow, unzipped his fly and pulled out his penis, first, it was alleged, asking the child to touch it and then attempting to make her take it into her mouth.

It is difficult to imagine a criminal charge that could more readily wreck a rehabilitation.

But the words had been set on the paper, and the allegations, coming from the mouths of the child's adoptive parents, considered by the district attorney to be valid, were distilled by the General Court of Justice of the County of Onslow into particulars: "1. That with respect to the acts in case number 80-CrS-18562, 80-CrC-18563, 81-CrS-3811 and 81-CrS-3812, the said acts occurred in the afternoon and early evening of August 7th, 1980. Further, the state's evidence will show that these acts occurred in the general vicinity of Swansboro."

Both sides always think they are right in a criminal case—but one is more believable, and on that simple formula men and women go to jail or walk free. The system seems to work remarkably well, so well that a person wrongly accused can almost breathe easy in the knowledge that when the key is turned on, the gears will mesh, the machine does work.

Yet in the first two, perhaps three days of the trial of Robert Garwood for the molestation of the girl, it seemed most certain that the saturnine, foreboding young ruin of a man would prove guilty as charged. So many things can happen to a person in prison—how much more likely in the prisons of Communist Asia?

The first reaction of Garwood's legal team was one of ghastly shock.

Garwood, it was remembered, was always affectionate with children. He hugged and kissed them, he played with them. One of his few successful roles was that of big brother, and now even that seemed to work against him.

They hauled Garwood in and grilled him. At first it looked grim. He had been staying at the house where the girl was lodged, he had often displayed affection to her; the prosecution sounded plausible. Garwood simply and glumly denied the charges.

Then someone remembered a peculiar hassle that had taken place on the base that day, August 7, involving the procurement of travel orders so that Garwood could go see Dr. Showalter, his psychiatrist, in Charlottesville, Virginia. A gunnery sergeant was found who remembered Garwood walking out of the office on the base where he worked at about 4:00 P.M. But Garwood had no money for airplane or train fare and decided to take his motorcycle the 320 miles from Jacksonville to Charlottesville, where he had found a bed in the apartment of a paralegal, Paul Patterson, who was working for John Lowe.

The defense team began to breathe easier, particularly when it found that a Patterson roommate, Howard Huntley, Jr., had found Garwood having a snack in the apartment kitchen at about 11:30 P.M. There simply hadn't been time for Garwood to have done what he was accused of and drive all the way up to Charlottesville by motorbike.

But what was devastating was that the case had been papered and prepared for trial anyway. The defense was not able to talk the prosecutor out of it—this sheds light enough on what Jacksonville, a place with one of the highest murder rates in the nation, thought of Robert Garwood. If it hadn't been for an almost airtight alibi, it would have been a very close thing indeed.

As quickly as the clouds had gathered in the trial, though, they disappeared. For even in the ghastly unseemliness of the charges there sounded a consistently ridiculous note. The father, for example, insisted that his daughter call the principal male sex organ a "tallywhacker," and similarly, she had been taught to name its opposite number a "tinkerbelle." The examination of the all-important details of the crimes, therefore, proceeded along bizarre linguistic lines.

The little girl herself, pretty and apparently composed, showed no animosity toward the defendant and acted as if she had been carefully rehearsed by her parents, who sat on the first benches of the courtroom visibly helping her with her answers. The whole questioning on direct examination was a farce.

It developed that Garwood knew the girl quite well, knew her parents, was a frequent visitor and for a while had stayed at the house where her parents had found a shelter after their own trailer had been burned; that the father, who at that point wore a huge bushy beard, wandered in the quarters he and assorted members of his family occupied in a Japanese kimono, reading issues of *Playboy* and *Hustler*.

If anyone saved Garwood it was the little girl herself, with her metronome answers, "Yes sir . . . No sir," to all the questions of prosecutor Andrews, and the answers remained the same as details were dragged past like odorous fish on a string.

The jury believed Garwood's alibi in spite of a detective's wife who swore she had seen Garwood's bright car outside a store near the scene of the alleged crime at approximately the correct time on the right day, and when the verdict came in "Not guilty" on all counts, her adoptive father stormed out of the court and nearly attacked the reporting corps, so great was his hostility.

The strangeness of the incident lingered. There was no rational explanation to it, unless one believed that Garwood might be liable to civil penalties—to wit, a suit for what was supposed to be huge sums from books and movies—if he were first found guilty of a felony. This was the theory put forward by Garwood himself and his lawyers.

The jury returned its verdict Saturday morning. There was never any question of Garwood's innocence, those newspersons polling it found. The little girl's testimony had not been believed.

Garwood walked out of the courtroom cleared of all charges and owing his lawyers another twenty thousand dollars for their skillfully conducted defense.

It was an important moment for the boy from Adams.

One of the defense witnesses had been Donna Long, still thought to be his fiancée, and indeed she had testified on the stand that the pair had intended to get married, ironically on the day the verdict was handed down.

But in fact, the romance between them was over and done with, at least from Garwood's point of view. Donna claims he did not know this at the time, and as they embraced in the courtroom it seemed likely that the next newspaper story about the Garwood case might include news of his marriage to the thirty-eight-year-old widow.

But what she didn't know was that Garwood's treatment at Dr. Showalter's primary office in Harrisonburg and his treatment at Rockingham Memorial Hospital provided him an easy way to see Margaret Kendal, a twenty-five-year-old woman who lived and worked near Harrisonburg, and whom he was courting.

Donna was never to get the full truth of it from Garwood himself, but things had begun to disintegrate between them the previous winter, while preparations for the court-martial were going on.

From the beginning it had been an affair of misinterpretations. In Garwood, Donna saw the personification of her cause, the man who could "prove" what she had known all along, namely that a conspiracy of silence kept the U.S. from revealing all it knew of the many men who were still in Vietnam, still in the prisons that Garwood described in the north, hostages for some obscure purpose.

In every way, she made herself helpful to him, tirelessly writing letters, talking on radio shows, finding witnesses, running gofer for the lawyers, driving cars, even giving forty thousand dollars of her own money to finance part of the legal costs.

The money had been a godsend at the time. It had kept the defense alive, and Donna thought that Garwood would never know of it. Throughout the trial she had relied on getting past the next day, and somewhere in a drawer of her house, well out of sight, lay the paper John Lowe had signed that June day:

"I have received from Donna Long $40,000. I agree to repay Donna Long, or in the event of her death, her surviving children, 40 percent of all payments received towards the fee to which I am entitled for the defense of Robert R. Garwood, until said $40,000 is fully repaid."

Garwood had no money, and Lowe saw no reason not to use someone else's. Or Donna may have pressed it on them so hard . . . who can tell, in memory, that hardest of things to know, the intent?

But the mischief was not only the loss of the money, which Donna came to resent as months and then seasons passed without repayment, without interest on the sum, and without Garwood.

Garwood had written to Donna about marriage, loving letters of maudlin tone with no indication at all that he was meeting another woman; yet if Donna had known, she would not have been surprised, in the soap opera sense, for she had enough confidence in the future, or at least she would not admit she did not have that confidence. She knew, she was convinced, what men were.

Yet late in the trial period, when everyone was under that frightening stress, Bobby discovered the forty-thousand-dollar loan note. Garwood, in the dark up to that point, was furious. In his street-corner pride, he was still free—though he was living on a modest wage from the law firm and the good will of a host of creditors who were willing to believe that somewhere he would get some money from the government and selling the rights to his story—and that Donna had used Dale's insurance, the death money, to pay legal expenses infuriated him. Worse than that, because he could do nothing about it, he blamed Donna. He decided, conveniently, that he could not trust her. Just as an adulterer is relieved and happy with the news of a spouse's corresponding adultery, Garwood was happy in his anger, for it gave him a way to be clear with Margaret.

So in Garwood's memory, the money was one of the things that drove them apart; for he stayed with Margaret Kendal after the sex charges trial, and he followed her up to the Washington suburbs and shared her house; he even mentioned marriage again.

Donna found it hard to believe that someone would simply walk away like that. "I didn't hear from Bobby," she wrote a year later, "but then, I wasn't really surprised. You know, to survive in Vietnam, Bobby had to be able to adapt to, and make the most of any situation he found himself in. After fourteen years of thinking of people in terms of how they affect your survival, it's not easy to change."

They hugged for the cameras in the courtroom at Onslow County, in the heat and exhaustion of the end of that trial, with the lawyers yet to pay and the innuendos still echoing that he had to have done something to that little girl.

It was only a few weeks later that the Associated Press carried an item announcing that the marriage of Garwood and Donna Long was off. In the meantime, he was toying with the idea of staying with John Lowe, in the basement apartment, and working through the summer as a driver for the law firm at minimum wage. Donna must have given him a hard time when she found she was holding the short end of the stick.

She said she was simply trying to get him to stand up to Lowe. "To take his own affairs into his own hands instead of letting money be doled out to him, and I told him to take away his [Lowe's] power of attorney, put his money in his own bank account. And he told me how he was going to live in his basement and be a chauffeur, and all this nonsense, and I just hit the ceiling, and I called him a slave, and I hurt him bad, I mean I overdid it, I just pushed him too far."

Their relationship, like a shipboard romance, was now without a place.

She saw him one last time, in the early spring of 1982, driving up from Jacksonville to Washington for a funeral service at Fort Myer, a funeral service for a man missing in action in Laos whose remains had been returned finally to his family.

They still award full military honors, even after all the years, and through POW/MIA activities, Donna had got to know the family quite well. She drove uneasily to the suburban gas station where Garwood was working as a pump jockey, but it was not at all what she had feared. He was warm and friendly. He took off the rest of the day so that they could go to the funeral together, and it was more than she could have hoped for. He even said he was still interested in POW/MIA affairs and asked that she continue the last of dead love's little errands, forwarding of mail from the organization to him. But he hadn't meant it, he had only meant to be kind.

29
The End of It

YOU SEE him and you hear him talk and you watch the play of girls and boys between Margaret and Bobby, and you hear the banter about the motorcycle, and the talk about going out to Indiana to see his folks, and later you remember his father saying, "I don't want to hurt Bob's feelings, but damn, I'm glad he got himself a place, it was like every time he came here, there was a get-together . . . and everyone's calling up and saying 'When's Bob coming home,' the press and all and I'm telling them, Hell, Bob's been home half a dozen times already . . . " and you wonder how he will ever find a way away from the name made of him because of whatever happened over there.

And the amazing thing, the thing that continues to strike you as you watch this young-old man and his young girl before the water, before that scene of the American summer, the summer of the sun, the summer that creates this country, is that Garwood never cared a damn for anything to do with that war, that he didn't know why we were fighting it, that he didn't have any feelings one way or the other when he was told he was going to Vietnam, but that he did like being a Marine. In 1965 he sent a picture to his real mother (not his stepmother) of himself sitting on the grass beside and behind a cast stone Marine Corps shield with anchor, eagle, globe, and robe. The boy in the picture doesn't look remotely like the man who returned in 1979. He is slighter, more fragile, his face a simple collection of plastic curves, a pudding under a shock of combed hair, with a windbreaker on his back, a pair of chino pants, white socks and black shoes—he looks like a puppy, not a soldier. He wrote on the back, "Mom & Bud it's just me. It ain't much but it's me anyway. Love your son Bob South Viet Nam, 3rd Marine Div."

There is another picture, this one with a tear in it, showing the same youth leaning casually against a tree, obviously some type of palm, with one hand on the tree and the other stuck in his back pocket, palm up. It is labeled "Taken in South Viet Nam near the village of Bingh Gih," and identifies the person pictured as Robert R. Garwood 2069669, and his station as Command Support Company, Headquarters Battalion, service and supply. It is the last known picture of Garwood before his disappearance.

The face is fuller now, the lines deeper, and there is the sense about Bobby Garwood that he is where he is going to be for some time. He emerged from the psychiatric wing of the Rockingham Memorial Hospital at Harrisonburg, Virginia, on a hot, humid and cloud-filled day, a young man with a past that was both an enormous weighty enigma and no past at all. That was in July of 1981, after the court-martial and the further trauma of the Onslow County trial on sex charges.

He was then under the care of a local psychiatrist, who recommended a course of psychotherapy to last two years. The care that Garwood required to get his head straight was a constant point of reference for his lawyers, who kept their statements tuned to the theme they had woven at the court-martial. The post-Vietnam syndrome, "a typical dissociative reaction" and the rest. But to Garwood, the sessions had only been worse than a waste of time. "This is the first time I've gone to a doctor," he was fond of saying that summer, "where you went in feeling good and came out feeling worse."

Once, the doctor arranged for Bobby to do some yard work for him, and Garwood labored all weekend, raking, shoveling, mowing, and moving furniture. He was paid seventy-five dollars, and the Monday after a one-hour psychiatric session with the doctor, all the money was to be owed back— eventually.

According to the patient, the course of therapy consisted of questions prompting Garwood to go over and over memories that were painful to him.

Garwood lived at the hospital in a view-favored room, looking out over the low hills and bluish ridges of that valley county. But he clung to the television and his cassette player in the smoky room, and yearned, not very effectively, to be free. His worries were both domestic and financial.

Donna Long had been fading from Garwood's mind, and his new romance with Margaret Kendal blooming. A college student taking a master's course in counseling, she had met Garwood during his stay at the hospital, while visiting a friend in the ward for depressives, where he was assigned.

Garwood's adaptation to the life of the ward was excellent, for in a way, it was his first real home, or his first familiar home, since Vietnam. As in prison in Asia, it was like an indeterminate sentence, he was under light supervision, but other than that, he was famous, something that adds enormously to Bobby Garwood's relish of life. "They didn't even know who I was!" he would burble enthusiastically about his stay and his friendships at the Rockingham Memorial Hospital, as he described how very well he got along with his fellow inmates. Depressive he was not, at least in his last days there, when he used to prowl the corridors asking everyone "How're ya doin'?" with an infectious grin and a puppy-dog swagger.

Garwood declared that he could no longer stay at the hospital, if only for financial reasons. Though he was still officially in the Marine Corps, the court-martial's sentence of forteiture of all pay and allowances included medical costs; but it was not until long after the trial had ended that he was first able to gauge his entire horrendous financial picture.

He owed his lawyer John Lowe an estimated $280,000 for the legal team that had defended him in the six-month court-martial. He was billed by his previous lawyer, Dermot Foley, for $130,000. He owed Jacksonville Attorney Ed Bailey $20,000 for the defense on the sex charges, and another $9,500 to Dr. Robert Showalter of Harrisonburg. A defense psychiatrist at the court-martial was suing for $12,000 in expenses and fees, and Donna Long was owed $40,000 that she had loaned to John Lowe.

The debts far outweighed the base sum he hoped to get from the Marine Corps if an administrative hearing on his back pay ruled favorably, and every day he spent in the hospital was increasing the bill.

Garwood had no marketable skills that he felt he could use. The attitude he held toward his skill in the Vietnamese language was a paradox. At this point he was still blanching at an Oriental face, though he would occasionally slip into Vietnamese, and would claim he still thought in Vietnamese. He could not see himself associating with Orientals, however. Instead, he looked for an entry-level job, always gravitating to the same skills that he knew as a youth and feeling, at the age of 33, like a boy of 18. Inevitably, he ended up pumping gas in the suburbs.

How this came about is a lesson in Garwoodiana. It is one of the contradictions of his character that though he suffered greatly from the loneliness he felt under the prison regimes, a new type of loneliness seized him on his return home, a loneliness more terrible and more lasting, since it was incurable. He had literally dropped out of his generation and then, after fourteen years of complete foreignness, dropped back into it.

The solution to this for him was to be attached to a series of people. For a while it was Dermot Foley, then the Longs, and perhaps for a while John Lowe. Finally it was Margaret, who when she met him did not know who he was, and then took him over like a kindly aunt.

Garwood was at first at the hospital, then staying with Margaret, and then with John C. Lowe. Lowe took more than a proprietary interest in Garwood, and for a time was speaking of himself as his client's father figure and social guide. The lawyer lived in nearby Charlottesville and had offered Garwood housing in his carefully restored, luxurious suburban home; he held out the promise of creating an apartment there for Garwood where he might live (albeit in the redecorated basement) and spend his days working for the Lowe and Gordon office in an undefined role. He became John Lowe's sometime chauffeur, and spent many hours idling around the comfortable Lowe office, where Margaret had been hired as a receptionist.

The young couple came to resent Lowe's intrusion into their lives, in spite of the many kindnesses he showed them.

It rubbed Garwood wrong, this mixture of social levels—one minute washing the dirt off Connie Lowe's new Jaguar sedan, and the next plunging into the swimming pool. John Lowe was paying him about six dollars an hour, and Garwood's most frequent duty was driving Lowe to business appointments out of town. He spent his evenings with Margaret, and when it became clear that there would not be a remodeled basement for Garwood to move into, they made arrangements to share an apartment with another female Lowe and Gordon employee.

It was only a matter of time before Garwood would sicken of Charlottesville; it was disheartening to plug away at six dollars an hour with a nearly half-million-dollar debt hanging over his head. Lowe's motives included caution as well as kindness. He had received a nasty shock six months earlier when Garwood had been charged with child molestation. Hypothetically, if the famous client had been living with him, he might never have become involved in the web of circumstances that led to the indictment.

Pushed this way by Lowe, and that by Margaret, he was also criticized by Donna Long, who saw the break-up of her relationship with Garwood as a result of her "trying to get Bobby to stand up to John Lowe." Donna, never a diplomat, let fly with both barrels when she got wind of Bob's affair with the other—much younger—woman. But she could not blame him outright, and significantly, does not hold him really accountable for his action. Bobby, she explains, is easily led and comes under influences.

To Garwood's credit, he did not curse all their houses and leave. Perhaps it would have been better if he had. Instead, he remained conciliatory, and chose to be guided by the person then closest to him, Margaret Kendal. She moved to northern Virginia, he moved too, finding a job at a gas station within a quarter of a mile of their rented home, a brick house that the couple shares with two other people on a quiet street. Margaret works as a legal secretary.

It is Garwood's instinct to thrust himself quickly under the direction of someone else, and when he is faced with the prospect of independence he will shun it. So it was with the gas station. He was dithering about the job, trying to choose between it and other possibilities, when the boss called him up and literally told him to take it—that was enough, the familiar voice giving orders, and he has been there since. The first job on his own in his native land is a distinct echo of his father's first job in faraway Michigan.

He had thought of becoming a messenger, a job pool that is wide and deep in the Washington area, where lawyers and bureaucrats by the thousands need papers and documents delivered, and always immediately. It is an independent life, where one can make good money, but where one must discipline oneself to put in the hours.

Though he had a motorcycle and a car, he couldn't accept the terms somehow.

Domestic tranquility, or at least inertia, overcame the couple. The house was really most advantageous. In the basement, garage doors opened onto the sloping driveway, which dove swiftly into the street. The place was perfect for the old Chevrolet, and nearby an ugly pipe-riddled basement room was soon tricked up with a pool table—one of Garwood's perpetual exaggerated bargains—to a sort of men's den. It was as if both young people, at twenty-five and thirty-four, were playing house, even to the complaints and petty bickering of televised marriage; certainly Garwood had no conception of how to behave. So they did as others they saw did, and the characters became set in that mold of American couples, with the wife as the real force, the person who humors the other, and the man a Dagwood.

In this case the roles seemed simple to fill. Basically Bobby wanted only to be taken care of, and in the barest, most humble way to have some kind of family that circulated around him. He took pleasure in calling Margaret his fiancée, a complete turnaround from the time a few months before when he was frightened by her possessiveness and her desire to make their relationship permanent.

Every morning, Bobby rises early to get to the station by 7:30. It is a clubbable place where the employees are allowed to use the two hydraulic lifts to work on their own cars and the customers, basically short-run commuters who are trying to keep their aging vehicles on the job jitney, are likely to have need of small repairs. The garage is expensive, inefficient, and charges about three cents more for gas than the lower-priced stations. On the other hand, it is close to the beltway, and near the intersection of several important suburban thoroughfares. The owner had trouble with employees and was delighted with Garwood, who took the job as seriously as a career.

He had spoken eagerly of getting a mechanic's certification at Northern Virginia Community College, but this talk faded with the routine of the job. Who could blame him for wanting more money, or overenthusiastically describing the course as taking six weeks, or thinking hopefully that he would be able to save money?

It seemed to Garwood that any income would be something of a miracle, and so conservative had he become, that even $3.50 per hour seemed to allow infinite savings. What did he have to buy except gas for his car, he asked? Ominously unprepared for the costs of running a home, the expenses of bringing money in, he had forgot the rent, the repairs, the clothes, the groceries, the bills that trickled in in a sad slow stream, belying the inefficiency of the post office.

Yet he liked the job, liked the hardship of pumping gas in all weather, the dirt and grease of it. And in the evening he would return to his home, dark with toil and exhausted by the irregular effort of wandering the paved gas station lot for hours like a museum-goer.

He claimed the job took no mental effort, and this made it acceptable, after the months of tension and uncertainty of the long trial, and the anxiety that still remained because of the administrative decision on his back pay. It also allowed him to discover people in his own generation, from backgrounds like his own, for among the other workers at the station were some of the lost and wandering sons, the dropouts, the unsteady and half-adequate to whom pumping gas would always appeal.

He had dropped low enough that he could shine, and among the other employees Garwood was singled out as the one who could "manage" the station. It meant being on duty, but it involved responsibility, and since the station's owner had been badly stung by a pair of "bad 'uns" who had made off with two thousand dollars in receipts, the compliment was double. Of course, in an establishment like this, there are some cautions. The first week's salary is withheld as a safety measure; it will be paid only when the employee moves on. Bobby took that in stride, and responded loyally when his boss told him they'd have to repossess a car.

The car was the best thing to happen, for somehow it connected, over fourteen years, the boy in Indianapolis with the thirty-five-year-old—the grinning Fonzie with his helmet of slicked hair and chain of keys to the same boy, now more tired and infinitely more confused, though wiser. The car came in for a transmission job in November, though one would have thought that a two-bay garage with a transient crew of gas jockeys would be the last place to take a big job. Perhaps the car could go no farther.

They finished the job—not Bob, but the mechanics he envied, men who got up to seven dollars per hour—and the cost to the owner came to $240.

The owner took the news with poor grace, and came back after business hours and removed the car with a spare set of keys without paying the bill.

When the garage boss told Bob to go out and get the car back, he was more thrilled than if he'd been given a raise, for he knew the job, like the times he had to surreptitiously make off with the car of his friends' parents, as one of life's great joys, a clean and stealthy bit of derring-do, with the added pleasure of being legal. At least he thought it was legal, or that was someone else's responsibility. To his way of thinking, he had been ordered to do it, it was a familiar excuse.

With the boss's secretary driving, the two stole out and in a minute or two removed the car while the owner, no doubt passing a slim congratulatory thought that evening, sat by his television. The next day the police were called and the owner became righteously indignant. Garwood, who had been promised ten percent of the money collected for taking the car, was less elated when he found that the garage owner had compromised on the bill, settling for half the $240. Garwood was to get twelve dollars for his efforts.

The money was nothing, only the icing. "I just drove that car off from in front of his house," Garwood said joyfully. "They could have arrested me or anything."

EPILOGUE

THERE IS a saying to the effect that the stones of justice grind slowly, but grind exceeding fine, and the first part of the saying would find Bob Garwood in agreement today.

The important parts of Bob Garwood's life are still frozen, still in limbo. He is neither married nor exactly single, but like many younger people, shares a house-space with Margaret Kendal in northern Virginia. Their life is quiet, their pleasures simple, perhaps an at-home beer party, a pizza, a trip in one of their cars. For they have three vehicles in various states of repair, and Bobby's red Chevrolet sits on the sloping drive that leads up to the garage of his rented home. The garage, of course, must be kept clear for work on Bobby's third vehicle, his motorcycle, also a gift from Donna Long. Bob recently bought a Volvo for two hundred dollars, and there are only a couple of things wrong with it, he says cheerfully.

But the present is not so bright. He left his first job and found another like it, pumping gas on an arterial road leading into Washington. It is a job of complete obscurity and only a few know who he is, where he has been, or that he is perhaps the most notorious veteran of the Vietnam War.

Bobby likes it that way.

He has broken off all communictions with Donna Long, and by simply ignoring her has managed little by little to shroud that chapter of his past in oblivion. His talk now is of cars and the problems on the job—and of the endless legal grind that still continues over him.

His legal case over the money the government may or may not owe him goes on, invisible, with a life and a time-scale of its own, apparently out of human control. The Marine Corps recommended denial of his claim for back pay in mid-1982, which does not affect his U.S. Court of Claims case on the matter, though the next decision in a line of decisions now rests with the secretary of the Navy.

Almost as soon as he arrived in America, Garwood was surrounded by those who wished to help or use him. No one who has helped him has yet been paid for their services—for which Garwood cannot be blamed. He came back to the U.S. utterly penniless, having given away his last few Vietnamese notes as souvenirs on the plane. The Marine Corps, after paying him the lowest salary the pay scale allows during the months he was stationed at Lejeune waiting trial, ordered his pay and allowances forfeit when the judgment of the court-martial was rendered.

It is puzzling that the Marines have denied pay—at least from the date of his capture in September 1965 to the date of the first alleged offense of which he was proven guilty, a period of about four years at the very minimum. That would be a help. Meantime, he has nearly completed work on his high school equivalent diploma.

Yet Garwood has little hope of getting even that small amount because of the legal bills piled up against him.

Dermot Foley, his original lawyer, has been able to force Putnam's to hold up payments of Garwood's share of book advances and royalties. Foley's claim: $130,000. Foley is no longer working for the POW/MIA organization.

John Lowe, of Lowe and Gordon, who claims a legal bill of in excess of two hundred thousand dollars (he refuses to disclose the exact amount), has also billed Garwood for the forty thousand dollars that has to be repaid to Donna Long. She is not on speaking terms with the tall Virginian and has had to mortgage her house. According to her, Lowe makes intermittent payments to her of five hundred dollars a month. He continues to practice and prosper in Charlottesville.

Dr. Tanay, the psychiatrist so vital to the defense, is suing Lowe and Gordon for $11,666 for witness fees, which are disputed and have never been paid.

Vaughn Taylor, the lawyer for the novel psychiatric defense, is not suing anyone—his only legal troubles have been a recent divorce. He has settled in Jacksonville, where he practices law on the base at Camp Lejeune and frequently takes on cases involving active military personnel all over the world.

Both Dale Miller and Lewis Olshin have separated from the service. Olshin has joined a Main Line Philadelphia law firm and Miller has started his own practice. He has become closely involved in POW/MIA affairs and has joined national committees for the organization.

Captain Werner Hellmer has been promoted to major and was named a military judge. He sits on courts-martial in Camp Lejeune.

Captain Theresa Wright, Hellmer's coprosecutor, has been posted to Okinawa.

Colonel R. E. Switzer, the Garwood trial judge, has retired his commission and now has a post as professor of law at Coastal Carolina Community College at Jacksonville. A recent student of his was Mrs. Donna Long, who took his military law course and received a high honors grade.

Donna Long is now a free-lance reporter and student. She plans a career as a paralegal after completing a degree program at Coastal Carolina.

Frank Anton, one of the prosecution's key witnesses, was a marcher in a POW/MIA Veteran's Day 1982 protest. He marched in New York City dressed as a prisoner in chains.

Mr. and Mrs. Jack Garwood, Sr., are living at Adams, Indiana, at the family home.

Code of Conduct for Members of the United States Armed Forces (1955 version—amended 1976)

1. I am an American fighting man. I serve in the forces which guard my country and our way of life. I am prepared to give my life in their defense.
2. I will never surrender of my own free will. If in command I will never surrender my men while they still have the means to resist.
3. If I am captured I will continue to resist by all means available. I will make every effort to escape and aid others to escape. I will accept neither parole nor special favors from the enemy.
4. If I become a prisoner of war, I will keep faith with my fellow prisoners. I will give no information or take part in any action which might be harmful to my comrades. If I am senior, I will take command. If not, I will obey the lawful orders of those appointed over me and will back them up in every way.
5. When questioned, should I become a prisoner of war, I am bound to give only name, rank, service number, and date of birth. I will evade answering further questions to the utmost of my ability. I will make no oral or written statements disloyal to my country and its allies or harmful to their causes.
6. I will never forget that I am an American fighting man, responsible for my actions, and dedicated to the principles which made my country free. I will trust in God and in the United States of America.

28

Due 14 Days From Latest Date

JAN 2 1 1986			
JAN 2 5 1986			
FEB 8 1986			
MAR 2 7 1986			
APR 8 1986			
JUL 1 1 1986			
AUG 2 9 1986			
SEP 1 6 1986	WITHDRAWN		

84B
.G899

Redwood Library and Athenaeum

Newport, R. I.